An Anthology
for
Creative Writers

An Anthology
for
Creative Writers
A GARDEN OF FORKING PATHS

Edited by

Beth Anstandig

Eric Killough

PEARSON

Prentice
Hall

Upper Saddle River, New Jersey 07458

Library of Congress Cataloging-in-Publication Data
An anthology for creative writers : a garden of forking paths / [collected by] Beth
Anstandig, Eric Killough.
   p. cm.
   Includes index.
   ISBN 0-13-113501-5
   1. College readers. 2. Creative writing—Problems, exercises, etc. I. Anstandig, Beth. II.
Killough, Eric.

PE1417.A58 2005
808'.0427—dc22   2005040199

Editor-in-Chief: Leah Jewell
Acquisitions Editor: Vivian Garcia
Editorial Assistant: Christina Volpe
Production Liaison: Joanne Hakim
Executive Marketing Manager: Brandy Dawson
Assistant Marketing Manager: Andrea Messineo
Manufacturing Buyer: Christina Helder
Permissions Specialist: Mary Dalton Hoffman
Cover Art Director: Jayne Conte
Cover Design: Bruce Kenselaar
Manager, Cover Visual Research & Permissions: Karen Sanatar
Cover Illustration/Photo: Marc Chagall, French (born Belarus), 1887–1985, Russian. Temptation
1912. Oil on canvas, 65-1/2 x 46 3/4 in. (166.4 x 118.7 cm). Signed l.l., in yellow paint: Chagall;
l.l., in brown paint: Chagall ("C" is obscured by frame). Painted: Paris, France, Europe. The Saint
Louis Art Museum. Gift of Morton D. May.
Composition/Full-Service Project Management: Donna Lee Lurker/GGS Book Services
Printer/Binder: The Courier Companies

Credits and acknowledgments borrowed from other sources and reproduced, with permission, in this
textbook appear on appropriate page within text.

Pearson Education LTD., London
Pearson Education Singapore, Pte. Ltd
Pearson Education, Canada, Ltd
Pearson Education–Japan
Pearson Education Australia PTY, Limited

Pearson Education North Asia Ltd
Pearson Educación de Mexico, S.A. de C.V.
Pearson Education Malaysia, Pte. Ltd
Pearson Education, Upper Saddle River, New Jersey

10 9 8 7 6 5 4 3 2 1
ISBN 0-13-113501-5

Contents

SECTION FOUR

Evolving Worlds and Disoriented Words: Experimental Writing 353

SECTION FIVE

The Mapmaker's Unmade Map: Writing About Writing 407

An Introduction to the Text

" 'I shall retire to write a book,' and at another point, 'I shall retire to construct a labyrinth.' Everyone pictured two projects; it occurred to no one that book and labyrinth were one and the same."

—Jorge Luis Borges

Excellent writing comes from excellent reading. As a student of creative writing, you must be prepared not only to constantly revise and rework your own writing but also to review, consider, and implement the work of other writers. We see farthest by standing on the shoulders of those who precede us. This book aims to compile, in one volume, innovative and inspirational writing from the last four decades. The works here defy traditional categorization while delivering accessible and instructive examples of the writer's creative art.

Jorges Luis Borges, the celebrated librarian, poet, essayist, and short story writer worked throughout his life to push the act of creative writing into strange and fruitful new territories. His work was necessitated both by his need to create as a writer and by his need to learn from what he created. As the narrator of his experimental short story "The Garden of Forking Paths" explains, the act of creating a new written work is often carried on between the acts of making decisions and of having decisions made for you. The writer must respond not only to his or her own need to write but also to the need of the subject to be written.

"In all fictions," he reminds us, "each time a man meets diverse alternatives, he chooses one and eliminates the others." However, in his story, we are offered an alternative. This story, "The Garden of Forking Paths," describes a book entitled *The Garden of Forking Paths*, in which the main character chooses not just one alternative, but, miraculously, all alternatives simultaneously and "creates, thereby, 'several futures,' several times, which themselves proliferate and fork."

We believe that our book is, itself, an immense (and perhaps labyrinthine) garden of forking paths into which all creative writers can enter, no matter what experience they bring. Wildly divergent writings have been selected for each genre, and their coexistence here provides proof that the act of writing can take many forms. This anthology aims to represent as many of those forms as possible. There are, we hope to show, as many paths into and through the garden as there are persons willing to enter, to explore, and to read. Furthermore, your participation in the world of creative writing will expand those paths and options even further.

Poet Theodore Roethke hated the term "creative writing" because he believed that all writing is creative. It is our hope that this anthology will provide undeniable evidence that this is true: *the possibility for creativity resides in every word.* Within these pages, you will find that the creative spirit rises above all genres and infuses every form with vitality and exuberance. Every aspiring writer—whether a poet, an essayist, a novelist, or none of the above—when faced with the impulse to create a piece of writing must choose the form that will best express his or her thoughts and ideas.

The beginning writer faces a single but two-sided problem: what *do I wish to create and* how *do I wish to create it?*

There is no right answer. Rather, in these pages, you will find that there are as many right answers as there are questions. We believe that you should approach the blank page with a working knowledge of as many approaches to writing as possible. We also believe that all writers learn their craft primarily by reading excellent and inspiring writing. Within these pages, you will find that we have gathered a representative sample of the most invigorating and creative writing today.

Guided by fiction writer, essayist, and poet Robert Creeley's belief that all writing is essentially the act of articulation and that "form is content, content form," we have brought together as many successful examples of ideas and styles as possible. We have grouped these writings by genre for ease of use so that *you* can choose how *you* want to spend your reading time. You will find in our garden that each author has labored to articulate at least one of the seemingly infinite possibilities that the creative spirit can bring into being. Many of the authors collected here have successfully created works of written art using more than one genre: Kim Addonizio, Jim Harrison, and Charles Simic, to name but a few. We hope their examples will inspire you as well to experiment in multiple genres.

Concerning the Structure of this Book

Understanding that the sheer weight of this volume may overwhelm you, we have attempted to group the writings in such a way that you can best make your way through the labyrinth. We balance the need for each new writer to feel *unconstrained* by tradition or "rules" with the need to feel *guided* by tradition and "rules." We hope that you will discover, through digesting this myriad of voices, a wide array of possible paths, goals, and perspectives—all of which will inform your own new writing. While we do not in any way wish to impose on you an order in which you should work through the book, we have organized the writings into five distinct groupings.

While there may be some disagreement over whether, for instance, Donald Hall's work of nonfiction on the subject of fiction should appear in Section One, Section Two, or Section Five, we hope you will agree that the most important point is that it appears at all. We have organized these items into the five groupings in order to simplify the browser's experience, not to pigeonhole the reading. We hope that our garden is so many-pathed and so well-tended that, as soon as you enter, you will want to stay for a very long time, exploring all five genres and their innumerable intersections.

The following five genres are represented in this text:

(1) Creative Nonfiction
(2) Short Fiction
(3) Poetry
(4) Experimental Writing
(5) Writing About Writing

Section One: More Than Just the Truth: Creative Nonfiction

A Garden of Forking Paths begins with "More Than Just the Truth: Creative Nonfiction." Over the past decade or so, the publishing industry has seen a remarkable proliferation of this kind of writing. Within, you will find essays on soccer, death, mothers, and liars. You will find memoirists, scientists, an undertaker, and humorists. You will find, perhaps, that the path of nonfiction is the surest beginning path for any human being, particularly for any writer. You will also find that the path of truth is no less exciting than other, more fanciful, paths, nor any less imaginative.

Creative nonfiction means to us, quite simply, writing done for the purposes of entertaining the reader with the truth. This is not technical writing, though it may be instructional; not political writing, though a political statement may be made; not journalism, though an event may be accurately related. This is writing written clearly and with its clear purpose clearly stated. Forking wildly to and from biography, comedy, autobiography, nature and travel writing, and many more subjects, these essays demonstrate the authors' abilities to convey experiences with feelings warmer than raw reportage. You will read memoirs of family dogs, a meditation on the desert tortoise, and Jim Harrison's passionate defense of eating. We have hoped to present to you convincing evidence that everything in our world that touches us can be the impetus for profound and creative new writing. The one thing all of these items have in common is that they report themselves as the truth. Some use satire, some use praise, some are dour, but all of these works have as their basis the world as we know it.

We hope that you will find evidence in these essays that your own life and your own interests are often the best starting places for your own new and creative writing.

Section Two: Telling Tales: Short Fiction

Having introduced you to the imaginative world that exists simultaneously with everyday life and thought, we invite you next to our Short Fiction section, titled "Telling Tales." Imagine that you take the darkest path in front of you—the path through the garden that never gets sunlight—this is where the imagination reigns supreme! The path of fiction. Unknown. Untrue. Unfathomable. The story that says to us, "I am a story" has admitted from the beginning that it is unpredictable. Fiction is a risk.

In this sampling from the last forty years of fiction, we have chosen risk-taking works from a diverse group of contemporary writers. Comprising work that pulls the reader along unfamiliar paths and in unfamiliar manners, our selection stretches from the Coeur d'Alene Indian reservation to a planet far away in the mind of Philip K. Dick. Bigfoot, the President, and the jilted work-a-day lover are all equal in the eyes of fiction writers and their readers. If you are taking or have taken a course in English, you are probably aware of the concept of a "willful suspension of disbelief" and are, therefore, prepared to enjoy each of these stories for what they are—works of creative and well-written tale-telling.

We hope that, by reading this section, you will come to believe that there is no one way to write rewarding fiction. We also hope, though, that you will find emotional, visionary, and exuberant commonalities in these works—crisp narration, vivid characterization, the element of surprise—which will resonate with you and will move you to pick up your own pen and to participate in the ongoing process of creating new fiction and new paths beyond the hard reality of truth.

Section Three: Making Lines: Poetry

Our poetry section, titled "Making Lines," will show you that there are innumerable ways to write a poem.

We believe that poetry defines itself, that poetry is more of a state of mind than a set of laws. You will not necessarily find sonnets or villanelles, or, for that matter, rhyme schemes or perfect meters. Rather, you will find singular voices voicing singular concerns in such a way that your own singular concerns will seem finally universal. Poetry is the path that appears underneath your feet as you walk ahead. While you may agree with us that there are a few things every poem should have, such as vivid voice, stunning imagery, and exceptional vocabulary, we hope you will also agree with us that no one poem will share these characteristics in the exact same way as another poem. We hope you will also agree with us that each poem in this book is as different as each writer, as unique as each moment that gave rise to each of these poems. The poem arrives to express the inexpressible.

The poems you will find in these pages come from nearly every corner of the writing life and the human dilemma. In reading Thomas Lux's "The Man Inside the Chipmunk Suit," one comes to weep when considering the life of a professional chipmunk-suit-wearer. After reading Beckian Fritz Goldberg's "Being Pharaoh," you will stay up all night with the poet considering her place and yours in the world as we know it. You will find that the spirit of language and the human need to express ourselves through poetry is inexhaustible and immeasurably varied. There is more than enough room in the world of poetry for anyone who cares to enter and take part, and we hope that this collection of poems will help you to take the path of the poem and to make new lines for yourself.

Section Four: Evolving Worlds and Disoriented Words: Experimental Writing

For those who feel confined by formal genres—maybe you are too poetic for poetry, too imaginative for fiction, or too creative for creative nonfiction—we offer you the wide-open world of alternative forms in our penultimate section, "Evolving Worlds and Disoriented Words." Take a path and jump off that path. Take another path and then jump off that one. Jump back to the first path and run it backwards. Do what you want to do, what you *need* to do.

We offer prose poems, flash fiction, false memoirs, dream landscapes, and unmade motion pictures. You will, for instance, jump out of an airplane with Stephen Dixon and live! Perhaps, like comedian Steve Martin, you will be visited late at night by cows on your doorstep. You have no idea what you will experience down any of these paths as you head down them. They may not even be paths at all. They may be scenes stolen from films never made or biographical sketches from a biography never written. Or, maybe, you'll find out, a few pages in, that poet Charles Simic is actually taking you on a prose tour of a Joseph Cornell exhibit.

Is it poetry? Is it prose? Is it a letter? Is it real? We offer no easy answers to the meanings of these works. We give you only this assurance: *you will find them inspiring and invigorating.* These works—call them experimental if you must—will inform your fiction, poetry, and memoirs in wild new ways. They will be short prose pieces and they will be large and unusually numbered meanderings. They will eschew character, form, or plot. They will do none of this, all of this, more of this and less.

Disorienting and evolving, hopefully, the ideas down this path will lead you to places you never thought you would go.

Section Five: The Mapmaker's Unmade Map: Writing About Writing

So, you've taken many paths. You've explored many options. You've unthought ideas you once thought you thought. Where do you go now? Now that you've learned enough to question everything you thought you knew, you might begin to wonder where all this started in the first place. Our garden ends with a section devoted to essays about the practice of writing (and the practice of reading), titled "The Mapmaker's Unmade Map," and you will find that, essentially, we end at the beginning. This section contains a wealth of essays meant both to illuminate the creative processes of others and to inspire you to engage in explorating your own writing process.

You'll consider the decision each writer makes to undertake the act of writing. You'll learn how to let an unruly prose poem happen. The writer is unusually lucky in that he or she can use his or her skills to investigate, evaluate, and improve those skills. Since writing is a record of thought, the ability to record thought about writing has enabled our thinking about writing to become very complex as well as to remain very simple. Simply, we have agreed that there are as many ways to write as there are writers willing to write.

We hope this section will provide you with a number of different ideas about writing which you can either accept or reject but, in some way, you will be moved to respond to them. These are ideas about how to make yourself write, why you should make yourself write, and what you should do if you cannot make yourself write. You are the mapmaker in the middle of unmapped woods. Writing is both your lure into the darkness and your light out of it.

We consider all writing to be creative and have found that writers in all fields have provided valuable insights into process and craft: for instance, you will learn here that when you feel that you cannot write, it may help you to write about how you feel about being unable to write.

The Toolbox

While we are certain that the writings in this garden of forking paths will speak to you for themselves, we have also incorporated a three-piece toolbox for each genre to help you focus your long journey through our many pages: Discussions of the Genres, Quintessentials, and Catalysts.

Discussions of the Genres

We have included brief introductory essays to each section in which we discuss the varied reasons for a writer coming to decide that this genre might be the most appropriate path toward articulating what he or she hopes to say. You will not find instruction on rhyme schemes, plotting, research, or character development here. Rather, you will find a lively discussion on the choices you will face as you head down the labyrinthine path of your choice. Should you take the path into darkness, the path that seems the wildest, the path not yet made? Making no claims for final authority on these subjects, we simply hope that these essays will serve as discussion points, perhaps "food for thought" in classroom or workshop situations or sources of private rumination at home or on the blank page before you.

Quintessentials

We include at the beginning of each section a Quintessential, a single work which we consider exemplary in illustrating the capacity of the genre. For each of these, we have written a brief, expository essay. Meant only as an example of how you could begin discussing whatever path you chose from the garden, we show you the product of our own written thought which may be nothing like your own. We hope these discussions will offer you a glimpse into what we consider to be the creative writer's creative reading process: the process by which we examine a written work and attempt to determine what there is to be determined of it. We hasten to add that any of the works included in this book could have been deemed *quintessential* by another reader.

These pieces have touched us in some way, and we hope they will also touch you. These are, in no way, however, the *best* pieces in this book. We would challenge any notion that one piece of writing here is better than any other; we hope that we have presented you with a wide range of excellent writing. These are the fruits of a single path each. They represent choices made and opportunities realized, but they should not be considered goals. They are inspirational examples, nothing more and nothing less.

We have chosen Thomas Lynch's "The Undertaking" to introduce our first section. A brilliant combination of first-person memoir and objective reporting, "The Undertaking" exemplifies the capacity of creative writing to both entertain and educate its audience with the dual truth of the writer's experience and of his emotional response to the experience.

In Melissa Pritchard's "A Private Landscape," we have found what we consider to be an ideal path for short fiction to take. In a family similar to many of our own, we find enacted the unspoken struggles of parent and child rendered passionately and with great sensitivity.

If the primary subjects of all great poetry are love and death, then there is no poem more quintessential in describing the capacity of poetry for feeling and evocation than Charles Wright's elegy for his fellow Southern poet Larry Levis. As if we are standing in Wright's shoes, we feel the loss of a beloved friend as if it were our own. And, in a way, his loss will become our own.

Similarly, in Section Four, when Carolyn Forché sits across from the inhumanly violent South American colonel in "The Colonel," we sit down with her. As poetry fails her and prose fails her, so poetry, prose, and narrative fail us when we are in the presence of her witnessing. "There is no other way to say it," she says.

Finally, at the end of the farthest and most winding path, we find ourselves ready to write about writing and what do we find? We find Patricia Hampl's "Memory and Imagination," which will challenge everything we think we know and have been bored by in the memoir. As with all of our quintessential examples, "Memory and Imagination" is more than just the sum of its parts.

CATALYSTS

Finally, we offer Catalysts, a set of three exercises at the end of each genre, designed not to dictate a form, but to suggest some possible approaches. These Catalysts are not necessarily intended to apply exclusively to one genre or another, although the suggested exercises in each genre have been created with that genre in mind.

Each Catalyst has two parts:

(1) a discussion of the theory behind the exercise
(2) an explanation of the exercise itself

Our intention has been to encourage you to think on your own about ways to trick out new writing and to get you started while you search for your own method or methods.

The Catalysts are suggestions, not prescriptions. We will send you out to sit on a park bench or to search the depths of your mind. We will do what we feel we have to do to prepare you to create your own imaginative work. The Catalysts hope not only to push you down the forking path but also to hold your arm as you lunge forward.

Some Final Comments

We hope that none of these tools from this toolbox will detract from your personal engagement with the *primary* sources included here. Instead, we hope these writings can inspire you to look at these works from a number of different perspectives. Ultimately, we hope that your creative process will lead you to brave new gardens in your own memory and in your own imagination.

There, we are certain that you will find your own paths through the limitless and sometimes labyrinthine world of creative writing.

Beth Anstandig and Eric Killough

More than Just the Truth:
Creative Nonfiction

I | *Discussion of the Genre*

This is who I am and this is my life. Our forking paths begin beneath our feet. For some writers, truth writing is an opportunity to gain insight and clarity where there was confusion before or maybe just a hunch. The act of writing itself is an occasion to learn, to understand better the self and the world it occupies. Every writer arrives at the blank page with an out-of-the-ordinary life experience. Each writer wishes to record, share, and subsequently enlighten his or her reader with this distinctive perspective on exceptional subjects.

The literary world has, for some time now, witnessed an increasing interest in creative nonfiction, particularly in the memoir. As readers, we are looking for some kind of truth and we are hoping that someone else's kind of truth will help us to understand our own. We are hoping that we can learn from someone else's mistakes and successes. The finest literary efforts at public self-exploration have more or less the same authentic intentions: to offer vividly a glimpse into an individual's human experience, to uncover new truths about the human condition as a whole, and to, thereby, better know what it means to be alive.

Of the abundance of writers publishing books of creative essays, interestingly, many have well-established reputations in other genres as well: for example, poet and novelist Jim Harrison, comedian Dave Barry, the versatile Ursula K. Le Guin, and playwright Tony Kushner. Because creative nonfiction has virtually no limitations, writers who are versed in other, more clearly defined forms of writing—such as short fiction or poetry or science writing—seem to find great liberty in experimenting with a genre which is both new to the writer and new to itself. With this freedom come some interesting challenges.

In this ever-changing and evolving written world of intersecting paths, we expect our contemporary writers to unearth a kind of originality that both shocks us and reminds us of the things we keep in common. Our daily experiences are filled with startling imagery and stimuli. Our newspapers are covered with disturbing headlines and graphic color photos. We turn on our computers and are bombarded with pop-up advertisements: words, images, sounds. And, of course, our televisions are always on.

For a written work to make an impression on our overstimulated brains, it must astonish and amaze. However, we commonly find recirculations of subject matter, character type, and language in our nonfiction literature: family, society, sports. As writers, and as humans, we eventually return to what we know—sometimes to uncover things we have forgotten, other times to find a new way of understanding that which we already know.

To communicate creatively a nonfiction in an engaging manner, you must find an imaginative way of communicating *your* experience, *your* life: *personal essay or narrative, travel essay, humor essay, social commentary,* or *memoir.* Strangely enough, these terms, while informative and sometimes accurate, are essentially useless in identifying one piece of writing from the next. We consider a piece of writing "creative nonfiction" if it is written in more or less traditional prose, if it attempts to embody a "true" or "real" experience, and if it is perhaps written in first person or represents the author's point of view.

Essentially, the subject matter is life as we are living it. Everything around us—the newspapers, televisions, the trees, your friends, family, and neighbors—can be the basis for exemplary nonfiction. The "creative" aspect of the genre is the writer's to provide. With vivid language, with surprising insight, and with openness to new understanding, the writer takes the raw elements of his or her factual life and "creates" a rich new landscape, a lush new garden.

We ask our subject matter to teach us something, and the act of writing is the act of discovering what's being taught. We hope to learn that which we do not yet know. We embrace our own mysteries. We rely on intuition. We ask our instincts to lead us.

In this section, you will find writers following their instincts down unusual paths. You will find the humor and social commentary of writers like David Sedaris and Sarah Vowell as they entertain and enlighten. You will read about Andre Dubus' experience of living in a wheelchair and Nancy Mairs' decision to refer to herself as "crippled." You will sit down with poet Donald Hall and consider the purposes of fiction. And you will find that the creative nonfiction writer often uses several elements from the many variations of the genre. The humor writer utilizes narrative. The travel essayist relies on the social perspective. And the memoirist who explores the sometimes painful moments of childhood finds emotional relief in employing humor.

This is a versatile and unpredictable genre, as versatile and unpredictable as reality itself. With each attempt at creative nonfiction, the definition experiences an evolution. As a reader and writer of this genre, you are part of the development of a new tradition.

Here is a great place to begin.

II | A Quintessential: "The Undertaking"

by Thomas Lynch

Every year I bury a couple hundred of my townspeople. Another two or three dozen I take to the crematory to be burned. I sell caskets, burial vaults, and urns for the ashes. I have a sideline in headstones and monuments. I do flowers on commission.

Apart from the tangibles, I sell the use of my building: eleven thousand square feet, furnished and fixtured with an abundance of pastel and chair rail and crown moldings. The whole lash-up is mortgaged and remortgaged well into the next century. My rolling stock includes a hearse, two Fleetwoods, and a minivan with darkened windows our pricelist calls a service vehicle and everyone in town calls the Dead Wagon.

I used to use the *unit pricing method*—the old package deal. It meant that you had only one number to look at. It was a large number. Now everything is itemized. It's the law. So now there is a long list of items and numbers and italicized disclaimers, something like a menu or the Sears Roebuck Wish Book, and sometimes the federally-mandated options begin to look like cruise control or rear-window defrost. I wear black most of the time, to keep folks in mind of the fact we're not talking Buicks here. At the bottom of the list there is still a large number.

In a good year the gross is close to a million, five percent of which we hope to call profit. I am the only undertaker in this town. I have a corner on the market.

The market, such as it is, is figured on what is called *the crude death rate*—the number of deaths every year out of every thousand persons.

Here is how it works.

Imagine a large room into which you coax one thousand people. You slam the doors in January, leaving them plenty of food and drink, color TVs, magazines, and condoms. Your sample should have an age distribution heavy on baby boomers and their children—1.2 children per boomer. Every seventh adult is an old-timer, who, if he or she wasn't in this big room, would probably be in Florida or Arizona or a nursing home. You get the idea. The group will include fifteen lawyers, one faith healer, three dozen real-estate agents, a video technician, several licensed counselors, and a Tupperware distributor. The rest will be between jobs, middle managers, ne'er-do-wells, or retired.

Now for the magic part—come late December when you throw open the doors, only 991.6, give or take, will shuffle out upright. Two hundred and sixty will now be selling Tupperware. The other 8.4 have become the crude death rate.

Here's another stat.

Of the 8.4 corpses, two-thirds will have been old-timers, five percent will be children, and the rest (slightly less than 2.5 corpses) will be boomers—realtors and attorneys likely—one of whom was, no doubt, elected to public office during the year. What's more, three will have died of cerebral-vascular or coronary difficulties, two of cancer, one each of vehicular mayhem, diabetes, and domestic violence. The spare change will be by act of God or suicide—most likely the faith healer.

The figure most often and most conspicuously missing from the insurance charts and demographics is the one I call The Big One, which refers to the number of people out of every hundred born who will die. Over the long haul, The Big One hovers right around . . . well, dead nuts on one hundred percent. If this were on the charts, they'd call it *death expectancy* and no one would buy futures of any kind. But it is a useful number and has its lessons. Maybe you will want to figure out what to do with your life. Maybe it will make you feel a certain kinship with the rest of us. Maybe it will make you hysterical. Whatever the implications of a one hundred percent death expectancy, you can calculate how big a town this is and why it produces for me a steady if unpredictable labor.

They die around the clock here, without apparent preference for a day of the week, month of the year; there is no clear favorite in the way of season. Nor does the alignment of the stars, fullness of moon, or liturgical calendar have very much to do with it. The whereabouts are neither here nor there. They go off upright or horizontally in Chevrolets and nursing homes, in bathtubs, on the interstates, in ERs, ORs, BMWs. And while it may be that we assign more equipment or more importance to deaths that create themselves in places marked by initials—ICU being somehow better than Greenbriar Convalescent Home—it is also true that the dead don't care. In this way, the dead I bury and burn are like the dead before them, for whom time and space have become mortally unimportant. This loss of interest is, in fact, one of the first sure signs that something serious is about to happen. The next thing is they quit breathing. At this point, to be sure, a *gunshot wound to the chest* or *shock and trauma* will get more ink than a CVA or ASHD, but no cause of death is any less permanent than the other. Any one will do. The dead don't care.

Nor does *who* much matter, either. To say, "I'm OK, you're OK, and by the way, he's dead!" is, for the living, a kind of comfort.

It is why we drag rivers and comb plane wrecks and bomb sites.

It is why MIA is more painful than DOA.

It is why we have open caskets and all read the obits.

Knowing is better than not knowing, and knowing it is you is terrifically better than knowing it is me. Because once I'm the dead guy, whether you're OK or he's OK won't much interest me. You can all go bag your asses, because the dead don't care.

Of course, the living, bound by their adverbs and their actuarials, still do. Now, there is the difference and why I'm in business. The living are careful and oftentimes caring. The dead are careless, or maybe it's care-less. Either way, they don't care. These are unremarkable and verifiable truths.

My former mother-in-law, herself an unremarkable and verifiable truth, was always fond of holding forth with Cagneyesque bravado—to wit: "When I'm dead, just throw me in a box and throw me in a hole." But whenever I would remind her that we did substantially that with everyone, the woman would grow sullen and a little cranky.

Later, over meatloaf and green beans, she would invariably give out with: "When I'm dead just cremate me and scatter the ashes."

My former mother-in-law was trying to make carelessness sound like fearlessness. The kids would stop eating and look at each other. The kids' mother would plead, "Oh Mom, don't talk like that." I'd take out my lighter and begin to play with it.

In the same way, the priest that married me to this woman's daughter—a man who loved golf and gold ciboria and vestments made of Irish linen; a man who drove a great black sedan with a wine-red interior and who always had his eye on the cardinal's job—this same fellow, leaving the cemetery one day, felt called upon to instruct me thus: "No bronze coffin for me. No sir! No orchids or roses or limousines. The plain pine box is the one I want, a quiet Low Mass and the pauper's grave. No pomp and circumstance."

He wanted, he explained, to be an example of simplicity, of prudence, of piety and austerity—all priestly and, apparently, Christian virtues. When I told him that he needn't wait, that he could begin his ministry of good example even today, that he could quit the country club and do his hacking at the public links and trade his brougham for a used Chevette; that free of his Florsheims and cashmeres and prime ribs, free of his bingo nights and building funds, he could become, for Christ's sake, the very incarnation of Francis himself, or Anthony of Padua; when I said, in fact, that I would be willing to assist him in this, that I would gladly distribute his savings and credit cards among the worthy poor of the parish, and that I would, when the sad duty called, bury him for free in the manner he would have, by then, become accustomed to; when I told your man these things, he said nothing at all, but turned his wild eye on me in the way that the cleric must have looked on Sweeney years ago, before he cursed him, irreversibly, into a bird.

What I was trying to tell the fellow was, of course, that being a dead saint is no more worthwhile than being a dead philodendron or a dead angelfish. Living is the rub, and always has been. Living saints still feel the flames and stigmata of this vale of tears, the ache of chastity and the pangs of conscience. Once dead, they let their relics do the legwork, because, as I was trying to tell this priest, the dead don't care.

Only the living care.

And I am sorry to be repeating myself, but this is the central fact of my business—that there is nothing, once you are dead, that can be done *to you* or *for you* or *with you* or *about you* that will do you any good or any harm; that any damage or decency we do accrues to the living, to whom your death happens, if it really happens to anyone. The living have to live with it. You don't. Theirs is the grief or gladness your death brings. Theirs is the loss or gain of it. Theirs is the pain and the pleasure of memory. Theirs is the invoice for services rendered and theirs is the check in the mail for its payment.

And there is the truth, abundantly self-evident, that seems, now that I think of it, the one most elusive to the old in-laws, the parish priest, and to perfect strangers who are forever accosting me in barber-shops and cocktail parties and parent-teacher conferences, hell-bent or duty bound to let me in on what it is they want done with them when they are dead.

Give it a rest is the thing I say.

Once you are dead, put your feet up, call it a day, and let the husband or the missus or the kids or a sibling decide whether you are to be buried or burned or blown out of a cannon or left to dry out in a ditch somewhere. It's not your day to watch it, because the dead don't care.

Another reason people are always rehearsing their obsequies with me has to do with the fear of death that anyone in their right mind has. It is healthy. It keeps us from playing in traffic. I say it's a thing we should pass on to the kids.

There is a belief—widespread among the women I've dated, local Rotarians, and friends of my children—that I, being the undertaker here, have some irregular fascination with, special interest in, inside information about, even attachment to, *the dead*. They assume, these people, some perhaps for defensible reasons, that I want their bodies.

It is an interesting concept.

But here is the truth.

Being dead is one—the worst, the last—but only one in a series of calamities that afflicts our own and several other species. The list may include, but is not limited to, gingivitis, bowel obstruction, contested divorce, tax audit, spiritual vexation, cash flow problems, political upheaval, and on and on and on some more. There is no shortage of misery. And I am no more attracted to the dead than the dentist is to your bad gums, the doctor to your rotten innards, or the accountant to your sloppy expense records. I have no more stomach for misery than the banker or the lawyer, the pastor or the politico—because misery is careless and is everywhere. Misery is the bad check, the ex-spouse, the mob in the street, and the IRS—who, like the dead, feel nothing and, like the dead, *don't care*.

Which is not to say that the dead do not matter.

They do. They do. Of course they do.

Last Monday morning Milo Hornsby died. Mrs. Hornsby called at 2 A.M. to say that Milo had *expired* and would I take care of it, as if his condition were like any other that could be renewed or somehow improved upon. At 2 A.M., yanked from my REM sleep, I am thinking, put a quarter into Milo and call me in the morning. But Milo is dead. In a moment, in a twinkling, Milo has slipped irretrievably out of our reach, beyond Mrs. Hornsby and the children, beyond the women at the laundromat he owned, beyond his comrades at the Legion Hall, the Grand Master of the Masonic Lodge, his pastor at First Baptist, beyond the mailman, zoning board, town council, and Chamber of Commerce; beyond us all, and any treachery or any kindness we had in mind for him.

Milo is dead.

X's on his eyes, lights out, curtains.

Helpless, harmless.

Milo's dead.

Which is why I do not haul to my senses, coffee and quick shave, Homburg and great coat, warm up the Dead Wagon, and make for the freeway in the early o'clock for Milo's sake. Milo doesn't have any sake anymore. I go for her—for she who has become, in the same moment and the same twinkling, like water to ice, the Widow Hornsby. I go for her—because she still can cry and care and pray and pay my bill.

The hospital that Milo died in is state-of-the-art. There are signs on every door declaring a part or a process or bodily function. I like to think that, taken together, the words would add up to The Human Condition, but they never do. What's left of Milo, the remains, are in the basement, between SHIPPING & RECEIVING and LAUNDRY ROOM. Milo would like that if he were still liking things. Milo's room is called PATHOLOGY.

The medical-technical parlance of death emphasizes disorder.

We are forever dying of failures, of anomalies, of insufficiencies, of dysfunctions, arrests, accidents. These are either chronic or acute. The language of death certificates—Milo's says "Cardiopulmonary Failure"—is like the language of weakness. Likewise, Mrs. Hornsby, in her grief, will be said to be breaking down or falling apart or going to pieces, as if there were something structurally awry with her. It is as if death and grief were not part of The Order of Things, as if Milo's failure and his widow's weeping were, or ought to be, sources of embarrassment. "Doing well" for Mrs. Hornsby would mean that she is bearing up, weathering the storm, or being strong for the children. We have willing pharmacists to help her with this. Of course, for Milo, doing well would mean he was back upstairs, holding his own, keeping the meters and monitors bleeping.

But Milo is downstairs, between SHIPPING & RECEIVING and LAUNDRY ROOM, in a stainless-steel drawer, wrapped in white plastic top to toe, and—because of his small head, wide shoulders, ponderous belly, and skinny legs, and the trailing white binding cord from his ankles and toe tag—he looks, for all the world, like a larger than life-size sperm.

I sign for him and get him out of there. At some level, I am still thinking Milo gives a shit, which by now, of course, we all know he doesn't—because the dead don't care.

Back at the funeral home, upstairs in the embalming room, behind a door marked PRIVATE, Milo Hornsby is floating on a porcelain table under florescent lights. Unwrapped, outstretched, Milo is beginning to look a little more like himself—eyes wide open, mouth agape, returning to our gravity. I shave him, close his eyes, his mouth. We call this *setting the features*. These are the features—eyes and mouth—that will never look the way they would have looked in life when they were always opening, closing, focusing, signaling, telling us something. In death, what they tell us is that they will not be doing anything anymore. The last detail to be managed is Milo's hands—one folded over the other, over the umbilicus, in an attitude of ease, of repose, of retirement.

They will not be doing anything anymore, either.

I wash his hands before positioning them.

When my wife moved out some years ago, the children stayed here, as did the dirty laundry. It was big news in a small town. There was the gossip and the goodwill that places like this are famous for. And while there was plenty of talk, no one knew exactly what to say to me. They felt helpless, I suppose. So they brought casseroles and beef stews, took the kids out to the movies or canoeing, brought their younger sisters around to visit me. What Milo did was send his laundry van around twice a week for two months, until I found a housekeeper. Milo would pick up five loads in the morning and return them by lunchtime, fresh and folded. I never asked him to do this. I hardly knew him. I had never been in his home or his laundromat. His wife had never known my wife. His children were too old to play with my children.

After my housekeeper was installed, I went to thank Milo and pay the bill. The invoices detailed the number of loads, the washers and the dryers, detergent, bleaches, fabric softeners. I think the total came to sixty dollars. When I asked Milo what the charges were for pick-up and delivery, for stacking and folding and sorting by size, for saving my life and the lives of my children, for keeping us in clean clothes and towels and bed linen, "Never mind that" is what Milo said. "One hand washes the other."

I place Milo's right hand over his left hand, then try the other way. Then back again. Then I decide that it doesn't matter. One hand washes the other either way.

The embalming takes me about two hours.

It is daylight by the time I am done.

Every Monday morning, Ernest Fuller comes to my office. He was damaged in some profound way in Korea. The details of his damage are unknown to the locals. Ernest Fuller has no limp or anything missing so everyone thinks it was something he saw in Korea that left him a little simple, occasionally perplexed, the type to draw rein abruptly in his day-long walks, to consider the meaning of litter, pausing over bottle caps and gum wrappers. Ernest Fuller has a nervous smile and a deadfish handshake. He wears a baseball cap and thick eyeglasses. Every Sunday night Ernest goes to the supermarket and buys up the tabloids at the checkout stands with headlines that usually involve Siamese twins or movie stars or UFOs. Ernest is a speed reader and a math whiz but because of his damage, he has never held a job and never applied for one. Every Monday morning, Ernest brings me clippings of stories under headlines like: 601 LB MAN FALLS THRU COFFIN—A GRAVE SITUATION or EMBALMER FOR THE STARS SAYS ELVIS IS FOREVER. The Monday morning Milo Hornsby died, Ernest's clipping had to do with an urn full of ashes, somewhere in East Anglia, that made grunting and groaning noises, that whistled sometimes, and that was expected to begin talking. Certain scientists in England could make no sense of it. They had run several tests. The ashes' widow, however, left with nine children and no estate, is convinced that her dearly beloved and greatly reduced husband is trying to give her winning numbers for the lottery. "Jacky would never leave us without good prospects," she says. "He loved his family more than anything." There is a picture of the two of them, the widow and the urn, the living and the dead, flesh and bronze, the Victrola and the Victrola's dog. She has her ear cocked, waiting.

We are always waiting. Waiting for some good word or the winning numbers. Waiting for a sign or wonder, some signal from our dear dead that the dead still care. We are gladdened when they do outstanding things, when they arise from their graves or fall through their caskets or speak to us in our waking dreams. It pleases us no end, as if the dead still cared, had agendas, were yet alive.

But the sad and well-known fact of the matter is that most of us will stay in our caskets and be dead a long time, and that our urns and graves will never make a sound. Our reason and requiems, our headstones or High Masses, will neither get us in nor keep us out of heaven. The meaning of our lives, and the memories of them, belong to the living, just as our funerals do. Whatever being the dead have now, they have by the living's faith alone.

We heat graves here for winter burials, as a kind of foreplay before digging in, to loosen the frost's hold on the ground before the sexton and his backhoe do the opening. We buried Milo in the ground on Wednesday. The mercy is that what we buried there, in an oak casket, just under the frost line, had ceased to be Milo. Milo had become the idea of himself, a permanent fixture of the third person and past tense, his widow's loss of appetite and trouble sleeping, the absence in places where we look for him, our habits of him breaking, our phantom limb, our one hand washing the other.

Discussion of a Quintessential

"The Undertaking"
by Thomas Lynch

This title essay of Thomas Lynch's book of "life studies," *The Undertaking*, is a particularly fine example of creative nonfiction. Lynch has a bountiful box of writing tools and he is deliberate and skillful in selecting from it. He utilizes the honesty of a direct but welcoming tone, a fascinating selection of facts and details, interesting narratives, and an analytical perspective on an unfamiliar topic. Even more strikingly, he confronts an authentic human dilemma—the relationship between the living and the dead—and he does so with emotional authenticity and the necessary reprieve of humor.

Thomas Lynch, an accomplished poet, has also written two books of essays, or "life studies" as he refers to his prose, and he serves as a consultant on the HBO television series *Six Feet Under*. As readers, we are already inclined to learn about others' lives. But Lynch offers us another enticing angle: he wants to tell us about others' deaths. Thomas Lynch is not only a poet and essayist, he is also an undertaker.

Lynch approaches essay writing with a built-in advantage: his topic is strikingly compelling. He is an expert on an unusual subject. Only an undertaker could authentically write about an undertaker's work. Lynch successfully isolates what is unique about his human experience and explores that experience on the page. Consequently, we learn from what he and few others know.

"Every year," he begins, "I bury a couple hundred of my townspeople. . . . I sell caskets, burial vaults, and urns for the ashes. . . . I do flowers on commission." While these are all "activities" involving the dead, Lynch does not handle them, as one might presume, with kid gloves. Instead, he demonstrates that his is an occupation like any other. He writes, "I am no more attracted to the dead than the dentist is to your bad gums, the doctor to your rotten innards, or the accountant to your sloppy expense records."

We, as readers, are allowed a rare glimpse into how we as a culture treat our dead: the very practice of preparing our bodies, our rituals, and our burials. We learn about crude death rates; we gather the vocabulary of undertaking like "setting the features" of a dead person's face; we become familiar with the "Dead Wagon" or Lynch's hearse. But, of course, Lynch's real gift to his readers is not simply his reportage of undertaking duties. His real gift is his articulation of his memorable and engaging voice. He may be an expert offering compelling details about an unusual subject, but we still have to trust him, to believe him.

What is most remarkable about Lynch's prose is his keen sense of this voice. It is with his familiar and comforting tone that he earns the trust of his readership. He uses phrases such as, "Here is how it works," and "Now for the magic part," and "Now that I think of it," and "But here is the truth," all of which exemplify his ability to carry a conversational tenor that engages the reader. He isn't afraid to expose his humanness in his writing. In fact, its exposure seems to be one of his primary concerns.

"The Undertaking" is an essay with a clear purpose, an intended outcome, and an intuited result. Lynch wishes to communicate an idea that he is still in the process of understanding; his thesis is "The dead don't care."

Acknowledging that this concept is difficult to accept, he repeats the thesis many times throughout the essay. He is working to internalize it. Trying to learn from his own experience, he examines his own knowledge of death, and, in doing so, examines his own writing process. We, as readers, become part of his development, his progress, his discovery.

He writes, "Once you are dead, put your feet up, call it a day, and let the husband or the missus or the kids or a sibling decide whether you are to be buried or burned or blown out of a cannon or left to dry out in a ditch somewhere." Ah, yes, he is discussing what to do with a person once he or she is dead, but he is also asking us to find lightness where otherwise we would not. It is as if he, an expert at death, knows that smiling or laughing will help us truly to realize and accept the difficult truths about life. He concludes, "The meaning of our lives, and the memories of them, belong to the living, just as our funerals do."

Essay writing, like all creative writing, requires a careful balance of three crucial elements: the emotional, the artistic, and the intellectual. "The Undertaking" is a sound example of how one writer comfortably carries the weight of these characteristics and creates a successful piece of literature. With the use of narrative and voice, Lynch portrays an authentic emotional self. With impeccably crafted images and stunning language, he maintains artistic integrity. Finally, he presents an intellectual component as he asks us to consider the quandary of living and dying.

III | *Reading Selections*

MITCH ALBOM

The Ninth Tuesday: We Talk About How Love Goes On

The leaves had begun to change color, turning the ride through West Newton into a portrait of gold and rust. Back in Detroit, the labor war had stagnated, with each side accusing the other of failing to communicate. The stories on the TV news were just as depressing. In rural Kentucky, three men threw pieces of a tombstone off a bridge, smashing the windshield of a passing car, killing a teenage girl who was traveling with her family on a religious pilgrimage. In California, the O. J. Simpson trial was heading toward a conclusion, and the whole country seemed to be obsessed. Even in airports, there were hanging TV sets tuned to CNN so that you could get an O. J. update as you made your way to a gate.

I had tried calling my brother in Spain several times. I left messages saying that I really wanted to talk to him, that I had been doing a lot of thinking about us. A few weeks later, I got back a short message saying everything was okay, but he was sorry, he really didn't feel like talking about being sick.

For my old professor, it was not the talk of being sick but the being sick itself that was sinking him. Since my last visit, a nurse had inserted a catheter into his penis, which drew the urine out through a tube and into a bag that sat at the foot of his chair. His legs needed constant tending (he could still feel pain, even though he could not move them, another one of ALS's cruel little ironies), and unless his feet dangled just the right number of inches off the foam pads, it felt as if someone were poking him with a fork. In the middle of conversations, Morrie would have to ask visitors to lift his foot and move it just an inch, or to adjust his head so that it fit more easily into the palm of the colored pillows. Can you imagine being unable to move your own head?

With each visit, Morrie seemed to be melting into his chair, his spine taking on its shape. Still, every morning he insisted on being lifted from his bed and wheeled to his study, deposited there among his books and papers and the hibiscus plant on the windowsill. In typical fashion, he found something philosophical in this.

"I sum it up in my newest aphorism," he said.

Let me hear it.

"When you're in bed, you're dead."

He smiled. Only Morrie could smile at something like that.

He had been getting calls from the "Nightline" people and from Ted Koppel himself.

"They want to come and do another show with me," he said. "But they say they want to wait."

Until what? You're on your last breath?

"Maybe. Anyhow, I'm not so far away."

Don't say that.

"I'm sorry."

That bugs me, that they want to wait until you wither.

"It bugs you because you look out for me."

He smiled. "Mitch, maybe they are using me for a little drama. That's okay. Maybe I'm using them, too. They help me get my message to millions of people. I couldn't do that without them, right? So it's a compromise."

He coughed, which turned into a long-drawn-out gargle, ending with another glob into a crushed tissue.

"Anyhow," Morrie said, "I told them they better not wait too long, because my voice won't be there. Once this thing hits my lungs, talking may become impossible. I can't speak for too long without needing a rest now. I have already canceled a lot of the people who want to see me. Mitch, there are so many. But I'm too fatigued. If I can't give them the right attention, I can't help them."

I looked at the tape recorder, feeling guilty, as if I were stealing what was left of his precious speaking time. "Should we skip it?" I asked. "Will it make you too tired?"

Morrie shut his eyes and shook his head. He seemed to be waiting for some silent pain to pass. "No," he finally said. "You and I have to go on."

"This is our last thesis together, you know."

Our last thesis.

"We want to get it right."

I thought about our first thesis together, in college. It was Morrie's idea, of course. He told me I was good enough to write an honors project—something I had never considered.

Now here we were, doing the same thing once more. Starting with an idea. Dying man talks to living man, tells him what he should know. This time, I was in less of a hurry to finish.

"Someone asked me an interesting question yesterday," Morrie said now, looking over my shoulder at the wallhanging behind me, a quilt of hopeful messages that friends had stitched for him on his seventieth birthday. Each patch on the quilt had a different message: STAY THE COURSE, THE BEST IS YET TO BE, MORRIE—ALWAYS NO.1 IN MENTAL HEALTH!

What was the question? I asked.

"If I worried about being forgotten after I died?"

Well? Do you?

"I don't think I will be. I've got so many people who have been involved with me in close, intimate ways. And love is how you stay alive, even after you are gone."

Sounds like a song lyric—"love is how you stay alive."

Morrie chuckled. "Maybe. But, Mitch, all this talk that we're doing? Do you ever hear my voice sometimes when you're back home? When you're all alone? Maybe on the plane? Maybe in your car?"

Yes, I admitted.

"Then you will not forget me after I'm gone. Think of my voice and I'll be there."

Think of your voice.

"And if you want to cry a little, it's okay."

Morrie. He had wanted to make me cry since I was a freshman. "One of these days, I'm gonna get to you," he would say.

Yeah, yeah, I would answer.

"I decided what I wanted on my tombstone," he said.

I don't want to hear about tombstones.

"Why? They make you nervous?"

I shrugged.

"We can forget it."

No, go ahead. What did you decide?

Morrie popped his lips. "I was thinking of this: A Teacher to the Last."

He waited while I absorbed it.

A Teacher to the Last.

"Good?" he said.

Yes, I said. Very good.

I came to love the way Morrie lit up when I entered the room. He did this for many people, I know, but it was his special talent to make each visitor feel that the smile was unique.

"Ahhhh, it's my buddy," he would say when he saw me, in that foggy, high-pitched voice. And it didn't stop with the greeting. When Morrie was with you, he was really with you. He looked you straight in the eye, and he listened as if you were the only person in the world. How much better would people get along if their first encounter each day were like this—instead of a grumble from a waitress or a bus driver or a boss?

"I believe in being fully present," Morrie said. "That means you should be *with* the person you're with. When I'm talking to you now, Mitch, I try to keep focused only on what is going on between us. I am not thinking about something we said last week. I am not thinking of what's coming up this Friday. I am not thinking about doing another Koppel show, or about what medications I'm taking.

"I am talking to you. I am thinking about you."

I remembered how he used to teach this idea in the Group Process class back at Brandeis. I had scoffed back then, thinking this was hardly a lesson plan for a university course. Learning to pay attention? How important could that be? I now know it is more important than almost everything they taught us in college.

Morrie motioned for my hand, and as I gave it to him, I felt a surge of guilt. Here was a man who, if he wanted, could spend every waking moment in self-pity, feeling his body for decay, counting his breaths. So many people with far smaller problems are so self-absorbed, their eyes glaze over if you speak for more than thirty seconds. They already have something else in mind—a friend to call, a fax to send, a lover they're daydreaming about. They only snap back to full attention when you finish talking, at which point they say "Uh-huh" or "Yeah, really" and fake their way back to the moment.

"Part of the problem, Mitch, is that everyone is in such a hurry," Morrie said. "People haven't found meaning in their lives, so they're running all the time look-ing for it. They think the next car, the next house, the next job. Then they find those things are empty, too, and they keep running."

Once you start running, I said, it's hard to slow yourself down.

"Not so hard," he said, shaking his head. "Do you know what I do? When someone wants to get ahead of me in traffic—when I used to be able to drive— I would raise my hand . . ."

He tried to do this now, but the hand lifted weakly, only six inches.

". . . I would raise my hand, as if I was going to make a negative gesture, and then I would wave and smile. Instead of giving them the finger, you let them go, and you smile.

"You know what? A lot of times they smiled back.

"The truth is, I don't have to be in that much of a hurry with my car. I would rather put my energies into people."

He did this better than anyone I'd ever known. Those who sat with him saw his eyes go moist when they spoke about something horrible, or crinkle in delight when they told him a really bad joke. He was always ready to openly display the emotion so often missing from my baby boomer generation. We are great at small talk: "What do you do?" "Where do you live?" But *really* listening to someone— without trying to sell them something, pick them up, recruit them, or get some kind of status in return—how often do we get this anymore? I believe many visitors in the last few months of Morrie's life were drawn not because of the attention they wanted to pay to him but because of the attention he paid *to them*. Despite his personal pain and decay, this little old man listened the way they always wanted someone to listen.

I told him he was the father everyone wishes they had.

"Well," he said, closing his eyes, "I have some experience in that area . . ."

The last time Morrie saw his own father was in a city morgue. Charlie Schwartz was a quiet man who liked to read his newspaper, alone, under a streetlamp on Tremont Avenue in the Bronx. Every night, when Morrie was little, Charlie would go for a walk after dinner. He was a small Russian man, with a ruddy complexion and a full head of grayish hair. Morrie and his brother, David, would look out the window and see him leaning against the lamppost, and Morrie wished he would come inside and talk to them, but he rarely did. Nor did he tuck them in, nor kiss them good-night.

Morrie always swore he would do these things for his own children if he ever had any. And years later, when he had them, he did.

Meanwhile, as Morrie raised his own children, Charlie was still living in the Bronx. He still took that walk. He still read the paper. One night, he went outside after dinner. A few blocks from home, he was accosted by two robbers.

"Give us your money," one said, pulling a gun.

Frightened, Charlie threw down his wallet and began to run. He ran through the streets, and kept running until he reached the steps of a relative's house, where he collapsed on the porch.

Heart attack.

He died that night.

Morrie was called to identify the body. He flew to New York and went to the morgue. He was taken downstairs, to the cold room where the corpses were kept.

"Is this your father?" the attendant asked.

Morrie looked at the body behind the glass, the body of the man who had scolded him and molded him and taught him to work, who had been quiet when Morrie wanted him to speak, who had told Morrie to swallow his memories of his mother when he wanted to share them with the world.

He nodded and he walked away. The horror of the room, he would later say, sucked all other functions out of him. He did not cry until days later.

Still, his father's death helped prepare Morrie for his own. This much he knew: there would be lots of holding and kissing and talking and laughter and no good-byes left unsaid, all the things he missed with his father and his mother.

When the final moment came, Morrie wanted his loved ones around him, knowing what was happening. No one would get a phone call, or a telegram, or have to look through a glass window in some cold and foreign basement.

DAVE BARRY

Borrrinnng!

I was at an airport, reading a newspaper, when the World's Three Most Boring People sat down next to me and started talking as loud as they could without amplifiers. They were so boring I took notes on their conversation. Here's an actual excerpt:

> FIRST PERSON (POINTING TO A BIG BAG): *That's a big bag.*
> SECOND PERSON: *That is a big bag.*
> FIRST PERSON: *You can hold a lot in a bag like that.*
> THIRD PERSON: *Francine has a big bag like that.*
> FIRST PERSON: *Francine does? Like that?*
> THIRD PERSON: *Yes. It holds everything. She puts everything in that bag.*
> SECOND PERSON: *It's a big bag.*
> THIRD PERSON: *She says whatever she has, she just puts it in that bag and just boom, closes it up.*
> FIRST PERSON: *Francine does?*
> SECOND PERSON: *This is a big bag.*

I want to stress that this was not all that they had to say about the big bag. They could have gone on for hours if they hadn't been interrupted by a major news development: namely, a person walking past pulling a wheeled suitcase. This inspired a whole new train of thought: ("There's one of those suitcases with those wheels." "Where?" "There, with those wheels." "John has one." "He does?" "With those wheels?" "Yes. He says you just roll it along." "John does?")

And so on. It occurred to me that a possible explanation for some plane crashes might be that people like these were sitting close enough to the cockpit for the flight crew to hear them talk ("There's a cloud." "Look, there's *another . . .*") and eventually the pilot deliberately flies into the ground to make them shut up.

The thing is, these people clearly didn't know they were boring. Boring people never do. In fact, no offense, even YOU could be boring. Ask yourself: When you talk to people, do they tend to make vague excuses—"Sorry! Got to run!"—and then walk briskly away? Does this happen even if you are in an elevator?

But even if people listen to you with what appears to be great interest, that doesn't mean you're not boring. They could be pretending. When Prince Charles speaks, everybody pretends to be fascinated, even though he has never said anything interesting except in that intercepted telephone conversation wherein he expressed the desire to be a feminine hygiene product.

And even if you're not Prince Charles, people might have to pretend you're interesting because they want to sell you something, or have intimate carnal knowledge of you, or because you hold some power over them. At one time I was a co-investor in a small aging apartment building with plumbing and electrical systems that were brought over on the *Mayflower;* my partner and I were regularly visited by the building inspector, who had the power to write us up for numerous minor building code infractions, which is why we always pretended to be fascinated when he told us—as he ALWAYS did—about the time he re-plumbed his house. His account of this event was as long as *The Iliad,* but with more soldering. I'm sure he told this story to everybody whose building he ever inspected; he's probably still telling it, unless some building owner finally strangled him, in which case I bet his wife never reported that he was missing.

The point is that you could easily be unaware that you're boring. This is why everybody should make a conscious effort to avoid boring topics. The problem here, of course, is that not everybody agrees on what "boring" means. For example, Person A might believe that collecting decorative plates is boring, whereas Person B might find this to be a fascinating hobby. Who's to say which person is correct?

I am. Person A is correct. Plate-collecting is boring. In fact, hobbies of any kind are boring except to people who have the same hobby. (This is also true of religion, although you will not find me saying so in print.) The New Age is boring, and so are those puzzles where you try to locate all the hidden words. Agriculture is important but boring. Likewise foreign policy. Also, come to think of it, domestic policy. The fact that your child made the honor roll is boring. Auto racing is boring except when a car is going at least 172 miles per hour upside down. Talking about golf is always boring. (*Playing* golf can be interesting, but not the part where you try to hit the little ball; only the part where you drive the cart.) Fishing is boring, unless you catch an actual fish, and then it is disgusting.

Speaking of sports, a big problem is that men and women often do not agree on what is boring. Men can devote an entire working week to discussing a single pass-interference penalty; women find this boring, yet can be fascinated by a four-hour movie with subtitles wherein the entire plot consists of a man and a woman yearning to have, but never actually having, a relationship. Men HATE that. Men can take maybe 45 seconds of yearning, and then they want everybody to get naked. Followed by a car chase. A movie called *Naked People in Car Chases* would do really well among men. I have quite a few more points to make, but I'm sick of this topic.

CHARLES BOWDEN

Tortoises

I once knew a woman who had a pet tortoise named Fluffy and I think of this fact as I face the action.

The blue air hangs over the room of clacking machines as people pack this casino hugging the banks of the Colorado River and wearily pull the levers on the slots.

I am hungry. I check my backpack with the doorman and rub my fingers across the stubble of my beard. The people are very intent and do not look up or around or at one another. Laughlin, Nevada, strings a half dozen casinos along the tame stream and is only a minute by boat from the Arizona shore. Outside the parking lots are packed with campers, trucks, and vans and every machine has a toy poodle yapping at the window. This is a blue collar Las Vegas.

I want bacon and eggs, but I hesitate on the floor of the casino. The players are men in caps and t-shirts, fat-hipped women in polyester stretch pants, retired folks plunging with dimes and quarters. I am pretty much dirty clothes, clumps of greasy hair, and hung-over eyes. Last night I slept in the hills overlooking the valley. Cottontails grazed around my head and hopped along the sides of my sleeping bag. All night the casino signs splashed color and form into the night sky and then at first light, lines of herons and ducks and geese slowly winged down the ribbon of river to the feeding grounds. In this big room of smoke, booze, and slots, sunrise and sunset count for nothing.

Clocks are kept from sight, the pit blocks all views of the outside and the women peddling drink to the players, God! Those women in black net stockings, thrusting breasts, fresh young faces, and ancient eyes. Well, the women strut through the blue air denying that time or age or bills or tomorrow exists or matters. I love the women and what they are doing for us all. Just savor them, I tell myself, don't speak to them, don't go home with them, just brush them with your eyes. In here, they are the promise of flesh and fun and smiles and I do not want to know about the two kids, the old man that skidaddled, the small trailer where everytime you turn around you bump into yourself.

I finally cross the casino floor and walk into the restaurant, a barren that is here and there dotted with tired people pumping coffee and reading the sports pages. I sit down, swallow a couple of cups and start nibbling at the pile of scientific papers I carry. I have come here to listen to experts consider the plight of the desert tortoise

"Tortoises" from Blue Desert *by Charles Bowden.* © 1986 The Arizona Board of Regents. Reprinted by permission *of the University of Arizona Press.*

and the experts have gathered here from the universities, from the Bureau of Land Management, from the fish and game departments, from all the small offices with gray desks and steady checks, because, hell, why not meet in a casino town?

The desert tortoise itself (*Gopherus agassizii*) has skipped this occasion. In the bright lights and big cities of the Sunbelt this small reptile is no big deal. Loving a desert tortoise is a little bit like bonding with a pet rock—scholars estimate that the beast spends 94.9 percent of its time in dormancy, which means just lying there in its burrow. Today they are being wiped out in the desert, and in Sunbelt cities survive mainly as pets and captives (at least twenty thousand in California and thousands in Tucson and Phoenix). Once upon a time they averaged from ten or twenty up to several hundred per square mile. But this is a new time and a new west.

I thumb through this leviathan study, an 838-page draft report being considered by the Desert Tortoise Council, the cabal of experts zeroing in on this casino for a conference. I discover that *Gopherus agassizii* runs six to fourteen inches, tops the scale at maybe ten pounds and hardly pesters anyone. They endure their slow lives for 50 to 100 years, and I am briefly bewitched by the notion that somewhere out there lumber Methuselah tortoises that have seen the whole western movie, all three reels, from Wyatt Earp to Palm Springs.

The eggs and bacon finally arrive and I devour them. This is a nickel-and-dime trip where I figure on skipping room rent by flopping in the desert, jotting notes during all the weighty sessions of tortoise papers, and hopefully, scribbling a story that will pay the rent.

The tortoise looks to be a perfect foil for a quick hit: they are the innocents, the benign nothings who do not attack cattle, sheep, or hikers, the little rascals who pack no venom and fire up all the fantasies of nature that people relish. Scientists tag them as an indicator species, meaning one that suggests the health of the ecosystem as a whole. Almost stationary in their habits, long-lived, low in reproduction rate and quiet, they function as witnesses to the way human beings in the Southwest treat the land and the forms of life woven into the land.

In short, tortoises have a high potential to evoke human guilt. Box office.

I have been counseled at length by a friend who for decades has flourished as a free-lance writer of nature stories. He warned me to avoid all colorful references to the casino ("none of those clinking ice cubes in glasses of whiskey," he fumed) and play it straight and be rich in technical information. This is good advice that I find hard to follow. I have yet to meet the casino that cannot seduce me. The pits are so full of human greed and human hope and always there are those little touches—the men in the glass room packing sacks of money and wearing smocks that have no pockets—that make me glad to be a human being. There are few places as honest as the rampant fraud and fantasy of a casino. Here we let down our hair, our pants, our everything and confess to all our secret hungers.

The women working the place are a problem also, busting out of their britches, bending down to pour coffee and slapping my face with deep cleavage. I can think of few things more pleasurable than to sleep on the desert, watch the rabbits bounce around and then at dawn walk into a casino where time has stopped and everything always promises to be juicy.

I pay the bill and move up the stairs to the meeting rooms where plump, contented tortoise experts gather over coffee and doughnuts. I strike up conversations with perfect strangers who are all friendly in this bastion of tortoise love. An elderly couple tells me of their son who is in the grocery business and has a kind of tortoise preserve at his home with eighteen of the beasts thriving on the wilted lettuce he brings home each night. A lady from Phoenix brags on her pet male who taps the patio doors when he wants in the house. The registration table for the conference is a gold mine of tortoise pendants, pens, pins, t-shirts, key chains, wind chimes.

Everyone seems satisfied after an evening of frolicking over steak dinners, trying their luck at blackjack, having a spin in this dab of sin—all at government expense. Finally, the session comes to order and I hunch in my chair busy noting the hard facts of *Gopherus* scholarship.

Being a desert tortoise may not constitute a full-time job. A calendar of the tortoise year, based on a daily time budget (DTB) and annual time budget (ATB), is not full of big events. The animals emerge from their holes in late March to late July when the days begin to be warm. At first, basking (tortoise sunbathing) takes up about 19 percent of the DTB, a figure which declines as the season advances, and only kills 1.5 percent of the ATB. Once out and about tortoises turn to foraging (1.5 percent ATB) and love-making (0.08 percent ATB). Even during the friskiest part of the summer season they go dormant 33 percent of the time.

Tortoises spend only three to six months a year actively feeding and moving, and even during this frisky period they devote most of their hours to snoozing in their burrows. Basically, *Gopherus agassizii* is not a Type A personality and this wonderful calm has prevented tortoise scholars from glimpsing much action.

A few tidbits have been gleaned. When picked up and alarmed they are liable to piss all over people. When two male tortoises meet, they bob their heads and often ram each other—the loser being toppled onto his back and left to die in the heat if he cannot right himself. When sprinting they can cover about six yards in a minute but they hardly ever move far from their burrows unless maddened by thirst.

They have very little to say. When disturbed or when mating, they sometimes hiss, grunt, and make pops and poinks. I hesitate in my note-taking and contemplate the ring of a hearty tortoise poink. Dominant males seem to pack a potent punch when they defecate and have been known to send the rest of the boys scurrying from a burrow with one mighty dump.

Sex occurs to a tortoise after reaching the age of fifteen or twenty and the first date begins with the male bobbing his head and then nipping the female a few times on the shell before mounting her. Tortoise women maintain an air of calm and sometimes keep right on eating during copulation. Eggs are laid, buried, and after 100 days, hatch. The young tortoise must face five years of desert life with a soft shell.

Generally, tortoises are homebodies and spend their lives within a few hundred yards of their burrows, wandering off mainly for a little dining, basking, or lovemaking. Specimens tagged during a study in the late thirties and early forties were found in the same area by scientists in the eighties. They chow down on green herbs, leaves, and blossoms of annuals, succulents, grasses, and cacti.

The papers come one after another and they stand in contrast to the sea of peace that constitutes normal tortoise life. Outside the casino walls in the desert we cannot see well (the meeting room, naturally, has no windows), out there it is holocaust time for tortoises. I look around at conference attendants and see a lot of grim faces.

People, it seems, have been wreaking havoc on tortoises for a long time—they were sold as dog food in Los Angeles during the 1890s—and from this fact has sprung the modern tortoise industry. We shoot them just for the hell of it, hack them to pieces, drive over them with cars, collapse their burrows with off-road vehicles, stomp them to death with our livestock, and starve them to death by running cattle and sheep on their range—beasts which devour all the forage tortoises crave.

Until the 1970s, nobody much cared. Then something new happened—all those federal laws about endangered species and all those new agency mandates demanding environmental impact statements. I take a closer look at the faces in the room and realize I am sitting with the new servants of the desert tortoise. Hacks from the BLM who suddenly must kowtow to a damn reptile because their beloved steers are destroying it. Biologists from game and fish departments who thought they would spend their days keeping tab on deer and antelope and bighorns and elk who now are here fat with statistics about tortoises and management plans for them.

I no longer like the room. I once had a professor who patiently explained to me that I never could stomach any cause once it had become successful. Well, there must be worse sins. I have heartily supported every law, executive order, and petition to salvage the dwindling biological wealth of the earth. But now I see what happens to every decent impulse in my society: they become that ugly thing, government.

I get up and wander out of the meeting. Downstairs time has passed, but mercifully everything has remained the same. I sidle up to the long bar which stares out at the river and sip whiskey as the afternoon sinks toward evening. Others at the bar amuse themselves with electronic poker games and there is an air of deadly serious sport about the place.

The hills bordering the valley bear the traces of Indian trails where tribes of the Colorado once raced north and south for hundreds and hundreds of miles exporting war, magic, and a few hard goods. The ground cover is scant and low and this is not the kind of country most Americans call beautiful. They storm across it in their machines from Phoenix, Tucson, Los Angeles, and more distant parts of the Republic so they, like their fathers before them, can gather at the river. And once here they drink, gamble and feed.

At my back, hunkered over the crap tables, poker tables, and slots, are my fellow citizens hailing from most states in the Union. And none of them are likely to waste much time pondering the plight of a desert tortoise. The couples, ma and pa, tend to wear matching caps and windbreakers. In the gift shop, there is practically nothing to read for sale. The casino seems dedicated to low-level aerobics and no slackers are allowed to pull back and pursue thick books or falter from doing their reps with the slot machines. No pain, no gain.

Denouncing this place would be like coming out against the tooth fairy.

I join the line for the casino cheap feed, a chicken dinner (all you can eat) for a few bucks. Three Indians sit down at my table. Their faces are brown, blank, and immobile. We chomp on the fried birds and slowly words drone from their mouths. They are Navajos working on a stretch of nearby railroad track and they find the casino curious and the food a great bargain. I arrived in the Southwest in 1957 and according to the best reports, my tablemates seized some local turf in the fifteenth century. But we seem to have wound up in the same situation. We ogle the girls, speculate on the thrill of guzzling a few drinks, and say the casino is a real pleasant puzzler.

The Southwest is a place where almost everyone slips their moorings and just drifts. The cities and towns are ugly, the populace footloose, the crime frequent, the marriages disasters, the plans pathetic gestures, the air electric with promise. There is so much space and so much ground that no one can for a single moment doubt the basic American dream that it is possible to make something worthwhile of life. Everything a desert tortoise is—calm, a homebody, long-lived, patient, quiet—the people of the Southwest are not. We don't stay in our burrows much anymore or limit our motion to the cycle of the sun. Just across the road from the casino, a huge powerplant belches smoke into the sky. The facility burns coal mined on Black Mesa in the Navajo and Hopi country of northern Arizona, coal that is piped as a slurry the 278 miles to Laughlin. The electricity generated here is then flashed outward to blaze in the lights of Southern California. Such grids of energy and rivers of energy-flows are the stuff of life in the Southwest and they do not produce a state of mind that cottons to the issue of endangered species. It is not that we are too busy building the empire to tend to details but simply that we are too busy running to ever look back at the ghosts trailing behind us or down at the ground where the writhing beasts shudder with their last convulsion of life. We haven't got time for this nature stuff. We were born to drive, not park.

I walk down the road to a store and buy a pint of whiskey, reclaim my backpack from the doorman, and head back into the hills for another night of stargazing. I lie amid the creosote with my head next to an Ajo lily and study tortoise papers under the flicker of my candle lantern. The documents are grim stuff with the reptile all but gone from the Mojave, being mowed down in Nevada and Utah, still legal game in Arizona. I pour my Sierra cup full of whiskey, blow out the light and witness a falling star.

When I was a kid I once stopped off in Goldfield, Nevada, a failed mining town that boomed around the turn of the century and since has whimpered along with a few cranks and loners lodging in the abandoned houses. The big hotel downtown had been shut for decades and I peered through the windows eyeing the tables all set with linen and silver and wondering if I could make off with some booty. The old man wanted a drink and we walked up the street and found a saloon. The barkeep was a grizzled prospector type with long, gray beard and fat, red nose. His name was Silver Dollar Kirby and his place boasted a plank on two saw horses for the bar and a couple of open bottles and glasses for his stock. My father pumped down a few shots and marveled at a place so free of expensive licenses and gruesome regulations that a fellow like Kirby could open for business with ten dollars worth of assets.

There is not much difference between the proud new Sunbelt cities and the old mining camps. They are both temporary Woodstocks of wanderers hell-bent on plundering. They will exhaust the place and then move on. I should say: we will exhaust the place and then move on. For my body may be sprawled in the desert tonight but a part of me is always seduced by the bright lights of the casino. All over the region I see my handiwork: the ghost towns, the mine scars, the butchered grazing tracts, the dull cities, the highways full of traffic racing to get nowhere, the crap tables, the dammed and maimed rivers. We have taken our main chance and the results only look good on the Dow Jones.

The night slips away and at gray light I march once again on the casino. A man stands outside his van shaving in the rearview mirror. He looks fresh and ready for the long odds offered by the slots. The restaurant is empty and I sit down and administer black coffee when a man joins me. He recognizes me from the conference— a fellow student of tortoise matters.

He is in his mid-thirties, fit and tanned and his beard is neatly trimmed. He works for a national wildlife organization and moves around the Southwest lobbying for this species and that. For him the casino is Babylon and he has spent his time, when not absorbing the scientific papers, sequestered in his room watching athletic events on cable television.

He is a man with a mission. Put simply, his organization is going to file suit against the federal government to make them obey their own laws about endangered species and spring to the defense of the tortoise. Since the reptiles can hardly cope with anything human beings or their livestock like to do, this means locking up big chunks of the Southwest to make them secure for tortoises. The tortoise in this cunning scenario becomes a wonderful tool that will smite many foes. The arrogant ranchers can be felled by the tortoises, the obscene power companies can be toppled, the crazed off-road vehicle freaks and all the minions of industrial life that are sacking the deserts can be chastened, banned, and outlawed.

I appreciate the elegance of the plan. Soon we move past such political stratagems and he begins to remember what got him into this wildlife business, this new religion of the mid- and late-twentieth century that seeks to stop the clock and perhaps wind it backwards to a time when the land was relatively unpeopled and the beasts held sway.

He worked for the National Park Service and saw Alaska, the Rockies, a lot of great country. He wound up in Yellowstone and grew interested in grizzly bears. During one management plan, the local dump was off limits and the bears feasted at the dump. He snuck in with another employee and sat high up on a hill. In the twilight he saw these dark blobs gliding over the grass toward the garbage and suddenly realized he was seeing bears, grizzly bears, the lords of all creation on the North American continent.

He stalls here in his retelling of that evening and searches for the right words, the right expressions. Behind us we can hear the early morning gamblers whacking away at the handles of the slots. But he is in Yellowstone on that hillside and his eyes have that thousand-yard stare.

The grass, the grass had this quality, this color, and the bears, the bears were big, wild and free and he was witnessing them. That is all he can say.

His bosses found out that he had broken the rules and he was promptly fired. That was okay. He had that memory of one evening and now he is in Laughlin, Nevada, representing the interests of desert tortoises and it is all the same thing to him.

I sip my coffee and mumble agreement. Actually, I am moved. I understand what he means. I sense myself on the same hillside. And I cannot explain it either.

The conference continues with a life of its own. I keep reading scientific papers and gorging myself on tortoise numbers. From time to time, I retreat to the bar and drink whiskey, one eye peeled for displays by the cocktail waitresses. I look out at the river and watch the powerboats race past and feel the burn of the booze sliding down my gullet.

The bears come back often, big forms of fur moving across the grass in the twilight. And the tortoises visit me also, hard cases snoring away a century, only to be periodically crushed, stolen, hacked, and shot by my kind.

The cocktail waitress brings me another drink—this time a scotch. I feel expansive. She has great legs, long firm stems sketched by the black net stockings. I want the river, the bear, the tortoise, and those legs.

I walk out the door and across the parking lot. The air hums with sound from the generators rumbling in all the campers, vans and mobile homes. The booze feels wonderfully warm in my gut and twilight slips down.

A line of geese V's up the river and I crane my neck to enjoy the sight. In the windows of the campers I can see the glow of the television screens.

BERNARD COOPER

101 Ways to Cook Hamburger

Theresa Sanchez sat behind me in ninth-grade algebra. When Mr. Hubbley faced the blackboard, I'd turn around to see what she was reading; each week a new book was wedged inside her copy of *Today's Equations*. The deception worked; from Mr. Hubbley's point of view, Theresa was engrossed in the value of *X*, but I knew otherwise. One week she perused *The Wisdom of the Orient*, and I could tell from Theresa's contemplative expression that the book contained exotic thoughts, guidelines handed down from on high. Another week it was a paperback novel whose title, *Let Me Live My Life*, appeared in bold print atop every page, and whose cover, a gauzy photograph of a woman biting a strand of pearls, her head thrown back in ecstasy, confirmed my suspicion that Theresa Sanchez was mature beyond her years. She was the tallest girl in school. Her bouffant hairdo, streaked with blond, was higher than the flaccid bouffants of other girls. Her smooth skin,

Bernard Cooper, "101 Ways to Cook Hamburger" from Truth Serum: Memoirs, *Mariner Books, 1997.*

plucked eyebrows, and painted fingernails suggested hours of pampering, a worldly and sensual vanity that placed her within the domain of adults. Smiling dimly, steeped in daydreams, Theresa moved through the crowded halls with a languid, self-satisfied indifference to those around her. "You are merely children," her posture seemed to say, "I can't be bothered." The week Theresa hid *101 Ways to Cook Hamburger* behind her algebra book, I could stand it no longer, and after the bell rang, ventured a question.

"Because I'm having a dinner party," said Theresa. "Just a couple of intimate friends."

No fourteen-year-old I knew had ever given a dinner party, let alone used the word "intimate" in conversation. "Don't you have a mother?" I asked.

Theresa sighed a weary sigh, suffered my strange inquiry. "Don't be so naive," she said. "Everyone has a mother." She waved her hand to indicate the brick school buildings outside the window. "A higher education should have taught you that." Theresa draped an angora sweater over her shoulders, scooped her books from the graffiti-covered desk, and just as she was about to walk away, turned and asked me, "Are you a fag?"

There wasn't the slightest hint of rancor or condescension in her voice. The tone was direct, casual. Still I was stunned, giving a sidelong glance to make sure no one had heard. "No," I said. Blurted really, with too much defensiveness, too much transparent fear in my response. Octaves lower than usual, I tried a "Why?"

Theresa shrugged. "Oh, I don't know. I have lots of friends who are fags. You remind me of them." Seeing me bristle, Theresa added, "It was just a guess." I watched her erect angora back as she sauntered out the classroom door.

She had made an incisive and timely guess. Only days before, I'd invited Grady Rogers to my house after school to go swimming. The instant Grady shot from the pool, shaking water from his orange hair, his freckled shoulders shining, my attraction to members of my own sex became a matter I could no longer suppress or rationalize. Sturdy and boisterous and gap-toothed, Grady was an inveterate back slapper, a formidable arm wrestler, a wizard at basketball. Grady was a boy at home in his body.

My body was a marvel I hadn't gotten used to; my arms and legs would sometimes act of their own accord, knocking over a glass at dinner or flinching at an oncoming pitch. I was never singled out as a sissy, but I could have been just as easily as Bobby Keagan, a gentle, intelligent, and introverted boy reviled by my classmates. And although I had always been aware of a tacit rapport with Bobby, a suspicion that I might find with him a rich friendship, I stayed away. Instead, I emulated Grady in the belief that being seen with him, being like him, would somehow vanquish my self-doubt, would make me normal by association.

Apart from his athletic prowess, Grady had been gifted with all the trappings of what I imagined to be a charmed life: a fastidious, aproned mother who radiated calm and maternal concern, a ruddy, stoic father with a knack for home repairs. Even the Rogerses' small suburban house in Hollywood, with its spindly Colonial furniture and chintz curtains, was a testament to normalcy.

Grady and his family bore little resemblance to my clan of Eastern European Jews, a dark and vociferous people who ate with abandon—matzo and halvah and gefilte fish; foods the goyim couldn't pronounce—who cajoled one another during endless games of canasta, making the simplest remark about the weather into a lengthy philosophical discourse on the sun and the seasons and the passage of time. My mother was a chain smoker, a dervish in a frowsy housedress. She showed her love in the most peculiar and obsessive ways, like spending hours extracting every seed from a watermelon before she served it in perfectly bite-sized geometric pieces. Preoccupied and perpetually frantic, my mother succumbed to bouts of absentmindedness so profound she'd forget what she was saying in midsentence, smile and blush and walk away. A divorce attorney, my father wore roomy, iridescent suits, and the intricacies, the deceits inherent in his profession, had the effect of making him forever tense and vigilant. He was "all wound up," as my mother put it. But when he relaxed, his laughter was explosive, his disposition prankish: "Walk this way," a waitress would say, leading us to our table, and my father would mimic the way she walked, arms akimbo, hips liquid, while my mother and I were wracked with laughter. Buoyant or brooding, my parents' moods were unpredictable, and in a household fraught with extravagant emotion it was odd and awful to keep my longing secret.

One day I made the mistake of asking my mother what a fag was. I knew exactly what Theresa had meant, but hoped against hope it was not what I thought; maybe *fag* was some French word, a harmless term like *naive*. My mother turned from the stove, flew at me, and grabbed me by the shoulders. "Did someone call you that?" she cried.

"Not me," I said. "Bobby Keagan."

"Oh," she said, loosening her grip. She was visibly relieved. And didn't answer. The answer was unthinkable.

For weeks after, I shook with the reverberations from that afternoon in the kitchen with my mother, pained by the memory of her shocked expression and, most of all, her silence. My longing was wrong in the eyes of my mother, whose hazel eyes were the eyes of the world, and if that longing continued unchecked, the unwieldy shape of my fate would be cast, and I'd be subjected to a lifetime of scorn.

During the remainder of the semester, I became the scientist of my own desire, plotting ways to change my yearning for boys into a yearning for girls. I had enough evidence to believe that any habit, regardless of how compulsive, how deeply ingrained, could be broken once and for all: the plastic cigarette my mother purchased at the Thrifty pharmacy (one end was red to approximate an ember, the other tan like a filter tip) was designed to wean her from the real thing. To change a behavior required self-analysis, cold resolve, and the substitution of one thing for another: plastic, say, for tobacco. Could I also find a substitute for Grady? What I needed to do, I figured, was kiss a girl and learn to like it.

This conclusion was affirmed one Sunday morning when my father, seeing me wrinkle my nose at the pink slabs of lox he layered on a bagel, tried to convince me of its salty appeal. "You should try some," he said. "You don't know what you're missing."

"It's loaded with protein," added my mother, slapping a platter of sliced onions onto the dinette table. She hovered above us, cinching up her housedress, eyes wet from onion fumes, a mock cigarette dangling from her lips.

My father sat there chomping with gusto, emitting a couple of hearty grunts to dramatize his satisfaction. And still I was not convinced. After a loud and labored swallow, he told me I may not be fond of lox today, but sooner or later I'd learn to like it. One's tastes, he assured me, are destined to change.

"Live," shouted my mother over the rumble of the Mixmaster. "Expand your horizons. Try new things." And the room grew fragrant with the batter of a spice cake.

The opportunity to put their advice into practice, and try out my plan to adapt to girls, came the following week when Debbie Coburn, a member of Mr. Hubbley's algebra class, invited me to a party. She cornered me in the hall, furtive as a spy, telling me her parents would be gone for the evening and slipping into my palm a wrinkled sheet of notebook paper. On it were her address and telephone number, the lavender ink in a tidy cursive. "Wear cologne," she advised, wary eyes darting back and forth. "It's a make-out party. Anything can happen."

The Santa Ana winds blew relentlessly the night of Debbie's party, careening down the slopes of the Hollywood Hills, shaking the road signs and stoplights in its path. As I walked down Beachwood Avenue, trees thrashed, surrendered their leaves, and carob pods bombarded the pavement. The sky was a deep but luminous blue, the air hot, abrasive, electric. I had to squint in order to check the number of the Coburns' apartment, a three-story building with glitter embedded in its stucco walls. Above the honeycombed balconies was a sign that read *Beachwood Terrace* in lavender script resembling Debbie's.

From down the hall, I could hear the plaintive strains of Little Anthony's "Goin' Out of My Head." Debbie answered the door bedecked in an empire dress, the bodice blue with orange polka dots, the rest a sheath of black and white stripes. "Op art," proclaimed Debbie. She turned in a circle, then proudly announced that she'd rolled her hair in frozen orange juice cans. She patted the huge unmoving curls and dragged me inside. Reflections from the swimming pool in the courtyard, its surface ruffled by wind, shuddered over the ceiling and walls. A dozen of my classmates were seated on the sofa or huddled together in corners, their whispers full of excited imminence, their bodies barely discernible in the dim light. Drapes flanking the sliding glass doors bowed out with every gust of wind, and it seemed that the room might lurch from its foundations and sail with its cargo of silhouettes into the hot October night.

Grady was the last to arrive. He tossed a six-pack of beer into Debbie's arms, barreled toward me, and slapped my back. His hair was slicked back with Vitalis, lacquered furrows left by the comb. The wind hadn't shifted a single hair. "Ya ready?" he asked, flashing the gap between his front teeth and leering into the darkened room. "You bet," I lied.

Once the beers had been passed around, Debbie provoked everyone's attention by flicking on the overhead light. "OK," she called. "Find a partner." This was the blunt command of a hostess determined to have her guests aroused in an orderly fashion. Everyone blinked, shuffled about, and grabbed a member of the opposite sex. Sheila Garabedian landed beside me (entirely at random, though I wanted to believe she was driven by passion), her timid smile giving way to plain fear as the light went out. Nothing for a moment but the heave of the wind and the distant banter of dogs. I caught a whiff of Sheila's perfume, as tangy and sweet as Hawaiian Punch. I probed her face with my own, grazing the small scallop of an ear, a velvety temple, and though Sheila's trembling made me want to stop, I persisted with my mission until I found her lips, as tightly sealed as a private letter. I held my mouth over hers and gathered her shoulders closer, resigned to the possibility that, no matter how long we stood there, Sheila was too scared to kiss me back. Still, she exhaled through her nose, and I listened to the squeak of every breath as though it were a sigh of inordinate pleasure. Diving within myself, I monitored my heartbeat and respiration, trying to will stimulation into being, and all the while an image intruded, an image of Grady erupting from our pool, rivulets of water sliding down his chest. "Change," shouted Debbie, switching on the light. Sheila thanked me, pulled away, and continued her routine of gracious terror with every boy throughout the room. It didn't matter whom I held—Margaret Sims, Betty Vernon, Elizabeth Lee—my experiment was a failure; I continued to picture Grady's wet chest, and Debbie would bellow "Change!" with such fervor, it could have been my own voice, my own incessant reprimand.

Our hostess commandeered the light switch for nearly half an hour. Whenever the light came on, I watched Grady pivot his head toward the newest prospect, his eyebrows arched in expectation, his neck blooming with hickeys, his hair, at last, in disarray. All that shuffling across the carpet charged everyone's arms and lips with static, and eventually, between low moans and soft osculations, I could hear the clack of tiny sparks and see them flare here and there in the dark like meager, short-lived stars.

I saw Theresa, as sultry and aloof as ever, read three more books—*North American Reptiles, Bonjour Tristesse,* and *MGM: A Pictorial History*—before she vanished early in December. Rumors of her fate abounded. Debbie Coburn swore that Theresa had been "knocked up" by an older man, a traffic cop, she thought, or a grocer. Nearly quivering with relish, Debbie told Grady and me about the home for unwed mothers in the San Fernando Valley, a compound teeming with pregnant girls who had nothing to do but touch their stomachs and contemplate their mistake. Even Bobby Keagan, who took Theresa's place behind me in algebra, had a theory regarding her disappearance colored by his own wish for escape; he imagined that Theresa, disillusioned with society, booked passage to a tropical island, there to live out the rest of her days without restrictions or ridicule. "No wonder she flunked out of school," I overheard Mr. Hubbley tell a fellow teacher one afternoon. "Her head was always in a book."

Along with Theresa went my secret, or at least the dread that she might divulge it, and I felt, for a while, exempt from suspicion. I was, however, to run across Theresa one last time. It happened during a period of torrential rain that, according to reports on the six o'clock news, washed houses from the hillsides and flooded the downtown streets. The halls of Joseph Le Conte Junior High were festooned with Christmas decorations: crepe-paper garlands, wreaths studded with plastic berries, and one requisite Star of David twirling above the attendance desk. In arts and crafts, our teacher, Gerald (he was the only teacher who allowed us, *required* us, to call him by his first name), handed out blocks of balsa wood and instructed us to carve them into bugs. We would paint eyes and antennae with tempera and hang them on a Christmas tree he'd made the previous night. "*Voilà*," he crooned, unveiling his creation from a burlap sack. Before us sat a tortured scrub, a wardrobe's worth of wire hangers that were bent like branches and soldered together. Gerald credited his inspiration to a Charles Addams cartoon he'd seen in which Morticia, grimly preparing for the holidays, hangs vampire bats on a withered pine. "All that red and green," said Gerald. "So predictable. So boring."

As I chiseled a beetle and listened to rain pummel the earth, Gerald handed me an envelope and asked me to take it to Mr. Kendrick, the drama teacher. I would have thought nothing of his request if I hadn't seen Theresa on my way down the hall. She was cleaning out her locker, blithely dropping the sum of its contents—pens and textbooks and mimeographs—into a trash can. "Have a nice life," she sang as I passed. I mustered the courage to ask her what had happened. We stood alone in the silent hall, the reflections of wreaths and garlands submerged in brown linoleum.

"I transferred to another school. They don't have grades or bells and you get to study whatever you want." Theresa was quick to sense my incredulity. "Honest," she said. "The school is progressive." She gazed into a glass cabinet that held the trophies of track meets and intramural spelling bees. "God," she said with a sigh, "this place is so . . . barbaric." I was still trying to decide whether to believe her story when she asked me where I was headed. "Dear," she said, her exclamation pooling in the silence, "that's no ordinary note, if you catch my drift." The envelope was blank and white; I looked up at Theresa, baffled. "Don't be so naive," she muttered, tossing an empty bottle of nail polish into the trash can. It struck bottom with a resolute thud. "Well," she said, closing her locker and breathing deeply, "bon voyage." Theresa swept through the double doors and in seconds her figure was obscured by rain.

As I walked toward Mr. Kendrick's room, I could feel Theresa's insinuation burrow in. I stood for a moment and watched Mr. Kendrick through the pane in the door. He paced intently in front of the class, handsome in his shirt and tie, reading from a thick book. Chalked on the blackboard behind him was THE ODYSSEY BY HOMER. I have no recollection of how Mr. Kendrick reacted to the note, whether he accepted it with pleasure or embarrassment, slipped it into his desk drawer or the pocket of his shirt. I have scavenged that day in retrospect, trying to see Mr. Kendrick's expression, wondering if he acknowledged me in any way as his liaison. All I recall is the sight of his mime through a pane of glass, a lone man mouthing an epic, his gestures ardent in empty air.

Had I delivered a declaration of love? I was haunted by the need to know. In fantasy, a kettle shot steam, the glue released its grip, and I read the letter with impunity. But how would such a letter begin? Did the common endearments apply?

This was a message between two men, a message for which I had no precedent, and when I tried to envision the contents, apart from a hasty, impassioned scrawl, my imagination faltered.

Once or twice I witnessed Gerald and Mr. Kendrick walk together into the faculty lounge or say hello at the water fountain, but there was nothing especially clandestine or flirtatious in their manner. Besides, no matter how acute my scrutiny, I wasn't sure, short of a kiss, exactly what to look for—what semaphore of gesture, what encoded word; I suspected there were signs, covert signs that would give them away, just as I'd unwittingly given myself away to Theresa.

In the school library, a *Webster's* unabridged dictionary lay on a wooden podium, and I padded toward it with apprehension; along with clues to the bond between my teachers, I risked discovering information that might incriminate me as well. I had decided to consult the dictionary during lunch period when most of the students would be on the playground. I clutched my notebook, moving in such a way as to appear both studious and nonchalant, actually believing that, unless I took precautions, someone would see me and guess what I was up to. The closer I came to the podium, the more obvious, I thought, was my endeavor; I felt like the model of the Visible Man in our science class, my heart's undulations, my overwrought nerves, legible through transparent skin. A couple of kids riffled through the card catalogue. The librarian, a skinny woman whose perpetual whisper and rubber-soled shoes caused her to drift through the room like a phantom, didn't seem to register my presence. Though I'd looked up dozens of words before, the pages felt strange beneath my fingers. *Homer* was the first word I saw. *Hominid. Homogenize.* I feigned interest and skirted other words before I found the word I was after. Following the boldfaced ho·mo·sex·u·al was this terse definition: *adj. Pertaining to, characteristic of, or exhibiting homosexuality.—n. A homosexual person.* I read the definition again and again, hoping the words would yield more than they could. I shut the dictionary, swallowed hard, and, none the wiser, hurried away.

As for Gerald and Mr. Kendrick, I never discovered evidence to prove or dispute Theresa's claim. By the following summer, however, I had overheard from my peers a confounding amount about homosexuals: they wore green on Thursday, couldn't whistle, hypnotized boys with a piercing glance. To this lore, Grady added a surefire test to ferret them out.

"A test?" I said.

"You ask a guy to look at his fingernails, and if he looks at them like this"—Grady closed his fingers into a fist and examined his nails with manly detachment—"then he's OK. But if he does this"—he held out his hands at arm's length, splayed his fingers, and coyly cocked his head—"you'd better watch out." Once he'd completed his demonstration, Grady peeled off his shirt and plunged into our pool. I dove in after him. It was early June, the sky immense, glassy, placid. My father was cooking spareribs on the barbecue, an artist with a basting brush. His apron bore the caricature of a frazzled French chef. Mother curled on a chaise longue, plumes of smoke wafting from her nostrils. In a stupor of contentment she took another drag, closed her eyes, and arched her face toward the sun.

Grady dog-paddled through the deep end, spouting a fountain of chlorinated water. Despite shame and confusion, my longing for him hadn't diminished; it continued to thrive without air and light, like a luminous fish in the dregs of the sea. In the name of play, I swam up behind him, encircled his shoulders, astonished by his taut flesh. The two of us flailed, pretended to drown. Beneath the heavy press of water, Grady's orange hair wavered, a flame that couldn't be doused.

I've lived with a man for eleven years. Some nights, when I'm half asleep and the room is suffused with blue light, I reach out to touch the expanse of his back, and it seems as if my fingers sink into his skin, and I feel the pleasure a diver feels the instant he enters a body of water.

I have few regrets. But one is that I didn't say to Theresa, "Of course I'm a fag." Maybe I'd have met her friends. Or become friends with her. Imagine the meals we might have concocted: hamburger Stroganoff, Swedish meatballs in a sweet translucent sauce, steaming slabs of Salisbury steak.

ANDRE DUBUS

A Woman in April

In New York city, the twenty-fifth of April 1988 was a warm and blue day, and daylight savings time held the sun in the sky after dinner and all the way from the restaurant to Lincoln Center, where we were supposed to be at eight o'clock. The way from the restaurant to Lincoln Center was sidewalks, nearly all of them with curbs and no curb cuts, and streets with traffic; and we were with my friend David Novak, and my friend and agent, Philip Spitzer, pushing my wheelchair and pulling it up curbs and easing it down them while I watched the grills and windshields of cars. I call David the Skipper because he was a Marine lieutenant then captain in Vietnam and led troops in combat, so I defer to his rank, although I was a peacetime captain while he was still a civilian. Philip is the brother I never had by blood.

Philip of course lives in New York. I happily do not. Neither does the Skipper. He lives here in Massachusetts, and he and his wife drove to New York that day, a Monday, and my daughter Suzanne and son Andre and friends and I came in two more cars, because Andre and I were reading that night at Lincoln Center with Mary Morris and Diana Davenport. In Massachusetts we had very little sun and

"A Woman in April" from Broken Vessels *by Andre Dubus. Reprinted by permission of David R. Godine, Publisher, Inc. Copyright © 1991 by Andre Dubus*

warmth during the spring, and that afternoon, somewhere in Connecticut, we drove into sunlight, and soon the trees along the road were green with leaves. We have not seen those either at home, only the promise of buds.

At close to eight o'clock the sky was still blue and the Skipper pushed me across the final street, then turned my chair and leaned it backward and pulled it up steps to the Plaza outside the Center. We began crossing the greyish white concrete floor and, as Philip spoke and pointed up, I looked at the tall buildings flanking the Plaza, angles of grey-white, of city color, against the sky, deepening now, but not much, still the bright blue of spring after such a long winter of short days, lived in bed, in the wheelchair, in physical therapy, in the courthouse losing my wife and two little girls. Philip told us of a Frenchman last year tightrope walking across the space between these buildings, without a net.

Then I looked at the people walking on the Plaza. My only good memories of New York are watching people walk on the streets, and watching people in bars and restaurants, and some meals or drinks with friends, and being with Philip. But one summer I spent five days with him and for the first time truly saw the homeless day after day and night after night, and from then on, whenever I went there, I knew the New York I was in, the penthouses and apartments and cabs and restaurants, were not New York, anymore than the Czar's Russia was the Russia of Chekhov's freed serfs, with their hopes destroyed long before they were born. Still on that spring Monday I loved watching the faces on the Plaza.

Like Boston, New York has beautiful women to look at, though in New York the women, in general, are made up more harshly, and they dress more self-consciously; there is something insular about their cosmetics and clothing, as if they have come to believe that sitting at a mirror with brushes and tubes and vials, and putting on a dress of a certain cut and color starts them on the long march to spiritual fulfillment with a second wind. And in New York the women walk as though in the rain; in Boston many women stroll. But then most New Yorkers walk like people in rain, leaving the stroll to police officers, hookers, beggars and wandering homeless, and teenagers who are yet unharried by whatever preoccupations preoccupy so many from their driving preoccupation with loneliness and death.

Women were on the Plaza, their pace slower as they neared the building, and looking to my right I saw a lovely one. She could have been thirty, or five years on either side of it. She wore a dark brown miniskirt, or perhaps it was black; I saw it and her strong legs in net stockings for only a moment, because they were in my natural field of vision from my chair. But a woman's face is what I love. She was in profile and had soft thick brown hair swaying at her shoulders as she strode with purpose but not hurry, only grace. She was about forty feet away, enough distance so that, when I looked up, I saw her face against the sky.

"Skipper," I said. "Accidently push me into *her*."

The forward motion of her legs and arms did not pause, but she immediately turned to me and, as immediately, her lips spread in a smile, and her face softened with it, and her eyes did, all at once from a sudden release in her heart that was soft too in her voice: "I heard that."

She veered toward me, smiling still, with brightened eyes.

"It was a compliment," I said.

The Skipper was pushing my chair, Philip was beside me, and she was coming closer. Then she said: "I know."

She angled back to her first path, as though it were painted there for her to follow, and Philip said: "That *never* happens in New York."

"It's the wheelchair," I said. "I'm harmless."

But I knew that was not true. There was no time to explain it then, and anyway I wanted to hold her gift for a while before giving it away with words.

Living in the world as a cripple allows you to see more clearly the crippled hearts of some people whose bodies are whole and sound. All of us, from time to time, suffer this crippling. Some suffer it daily and nightly; and while most of us, nearly all of us, have compassion and love in our hearts, we cannot or will not see these barely visible wounds of other human beings, and so cannot or will not pick up the telephone or travel to someone's home or write a note or make some other seemingly trifling gesture to give to someone what only we, and God, can give: an hour's respite, or a day's, or a night's; and sometimes more than respite: sometimes joy.

Yet in a city whose very sidewalks show the failure of love, the failure to make agape a bureaucracy, a young woman turned to me with instinctive anger or pride, and seeing me in a wheelchair she at once felt not pity but lighthearted compassion. For seeing one of her kind wounded, she lay down the shield and sword she had learned to carry (*I dried my tears/ And armed my fears/ With ten thousand/ shields and spears*, William Blake wrote), and with the light of the sun between us, ten or fifteen feet between us, her face and voice embraced me.

For there is a universality to a wounded person: again and again, for nearly two years, my body has drawn sudden tenderness from men and women I have seen for only those moments in their lives when they helped me with their hands or their whole bodies or only their eyes and lips and tongues. They see, in their short time with me, a man injured, as they could be; a man always needing the care of others, as they could too. Only the children stare with frightened curiosity, as they do at funeral processions and the spoken news of death, for they know in their hearts that they too will die, and they believe they will grow up and marry and have children, but they cannot yet believe they will die.

But I am a particular kind of cripple. In New York I was not sitting on a sidewalk, my back against a wall, and decades of misfortune and suffering in my heart. I was not wearing dirty clothes on an unwashed body. Philip and the Skipper wore suits and ties. I rode in a nine-hundred-dollar wheelchair, and rolled across the Plaza at Lincoln Center. Yet I do not ask that woman, on seeing my body, to be struck there in the sunlight, to stand absolutely still and silent and hear like rushing tide the voices of all who suffer in body and in spirit and in both, then to turn before my dazzled eyes and go back to her home and begin next morning to live as Mother Teresa, as Dorothy Day. No: she is one of us, and what she said and did on that April evening was, like the warm sunlit sky, enough: for me, for the end of winter, for the infinite possibilities of the human heart.

LARS EIGHNER

Austin to Tucson: Hitting the Road

Billy inelegantly brought his little black Scirocco about and drove back toward Austin. That car was Billy's shibboleth; he never learned to pronounce its name although he was frequently corrected by parts dealers, his mechanic, and me. Never mind. In Billy's mind it was a Porsche and that was the way he drove it.

There we were, Lizbeth the bitch and I, with a pile of gear I could carry only a few yards at a time, by the side of the road in what seemed to me to be a desolate area. I had not been to the desert yet.

At that moment I had my first doubts that moving to California was the best idea I had ever had and that my plans were entirely adequate.

My plans, so far as they went, were in three parts.

My friend Rufus was in prison in Las Vegas on a charge of "gross and public lewdness"—a picturesque title for a crime, I thought. He had propositioned a minor, but as it was known that the minor was a prostitute, Rufus had been allowed to plead to the lesser charge. He was due to be released soon—exactly when, I was not sure—and he had mentioned in writing that I might visit him and his benefactor, an older man I had never met, at their home in La Puente, California.

I could see from my map that La Puente was not so far from Los Angeles. Rufus always seemed happy to see me and owed me some hospitality. But as I stood by the side of the road it occurred to me that Rufus had nothing of his own and perhaps his companion, who owed me nothing, would not be so happy to see me.

The second part of my plan was to obtain a position with one of the gay men's magazines that had bought my short stories. I had been writing short stories for the gay men's market for about five years. A collection of my stories had been published and had been a critical success. One of the magazines in Southern California had recently advertised in its own pages for an assistant editor, and thinking myself exceptionally qualified for such work, I had sent a résumé. That periodical had not had time to respond, but I took the fact of the advertisement as evidence that the demand for literary talent was brisk in the Los Angeles area.

By the side of the road I reflected on my lack of experience in layout, copy fitting, and all the other aspects of magazine work, except copy- and proofreading. But I was just as willing to start in the mail room.

My third thought was to seek a position working with PWAs (people with AIDS). For this I had fifteen years of related work experience. I had kept books and filed tax forms for a nonprofit eleemosynary corporation, I had maintained medical records, I had stalked the elusive third-party payment, I had wrestled with budgets and written parts of proposals, I had tiptoed—not always successfully—through the minefield of alternative agency collective decision-making, I had directed a suicide-prevention and drug-crisis center, I had carried bedpans and changed linens on occupied beds, and I had ruthlessly manipulated other agencies into providing the services they were supposed to provide for my clients. I thought if there were any order in the universe at all, I had been provided with this particular combination of skills and experience to be of some use in the AIDS crisis.

The only drawback I could see here was that in Southern California such work would probably entail lots of sensitivity training, encounter groups, and similar things that always make me want to throw up.

Perhaps the idea of moving to California was not so wonderful after all, but remaining in Austin certainly offered no better prospects.

By exploiting the formalities of the eviction process, I might have remained in the little shack on Avenue B a few weeks longer. But I had been without a job for almost a year. The shack had changed hands in the height of Austin's real estate boom. My new landlord had taken out an enormous loan to acquire the property and was in no position to extend me any more credit.

I had resigned from the state lunatic asylum under threat of being fired. I had always been in trouble at the asylum, for the humane published policies of the institution conflict with the abusive habits of some of the staff, and I often found myself in an unpopular position. But in the event, I was in trouble for complaining of being assigned to vegetative patients who had been warehoused at the institution since birth. That was not the work I had been hired to do and I found it emetic.

I sought work elsewhere. I knew I could do many things that might turn a profit for anyone who would employ me. But I had no documentary evidence of my skills. I had made a point of attending staff-development classes at the asylum. Those classes qualified me for more advanced positions at the asylum but provided me with no credentials that would be accepted elsewhere. My previous experience had been with a so-called alternative agency that did not believe in documents of any sort. What I knew of computers and electronics I had learned as a hobbiest. I had qualified as a first-class radio-television engineer, but my FCC license had not proved useful when I first got it and had long since lapsed. I knew I could write, but whenever I learned of a position for a staff writer, the position required a college degree, which I did not have.

I went to the state unemployment commission. In past years when I had been unemployed the commission had provided me with inappropriate referrals. Now it was too swamped to do even that. The bust had hit Austin. Only those who claimed unemployment compensation could see a counselor. I did not qualify for unemployment compensation because I had resigned my last position, and it would have been the same if I had been fired for cause. Since I was not a drain on the state fund, I would not get any help in looking for a job.

As for public assistance, it is like credit—easier to get if you have had it before. That you have qualified for one sort of benefit is often taken as evidence that you are eligible for another. Documents from one agency are accepted as proof of need at another agency. But as I had never received any form of public assistance before, I had no documents. When I was asked to provide documents to prove I had no income, I could not do so. I still do not know how to prove lack of income.

The private charities had organized a clearing house, orginally under the direction of the Catholic Church and still dominated by it. There I was told plainly that having neglected to produce children I could not support, I was disqualified for any benefit. Single men, I was told, were persons of sacred worth, but if only I could come up with a few mewling little wretches, illegitimate would do, then something might be done for me.

Sadly I had neglected to become addicted to drugs or alcohol and had not committed a serious crime. Rehabilitation was out of the question. But some hope was held out if I were to become maimed before funds ran out in that category.

Wherever I went I noticed an enormously fat blond woman, at least twice my size, with two screaming, undernourished brats. She fared better than I at the public and private agencies; they could hardly do enough for her. The waifs were about three and five years of age. The peculiar thing was they were never the same children. She had a different pair with her every day. So I must assume she had at least sixteen children under the age of six, and I can hardly begrudge her all the assistance she received.

I continued to write and to send my stories to the gay magazines that had bought them in the past. I had not yet learned to write when I was uninspired, and at three cents a word, paid six to eight months after I had finished a story, I could not make a living, though I sold all the stories I wrote.

Nearly every block in Hyde Park, as my neighborhood in Austin was called, had at least one foreclosure sign. The banks and the savings and loans were beginning to go belly up. The bust might not have been so bad if it had not been for the boom. Once, Austin had many old roomy houses that were inhabited by musicians and artists, students, punks, and latter-day hippies. The rents were low and such households stayed afloat so long as the law of averages prevented all of the occupants being out of work at once. Years before I had survived in Austin on a low income by living in such places. But during the boom many of these old houses were replaced with condos. When the bust hit, the condos went into receivership and housed no one.

As I watched the vacant condos deteriorate I understood the depression stories, stories that always seemed incredible to me, of people waiting in lines for thin soup while food rotted on the docks.

Going to California seemed to me to be something I could do, and I wanted to do something rather than to wait for the sheriff to come to put my things on the street. As I stood by the side of the road, weighing the uncertainties, I wondered whether the urge to do something had not led me to do the wrong thing.

While I had my second thoughts about our traveling to California, Lizbeth became fascinated by the sheep.

The eastern extreme of the Edwards plateau, where Billy had let us out, consists of small rolling limestone hills with grasses, low shrubs, and even the occasional tree. While hardly the picture of fertility, such land can support life as we know it, to wit: sheep, deer, and less-fortunate cattle.

I walked Lizbeth to the fence. The sheep did not tarry. Nonetheless Lizbeth found many smellworthy things and I did not hurry her. I took off my heavy jacket. Billy and I had agreed that I should get an early start, but in the way such things go with Billy, it was afternoon when he dropped Lizbeth and me by the road. Although the date was January 20, 1988, the sky was bright and clear and the temperature would reach into the eighties.

I counted the change in my pocket: less than a quarter, mostly in pennies. I smoked one of Billy's cigarettes. I arranged the gear and tightened the straps. I knew I was overpacked. Having never been to the desert before, I discarded the three-liter plastic Coke bottle filled with water which fit nowhere because Billy had suggested it at the last moment. I did have a canteen.

I made Lizbeth sit up on things where she could be seen. Then there was nothing to do except to begin hitchhiking. My sign read: TO L.A. WITH DOG. I did not want people to stop and then decline to take Lizbeth when they discovered her.

The problem was to get to the interstate.

Interstate 10, which goes to Los Angeles, runs northwest from San Antonio. We were on Highway 290, which to the east of Austin is a major highway joining the state's largest city to its capital, but to the west, where we were, goes 143 miles to meet the interstate in the middle of nowhere. There is little traffic and most of it is local. A local in a pickup with farm plates gave us a ride of less than five miles. Lizbeth rode in the cab. We were let out on a curve, just over a rise, so anyone going our way could not see us until he was as good as past us.

I had a large, square backpack that contained close to twenty-five pounds of dog food and some other odds and ends. Tied to the bottom of the pack was a bedroll consisting of a large comforter and several blankets wrapped around a hospital scrub suit and a large, heavy caftan that had been made for me by the former housemate who had brought Lizbeth, as a puppy, into the shack on Avenue B. The backpack would have been a load for me in any event, but the lack of a frame made it all the more unwieldy. I could only get the pack on my back by reclining on it, hooking my arms through the straps, and thrashing my limbs like a supine cockroach to right myself.

Besides the backpack there was also a rollbag in a trendy color that I found with several like it in a Dumpster behind a gift shop, the lot having been discarded, I soon discovered, because their nylon zippers were wholly inadequate. In addition, I had hooked another, smaller bookbag through the handles of the rollbag. I had also the heavy pea jacket I had been wearing, which I laid along the length of the rollbag.

Thus the most efficient way to move a few hundred yards was to leapfrog the various pieces of luggage a few score yards at a time until everything was past the first highway sign, which I supposed had been placed with some regard for its visibility. The move being made, it was still many hours until we got another ride. This was Wednesday and on a weekday most of the local traffic was single women, whom one never expects to stop. Late enough in the afternoon that he had already got off work in Austin, an electrician in a pickup stopped and again Lizbeth rode in the cab.

In this part of Texas it is often difficult to distinguish unreformed hippies from country types of about the same age, and indeed they are often the same. This driver had a great bushy red beard and recalled hitchhiking with a dog in the late Sixties, particularly in the Pacific Northwest. Perhaps this was the first ride Lizbeth got for us. The driver offered me a part of a tiny roach and was surprised I did not smoke marijuana.

I had shaved closely that morning and had been given for the trip an excellent short haircut by a former companion who was a professional hairdresser. Perhaps anyone of my obvious age and station was to be presumed to smoke marijuana. I had forced myself to smoke it for a number of years, but I always found it dysphoric and at last learned to refuse it in spite of the social consequences. The driver went a few miles out of his way to leave us in Johnson City.

We were let out at a Circle K, one of a chain of convenience stores found throughout the Southwest. The clerk let me water Lizbeth from the tap at the side of the building. I refreshed myself at the same time.

Eventually a semitrailer stopped and I gathered up my gear, but the driver meant only to go into the store. Having got the gear together, I decided to walk to the out-skirts of town. Sunset was approaching and several carloads of local youth had already yelled insults at me. I could see from the increasing speed-limit signs that I was near the edge of town. I hoped to find an inconspicuous spot to lay out the bedroll.

We had gone only a few blocks when a young couple in an old car offered us a ride. They whispered among themselves as if there were some reason besides ordinary etiquette not to invite me to join the party. From the way the male spoke, hardly able to pack enough words into a sentence, I would guess the reason was methamphetamines.

They are popular drugs in Central Texas and the labs are often located in the country because the synthesis is very smelly. However that may be, this ride put Lizbeth and me far enough out in the country that I might lay out the bedroll without fear of being disturbed. I sat on the gear and wrote a postcard in the last moments of twilight.

Then Lizbeth got us the first ride I am sure she was responsible for. A man, perhaps in his fifties, said he had passed us and seen the dog and come back for us. He drove us to his home in Fredricksburg. His wife, he told me, worked in a veterinary clinic in Austin and they both rather fancied dogs. This last I might have concluded for myself. They had, it turned out, four house dogs of various sizes and many yard dogs.

Lizbeth does not suffer other dogs to come near me, but this problem was evidently not new to my hosts for they had an improvised system of runs and gates so that Lizbeth could be accommodated and fed by herself.

This couple lived with the aged female parent of one of them. She reminded me of all the wives of my granduncles in that it was impossible to tell whether she was becoming senile or simply had always been a nitwit. My granduncles, I have always supposed, chose fluff-brained flappers in reaction to my grandaunts-by-blood, who were intelligent and level-headed, if not domineering and obstinate. I was given dinner of chicken à la king of a sort, based on Miracle Whip. I remarked on how beautiful Fredricksburg is, speaking from memory because I had hardly seen any of it in the dark. I related the story of my grandmother's Germans.

In the first part of the nineteenth century, an association of German princes in hopes of eliminating poverty deported large numbers of poor people, some of them to the Texas coast. Although this was supposed to be colonization, in fact the people were more or less dumped on the shore, sometimes by shipwreck, but inadequately provisioned at best. Malaria was then very common on the Texas coast and the immigrant population was decimated many times over. The Germans moved inland and settled in various parts of Central Texas. Fredricksburg was one of these settlements. This much of the story any native knows. Few, however, know of the orphan colony. A large band of children removed afoot from the coast to Fredricksburg, but there is no historical record of how they made their way.

The research was done before I could remember, but a central fact of my childhood, aside from the boxes of bond paper, typewriter erasers, eraser shields, and the upright Underwood, was my grandmother's composition of her book-length narrative poem that told how the children may have made it and then followed them up to the outbreak of the Civil War. Grandmother was no hearts-and-flowers old-lady poet, and some parts of her work were thought too racy for me when I was younger. I never read the manuscript when I was older. But I became perfectly familiar with the historic bones of the plot.

I should say this was my maternal grandmother, who, so far as I know, had no particular reason to choose this subject except that it seemed to her a good one. My own surname, if it is German, has no Texas connection.

Unfortunately my hosts, although they listened to my story patiently enough, were not natives and could not amplify any of the details. They agreed that Fredricksburg is beautiful—the oldest stone buildings being picturesque and pristine not so much for restoration as for maintenance. The gentleman agreed to drive us to the interstate. By the time we left, Lizbeth was frantic. She had never been away from her puppyhood home before and the separation from me and the presence of all the other dogs left her in a dither. She jumped from the backseat into my lap and licked me wherever she could reach until we were let out.

I thought we were let out at the junction of Highway 290 and I-10, sixty-three miles to the west of Fredricksburg. But in fact we had been taken twenty-three miles due south where I-10 passes through Comfort, Texas. The difference on I-10 was one mile more than the Pythagorean sixty-seven miles, but at least we had made it to the road that went right through to L.A. We might even get a ride all the way. But not that night.

No cars were using the entrance ramp. We walked along the ramp, but when we reached the highway there were no lights and the night was dark and moonless. We could not be seen. I was tired. I had not slept much the night before. The frontage road was above our heads and on it was a well-lit auto dealership. Beyond that was darkness and perhaps a place to sleep. With some difficulty Lizbeth and I scaled the grassy incline to the frontage road. Here was a guard rail. Lizbeth would not go under it, nor could she jump over it. To lift her over the rail I had to remove the backpack or else its weight would have dumped me over.

Past the auto dealership on the frontage road we found a curious little grassy spot. Even in the morning I could not make out what it was. It was landscaped. A gravel road looped around it but did not go off anywhere. I did not really care what it was except that it seemed unlikely we would be disturbed there for the rest of the night. I laid out the bedroll, put on the heavy caftan, and crawled in.

Naturally Lizbeth crawled into the bedroll too, but she found it too cold at her usual station behind my knees. She got under the caftan and wiggled up until her nose just stuck out of the neckhole. This might have been cozy enough except that she detected the security guard at the auto dealership whenever he made his rounds. She barked.

As concealment seemed to me the most logical first strategy in providing for our safety, I was concerned that I could hardly control Lizbeth, although the guard never came closer to us than a couple of hundred yards. Discovery where we were might not have been so bad, but I thought surely we would come to times that our survival would depend upon Lizbeth's not giving away our position. I got little sleep. We were up at first light. After the burst of hope and energy that comes with dawn, my mood sharply declined. Getting the pack on my back had been a struggle when I first tried it. Now moving at all was becoming difficult.

Lizbeth would not eat. I dumped most of her food. Twenty-five pounds was more than she would eat in a month. Of course she would not eat that morning because she had gorged herself the night before in Fredricksburg—our hosts had mixed meat in with her food. She would not be hungry enough to eat plain, dry dog food for a day or two, although she would be happy to have any little scrap of human food she could get. I knew her eating habits as well then as I know them now. But at the time I took her refusal to eat as a vote of no confidence. I do not think I was mistaken in perceiving a number of quizzical looks from her quarter.

I discarded my boots next. Although I walked a great deal in town and the boots were broken in perfectly well, they were not the thing for the road. Everyone advises the traveler to wear sensible shoes, and I have not found a better piece of advice.

We were in Comfort for most of the day. Several other hitchhikers appeared and got rides. I got a short ride late in the afternoon and made five dollars in the process. The driver offered to let me out at a rest stop or to drive me a few miles farther. As I did not then know the advantages of hitchhiking from a rest area, I asked to be driven the few miles farther.

We were let off at a crossover near the little town of Mountain Home. Here the median of the interstate expanded to several hundred yards and there were several shady trees. I left our gear under a tree and Lizbeth and I walked over the crossover to a store the last driver had said would be there.

It was a little country store with sparsely stocked, unfinished wood shelves. They were discontinuing cigarettes and had only a few stale packs of unfiltered Camels. I bought two packs and a Big Red, a caffeine-laced cream soda popular in Oklahoma and Texas, and I watered Lizbeth from the hose outside. Thursday afternoon had become very warm.

We returned to the tree where I had stashed our gear and I drank the Big Red and wrote a letter to Billy. Then I tried thumbing until dark, but it was useless.

I still do not know whether it is better to have a sign or not, if it is worth the effort of standing all the while, whether to look as presentable as possible or to try to appear down on my luck. I think perhaps none of that matters. Many, many people still pass by.

I was not so discouraged that night when I decided it was time to lie down. I was better off than when the day had started. I had smokes and some change in my pocket.

About dark we walked back on a little rise through which the road cut. When we were about sixteen feet above the road I decided to stop. I dropped the gear, left Lizbeth strapped to the gear, and raced another twenty or thirty yards.

When you live out of Dumpsters, dysentery is an occasional fact of life, although it is less frequent in cool weather. I had eaten nothing save the chicken à la king since we left Austin, but the day before that I had eaten some suspicious Dumpster pizza. In the middle of nowhere the result was inconvenient. In the city, as I had yet to discover, intestinal distress and the dearth of truly public rest rooms provide a number of unpretty options.

I had a magazine-premium battery-powered radio. From it I got enough of a weather report to hear that a low of twenty-eight degrees was expected somewhere, but the station faded before I learned its location. Suddenly Lizbeth broke loose from her moorings and ran across the rise. A white tail disappeared over a fence. Lizbeth had discovered deer.

Friday morning was overcast with high clouds. The grass was very dewy and, in patches, frosty. Because I was bigger and stronger I eventually dislodged Lizbeth from the bedroll. As we were up at first light, I believe I had packed and we were down at the road before sunrise. Very many semitrailers passed us. I tipped my cap or waved at most of them and a few of them sounded their horns. So far as I know, no trucker has ever done me any good in my travels, but I had heard it was a good idea to be friendly toward the truckers, so I was. Lizbeth curled up on the gear and shivered. I hate it when she shivers.

Quite soon, although at the time it seemed not so soon, we got another ride. I did not notice him until he had passed us and stopped and honked his horn.

The old pickup was very battered, mostly lime green, with a Florida license plate taped in the rear window of the cab. It sat on the shoulder under the crossover some two or three hundred yards beyond us. As fast as I could move with all the gear was hardly more than a brisk walk, even with Lizbeth towing me as hard she was able. The truck did not pull away as sometimes happens in these situations. The cab was nearly full of gear and delicately balanced arrangements for brewing coffee with power from the cigarette lighter. The bed of the pickup was loaded with exactly what all I never discovered, but Lizbeth would have to ride there.

Lizbeth is a fool. Off her leash she cannot be trusted not to dart out into traffic. In the last couple of days she had ridden more than she had in her whole life before and she had never been in the back of a pickup alone. I tied her leash to the hub of a loose spare tire in the bed of the pickup.

It was far from clear that she could not hang herself by jumping overboard or be lost over the side by slipping her collar. There was not room for me to ride with her. I worried about her constantly for she rode standing on various objects and precariously balanced. The worst was when we would overtake a livestock truck. She clearly appreciated only the very slight relative motion of the vehicles and gave every appearance of being willing to dash herself against the slats of the livestock trucks, just as she might jump against a stationary fence.

The driver's story was that he had been a couple of years in Florida with a girlfriend, but the relationship had gone sour. So he was returning to Tucson, his hometown, and a previous girlfriend.

To Tucson seemed quite a ways and I was very much encouraged. I had pored over the map without absorbing many facts of geography. I thought, for example, that the continental divide was somewhere in California, rather near the San Gabriel Mountains. I was not entirely sure how far I would have got when I reached Tucson, but from the mile markers I could see this ride would put at least five hundred miles of Texas behind me.

We stopped fairly soon at a rest stop. I scraped a razor over my face, washed my neck and forearms, and since I had a ride already, changed into my most ragged jeans. The driver wanted to be sure that Lizbeth was walked. She seldom wants walking more than twice a day. But I welcomed the chance to lash her to the tire again, this time with much less slack. Nonetheless, she managed to get up and about and to keep my heart in my throat for the rest of the ride.

The last of the grass and the trees petered out a little past Junction, Texas, and then for many miles there was nothing except what is called cedar in Austin but elsewhere is known as juniper scrub. This is a long and desolate stretch, but what is more, the few wretched settlements that exist are several miles from the highway and no cafés, gas stations, or even tourist traps are visible from the road. I was set to work brewing coffee. The driver was well into his second day on the road without stopping and had no intention resting until he reached Tucson. Again I was offered a part of a roach from the ashtray, but once it was clear I had no interest in mari-juana, I was given the job of rolling joints for the driver from a stash in a Bull Durham bag. We did not talk much. The driver was determined to coax something out of the radio. For the most part we got static and whenever he did pick up something he overpowered his speakers so the result to me was little different from static.

I was suitably impressed by the mountains as we got to them. I had seldom seen mountains and never such as these, young and rising from a treeless landscape.

It was another hot day and we were climbing. The temperature gauge in the old pickup read hot, but the driver insisted it was stuck. We pulled into Las Cruces to get gas and the radiator blew.

The cap is supposed to blow first, just as a safety valve on a boiler blows before the boiler reaches the bursting point. But this cap had not. Yet as the steam dissipated and things cooled off, it appeared the radiator had only split a seam. A welder was found who would draw a bead down the seam for seven dollars.

This exhausted our folding cash and I was set to the task of sorting through the driver's change pot. There was enough for a couple of packs of cigarettes and, perhaps, gasoline to get to Tucson. I had about three quarters besides of my own, which I did not mention. We would press on.

As we pulled out of the service station in Las Cruces, Lizbeth finally managed to hang herself, but inadequately. She was attempting to get from the back of the pickup to the cab window. I made a bed for her in the hub of the spare tire and then lashed her to it again with as little slack as I thought possible. Night was falling and I knew it would be cold. I hoped she would nest in the tire. Of course she did not. I was set back to square one in worrying about her. I became accustomed to the shadow of her head in the lights of the vehicles that overtook us, only to be alarmed again by the absence of the shadow when she finally fell asleep.

The sun set as we passed Vail, Arizona. We were climbing again. The driver explained that Tucson was in a box canyon and if we reached the top of this climb we could coast into town. This was far from an idle observation, for fuel was precariously low. Eventually the truck did make it to the top and it was all downhill from there.

The driver let us off about 9:00 P.M. at a truck stop south of town. I have since learned that this was a famous truck stop and elegantly appointed as these things go, but I had no chance of learning that firsthand. Immediately Lizbeth sat on a prickly pear and thus struck the keynote of our tenure in Tucson.

The shoulder of the frontage road was under construction for as far ahead as I could see. That would pose a problem in getting away from the truck stop.

I know now what I should have done. I should have found a dark spot and gone to sleep. Our situation did not appear to me to be good, but it was far from desperate and unlikely to deteriorate overnight. "Things will look brighter in the morning" was the sort of adage I always sneered at. Now I was to learn it was valuable advice and in Tucson it was a dear lesson. A long ride is such a piece of luck that one is tempted to try to press on before fortune shows its other face. I suppose that was why I hoped to get farther that night. But instead, Lizbeth and I were fallen upon by thieves.

A young Latin man distracted me with some discussion that I never understood. I was holding Lizbeth and we were not more than twenty feet from our gear. When I turned to the gear, it was gone, and when I turned again, so was the young man.

His confederates must have had a car, for there was no other way they could have made such a pile of gear disappear in so short a time. Naturally, I had laid my heavy coat on the bundle.

I find it hard to believe that anyone would have thought I had anything of much value. My clothes, besides being worn, would not fit many other people, and this should have been obvious to look at me. The little radio was of no appreciable value. Besides my papers, most of the bulk of what was taken was the remainder of Lizbeth's food and the bedding, which was warm enough, but could not have been sold. Other than a few dollars in postage, nothing could have been readily converted to cash. I was left with what I was wearing, a football practice jersey and my most ragged pair of jeans, and Lizbeth.

My mistake, besides not getting us out of harm's way after dark, was in not lashing Lizbeth to the gear the minute I set it down. While Lizbeth is harmless, most people would require some time to discover the fact and in the meanwhile she would make noise.

Tired and disheartened, I sat by a telephone pole, and in spite of the cold I must have dozed sitting up.

When I awoke I discovered a further disaster. Lizbeth had curled up at the base of the telephone pole, and cold as it was, she had heated the tar on the pole until it flowed all over her back. Clearly no one would want this mess in his vehicle. When the sun rose I saw it was even worse than it had first appeared.

My own stamps and envelopes had gone with our gear. But just before I left Austin, Billy gave me a whole book of stamps with a face value of $4.40, which I had put in my wallet. By chance the wallet was in my jeans and not in the pocket of the coat that had been stolen.

Billy had told me his phone credit card number and I used it to call a bookstore that was listed in the copied pages of a gay travelers' guide that Billy had given me with the stamps. I supposed the bookstore was a gay one, and in my experience these little stores, which are not to be confused with adult bookstores, take a proprietary interest in their authors. The clerk I spoke to, however, seemed less than gracious and only grudgingly agreed to give me cash for the stamps. My object was to buy some rubbing alcohol to clean the tar off Lizbeth's back.

The immediate problem was to get to the bookstore.

South Tucson consists of huts and shacks and sand dunes, with here and there the occasional obvious federal housing project. It is unremittingly barren and ugly. There are few improvements of any kind. Street signs are restricted to the housing projects where they identify various *stravs*. Using the dictionaries of several languages, I have been unable to discover what a *strav* is, and have concluded that it is a compromise between *street* and *avenue*.

South Tucson simply has no sidewalks. I thought at first this was merely in keeping with the general wretchedness of the place, but eventually it seemed to me that the public policy in Tucson is to impede pedestrians as much as possible. In particular, I could find no way to walk to the main part of town in the north except in the traffic lanes of narrow highway ramps.

I could not believe this at first, and Lizbeth and I spent several hours wandering on the south bank of the dry gash that divides Tucson as I looked for a walkway. More than anywhere we have been, adults like teenagers shouted threats as well as insults at us in Tucson, and did so whether I was trying to hitchhike or was merely walking. More than one man found it necessary to brandish a firearm at us although we were afoot and presented no conceivable threat to those cruising past us at upward of fifty miles per hour. This atmosphere did not make the walk across the high ramp in the traffic lane any less exciting.

The usual medium in Tucson for vulgar displays of wealth appeared to be the conspicuous and wasteful consumption of water. As we walked north things got greener and more affluent. The ritziest neighborhoods were positively swamp-like. Lizbeth could drink from the runoff of the sprinkler systems that ran throughout the heat of the day. Still, there were no continuous sidewalks.

Perhaps the bookstore was no more than seven miles north of the gorge, but it was late in the afternoon when Lizbeth and I got there. The bookstore was not of the sort I expected. It was not after all a little gay bookstore, but was a very large general-interest bookstore with a gay-interest section.

The clerk took the book of stamps and said he would have to check with the owner, although I mentioned having phoned earlier. I suppose they counted the stamps each and every one, for it was some time before he returned to give me $4.40. I noticed that a couple of magazines that contained my stories were on display behind the counter, over the clerk's head.

I took the money to a nearby drugstore to get some rubbing alcohol.

If I had then had a better grasp of the geography I might have saved us considerable trouble and heartbreak. The bookstore was not so very far to the east of the interstate. But as we had crossed the gorge, the interstate appeared to veer off sharply to the west. I thought the nearest point of the highway was in the south, and to the south we returned.

We were quite in darkness by the time we crossed the gorge again. Lizbeth could no longer walk.

We were far enough west now that convenience stores no longer had faucets and hoses on the outside. I went into a convenience store and bought a gallon of water. I returned to Lizbeth and carried her a few feet from the road, behind a sand dune.

I would never have thought a stout middle-aged man could outwalk a healthy young dog. I have since learned I cannot expect much more than five miles a day out of Lizbeth on a consistent basis, and then only when conditions are favorable. In Tucson conditions are not favorable. Without sidewalks or grass, she had walked on cinders, sand, and rocks. The trip to the bookstone had worn the pads off her paws.

VIVIAN GORNICK

From Fierce Attachments

I'm eight years old. My mother and I come out of our apartment onto the second-floor landing. Mrs. Drucker is standing in the open doorway of the apartment next door, smoking a cigarette. My mother locks the door and says to her, "What are you doing here?" Mrs. Drucker jerks her head backward toward her own apartment. "He wants to lay me. I told him he's gotta take a shower before he can touch me." I know that "he" is her husband. "He" is always the husband. "Why? He's so dirty?" my mother says. "He feels dirty to *me*," Mrs. Drucker says. "Drucker, you're a whore," my mother says. Mrs. Drucker shrugs her shoulder. "I can't ride the subway," she says. In the Bronx "ride the subway" was a euphemism for going to work.

I lived in that tenement between the ages of six and twenty-one. There were twenty apartments, four to a floor, and all I remember is a building full of women. I hardly remember the men at all. They were everywhere, of course—husbands, fathers, brothers—but I remember only the women. And I remember them all crude like Mrs. Drucker or fierce like my mother. They never spoke as though they knew who they were, understood the bargain they had struck with life, but they often acted as though they knew. Shrewd, volatile, unlettered, they performed on a Dreiserian scale. There would be years of apparent calm, then suddenly an outbreak of panic and wildness: two or three lives scarred (perhaps ruined), and the turmoil would subside. Once again: sullen quiet, erotic torpor, the ordinariness of daily denial. And I—the girl growing in their midst, being made in their image—I absorbed them as I would chloroform on a cloth laid against my face. It has taken me thirty years to understand how much of them I understood.

My mother and I are out walking. I ask if she remembers the women in that building in the Bronx. "Of course," she replies. I tell her I've always thought sexual rage was what made them so crazy. "Absolutely," she says without breaking her stride. "Remember Drucker? She used to say if she didn't smoke a cigarette while she was having intercourse with her husband she'd throw herself out the window. And Zimmerman, on the other side of us? They married her off to him when she was sixteen, she hated his guts, she used to say if he'd get killed on the job (he was a construction worker) it would be a *mitzvah*." My mother stops walking. Her voice drops in awe of her own memory. "He actually used to take her by physical force," she says. "Would pick her up in the middle of the living-room floor and carry her off to the bed." She stares into the middle distance for a moment. Then she says to me, "The European men. They were animals. Just plain animals." She starts walking again. "Once, Zimmerman locked him out of the house. He rang our bell. He could hardly look at me. He asked if he could use our fire-escape window. I didn't speak one word to him. He walked through the house and climbed out the window." My mother laughs. "That fire-escape window, it did some business! Remember Cessa upstairs? Oh no, you couldn't remember her, she only lived there one year after we moved into the house, then the Russians were in that apartment. Cessa and I were very friendly. It's so strange, when I come to think of it. We hardly knew each other, any of us, sometimes we didn't talk to each other at all. But we lived on top of one another, we were in and out of each other's house. Everybody knew everything in no time at all. A few months in the building and the women were, well, *intimate*.

"This Cessa. She was a beautiful young woman, married only a few years. She didn't love her husband. She didn't hate him, either. He was a nice man, actually. What can I tell you, she didn't love him, she used to go out every day, I think she had a lover somewhere. Anyway, she had long black hair down to her ass. One day she cut it off. She wanted to be modern. Her husband didn't say anything to her, but her father came into the house, took one look at her cut hair, and gave her a slap across the face she saw her grandmother from the next world. Then he instructed her husband to lock her in the house for a month. She used to come down the fire escape into my window and out my door. Every afternoon for a month. One day she comes back and we're having coffee in the kitchen. I say to her, 'Cessa, tell your father this is America, Cessa, America. You're a free woman.' She looks at me and she says to me, 'What do you mean, tell my father this is America? He was born in Brooklyn.'"

My relationship with my mother is not good, and as our lives accumulate it often seems to worsen. We are locked into a narrow channel of acquaintance, intense and binding. For years at a time there is an exhaustion, a kind of softening, between us. Then the rage comes up again, hot and clear, erotic in its power to compel attention. These days it is bad between us. My mother's way of "dealing" with the bad times is to accuse me loudly and publicly of the truth. Whenever she sees me she says, "You hate me. I know you hate me." I'll be visiting her and she'll say to anyone who happens to be in the room—a neighbor, a friend, my brother, one of my nieces—"She hates me. What she has against me I don't know, but she hates me." She is equally capable of stopping a stranger on the street when we're out walking and saying, "This is my daughter. She hates me." Then she'll turn to me and plead, "What did I do to you, you should hate me so?" I never answer. I know she's burning and I'm glad to let her burn. Why not? I'm burning, too.

But we walk the streets of New York together endlessly. We both live in lower Manhattan now, our apartments a mile apart, and we visit best by walking. My mother is an urban peasant and I am my mother's daughter. The city is our natural element. We each have daily adventures with bus drivers, bag ladies, ticket takers, and street crazies. Walking brings out the best in us. I am forty-five now and my mother is seventy-seven. Her body is strong and healthy. She traverses the island easily with me. We don't love each other on these walks, often we are raging at each other, but we walk anyway.

Our best times together are when we speak of the past. I'll say to her, "Ma, remember Mrs. Kornfeld? Tell me that story again," and she'll delight in telling me the story again. (It is only the present she hates; as soon as the present becomes the past, she immediately begins loving it.) Each time she tells the story it is both the same and different because each time I'm older, and it occurs to me to ask a question I didn't ask the last time around.

The first time my mother told me that her uncle Sol had tried to sleep with her I was twenty-two and I listened silently: rapt and terrified. The background I knew by heart. She was the youngest of eighteen children, eight of whom survived into adult life. (Imagine. My grandmother was pregnant for twenty years.) When the family came to New York from Russia, Sol, my grandmother's youngest brother and the same age as her own oldest child (her mother had *also* been pregnant for twenty years), came along with them. My mother's two oldest brothers had preceded the family by some years, had gone to work in the rag trade, and had rented a cold-water flat on the Lower East Side for all eleven of them: bathroom in the hall, coal stove in the kitchen, a train of dark cubbyhole inner rooms. My mother, then a ten-year-old child, slept on two chairs in the kitchen, because my grandmother took in a boarder.

Sol had been drafted into the army during the First World War and sent to Europe. When he returned to New York my mother was sixteen years old and the only child left at home. So here he comes, a glamorous stranger, the baby niece he left behind now womanly and dark-eyed, with glossy brown hair cut in a stylish bob and a transforming smile, all of which she pretends she doesn't know how to use (that was always my mother's style: outrageous coquettishness unhampered by the slightest degree of self-consciousness), and he begins sleeping in one of those cubbyholes two walls away from her, with the parents snoring loudly at the farthest end of the apartment.

"One night," my mother said, "I jumped up from sleep, I don't know why, and I see Sol is standing over me. I started to say, 'What is it?' I thought something was wrong with my parents, but then he looked so funny I thought maybe he was sleepwalking. He didn't say a word to me. He picked me up in his arms and he carried me to his bed. He laid us both down on the bed, and he held me in his arms, and he began to stroke my body. Then he lifted my nightgown and he began to stroke my thigh. Suddenly he pushed me away from him and said, 'Go back to your bed.' I got up and went back to my bed. He never spoke one word about what happened that night, and I didn't either."

The second time I heard the story I was thirty. She repeated it nearly word for word as we were walking up Lexington Avenue somewhere in the Sixties. When she came to the end I said to her, "And you didn't say anything to him, throughout the whole time?" She shook her head no. "How come, Ma?" I asked. Her eyes widened, her mouth pursed. "I don't know," she puzzled. "I only know I was very scared." I looked at her, as she would say, *funny*. "Whatsamatter?" she said. "You don't like my answer?" "No," I protested, "it's not that. It just seems odd not to have uttered a sound, not to have indicated your fears at all."

The third time she told the story I was nearly forty. We were walking up Eighth Avenue, and as we neared Forty-second Street I said to her, "Ma, did it ever occur to you to ask yourself *why* you remained silent when Sol made his move?" She looked quickly at me. But this time she was wise to me. "What are you getting at?" she asked angrily. "Are you trying to say I *liked* it? Is that what you're getting at?" I laughed nervously, gleefully. "No, Ma, I'm not saying that. I'm just saying it's *odd* that you didn't make a sound." Again, she repeated that she had been very frightened. "Come off it," I said sharply. "You are disgusting!" she raged at me in the middle of the street. "My brilliant daughter. I should send you to college for another two degrees you're so brilliant. I *wanted* my uncle to rape me, is that it? A new thought!" We didn't speak for a month after that walk.

The Bronx was a patchwork of invaded ethnic territories: four or five square blocks dominated by Irish or Italians or Jews, but each section with its quota of Irish living in a Jewish block or Jews in an Italian block. Much has been made of this change rung on the New York neighborhood register, but those who grew up running the

Irish or Italian gauntlet, or being frozen out by Jewish neighbors, are not nearly so marked by their extra portion of outsidedness as they are leveled by the shared street life. Our family had lived for a year in an Italian neighborhood. My brother and I had been the only Jewish children in the school, and we had indeed been miserable. That's all: miserable. When we moved back into a Jewish neighborhood, my brother was relieved at no longer having to worry that he'd be beaten up every afternoon by kids who called him the Jewish genius, but the outline and substance of his life were not fundamentally altered. The larger truth is that the "otherness" of the Italians or the Irish or the Jews among us lent spice and interest, a sense of definition, an exciting edge to things that was openly feared but secretly welcomed.

Our building was all Jewish except for one Irish family on the first floor, one Russian family on the third floor, and a Polish superintendent. The Russians were tall and silent: they came and went in the building in a manner that seemed mysterious. The Irish were all thin and blond: blue eyes, narrow lips, closed faces. They, too, were a shadowy presence among us. The super and his wife were also quiet. They never spoke first to anyone. That's the main thing, I guess, about being a few among the many: it silences you.

My mother might have been silenced, too, had she remained living among the Italians, might have snatched her children up in wordless anxiety when a neighbor befriended one of us, just as Mrs. Cassidy did whenever a woman in our building smoothed the hair of one of the "Irish blondies." But my mother was not one among the many. Here, in this all-Jewish building, she was in her element, had enough room between the skin of social presence and the flesh of an unknowing center in which to move around, express herself freely, be warm and sarcastic, hysterical and generous, ironic and judgmental, and, occasionally, what she thought of as affectionate: that rough, bullying style she assumed when overcome with the tenderness she most feared.

My mother was distinguished in the building by her unaccented English and the certainty of her manner. Although our apartment door was always closed (a distinction was made between those educated enough to value the privacy of a closed door and those so peasant-like the door was always half open), the neighbors felt free to knock at any time: borrow small kitchen necessities, share a piece of building gossip, even ask my mother to act as arbiter in an occasional quarrel. Her manner at such times was that of a superior person embarrassed by the childlike behavior of her inferiors. "*Oy*, Zimmerman." She would smile patronizingly when Mrs. Zimmerman, beside herself over some slight, real or imagined, came to tell her of the perfidy of one or another of our neighbors. "Such foolishness." Or, "That's ridiculous," she would rap out sharply when a tale she considered base or ignorant was repeated to her. She seemed never to be troubled by the notion that there might be two sides to a story, or more than one interpretation of an event. She knew that, compared with the women around her, she was "developed"—a person of higher thought and feeling—so what was there to think about? "Developed" was one of her favorite words. If Mrs. Zimmerman spoke loudly in the hall on a Saturday morning, we, sitting in the kitchen just behind our apartment door, would stare at each other and, inevitably, my mother would shake her head and pronounce, "An undeveloped woman." If someone made a crack about the *schvartzes*, my mother would carefully explain to me that such sentiments were "undeveloped." If there was a dispute in the grocery store over price or weight, again I would hear the word "undeveloped." My father smiled at her when she said "undeveloped," whether out of indulgence or pride I never did know. My brother, on his guard from the age of ten, stared without expression. But I, I absorbed the feel of her words, soaked up every accompanying gesture and expression, every complicated bit of impulse and intent. Mama thinking everyone around was undeveloped, and most of what they said was ridiculous, became imprinted on me like dye on the most receptive of materials.

The apartment was a five-room flat, with all the rooms opening onto each other. It was a tenement flat not a railroad flat: not one window looked into an airshaft. The apartment door opened into a tiny foyer that gave directly onto the kitchen. To the right of the kitchen, in the foyer, stood the refrigerator, propped against a wall at right angles to the bathroom: a tiny rectangle with a painted wooden door whose upper half was frosted glass. Beyond the foyer stood two rooms of equal size separated by a pair of curtained glass doors. The second of these rooms faced the street and was flooded with afternoon sunlight. Off this front room, at either end, were two tiny bedrooms, one of which also faced the street, the other the back of the building.

Because the front room and one of the bedrooms faced the street, ours was considered a desirable apartment, an apartment "to the front." A few years ago a man who had also grown up on my block said to me, "I always thought you were richer than us because you lived to the front." Although living to the front usually did mean that the husbands made more money than did the husbands of those living *tief, teier in draird* (deeply, dearly in hell) to the back, we lived to the front because part of my mother's claim to a superior grasp of life's necessities rested on her insistence that, unless we stood nose to nose with welfare, an apartment to the back was not within the range of domestic consideration. Nevertheless, it was "to the back" that we—that is, she and I—actually lived.

The kitchen window faced the alley in the back of the building, as did the kitchen windows of the building next to ours, and those of two other buildings whose entrances were on the opposite side of the square block these apartment houses shared. There were no trees or bushes or grasses of any kind in the alley—only concrete, wire fencing, and wooden poles. Yet I remember the alley as a place of clear light and sweet air, suffused, somehow, with a perpetual smell of summery green.

The alley caught the morning sun (our kitchen was radiant before noon), and it was a shared ritual among the women that laundry was done early on a washboard in the sink and hung out to dry in the sun. Crisscrossing the alley, from first floor to fifth, were perhaps fifty clotheslines strung out on tall wooden poles planted in the concrete ground. Each apartment had its own line stretching out among ten others on the pole. The wash from each line often interfered with the free flap of the wash on the line above or below, and the sight of a woman yanking hard at a clothesline, trying to shake her wash free from an indiscriminate tangle of sheets and trousers, was common. While she was pulling at the line she might also be calling. "Berth-a-a. Berth-a-a. Ya home, Bertha?" Friends were scattered throughout the buildings on the alley, and called to one another all during the day to make various arrangements ("What time ya taking Harvey to the doctor?" Or, "Got sugar in the house? I'll send Marilyn over." Or, "Meetcha on the corner in ten minutes"). So much stir and animation! The clear air, the unshadowed light, the women calling to each other, the sounds of their voices mixed with the smell of clothes drying in the sun, all that texture and color swaying in open space. I leaned out the kitchen window with a sense of expectancy I can still taste in my mouth, and that taste is colored a tender and brilliant green.

For me, the excitement in the apartment was located in the kitchen and the life outside its window. It was a true excitement: it grew out of contradiction. Here in the kitchen I did my homework and kept my mother company, watched her prepare and execute her day. Here, also, I learned that she had the skill and vitality to do her work easily and well but that she disliked it, and set no store by it. She taught me nothing. I never learned how to cook, clean, or iron clothes. She herself was a boringly competent cook, a furiously fast housecleaner, a demonic washerwoman.

Still, she and I occupied the kitchen fully. Although my mother never seemed to be listening to what went on in the alley, she missed nothing. She heard every voice, every motion of the clothesline, every flap of the sheets, registered each call and communication. We laughed together over this one's broken English, that one's loudmouthed indiscretion, a screech here, a fabulous curse there. Her running commentary on the life outside the window was my first taste of the fruits of intelligence: she knew how to convert gossip into knowledge. She would hear a voice go up one octave and observe: "She had a fight with her husband this morning." Or it would go down an octave and, "Her kid's sick." Or she'd catch a fast exchange and diagnose a cooling friendship. This skill of hers warmed and excited me. Life seemed fuller, richer, more interesting when she was making sense of the human activity in the alley. I felt a live connection, then, between us and the world outside the window.

The kitchen, the window, the alley. It was the atmosphere in which she was rooted, the background against which she stood outlined. Here she was smart, funny, and energetic, could exercise authority and have impact. But she felt contempt for her environment. "Women, yech!" she'd say. "Clotheslines and gossip," she'd say. She knew there was another world—*the* world—and sometimes she thought she wanted that world. Bad. She'd stop dead in the middle of a task, staring for long minutes at a time at the sink, the floor, the stove. But where? how? what?

So this was her condition: here in the kitchen she knew who she was, here in the kitchen she was restless and bored, here in the kitchen she functioned admirably, here in the kitchen she despised what she did. She would become angry over the "emptiness of a woman's life" as she called it, then laugh with a delight I can still hear when she analyzed some complicated bit of business going on in the alley. Passive in the morning, rebellious in the afternoon, she was made and unmade daily. She fastened hungrily on the only substance available to her, became affectionate toward her own animation, then felt like a collaborator. How could she not be devoted to a life of such intense division? And how could I not be devoted to her devotion?

DONALD HALL

To Read Fiction

When we learn to read fiction, we acquire a pleasure and a resource we never lose. Although literary study is impractical in one sense—few people make their living reading books—in another sense it is almost as practical as breathing. Literature records and embodies centuries of human thought and feeling, preserving for us the minds of people who lived before us, who were like us and unlike us, against whom we can measure our common humanity and our historical difference. And when we read the stories of our contemporaries, they illuminate the world all of us share.

When we read great literature, something changes in us that stays changed. Literature remembered becomes material to think with. No one who has read *The Death of Ivan Ilych* well is quite the same again. Reading adds tools by which we observe, measure, and judge the people and the properties of our universe, we understand the actions and motives of others and of ourselves.

In the fable of the ant and the grasshopper, the wise ant builds his storehouse against winter and prospers; the foolish grasshopper saves nothing and perishes. Anyone who dismisses the study of literature on the ground that it will not be useful—to a chemist or an engineer, to a foreman or an X-ray technician—imitates the grasshopper. When we shut from our lives everything except food and shelter, part of us starves to death. Food for this hunger is music, painting, film, plays, poems, stories, and novels. Much writing in newspapers, magazines, and popular novels is not literature, if we reserve that word for work of high quality. This reading gives us as little nourishment as most television and most fast food. For the long winters and energetic summers of our lives, we require the sustenance of literature.

Reading fiction old and new—taking into ourselves the work of nineteenth-century Russian, contemporary English, Irish, and especially American storytellers—we build a storehouse of knowledge and we entertain ourselves as well. But to take pleasure and understanding from fiction we have to learn how to read it. No one expects to walk up to a computer and be able to program it without first learning something about computers. For some reason—perhaps because we are familiar with words from childhood and take them for granted—we tend to think that a quick glance at the written word should reward us and that if we do not take instant satisfaction the work is beyond us, or not worth it, or irrelevant or boring. But all our lives, in other skills, we have needed instruction and practice—to be able to ride a bicycle, drive a car, play guitar, shoot baskets, typewrite, dance.

The knowledge we derive from literature can seem confusing. Equally great works may contradict each other in the generalizations we derive from them. One work may recommend solitude, another society. One may advise us to seize the moment, another to live a life of contemplation. Or, two good readers may disagree about the implication of a work and each argue convincingly, with detailed references to the writing, in support of contrary interpretations. A complex work of fiction cannot be reduced to a simple, correct meaning. In an elementary arithmetic text, the answers may be printed in the back of the book. There are no answers to be printed in the back of . . . any collection of literature.

Such nebulousness, or ambiguity, disturbs some students. After an hour's class discussion of a short story, with varying interpretations offered, they want to know, "But what does it mean?" We must admit that literature is inexact, and its truth is not easily verifiable. Probably the story means several things at once, and not one thing at all. This is not to say, however, that it means anything that anybody finds in it. Although differing, equally defensible opinions are common, error is even more common.

When we speak of truth in the modern world, we usually mean something scientific or tautological. Arithmetic contains the truth of tautology; two and two make four because our definitions of two and four say so. In laboratories we encounter the truth of statistics and the truth of observation. If we smoke cigarettes heavily, it is true that we have one chance in four to develop lung cancer. When we heat copper wire over a Bunsen burner, the flame turns blue.

But there is an older sense of truth, in which statements apparently opposite can be valid. In this older tradition, truth is dependent on context and circumstance, on the agreement of sensible men and women—like the "Guilty" or "Not guilty" verdict of a jury. Because this literary (or philosophical, or legal, or historical) truth is inexact, changeable, and subject to argument, literature can seem nebulous to minds accustomed to arithmetical certainty.

Let me argue this: If literature is nebulous or inexact; if it is impossible to determine, with scientific precision, the value or the meaning of a work of art, this inexactness is the price literature pays for representing whole human beings. Human beings themselves, in their feelings and thoughts, in the wandering of their short lives, are ambiguous and ambivalent, shifting mixtures of permanence and change, direction and disorder. Because literature is true to life, true to the complexities of human feeling, different people will read the same work with different responses. And the storyteller's art will sometimes affirm that opposite things are both true because they are. Such a condition is not tidy; it is perhaps regrettable—but it is human nature.

What's Good, What's Bad

The claims I make for fiction are large: that it alters and enlarges our minds, our connections with each other past and present, our understanding of our own feelings. These claims apply to excellent literature only. This . . . suggests that some fiction is better than other fiction, and that some narratives are not literature at all. Even if judgments are always subject to reversal, even if there is no way we can be certain of being correct, evaluation lives at the center of literary study.

When I was nineteen, I liked to read everything: science fiction, Russian novels, mystery stories, great poems, adventure magazines. Then for six months after an accident, sentenced to a hospital bed and a body cast, I set myself a reading list, all serious books I had been thinking about getting to. Of course there was a background to this choice: I had been taught by a good teacher who had directed and encouraged and stimulated my reading. I read through Shakespeare, the Bible in the King James version, novels by Henry James and Ernest Hemingway and William Faulkner. Toward the end of six months, taking physical therapy, I hurried to finish the books I had assigned myself; I looked forward to taking a vacation among private detectives and adventures of the twenty-fourth century. I thought I would take a holiday of light reading.

When I tried to read the light things, I experienced one of those "turning points in life" we are asked to describe in freshman composition. I remember the dismay, the abject melancholy that crept over me as I realized—restless, turning from book to book in search of entertainment—that these books bored me; that I was ruined for life, that I would never again lose myself to stick-figure characters and artificial suspense. Literature ruined me for light reading. . . .

I don't mean to say that I was able to give reasons why Fyodor Dostoyevsky's novel about a murder was better than Agatha Christie's or why Aldous Huxley's view of the future, though less exciting, was more satisfying than Astounding Science Fiction's. But I began a lifetime of trying to figure out why. What is it that makes Checkhov so valuable to us? The struggle to name reasons for value—to evaluate works of art—is lifelong, and although we may never arrive at satisfactory explanations, the struggle makes the mind more sensitive, more receptive to the next work of literature it encounters. And as the mind becomes more sensitive and receptive to literature, it may become more sensitive and receptive to all sorts of things.

JIM HARRISON

Eat or Die

In no department of life, in no place, should indifference be allowed to creep; into none less than the domain of cookery.

—Yuan Mei

It is a few degrees above zero and I'm far out on the ice of Bay de Noc near Escanaba in the Upper Peninsula of Michigan, beyond the last of the fish shanties. It doesn't matter how far it is but how long it takes to get there—an hour out, and an hour back to my hotel, the House of Ludington. Unfortunately, I've been caught in a whiteout, a sudden snow squall out of the northwest, and I can't see anything but my hands and cross-country skis, a short, broad type called Bushwhackers, which allow you to avoid the banality of trails. I turn myself around and try to retrace my path but it has quickly become covered with the fresh snow. Now I have to stand here and wait it out because, last evening, a tanker and Coast Guard icebreaker came into the harbor, which means there is a long path of open water or some very thin ice out there in the utter whiteness. I would most certainly die if I fell in and that would mean, among other things, that I would miss a good dinner, and that's what I'm doing out here in the first place—earning, or deserving, dinner.

I become very cold in the half hour or so it takes for the air to clear. I think about food and listen to the plane high above, which has been circling and presumably looking for the airport. With the first brief glimpse of shore in the swirling snow I creak into action, and each shoosh of ski speaks to me: Oysters, snails, maybe a lobster or the *Kassler Rippchen*, the braised lamb shanks, a simple porterhouse or Delmonico, with a bottle or two of the Firestone Merlot, or the Freemark Abbey Cabernet I had for lunch . . .

The idea is to eat well and not die from it—for the simple reason that that would be the end of your eating. At age fifty that means I have to keep a cholesterol count down around 170. There is abundant dreariness in even the smallest health detail. Skip butter and desserts and toss all the obvious fat to your bird dogs.

Small portions are for smallish and inactive people. When it was all the rage, I was soundly criticized for saying that *cuisine minceur* was the moral equivalent of the fox-trot. Life is too short for me to approach a meal with the mincing steps of a

Japanese prostitute. The craving is for the genuine rather than the esoteric. It is far better to avoid expense-account restaurants than to carp about them; who wants to be a John Simon of the credit-card feedbag? I'm afraid that eating in restaurants reflects one's experiences with movies, art galleries, novels, music—that is, characterized by mild amusement but with an overall feeling of stupidity and shame. Better to cook for yourself.

As for the dinner that was earned by the brush with death, it was honest rather than great. As with Chinese food, any Teutonic food, in this case smoked pork loin, seems to prevent the drinking of good wine. In general I don't care for German wines for the same reason I don't like the smell down at the Speedy Car Wash, but both perhaps are acquired tastes. The fact is, the meal demanded a couple of Heileman's Exports, even Budweisers, but that occurred to me only later.

Until recently my home base in Leelanau County, in northern Michigan, was more than sixty miles from the nearest first-rate restaurant, twice the range of the despised and outmoded atomic cannon. This calls for resourcefulness in the kitchen, or what the *tenzo* in a Zen monastery would call "skillful means." I keep an inventory taped to the refrigerator of my current frozen possibilities: local barnyard capons; the latest shipment of prime veal from Summerfield Farms, which includes sweetbreads, shanks for osso bucco, liver chops, kidneys; and a little seafood from Charles Morgan in Destin, Florida—triggerfish, a few small red snapper, conch for chowder and fritters. There are also two shelves of favorites—rabbit, grouse, woodcock, snipe, venison, dove, chukar, duck, and quail—and containers of fish fumet, various glacés and stocks, including one made from sixteen woodcock that deserves its own armed guard. I also traded my alfalfa crop for a whole steer, which is stored at my secretary's home due to lack of space.

In other words, it is important not to be caught short. It is my private opinion that many of our failures in politics, art, and domestic life come from our failure to eat vividly, though for the time being I will lighten up on this pet theory. It is also one of a writer's neuroses not to want to repeat himself—I recently combed a five-hundred-page galley proof of a novel in terror that I may have used a specific adjective twice—and this urge toward variety in food can be enervating. If you want to be loved by your family and friends it is important not to drive them crazy; thus the true outer limits of this compulsion are rested only in the month of eating during the fall bird season when we are visited by artist Russell Chatham and the writer and Frenchman Guy de la Valdene, as well as during a few other brief spates throughout the year.

The flip side of the Health Bore is, after all, the Food Bully. Several years ago, when my oldest daughter visited from New York City, I overplanned and finally drove her to tears and illness by Christmas morning (grilled woodcock and truffled eggs). At the time she was working at Dean & DeLuca, so a seven-day feast was scarcely necessary. (New Yorkers, who are anyway a thankless lot, have no idea of the tummy thrills and quaking knees an outlander feels walking into Dean & DeLuca, Balducci's, Zabar's, Manganaro's, Lobel's, Schaller & Weber, etc.) I respected my daughter's tears, albeit tardily, having been brought to a similar condition by

Orson Welles over a number of successive meals at Ma Maison, the last of which he "designed" and called me at dawn with the tentative menu as if he had just written the Ninth Symphony. We ate a half-pound of beluga with a bottle of Stolichnaya, a salmon in sorrel sauce, sweetbreads *en croûte*, a miniature leg of lamb (the whole thing) with five wines, desserts, cheeses, ports. I stumbled to the toilet for a bit of nose powder, a vice I've abandoned, and rested my head in a greasy faint against the tiled walls. Welles told me to avoid hatcheck girls as they always prefer musicians. That piece of wisdom was all that Warner Brothers got for picking up the tab. Later John Huston told me that he and Welles were always trying to stick each other with the tab and once faked simultaneous heart attacks at a restaurant in Paris. In many respects, Orson Welles was the successor to the Great Curnonsky, Prince of Gourmands. This thought occurred to me as I braced my boots against the rocker panel to haul the great director from his limousine.

Last week when my oldest daughter, who has since moved to Montana (where the only sauce is a good appetite), came home to plan her May wedding, her mother cautioned the Food Bully, threatening the usual fire extinguisher full of lithium kept in the kitchen for such purposes. While dozing, I heard my daughter go downstairs to check out the diminishing wine cellar. (I can't hear an alarm clock but I can hear this.) Certain bottles have been preserved for a few guests the evening before the wedding: a '49 Latour, a '61 Lafite, a '47 Meursault (probably turned, but the disappointment will be festive), a '69 Yquem, and a couple of '68 Heitz Martha's Vineyards for a kicker. It is a little bizarre to consider that these bottles are worth more than I made during the year she was born.

The first late evening, after a nasty January flight, we fed her a winter vegetable soup with plenty of beef shanks and bone marrow. By the next evening she was soothed enough for quail stuffed with lightly braised sweetbreads, followed by some gorgeous roasted wood ducks. I had shot the quail and wood ducks earlier in the month down south, and we especially enjoyed the latter because I will never shoot another in my life. Wood duck are the most beautiful (and tasty) of all ducks, and are very simpleminded in the way they flutter down through the trees. I felt I deserved to be bitten by the six-foot water moccasin sleeping off the cold under a nearby log. I don't feel this preventive remorse over hunting other birds, just ducks and geese.

This meal was a tad heavy so we spent the next afternoon making some not-exactly-airy cannelloni from scratch. Late that evening, I pieced up two rabbits and put them in a marinade of an ample amount of Tabasco and a quart of buttermilk, using the rabbit scraps to make half a cup of stock. The recipe is an altered version of a James Villas recipe for chicken (attribution is important in cooking).

The next evening, we floured and fried the rabbit, serving it with a sauce of the marinade, stock, and the copious brown bits from the skillet. I like the dish best with simple mashed potatoes and succotash made from frozen tiny limas and corn from the garden. The rabbit gave one a thickish feeling so the next evening I broiled two small red snappers with a biting Thai hot-and-sour sauce, which left one refreshingly hungry by midnight. My wife had preserved some lemon, so

I went to the cellar for a capon as she planned a Paula Wolfert North African dish. Wolfert and Villas are food people whom you tend to "believe" rather than simply admire. In this same noble lineage is Patience Gray, a wandering Bruce Chatwin of food.

Naturally, I had been floundering through the deep snow an hour or two a day with my bird dogs to deserve such meals. My system had begun to long for a purging meal of a mixed-grain concoction called Kashi, plus a pot of mustard and collard greens with a lump of locally made salt pork. This meal can be stretched into something bigger by adding barbecued chicken laved in a tonic sauce, which I call the sauce of Lust and Violence. The name refers to what it does to the palate rather than a motivation of behavior.

We weren't exactly saving up for the big one when the few guests begin to arrive the following evening. The cautionary note was something Jack Nicholson had said to me more than a decade ago after I had overfed a group in his home: "Only in the Midwest is overeating still considered an act of heroism." Still, the winter weather was violent, and lacking the capacity to hibernate it was important to go on with the eating, not forgetting the great Lermontov's dictum: "Eat or die."

We made a simple, nonauthentic "scampi" as an appetizer. Garlic is a vegetable and should be used in quantity, and must never be burned. To avoid this I broil the shrimp for two minutes in the shells, then add the garlic, oil, butter, and lemon juice. Infantile but good with sourdough bread. Next came the innovation of the evening, an idea that came after talking to my neighbor and hunting friend Nick. We breasted eighteen doves and my wife made a clear stock of the carcasses. Each whole breast was cut in four pieces. We added finely julienned red pepper, mostly for color, and a little shredded endive to the clear stock. We poached the pieces of dove breast briefly so they would be soft and pinkish in the center. It was a delicious soup and we looked forward to making it with surplus woodcock in the fall. The final course, rare venison steaks with a sauce made of venison marrow bones and a little of my prized woodcock stock, was almost an afterthought. Enough is enough.

The final evening we went to a restaurant called Hattie's in the small nearby town of Suttons Bay. I wondered if we had actually planned a wedding but didn't want to ask. My wife and two daughters were in good humor and ate lightly. I couldn't resist the cassoulet with an enormous preserved goose thigh smack dab in the middle—true homemade confit here in northern Michigan when it is hard to find even in New York! I would resume running at night, all night long across frozen lakes, were it not for the dangerous holes left by the ice fisherman.

LINDA HOGAN

Walking

It began in dark and underground weather, a slow hunger moving toward light. It grew in a dry gulley beside the road where I live, a place where entire hillsides are sometimes yellow, windblown tides of sunflower plants. But this plant was different. It was alone and larger than the countless others that had established their lives farther up the hill. This one was a traveler, a settler, and like a dream beginning in conflict, it grew where the land had been disturbed.

I saw it first in early summer. It was a green and sleeping bud, raising itself toward the sun. Ants worked around the unopened bloom, gathering aphids and sap. A few days later, it was a tender young flower, soft and new, with a pale green center and a troop of silver-gray insects climbing up and down the stalk. Over the summer this sunflower grew into a plant of incredible beauty, turning its face daily toward the sun in the most subtle of ways, the black center of it dark and alive with a deep blue light, as if flint had sparked an elemental fire there, in community with rain, mineral, mountain air, and sand.

As summer changed from green to yellow there were new visitors daily, the lace-winged insects, the bees whose legs were fat with pollen, and grasshoppers with their clattering wings and desperate hunger. There were other lives I missed, those too small or hidden to see. It was as if this plant with its host of lives was a society, one in which moment by moment, depending on light and moisture, there was great and diverse change.

There were changes in the next larger world around the plant as well. One day I rounded a bend in the road to find the disturbing sight of a dead horse, black and still against a hillside, eyes rolled back. Another day I was nearly lifted by a wind and sandstorm so fierce and hot that I had to wait for it to pass before I could return home. On this day the faded dry petals of the sunflower were swept across the land. That was when the birds arrived to carry the new seeds to another future.

In this one plant, in one summer season, a drama of need and survival took place. Hungers were filled. Insects coupled. There was escape, exhaustion, and death. Lives touched down a moment and were gone.

I was an outsider. I only watched. I never learned the sunflower's golden language or the tongues of its citizens. I had a small understanding, nothing more than a shallow observation of the flower, insects, and birds. But they knew what to do, how to live. An old voice from somewhere, gene or cell, told the plant how to evade the pull of gravity and find its way upward, how to open. It was instinct, intuition, necessity. A certain knowing directed the seed-bearing birds on paths to ancestral homelands they had never seen. They believed it. They followed.

There are other summons and calls, some even more mysterious than those commandments to birds or those survival journeys of insects. In bamboo plants, for instance, with their thin green canopy of light and golden stalks that creak in the wind. Once a century, all of a certain kind of bamboo flower on the same day. Neither the plants' location, in Malaysia or in a greenhouse in Minnesota, nor their age or size make a difference. They flower. Some current of an inner language passes among them, through space and separation, in ways we cannot explain in our language. They are all, somehow, one plant, each with a share of communal knowledge.

John Hay, in *The Immortal Wilderness*, has written: "There are occasions when you can hear the mysterious language of the Earth, in water, or coming through the trees, emanating from the mosses, seeping through the undercurrents of the soil, but you have to be willing to wait and receive."

Sometimes I hear it talking. The light of the sunflower was one language, but there are others more audible. Once, in the redwood forest, I heard a beat, something like a drum or heart coming from the ground and trees and wind. That underground current stirred a kind of knowing inside me, a kinship and longing, a dream barely remembered that disappeared back to the body. Another time, there was the booming voice of an ocean storm thundering from far out at sea, telling about what lived in the distance, about the rough water that would arrive, wave after wave revealing the disturbance at center.

Tonight I walk. I am watching the sky. I think of the people who came before me and how they knew the placement of stars in the sky, watched the moving sun long and hard enough to witness how a certain angle of light touched a stone only once a year. Without written records, they knew the gods of every night, the small, fine details of the world around them and of immensity above them.

Walking, I can almost hear the redwoods beating. And the oceans are above me here, rolling clouds, heavy and dark, considering snow. On the dry, red road, I pass the place of the sunflower, that dark and secret location where creation took place. I wonder if it will return this summer, if it will multiply and move up to the other stand of flowers in a territorial struggle.

It's winter and there is smoke from the fires. The square, lighted windows of houses are fogging over. It is a world of elemental attention, of all things working together, listening to what speaks in the blood. Whichever road I follow, I walk in the land of many gods, and they love and eat one another. Walking, I am listening to a deeper way. Suddenly all my ancestors are behind me. Be still, they say. Watch and listen. You are the result of the love of thousands.

NICK HORNBY

Home Début

I fell in love with football as I was later to fall in love with women: suddenly, inexplicably, uncritically, giving no thought to the pain or disruption it would bring with it.

In May '68 (a date with connotations, of course, but I am still more likely to think of Jeff Astle than of Paris), just after my eleventh birthday, my father asked me if I'd like to go with him to the FA Cup Final between West Brom and Everton; a colleague had offered him a couple of tickets. I told him that I wasn't interested in football, not even in the Cup Final—true, as far as I was aware, but perversely I watched the whole match on television anyway. A few weeks later I watched the Man Utd–Benfica game, enthralled, with my mum, and at the end of August I got up early to hear how United had got on in the final of the World Club Championship. I loved Bobby Charlton and George Best (I knew nothing about Denis Law, the third of the Holy Trinity, who had missed the Benfica match through injury) with a passion that had taken me completely by surprise; it lasted three weeks, until my dad took me to Highbury for the first time.

My parents were separated by 1968. My father had met someone else and moved out, and I lived with my mother and my sister in a small detached house in the Home Counties. This state of affairs was unremarkable enough in itself (although I cannot recall anyone else in my class with an absent parent—the sixties took another seven or eight years to travel the twenty-odd miles down the M4 from London), but the break-up had wounded all four of us in various ways, as break-ups are wont to do.

There were, inevitably, a number of difficulties that arose from this new phase of family life, although the most crucial in this context was probably the most banal: the commonplace but nevertheless intractable one-parent Saturday-afternoon-at-the-zoo problem. Often Dad was only able to visit us midweek; no one really wanted to stay in and watch TV, for obvious reasons, but on the other hand there wasn't really anywhere else a man could take two children under twelve. Usually the three of us drove to a neighbouring town, or up to one of the airport hotels, where we sat in a cold and early-evening deserted restaurant, and where Gill and I ate steak or chicken, one or the other, in more or less complete silence (children are not great dinner conversationalists, as a rule, and in any case we were used to eating with the TV on), while Dad watched. He must have been desperate to find something else to do with us, but the options in a commuter-belt town between 6.30 and 9.00 on a Monday night were limited.

That summer, Dad and I went to a hotel near Oxford for a week, where in the evenings we sat in a deserted hotel dining room, and where I ate steak or chicken, one or the other, in more or less complete silence. After dinner we went to watch TV with the other guests, and Dad drank too much. Things had to change.

My father tried again with the football that September, and he must have been amazed when I said yes. I had never before said yes to any suggestion of his, although I rarely said no either. I just smiled politely and made a noise intended to express interest but no commitment, a maddening trait I think I invented especially for that time in my life but which has somehow remained with me ever since. For two or three years he had been trying to take me to the theatre; every time he asked I simply shrugged and grinned idiotically, with the result that eventually Dad would get angry and tell me to forget it, which was what I wanted him to say. And it wasn't just Shakespeare, either: I was equally suspicious of rugby matches and cricket matches and boat trips and days out to Silverstone and Longleat. I didn't want to do anything at all. None of this was intended to punish my father for his absence: I really thought that I would be happy to go anywhere with him, apart from every single place he could think of.

1968 was, I suppose, the most traumatic year of my life. After my parents' separation we moved into a smaller house, but for a time, because of some sort of chain, we were homeless and had to stay with our neighbours; I became seriously ill with jaundice; and I started at the local grammar school. I would have to be extraordinarily literal to believe that the Arsenal fever about to grip me had nothing to do with all this mess. (And I wonder how many other fans, if they were to examine the circumstances that led up to their obsession, could find some sort of equivalent Freudian drama? After all, football's a great game and everything, but what is it that separates those who are happy to attend half a dozen games a season—watch the big matches, stay away from the rubbish, surely the sensible way—from those who feel compelled to attend them all? Why travel from London to Plymouth on a Wednesday, using up a precious day's holiday, to see a game whose outcome was effectively decided in the first leg at Highbury? And, if this theory of fandom as therapy is anywhere near the mark, *what the hell is buried in the subconscious of people who go to Leyland DAF Trophy games?* Perhaps it is best not to know.)

There is a short story by the American writer Andre Dubus entitled 'The Winter Father', about a man whose divorce has separated him from his two children. In the winter his relationship with them is tetchy and strained: they move from afternoon jazz club to cinema to restaurant, and stare at each other. But in the summer, when they can go to the beach, they get on fine. 'The long beach and the sea were their lawn; the blanket their home; the ice chest and thermos their kitchen. They lived as a family again.' Sitcoms and films have long recognised this terrible tyranny of place, and depict men traipsing round parks with fractious kids and a frisbee. But 'The Winter Father' means a lot to me because it goes further than that: it manages to isolate what is valuable in the relationship between parents and children, and explains simply and precisely *why* the zoo trips are doomed.

In this country, as far as I know, Bridlington and Minehead are unable to provide the same kind of liberation as the New England beaches in Dubus's story; but my father and I were about to come up with the perfect English equivalent. Saturday afternoons in north London gave us a context in which we could be together. We could talk when we wanted, the football gave us something to talk about (and anyway the silences weren't oppressive), and the days had a structure, a routine. The Arsenal pitch was to be our lawn (and, being an English lawn, we would usually peer at it mournfully through driving rain); the Gunners' Fish Bar on Blackstock Road our kitchen; and the West Stand our home. It was a wonderful set-up, and changed our lives just when they needed changing most, but it was also exclusive: Dad and my sister never really found anywhere to live at all. Maybe now that wouldn't happen; maybe a nine-year-old girl in the nineties would feel that she had just as much right to go to a game as we did. But in 1969 in our town, this was not an idea that had much currency, and my sister had to stay at home with her mum and her dolls.

I don't recall much about the football that first afternoon. One of those tricks of memory enables me to see the only goal clearly: the referee awards a penalty (he runs into the area, points a dramatic finger, there's a roar); a hush as Terry Neill takes it, and a groan as Gordon Banks dives and pushes the ball out; it falls conveniently at Neill's feet and this time he scores. But I am sure this picture has been built up from what I have long known about similar incidents, and actually I was aware of none of this. All I really saw on the day was a bewildering chain of incomprehensible incidents, at the end of which everyone around me stood and shouted. If I did the same, it must have been an embarrassing ten seconds after the rest of the crowd.

But I do have other, more reliable, and probably more meaningful memories. I remember the overwhelming *maleness* of it all—cigar and pipe smoke, foul language (words I had heard before, but not from adults, not at that volume), and only years later did it occur to me that this was bound to have an effect on a boy who lived with his mother and his sister; and I remember looking at the crowd more than at the players. From where I was sitting I could probably have counted twenty thousand heads; only the sports fan (or Mick Jagger or Nelson Mandela) can do that. My father told me that there were nearly as many people in the stadium as lived in my town, and I was suitably awed.

(We have forgotten that football crowds are still astonishingly large, mostly because since the war they have become progressively smaller. Managers frequently complain about local apathy, particularly when their mediocre First or Second Division team has managed to avoid a good hiding for a few weeks; but the fact that, say, Derby County managed to attract an average crowd of nearly seventeen thousand in 1990/91, the year they finished bottom of the First Division, is a miracle. Let's say that three thousand of these are away supporters; that means that among the remaining fourteen thousand from Derby, there were a number of people who went at least *eighteen times* to see the worst football of last or indeed most other seasons. Why, really, should anyone have gone at all?)

It wasn't the size of the crowd that impressed me most, however, or the way that adults were allowed to shout the word 'WANKER!' as loudly as they wanted without attracting any attention. What impressed me most was just how much most of the men around me *hated*, really *hated*, being there. As far as I could tell, nobody seemed to enjoy, in the way that I understood the word, anything that happened during the entire afternoon. Within minutes of the kick-off there was real anger ('You're a DISGRACE, Gould. He's a DISGRACE!' 'A hundred quid a week? A HUNDRED QUID A WEEK! They should give that to me for watching you.'); as the game went on, the anger turned into outrage, and then seemed to curdle into sullen, silent discontent. Yes, yes, I know all the jokes. What else could I have expected at Highbury? But I went to Chelsea and to Tottenham and to Rangers, and saw the same thing: that the natural state of the football fan is bitter disappointment, no matter what the score.

I think we Arsenal fans know, deep down, that the football at Highbury has not often been pretty, and that therefore our reputation as the most boring team in the entire history of the universe is not as mystifying as we pretend: yet when we have a successful side much is forgiven. The Arsenal team I saw on that afternoon had been spectacularly unsuccessful for some time. Indeed they had won nothing since the Coronation and this abject and unambiguous failure was simply rubbing salt into the fans' stigmata. Many of those around us had the look of men who had seen every game of every barren season. The fact that I was intruding on a marriage that had gone disastrously sour lent my afternoon a particularly thrilling prurience (if it had been a real marriage, children would have been barred from the ground): one partner was lumbering around in a pathetic attempt to please, while the other turned his face to the wall, too full of loathing even to watch. Those fans who could not remember the thirties (although at the end of the sixties a good many of them could), when the club won five Championships and two FA Cups, could remember the Comptons and Joe Mercer from just over a decade before; the stadium itself, with its beautiful art deco stands and its Jacob Epstein busts, seemed to disapprove of the current mob even as much as my neighbours did.

I'd been to public entertainments before, of course; I'd been to the cinema and the pantomime and to see my mother sing in the chorus of the *White Horse Inn* at the Town Hall. But that was different. The audiences I had hitherto been a part of had paid to have a good time and, though occasionally one might spot a fidgety child or a yawning adult, I hadn't ever noticed faces contorted by rage or despair or frustration. Entertainment as pain was an idea entirely new to me, and it seemed to be something I'd been waiting for.

It might not be too fanciful to suggest that it was an idea which shaped my life. I have always been accused of taking the things I love—football, of course, but also books and records—much too seriously, and I do feel a kind of anger when I hear a bad record, or when someone is lukewarm about a book that means a lot to me. Perhaps it was these desperate, bitter men in the West Stand at Arsenal who taught me how to get angry in this way; and perhaps it is why I earn some of my living as a critic—maybe it's those voices I can hear when I write. 'You're a WANKER, X.' 'The Booker Prize? THE BOOKER PRIZE? They should give that to me for having to read you.'

Just this one afternoon started the whole thing off—there was no prolonged courtship—and I can see now that if I'd gone to White Hart Lane or Stamford Bridge the same thing would have happened, so overwhelming was the experience the first time. In a desperate and percipient attempt to stop the inevitable, Dad quickly took me to Spurs to see Jimmy Greaves score four against Sunderland in a 5–1 win, but the damage had been done, and the six goals and all the great players left me cold: I'd already fallen for the team that beat Stoke 1–0 from a penalty rebound.

MARY KARR

From The Liars' Club

CHAPTER 1

My sharpest memory is of a single instant surrounded by dark. I was seven, and our family doctor knelt before me where I sat on a mattress on the bare floor. He wore a yellow golf shirt unbuttoned so that sprouts of hair showed in a V shape on his chest. I had never seen him in anything but a white starched shirt and a gray tie. The change unnerved me. He was pulling at the hem of my favorite nightgown—a pattern of Texas bluebonnets bunched into nosegays tied with ribbon against a field of nappy white cotton. I had tucked my knees under it to make a tent. He could easily have yanked the thing over my head with one motion, but something made him gentle. "Show me the marks," he said. "Come on, now. I won't hurt you." He had watery blue eyes behind thick glasses, and a mustache that looked like a caterpillar. "Please? Just pull this up and show me where it hurts," he said. He held a piece of hem between thumb and forefinger. I wasn't crying and don't remember any pain, but he talked to me in that begging voice he used when he had a long needle hidden behind his back. I liked him but didn't much trust him. The room I shared with my sister was dark, but I didn't fancy hiking my gown up with strangers milling around in the living room.

It took three decades for that instant to unfreeze. Neighbors and family helped me turn that one bright slide into a panorama. The bed frame tilted against the wall behind the doctor had a scary, spidery look in the dark. In one corner, the tallboy was tipped over on its back like a stranded turtle, its drawers flung around. There were heaps of spilled clothes, puzzles, comics, and the Golden Books I could count on my mom to buy in the supermarket line if I'd stayed in the carriage. The doorway framed the enormous backlit form of Sheriff Watson, who held my sister, then nine, with one stout arm. She had her pink pajamas on and her legs wrapped around his waist. She fiddled with his badge with a concentration too intense for the actual interest such a thing might hold for her. Even at that age she was cynical about authority in any form. She was known for mocking nuns in public and sassing teachers. But I could see that she had painted a deferential look on her face. The sheriff's cowboy hat kept the details of his expression in deep shadow, but I made out a sort of soft half-smile I'd never seen on him.

I had a knee-jerk fear of the sheriff based on my father's tendency to get in fights. He'd pull open the back screen with knuckles scraped and bleeding, then squat down to give instructions to me and Lecia (pronounced, she would have me tell you, "Lisa"). "If the sheriff comes by here, you just tell him you ain't seen me in a few days." In fact, the sheriff never came by, so my ability to straight-faced lie to the law was never tested. But just his presence that night flooded me with an odd sense: *I done something wrong and here's the sheriff.* If I had, that night, possessed a voice, or if anyone nearby felt like listening, that's what I might have said. But when you're a kid and something big is going on, you might as well be furniture for all anybody says to you.

It was only over time that the panorama became animate, like a scene in some movie crystal ball that whirls from a foggy blur into focus. People developed little distinct motions; then the whole scene jerked to smooth and sudden life. Sheriff Watson's jaw dipped into the light and returned to shadow with some regularity as he said things that I couldn't hear to my blond, suddenly cherubic-acting sister. Some firemen wearing canary-colored slickers started to move through the next room, and Dr. Boudreaux's thick fingers came again to rub the edge of my speckled nightgown the way old ladies at the five-and-dime tested yard goods. There must have been an ambulance outside, because at intervals big triangles of red light slashed across the room. I could almost feel them moving over my face, and in the window, through a web of honeysuckle, I saw in my own backyard flames like those of a football bonfire.

And the volume on the night began to rise. People with heavy boots stomped through the house. Somebody turned off the ambulance siren. The back screen opened and slammed. My daddy's dog, Nipper, was growling low and making his chain clank in the yard. He was a sullen dog trained to drink beer and bite strangers. He'd been known to leap from a speeding truck's window to chase down and fight any hound he saw. He'd killed one lady's Chihuahua, then just shook it like a rag while Daddy tried to coax him out of her garage and she hollered and cried. When a voice I didn't know told some sonofabitch to get out of the way, I knew it meant Nipper, who disappeared that night into the East Texas bayou—or more likely, my sister later figured out, the gas chamber at the local pound. Anyway, we never saw him again, which was okay by me. That dog had bitten me more than once.

More door slams, the noise of boots, and some radio static from the cruiser in the road. "Come on, baby," Dr. Boudreaux said, "show me the marks. I'm not about to hurt you." I kept waiting to make eye contact with my sister to get some idea of how to handle this, but she was dead set on that badge.

I don't remember talking. I must eventually have told Dr. Boudreaux there weren't any marks on me. There weren't. It took a long time for me to figure that out for certain, even longer to drive my memory from that single place in time out toward the rest of my life.

The next thing I knew, I was being led away by Sheriff Watson. He still held Lecia, who had decided to pretend that she was asleep. My eyes were belt-level with his service revolver and a small leather sap that even then must have been illegal in the state of Texas. It was shaped like an enormous black tear. I resisted the urge to touch it. Lecia kept her face in his neck the whole time, but I knew she was scudging sleep. She slept like a cat, and this was plenty of hoopla to keep her awake. The sheriff held my left hand. With my free one, I reached up and pinched her dirty ankle. Hard. She kicked out at me, then angled her foot up out of reach and snuggled back to her fake sleep on his chest.

The highway patrolmen and firemen stood around with the blank heaviness of uninvited visitors who plan a long stay. Somebody had made a pot of coffee that laid a nutty smell over the faint chemical stink from the gasoline fire in the backyard. The men in the living room gave our party a wide berth and moved toward the kitchen.

I knew that neither of my parents was coming. Daddy was working the graveyard shift, and the sheriff said that his deputy had driven out to the plant to try and track him down. Mother had been taken Away—he further told us—for being Nervous.

I should explain here that in East Texas parlance the term Nervous applied with equal accuracy to anything from chronic nail-biting to full-blown psychosis. Mr. Thibideaux down the street had blown off the heads of his wife and three sons, then set his house on fire before fixing the shotgun barrel under his own jaw and using his big toe on the trigger. I used to spend Saturday nights in that house with his daughter, a junior high twirler of some popularity, and I remember nothing more of Mr. Thibideaux than that he had a crew cut and a stern manner. He was a refinery worker like Daddy, and also a deacon at First Baptist.

I was in my twenties when Mr. Thibideaux killed his family. I liked to call myself a poet and had affected a habit of reading classical texts (in translation, of course—I was a lazy student). I would ride the Greyhound for thirty-six hours down from the Midwest to Leechfield, then spend days dressed in black in the scalding heat of my mother's front porch reading Homer (or Ovid or Virgil) and waiting for someone to ask me what I was reading. No one ever did. People asked me what I was drinking, how much I weighed, where I was living, and if I had married yet, but no one gave me a chance to deliver my lecture on Great Literature. It was during one of these visits that I found the Thibideauxs' burned-out house, and also stumbled on the Greek term *ate*. In ancient epics, when somebody boffs a girl or slays somebody or just generally gets heated up, he can usually blame *ate*, a kind of raging passion, pseudo-demonic, that banishes reason. So Agamemnon, having robbed Achilles of his girlfriend, said, "I was blinded by *ate* and Zeus took away my understanding." Wine can invoke *ate*, but only if it's ensorcered in some way. Because the *ate* is supernatural, it releases the person possessed of it from any guilt for her actions. When neighbors tried to explain the whole murder-suicide of the Thibideaux clan after thirty years of grass-cutting and garbage-taking-out and dutiful church-service attendance, they did so with one adjective, which I have since traced to the Homeric idea of *ate*: Mr. Thibideaux was Nervous. No amount of prodding on my part produced a more elaborate explanation.

On the night the sheriff came to our house and Mother was adjudged more or less permanently Nervous, I didn't yet understand the word. I had only a vague tight panic in the pit of my stomach, the one you get when your parents are nowhere in sight and probably don't even know who has a hold of you or where you'll wind up spending the night.

I could hear the low hum of neighbor women talking as we got near the front door. They had gathered on the far side of the ditch that ran before our house, where they stood in their nightclothes like some off-duty SWAT team waiting for orders. The sheriff let go of my hand once we were outside. From inside the tall shadow of his hat, with my sister still wrapped around him in bogus slumber, he told me to wait on the top step while he talked to the ladies. Then he went up to the women, setting in motion a series of robe-tightenings and sweater-buttonings.

The concrete was cold on my bottom through the thin nightgown. I plucked two june bugs off the screen and tried to line them up to race down a brick, but one flew off, and the other just flipped over and waggled its legs in the air.

At some point it dawned on me that my fate for the night was being decided by Sheriff Watson and the neighbor ladies. It was my habit at that time to bargain with God, so I imagine that I started some haggling prayer about who might take us home. *Don't let it be the Smothergills*, I probably prayed. They had six kids already and famously strict rules about who ate what and when. The one time we'd spent the night there, Lecia and I wound up in the bathroom eating toothpaste past midnight. We'd eaten a whole tube, for which we had been switch-whipped in the morning by a gray-faced Mr. Smothergill. He was undergoing weekly chemotherapy treatments for mouth cancer at the time, and every kid in the neighborhood had an opinion about when he would die. Cancer and death were synonymous. His sandpaper voice and bleak disposition scared us more than any whipping. His kids called him Cheerful Chuck behind his back. The oldest Smothergill daughter had been permitted to visit my house only once. (Our house was perceived as Dangerous, a consequence of Mother's being Nervous.) She was so tickled by the idea that we could open the refrigerator at will that she melted down a whole stick of butter in a skillet and drank it from a coffee mug. *Lord, I would rather eat a bug than sleep on that hard pallet at the Smothergills'. Plus in the morning the boys get up and stand around the TV in their underpants doing armpit farts. Let it be the Dillards', and I'll lead a holy life forever from this day. I will not spit or scratch or pinch or try to get Babby Carter to eat doo-doo.* Mrs. Dillard stood with the other ladies in her pale blue zip-front duster, her arms folded across her chest. She made Pillsbury cinnamon rolls in the morning and let me squiggle on the icing. Plus her boys had to wear pajama pants when we were there. But the Dillards had space for only one of us, and that on the scratchy living room sofa. *Maybe Lecia could go to the Smothergills'*, I proposed to whatever God I worshiped, *and I could take the Dillards*. I wished Lecia no particular harm, but if there was only one banana left in the bowl, I would not hesitate to grab it and leave her to do without. I decided that if the june bug could be herded the length of a brick before I could count five I'd get what I wanted. But the june bug kept flipping and waggling before it had even gone an inch, and Mrs. Dillard went out of her way, it seemed, not to look at me.

I don't remember who we got farmed out to or for how long. I was later told that we'd stayed for a time with a childless couple who bred birds. Some memory endures of a screened-in breezeway with green slatted blinds all around. The light was lemon-colored and dusty, the air filled with blue-and-green parakeets, whose crazy orbits put me in mind of that Alfred Hitchcock movie where birds go nuts and start pecking out people's eyeballs. But the faces of my hosts in that place—no matter how hard I squint—refuse to be conjured.

Because it took so long for me to paste together what happened, I will leave that part of the story missing for a while. It went long unformed for me, and I want to keep it that way here. I don't mean to be coy. When the truth would be unbearable the mind often just blanks it out. But some ghost of an event may stay in your head. Then, like the smudge of a bad word quickly wiped off a school blackboard, this ghost can call undue attention to itself by its very vagueness. You keep studying the dim shape of it, as if the original form will magically emerge. This blank spot in my past, then, spoke most loudly to me by being blank. It was a hole in my life that I both feared and kept coming back to because I couldn't quite fill it in.

I did know from that night forward that things in my house were Not Right, this despite the fact that the events I have described so far had few outward results. No one ever mentioned the night again. I don't remember any subsequent home visits from any kind of social worker or concerned neighbor. Dr. Boudreaux seemed sometimes to minister to my health with an uncharacteristic tenderness. And neighbors dragged my sister and me to catechism classes and Vacation Bible School and to various hunting camps, never mentioning the fact that our family never reciprocated. I frequently showed up on doorsteps at suppertime; foraging, Daddy called it. He said it reminded him of his rail-riding days during the Depression. But no one ever failed to hand me a plate, though everybody knew that I had plenty to eat at home, which wasn't always true for the families I popped in on.

The night's major consequences for me were internal. The fact that my house was Not Right metastasized into the notion that I myself was somehow Not Right, or that my survival in the world depended on my constant vigilance against various forms of Non-Rightness. Whenever I stepped into the road at Leechfield's one traffic light, I usually expected to get plowed down by a Red Ball truck flying out of nowhere (unlikely, given the lack of traffic). I became both a flincher and a fighter.

I was quick to burst into tears in the middle of a sandlot baseball game and equally quick to whack someone in the head without much provocation. Neighborhood myth has it that I once coldcocked a five-year-old playmate with an army trench shovel, then calmly went back to digging. Some of this explosiveness just came from a naturally bad temperament, of course. But some stems from that night, when my mind simply erased everything up until Dr. Boudreaux began inviting me to show him marks that I now know weren't even there.

The missing story really starts before I was born, when my mother and father met and, for reasons I still don't get, quickly married.

My mother had just arrived in Leechfield. She'd driven down from New York with an Italian sea captain named Paolo. He was fifty to her thirty, and her fourth husband. My mother didn't date, she married. At least that's what we said when I finally found out about all her marriages before Daddy. She racked up seven weddings in all, two to my father. My mother tended to blame the early marriages on her own mother's strict Methodist values, which didn't allow for premarital fooling around, of which she was fond. She and Paolo had barely finished the honeymoon and set up housekeeping in Leechfield, where he was fixing to ship out, than they began fighting.

So it was on a wet winter evening in 1950 that she threw her dresses, books, and hatboxes in the back of an old Ford and laid rubber out of Leechfield, intending never to return. She was heading for her mother's cotton farm about five hundred miles west. Just outside of Leechfield, where Highway 73 yields up its jagged refinery skyline to bayous and rice fields, she blew a tire. She was about twenty yards from the truck stop where Daddy happened to be working. He had a union job as an apprentice stillman at Gulf Oil, but he was filling in at the station that night for his friend Cooter, who'd called him in desperation from a crap game in Baton Rouge where he was allegedly on a roll.

All Mother's marriages, once I uncovered them in my twenties, got presented to me as accidents. Her meeting Daddy was maybe the most unlikely. Had Cooter not gotten lucky with the dice in a Baton Rouge honky-tonk, and had Paolo not perturbed Mother in the process of unpacking crates, and had the tire on the Ford not been worn from a recent cross-country jaunt (Paolo's mother lived in Seattle, and they'd traveled there from New York, then down to Texas, where divorce laws permitted Mother to quickly get rid of husband number three before signing up with number four). . . . All these events conspired to strand my mother quite literally at my father's feet on Highway 73 that night.

He said there was a General Electric moon shining the first time he saw her, so bright it was like a spotlight on her. She refused his help jacking up the car and proceeded to cuss like a sailor when she couldn't get the lug nuts loose. My mother claims that she had only recently learned to cuss, from Paolo. Daddy said her string of practiced invectives, which seemed unlikely given her fancy clothes (she had on a beige silk suit) and New York license plates, impressed him no end. He'd never heard a woman cuss like that before.

She changed the tire and must have made some note of his raw good looks. He was some part Indian—we never figured out which tribe—black-haired and sharp-featured. His jug-eared grin reminded her of Clark Gable's. Since she fancied herself a sort of Bohemian Scarlett O'Hara, the attraction was deep and sudden. I should also note that Mother was prone to conversion experiences of various kinds, and had entered a fervent Marxist stage. She toted *Das Kapital* around in her purse for years. Daddy was active in the Oil Chemical and Atomic Workers Union. Whenever they renegotiated a contract—every two years—he was known as an able picket-line brawler. He was, in short, a Texas working man, with a smattering of Indian blood and with personality traits that she had begun to consider heroic.

Out in Lubbock, Grandma was rolling a cobbler crust for Mother's homecoming dinner when the call came that she had been detained in Leechfield. Grandma had prayed for her to make up with Paolo. She'd started auctioning Mother off to various husbands when she was only fifteen. Like some prize cow, Mother liked to say, fattened for the highest bidder. With a paid-for Ford and a ship waiting for him in the Gulf, Paolo had what Grandma thought of as the Ability to Provide. Plus he had dragged Mother out of New York, where God knew what-all went on, and relocated her in Texas. Grandma subsequently viewed my father as some slick-talking hick who had buffaloed her only child into settling for a two-bedroom tract house when she deserved a big ranch. In fact, Paolo was the only husband of Mother's whose existence Grandma would acknowledge—other than Daddy, of course, and him she couldn't very well ignore. She felt that Paolo's story would teach me a lesson, the punch line of which was something like divorcing a salary man for somebody who punches a clock was bad manners. At least Grandma told me a few stories about Paolo. Pressing Mother for details of her past always led to eye-rolling and aspirin-taking and long afternoon naps.

To Paolo's credit, he didn't give Mother up as easily as the others had. He chased her—so the saying goes—like a duck would a june bug. He sent yellow roses to her hotel room every week, and Daddy finally took to setting the boxes of chocolate-covered cherries that kept arriving for her in the common parlor of his boarding house, where his roommates ate them by the fistful. Paolo finally got up enough courage or desperation to appear there for a final showdown. For some reason, I picture Daddy stretched out on a narrow bed in a string T-shirt and boxer shorts, his eyes narrowing like a snake's when Paolo, whom I imagine in the seersucker suit he wore for his wedding snapshot, ducked into the room with slanty ceilings. Mother was there to watch all this. At some point the talk got heated, and Paolo called Mother a strumpet, for which Daddy was said to have stomped a serious mudhole in Paolo's ass. It was the first time Mother saw Daddy fight. (In fact, there wasn't ever much fighting to it, at least that I ever saw. Daddy hit people, and then they fell down. End of fight.) After that, I picture Paolo more or less crawling down the stairs. He shipped out to Saudi Arabia, never to be seen again until his picture cropped up in a box some decades later and I asked Mom who the hell that was.

At my parents' wedding in the Leechfield Town Hall, Daddy concluded the ceremony by toasting Mother with the silver flask she'd bought him for a present. "Thank you for marrying poor old me," he said. He was used to carhops and cowgirls, and said Mother represented a new and higher order of creature altogether.

The truth seems to be that Mother married Daddy at least in part because she'd gotten scared. As much as she liked to brag about being an art student in Greenwich Village during the war—and believe me, in Leechfield she stood out— she had racked up a frightening number of husbands, so frightening that she did her best to keep them secret. And her economic decline had been steady: over fifteen years she'd gone from a country house in Connecticut to a trailer park in Leechfield. Somehow all her wildness just didn't wash in the anesthetized fifties. She'd lost some things along the way, and losing things scared her. Daddy was handsome enough and the proper blend of outlaw and citizen. And he didn't bow much to the mannerisms she'd picked up to impress her cold-blooded Yankee husbands. The only Marx he knew was Groucho, the only dance the Cajun two-step. The first night he slept with her, he took a washrag and a jug of wood alcohol to get rid of her makeup, saying he wanted to see what he was getting into.

Their early time sounded happy. With the G.I. Bill, they bought a small house in a line of identical small houses. It was more than Daddy had ever dreamed of owning. He was so proud that she had more going on north of her neck than her hairdo that he built bookshelves for her art books, hung her paintings all over the house, and promised someday to construct a studio so she wouldn't have to keep her easel propped in the dining room.

My daddy had grown up with three loud brothers and a sister in a logging camp in the piney section of East Texas called The Big Thicket. His family lived mostly without hard currency, buying coffee and sugar with credit vouchers at the Kirby Lumber Company Store. Other than that and such luxuries as calico for dresses, they grew and shot and caught what they needed.

That world was long gone before my birth, but I remember it. In fact, my father told me so many stories about his childhood that it seems in most ways more vivid to me than my own. His stories got told and retold before an audience of drinking men he played dominoes with on days off. They met at the American Legion or in the back room of Fisher's Bait Shop at times when their wives thought they were paying bills or down at the union hall. Somebody's pissed-off wife eventually christened them the Liars' Club, and it stuck. Certainly not much of the truth in any technical sense got told there.

Except for Christmas Eve morning, when they met in the Legion parking lot at dawn to exchange identical gift bottles of Jack Daniel's from the windows of their pickups, the men had no official meeting time and place. I never saw evidence of any planning. They never called each other on the phone. No one's wife or kids ever carried a message to meet at thus-and-such a place. They all just seemed to meander together, seemingly by instinct, to a given place and hour that had magically planted itself in their collective noggins. No women ever came along. I was the only child allowed, a fact frequently held up as proof that I was hopelessly spoiled. I would ask Daddy for money for a Coke or shuffleboard or to unlock the pool table, and it was only a matter of time before somebody piped over at us that he was spoiling me and that if he kept it up, I wasn't going to be worth a shit. Comments like that always rang a little too true to me. Sometimes I'd even fake starting to give the coin back or shying away from the pool table. But Daddy would just wag his head at whoever spoke. "Leave her alone. She can do anything she's big enough to do, cain't you, Pokey?" And then I would say I guessed I could.

Of all the men in the Liars' Club, Daddy told the best stories. When he started one, the guys invariably fell quiet, studying their laps or their cards or the inner rims of their beer mugs like men in prayer. No matter how many tangents he took or how far the tale flew from its starting point before he reeled it back, he had this gift: he knew how to be believed. He mastered it the way he mastered bluffing in poker, which probably happened long before my appearance. His tough half-breed face would move between solemn blankness and sudden caricature. He kept stock expressions for stock characters. When his jaw jutted and stiffened and his eyes squinted, I expected to hear the faint brogue of his uncle Husky. A wide-eyed expression was the black man Ugh, who taught him cards and dice. His sister pursed her lips in steady disapproval. His mother wore an enormous bonnet like a big blue halo, so he'd always introduce her by fanning his hands behind his head, saying *Here comes Momma.*

My father comes into focus for me on a Liars' Club afternoon. He sits at a wob-bly card table weighed down by a bottle. Even now the scene seems so real to me that I can't but write it in the present tense.

I am dangling my legs off the bar at the Legion and shelling unroasted peanuts from a burlap bag while Daddy slides the domino tiles around the table. They make a clicking sound. I haven't started going to school yet, so the day seems without beginning or end, stalled in the beer-smelling dark of the Legion.

Cooter has just asked Daddy if he had planned to run away from home. "They wasn't no planning to it," Daddy says, then lights a cigarette to stall, picking a few strands of tobacco off his tongue as if that gesture may take all the time in the world. "Poppa had give me a silver dollar and told me to get into town and buy some coffee. Had to cross the train tracks to get there. When that old train come around the turn, it had to slow up. Well, when it slowed up, I jumped, and that dollar come with me.

"Got a job threshing wheat up to Kansas. Slept at night with some other old boys in this fella's barn. Man by the name of Hamlet. Sorriest sonofabitch ever to tread shoe leather. Wouldn't bring you a drink from sunup to lunch. And married to the prettiest woman you ever seen. A butt like two bulldogs in a bag." This last makes everybody laugh.

I ask him how he got home, and he slides the story back on track. While I'm waiting for his answer, I split open a fresh peanut with my fingernail. The unroasted shell is soft as skin, the meat of the nut chewy and almost tasteless with-out salt. Daddy finishes his drink and moves a domino. "About didn't make it. Hopped the Double-E train from Kansas City to New Orleans. Cold?" He glares at each of us as if we might doubt the cold. "That wind come inching in those boxcar cracks like a straight razor. It'll cut your gizzard out, don't think it won't. They finally loaded some cattle on somewhere in Arkansas, and I cozied up to this old heifer. I'd of froze to death without her. Many's the time I think of that old cow. Tried milking her, but it come out froze solid. Like a Popsicle."

"It's getting high and deep in here," Shug says. He's the only black man I've ever seen in the Legion, and then only when the rest of the guys are there. He wears a forest-green porkpie hat with the joker from a deck of cards stuck on the side. He's famously intolerant of Daddy's horseshit, and so tends to up the credibility factor when around.

"I shit you not," Daddy says and sprinkles some salt in the triangular hole in his beer can. "You hop one of those bastards some January and ride her. You'll be pissing ice cubes. I guarangoddamntee you that." They shake their heads, and I can see Daddy considering his next move by pretending to study his dominoes. They're lined up like bricks in a wall, and after he chooses one, he makes a show of lining it up right on the tabletop, then marking down his score. "They unloaded one old boy stiff as a plank from down off the next car over. He was a old one. Didn't have no business riding trains that old. And when we tipped him down to haul him off—they was four or five of us lifting him—about a dozen of these round fuzzy things rolled out his pant leg. Big as your thumb, and white," He measures off the right length on his thumb.

"Those were the crown pearls, no doubt," Shug says.

Daddy stares seriously into the middle distance, as if the old man in question were standing there himself, waiting for his story to get told properly and witnessing the ignorance that Daddy had to suffer in the process. "Wasn't no such thing. If you shut up, I can tell your thickheaded self what they was."

"Let him tell it," Cooter says, then lowers his head into a cloud of cigar smoke. Cooter is bothered by the fact that Shug is colored, and takes any chance to scold him, which the other guys tend to ignore. Shug gives me Fig Newtons out of his glove compartment, and I feel evil seeing him scolded for no reason and not saying anything. But I know the rules and so lay low.

"One old boy had a big black skillet in his gear. So we built a fire on the edge of the freight yard. It was a kind of hobo camp already there, some other guys set up all around, Nobody bothered us. This old fella's stretched out behind us stiff as this bench I'm sitting on here."

"The dead one?" I ask, and the men shift around in their chairs, a signal for me to shut up, so I do.

"That's right. And you ain't never gonna guess what happens when they thaw." This is the turning point. Daddy cocks his head at everybody to savor it. The men don't even fake indifference. The domino tiles stop their endless clicking. The cigar smoke might even seem to quit winding around on itself for a minute. Nobody so much as takes a drink. "They pop like firecrackers and let off the biggest stink you ever smelled."

"They was farts?" Cooter finally screams, more high-pitched than is masculine, and at that the men start to laugh. Daddy's Adam's apple googles up and down, and Ben slaps the table, and Shug has to wipe his eyes after a minute.

When everybody settles down, Daddy passes the bottle around again and jumps back to the story of his coming home without even a stab at a segue. "Ain't nothing else to tell. I just walked up through the razor grass to Daddy's old dirt yard. And there's the old man, sitting on the porch. Just exactly like I left him the year before. And he looks up at me serious as polio and says, 'You git the coffee?'"

To Mother, such stories showed that Daddy offered steadiness. He always returned to the logging camp at the end of whatever journey, and coming back was something she'd begun to need from a man, badly. He was a rock. Guys he worked with claimed you could set a watch by when he pulled into the parking lot or what time he clicked open his lunch box. When Mother described Daddy's childhood to us, she would sometimes fake horror at how savage it all sounded—boiling the bristles off a live hog and so forth. But really she admired this world, as she admired the scratchy misery of the blues she listened to on her Bessie Smith records.

Mother was also desperate to get pregnant when she met Daddy. She was thirty, and back then that was late. And Daddy was a fool for kids. During World War II, he wrote in hilarious detail to his sister's kids, Bob Earl and Patty Ann, whom he nicknamed Booger Red and Shadow, respectively. The letters were infrequent, but he made boot camp—and later the war—sound like giant camping trips. "Well Booger you ought to have heard the 50 cal. machine gun I fired at a plane today. Of corse it was radio operated thats a wonderful thing to send a plane up and no one in it. Tell my shadow to eat plenny of pinto beans so she can grow big enuff for the air force and stay out of the stinking army. Ha Ha." About the same time, he wrote his sister about wanting some kids. "I'm too old to start a famly now I gess but I had my day. I got a 48 hour pass to London and shore like them English girls." A car later postmarked Paris is more cryptic: "I way 176 pounds and am mean as hell."

The war letters were passed on to me by my aunt Iris, Daddy's sister, during one of my rare forays down south from grad school. I kept them in a cigar box I'd spray-painted gold for Father's Day once, and which he'd stuffed with old pay stubs from Gulf Oil and then rat-holed in the army footlocker we didn't open till after his memorial service.

I can still smell the odor that came out of the trunk when we'd crowbarred the padlock off and opened it. The smell had seeped into the letters and endures there—damp paper, and gun oil, and chalk from the edges of a puzzling cedar box, which we eventually figured out was a turkey call. (Its lid, held in place by a wooden peg at one end, gives a jagged gobble when you slide it back and forth across the chalked edges of the box.) He kept his Colt pistol wrapped in a flesh-colored chamois cloth. Though he'd preached to me about the dangers of loaded weapons when I first learned to shoot, I found a single bullet in the firing chamber, which to this day I don't believe he'd left there by accident. He was too careful for that. He put the bullet in there deliberately, for a reason I would today give a lot to know. Whose face was floating in your mind, Daddy, yours or some other's, when you snapped the chamber into place and after some thought, perhaps, put the safety on? Even if I'd had the wherewithal to ask this question before his death, he would have probably answered with a shrug, staring into a cloud of Camel smoke. Maybe he would have started a story about his first squirrel gun, or a lecture about how much to lead a mallard with a shotgun before you picked it off. Like most people, he lied best by omission, and what he didn't want you to know there was no point asking about.

The envelopes are smudged with gun oil that's turned the army-issue paper a transparent gray in spots. After the Normandy invasion, the envelopes are of uniform size, dated weekly with few exceptions. The story had it that my father's mother had written his commanding officer complaining that she hadn't heard from Daddy since he'd been shipped overseas. So Captain Pearse, a blue-eyed West Point grad who would eventually arrange to have my father offered a battlefield commission, ordered him to write her every Sunday. On the seal you can see the young man's mark, "Capt. P.," his matter-of-fact block print the opposite of Daddy's wobbly scrawl. Daddy's hands always shook, so maybe he was himself some form of Nervous and just hid it better than most.

The envelopes have no stamps, just the black cancellation mark of the army postal service, and the ones dated after 1944 have "Passed by the Base Censors" in one corner. The censors have razored out some words, leaving oblong slots in the pages where Daddy had tried dropping hints of his whereabouts to folks back home. The tone of the letters progresses from the early farm-boy bragging to a soldier's gravity: "I gess you will faint when I tell you I saw [blank] a few days ago and today I run into some of his outfit and they said he'd [blank]. I sure hated to hear it. Plese tell his Daddy that I cut his name on a piss elum tree right where it happened near the [blank] River. Tell him it was sure a pretty place. I'll talk to him about it when I get home."

The trunk help sepia photos wrapped in cheesecloth from his childhood during the early part of this century. My favorite shows Aunt Iris with the four boys— Uncle A.D., Daddy (who also received no name, only initials—J.P.), Uncle Pug, and Uncle Tim. The boys range from just under six feet (Pug) to six four (A.D.). They are shirtless under their bib overalls; their matching close-cropped haircuts, which Daddy claimed you could rub the river water out of with three strokes of a flat palm, are dark and sleek as seals. With odd solemnity, they hold a single boat oar like a totem. And strung from the giant pecan tree behind them are half a dozen dead alligators, which they hunted for the hides. I remember Daddy's description of swamp gas circling their flat-bottomed boat. Baby Tim usually sat at the prow with a bull's-eye lantern that turned a gator's eyes an eerie reflecting red. In another picture, his mother—her face partly obscured by the huge bonnet—holds the halter of a mule my grandfather allegedly beat to death one day for its stubbornness in the field. My grandfather's picture resembles a younger, stouter version of what I had watched him calcify into before he finally died at eighty-six—a hard brown man in a Stetson, planted in a cane-bottomed rocker on a porch with three equally taciturn-looking bird dogs.

We found a clipping from *Life* on Normandy. Daddy had taken a pen to the spread, writing names underneath many of the men walking away from boats in the surf and holding their rifles up out of the spray. Others posed on tanks. Daddy had scribbled names under certain faces—Rogers, Kinney, Brown, Gustitus, and some faces he had inked out with a simple X.

The trunk also held just about every receipt from every bill he ever paid. He didn't trust banks and believed checking accounts and credit cards were big-company traps to make a man spend money he didn't have without even knowing it. If a Southwestern Gas representative ever had the gall to knock on our door to claim that Daddy owed three dollars for a 1947 gas bill, he would have met with one of the elastic-bound bundles of receipts from that year, then a rectangular piece of faded onionskin stamped PAID. It was a feat Daddy never got to perform, but on nights when he spread the receipts out chronologically, he made it clear to my sister and me that every day some suit-wearing, Republican sonofabitch (his term) weaseled a working man out of an extra three dollars for lack of a receipt. He would not be caught short.

These notorious Republicans were the bogeymen of my childhood. When I asked him to define one (I think it was during the Kennedy-Nixon debate), Daddy said a Republican was somebody who couldn't enjoy eating unless he knew somebody else was hungry, which I took to be gospel for longer than I care to admit. Maybe the only thing worse than being a Republican was being a scab.

Scabs were the cornerstones of one of Daddy's favorite lectures. For some reason, I remember him delivering it one particular morning when I was just old enough to drive and had picked him up from the night shift in his truck. I slid over so he could take the wheel. He brought into the cab the odors of stale coffee and of the cleaning solvent he used to get the oil off his hands. "Now you take me," he said. "Any kind of ciphering I could always do. Math or anything. I could have had that shift foreman's job right over there." He titled his hard hat toward the white oil-storage tanks and the flaming towers by the roadside. "Twelve thousand dollars a year, straight salary. Mr. Briggs called me in. His secretary got me coffee like I like. And he had a desk near as wide as this highway, solid mahogany. 'Pete,' he tells me, 'if you'll stop worrying about crossing a picket line you'll do a helluva lot better by your family.' Well I thanked him just the same. Shook his hand. And a few days later I hear they give it to old Booger." Who old Booger was I had no idea, but this lecture had its own velocity, so there was no point in interrupting. "Pretty soon old Booger gets to feeling poorly. He's got the headache and the sore back. Pretty soon his belly's swelled out over the top of his britches. He's got the mulligrubs." Maybe Daddy thumped his cigarette butt out the triangular side window at this point to buy a minute of thought. "See, Pokey, there was more job there than there was man. And you don't believe me, his wife's a widow today.

"More money, my rosy red ass. That ignorant scab sonofabitch." When he said the word *scab* his knuckles would get white where he gripped the wheel. "Pokey, anybody cross a picket line—and not just here. I mean any picket line. I don't care if it's the drugstore or the carpenters or whoever . . ." What followed would be a grisly portrayal of people prying open children's mouths to steal the bread from them.

In the trunk's very bottom, under the stack of plastic-wrapped dress shirts we bought from Sears or Penney's each Christmas and never saw him even unwrap, we found a stock with a roll of bills adding up to some three thousand dollars— gambling money, I guess, his version of security.

TONY KUSHNER

American Things

Summer is the season for celebrating freedom, summer is the time when we can almost believe it is possible to be free. American education conditions us for this expectation: School's out! The climate shift seductively whispers emancipation. Warmth opens up the body and envelops it. The body in summer is most easily at home in the world. This is true even when the summer is torrid. I have lived half my life in Louisiana and half in New York City. I know from torrid summers.

On my seventh birthday, midsummer 1963, my mother decorated my cake with sparklers she'd saved from the Fourth of July. This, I thought, was extraordinary, fantastic, sparklers spitting and smoking, dangerous and beautiful atop my birthday cake. In one indelible, ecstatic instant my mother completed a circuit of identification for me, melding two iconographies, of self and of liberty: of birthday cake, delicious confectionery emblem of maternal enthusiasm about my existence, which enthusiasm I shared; and of the nighttime fireworks of pyro-romantic Americana, fireworks-liberty-light which slashed across the evening sky, light which thrilled the heart, light which exclaimed loudly in the thick summer air, light which occasionally tore off fingers and burned houses, the fiery fierce explosive risky light of Independence, of Freedom.

Stonewall, the festival day of lesbian and gay liberation, is followed closely by the Fourth of July; they are exactly one summer week apart. The contiguity of these two festivals of freedom is important, at least to me. Each adds piquancy and meaning to the other. In the years following my seventh birthday I had lost some of my enthusiasm for my own existence, as most queer kids growing up in a hostile world will do. I'd certainly begun to realize how unenthusiastic others, even my parents, would be if they knew I was gay. Such joy in being alive as I can now lay claim to has been returned to me largely because of the successes of the political movement which began, more or less officially, twenty-five years ago on that June night in the Village. I've learned how absolutely essential to life freedom is.

Lesbian and gay freedom is the same freedom celebrated annually on the Fourth of July. Of this I have no doubt; my mother told me so, back in 1963, by putting sparklers on that cake. She couldn't have made her point more powerfully if she'd planted them on my head. Hers was a gesture we both understood, though at the time neither could have articulated it: "This fantastic fire is yours." Mothers and fathers should do that for their kids: give them fire, and link them proudly and durably to the world in which they live.

One of the paths down which my political instruction came was our family Seder. Passover, too, is a celebration of Freedom in sultry, intoxicating heat. (Passover actually comes in the spring, but in Louisiana the distinction between spring and summer was never clear.) Our family read from Haggadahs written by a New Deal Reform rabbinate which was unafraid to draw connections between Pharaonic and modern capitalist exploitations; between the exodus of Jews from Goshen and the journey towards civil rights of African-Americans; unafraid to make of the yearning which Jews have repeated for thousands of years a democratic dream of freedom for all peoples. It was impressed upon us, as we sang "America the Beautiful" at the Seder's conclusion, that the dream of millennia was due to find its ultimate realization not in Jerusalem but in this country.

The American political tradition to which my parents made me an heir is mostly an immigrant appropriation of certain features and promises of our Constitution, and of the idea of democracy and federalism. This appropriation marries freedom—up-for-grabs, morally and ideologically indeterminate freedom—to the more strenuous, grave and specific mandates of justice. It is the aggressive, unapologetic, progressive liberalism of the thirties and forties, a liberalism strongly spiced with socialism, trade unionism and the ethos of internationalism and solidarity.

This liberalism at its best held that citizenship was bestowable on everyone, and sooner or later it would be bestowed. Based first and foremost on reason, and then secondarily on protecting certain articles of faith such as the Bill of Rights, democratic process would eventually perform the action of shifting power from the mighty to the many, in whose hands, democratically and morally speaking, it belongs. Over the course of two hundred years, brave, visionary activists and ordinary, moral people had carved out a space, a large sheltering room from which many were now excluded, but which was clearly intended to be capable of multitudes. Within the space of American Freedom there was room for any possibility. American Freedom would become the birthplace of social and economic Justice.

Jews who came to America had gained entrance into this grand salon, as had other immigrant groups: Italians, Irish. Black people, Chicanos and Latinos, Asian-Americans would soon make their own ways, I was told, as would women, as would the working class and the poor—it could only be a matter of time and struggle.

People who desired sex with people of their own gender, transgender people, fags and dykes, drag kings and drag queens, queers, deviants from heterosexual normality were not discussed. There was identity, and then there was illness.

I am nearly thirty-eight, and anyone who's lived thirty-eight years should have made generational improvements on the politics of his or her parents. For any gay man or lesbian since Stonewall, the politics of homosexual enfranchisement is part of what is to be added to the fund of human experience and understanding, to the cosmologies, described and assumed, that we pass on to the next generation—upon which we hope improvements will be made.

The true motion of freedom is to expand outward. To say that lesbian and gay freedom is the same freedom celebrated annually on the Fourth of July is simply to say that queer and other American freedoms have changed historically, generally in a healthy direction (with allowances for some costly periods of faltering, including recently), and must continue to change if they are to remain meaningful. No freedom that fails to grow will last.

Lesbians and gay men of this generation have added homophobia to the consensus list of social evils: poverty, racism, sexism, exploitation, the ravaging of the environment, censorship, imperialism, war. To be a progressive person is to believe that there are ways to actively intervene against these evils. To be a progressive person is to resist Balkanization, tribalism, separatism, is to resist the temptation to bunker down; to be progressive is to seek out connection. I am homosexual, and this ought to make me consider how my experience of the world, as someone who is not always welcome, resembles that of others, however unlike me, who have had similar experiences. I demand to be accorded my rights by others; and so I must be prepared to accord to others their rights. The truest characteristic of freedom is generosity, the basic gesture of freedom is to include, not to exclude.

That there would be a reasonably successful movement for lesbian and gay civil rights was scarcely conceivable a generation ago. In spite of these gains, much of the social progress, which to my parents seemed a foregone conclusion, has not yet been made, and much ground has been lost. Will racism prove to be more intractable, finally, than homophobia? Will the hatred of women, gay and straight, continue to find new and more violent forms of expression, and will gay men and women of color remain doubly, or triply oppressed, while white gay men find greater measures of acceptance, simply because they are white men?

Along with the principle of freedom, much that is gory and disgraceful is celebrated on the Fourth of July, much that is brutal and oppressive. American history is the source for some people of a belief in the inevitable triumph of justice; for others it is the source of a sense of absolute power and ownership which obviates the need to be concerned about justice; while for still others American history is a source of despair that anything like justice will ever come. The can-do liberalism of an earlier day may be faulted for having failed to consider the awesome weight of the crimes of the past, the propensity for tragedy in history, the river of spilled blood that precedes us into the future.

The tensions that have defined American history and American political consciousness have most often been those existing between the margin and the center, the many and the few, the individual and society, the dispossessed and the possessors. It is a peculiar feature of our political life that some of these tensions are frequently discussed and easily grasped, such as those existing between the states and the federal government, or between the rights of individuals and any claim society might make upon them; while other tensions, especially those which are occasioned by the claims of minorities, of marginalized peoples, are regarded with suspicion and fear. Listing the full catalogue of the complaints of the disenfranchised is sure to raise howls decrying "victimology" and "political correctness" from those who need desperately to believe that democracy is a simple thing.

Democracy isn't simple and it doesn't mean that majorities tyrannize minorities. We learned this a long time ago, from, among others, the demi-Moses of that Jewish-American Book of Exodus, Louis Dembitz Brandeis, or in more recent times from Thurgood Marshall. In these days of demographic shifts, when majorities are disappearing, this knowledge is particularly useful, and it needs to be expanded. There are in this country political traditions congenial to the idea that democracy is multi-color and multicultural and also multigendered, that democracy is about returning to individuals the fullest range of their freedoms, but also about the sharing of power, about the rediscovery of collective responsibility. There are in this country political traditions—from organized labor, from the civil rights and black power movements, from feminist and homosexual liberation movements, movements for economic reform—which postulate democracy as an ongoing project, as a dynamic process. These traditions exist in opposition to those which make fixed fetishes of democracy and freedom, talismans for Reaction.

These traditions, which constitute the history of progressive and radical America, have been shunted to the side, covered over in an attempt at revisionism that began during the McCarthy era. Over the course of American history since the Second World War, the terms of the national debate have subtly, insidiously shifted. What used to be called liberal is now called radical; what used to be called radical is now called insane. What used to be called reactionary is now called moderate, and what used to be called insane is now called solid conservative thinking.

The recovery of antecedents is immensely important work. Historians are reconstructing the lost history of homosexual America, along with all the other lost histories. Freedom, I think, is finally being at home in the world, it is a returning—to an enlargement of the best particulars of the home you came from, or the arrival, after a lengthy and arduous journey, at the home you never had, which your dreams and desires have described for you.

I have a guilty confession to make. When I am depressed, when nerve or inspiration or energy flags, I put Dvořák's Ninth Symphony, *From the New World*, on the CD player; I get teary listening to the Largo. It's become classical Muzak, one of the all-time most shopworn musical cliches, which I think is regrettable. My father, who is a symphony conductor, told me that Dvořák wrote it in Spillville, Iowa. The National Conservatory of Music brought him to America to start a nationalist school of American composers. Dvořák contributed all the money for the *New World* Symphony's premiere to a school for former slaves. But then his daughter fell in love with a Native American from the Spillville reservation and Dvořák freaked and took the whole family back to Bohemia.

Like many Americans, I'm looking for home. Home is an absence, it is a loss that impels us. I want this home to be like the Largo from the *New World* Symphony. But life most frequently resembles something by Schoenberg, the last quartet, the one he wrote after his first heart attack and they had to stick a five-inch needle into his heart to revive him. Life these days is played out to the tune of that soundtrack. Or something atonal, anyway, something derivative of Schoenberg, some piece written by one of his less talented pupils, something else.

The only politics that can survive an encounter with this world, and still speak convincingly of freedom and justice and democracy, is a politics that can encompass both the harmonics and the dissonance. The frazzle, the rubbed raw, the unresolved, the fragile and the fiery and the dangerous: These are American things. This jangle is our movement forward, if we are to move forward; it is our survival, if we are to survive.

URSULA K. LE GUIN

The Creatures on My Mind

I. THE BEETLE

When I stayed for a week in New Orleans, out near Tulane, I had an apartment with a balcony. It wasn't one of those cast-iron-lace showpieces of the French Quarter, but a deep, wood-railed balcony made for sitting outside in privacy, just the kind of place I like. But when I first stepped out on it, the first thing I saw was a huge beetle. It lay on its back directly under the light fixture. I thought it was dead, then saw its legs twitch and twitch again. No doubt it had been attracted by the light the night before, and had flown into it, and damaged itself mortally.

Big insects horrify me. As a child I feared moths and spiders, but adolescence cured me, as if those fears evaporated in the stew of hormones. But I never got enough hormones to make me easy with the large, hard-shelled insects: wood roaches, June bugs, mantises, cicadas. This beetle was a couple of inches long; its abdomen was ribbed, its legs long and jointed; it was dull reddish brown; it was dying. I felt a little sick seeing it lie there twitching, enough to keep me from sitting out on the balcony that first day.

Next morning, ashamed of my queasiness, I went out with the broom to sweep it away. But it was still twitching its legs and antennae, still dying. With the end of the broom handle I pushed it very gently a little farther toward the corner of the balcony, and then I sat to read and make notes in the wicker chair in the other corner, turned away from the beetle because its movements drew my eyes. My intense consciousness of it seemed to have something to do with my strangeness in that strange city, New Orleans, and my sense of being on the edge of the tropics—a hot, damp, swarming, fetid, luxuriant existence—as if my unease took the beetle as its visible sign. Why else did I think of it so much? I weighed maybe two thousand times what it weighed, and lived in a perceptual world utterly alien from its world. My feelings were quite out of proportion.

And if I had any courage or common sense, I kept telling myself, I'd step on the poor damned creature and put it out of its misery. We don't know what a beetle may or may not suffer, but it was, in the proper sense of the word, in agony, and the agony had gone on two nights and two days now. I put on my leather-soled loafers. But then I couldn't do it. It would crunch, ooze, squirt under my shoe. Could I hit it with the broom handle? No, I couldn't. I have had a cat with leukemia put down, and have stayed with a cat while he died; I think that if I were hungry, if I had reason to, I could kill for food, wring a chicken's neck, as my grandmothers did, with no more guilt and no less fellow feeling than they. My inability to kill this creature had nothing ethical about it, and no kindness in it. It was mere squeamishness. It was a little rotten place in me, like the soft brown spots in fruit; a sympathy that came not from respect but from loathing. It was a responsibility that would not act. It was guilt itself.

On the third morning the beetle was motionless, shrunken, dead. I got the broom again and swept it into the gutter of the balcony among dry leaves. And there it still is in the gutter of my mind, among dry leaves, a tiny dry husk, a ghost.

II. THE SPARROW

In the humid New England summer the small cooling plant ran all day, making a deep, loud noise. Around the throbbing machinery was a frame of coarse wire net. I thought the bird was outside that wire net, then I hoped it was, then I wished it was. It was moving back and forth with the regularity of the trapped: the zoo animal that paces twelve feet east and twelve feet west and twelve feet east and twelve feet west, hour after hour; the heartbeat of the prisoner in the cell before the torture; the unending recurrence; the silent, steady panic. Back and forth, steadily fluttering between two wooden uprights just above a beam that supported the wire screen: a sparrow, ordinary, dusty, scrappy. I've seen sparrows fighting over territory till the feathers fly, and fucking cheerfully on telephone wires, and in winter gathering in trees in crowds like dirty little Christmas ornaments and talking all together like noisy children, chirp, charp, chirp, charp! But this sparrow was alone, and back and forth it went in terrible silence, trapped in wire and fear. What could I do? There was a door to the wire cage, but it was padlocked. I went on. I tell you I felt that bird beat its wings right here, here under my breastbone in the hollow of my heart. I said in my mind, Is it my fault? Did I build the cage? Just because I happened to see it, is it my sparrow? But my heart was low already, and I knew now that I would be down, down like a bird whose wings won't bear it up, a starving bird.

Then on the path I saw the man, one of the campus managers. The bird's fear gave me courage to speak. "I'm so sorry to bother you," I said. "I'm just visiting here at the librarians' conference—we met the other day in the office. I didn't know what to do, because there's a bird that got into the cooling plant there, inside the screen, and it can't get out." That was enough, too much, but I had to go on. "The noise of the machinery, I think the noise confuses it, and I didn't know what to do. I'm sorry." Why did I apologize? For what?

"Have a look," he said, not smiling, not frowning.

He turned and came with me. He saw the bird beating back and forth, back and forth in silence. He unlocked the padlock. He had the key.

The bird didn't see the door open behind it. It kept beating back and forth along the screen. I found a little stick on the path and threw it against the outside of the screen to frighten the bird into breaking its pattern. It went the wrong way, deeper into the cage, toward the machinery. I threw another stick, hard, and the bird veered and then turned and flew out. I watched the open door, I saw it fly.

The man and I closed the door. He locked it. "Be getting on," he said, not smiling, not frowning, and went on his way, a man with a lot on his mind, a hardworking man. But did he have no joy in it? That's what I think about now. Did he have the key, the power to set free, the will to do it, but no joy in doing it? It is his soul I think about now, if that is the word for it, the spirit, that sparrow.

III. THE GULL

They were winged, all the creatures on my mind.

This one is hard to tell about. It was a seagull. Gulls on Klatsand Beach, on any North Pacific shore, are all alike in their two kinds: white adults with black wingtips and yellow bills; and yearlings, adult-sized but with delicately figured brown features. They soar and cry, swoop, glide, dive, squabble, and grab; they stand in their multitudes at evening in the sunset shallows of the creek mouth before they rise in silence to fly out to sea, where they will sleep the night afloat on waves far out beyond the breakers, like a fleet of small white ships with sails furled and no riding lights. Gulls eat anything, gulls clean the beach, gulls eat dead gulls. There are no individual gulls. They are magnificent flyers, big, clean, strong birds, rapacious, suspicious, fearless. Sometimes as they ride the wind I have seen them as part of the wind and the sea, exactly as the foam, the sand, the fog is part of the wind and the sea, exactly as the foam, the sand, the fog is part of it all, all one, and in such moments of vision I have truly seen the gulls.

But this was one gull, an individual, for it stood alone near the low-tide water's edge with a broken wing. I saw first that the left wing dragged, then saw the naked bone jutting like an ivory knife up from blood-rusted feathers. Something had attacked it, something that could half tear away a wing, maybe a shark when it dove to catch a fish. It stood there. As I came nearer, it saw me. It gave no sign. It did not sidle away, as gulls do when you walk toward them, and then fly if you keep coming on. I stopped. It stood, its flat red feet in the shallow water of a tidal lagoon above the breakers. The tide was on the turn, returning. It stood and waited for the sea.

The idea that worried me was that a dog might find it before the sea did. Dogs roam that long beach. A dog chases gulls, barking and rushing, excited; the gulls fly up in a rush of wings; the dog trots back, maybe a little hangdog, to its owner strolling far down the beach. But a gull that could not fly and the smell of blood would put a dog into a frenzy of barking, lunging, teasing, torturing. I imagined that. My imagination makes me human and makes me a fool; it gives me all the world and exiles me from it. The gull stood waiting for the dog, for the other gulls, for the tide, for what came, living its life completely until death. Its eye looked straight through me, seeing truly, seeing nothing but the sea, the sand, the wind.

BARRY LOPEZ

Children in the Woods

When I was a child growing up in the San Fernando Valley in California, a trip into Los Angeles was special. The sensation of movement from a rural area into an urban one was sharp. On one of these charged occasions, walking down a sidewalk with my mother, I stopped suddenly, caught by a pattern of sunlight trapped in a spiraling imperfection in a windowpane. A stranger, an elderly woman in a cloth coat and a dark hat, spoke out spontaneously, saying how remarkable it is that children notice these things.

I have never forgotten the texture of this incident. Whenever I recall it I am moved not so much by any sense of my young self but by a sense of responsibility toward children, knowing how acutely I was affected in that moment by that woman's words. The effect, for all I know, has lasted a lifetime.

Now, years later, I live in a rain forest in western Oregon, on the banks of a mountain river in relatively undisturbed country, surrounded by 150-foot-tall Douglas firs, delicate deer-head orchids, and clearings where wild berries grow. White-footed mice and mule deer, mink and coyote move through here. My wife and I do not have children, but children we know, or children whose parents we are close to, are often here. They always want to go into the woods. And I wonder what to tell them.

In the beginning, years ago, I think I said too much. I spoke with an encyclopedic knowledge of the names of plants or the names of birds passing through in season. Gradually I came to say less. After a while the only words I spoke, beyond answering a question or calling attention quickly to the slight difference between a sprig of red cedar and a sprig of incense cedar, were to elucidate single objects.

I remember once finding a fragment of a raccoon's jaw in an alder thicket. I sat down alongside the two children with me and encouraged them to find out who this was—with only the three teeth still intact in a piece of the animal's maxilla to guide them. The teeth told by their shape and placement what this animal ate. By a kind of visual extrapolation its size became clear. There were other clues, immediately present, which told, with what I could add of climate and terrain, how this animal lived, how its broken jaw came to be lying here. Raccoon, they surmised. And tiny tooth marks along the bone's broken edge told of a mouse's hunger for calcium.

Barry Lopez, "Children in the Woods" is reprinted by permission of SLL/Sterling Lord Literistic, Inc. Copyright 1988 by Barry Lopez.

We set the jaw back and went on.

If I had known more about raccoons, finer points of osteology, we might have guessed more: say, whether it was male or female. But what we deduced was all we needed. Hours, later, the maxilla, lost behind us in the detritus of the forest floor, continued to effervesce. It was tied faintly to all else we spoke of that afternoon.

In speaking with children who might one day take a permanent interest in natural history—as writers, as scientists, as filmmakers, as anthropologists—I have sensed that an extrapolation from a single fragment of the whole is the most invigorating experience I can share with them. I think children know that nearly anyone can learn the names of things; the impression made on them at this level is fleeting. What takes a lifetime to learn, they comprehend, is the existence and substance of myriad relationships: it is these relationships, not the things themselves, that ultimately hold the human imagination.

The brightest children, it has often struck me, are fascinated by metaphor—with what is shown in the set of relationships bearing on the raccoon, for example, to lie quite beyond the raccoon. In the end, you are trying to make clear to them that everything found at the edge of one's senses—the high note of the winter wren, the thick perfume of propolis that drifts downwind from spring willows, the brightness of wood chips scattered by beaver—that all this fits together. The indestructibility of these associations conveys a sense of permanence that nurtures the heart, that cripples one of the most insidious of human anxieties, the one that says, you do not belong here, you are unnecessary.

Whenever I walk with a child, I think how much I have seen disappear in my own life. What will there be for this person when he is my age? If he senses something ineffable in the landscape, will I know enough to encourage it?—to somehow show him that, yes, when people talk about violent death, spiritual exhilaration, compassion, futility, final causes, they are drawing on forty thousand years of human meditation on *this*—as we embrace Douglas firs, or stand by a river across whose undulating back we skip stones, or dig out a camas bulb, biting down into a taste so much wilder than last night's potatoes.

The most moving look I ever saw from a child in the woods was on a mud bar by the footprints of a heron. We were on our knees, making handprints beside the footprints. You could feel the creek vibrating in the silt and sand. The sun beat down heavily on our hair. Our shoes were soaking wet. The look said: I did not know until now that I needed someone much older to confirm this, the feeling I have of life here. I can now grow older, knowing it need never be lost.

The quickest door to open in the woods for a child is the one that leads to the smallest room, by knowing the name each thing is called. The door that leads to the cathedral is marked by a hesitancy to speak at all, rather to encourage by example a sharpness of the senses. If one speaks it should only be to say, as well as one can, how wonderfully all this fits together, to indicate what a long, fierce peace can derive from this knowledge.

NANCY MAIRS

On Being a Cripple

To escape is nothing. Not to escape is nothing.

—Louise Bogan

The other day I was thinking of writing an essay on being a cripple. I was thinking hard in one of the stalls of the women's room in my office building, as I was shoving my shirt into my jeans and tugging up my zipper. Preoccupied, I flushed, picked up my book bag, took my cane down from the hook, and unlatched the door. So many movements unbalanced me, and as I pulled the door open I fell over backward, landing fully clothed on the toilet seat with my legs splayed in front of me: the old beetle-on-its-back routine. Saturday afternoon, the building deserted, I was free to laugh aloud as I wriggled back to my feet, my voice bouncing off the yellowish tiles from all directions. Had anyone been there with me, I'd have been still and faint and hot with chagrin. I decided that it was high time to write the essay.

First, the matter of semantics. I am a cripple. I choose this word to name me. I choose from among several possibilities, the most common of which are "handicapped" and "disabled." I made the choice a number of years ago, without thinking, unaware of my motives for doing so. Even now, I'm not sure what those motives are, but I recognize that they are complex and not entirely flattering. People—crippled or not—wince at the word "cripple," as they do not at "handicapped" or "disabled." Perhaps I want them to wince. I want them to see me as a tough customer, one to whom the fates/gods/viruses have not been kind, but who can face the brutal truth of her existence squarely. As a cripple, I swagger.

But, to be fair to myself, a certain amount of honesty underlies my choice. "Cripple" seems to me a clean word, straightforward and precise. It has an honorable history, having made its first appearance in the Lindisfarne Gospel in the tenth century. As a lover of words, I like the accuracy with which it describes my condition: I have lost the full use of my limbs. "Disabled," by contrast, suggests any incapacity, physical or mental. And I certainly don't like "handicapped," which implies that I have deliberately been put at a disadvantage, by whom I can't imagine (my God is not a Handicapper General), in order to equalize chances in the great race of life. These words seem to me to be moving away from my condition, to be widening the gap between word and reality. Most remote is the recently coined euphemism "differently abled," which partakes of the same semantic hopefulness that transformed countries from "undeveloped" to "underdeveloped," then to "less developed," and finally to "developing" nations. People have continued to starve in those countries during the shift. Some realities do not obey the dictates of language.

Mine is one of them. Whatever you call me, I remain crippled. But I don't care what you call me, so long as it isn't "differently abled," which strikes me as pure verbal garbage designed, by its ability to describe anyone, to describe no one. I subscribe to George Orwell's thesis that "the slovenliness of our language makes it easier for us to have foolish thoughts." And I refuse to participate in the degeneration of the language to the extent that I deny that I have lost anything in the course of this calamitous disease; I refuse to pretend that the only differences between you and me are the various ordinary ones that distinguish any one person from another. But call me "disabled" or "handicapped" if you like. I have long since grown accustomed to them; and if they are vague, at least they hint at the truth. Moreover, I use them myself. Society is no readier to accept crippledness than to accept death, war, sex, sweat, or wrinkles. I would never refer to another person as a cripple. It is the word I use to name only myself.

I haven't always been crippled, a fact for which I am soundly grateful. To be whole of limb is, I know from experience, infinitely more pleasant and useful than to be crippled; and if that knowledge leaves me open to bitterness at my loss, the physical soundness I once enjoyed (though I did not enjoy it half enough) is well worth the occasional stab of regret. Though never any good at sports, I was a normally active child and young adult. I climbed trees, played hopscotch, jumped rope, skated, swam, rode my bicycle, sailed. I despised team sports, spending some of the wretchedest afternoons of my life, sweaty and humiliated, behind a field-hockey stick and under a basketball hoop. I tramped alone for miles along the bridle paths that webbed the woods behind the house I grew up in. I swayed through countless dim hours in the arms of one man or another under the scattered shot of light from mirrored balls, and gyrated through countless more as Tab Hunter and Johnny Mathis gave way to the Rolling Stones, Creedence Clearwater Revival, Cream. I walked down the aisle. I pushed baby carriages, changed tires in the rain, marched for peace.

When I was twenty-eight I started to trip and drop things. What at first seemed my natural clumsiness soon became too pronounced to shrug off. I consulted a neurologist, who told me that I had a brain tumor. A battery of tests, increasingly disagreeable, revealed no tumor. About a year and a half later I developed a blurred spot in one eye. I had, at last, the episodes "disseminated in space and time" requisite for a diagnosis: multiple sclerosis. I have never been sorry for the doctor's initial misdiagnosis, however. For almost a week, until the negative results of the tests were in, I thought that I was going to die right away. Every day for the past nearly ten years, then, has been a kind of gift. I accept all gifts.

Multiple sclerosis is a chronic degenerative disease of the central nervous system, in which the myelin that sheathes the nerves is somehow eaten away and scar tissue forms in its place, interrupting the nerves' signals. During its course, which is unpredictable and uncontrollable, one may lose vision, hearing, speech, the ability to walk, control of bladder and/or bowels, strength in any or all extremities, sensitivity to touch, vibration, and/or pain, potency, coordination of movements—the list of possibilities is lengthy and, yes, horrifying. One may also lose one's sense of humor. That's the easiest to lose and the hardest to survive without.

In the past ten years, I have sustained some of these losses. Characteristic of MS are sudden attacks, called exacerbations, followed by remissions, and these I have not had. Instead, my disease has been slowly progressive. My left leg is now so weak that I walk with the aid of a brace and a cane; and for distances I use an Amigo, a variation on the electric wheelchair that looks rather like an electrified kiddie car. I no longer have much use of my left hand. Now my right side is weakening as well. I still have the blurred spot in my right eye. Overall, though, I've been lucky so far. My world has, of necessity, been circumscribed by my losses, but the terrain left me has been ample enough for me to continue many of the activities that absorb me: writing, teaching, raising children and cats and plants and snakes, reading, speaking publicly about MS and depression, even playing bridge with people patient and honorable enough to let me scatter cards every which way without sneaking a peek.

Lest I begin to sound like Pollyanna, however, let me say that I don't like having MS. I hate it. My life holds realities—harsh ones, some of them—that no right-minded human being ought to accept without grumbling. One of them is fatigue. I know of no one with MS who does not complain of bone-weariness; in a disease that presents an astonishing variety of symptoms, fatigue seems to be a common factor. I wake up in the morning feeling the way most people do at the end of a bad day, and I take it from there. As a result, I spend a lot of time *in extremis* and, impatient with limitation, I tend to ignore my fatigue until my body breaks down in some way and forces rest. Then I miss picnics, dinner parties, poetry readings, the brief visits of old friends from out of town. The offspring of a puritanical tradition of exceptional venerability, I cannot view these lapses without shame. My life often seems a series of small failures to do as I ought.

I lead, on the whole, an ordinary life, probably rather like the one I would have led had I not had MS. I am lucky that my predilections were already solitary, sedentary, and bookish—unlike the world-famous French cellist I have read about, or the young woman I talked with one long afternoon who wanted only to be a jockey. I had just begun graduate school when I found out something was wrong with me, and I have remained, interminably, a graduate student. Perhaps I would not have if I'd thought I had the stamina to return to a full-time job as a technical editor; but I've enjoyed my studies.

In addition to studying, I teach writing courses. I also teach medical students how to give neurological examinations. I pick up freelance editing jobs here and there. I have raised a foster son and sent him into the world, where he has made me two grandbabies, and I am still escorting my daughter and son through adolescence. I go to Mass every Saturday. I am a superb, if messy, cook. I am also an enthusiastic laundress, capable of sorting a hamper full of clothes into five subtly differentiated piles, but a terrible housekeeper. I can do italic writing and, in an emergency, bathe an oil-soaked cat. I play a fiendish game of Scrabble. When I have the time and the money, I like to sit on my front steps with my husband, drinking Amaretto and smoking a cigar, as we imagine our counterparts in Leningrad and make sure that the sun gets down once more behind the sharp childish scrawl of the Tucson Mountains.

This lively plenty has its bleak complement, of course, in all the things I can no longer do. I will never run again, except in dreams, and one day I may have to write that I will never walk again. I like to go camping, but I can't follow George and the children along the trails that wander out of a campsite through the desert or into the mountains. In fact, even on the level I've learned never to check the weather or try to hold a coherent conversation: I need all my attention for my wayward feet. Of late, I have begun to catch myself wondering how people can propel themselves without canes. With only one usable hand, I have to select my clothing with care not so much for style as for ease of ingress and egress, and even so, dressing can be laborious. I can no longer do fine stitchery, pick up babies, play the piano, braid my hair. I am immobilized by acute attacks of depression, which may or may not be physiologically related to MS but are certainly its logical concomitant.

These two elements, the plenty and the privation, are never pure, nor are the delight and wretchedness that accompany them. Almost every pickle that I get into as a result of my weakness and clumsiness—and I get into plenty—is funny as well as maddening and sometimes painful. I recall one May afternoon when a friend and I were going out for a drink after finishing up at school. As we were climbing into opposite sides of my car, chatting, I tripped and fell, flat and hard, onto the asphalt parking lot, my abrupt departure interrupting him in mid-sentence. "Where'd you go?" he called as he came around the back of the car to find me hauling myself up by the door frame. "Are you all right?" Yes, I told him, I was fine, just a bit rattly, and we drove off to find a shady patio and some beer. When I got home an hour or so later, my daughter greeted me with "What have you done to yourself?" I looked down. One elbow of my white turtleneck with the green froggies, one knee of my white trousers, one white kneesock were blood-soaked. We peeled off the clothes and inspected the damage, which was nasty enough but not alarming. That part wasn't funny: The abrasions took a long time to heal, and one got a little infected. Even so, when I think of my friend talking earnestly, suddenly, to the hot thin air while I dropped from his view as though through a trap door, I find the image as silly as something from a Marx Brothers movie.

I may find it easier than other cripples to amuse myself because I live propped by the acceptance and the assistance and, sometimes, the amusement of those around me. Grocery clerks tear my checks out of my checkbook for me, and sales clerks find chairs to put into dressing rooms when I want to try on clothes. The people I work with make sure I teach at times when I am least likely to be fatigued, in places I can get to, with the materials I need. My students, with one anonymous exception (in an end-of-the-semester evaluation), have been unperturbed by my disability. Some even like it. One was immensely cheered by the information that I paint my own fingernails; she decided, she told me, that if I could go to such trouble over fine details, she could keep on writing essays. I suppose I became some sort of bright-fingered muse. She wrote good essays, too.

The most important struts in the framework of my existence, of course, are my husband and children. Dismayingly few marriages survive the MS test, and why should they? Most twenty-two- and nineteen-year-olds, like George and me, can vow in clear conscience, after a childhood of chicken pox and summer colds, to keep one another in sickness and in health so long as they both shall live. Not many are equipped for catastrophe: the dismay, the depression, the extra work, the boredom that a degenerative disease can insinuate into a relationship. And our society, with its emphasis on fun and its association of fun with physical performance, offers little encouragement for a whole spouse to stay with a crippled partner. Children experience similar stresses when faced with a crippled parent, and they are more helpless, since parents and children can't usually get divorced. They hate, of course, to be different from their peers, and the child whose mother is tacking down the aisle of a school auditorium packed with proud parents like a Cape Cod dinghy in a stiff breeze jolly well stands out in a crowd. Deprived of legal divorce, the child can at least deny the mother's disability, even her existence, forgetting to tell her about recitals and PTA meetings, refusing to accompany her to stores or church or the movies, never inviting friends to the house. Many do.

But I've been limping along for ten years now, and so far George and the children are still at my left elbow, holding tight. Anne and Matthew vacuum floors and dust furniture and haul trash and rake up dog droppings and button my cuffs and bake lasagna and Toll House cookies with just enough grumbling so I know that they don't have brain fever. And far from hiding me, they're forever dragging me by racks of fancy clothes or through teeming school corridors, or welcoming gaggles of friends while I'm wandering through the house in Anne's filmy pink babydoll pajamas. George generally calls before he brings someone home, but he does just as many dumb thankless chores as the children. And they all yell at me, laugh at some of my jokes, write me funny letters when we're apart—in short, treat me as an ordinary human being for whom they have some use. I think they like me. Unless they're faking. . . .

Faking. There's the rub. Tugging at the fringes of my consciousness always is the terror that people are kind to me only because I'm a cripple. My mother almost shattered me once, with that instinct mothers have—blind, I think, in this case, but unerring nonetheless—for striking blows along the fault-lines of their children's hearts, by telling me, in an attack on my selfishness, "We all have to make allowances for you, of course, because of the way you are." From the distance of a couple of years, I have to admit that I haven't any idea just what she meant, and I'm not sure that she knew either. She was awfully angry. But at the time, as the words thudded home, I felt my worst fear, suddenly realized. I could bear being called selfish: I am. But I couldn't bear the corroboration that those around me were doing in fact what I'd always suspected them of doing, professing fondness while silently putting up with me because of the way I am. A cripple. I've been a little cracked ever since.

Along with this fear that people are secretly accepting shoddy goods comes a relentless pressure to please—to prove myself worth the burdens I impose, I guess, or to build a substantial account of goodwill against which I may write drafts in times of need. Part of the pressure arises from social expectations. In our society, anyone who deviates from the norm had better find some way to compensate. Like fat people, who are expected to be jolly, cripples must bear their lot meekly and cheerfully. A grumpy cripple isn't playing by the rules. And much of the pressure is self-generated. Early on I vowed that, if I had to have MS, by God I was going to do it well. This is a class act, ladies and gentlemen. No tears, no recriminations, no faint-heartedness.

One way and another, then, I wind up feeling like Tiny Tim, peering over the edge of the table at the Christmas goose, waving my crutch, piping down God's blessing on us all. Only sometimes I don't want to play Tiny Tim. I'd rather be Caliban, a most scurvy monster. Fortunately, at home no one much cares whether I'm a good cripple or a bad cripple as long as I make vichyssoise with fair regularity. One evening several years ago, Anne was reading at the dining-room table while I cooked dinner. As I opened a can of tomatoes, the can slipped in my left hand and juice spattered me and the counter with bloody spots. Fatigued and infuriated, I bellowed, "I'm so sick of being crippled!" Anne glanced at me over the top of her book. "There now," she said, "do you feel better?" "Yes," I said, "yes, I do." She went back to her reading. I felt better. That's about all the attention my scurviness ever gets.

Because I hate being crippled, I sometimes hate myself for being a cripple. Over the years I have come to expect—even accept—attacks of violent self-loathing. Luckily, in general our society no longer connects deformity and disease directly with evil (though a charismatic once told me that I have MS because a devil is in me) and so I'm allowed to move largely at will, even among small children. But I'm not sure that this revision of attitude has been particularly helpful. Physical imperfection, even freed of moral disapprobation, still defies and violates the ideal, especially for women, whose confinement in their bodies as objects of desire is far from over. Each age, of course, has its ideal, and I doubt that ours is any better or worse than any other. Today's ideal woman, who lives on the glossy pages of dozens of magazines, seems to be between the ages of eighteen and twenty-five; her hair has body, her teeth flash white, her breath smells minty, her underarms are dry; she has a career but is still a fabulous cook, especially of meals that take less than twenty minutes to prepare; she does not ordinarily appear to have a husband or children; she is trim and deeply tanned; she jogs, swims, plays tennis, rides a bicycle, sails, but does not bowl; she travels widely, even to out-of-the-way places like Finland and Samoa, always in the company of the ideal man, who possesses a nearly identical set of characteristics. There are a few exceptions. Though usually white and often blonde, she may be black, Hispanic, Asian, or Native American, so long as she is unusually sleek. She may be old, provided she is selling a laxative or is Lauren Bacall. If she is selling a detergent, she may be married and have a flock of strikingly messy children. But she is never a cripple.

Like many women I know, I have always had an uneasy relationship with my body. I was not a popular child, largely, I think now, because I was peculiar: intelligent, intense, moody, shy, given to unexpected actions and inexplicable notions and emotions. But as I entered adolescence, I believed myself unpopular because I was homely; my breasts too flat, my mouth too wide, my hips too narrow, my clothing never quite right in fit or style. I was not, in fact, particularly ugly, old photographs inform me, though I was well off the ideal; but I carried this sense of self-alienation with me into adulthood, where it regenerated in response to the depredations of MS. Even with my brace I walk with a limp so pronounced that, seeing myself on the videotape of a television program on the disabled, I couldn't believe that anything but an inchworm could make progress humping along like that. My shoulders droop and my pelvis thrusts forward as I try to balance myself upright, throwing my frame into a bony S. As a result of contractures, one shoulder is higher than the other and I carry one arm bent in front of me, the fingers curled into a claw. My left arm and leg have wasted into pipe-stems, and I try always to keep them covered. When I think about how my body must look to others, especially to men, to whom I have been trained to display myself, I feel ludicrous, even loathsome.

At my age, however, I don't spend much time thinking about my appearance. The burning egocentricity of adolescence, which assures one that all the world is looking all the time, has passed, thank God, and I'm generally too caught up in what I'm doing to step back, as I used to, and watch myself as though upon a stage. I'm also too old to believe in the accuracy of self-image. I know that I'm not a hideous crone, that in fact, when I'm rested, well dressed, and well made up, I look fine. The self-loathing I feel is neither physically nor intellectually substantial. What I hate is not me but a disease.

I am not a disease.

And a disease is not—at least not singlehandedly—going to determine who I am, though at first it seemed to be going to. Adjusting to a chronic incurable illness, I have moved through a process similar to that outlined by Elizabeth Kübler-Ross in *On Death and Dying.* The major difference—and it is far more significant than most people recognize—is that I can't be sure of the outcome, as the terminally ill cancer patient can. Research studies indicate that, with proper medical care, I may achieve a "normal" life span. And in our society, with its vision of death as the ultimate evil, worse even than decrepitude, the response to such news is, "Oh well, at least you're not going to *die*." Are there worse things than dying? I think that there may be.

I think of two women I know, both with MS, both enough older than I to have served me as models. One took to her bed several years ago and has been there ever since. Although she can sit in a high-backed wheelchair, because she in incontinent she refuses to go out at all, even though incontinence pants, which are readily available at any pharmacy, could protect her from embarrassment. Instead, she stays at home and insists that her husband, a small quiet man, a retired civil servant, stay there with her except for a quick weekly foray to the supermarket. The other woman, whose illness was diagnosed when she was eighteen, a nursing student engaged to a young doctor, finished her training, married her doctor, accompanied him to Germany when he was in the service, bore three sons and a daughter, now grown and gone. When she can, she travels with her husband; she plays bridge, embroiders, swims regularly; she works, like me, as a symptomatic-patient instructor of medical students in neurology. Guess which woman I hope to be.

At the beginning, I thought about having MS almost incessantly. And because of the unpredictable course of the disease, my thoughts were always terrified. Each night I'd get into bed wondering whether I'd get out again the next morning, whether I'd be able to see, to speak, to hold a pen between my fingers. Knowing that the day might come when I'd be physically incapable of killing myself, I thought perhaps I ought to do so right away, while I still had the strength. Gradually I came to understand that the Nancy who might one day lie inert under a bedsheet, arms and legs paralyzed, unable to feed or bathe herself, unable to reach out for a gun, a bottle of pills, was not the Nancy I was at present, and that I could not presume to make decisions for that future Nancy, who might well not want in the least to die. Now the only provision I've made for the future Nancy is that when the time comes—and it is likely to come in the form of pneumonia, friend to the weak and the old—I am not to be treated with machines and medications. If she is unable to communicate by then, I hope she will be satisfied with these terms.

Thinking all the time about having MS grew tiresome and intrusive, especially in the large and tragic mode in which I was accustomed to considering my plight. Months and even years went by without catastrophe (at least without one related to MS), and really I was awfully busy, what with George and children and snakes and students and poems, and I hadn't the time, let alone the inclination, to devote myself to being a disease. Too, the richer my life became, the funnier it seemed, as though there were some connection between largesse and laughter, and so my tragic stance began to waver until, even with the aid of a brace and a cane, I couldn't hold it for very long at a time.

After several years I was satisfied with my adjustment. I had suffered my grief and fury and terror, I thought, but now I was at ease with my lot. Then one summer day I set out with George and the children across the desert for a vacation in California. Part way to Yuma I became aware that my right leg felt funny. "I think I've had an exacerbation," I told George. "What shall we do?" he asked. "I think we'd better get the hell to California," I said, "because I don't know whether I'll ever make it again." So we went on to San Diego and then to Orange, up the Pacific Coast Highway to Santa Cruz, across to Yosemite, down to Sequoia and Joshua Tree, and so back over the desert to home. It was a fine two-week trip, filled with friends and fair weather, and I wouldn't have missed it for the world, though I did in fact make it back to California two years later. Nor would there have been any point in missing it, since in MS, once the symptoms have appeared, the neurological damage has been done, and there's no way to predict or prevent that damage.

The incident spoiled my self-satisfaction, however. It renewed my grief and fury and terror, and I learned that one never finishes adjusting to MS. I don't know now why I thought one would. One does not, after all, finish adjusting to life, and MS is simply a fact of my life—not my favorite fact, of course—but as ordinary as my nose and my tropical fish and my yellow Mazda station wagon. It may at any time get worse, but no amount of worry or anticipation can prepare me for a new loss. My life is a lesson in losses. I learn one at a time.

And I had best be patient in the learning, since I'll have to do it like it or not. As any rock fan knows, you can't always get what you want. Particularly when you have MS. You can't, for example, get cured. In recent years researchers and the organizations that fund research have started to pay MS some attention even though it isn't fatal; perhaps they have begun to see that life is something other than a quantitative phenomenon, that one may be very much alive for a very long time in a life that isn't worth living. The researchers have made some progress toward understanding the mechanism of the disease: It may well be an autoimmune reaction triggered by a slow-acting virus. But they are nowhere near its prevention, control, or cure. And most of us want to be cured. Some, unable to accept incurability, grasp at one treatment after another, no matter how bizarre: megavitamin therapy, gluten-free diet, injections of cobra venom, hypothermal suits, lymphocytopharesis, hyperbaric chambers. Many treatments are probably harmless enough, but none are curative.

The absence of a cure often makes MS patients bitter toward their doctors. Doctors are, after all, the priests of modern society, the new shamans, whose business is to heal, and many an MS patient roves from one to another, searching for the "good" doctor who will make him well. Doctors too think of themselves as healers, and for this reason many have trouble dealing with MS patients, whose disease in its intransigence defeats their aims and mocks their skills. Too few doctors, it is true, treat their patients as whole human beings, but the reverse is also true. I have always tried to be gentle with my doctors, who often have more at stake in terms of ego than I do. I may be frustrated, maddened, depressed by the incurability of my disease, but I am not diminished by it, and they are. When I push myself up from my seat in the waiting room and stumble toward them, I incarnate the limitation of their powers. The least I can do is refuse to press on their tenderest spots.

This gentleness is part of the reason that I'm not sorry to be a cripple. I didn't have it before. Perhaps I'd have developed it anyway—how could I know such a thing?—and I wish I had more of it, but I'm glad of what I have. It has opened and enriched my life enormously, this sense that my frailty and need must be mirrored in others, that in searching for and shaping a stable core in a life wrenched by change and loss, change and loss, I must recognize the same process, under individual conditions, in the lives around me. I do not deprecate such knowledge, however I've come by it.

All the same, if a cure were found, would I take it? In a minute. I may be a cripple, but I'm only occasionally a loony and never a saint. Anyway, in my brand of theology God doesn't give bonus points for a limp. I'd take a cure; I just don't need one. A friend who also has MS startled me once by asking, "Do you ever say to yourself, 'Why me, Lord?' " "No, Michael, I don't," I told him, "because whenever I try, the only response I can think of is 'Why not?' " If I could make a cosmic deal, who would I put in my place? What in my life would I give up in exchange for sound limbs and a thrilling rush of energy? No one. Nothing. I might as well do the job myself. Now that I'm getting the hang of it.

From The Same River Twice

The guts of America unfolded in every direction as I traveled the interstate blood-stream, dodging the white corpuscles of perverts, cops, and outlaws. Thumbing induced a peculiar form of freedom linked to terror. I could go anywhere, sleep anywhere, be killed anywhere. The only restrictions were fear and rain. Mine was the indifferent life of a barnacle: temporary attachment to a larger object at a pace dependent upon the ride. Lacking plan or destination, I was at last content. A job became as meaningless as food and shelter, a drab necessity.

I was roaming with my brethren, all the ragtag bums and bandits moving through the nation. Occasionally we met at a cloverleaf. After a visual sizing up, in which each of us tried to look menacing in case the other was an escaped convict, we claimed our hitching spots. Existence was reduced to a backpack, the highway, and the benevolence of utter strangers. I kept my journal buttoned inside my shirt. The pack and everything in it could be abandoned.

I slalomed the past, searching for a genetic base to my wandering. Dad had grown up in a genuine log cabin and had inherited a fraction of crackpottery. My own fisticuffs with the world proved that I bore my generation's share of the family darkness. When I was twelve, Dad quit his job as a traveling salesman and came home for good. He grew a beard and wore mail order African dashikis. He tuned in to distant airwaves, turned on with bourbon, and dropped into the family. Our absent father had become a stranger who never left the house.

My brother and I spent all our time outside playing baseball, using plates from the kitchen as bases. Soon we ran out of plates, a fact that Mom accepted with an equanimity fed by years of facing cryptic boy-stuff. Lacking brothers, she'd had no experience with young boys. She was like a straw boss of immigrant workers—she didn't speak our language, and regarded our alien ways as best left alone. Mom preferred not to tell Dad about the plate shortage until he was in a receptive mood, a wait that could conceivably require the passage of a season. He'd blame her, and we were too broke to buy new dishes.

Mom's grand solution was paper plates. She'd gotten hold of a dozen some-how, probably through VISTA, since they prowled the hills giving away combs, key chains, and toothbrushes. To make the paper plates last, we used them over and over until they were heavy as hubcaps. Every Saturday we ate fried chicken, Dad's favorite meal. For dessert he split the bones and sucked the marrow. He finally lifted his plate for seconds and the bottom dropped like a trapdoor, dumping

Excerpt from pp. 59–71 is reprinted with permission of Simon & Schuster Adult Publishing Group from The Same River Twice *by Chris Offutt. Copyright © 1993 by Chris Offutt.*

his cache of bones to the table. He immediately accused me of having booby-trapped his plate.

"No," I said. "Mine's the same way."

I lifted my plate and a chunk of mashed potato slid through the opening. My siblings followed suit, attempting to head off Dad's phenomenal and unpredictable rage. When he got mad, which was not infrequent, the house was tense as a cancer ward until everyone apologized. To avoid these awful times, we coalesced to maintain the illusion of normalcy at any cost.

Dad hunched his bony shoulders, preparing for either a ten-hour tirade or face-saving laughter. His greatest fear was of duplicating Caesar's deathbed epiphany, and each of us was a potential Brutus, Judas, or Delilah. Everyone looked at Mom. Affairs didn't often come to this, but when they did, her reaction was crucial. She hated to take a side. Her usual stance was a balancing act between loyalty to her children and to her husband. She raised us, but Dad controlled us. If so much as a hound dog refused fealty, it disappeared in a South American fashion and was never mentioned.

Mom calmly tipped over a bowl of peaches. Thick juice ran across the old formica. Dad plucked a peach from the table and ate it. I stuffed a handful of beans down my gullet and we finished the meal eating like Romans.

It was late that night, lying in bed, when I decided to save my money and head into the world.

A decade later I was in it, facing the end of autumn. During cold weather bums and birds headed south, and I wintered in West Texas, working as a painter of houses built rapidly during the oil boom. Entire towns were materializing near oilfields. Trucks brought stud walls and rafter frames, predrilled for electrical wires. Young trees waited for holes, their root balls wrapped in cheesecloth. Mats of damp sod arrived by flatbed truck. As soon as the interior work was complete, a family moved into the house.

Outdoor painting was the last stage, and I hired with a contractor named Bill, a former gunnery sergeant in Vietnam. Half the crew was Mexican and the rest were ex-cons or marginal ruffians. Bill paid us in cash at the end of each day, saying, "You have two choices, boys. You can save for a convertible or spend it on poontang. I'll go your bail once. Just once."

Bill always wore some article of military clothing—a hat one day, boots the next, a web belt on another day. He was prone to silent crying, apropos of nothing. No one mentioned it. He was also good-looking and gentle, very popular with the women whose houses we colored. After an incident in which a woman exposed her breasts to me while I was on a ladder, I asked him if he'd ever gotten laid on a job.

"The problem is what to do with your wet brush," he said. "If you lay it on top of the bucket, it gets too dry. And if you stick it in the bucket, the paint gets up into the handle and ruins the bristles." He glanced at the bleak landscape beyond the carefully watered lawns. "Indoor work with latex is the best."

The woman whose house we were painting couldn't decide what color she wanted. We had several different buckets, and were instructed to paint giant swatches on the front of the house. After lunch, the crew lounged in the shade while the other wives in the community congregated to give opinion. They carried infants, whom they regarded with the same detachment as they did the patches of color on the siding.

"You know, Judy's baby has already got a suntan," one mother said. "I'm going to get mine in the sun today."

"I can't make mine shut up crying long enough to dress it," said another.

"Take and push half a Tylenol up its butt. That quiets mine right down. Regular, not extra-strength."

The husbands took little interest in their homes, confining their aesthetic concerns to clothing. Boot toes ran to amazing points, as if designed to spindle a spider in a corner. They wore the biggest hats in the West, decorated with huge feathers. In local bars, the men spent most of their time accusing each other of having "knocked my feather." Such an insult was tantamount to a Kentucky warning shot, the French musketeer's slap in the face, or the New York faux pas of daring to look someone in the eyes for more than ten seconds.

"Hey!" someone would yell. "You knocked my feather."

People backed away from the victim, who stroked his feather while glaring at the perpetrator. The accused man started back. Each stretched his body to full height, squinting, jaw thrust out, gauging his chances in case things got downright western. After a minute of staring, both men turned slowly away feigning reluctance. After witnessing this rite, I spoke with the men involved. Each claimed to be a descendant of original settlers. One was a dentist. The other worked as an accountant. Both were a little put out that oil hadn't been discovered on their land.

When occasional trouble actually erupted, it was the wrestling-across-the-floor sort, until one man exposed his genitals in surrender. A little while later they'd be drinking together. The Kentucky style of brawling is similar to the Viking berserker—all out, using whatever is at hand, aiming for the throat and crotch. Texans seemed to consider anything shy of a gunfight little more than sport. Since I couldn't trust myself to follow house rules, I spent the better part of four months dodging feathers.

After work one Friday, Bill and I were in a tavern drinking beer and shooting pool. A neckless man with a body like a wedge called Bill a feather knocker. Bill turned away. The man followed, saying that Bill was a chicken with a yellow stripe up his back a mile wide. There were three guys backing him up. As casually as possible, I picked up an empty beer mug in each hand. Bill saw me and shook his head. The man stepped close, yelling so fiercely that saliva sprayed the air. Bill leaned to the man, their chests nearly touching, and began talking in a low voice. Then he walked back to the pool table and sank a combination shot as if he'd been concentrating on the game all along. The other man stood immobile for a couple of minutes before returning to his bar stool.

I asked Bill what he'd said.

"Simple," he said. "I told him that if we fought, all we'd do was rip our clothes, and women didn't favor men wearing tore-up shirts. I said there was nothing wrong with fighting but I didn't feel like it today."

"That's all it took?"

"No," Bill said. "I kindly had hold of his balls the whole time, squeezing tighter and tighter."

After the war, Bill had stayed drunk for three years, then tried the rodeo circuit as a bull rider. He described it as wrapping your arm around a chain tied to the bumper of a car, then having the driver pop the clutch. The first two seconds were the worst. It didn't compare to the exhilaration of combat, though, and it wasn't until recently that he'd found an activity that did.

Twice a month, Bill went skydiving. He offered to pay the fee if I accompanied him, and we drove an hour to a small airstrip near a cattle ranch. Two other customers were there. Like us, one was an aficionado, the other a novice. An instructor outfitted us with boots and coveralls, then spent two hours teaching us to land and roll.

The four of us flew into the sky with the instructor. The main chute was strapped to my back. A spare on my chest made me realize the extent to which I'd finally taken the irrational. The little plane leveled out at three thousand feet, circling above a scrubby pasture. The noise made talking impossible. Wind rushed through the open hatch. Bill winked at me and left the aircraft half a mile above the earth. He was simply not there anymore. I knew instantly that this was the stupidest idea I'd ever had. I decided to stay in the plane, and shifted position to go last so the others would not witness my decision. Once they were gone, I'd feign cramps, a headache, or a case of the vapors.

The second man gave his buddy the thumbs-up signal and jumped. The next guy balked at the door. He fought the instructor, kicking and scrabbling, and huddled in the rear of the fuselage, his face wet with tears. The instructor looked at me, shrugged, and rolled his eyes. I realized that I had to go. I wasn't as afraid as the other guy, but the instructor's look of contempt would place me in the same category. Very slowly, I moved to the hatch.

Ten million years of genetic conditioning screamed in outrage and protest. Every molecule in me forbade the jump. I gripped a handle beside the door and closed my eyes. The plane was shaking and so were my knees, but I was too scared to be a coward. I leaned through the hole. Open fields flashed below. Freefall lasted all of four seconds, but they were long ones, rushing to earth at thirty-two feet per second. I yelled and the rush of air kept my mouth wide. The chute jerked open with a hard thump, and I squeezed the ropes as tightly as possible. There was a brief period of intense joy in which I realized that the only way to increase the feeling was to jump from higher up. Briefly I wished we had. I was already halfway down, and instead of wafting like a leaf, I seemed to be dropping at an incredible rate. Some huge mechanism was pushing the land rapidly in my direction.

I hit the earth, rolled as I'd been taught, and came up covered with flakes of last year's cow droppings. Wind caught the parachute and wrapped me with lines. Bill bounded across the field, his face stained with manure.

"Did you piss?" he yelled.

I was so grateful to be sitting in dirt that I didn't understand what he was talking about. He helped me out of the straps. I could smell dust and urine.

"I knew you would," he said, pointing to the wet fly of my coveralls. "Some guys load their britches. It happens at impact. After another couple of jumps, you won't anymore."

A waiting truck trundled us back to the airstrip. When the plane landed, the guy who'd stayed aboard climbed out with his head down. No one looked at him. His presence was a reminder of our own unclaimed fear.

Bill clapped me across the shoulders. "That's why you have to pay in advance," he said. "Next time you and me'll go at a higher altitude."

He told me about his first brush with the enemy, an experience that had led him to reenlist. He was the first man behind the soldier walking point, leading their platoon through jungle. The point man gave the hand signal for VC and motioned Bill forward. Six enemy were walking toward a pond in a clearing at the bottom of the slight hill. They each carried a bucket in one hand, a weapon in the other.

The point man whispered to Bill, "Cover me with single fire. I'll be on rock and roll."

When the hostiles moved close, the point man began spraying bursts of automatic fire. Bill plugged away. His last thought, he told me, was wishing he was the one who got to use automatic. It seemed like more fun. After that, he always volunteered to walk point.

A month later, Bill didn't show up for work, an unprecedented event. He didn't answer the phone and none of us knew where he lived. A police car arrived at the work site. The cop told us that the night before, Bill had removed his clothes and stacked them neatly. He then drank a pint of kerosene, and Zippoed his mouth— reversing the favored method of Vietnamese monks protesting the war. There was no note.

He'd once told me that when a man died in combat, the survivors never eulogized him. Instead they insulted him for days, talking about how well rid they were of his presence, no matter how close they'd been. I considered taking his paintbrush, but decided it would be an affront. Sentiment, he'd said, only made you vulnerable.

I aimed myself north, a tricky move without benefit of interstates. Five days later a gay black man picked me up at an isolated exit along the North Platte River in Nebraska. He claimed to eat white boys like me for lunch. I told him I wasn't fit for a meal. He laughed and left my lingam alone, nestled and trembling deep in its fur. A cornholing on the road was my greatest fear, worse than murder. He said his single regret was being born black in the South instead of red on the Plains, because the Indians accepted homosexuality in a more civilized manner. Then he laughed and said it really didn't matter because they both got fucked hard.

He dropped me off near Omaha, where I found slaughterhouse work, herding huge steers down a narrow ramp to death. They walked steadily, without curiosity or comprehension. A man placed an electrical rod against their foreheads and literally zapped the crap out of them. It was boring and professional; at home we used a rifle. After one stench-filled day, I quit and walked to the vacant prairie at the edge of town, hoping to hear a coyote. There was nothing but bugs. Constellations spanned the sky. The moon moldered like a gnawed bone. Two hundred years back, someone asked Boone if he had ever been lost. He answered no, but that he'd once been bewildered for three days. I knew exactly how he felt.

Buried beneath my sleeping bag lay dinosaur bones mixed with bison, antelope, and Sioux. The barometer of intelligence is the innate ability to adapt, to tame for the conqueror. Maybe wild and dead was better, like bison, Crazy Horse, and wolves. I watched the sky, wondering if I was living at the edge of adaptability, cherishing the residue of death.

I thought of Bill's belief that America's greatest contributions to world culture came from the West.

"The all-night diner," he'd said. "And the billboard. You can get coffee and talk at any time you want. The billboard always tells you where you are."

"Time and space. Cowboy science."

"That's what I like about you, Chris. You're so damn dumb you don't know you're smart. Like Mr. Charles in the Nam."

He turned his head slightly away, enough so that I knew to avert my gaze. The tears were coming down his face. His breathing was normal and he didn't sob. It was as if his head was so filled with sorrow that it had sprung a couple of leaks. When it passed he looked at me, his eyes hard and ancient as a trilobite's. "The West wasn't tamed," he said. "It was corralled for slaughter."

I woke early and on the move, despising Nebraskans for their cultural politesse. A man couldn't buy a pack of smokes without being offered a lighter, exhorted to have a good day, and in general made to feel inferior for not being aggressively cheerful enough. Nebraska was symmetric as an equation, the pathetic result of living on land emptied of buffalo. Prairie dog towns had been reduced to tourist attractions.

I tarried hard in the West, eager to find a home. American boys are raised knowing that a horse between your legs and a low-slung pistol are a guarantee of manhood. It worked for Billy the Kid, who shot seventeen men in the back before he reached legal age. Montana was a beautiful state, but lacked employment. I met a guy with a graduate degree who felt lucky to have work mending fence. A waitress told me that if I planned to settle there, I should bring a woman with me. I was unable to find work in Wyoming either, which made me want to stay, believing that the citizens shared my propensity for freedom. The difference was that they had places to sleep. The people were open to strangers, perhaps because they saw so few. Instead of viewing me with eastern scorn or southern suspicion, they recognized me for what I was, more or less a damn fool.

In Colorado I got a job chipping mortar from bricks with a hammer and chisel. I sat in the dirt beside a pile of brick, making a new pile in a primitive form of recycling. The wage was fourteen cents a brick. After two days of squatting in the sun, my hands ached from gripping the tools, and my fingers were scabbed from mislicks with the hammer.

I collected my pay and moved south, crisscrossing the Continental Divide, trying to find the actual border. Rivers run east on one side, west on the other. My goal was to straddle it. Since we are three-quarters water, I figured that the simultaneous tow of both oceans would rip a hole in my soul for something worthwhile to enter. Black Elk said the central mountain is everywhere. From my vantage alone in the

Rockies, centrality always seemed elsewhere. More and more, I depended on my journal. It was organic, I believed, even sentient. I came to regard the process of recording a lived life as the only material fit for writing. Somewhere in the Rockies, this shifted into a belief that the journal was my life, and the rest of existence only a fiction.

After two days of walking south, I was lucky enough to catch a ride to Flagstaff, and from there found a job washing dishes at the Grand Canyon. The administrative staff took my photograph and sent me to a lightless cabin with no water. Each morning I joined the other workers in public showers at the end of our dead-end lane. At night we drank in the employee bar.

Washing dishes was the ideal work of freedom, requiring no focus save the immediate cleaning of a mottled pot or plate. It also provided food. The occupation was of such wretched status that no one bothered me. Cooks labored in hundred-degree temperatures, while busboys staggered beneath enormous loads. The best waiters were able to change demeanor extremely fast. Seconds after battling a cook or debasing themselves before a tyrannical boss, they had to be sweetly sensitive to a customer. Bartenders enjoyed a slightly higher rank, but the job entailed steady recruitment and coddling of one's private circle of alcoholics. The dishwasher, in his perpetually soggy and food-flecked state, could remain true to himself.

The canyon gift shops employed Hopi women who sold copper-hued plastic dolls dressed in fringed felt. The hollow foot of each bore an inked stamp that read "Made in Japan." A few yards away was a hole in the ground a mile deep and ten miles wide. Somebody jumped once a month. Every week, a foreign tourist clutching a camera raced through the pines with skunk stench trailing behind. Apparently the Old World has not a polecat to its name. They are cute, graceful creatures, ripe for a photograph. Sometimes an entire family received the spray.

After supper I watched the sunset from the canyon's rim, sitting on the narrowest lip of rock protruding over the hole. I wrote in my diary there, looking down on clouds, trying to understand the strange impulse to step into space. It was not death that pulled me, it was the canyon itself. A jump was an urge to fill the void. Just before dusk, I witnessed an electrical storm from above, actually seeing the ignition of lightning and smelling the discharge. A sudden lance of fire cracked into the canyon's bowels and disappeared. The air smelled of ozone. It cured me of the itch to jump.

Weekends, I walked to the bottom where the Colorado River continued to cut a path. The river has never actually sunk but remains in place, cutting the land as the earth rises against the water. My treks down were a passage backwards through time, descending through millennia layered in the geology of the canyon walls. Color marked each era. Red at the top faded to pink, brown, a delicate green, and finally the slates and violets of the bottom. Naturally there was a bar and restaurant beside the river. Every Sunday, I climbed out to my work.

I was the only dishwasher who was not black, Mexican, or Indian. We worked in teams posted at either end of a colossal automatic washer and rinser. One man fed the beast while two others stacked the clean plates. A fourth dried silverware. Since I was new, my chore was the worst—scraping food into plastic barrels.

I saved the good parts to divide later among the crew. Willie, the head cook, offered me a job as short-order breakfast cook. I refused, preferring the simple world of water and dishes. Willie didn't quite understand this. Each day, he asked if I'd changed my mind yet. He eventually offered a higher wage, but I remained loyal to freedom.

A new manager was shifted to the restaurant, a sneering spud named Jackie Jr. Like many dwellers of the West, he pretended to be a cowboy, in hand-tooled boots, expensive hats, and tailored shirts with pearl snaps. Accustomed to calling all dish-washers "boy," Jackie Jr. enjoyed referring to me as a "hillbilly," a term that put me off my feed. Hillbilly was what the people in town called us at home; that and worse—hick, ridgerunner, redneck, inbred ingrate, and my personal favorite, pig-fucker. My mother is my sixth cousin. My brother and sister are also my cousins but nobody in my family ever seduced a hog.

I decided to quit after a week beneath the rule of Jackie Jr. On my final shift, he sauntered through the kitchen, amused at our miserable condition. I turned off the dishwashing machine and told him it was broken.

"What's the matter, hillfuck?" he said. "Even Meskins know how to crank this sucker on."

As he pushed the mechanized button, I opened the metal trapdoor that housed the soap jets. Jackie Jr. screeched like a kicked cat. Suds and water ruined his splen-did clothes. I stepped past him and out the back door, willie my pack waited beside a dumpster surrounded by skunks and ravens. Willie followed me. I turned with my arms spread and low, unsure what to expect. His face was lined as a washboard. He eyed the backpack strapped to my shoulders, opened his wallet, and handed me two twenty-dollar bills.

"Go while you can, kid. I'll slow him down some."

"I don't need your money, Willie."

"Don't be a fool, kid. You're too puny to back it up." He shook his head, chuck-ling. "I was a goddam drifter once."

He waited till I took the money, then stepped into the kitchen. I tried to imagine white-haired Willie being young. It was easier than seeing myself as old. I'd begun traveling with the vague belief that I sought something tangible. Now I wondered if I was actually running away, not toward. The legendary West, with its vast and empty spaces, had boiled down to just that—vast and empty, filled with people trying desperately to plug the gap with labor.

I carried my backpack to the single road that led away from the canyon's south rim. In another era, Bill might have been a Texas Ranger fighting the Comanche, or a mountain man scouting the Rockies. People of the West suffer from a historical malady similar to that of Appalachians. They are deprived of the old outlets, but stuck with the need to live up to their heritage.

While waiting for a ride out of the park, I resolved to live in the West—settle rather than pass through—but not yet. I was still an outrider of the self. If I stayed, I knew that I'd become a feral hermit, climbing like the end of a species to higher ground. I didn't want my bones discovered on a rocky ledge at thin altitude. There was still California to explore, the edge of the continent.

SHARMAN APT RUSSELL

Not a Butterfly

Concealed among the flowers, the Goldenrod Stowaway flutters up, a dab of butter in the sun. Its shiny yellow wings are streaked with orange. It is not a butterfly.

The Grapevine Epimenis is black with a large red patch on its hindwing and a large white patch on its forewing. During the day, it feeds on wild grapes in the dappled woods of eastern North America. It is commonly mistaken for a butterfly.

The upper green forewings of the Scarlet Tiger moth are speckled in yellow. Its hindwings are matador red.

A moth in India is laced with patterns of green, black, orange, and white, overlaid with a blue metallic sheen.

One day-flying moth looks like a swallowtail.

Another shimmers like a rainbow.

What is the difference between a moth and a butterfly?

Entomologists find the question tiresome. According to their nature, they look defensive or chagrined. There is often too little difference, and scientists understand how unscientific this must seem.

Of some 165,000 species of Lepidoptera, we have decided that about 11 percent are butterflies. The rest are moths, and the majority of these are micromoths, or microlepidoptera, usually small and primitive in the sense that they evolved first, before butterflies. From 50 to 100 million years ago, butterflies and a few other families of moths, called the macromoths, or macrolepidoptera, developed from this original group.

The two superfamilies of butterflies, the Papilionoidea and Hesperiodea, have distinct traits separate from most macromoths.

Notably, most butterflies are active during the day. They rely on sight to find food, host plants, and each other, and they use visual signals, design and color, to communicate with friends and enemies.

Some researchers believe that butterflies moved into the sun to escape predation by bats; that, in effect, bats invented butterflies.

Certainly, bats helped shape moths. Bats emit ultrasonic cries and use echolocation to zero in on night-flying insects. In response, night-flying moths tend to be furry, which may obscure their radar profile. Some moths also developed "ears" on the wings, thorax, and abdomen that are sensitive to ultrasonic sound. Hearing a bat close by, the moth dive-bombs to the ground. Some moths produce their own ultrasonic squeaks and clicking noises that may confuse the bat's radar system. Just as likely, these sounds warn the bat that the moth is toxic, an audio form of the Monarch's wings.

Spiders also prey on moths, fishing with their webs as the insects careen blindly in the dark. Moths and butterflies escape spider silk by shedding their wing scales (which detach easily) and slipping free. Spiders have learned to distinguish the vibration of a fluttering moth from that of a fly or a bee, and they rush immediately to bite the former before it can escape.

Some spiders build their webs in columns, towers of silk, catching and recatching the moth as it flutters free and up, free and up, until its wing scales are gone, and the bald wings are easily caught and held.

Flying at night means that moths rely heavily on scent to find food and mates. Spiders take advantage of this, too, by sending out a lure of fake sex pheromones. Male moths hurry to the bait, where they are caught with strands of specially prepared superstrength glue.

As a group, butterflies exchanged these night dangers for the new dangers of daylight, a world of birds with excellent eyesight and color vision. Some moth species in different families chose to do the same thing, and so we have a bright day-flying moth in the same family as a dull night-flying cousin.

Antennae also distinguish butterflies from moths. A butterfly's antenna will end in a thickened knob, or club. A moth's antenna may taper to a point, or look saw-toothed, or resemble a feather or a palm frond. Antennae are mainly used for smell, and moths are champion smellers. Moths win all the smelling bees. From experiments in the lab, we know that male hawkmoths can smell and distinguish almost every compound we throw at them. We know that the male silkmoth, with its huge plumose antennae, can detect the sexual attractant of a female silkmoth at volumes of only a thousand *molecules* per cubic centimeter. We know that some male moths can scent and track a female from over a mile away.

In the dark world of moths, females do most of the calling for mates, sending out their chemical bouquet from a gland on the abdomen. According to her species, the female calls at certain times under certain conditions in certain places. The males are poised to receive the message, their antennae sweeping and filtering the air. The male smells the call, follows the odor plume, finds the female, and emits his own chemical signal. With the female already in charge, courtship is usually quick and easy. So is copulation.

A third way to distinguish butterflies from moths is to look for a tiny bit of carpentry in the structure of the wings. Butterflies lack the catch-and-bristle arrangement, common to most moths, that hooks the fore- and hindwing together. In flight, this helps the wings beat together as a unit.

Also, butterflies tend to rest with their wings closed over their backs. They fly or bask in the sun with wings spread out horizontally. Moths tend to rest with their wings either folded up in an angled tent or flat and horizontal like a basking butterfly.

Eggs and larvae have their own peculiarities: the position of a pore, a special gland in the neck, various tufts of hair.

Exceptions abound. Skipper butterflies can be drab and small, fold their wings in a tentlike position, and have barely thickened antennae. Burnet moths are red-spotted day-fliers whose antennae seem noticeably clublike.

One group of "butterfly-moths" is such a mix that taxonomists recently added them to the butterfly family. The neotropical Hedyloidae have ears on their wings and are mostly dull-colored and small. They include day-flying and night-flying species. They do not have clubbed antennae, but, like swallowtails, they spin girdles and their eggs and caterpillars seem very butterflyish.

Another group of larger tropical "butterfly-moths" fly mostly during the day, are boldly colored, and have clubbed antennae; their caterpillars are distinctly moth-like.

For now, they are not butterflies.

Count up the mammal, bird, reptile, amphibian, and fish species. Add them together. There are still more moths. In such a large group, you are guaranteed a range of adaptation.

You can anticipate the fun.

Some moths are so small that they spend their entire larval lives mining the inner cells of a leaf. The tunnels of these leaf miners create characteristic designs: a delicate spiral, a simple maze.

Other larvae excavate tree trunks, feeding lugubriously on wood pulp for as long as four years and emitting strong-smelling frass in great quantity from their burrows.

There are moth larvae that live in ponds, eat pondweed, make shelters from aquatic leaves, and use feathery tracheal gills to draw oxygen from the water.

There are moth larvae that build silk "bags," which they carry about and camouflage with debris and evergreen needles. As an adult, the male escapes from his shelter. The adult female does not. Even after metamorphosis, she lacks legs or wings or eyes and is not much more than a sack of eggs waiting to be found and fertilized.

The caterpillars of a moth in Arizona feed on the small flowers of oak trees, which they mimic with yellow-green skin and fake pollen sacs. Later in summer, after the flowers are gone, the next generation of larvae look like oak twigs, with bigger and heavier jaws for eating leaves. Scientists once thought these were two species. They are, instead, the different costumes of one.

The largest moth, from South America, has a wingspan of a foot.

A hawkmoth in Madagascar uncurls a foot-long proboscis to fit into the foot-long nectary tube of the orchid it pollinates.

A moth in Asia pierces skin and sucks blood.

A luna moth has no mouth.

The ascetic Yucca moth also does not eat or drink but pollinates the yucca flower by collecting pollen, flying to another yucca plant, and depositing her load on the waiting stigma. At that point, the female lays her eggs in the flower's ovary.

The flower becomes a pod full of seeds. When the larvae hatch, they consume a percentage of these, burrow out, fall to the ground, and pupate. The Yucca moth is one of the few insects that pollinates actively, deliberately, as a way to ensure food for her young.

Hornet moths are a caricature of what they imitate, with the long, translucent wings of a wasp and a fat yellow-and-black-striped abdomen. These moths buzz viciously and pump out their stomachs as though about to sting.

Other moths resemble bumblebees.

Some hover like hummingbirds.

A moth in Venezuela imitates a cockroach.

In their great range and number, moths have a greater influence than butterflies. They are better and more important pollinators of flowers and crops. Their caterpillars feed the world. We have even domesticated moths, as we have sheep, turning them into small silk factories. We wear their excretions proudly.

Moths are bigger pests, too. They eat flour and clothes. They devour crops and gardens. The Gypsy moth has defoliated forests.

Our cultural associations with moths tend to the negative. Like butterflies, they represent the souls of the dead, but their visitations are less benign. Moths bring bad luck. They foretell mischief. They come from the shadows. They are hairy and gray. They fly grotesquely, suicidally, into candles and lamps and porch lights. (Their compound eyes may actually be seeing a very dark area next to the bright light; they are trying to fly into that dark zone.)

Think of the Death's-head Hawk moth. Patterned in yellow and black, it weighs as much as a mouse and has the design of a skull on its upper back. Its name, *Acherontia atropos*, comes from the Greek *Acheron*, the river of pain in the underworld, and *atropos*, one of the three Fates who cut the thread of life. The moth squeaks when disturbed and uses its short pointed proboscis to pierce through the wax of beehives, from which it steals honey. The skull mark may mimic a queen bee's face, so that bee workers will not attack the intruder. The moth's squeak may further pacify the insects.

In the movie *The Silence of the Lambs*, a serial killer breeds Death's head Hawk moths and places their pupae in the throats of his victims.

In a fifteenth-century manuscript, a Death's-head Hawk moth is painted in the corner of the page dedicated to Saint Vincent, who represents immortality, the triumph over death.

Moths represent the dying that comes before eternal life, the gloomier side of resurrection.

Give them their due. Moths are beautiful. Moths are complex.

But they are not butterflies.

DAVID SEDARIS

The Youth in Asia

In the early 1960s, during what my mother referred to as "the tail end of the Lassie years," my parents were given two collies, which they named Rastus and Duchess. We were living in New York State, out in the country, and the dogs were free to race through the forest. They napped in meadows and stood knee-deep in frigid streams, costars in their own private dog-food commercial. According to our father, anyone could tell that the two of them were in love.

Late one evening, while lying on a blanket in the garage, Duchess gave birth to a litter of slick, potato-size puppies. When it looked as though one of them had died, our mother arranged the puppy in a casserole dish and popped it in the oven, like the witch in Hansel and Gretel.

"Oh, keep your shirts on," she said. "It's only set on two hundred. I'm not *baking* anyone, this is just to keep him warm."

The heat revived the sick puppy and left us believing that our mother was capable of resurrecting the dead.

Faced with the responsibilities of fatherhood, Rastus took off. The puppies were given away and we moved south, where the heat and humidity worked against a collie's best interests. Duchess's once beautiful coat now hung in ragged patches. Age set in and she limped about the house, clearing rooms with her suffocating farts. When finally, full of worms, she collapsed in the ravine beside our house, we reevaluated our mother's healing powers. The entire animal kingdom was beyond her scope; apparently she could resurrect only the cute dead.

The oven trick was performed on half a dozen peakish hamsters but failed to work on my first guinea pig, who died after eating a couple of cigarettes and an entire pack of matches.

"Don't take it too hard," my mother said, removing her oven mitts. "The world is full of guinea pigs: you can get another one tomorrow."

Eulogies tended to be brief, our motto being Another day, another collar.

A short time after Duchess died, our father came home with a German shepherd puppy. For reasons that were never fully explained, the privilege of naming the dog went to a friend of my older sister's, a fourteen-year-old girl named Cindy. She was studying German at the time, and after carefully examining the puppy and weighing it in her hands, she announced that it would be called Mädchen, which apparently meant "girl" to the Volks back in the Vaterland. We weren't wild about the name but considered ourselves lucky that Cindy wasn't studying one of the hard-to-pronounce Asian languages.

When she was six months old, Mädchen was hit by a car and killed. Her food was still in the bowl when our father brought home an identical German shepherd, which the same Cindy thoughtfully christened Mädchen II. This tag-team progression was disconcerting, especially to the new dog, which was expected to possess both the knowledge and the personality of her predecessor.

"Mädchen One would never have wet the floor like that," my father would scold, and the dog would sigh, knowing she was the canine equivalent of a rebound.

Mädchen Two never accompanied us to the beach and rarely posed in any of the family photographs. Once her puppyhood was spent, we lost all interest. "We ought to get a dog," we'd sometimes say, completely forgetting that we already had one. She came inside to eat, but most of her time was spent outside in the pen, slumped in the A-frame doghouse our father had designed and crafted from scrap pieces of redwood.

"Hey," he'd ask, "how many dogs can say they live in a redwood house?"

This always led to my mother's exhausted "Oh, Lou, how many dogs can say that they *don't* live in a goddamn redwood house?"

Throughout the collie and shepherd years we kept a succession of drowsy, secretive cats that seemed to enjoy a unique bond with our mother. "It's because I open their cans," she'd say, though we all knew it ran deeper than that. What they really had in common was their claws. That and a primal urge to destroy my father's golf bags. The first cat ran away, and the second one was hit by a car. The third passed into a disagreeable old age and died hissing at the kitten that had prematurely arrived to replace her. When, at the age of seven, the fourth cat was diagnosed with feline leukemia, my mother was devastated.

"I'm going to have Sadie put to sleep," she said. "It's for her own good, and I don't want to hear a word about it from any of you. This is hard enough as it is."

The cat was put down, and then came a series of crank phone calls and anonymous postcards orchestrated by my sisters and me. The cards announced a miraculous new cure for feline leukemia, and the callers identified themselves as representatives from *Cat Fancy* magazine. "We'd like to use Sadie as our September cover story and were hoping to schedule a photo shoot as soon as possible. Do you think you could have her ready by tomorrow?"

We thought a kitten might lift our mother's spirits, but she declined all offers. "That's it," she said. "My cat days are over."

When Mädchen Two developed splenic tumors, my father dropped everything and ran to her side. Evenings were spent at the animal hospital, lying on a mat outside of her cage and adjusting her IV. He'd never afforded her much attention when she was healthy, but her impending death awoke in him a great sense of duty. He was holding her paw when she died, and he spent the next several weeks asking us how many dogs could say they'd lived in a redwood house.

Our mother, in turn, frequently paused beside my father's tattered, urine-stained golf bag and relived memories of her own.

After spending a petless year with only one child still living at home, my parents visited a breeder and returned with a Great Dane they named Melina. They loved this dog in proportion to its size, and soon their hearts had no room for anyone else. In terms of mutual respect and admiration, their six children had been nothing more than a failed experiment. Melina was the real thing. The house was given over to the dog, rooms redecorated to suit her fancy. Enter your former bedroom and you'd be told, "You'd better not let Melina catch you in here," or, "This is where we come to peepee when there's nobody home to let us outside, right, girl!" The knobs on our dressers were whittled down to damp stumps, and our beds were matted with fine, short hairs. Scream at the mangled leather carcass lying at the foot of the stairs, and my parents would roar with laughter. "That's what you get for leaving your wallet on the kitchen table."

The dog was their first genuine common interest, and they loved it equally, each in his or her own way. Our mother's love tended toward the horizontal, a pet being little more than a napping companion, something she could look at and say, "That seems like a good idea. Scoot over, why don't you." A stranger peeking through the window might think that the two of them had entered a suicide pact. She and the dog sprawled like corpses, their limbs arranged in an eternal embrace. "God, that felt good," my mom would say, the two of them waking for a brief scratch. "Now let's go try it on the living-room floor."

My father loved the Great Dane for its size, and frequently took her on long, aimless drives, during which she'd stick her heavy, anvil-sized head out the window and leak great quantities of foamy saliva. Other drivers pointed and stared, rolling down their windows to shout, "Hey, you got a saddle for that thing?" When out for a walk there was the inevitable "Are you walking her, or is it the other way 'round?"

"Ha-ha!" our father always laughed, as if it were the first time he'd heard it. The attention was addictive, and he enjoyed a pride of accomplishment he never felt with any of us. It was as if he were somehow responsible for her beauty and stature, as if he'd personally designed her spots and trained her to grow to the size of a pony. When out with the dog, he carried a leash in one hand and a shovel in the other. "Just in case," he said.

"Just in case, what, she dies of a heart attack and you need to bury her?" I didn't get it.

"No," he said, "the shovel is for, you know, her . . . business."

My father was retired, but the dog had business.

I was living in Chicago when they first got Melina, and every time I came home the animal was bigger. Every time, there were more Marmaduke cartoons displayed on the refrigerator, and every time, my voice grew louder as I asked, "Who *are* you people?"

"Down, girl," my parents would chuckle as the dog jumped up, panting for my attention. Her great padded paws reached my waist, then my chest and shoulders, until eventually, her arms wrapped around my neck and, her head towering above my own, she came to resemble a dance partner scouting the room for a better offer.

"That's just her way of saying hello," my mother would chirp, handing me a towel to wipe off the dog's bubbling seepage. "Here, you missed a spot on the back of your head."

Among us children, Melina's diploma from obedience school was seen as the biggest joke since our brother's graduation from Sanderson High.

"So she's not book-smart," our mother said. "Big deal. I can fetch my own goddamn newspaper."

The dog's growth was monitored on a daily basis and every small accomplishment was captured on film. One could find few pictures of my sister Tiffany, but Melina had entire albums devoted to her terrible twos.

"Hit me," my mother said on one of my return visits home from Chicago. "No, wait, let me go get my camera." She left the room and returned a few moments later. "Okay, now you can hit me. Better yet, why don't you just *pretend* to hit me."

I raised my hand, and my mother cried out in pain. "Ow!" she yelled. "Somebody help me. This stranger is trying to hurt me and I don't know why."

I caught an advancing blur moving in from the left, and the next thing I knew I was down on the ground, the dog ripping significant holes in the neck of my sweater.

The camera flashed and my mother screamed with delight. "God, I love that trick."

I rolled over to protect my face. "It's not a trick."

My mother snapped another picture. "Oh, don't be so critical. It's close enough."

With us grown and out of the house, my sisters and I reasonably expected our parents' lives to stand still. Their assignment was to stagnate and live in the past. We were supposed to be the center of their lives, but instead, they had constructed a new family consisting of Melina and the founding members of her fan club. Someone who obviously didn't know her too well had given my mother a cheerful stuffed bear with a calico heart stitched to its chest. According to the manufacturer, the bear's name was Mumbles, and all it needed in order to thrive were two double-A batteries and a regular diet of hugs.

"Where's Mumbles?" my mother would ask, and the dog would jump up and snatch the bear from its hiding place on top of the refrigerator, yanking its body this way and that in hopes of breaking its neck. Occasionally her teeth would press against the on switch, and the doomed thing would flail its arms, whispering one of its five recorded messages of goodwill.

"That's my girl," my mother would say. "We don't like Mumbles, do we?"

"*We?*"

During the final years of Mädchen Two and the first half of the Melina administration, I lived with a female cat named Neil. Dull gray in color, she'd been abandoned by a spooky alcoholic with long fingernails and a large collection of kimonos. He was a hateful man, and after he moved, the cat was taken in and renamed by my sister Gretchen, who later passed the animal on to me. My mother looked after Neil when I moved from Raleigh, and flew her to Chicago once I'd found a place and settled in. I'd taken the cheapest apartment I could find, and it showed. Though they were nice, my immigrant neighbors could see no connection between their personal habits and the armies of mice and roaches aggressively occupying the building. Welcoming the little change of scenery, entire families would regularly snack and picnic in the hallways, leaving behind candied fruits and half-eaten tacos. Neil caught fourteen mice, and scores of others escaped with missing limbs and tails. In Raleigh she'd just lain around the house doing nothing, but now she had a real job.

Her interests broadened and she listened intently to the radio, captivated by the political and financial stories, which failed to engage me. "One more word about the Iran-Contra hearings, and you'll be sleeping next door with the aliens," I'd say, though we both knew that I didn't really mean it.

Neil was old when she moved to Chicago, and then she got older. The Oliver North testimony now behind her, she started leaving teeth in her bowl and developed the sort of breath that could remove paint. She stopped cleaning herself, and I took to bathing her in the sink. When she was soaking wet, I could see just how thin and brittle she really was. Her kidneys shrank to the size of raisins, and although I wanted what was best for her, I naturally assumed the vet was joking when he suggested dialysis. In addition to being elderly, toothless, and incontinent, it seemed that, for the cost of a few thousand dollars, she could also spend three days a week hooked up to a machine. "Sounds awfully tempting," I said. "Just give us a few days to think it over." I took her for a second opinion. Vet number two tested her blood and phoned me a few days later suggesting I consider euthanasia.

I hadn't heard that word since childhood and immediately recalled a mismatched pair of Japanese schoolboys standing alone in a deserted school yard. One of the boys, grossly obese, was attempting to climb a flagpole that towered high above him. Silhouetted against the darkening sky, he hoisted himself a few feet off the ground and clung there, trembling and out of breath. "I can't do it." he said. "This is too hard for me."

His friend, a gaunt and serious boy named Komatsu, stood below him, offering encouragement. "Oh, but you *can* do it. You must," he said. "It is required."

This was a scene I had long forgotten, and thinking of it made me unbearably sad. The boys were characters from *Fatty and Skinny*, a Japanese movie regularly presented on *The CBS Children's Film Festival*, a weekly TV series hosted by two puppets and a very patient woman who pretended to laugh at their jokes. My sisters and I had watched the program every Saturday afternoon, our gasbag of a collie imposing frequent intermissions.

Having shimmied a few more inches up the flagpole, Fatty lost his grip and fell down into the sand. As he brushed himself off, Skinny ran down the mountain toward the fragile, papery house he shared with his family. This had been Fatty's last chance to prove himself. He'd thought his friend's patience was unlimited, but now he knew he was wrong. "Komatsuuuuuuuuuu!" he yelled. "Komatsu, please give me one more chance."

The doctor's voice called me back from the Japanese playground. "So the euthanasia," he said. "Are you giving it some thought?"

"Yes," I said. "As a matter of fact, I am."

In the end I returned to the animal hospital and had her put to sleep. When the vet injected the sodium pentobarbital, Neil fluttered her eyes, assumed a nap position, and died. My then boyfriend stayed to make arrangements, and I ran outside to blubber beside the parked and, unfortunately, locked car. Neil had gotten into her cat carrier believing she would eventually return to our apartment, and that tore me up. Someone had finally been naive enough to trust me, and I'd rewarded her with death. Racked by guilt, the youth in Asia sat at their desks and wept bitter tears.

A week after putting her to sleep, I received Neil's ashes in a forest green can. She'd never expressed any great interest in the outdoors, so I scattered her remains on the carpet and then vacuumed her back up. The cat's death struck me as the end of an era. It was, of course, the end of *her* era, but with the death of a pet there's always that urge to string black crepe over an entire ten- or twenty-year period. The end of my safe college life, the last of my thirty-inch waist, my faltering relationship with my first real boyfriend: I cried for it all and wondered why so few songs were written about cats.

My mother sent a consoling letter along with a check to cover the cost of the cremation. In the left-hand corner, on the line marked MEMO, she'd written, "Pet Burning." I had it coming.

When my mother died and was cremated herself, we worried that, acting on instinct, our father might run out and immediately replace her. Returning from the funeral, my brother, sisters, and I half expected to find some vaguely familiar Sharon Two standing at the kitchen counter and working the puzzle in TV *Guide.* "Sharon One would have gotten five across," our father would have scolded. "Come on, baby, get with it."

With my mother gone, my father and Melina had each other all to themselves. Though she now occupied the side of the bed left vacant by her former mistress, the dog knew she could never pass as a viable replacement. Her love was too fierce and simple, and she had no talent for argument. Yet she and my father honored their pledge to adore and protect each other. They celebrated anniversaries, regularly renewed their vows, and growled when challenged by outside forces.

"You want me to go *where?*" When invited to visit one of his children, my father would beg off, saying, "But I can't leave town. Who'd take care of Melina?" Mention a kennel, and he'd laugh. "You've got to be out of your mind. A kennel, ha! Hey, did you hear that, Melina? They want me to put you in prison."

Due to their size, Great Danes generally don't live very long. There are cheeses with a longer shelf life. At the age of twelve, gray bearded and teetering, Melina was a wonder of science. My father massaged her arthritic legs, carried her up the stairs, and lifted her in and out of bed. He treated her the way that men in movies treat their ailing wives, the way he might have treated my mother had she allowed such naked displays of helplessness and affection. Melina's era spanned the final dozen years of his married life. The dog had ridden in the family's last station wagon, attended my father's retirement party, and celebrated the elections of two Republican presidents. She grew weaker and lost her appetite, but against all advice, my father simply could not bear to let her go.

The youth in Asia begged him to end her life.

"I can't," he said. "This is too hard for me."

"Oh, but you must do it," said Komatsu. "It is required."

A month after Melina was put to sleep, my father returned to the breeder and came home with another Great Dane. A female like Melina, gray spots like Melina, only this one is named Sophie. He tries to love her but readily admits that he may have made a mistake. She's a nice enough dog, but the timing is off.

When walking Sophie through the neighborhood, my father feels not unlike the newly married senior stumbling behind his capricious young bride. The puppy's stamina embarrasses him, as does her blatant interest in young men. Passing drivers slow to a stop and roll down their windows. "Hey," they yell, "are you walking her, or is it the other way 'round?" Their words remind him of a more gracious era, of gentler forces straining against the well-worn leash. He still gets the attention, but now, in response, he just lifts his shovel and continues on his way.

SARAH VOWELL

Shooting Dad

If you were passing by the house where I grew up during my teenage years and it happened to be before Election Day, you wouldn't have needed to come inside to see that it was a house divided. You could have looked at the Democratic campaign poster in the upstairs window and the Republican one in the downstairs window and seen our home for the Civil War battleground it was. I'm not saying who was the Democrat or who was the Republican—my father or I—but I will tell you that I have never subscribed to *Guns & Ammo*, that I did not plaster the family vehicle with National Rifle Association stickers, and that hunter's orange was never my color.

About the only thing my father and I agree on is the Constitution, though I'm partial to the First Amendment, while he's always favored the Second.

I am a gunsmith's daughter. I like to call my parents' house, located on a quiet residential street in Bozeman, Montana, the United States of Firearms. Guns were everywhere: the so-called pretty ones like the circa 1850 walnut muzzleloader hanging on the wall, Dad's clients' fixer-uppers leaning into corners, an entire rack right next to the TV. I had to move revolvers out of my way to make room for a bowl of Rice Krispies on the kitchen table.

I was eleven when we moved into that Bozeman house. We had never lived in town before, and this was a college town at that. We came from Oklahoma—a dusty little Muskogee County nowhere called Braggs. My parents' property there included an orchard, a horse pasture, and a couple of acres of woods. I knew our lives had changed one morning not long after we moved to Montana when, during breakfast, my father heard a noise and jumped out of his chair. Grabbing a BB gun, he rushed out the front door. Standing in the yard, he started shooting at crows. My mother sprinted after him screaming, "Pat, you might ought to check, but I don't think they do that up here!" From the look on his face, she might as well have told him that his American citizenship had been revoked. He shook his head, mumbling, "Why, shooting crows is a national pastime, like baseball and apple pie." Personally, I preferred baseball and apple pie. I looked up at those crows flying away and thought, I'm going to like it here.

Dad and I started bickering in earnest when I was fourteen, after the 1984 Democratic National Convention. I was so excited when Walter Mondale chose Geraldine Ferraro as his running mate that I taped the front page of the newspaper with her picture on it to the refrigerator door. But there was some sort of mysterious gravity surge in the kitchen. Somehow, that picture ended up in the trash all the way across the room.

Nowadays, I giggle when Dad calls me on Election Day to cheerfully inform me that he has once again canceled out my vote, but I was not always so mature. There were times when I found the fact that he was a gunsmith horrifying. And just *weird*. All he ever cared about were guns. All I ever cared about was art. There were years and years when he hid out by himself in the garage making rifle barrels and I holed up in my room reading Allen Ginsberg poems, and we were incapable of having a conversation that didn't end in an argument.

Our house was partitioned off into territories. While the kitchen and the living room were well within the DMZ, the respective work spaces governed by my father and me were jealously guarded totalitarian states in which each of us declared ourselves dictator. Dad's shop was a messy disaster area, a labyrinth of lathes. Its walls were hung with the mounted antlers of deer he'd bagged, forming a makeshift museum of death. The available flat surfaces were buried under a million scraps of paper on which he sketched his mechanical inventions in blue ball-point pen. And the floor, carpeted with spiky metal shavings, was a tetanus shot waiting to happen. My domain was the cramped, cold space known as the music room. It was also a messy disaster area, an obstacle course of musical instruments—piano, trumpet, baritone horn, valve trombone, various percussion doodads (bells!), and recorders. A framed portrait of the French composer Claude Debussy was nailed to the wall. The available flat surfaces were buried under piles of staff paper, on which I penciled in the pompous orchestra music given titles like "Prelude to the Green Door" (named after an O. Henry short story by the way, not the watershed porn flick *Behind the Green Door*) I starting writing in junior high.

It has been my experience that in order to impress potential suitors, skip the teen Debussy anecdotes and stick with the always attention-getting line "My dad makes guns." Though it won't cause the guy to like me any better, it will make him handle the inevitable breakup with diplomacy—just in case I happen to have any loaded family heirlooms lying around the house.

But the fact is, I have only shot a gun once and once was plenty. My twin sister, Amy, and I were six years old—six—when Dad decided that it was high time we learned how to shoot. Amy remembers the day he handed us the gun for the first time differently. She liked it.

Amy shared our father's enthusiasm for firearms and the quick-draw cowboy mythology surrounding them. I tended to daydream through Dad's activities—the car trip to Dodge City's Boot Hill, his beloved John Wayne Westerns on TV. My sister, on the other hand, turned into Rooster Cogburn Jr., devouring Duke movies with Dad. In fact, she named her teddy bear Duke, hung a colossal John Wayne portrait next to her bed, and took to wearing one of those John Wayne shirts that button on the side. So when Dad led us out to the backyard when we were six and, to Amy's delight, put the gun in her hand, she says she felt it meant that Daddy trusted us and that he thought of us as "big girls."

But I remember holding the pistol only made me feel small. It was so heavy in my hand. I stretched out my arm and pointed it away and winced. It was a very long time before I had the nerve to pull the trigger and I was so scared I had to close my eyes. It felt like it just went off by itself, as if I had no say in the matter, as if the gun just had this *need*. The sound it made was as big as God. It kicked little me back to the ground like a bully, like a foe. It hurt. I don't know if I dropped it or just handed it back over to my dad, but I do know that I never wanted to touch another one again. And, because I believed in the devil, I did what my mother told me to do every time I felt an evil presence. I looked at the smoke and whispered under my breath, "Satan, I rebuke thee."

It's not like I'm saying I was traumatized. It's more like I was decided. Guns: Not For Me. Luckily, both my parents grew up in exasperating households where children were considered puppets and/or slaves. My mom and dad were hell-bent on letting my sister and me make our own choices. So if I decided that I didn't want my father's little death sticks to kick me to the ground again, that was fine with him. He would go hunting with my sister, who started calling herself "the loneliest twin in history" because of my reluctance to engage in family activities.

Of course, the fact that I was allowed to voice my opinions did not mean that my father would silence his own. Some things were said during the Reagan administration that cannot be taken back. Let's just say that I blamed Dad for nuclear proliferation and Contra aid. He believed that if I had my way, all the guns would be confiscated and it would take the commies about fifteen minutes to parachute in and assume control.

We're older now, my dad and I. The older I get, the more I'm interested in becoming a better daughter. First on my list: Figure out the whole gun thing.

Not long ago, my dad finished his most elaborate tool of death yet. A cannon. He built a nineteenth-century cannon. From scratch. It took two years.

My father's cannon is a smaller replica of a cannon called the Big Horn Gun in front of Bozeman's Pioneer Museum. The barrel of the original has been filled with concrete ever since some high school kids in the '50s pointed it at the school across the street and shot out its windows one night as a prank. According to Dad's historical source, a man known to scholars as A Guy at the Museum, the cannon was brought to Bozeman around 1870, and was used by local white merchants to fire at the Sioux and Cheyenne Indians who blocked their trade access to the East in 1874.

"Bozeman was founded on greed," Dad says. The courthouse cannon, he continues, "definitely killed Indians. The merchants filled it full of nuts, bolts, and chopped-up horseshoes. Sitting Bull could have been part of these engagements. They definitely ticked off the Indians, because a couple of years later, Custer wanders into them at Little Bighorn. The Bozeman merchants were out to cause trouble. They left fresh baked bread with cyanide in it on the trail to poison a few Indians."

Because my father's sarcastic American history yarns rarely go on for long before he trots out some nefarious ancestor of ours—I come from a long line of moonshiners, Confederate soldiers, murderers, even Democrats—he cracks that the merchants hired some "community-minded Southern soldiers from North Texas." These soldiers had, like my great-great-grandfather John Vowell, fought under pro-slavery guerrilla William C. Quantrill. Quantrill is most famous for riding into Lawrence, Kansas, in 1863 flying a black flag and commanding his men pharaohlike to "kill every male and burn down every house."

"John Vowell," Dad says, "had a little rep for killing people." And since he abandoned my great-grandfather Charles, whose mother died giving birth to him in 1870, and wasn't seen again until 1912, Dad doesn't rule out the possibility that John Vowell could have been one of the hired guns on the Bozeman Trail. So the cannon isn't just another gun to my dad. It's a map of all his obsessions—firearms, certainly, but also American history and family history, subjects he's never bothered separating from each other.

After tooling a million guns, after inventing and building a rifle barrel boring machine, after setting up that complicated shop filled with lathes and blueing tanks and outmoded blacksmithing tools, the cannon is his most ambitious project ever. I thought that if I was ever going to understand the ballistic bee in his bonnet, this was my chance. It was the biggest gun he ever made and I could experience it and spend time with it with the added bonus of not having to actually pull a trigger myself.

I called Dad and said that I wanted to come to Montana and watch him shoot off the cannon. He was immediately suspicious. But I had never taken much interest in his work before and he would take what he could get. He loaded the cannon into the back of his truck and we drove up into the Bridger Mountains. I was a little worried that the National Forest Service would object to us lobbing fiery balls of metal onto its property. Dad laughed, assuring me that "you cannot shoot fireworks, but this is considered a fire*arm*."

It is a small cannon, about as long as a baseball bat and as wide as a coffee can. But it's heavy—110 pounds. We park near the side of the hill. Dad takes his gunpowder and other tools out of this adorable wooden box on which he has stenciled "PAT G. VOWELL CANNONWORKS." Cannonworks: So that's what NRA members call a metal-strewn garage.

Dad plunges his homemade bullets into the barrel, points it at an embankment just to be safe, and lights the fuse. When the fuse is lit, it resembles a cartoon. So does the sound, which warrants Ben Day dot words along the lines of *ker-pow!* There's so much Fourth of July smoke everywhere I feel compelled to sing the national anthem.

I've given this a lot of thought—how to convey the giddiness I felt when the cannon shot off. But there isn't a sophisticated way to say this. It's just really, really cool. My dad thought so, too.

Sometimes, I put together stories about the more eccentric corners of the American experience for public radio. So I happen to have my tape recorder with me, and I've never seen levels like these. Every time the cannon goes off, the delicate needles which keep track of the sound quality lurch into the bad, red zone so fast and so hard I'm surprised they don't break.

The cannon was so loud and so painful, I had to touch my head to make sure my skull hadn't cracked open. One thing that my dad and I share is that we're both a little hard of hearing—me from Aerosmith, him from gunsmith.

He lights the fuse again. The bullet knocks over the log he was aiming at. I instantly utter a sentence I never in my entire life thought I would say. I tell him, "Good shot, Dad."

Just as I'm wondering what's coming over me, two hikers walk by. Apparently, they have never seen a man set off a homemade cannon in the middle of the wilderness while his daughter holds a foot-long microphone up into the air recording its terrorist boom. One hiker gives me a puzzled look and asks, "So you work for the radio and that's your dad?"

Dad shoots the cannon again so that they can see how it works. The other hiker says, "That's quite the machine you got there." But he isn't talking about the cannon. He's talking about my tape recorder and my microphone—which is called a *shotgun* mike. I stare back at him, then I look over at my father's cannon, then down at my microphone, and I think, Oh. My. God. My dad and I are the same person. We're both smart-alecky loners with goofy projects and weird equipment. And since this whole target practice outing was my idea, I was no longer his adversary. I was his accomplice. What's worse, I was liking it.

I haven't changed my mind about guns. I can get behind the cannon because it is a completely ceremonial object. It's unwieldy and impractical, just like everything else I care about. Try to rob a convenience store with this 110-pound Saturday night special, you'd still be dragging it in the door Sunday afternoon.

I love noise. As a music fan, I'm always waiting for that moment in a song when something just flies out of it and explodes in the air. My dad is a one-man garage band, the kind of rock 'n' roller who slaves away at his art for no reason other than to make his own sound. My dad is an artist—a pretty driven, idiosyncratic one, too. He's got his last *Gesamtkunstwerk* all planned out. It's a performance piece. We're all in it—my mom, the loneliest twin in history, and me.

When my father dies, take a wild guess what he wants done with his ashes. Here's a hint: It requires a cannon.

"You guys are going to love this," he smirks, eyeballing the cannon. "You get to drag this thing up on top of the Gravellies on opening day of hunting season. And looking off at Sphinx Mountain, you get to put me in little paper bags. I can take my last hunting trip on opening morning."

I'll do it, too. I will have my father's body burned into ashes. I will pack these ashes into paper bags. I will go to the mountains with my mother, my sister, and the cannon. I will plunge his remains into the barrel and point it into a hill so that he doesn't take anyone with him. I will light the fuse. But I will not cover my ears. Because when I blow what used to be my dad into the earth, I want it to hurt.

IV | *Catalysts*

1. The Autobiographical Object

Discussion

We surround ourselves with things. Our houses are full of objects which we have carefully, and sometimes not so carefully, chosen. Yet, the "stuff" of our lives is almost never careless. More often than not, the objects that line our shelves, rest on our coffee tables, sit atop our kitchen counters, and decorate our dressers communicate a whole lot about who we are. These "things" illustrate our personalities, and our identities are made more tangible when we examine our material belongings.

We belong to our belongings.

Because of this inextricable relationship we have with our possessions, there is a wealth of narratives associated with each and every object we own. There are stories that describe how we acquired certain items, and there are objects that remind us of other stories. There are people who have brought important objects into our lives, and there are objects that, for certain reasons, remind us of significant people.

This exercise will help you develop a closer relationship with your possessions and fully explore the way in which most objects carry narrative value, as well as offer the possibility of insight into your identity.

Exercise

First, spend some time wandering around your living space. Study what you have chosen to hang on your walls. Pick up and examine the artifacts that you have displayed on your surfaces. Look through your drawers and cabinets and study the things you have collected and stored.

Now, choose one object to which you seem especially connected.

Investigate how this item represents the many characteristics that define your personality. Ask yourself some questions about the object: *Where did this object come from? Why have I kept it? What else does it remind me of? Does this object cause me to think of any significant people in my life? Does this object cause me to think of any significant events in my life?*

To begin the writing process, start recording the answers to these questions. Then, try to write a full page describing the object. Explore every possibility of description: *What does this object look similar to? What kind of action can this object take? Does it have a smell and, if so, how does the smell make me feel? Can the object make noise? Does the object itself exhibit any emotional or human qualities?*

Your task is to construct a piece of memoir or a personal narrative with this object at its center. It will most likely evoke several narratives, and your job is to find the connection between them. Most likely, you won't see the connections right away. But this is where the magic happens. Allow yourself to travel away from the object, to explore all of the paths available, even if they seem completely unrelated. Write yourself as far away from the object as possible.

Finally, try to return to the object after you have strayed from it. Remember that all paths lead back to the object. After all, this is your autobiographical object, your experience of self made tangible in the material world, your "self" found in "stuff."

2. Pushing a Metaphor to Its Limits

Discussion

In her book-length meditation *The Writing Life*, Annie Dillard must learn, out of the necessity for warmth, to chop wood for a fire. Ultimately, Dillard discovers that in order to hit the piece of wood successfully, one must aim for the chopping block, not for the piece of wood itself. In essence, one must trick the brain and its perception of space, of concentration. From this lesson, she realizes that the same concept is true for the process of writing. To produce authentic writing, one must avoid too much attention to the actual subject. Writing around the subject, actually focusing on everything but the subject, will allow it to come organically into consciousness.

The goal of this exercise is to do the same. Many times, the activities in our lives are more connected than we realize. This writing exercise can help illuminate some of those relationships.

Exercise

Start by making a list of ordinary activities, things that you do throughout your normal daily life, such as washing dishes, walking the dog, taking a bath, cooking a meal, shaving, mowing the lawn, or grocery shopping. You may find yourself listing things that you do to make a living, such as building houses, serving food to others, fighting fires, or answering phones.

Next, pick one of these activities and explore every aspect of it. Write down all of the stages of the action, describing with vivid details what it is like to do this activity. Try to fill an entire page, simply illustrating this activity, as if your reader has never seen a person clean a house or do laundry or the thing that at which you are "an expert."

Now, it is time to find the metaphor. Try to make a single statement that brings your chosen activity together with another activity. For instance, one might find that constructing rock walls is similar to revising poems. One must examine all of the sides of each rock and choose the most aesthetically pleasing one. Yet, the rock must be able to fit with the others, just like one line in a poem. It must be individually evaluated and held up next to all of the other lines as well.

Once you have made this single metaphorical statement, spend some time discovering all of the similarities between the two actions. Write about both actions almost as if you were comparing and contrasting them. Push the metaphor to its limits. Continue doing so until you feel the impulse to include your own experience. At some point, you will be compelled to make "I" statements. When this happens, let yourself enter the exploration of these two actions and start looking for the narrative. Most likely, you have a story associated with one or both of these activities. If you built rock walls with your grandfather and later realized that this activity was significant in how you came to understand the writing of poems, you might write a story, or several stories, about your experiences with your grandfather.

Allow the narrative to become central to the piece. Let the story take over. Ultimately, the story will serve you better than a discussion of the metaphor. Aim for the chopping block, a well-told tale. Don't worry about the metaphor. You will inadvertently hit the wood.

3. Finding Humor in Heartache

Discussion

A keen observer of the human condition, essayist David Sedaris writes about our profoundly disturbing and sometimes deeply sad behaviors. Of his subject matter, readers commonly remark that nothing is sacred. He will write about virtually anything that strikes his fancy. And while this seems a dismal trade, Sedaris' saving grace is his wit and razor sharp humor. His ability to find humor in heartache exemplifies his very original and recognizable style as a writer.

In an essay titled "Go Carolina," Sedaris writes of his speech impediment as an adolescent boy and isn't afraid to explore the humiliation and frustration he felt in his youth. Yet, it's almost so heartbreaking a story that we need relief from it, reprieve from what is so desperately true about our humanness. In another essay, "The Youth in Asia," Sedaris describes the many family pets that lived and died during his childhood, an inherently painful topic; however, he illustrates the absurdity of how we sometimes handle the deaths of pets. He describes his mother placing sick and dying animals in the oven in an effort to revive them!

Sedaris has become a master at recognizing moments that will enlighten the human condition, telling vivid stories about these moments, and balancing our difficulty in accepting truth with our willingness to laugh at ourselves.

Exercise

For this exercise, make a list of difficult and painful situations that you have endured. Think of moments of embarrassment, shame, and loss. Consider times that you have gotten physically hurt or have been in extreme danger. Look over this list and try to decipher which of these circumstances might have humorous elements in retrospect.

Once you have chosen an experience, begin by writing its basic narrative. Avoid dramatizing the negative aspects of the situation. Instead, just relay the essentials. Once you have a skeleton of the story, read what you have written. Try to emotionally remove yourself from the narrative. Pretend that this experience did not happen to you and that you are someone else, someone with a dark sense of humor, maybe even someone slightly cruel. Go looking for the ridiculous, the silly, the absurd. Find places in the story where you can laugh at yourself, at the other characters. Find what is funny about the story now and determine why humor was impossible then.

Start inserting those humorous moments into the narrative. Play with tone and cadence. Try playing with dialogue. Allow your characters to come alive. You may even find yourself "re-inventing" details from the experience. Your characters might become more vibrant and outlandish than they were in "real life." Your conversations might be slightly altered to reflect those exaggerated characters. Remember that this is creative nonfiction, and that "creative" allows for some fabrication. One of your goals is to entertain. But be mindful of your primary goal. Like any authentic humor writer, you should be able to isolate what is painfully true and make it laughably tolerable.

Telling Tales:
Short Fiction

I | *Discussion of the Genre*

With the wealth of creative opportunities presented to us by the natural world of our memories and our factual observations, why create fiction? Why tell tales? With the confusions presented to us by the most routine events of daily lives, why create more confusions with fictions? Why take the path of the unreal? Why the unknown? Why bother with the unreal when the real is complicated enough? Why take the darkest path through the garden?

We simply suggest this: *sometimes the real is too real.* Sometimes we come too close to the light and are blinded by it. Sometimes only an untruth can point us toward the truths that have always been with us. Sometimes, fiction is the clearest mirror to reality.

In this section, you will find characters struggling with plots both mundane and fantastic, with truths both explicit and hidden, and with resolutions both final and open ended. In short, you will find the whole of human experience in five- to-thirty page glimpses. While a memoirist must grapple with the truth of his or her own biography and his or her place in it, the short story writer can create a parallel world in which the emotional truths of his or her own life may play out without the often painful burden of working with the truth. As Thomas Wolfe found, you may not be able to go home again, but you can surely create a new home just like it with fictional characters who are a close approximation to your truth and who are every bit as real as the characters of your daily life, and, in this fictional space, you can begin to work out the issues that are too painful or too obvious to work out in "the real world."

How does this happen? If you consider your life and the life of those around you, you will find that all of the elements of successful fiction are present at all times: personality conflicts, disturbing surprises, recurrent patterns of behavior, vivid locations, and poignant images. If you are a student, consider your classmates and your classroom. If you are a worker, consider your coworkers and your workplace. Consider your relatives and your home. Consider your hometown. All of these contain what the most essential works of short fiction also contain: lives as works in progress, humans working with the very notion of how to be humans and how to interact with others. Maybe, as in Chester Himes' "Prediction," it's an alternate universe. Maybe, as in Philip K. Dick's "Beyond Lies the Wub," it's another planet entirely. Maybe, as in Melissa Pritchard's "A Private Landscape," it's a suburban home not unlike most other contemporary, Earth-bound homes. In every instance, you will find that the core of the story is built around the human characters that inhabit it.

If you are considering the many stations of life that we've just suggested, consider looking down on them from above. What do you see? When you sit on a bench in a public area, what do you see around you? You see characters interacting with an unpredictable world disguised as predictable. If you are watching a man with a wireless telephone crossing a street in front of red-lighted traffic, ask yourself: To whom is he talking? Where is he headed? From where did he just leave? Does the person with whom he's talking know where he's just been? What if he trips just as the light changes? What would the drivers do? Where are they headed anyway? The answer to any of these questions could be a perfect seed for a perfect new fiction. You do not need to know which direction the path will take you; you only need to keep moving down it. You do not need to know the answer . . . *you only need to ask the question.*

In this section, the finest examples of the tale-teller's art do not offer answers to life's questions. Rather, they ask questions in ways not quite like any other questions before them. They posit "what ifs" where before there were only "whatevers." It is fine and well to live one's life according to "whatever," but the energy generated by a well-pursued "what if" can lead your life to surprising and fascinating places.

A Quintessential: "A Private Landscape"

by Melissa Pritchard

MELISSA PRITCHARD

A Private Landscape

Slouched in the window seat, Deirdre dutifully reads a novel for her schoolwork. Her young face is remote, attending to more complex characters than mine.

"Tea?" I ask again.

She hesitates. "No. What are you making?"

I smack two eggs one-handedly against the bowl, a trick Mother insisted I inherit.

"Carrot cake. These carrots from last year's garden are crying to be done away with."

Deirdre's slight smile indicates that I am simple, overly concerned with food and trivialities; she goes back to her reading, her education.

I shall wind up swallowing this cake myself. Deirdre is on a health kick this week, claiming that yogurt and grapefruit juice are all she needs. Martin, in an uncharacteristically vain humor, has also gone off his feed.

Last night he commented on my weight problem. Undressing with no eye toward pleasing anybody, dropping my frayed nightgown over my head, I was unaware, until I heard his soft but disapproving words, that I was being observed from our bed, my flesh critically measured. Martin's aesthetics, I tell myself, were always sadly predictable. He wistfully watches Deirdre these days, hugs her waist tightly, strokes her long black hair while I scrape dishes and carry up laundry from the basement. Perhaps I'll move back into the guest room whenever I undress, fetch back the humble privacy I had trustingly set aside upon my marriage.

"Deirdre? Kindly remember to keep your legs together when you wear a dress."

She sighs over my prudery, and with intense exaggeration rearranges herself in the window seat. Yesterday I requested that she not loll about the house in her bikini underwear when her father was expected home. "You're nearly fourteen years old," I said by way of justification. She shrugged and brushed wearily past me; her skin, I thought, smelled strongly of my best perfume.

After driving alongside miles of immaculate white fencing, I turn into the graveled driveway of the horse farm and pull up near the house. I walk over to the fence, rest my arms upon the top railing, watch the horses, their necks languidly dropped, mouths tearing the grass in small arcs. That bowing curve of a horse's neck suggests the prehistoric, an era comfortably free of human conflict. I wonder at such powerful animals, content to move listlessly within expensive but brittle fencing.

The owner steps out from her house and we walk across to the green and white stables. Inside, it is dim and smells strongly of hay and salt. Crossing bands of sunlight are flecked, like coarse tweed, with bits of hay and dust. Most of the stalls are vacant, but a few horses turn their heads towards us as we approach, their eyes white-rimmed, shining past us towards the open doors.

We stop in front of one stall where a dark red horse holds his head suspiciously high and tight, his ears laid back. I tentatively proffer my hand, and then withdraw it as his square lip curls back. Foul-tempered, I think, succumbing to a private notion about red horses, red anything. His eyes pitch back defiantly and I shake my head, no, not this one.

The stable phone rings, the woman excuses herself, and shielding my eyes from the cutting sunlight I walk outside again. The pasture is sprinkled with the yellow blurs of dandelion and mild blue wheels of chicory. Sparrows skim and cry out over the glistening backs of grazing horses. I climb a white railing and watch as a stocky black mare trots over to another horse and gives it a sly, aggressive nip in the rear. The bitten horse mildly moves aside and continues grazing. Over by the highway, reduced to a fine porcelain-like figure, stands a white horse, head lifted as though reading the fertile spring wind. He crosses the pasture and stops within a few yards of me. His expression is peculiarly intelligent. I notice that his underbelly is a soft gray.

"I would like to purchase this white horse," I say as soon as the owner finds me. We agree on a price, more than I had intended to spend, but I know better than to bargain with fate. We discuss terms of payment, veterinarians, places to buy tack and feed. She promises to deliver the horse to me on the day before my daughter's fourteenth birthday.

On the drive back home I consider how Deirdre will look sitting upon the back of a pale, galloping horse, her dark hair lifting and falling. I imagine them set against the black and green tracery of the woods behind our property.

The box with the monogrammed blouse lies unwrapped beside Deirdre's dinner plate. In the bathroom, all the faucets are turned on, absorbing her disappointed sobs.

Martin is looking worried, so I finally whisper, "Go in and comfort her, tell her next year we promise her a horse, we couldn't afford one this year, and I'll go up to the barn and get him."

From running the slight uphill to the barn, I am breathless, sliding back the wooden bar and stepping into the darkness. The barn is old, with loose tongues of air between the sagging plankings; it has been empty for the two years we've owned it. We are not farmers or husbandmen, our possessions fit neatly into the house. My garden tools stand upright in a small metal shed. Nothing overlaps.

I pick out the gleam of the white horse before the electric light abruptly halos him, his neck curved around, his eyes fixed on me. Unhitching the rope, I lead him out of the barn and down the soft, grassy path into the corral. I stroke his back, comparing its milky tint to that of the moon overhead, neither of them purely white. Against his flesh, my hand feels heavy, forgetful, and with a small, bitter feeling in me, I go back to the house.

Deirdre sits at the kitchen table, Martin holds one of his hands over hers, grateful for any contact she allows him. Eye shadow is smudged on the lids of her lowered eyes. Martin's hand is covering hers. She smiles thinly, her face blotched.

"Sorry, Mom. Still a baby about some things I guess." She looks ready to cry again, but, brave girl, crunches up another flowered Kleenex, adds it to the pile in front of her, and thanks me for the blouse.

"That's all right, darling." I bend down, kiss the top of her head.

Martin says, "Come on down to the creek with us. I'll get the flashlights and afterwards we can drive in to town for some ice cream."

She winces but, still subdued from her own outburst, answers, "Sure, Dad."

The moon shines upon our property, exposing our small family. I tell Deirdre that she must shut her eyes for a minute or two. She stumbles between us and when Martin opens the corral gate I think she has guessed, but her eyes remain shut. We place her a few feet from the white horse.

"Open your eyes, darling." I am crying now. "And happy birthday!"

My original feeling for the horse had minimized; he became, for a time, an oversized pet I watched from a distance as I worked in the garden or as I backed the car down the driveway. I paid a number of expensive vet bills. My daughter persuaded me into one disastrous riding lesson under her instruction, with Martin looking on. I contrasted her vital buoyant manner with my own clumsy ability and did not ride again.

At some moment during summer's peak, the garden overreaches its own ripeness; vegetation hangs exhausted, overcome by its own lush growth. This is my least favorite time of year, when the harvest is forgotten; unpicked tomatoes split open on trailing, imperfect vines. This is also my least favorite wedge of the afternoon, between noon and four o'clock, an empty glaring period for me. I can, with some accuracy, match my own age and season to this month and this hour. From the porch where I sit, pinned to my chair by a humidity more potent than gravity, I see the white horse, standing inert and passive. I always envisioned horses as magnificent dreamlike creatures, rearing heavenward, manes swirling like seagrass. It is not so. A horse passes its time like most anything else, placid, concerned only with whatever passes before its eyes. The horse, sapped by domesticity, confined by fences, has disillusioned me. I expected more from it.

Deirdre and Martin quarreled again last night. Instinctively, I stayed clear of their conflict, scenting its primitive, disturbing theme. The omnipotent, adored father, supplanted in the child's affections by a young stranger, in this case our neighbor's pleasant-mannered, nice-looking son.

They argued over the horse, over Deirdre's neglect of him. She goes out with her young friend, forgets to groom the horse. She rides him less and less. Martin says he is upset with her for so casually abandoning a creature who depends on her for care and affection. Of course, he has a point.

I have gone out myself to groom the horse, tugging at his mane with the metal comb, plucking out burrs from his tail, and with the curved pick prying rocks from the greenish, mossy trenches of his hooves. I brush along the supple hills of hips, following the direction, the grain. I remind myself that the horse was a gift to my daughter and that I should not long for a thing which lies beyond my personal, private landscape.

I prattle on about a letter from an old school friend, about a greedy crow I chased from the garden. Deirdre licks yogurt off the tip of her spoon, then excuses herself to go and dress for her date. Martin eats in order to be done with eating, then says he is going out for a walk. I praise myself for not feeling hurt that I am uninvited and dump dishes in the sink, wipe down counters, and feel vexed that no one thought to help me. But I never ask for help, or even demand it; I wish to appear self-sufficient before my family, because I suspect I am not. Damn. I turn off the water, leave the kitchen undone, and go after my husband in the summer twilight.

In the middle of the creek we sit on rocks as bleached and flattened as the horse's flank I brushed this morning. Martin snaps a dry stick into pieces, letting each bit drop into the swirling water and take its course. He flicks the last chip of wood; it lodges between our two stones, resisting the current of water.

Martin looks tired. The loss of weight from his recent diet has not improved him; it has left him slack, gaunt.

Plunging my arm into the softly buckling water, I am shocked by its coldness.

"I asked Deirdre to stop going about the house in her underwear when you're home."

I am remembering Martin's criticisms as I undressed in our bedroom that night, and hold my wet, reddened hand up to the sky.

"Sometimes I almost hate her."

I climb awkwardly over to my husband and crouch down. He puts an arm around me, draws me close. Needing comfort, we sit upon a large flat stone, until we become cramped and stiff from sitting so motionless, surrounded by water.

Walking home in the dark, without a flashlight, I trip across a fallen cotton-wood tree, bruising my shin on its upreaching tangled root. Martin is concerned and helps me up.

Back home, relieved that our house is emptied of her, we make oddly exuberant love. Afterward we are reserved toward one another, sitting up late, drinking brandies, and reading fiction, the light steady between our two chairs, waiting for Deirdre.

One-thirty and she has not come home. Martin, furious with me for not knowing the address of the party she has gone to, is in the kitchen, watching television and thinking about calling the police. In the living room I am trying to understand the jealousy and resentment I feel towards my only child. When the telephone rings, Martin answers, comes into the doorway.

"She wants you. She wants to talk to you."

In a crisis she has always reached for me.

I wave a signal to Martin that she is all right.

"Deirdre, please, stop it. Stop crying now. It's all right."

Martin sets down a pencil, a pad of paper, and I write down the address she gives me.

"Ok, honey, hang on, we'll be there in about twenty minutes. Yes, Daddy's fine. He's right here and he's just fine."

Martin is gone. Looking through the house, I discover him in Deirdre's room, a place he has seldom entered, respectful of his child's privacy. Now he is bent over her dressing table, holding open a grocery sack, and all of it, cosmetics, mirrors, ribbons, hair rollers, all the paraphernalia of a young female, is tumbling into the bag. When the dressing table is bare, he goes to the bulletin board above her bed and tears down pictures of rock stars and movie stars. They float, without a change of expression, into the grocery bag. Martin takes the bag outside, sets it inside the garbage can, and we drive into town to find Deirdre. She sits in the back seat on the way home, and none of us says anything.

Sitting on the edge of her bed, I apologize and try to explain for Martin, and I am the one who smooths her dark hair. She has lately denied me this power to comfort her and hungrily I draw her back into myself. She relates a small, scattered story of betrayal and jealousy at a teenage party. I am proud that she defended the values we taught her, but with apprehension I read her expression, which tells me that one day she will risk a different choice, hurting us in the process. But now she says she loves me and, believing her, I leave Deirdre sleeping and safe again, a recovered part of my own self.

In the dark living room Martin, at a loss in his own house, is staring out of a window.

"She's fine," I say lightly. "You'd be proud of her." I feel myself the center of the family once again, though this is temporary power, splinted and artificial. He answers only that he is exhausted and is going to bed.

The late summer moon, like a veined marble bowl, spills out an abundance of light. I walk up the hill to the barn, take down the saddle, the bridle, and go back down to the corral. "Here," I say, "come here, hey," and the white horse, splashed with shadow, moves over to me. Calmly, I slip the bit and the bridle over him and cinch up the saddle. I have watched Deirdre do this many times. He absorbs my clumsiness as I climb up on his broad back.

Passing out of the corral gate, I see the house where my daughter and my husband sleep in rooms broken off from each other. I turn away from them and ride unburdened through damp grasses, straying from those boundaries set by daylight, by marriage, by family, by the erosion of time upon my private life.

With an urge to swiftness, the horse gallops forward and forward into the humid and calling darkness. A wildness begins to rise up in me when I glimpse the uprooted cottonwood, the tree I had fallen across earlier this evening.

In steady, lulling rhythm the white horse goes straight for it, his breath drawing in and out of the moist swell of his lungs. We rise dreamlike, above the tree, both of us soaring up, freed from the heavy, clinging earth.

Not far away, glittering like falseness, runs the silver and black cord of creek water, which, even in this particular season, is considered pure, quite excellent for our family to drink.

Discussion of a Quintessential

"A Private Landscape"
by Melissa Pritchard

A world within the world, successful short fiction invites both the reader and the writer to peek behind the curtain of reality and into the essence of reality: characters reacting to unforeseen, but perhaps predicted, events. As we all have experienced, the nature of a person can often be irrevocably revealed in an instant of honest interaction with the environment. In Melissa Pritchard's fine short story "A Personal Landscape," a family of three unwittingly grapples with the changing dynamic of their threesome while attempting to carry on with the daily business of living.

The piece begins, appropriately enough, in a kitchen. Dierdre, the teen-aged daughter of the story's narrator, is "dutifully" reading a novel which finds her, as her mother points out, "attending to more complex characters than mine." The mother, who remains tellingly nameless throughout the story, works to maintain the daily necessities of the home while observing the developing psyches of both her daughter and her husband in their uncomfortably changing relationship. Pritchard, with a soft touch, allows the reader access to the most private of spaces: the unguarded thoughts of her narrator.

The short story writer has many tools at his or her disposal—narration, characterization, and visualization, to name but a few—and the most effective will utilize all of these and many more. In "A Personal Landscape," Pritchard does just this. Consider the following passage, only a few paragraphs in:

> I shall wind up swallowing this cake myself. Deirdre is on a health kick this week, claiming that yogurt and grapefruit juice are all she needs. Martin, in an uncharacteristically vain humor, has also gone off his feed.

In this deceptively simple passage, we learn a great deal about the three main characters. First, we learn that Deirdre is prone to the same "kicks"—wild character shifts which occur on a weekly basis—to which all adolescents are prone. We also learn that Martin, the father, is normally guilty of that selfless/lazy approach to hygiene and health to which many middle-aged males are prone. And, most important, we learn very quickly of the narrator's attitudes to these character experimentations: Deirdre is "on a . . . kick" and she is "claiming." Martin is "off his feed."

The narrator "shall wind up swallowing" the cake herself. Pritchard's tone and word choice contribute to a very telling moment in the story. From this carefully crafted series of sentences, we learn quite a bit about the nature of these personalities, their relationships to one another, and about the inner workings of the main character, the story's protagonist.

In the very next passage, we get a glimpse behind the metaphorical curtain of the speaker's voice and we see what might be motivating her. Martin has, recently, "commented" on her "weight problem." She relates the following scene, a scene of heartbreaking honesty:

> Undressing with no eye toward pleasing anybody, dropping my frayed nightgown over my head, I was unaware, until I heard his soft but disapproving words, that I was being observed from our bed, my flesh critically measured. Martin's aesthetics, I tell myself, were always sadly predictable.

Here we see a saddeningly human response to a saddeningly human rebuke. Martin has coldly quantified the beauty of the mother of his child, his wife, and she is left to comfort herself with the rationalization that his judgment of her is "sadly predictable." Perhaps a lesser author would have let this moment stand alone, or perhaps a first-person memoirist would have felt that this moment was realization enough, but Pritchard pursues the point further. She allows her narrator to connect with a more primitive and disturbing idea, that Martin "wistfully watches Deirdre these days, hugs her waist tightly, strokes her long black hair while I scrape dishes and carry up laundry from the basement."

This is not to say that the story goes on to posit a domestic abuse situation or that Martin will sexually exploit his daughter. This is not that story. Rather, what this story dares to say, dangerously enough, is that Martin covets in his daughter the physical beauty that his wife may have naturally lost. And, whether she is aware of it or not, the wife and mother experiences and resents this taboo as it creates a distance from both her husband and her child.

The section ends with the narrator asking Deirdre to keep her legs together when wearing a dress:

> She sighs over my prudery, and with intense exaggeration rearranges herself in the window seat. Yesterday I requested that she not loll about the house in her bikini underwear when her father was expected home. "You're nearly fourteen years old," I said by way of justification. She shrugged and brushed wearily past me; her skin, I thought, smelled strongly of my best perfume.

In this and similar passages, Pritchard probes deep into the often disturbing psychological depths that separate parents and children—mothers and daughters, fathers and sons—and also the psychosexual dynamics between them. We do not have to ask ourselves if the author's family was like this or if she is telling the truth. Rather we ask ourselves, "Is my family like this?" or maybe "How many families are like this?"

Pritchard does all of this in just the first two pages of the story. As the narrative progresses, we will observe the members of this family as they undergo and adapt to changes, and they clumsily figure out how to remain together. We will see the parents give their child what they imagine is her wildest dream—a horse—and we will see the teenaged child abandon that horse for a boyfriend. We will see the father dote on his daughter, and then we will see that same father in a rage, tearing posters down from her wall when she misses curfew. We see the husband neglect and take for granted his wife, and then we will see him put his arm unexpectedly around her before they go home to make "oddly exuberant love." In short, we see the entirety of their shared lives in the short time we have to spend with them.

Pritchard uses one of the most important tools available to the fiction writer: the vivid description of a physical world. She writes, "In the middle of the creek we sit on rocks as bleached and flattened as the horse's flank I brushed this morning." She also opens for us emotional windows into the heart of her speaker: "In the living room I am trying to understand the jealousy and resentment I feel towards my only child." She offers telling observations through her speaker's eyes and glimpses into the hearts of her other characters as well: "Passing out of the corral gate, I see the house where my daughter and my husband sleep in rooms broken off from each other."

Finally, what Pritchard offers to her reader is much more than simply the sum of these narrative gifts. Sure, this is a story simply about a mother and father who give their daughter a horse which goes underappreciated, but each seemingly incidental anecdote carries an emotional surplus, a heaviness of feeling which ultimately outweighs the lightness of this easily summarized plot.

Quintessentially, this is what the best fiction can and should do: make the most out of every element in the story by choosing the most vivid narrative perspective, visual language, and evocative dialogue in the hopes of leading the reader somewhere new. Somewhere new, but somewhere powerfully familiar as well.

III | *Reading Selections*

KIM ADDONIZIO

In the Box Called Pleasure

My husband left me because he felt like he had no power. Now he has it; I call him up and beg him to come over and fuck me. I've just quit cigarettes, and all I can think about is how good it would feel to take a deep drag of smoke into my lungs. He pushes his cock down my throat until I gag on it, makes me keep it there until I have to relax; if I don't I'll choke. I relax. Everything is fine between us.

I have papers on my desk that read Dissolution of Marriage. I call and ask my husband for his Social Security number so I can fill them out, then I scream at him, then I don't do anything. I am having a crisis of self-esteem because I am ugly and stupid, with a bad memory to boot. I forget names, including my own, and most of what happened in books I read. *Madame Bovary*, for example. I remember that Emma kills herself, but not how. *Sentimental Education*: someone named Frédéric rides in a carriage and complains and is in love with a married woman. This is in the box called Flaubert. Also: origins of the modern novel. The Seine. Someone making love. A view of mist-covered pines from the apartment I rented one summer. End of box.

After I phone my husband he comes over and mashes me against the wall with his body. I love the feeling of being physically trapped. It's my worst fear, psychologically, why I ran from all my lovers before him. I realize I've lived by definitions; now there aren't any and it's impossible to function. Nature isn't friendly, but it exhibits a profound order. I think that if I could somehow stir myself into it as one more ingredient, I would know how to get through this. He's silent on the other end of the phone and I wonder what he's thinking, if he gives a shit if I live or die. The only way I can get over him is if I die.

I don't die.

Kim Addonizio, "In the Box Called Pleasure" from In the Box Called Pleasure: Stories, *Northwestern University Press, 1999. Reprinted by permission of the author.*

I live in a mansion with ghosts. At night the former lady of the house floats, transparent, over the lawn, calling each of her children by name. Sometimes they answer. It's that or cats. A frieze over my fireplace shows a naked man in a chariot, a horse, cherubs, women in filmy robes. I don't touch anything for fear I'll break it. I can't remember how I got here, but it's pleasant enough. The floor shines, and there are windows all around, and a piece of furniture called a swooning couch. After a discrete knock, food appears on a tray outside my door; I never see the servants. Mostly I stay in my room, but sometimes I go down the wide red-carpeted staircase and into the drawing room, which is dark and filled with gloomy paintings of people I don't know in elaborate gold frames.

I masturbate constantly, imagining that my husband is ordering me to spread my legs. He slaps my thighs; if I try to close them he slaps them harder. He ties me to the brass bed, and I can't get up to answer the servants' knock. After he fucks me he throws a fire ladder out the window, climbs down it, and doesn't come back.

I call for help the first few days but nobody comes; nobody even knocks on the door anymore. After a few weeks I starve to death. I rise above my body, and it looks so pathetic I can't believe I didn't get rid of it sooner; my mouth is open, my eyes have a scummy film over them, there's shit and piss everywhere, not to mention blood because I got my period. I'm glad my ugly, filthy body can't drag me down any longer; now I'm light as a feather, I spin around near the ceiling feeling like I've just chain-smoked an entire pack of cigarettes. At first it's fun, but then I start to get bored with being dead and wonder what else there is to do. I decide to try masturbating, and guess what, it's great: when I come I fly into a million pieces, and it takes hours to collect myself from the corners of the room. I notice I can't go through walls, though, and that worries me. I don't want to be stuck here in this room with my body forever. It stinks, for one thing. A fly crawls over my cheek and into my mouth.

I'm lonely here, and I miss my husband. I write him a long letter, a letter full of questions about us. What is there between us, I ask him, besides our sex? Is there any point to staying married? What does that mean, anyway? We don't live together. We rarely see each other. I wear my wedding band on my right hand, if I wear it at all. His name is engraved on the inside so I won't forget it. Marriage is *a)* a capitalist institution for the subjugation of women and preservation of male power and authority, *b)* an anachronism, *c)* a way to get health insurance, *d)* a species of insect.

> Dear, Darling, Sweetheart:
> How I miss your hands on me, the smell of your skin, your tattoos, the harsh tobacco taste of your tongue. Though you should try not to smoke so much. I wish we could talk sometimes, instead of just fucking. You've become a total stranger to me except in bed, where I feel like we're the same person. I known it's the same for you. Marriage

didn't kill our desire. Why can't we be friends? Don't you like me, just a little?

Love,

Your Wife

Every day I walk past the table in the hall where the servants leave the mail. There's nothing yet. Long-distance relationships suck. I wish there were someone here to fuck, but I'm too hung up on my husband to even consider it. Most men are lousy fucks anyway; that box is crammed full. Can't get it up, can't keep it up, won't eat pussy, comes in three seconds, holds me like I'm made of glass, can't find my clit, won't use a condom, fucks in total silence, expects me to do all the work, thinks of it as work, as proof of his power, as pure release: I have to come, there's a hole, I'd like to come in that but shit there's a person attached to it. My husband is an incredible fuck. I'm not sure what we do should even be called fucking. How can I give that up?

My husband left me to punish me; I wasn't behaving like A Wife. Fuck that. We didn't know each other very well. I'm starting to enjoy my freedom, even though my heart is a crushed useless lump of tissue that gurgles constantly like bad plumbing. I blame him for everything. Then I blame myself. Then I blame my father, my brothers, and God. It's impossible to have a relationship, nothing lasts anyway, there are no models, men go into the woods and beat little drums and scream, gender is meaningless, or it's everything; I want a partner, I need to be strong alone since we live and die alone anyway. I want someone to love me. That's what everybody wants, right? Besides being stupid, ugly, and amnesiac I am incapable of seeing beyond my own selfish ego. Until I do, I'll never get what I want.

Once we were happy.

Once he looked at me and I knew he loved and wanted me and I wasn't scared he would stop.

Once there was a queen who was the most beautiful woman in the land; everyone said so. Secretly, though, she knew she was a disgusting, hideous creature who had fooled everyone. Either that or she was totally insane. She didn't know which would be worse, to find out she was really a monster or really a crazy nut, so she ordered her subjects to remove all the mirrors from the kingdom. Her husband the king humored her, but every year on her birthday he tried to give her a mirror as a present, figuring it was a phobia she would overcome in time. Every year the queen refused the present and ordered the mirror taken out to the forest and smashed with a hammer.

One year the king found such a gorgeously exquisite mirror that the entire court urged the queen to accept it, but it was the same old story: smash the shit out of it. The woodsman whose job it was to do this took it out to the forest, but he couldn't bring himself to ruin such a beautiful object. He went deep into the forest, and there he found a small house where he hid the mirror. He broke a window in the house and brought the pieces back in a leather bag, to prove to the queen that he had done her bidding, and the queen put the bag in the bottom drawer of her dresser with all the other bags from previous years.

One afternoon when she was out jogging, the queen ran farther than she had ever run before, and came upon the little house hidden deep in the forest. Being extremely thirsty, she went inside to look for something to drink. As soon as she entered the house she saw the mirror, leaning against the wall under the broken window. She wanted to leave, but it was too late; as soon as she caught a glimpse of herself she stopped, transfixed, and couldn't look away.

I think all this has something to do with Lacan, whose theories I've forgotten.

Once we were fucking, I was on top, and between one thrust and the next I felt I didn't love him anymore. Suddenly I was just fucking a male body, not his body, and I felt a sense of freedom and power: now I could fuck anyone, do anything, create my own life. Then I was in love with him again, and I thought maybe I'd imagined it; can love go in and out like breath?

I've got to find a way to get out of here and get to town. In town there's a store: nail polish. Tampax. Liquor. Cigarettes. Lipstick. I don't have to wait here passively for something to happen. Do you think she saw a monster in the mirror? Makeup, in the seventies, meant slavery to imposed definitions of beauty; now it's assertive, self-adornment, a hip feminist statement.

I hate it that everything changes.

Themes so far: loss of power; loss of memory; self-hatred; definitions. A large crow lands on the lawn. In the box called pleasure:

I'm riding my bike around the streets of our neighborhood. My mom, who happens to be queen of the kingdom, has given me a letter to mail. I'm proud of being chosen to do this, especially since my mom never speaks to me; she spends most of her time shut up in her room, she's beautiful but crazy as a loon. But this morning she called me in, handed me a letter. Her stunning black hair was loose around her shoulders. She used to jog and work out and play tennis, but now she just lies around watching TV all day, and she's starting to get fat. I don't think she realizes this because there aren't any mirrors in the house; I have to go over to friends' houses to see what I look like. I'm blonde; I don't look a thing like my mother, but I'm cute as hell. I'm six years old and I want to be on TV. My name is Buffie. I adore my mother. When she gives me the letter I feel warm and happy; she hands it to me and kisses me on my forehead.

"Don't tell your brothers," she whispers. "Or your father, either. This will be our little secret. All right, darling?"

When she calls me "darling" I think I'll pass out from being so thrilled. I tuck the letter into a pocket of my dress. She turns back to "One Life to Live," and I go out of her room and down the stairs.

On the second floor I run into one of my seven brothers.

"C'mere, Buffie," he says. "I've got something in my room for you."

My seven brothers are all older than I am. They take me for pizza and ice cream, or ignore me; sometimes they protect me from our violent father, the king, and sometimes they tie me up and torment me.

"What've you got?" I say, suspicious. "I have to go do something for mom."

"It will only take a sec," my brother says.

I follow him into his room. My brother's room is filled with rats: cages and cages of them, sleeping in wood chips or running on treadmills or staring out at me, their tiny hands clawing at the wire mesh. They give me the creeps, like my brother. I don't trust him.

"Sit down there," my brother says, pointing to his bed. He has a can of Pam— spray-on cooking oil—in his right hand. He takes a baggie, sprays the Pam into the baggie, and holds it over my nose and mouth.

"Breathe, Buffie," my brother says.

I take a breath. Immediately my ears start ringing, the room recedes, I know I'm still in it, but I'm miles away; I can't find my body. I try to lift my hand, fall backwards on the bed; it takes hours to fall, I keep expecting to feel the bed but don't. I can hear my brother laughing somewhere. Then there's something hot between my legs and I feel like I have to pee, or maybe I am peeing; it's sticky, my underwear is wet; I try to move, but I'm trapped under something I can't see. I'm blind. I start to scream; I open my mouth and something cold rushes into my lungs, and I feel fantastic, I'm a big balloon, I start to giggle imagining myself as a balloon in a dress, my skin stretched tight over my enormous face I'm laughing so hard now I ache, more cold air filling me up I'm rocking back and forth in a rowboat in the middle of an ocean, rats are swimming by, their hairless tails whipping the water. The boat goes under.

I'm in my brother's room again. My head aches, I'm lying on his bed with my legs twisted open and my underwear off. He's standing over at the wall of cages, his back to me. He takes out a rat and brings it over to the bed.

"Ugh," I say. "Get it away from me." He knows I hate his rats.

"You'd better run," he says, smiling. He makes like he's going to toss the rat at me, but doesn't. I start crying. It hurts between my legs now. I jump up from his bed and run out, leaving my underwear.

I run downstairs to the garage and get on my bicycle. It's a pink five-speed Schwinn with streamers on the handles. As I ride, I feel more wetness come out of me. I press my crotch against the bike seat, rub it back and forth.

At the mailbox on the corner I jump off my bike, then throw myself onto the grass. I lie on my stomach and put my fist under my cunt, between it and the ground, and grind against it. Cars drive by. I can't stop; I hope nobody pulls over. Finally I come. I've never masturbated before this. I don't understand what's just happened.

I remember my mother's letter and find it in my pocket, all wrinkled and creased. I smooth it as well as I can, then open the mailbox and drop the letter into its mouth.

Dear Woodsman:

I hate my husband, the king. Unless you become my lover I'm going to kill myself. I can't divorce him because I'm terrified to live on my own, without money. If I could look forward to seeing you each week, death wouldn't exert such a powerful pull. I can't live for my children; they're on their own. Meet me at the house in the woods, and bring condoms.

Your Queen

Letters are a woman's form. And diaries. The domestic isn't historical; in most of history women don't exist. The self is constituted in memory, so I don't have a self, just a few ideas for one. I sit for hours in the room that used to be my mother's, looking out at the lawn and the enormous fountain; it's the size of an Olympic swimming pool. I'm dying for a cigarette. I drink too much coffee, chew gum, bite my fingernails; I'm not going to make it. I pull Dante's box out of the closet. Open it a crack, flames and shit and vomit spill out; I've only read the *Inferno*. My mom's in there. The Geryon flies past my window, or maybe it's an eagle; I should get a bird book. I wonder why birds sing, anyway. Is it necessary for their survival? There's one here that drives me crazy every morning, waking me at dawn. I'd like to sleep in, just once. All night it's ghosts, and then this fucking bird.

Dear Mom,

I don't know what the mail service is like down there, but I hope you get this in time for your birthday. Even though you were a lousy mother I loved you; I couldn't help it. I was only ten when you died. Why did you leave me? Why didn't you protect me from my brothers, those shits? My childhood was one long molestation. It's all your fault. How am I supposed to get past this and stop being a victim? Happy Birthday. I'm sorry there's no present but you were always so hard to buy for.

Love,

Buffie

p.s. Would you please stop calling my brothers' names every night? They are all doing fine. They have wives and ex-wives and girlfriends and kids and cocaine habits and big-screen TV's. You're the one that's dead.

I'm so depressed. I try to live as though life has meaning; I know it doesn't mean anything. You get old and sexually undesirable and then you die, or you kill yourself before that. Before my husband left me I felt loved, attractive, sexy: he grabs me by my cunt in the kitchen, leads me to the hall and fucks me on the floor, we're two animals; I love that he never thinks during sex or at least never seems to; I love being the instrument of his pleasure; I love the tiny space on his left eyelid—I think it's his left—where a lash is missing. I can't remember now. I've been abandoned. Or I set things up so he would abandon me; I didn't love him enough, my ex-lovers came out of the woodwork to have lunch and flirt, my husband was jealous, I didn't reassure him. Now I'm suffering

In that box:

A six-year old boy on his way to school in LA gets caught in the crossfire between two gangs and dies. A man with a Serbian mother and Croatian father gets drafted into both armies, runs away to America; in America he drives a taxi in New York City in summer, a lower circle of hell. In the Wood of Suicides my mother moans. A woman answers an ad for a maid, goes to the door; it's a Hell's Angels house, they pull her inside and rape her, later she escapes out a window and goes home to her alcoholic mother. She's seventeen when all this happens, then finds out she's pregnant and gets an abortion, but it turns out she's carrying twins and the doctor has only aborted one. That night at home she's feverish, delirious, the second fetus comes out, she's hallucinating, passing out; she wakes up, blood all over the sheets. Before this her father fucked her for years; she finally told her mother, who had her committed. She's my best friend.

It is, after all, the love of women that sustains me.

Another friend says, "Do you feel that sex saved your life?" She means boys. Actually I think art saved my life at the time it needed saving, when I was doing too much heroin and fucking junkies and living in roach-filled apartments with gunshots in the street every night and the guy upstairs beating the shit out of his girlfriend. Now art isn't enough; I have that, and friends who love me—they write me letters, even if my husband doesn't—and I'm miserable.

One day I'm whining about my life and a girlfriend looks at me and says, "Well, Buffie, the important thing is to feel bad." She's right; I'm complaining about nothing, I should be grateful.

I'm still miserable.

There's a knock on the door. It's my husband, finally; he's come all this way to see me, he says he's sorry for everything and it doesn't matter what happened between us, whatever it was—who knows what's true or real anyway—he says, "I feel the pain and love and desire in your words to me and you're right, darling, sometimes it seems so perfectly simple and natural and right between us, even out of bed on occasion," he pushes me down on the bed, begins to rip my clothes off, *rip* my troubles are over *rip* this is a work of fiction and any resemblance to actual persons can't be helped, *rip rip* my underwear flies across the room, a bird goes up to heaven in a rush of wings and it starts raining, sheets of rain over the lawn and fountain, the roof of the house, the windows are streaming, *rip, rip, rip*, I can't stop remembering love.

SHERMAN ALEXIE

Because My Father Always Said He Was the Only Indian Who Saw Jimi Hendrix Play "The Star-Spangled Banner" at Woodstock

During the sixties, my father was the perfect hippie, since all the hippies were trying to be Indians. Because of that, how could anyone recognize that my father was trying to make a social statement?

But there is evidence, a photograph of my father demonstrating in Spokane, Washington, during the Vietnam war. The photograph made it onto the wire service and was reprinted in newspapers throughout the country. In fact, it was on the cover of *Time*.

In the photograph, my father is dressed in bell-bottoms and flowered shirt, his hair in braids, with red peace symbols splashed across his face like war paint. In his hands my father holds a rifle above his head, captured in that moment just before he proceeded to beat the shit out of the National Guard private lying prone on the ground. A fellow demonstrator holds a sign that is just barely visible over my father's left shoulder. It read MAKE LOVE NOT WAR.

The photographer won a Pulitzer Prize, and editors across the country had a lot of fun creating captions and headlines. I've read many of them collected in my father's scrapbook, and my favorite was run in the *Seattle Times*. The caption under the photograph read DEMONSTRATOR GOES TO WAR FOR PEACE. The editors capitalized on my father's Native American identity with other headlines like ONE WARRIOR AGAINST WAR and PEACEFUL GATHERING TURNS INTO NATIVE UPRISING.

Anyway, my father was arrested, charged with attempted murder, which was reduced to assault with a deadly weapon. It was a high-profile case so my father was used as an example. Convicted and sentenced quickly, he spent two years in Walla Walla State Penitentiary. Although his prison sentence effectively kept him out of the war, my father went through a different kind of war behind bars.

"There was Indian gangs and white gangs and black gangs and Mexican gangs," he told me once. "And there was somebody new killed every day. We'd hear about somebody getting it in the shower or wherever and the word would go down the line. Just one word. Just the color of his skin. Red, white, black, or brown. Then we'd chalk it up on the mental scoreboard and wait for the next broadcast."

My father made it through all that, never got into any serious trouble, somehow avoided rape, and got out of prison just in time to hitchhike to Woodstock to watch Jimi Hendrix play "The Star-Spangled Banner."

"After all the shit I'd been through," my father said, "I figured Jimi must have known I was there in the crowd to play something like that. It was exactly how I felt."

Twenty years later, my father played his Jimi Hendrix tape until it wore down. Over and over, the house filled with the rockets' red glare and the bombs bursting in air. He'd sit by the stereo with a cooler of beer beside him and cry, laugh, call me over and hold me tight in his arms, his bad breath and body odor covering me like a blanket.

Jimi Hendrix and my father became drinking buddies. Jimi Hendrix waited for my father to come home after a long night of drinking. Here's how the ceremony worked:

1. I would lie awake all night and listen for the sounds of my father's pickup.
2. When I heard my father's pickup, I would run upstairs and throw Jimi's tape into the stereo.
3. Jimi would bend his guitar into the first note of "The Star-Spangled Banner" just as my father walked inside.
4. My father would weep, attempt to hum along with Jimi, and then pass out with his head on the kitchen table.
5. I would fall asleep under the table with my head near my father's feet.
6. We'd dream together until the sun came up.

The days after, my father would feel so guilty that he would tell me stories as a means of apology.

"I met your mother at a party in Spokane," my father told me once. "We were the only two Indians at the party. Maybe the only two Indians in the whole town. I thought she was so beautiful. I figured she was the kind of woman who could make buffalo walk on up to her and give up their lives. She wouldn't have needed to hunt. Every time we went walking, birds would follow us around. Hell, tumbleweeds would follow us around."

Somehow my father's memories of my mother grew more beautiful as their relationship became more hostile. By the time the divorce was final, my mother was quite possibly the most beautiful woman who ever lived.

"Your father was always half crazy," my mother told me more than once. "And the other half was on medication."

But she loved him, too, with a ferocity that eventually forced her to leave him. They fought each other with the kind of graceful anger that only love can create. Still, their love was passionate, unpredictable, and selfish. My mother and father would get drunk and leave parties abruptly to go home and make love.

"Don't tell your father I told you this," my mother said. "But there must have been a hundred times he passed out on top of me. We'd be right in the middle of it, he'd say *I love you*, his eyes would roll backwards, and then out went his lights. It sounds strange, I know, but those were good times."

I was conceived during one of those drunken nights, half of me formed by my father's whiskey sperm, the other half formed by my mother's vodka egg. I was born a goofy reservation mixed drink, and my father needed me just as much as he needed every other kind of drink.

One night my father and I were driving home in a near-blizzard after a basketball game, listening to the radio. We didn't talk much. One, because my father didn't talk much when he was sober, and two, because Indians don't need to talk to communicate.

"Hello out there, folks, this is Big Bill Baggins, with the late-night classics show on KROC, 97.2 on your FM dial. We have a request from Betty in Tekoa. She wants to hear Jimi Hendrix's version of 'The Star-Spangled Banner' recorded live at Woodstock."

My father smiled, turned the volume up, and we rode down the highway while Jimi led the way like a snowplow. Until that night, I'd always been neutral about Jimi Hendrix. But, in that near-blizzard with my father at the wheel, with the nervous silence caused by the dangerous roads and Jimi's guitar, there seemed to be more to all that music. The reverberation came to mean something, took form and function.

That song made me want to learn to play guitar, not because I wanted to be Jimi Hendrix and not because I thought I'd ever play for anyone. I just wanted to touch the strings, to hold the guitar tight against my body, invent a chord, and come closer to what Jimi knew, to what my father knew.

"You know," I said to my father after the song was over, "my generation of Indian boys ain't ever had no real war to fight. The first Indians had Custer to fight. My great-grandfather had World War I, my grandfather had World War II, you had Vietnam. All I have is video games."

My father laughed for a long time, nearly drove off the road into the snowy fields.

"Shit," he said. "I don't know why you're feeling sorry for yourself because you ain't had to fight a war. You're lucky. Shit, all you had was that damn Desert Storm. Should have called it Dessert Storm because it just made the fat cats get fatter. It was all sugar and whipped cream with a cherry on top. And besides that, you didn't even have to fight it. All you lost during that war was sleep because you stayed up all night watching CNN."

We kept driving through the snow, talked about war and peace.

"That's all there is," my father said. "War and peace with nothing it between. It's always one or the other."

"You sound like a book," I said.

"Yeah, well, that's how it is. Just because it's in a book doesn't make it not true. And besides, why the hell would you want to fight a war for this country? It's been trying to kill Indians since the very beginning. Indians are pretty much born soldiers anyway. Don't need a uniform to prove it."

Those were the kinds of conversations that Jimi Hendrix forced us to have. I guess every song has a special meaning for someone somewhere. Elvis Presley is still showing up in 7–11 stores across the country, even though he's been dead for years, so I figure music just might be the most important thing there is. Music turned my father into a reservation philosopher. Music had powerful medicine.

"I remember the first time your mother and I danced," my father told me once. "We were in this cowboy bar. We were the only real cowboys there despite the fact that we're Indians. We danced to a Hank Williams song. Danced to that real sad one, you know. 'I'm So Lonesome I Could Cry.' Except your mother and I weren't lonesome or crying. We just shuffled along and fell right goddamn down into love."

"Hank Williams and Jimi Hendrix don't have much in common," I said.

"Hell, yes, they do. They knew all about broken hearts," my father said.

"You sound like a bad movie."

"Yeah, well, that's how it is. You kids today don't know shit about romance. Don't know shit about music either. Especially you Indian kids. You all have been spoiled by those drums. Been hearing them beat so long, you think that's all you need. Hell, son, even an Indian needs a piano or guitar or saxophone now and again."

My father played in a band in high school. He was the drummer. I guess he'd burned out on those. Now, he was like the universal defender of the guitar.

"I remember when your father would haul that old guitar out and play me songs," my mother said. "He couldn't play all that well but he tried. You could see him thinking about what chord he was going to play next. His eyes got all squeezed up and his face turned all red. He kind of looked that way when he kissed me, too. But don't tell him I said that."

Some nights I lay awake and listened to my parents' lovemaking. I know white people keep it quiet, pretend they don't ever make love. My white friends tell me they can't even imagine their own parents getting it on. I know exactly what it sounds like when my parents are touching each other. It makes up for knowing exactly what they sound like when they're fighting. Plus and minus. Add and subtract. It comes out just about even.

Some nights I would fall asleep to the sounds of my parents' lovemaking. I would dream Jimi Hendrix. I could see my father standing in the front row in the dark at Woodstock as Jimi Hendrix played "The Star-Spangled Banner." My mother was at home with me, both of us waiting for my father to find his way back home to the reservation. It's amazing to realize I was alive, breathing and wetting my bed, when Jimi was alive and breaking guitars.

I dreamed my father dancing with all these skinny hippie women, smoking a few joints, dropping acid, laughing when the rain fell. And it did rain there. I've seen actual news footage. I've seen the documentaries. It rained. People had to share food. People got sick. People got married. People cried all kinds of tears.

But as much as I dream about it, I don't have any clue about what it meant for my father to be the only Indian who saw Jimi Hendrix play at Woodstock. And maybe he wasn't the only Indian there. Most likely there were hundreds but my father thought he was the only one. He told me that a million times when he was drunk and a couple hundred times when he was sober.

"I was there," he said. "You got to remember this was near the end and there weren't as many people as before. Not nearly as many. But I waited it out. I waited for Jimi."

A few years back, my father packed up the family and the three of us drove to Seattle to visit Jimi Hendrix's grave. We had our photograph taken lying down next to the grave. There isn't a gravestone there. Just one of those flat markers.

Jimi was twenty-eight when he died. That's younger than Jesus Christ when he died. Younger than my father as we stood over the grave.

"Only the good die young," my father said.

"No," my mother said. "Only the crazy people choke to death on their own vomit."

"Why you talking about my hero that way?" my father asked.

"Shit," my mother said. "Old Jesse WildShoe choked to death on his own vomit and he ain't anybody's hero."

I stood back and watched my parents argue. I was used to these battles. When an Indian marriage starts to fall apart, it's even more destructive and painful than usual. A hundred years ago, an Indian marriage was broken easily. The woman or man just packed up all their possessions and left the tipi. There were no arguments, no discussions. Now, Indians fight their way to the end, holding onto the last good thing, because our whole lives have to do with survival.

After a while, after too much fighting and too many angry words had been exchanged, my father went out and bought a motorcycle. A big bike. He left the house often to ride that thing for hours, sometimes for days. He even strapped an old cassette player to the gas tank so he could listen to music. With that bike, he learned something new about running away. He stopped talking as much, stopped drinking as much. He didn't do much of anything except ride that bike and listen to music.

Then one night my father wrecked his bike on Devil's Gap Road and ended up in the hospital for two months. He broke both his legs, cracked his ribs, and punctured a lung. He also lacerated his kidney. The doctors said he could have died easily. In fact, they were surprised he made it through surgery, let alone survived those first few hours when he lay on the road, bleeding. But I wasn't surprised. That's how my father was.

And even though my mother didn't want to be married to him anymore and his wreck didn't change her mind about that, she still came to see him every day. She sang Indian tunes under her breath, in time with the hum of the machines hooked into my father. Although my father could barely move, he tapped his finger in rhythm.

When he had the strength to finally sit up and talk, hold conversations, and tell stories, he called for me.

"Victor," he said. "Stick with four wheels."

After he began to recover, my mother stopped visiting as often. She helped him through the worst, though. When he didn't need her anymore, she went back to the life she had created. She traveled to powwows, started to dance again. She was a champion traditional dancer when she was younger.

"I remember your mother when she was the best traditional dancer in the world," my father said. "Everyone wanted to call her sweetheart. But she only danced for me. That's how it was. She told me that every other step was just for me."

"But that's only half of the dance," I said.

"Yeah," my father said. "She was keeping the rest for herself. Nobody can give everything away. It ain't healthy."

"You know," I said, "sometimes you sound like you ain't even real."

"What's real? I ain't interested in what's real. I'm interested in how things should be."

My father's mind always worked that way. If you don't like the things you remember, then all you have to do is change the memories. Instead of remembering the bad things, remember what happened immediately before. That's what I learned from my father. For me, I remember how good the first drink of that Diet Pepsi tasted instead of how my mouth felt when I swallowed a wasp with the second drink.

Because of all that, my father always remembered the second before my mother left him for good and took me with her. No. I remembered the second before my father left my mother and me. No. My mother remembered the second before my father left her to finish raising me all by herself.

But however memory actually worked, it was my father who climbed on his motorcycle, waved to me as I stood in the window, and rode away. He lived in Seattle, San Francisco, Los Angeles, before he finally ended up in Phoenix. For a while, I got postcards nearly every week. Then it was once a month. Then it was on Christmas and my birthday.

On a reservation, Indian men who abandon their children are treated worse than white fathers who do the same thing. It's because white men have been doing that forever and Indian men have just learned how. That's how assimilation can work.

My mother did her best to explain it all to me, although I understood most of what happened.

"Was it because of Jimi Hendrix?" I asked her.

"Part of it, yeah," she said. "This might be the only marriage broken up by a dead guitar player."

"There's a first time for everything, enit?"

"I guess. Your father just likes being alone more than he likes being with other people. Even me and you."

Sometimes I caught my mother digging through old photo albums or staring at the wall or out the window. She'd get that look on her face that I knew meant she missed my father. Not enough to want him back. She missed him just enough for it to hurt.

On those nights I missed him most I listened to music. Not always Jimi Hendrix. Usually I listened to the blues. Robert Johnson mostly. The first time I heard Robert Johnson sing I knew he understood what it meant to be Indian on the edge of the twenty-first century, even if he was black at the beginning of the twentieth. That must have been how my father felt when he heard Jimi Hendrix. When he stood there in the rain at Woodstock.

Then on the night I missed my father most, when I lay in bed and cried, with that photograph of him beating that National Guard private in my hands, I imagined his motorcycle pulling up outside. I knew I was dreaming it all but I let it be real for a moment.

"Victor," my father yelled. "Let's go for a ride."

"I'll be right down. I need to get my coat on."

I rushed around the house, pulled my shoes and socks on, struggled into my coat, and ran outside to find an empty driveway. It was so quiet, a reservation kind of quiet, where you can hear somebody drinking whiskey on the rocks three miles away. I stood on the porch and waited until my mother came outside.

"Come on back inside," she said. "It's cold."

"No," I said. "I know he's coming back tonight."

My mother didn't say anything. She just wrapped me in her favorite quilt and went back to sleep. I stood on the porch all night long and imagined I heard motorcycles and guitars, until the sun rose so bright that I knew it was time to go back inside to my mother. She made breakfast for both of us and we ate until we were full.

DONALD BARTHELME

A Shower of Gold

Because he needed the money Peterson answered an ad that said *"We'll pay you to be on TV if your opinions are strong enough or your personal experiences have a flavor of the unusual."* He called the number and was told to come to Room 1551 in the Graybar Building on Lexington. This he did and after spending twenty minutes with a Miss Arbor who asked him if he had ever been in analysis was okayed for a program called *Who Am I?* "What do you have strong opinions about?" Miss Arbor asked. "Art," Peterson said, "life, money." "For instance?" "I believe," Peterson said, "that the learning ability of mice can be lowered or increased by regulating the amount of serotonin in the brain. I believe that schizophrenics have a high incidence of unusual fingerprints, including lines that make almost complete circles. I believe that the dreamer watches his dream in sleep, by moving his eyes." *"That's very interesting!"* Miss Arbor cried. "It's all in the *World Almanac*," Peterson replied.

Donald Barthelme, "A Shower of Gold," from Sixty Stories, *Putnam Publishing Group, 1995. © 1995 by Donald Barthelme, reprinted with the permission of the Wylie Agency Inc.*

"I see you're a sculptor," Miss Arbor said. "that's wonderful." "What is the nature of the program?" Peterson asked. "I've never seen it." "Let me answer your question with another question," Miss Arbor said. "Mr. Peterson, are you absurd?" Her enormous lips were smeared with a glowing white cream. "I beg your pardon?" "I mean," Miss Arbor said earnestly, "do you encounter your own existence as gratuitous? Do you feel *de trop*? Is there nausea?" "I have an enlarged liver," Peterson offered. "That's *excellent!*" Miss Arbor exclaimed. "That's a *very* good beginning. *Who Am I?* tries, Mr. Peterson, to discover what people *really are*. People today, we feel, are hidden away inside themselves, alienated, desperate, living in anguish, despair and bad faith. Why have we been thrown here, and abandoned? That's the question we try to answer, Mr. Peterson. Man stands alone in a featureless, anonymous landscape, in fear and trembling and sickness unto death. God is dead. Nothingness everywhere. Dread. Estrangement. Finitude. *Who Am I?* approaches these problems in a root radical way." "On television?" "We're interested in basics, Mr. Peterson. We don't play around." "I see," Peterson said, wondering about the amount of the fee. "What I want to know now, Mr. Peterson, is this: are you *interested* in absurdity?" "Miss Arbor," he said, "to tell you the truth, I don't know. I'm not sure I believe in it." "Oh, Mr. Peterson!" Miss Arbor said, shocked. "Don't *say* that! You'll be . . . " "Punished?" Peterson suggested. "*You* may not be interested in absurdity," she said firmly, "but absurdity is interested in *you*." "I have a lot of problems, if that helps," Peterson said. "Existence is problematic for you," Miss Arbor said, relieved. "The fee is two hundred dollars"

"I'm going to be on television," Peterson said to his dealer. "A terrible shame," Jean-Claude responded. "Is it unavoidable?" "It's unavoidable," Peterson said, "if I want to eat." "How much?" Jean-Claude asked and Peterson said: "Two hundred." He looked around the gallery to see if any of his works were on display. "A ridiculous compensation considering the infamy. Are you using your own name?" "You haven't by any chance . . ." "No one is buying," Jean-Claude said. "Undoubtedly it is the weather. People are thinking in terms of—what do you call those things?— Chris-Crafts. To boat with. You would not consider again what I spoke to you about before?" "No," Peterson said, "I wouldn't consider it." "Two little ones would move much, much faster than a single huge big one," Jean-Claude said, looking away. "To saw it across the middle would be a very simple matter." "It's supposed to be a work of art," Peterson said, as calmly as possible. "You don't go around sawing works of art across the middle, remember?" "That place where it saws," Jean-Claude said, "is not very difficult. I can put my two hands around it." He made a circle with his two hands to demonstrate. "Invariably when I look at that piece I see two pieces. Are you absolutely sure you didn't conceive it wrongly in the first instance?" "Absolutely," Peterson said. Not a single piece of his was on view, and his liver expanded in rage and hatred. "You have a very romantic impulse," Jean-Claude said. "I admire, dimly, the posture. You read too much in the history of art. It estranges you from those possibilities for authentic selfhood that inhere in the present century." "I know," Peterson said, "could you let me have twenty until the first?"

Peterson sat in his loft on lower Broadway drinking Rheingold and thinking about the President. He had always felt close to the President but felt now that he had, in agreeing to appear on the television program, done something slightly disgraceful, of which the President would not approve. But *I needed the money,* he told himself, *the telephone is turned off and the kitten is crying for milk. And I'm running out of beer.* The President feels that the arts should be encouraged, Peterson reflected, *surely he doesn't want me to go without beer?* He wondered if what he was feeling was simple guilt at having sold himself to television or something more elegant: nausea? His liver groaned within him and he considered a situation in which his new relationship with the President was announced. He was working in the loft. The piece in hand was to be called *Season's Greetings* and combined three auto radiators, one from a Chevrolet Tudor, one from a Ford pickup, one from a 1932 Essex, with part of a former telephone switchboard and other items. The arrangement seemed right and he began welding. After a time the mass was freestanding. A couple of hours had passed. He put down the torch, lifted off the mask. He walked over to the refrigerator and found a sandwich left by a friendly junk dealer. It was a sandwich made hastily and without inspiration: a thin slice of ham between two pieces of bread. He ate it gratefully nevertheless. He stood looking at the work, moving from time to time so as to view it from a new angle. Then the door to the loft burst open and the President ran in, trailing a sixteen-pound sledge. His first blow cracked the principal weld in *Season's Greetings,* the two halves parting like lovers, clinging for a moment and then rushing off in opposite directions. Twelve Secret Service men held Peterson in a paralyzing combination of secret grips. *He's looking good,* Peterson thought, *very good, healthy, mature, fit, trustworthy. I like his suit.* The President's second and third blows smashed the Essex radiator and the Chevrolet radiator. Then he attacked the welding torch, the plaster sketches on the workbench, the Rodin cast and the Giacometti stickman Peterson had bought in Paris. "*But Mr. President!*" Peterson shouted. "*I thought we were friends!*" A Secret Service man bit him in the back of the neck. Then the President lifted the sledge high in the air, turned toward Peterson, and said: "Your liver is diseased? That's a good sign. You're making progress. You're thinking."

"I happen to think that guy in the White House is doing a pretty darn good job." Peterson's barber, a man named Kitchen who was also a lay analyst and the author of four books titled *The Decision to Be,* was the only person in the world to whom he had confided his former sense of community with the President. "As far as his relationship with you personally goes," the barber continued, "it's essentially a kind of I-Thou relationship, if you know what I mean. You got to handle it with full awareness of the implications. In the end one experiences only oneself, Nietzsche said. When you're angry with the President, what you experience is self-as-angry-with-the-President. When things are okay between you and him, what you experience is self-as-swinging-with-the-President. Well and good. *But,*" Kitchen said, lathering up, "you want the relationship to be such that what you experience is the-President-as-swinging-with-you. You want *his* reality, get it? So that you can break out of the hell of solipsism. How about a little more off the sides?" "Everybody knows the language but me," Peterson said irritably. "Look," Kitchen said, "when you talk about me to somebody else, you say 'my barber,' don't you? Sure you do. In the same way, I look on you as being 'my customer,' get it? But you don't regard yourself as being 'my' customer and I don't regard myself as 'your' barber. Oh, it's hell all right." The razor moved like a switchblade across the back of Peterson's neck. "Like Pascal said: 'The natural misfortune of our mortal and feeble condition is so wretched that when we consider it closely, nothing can console us.'" The razor rocketed around an ear. "Listen," Peterson said, "what do you think of this television program called *Who Am I?* Ever seen it?" "Frankly," the barber said, "it smells of the library. But they do a job on those people, I'll tell you that." "What do you mean?" Peterson said excitedly. "What kind of a job?" The cloth was whisked away and shaken with a sharp popping sound. "It's too horrible even to talk about," Kitchen said. "But it's what they deserve, those crumbs." "Which crumbs?" Peterson asked.

That night a tall foreign-looking man with a switchblade big as a butcherknife open in his hand walked into the loft without knocking and said "Good evening, Mr. Peterson, I am the cat-piano player, is there anything you'd particularly like to hear?" "Cat-piano?" Peterson said, gasping, shrinking from the knife. "What are you talking about? What do you want?" A biography of Nolde slid from his lap to the floor. "The cat-piano," said the visitor, "is an instrument of the devil, a diabolical instrument. You needn't sweat quite so much," he added, sounding aggrieved. Peterson tried to be brave. "I don't understand," he said. "Let me explain," the tall foreign-looking man said graciously. "The keyboard consists of eight cats—the octave—encased in the body of the instrument in such a way that only their heads and forepaws protrude. The player presses upon the appropriate paws, and the appropriate cats respond—with a kind of shriek. There is also provision made for pulling their tails. A tail-puller, or perhaps I should say tail *player*" (he smiled a disingenuous smile) "is stationed at the rear of the instrument, where the tails are. At the correct moment the tail-puller pulls the correct tail. The tail-note is of course quite different from the paw-note and produces sound in the upper registers. Have you ever seen such an instrument, Mr. Peterson?" "No, and I don't believe it exists," Peterson said heroically. "There is an excellent early seventeenth-century engraving by Franz van der Wyngaert, Mr. Peterson, in which a cat-piano appears. Played, as it happens, by a man with a wooden leg. You will observe my own leg." The cat-piano player hoisted his trousers and a leglike contraption of wood, metal and plastic appeared. "And now, would you like to make a request? 'The Martyrdom of St. Sebastian'? The 'Romeo and Juliet' overture? 'Holiday for Strings'?" "But why—" Peterson began. "The kitten is crying for milk, Mr. Peterson. And whenever a kitten cries, the cat-piano plays." "But it's not my kitten," Peterson said reasonably. "It's just a kitten that wished itself on me. I've been trying to give it away. I'm not sure it's still around. I haven't seen it since the day before yesterday." The kitten appeared, looked at Peterson reproachfully, and then rubbed itself against the cat-piano player's mechanical leg. "Wait a minute!" Peterson exclaimed. "This thing is rigged! That cat hasn't been here in two days. What do you want from me? What am I supposed to do?" "Choices, Mr. Peterson, choices. You *chose* that kitten as a way of encountering that which you are not, that is to say, kitten. An effort on the part of the *pour-soi* to—" "But it chose me!" Peterson cried, "the door was open and the first thing I knew it was lying in my bed, under the Army blanket. I didn't have anything to do with it!" The cat-piano player repeated his disingenuous smile. "Yes, Mr. Peterson, I know, I know. Things are done to you, it is all a gigantic conspiracy. I've heard the story a hundred times. But the kitten is here, is it not? The kitten is weeping, is it not?" Peterson looked at the kitten, which was crying huge tigerish tears into its empty dish. "*Listen*, Mr. Peterson," the cat-piano player said, "*listen!*" The blade of his immense knife jumped back into the handle with a thwack! and the hideous music began.

The day after the hideous music began the three girls from California arrived. Peterson opened his door, hesitantly, in response to an insistent ringing, and found himself being stared at by three girls in blue jeans and heavy sweaters, carrying suitcases. "I'm Sherry," the first girl said, "and this is Ann and this is Louise. We're from California and we need a place to stay." They were homely and extremely purposeful. "I'm sorry," Peterson said, "I can't—" "We sleep anywhere," Sherry said, looking past him into the vastness of his loft," on the floor if we have to. We've done it before." Ann and Louise stood on their toes to get a good look. "What's that funny music?" Sherry asked, "it sounds pretty far-out. We really won't be any trouble at all and it'll just be a little while until we make a connection." "Yes," Peterson said, "but why me?" "You're an artist," Sherry said sternly, "we saw the AIR sign downstairs." Peterson cursed the fire laws which made posting of the signs obligatory. "Listen," he said, "I can't even feed the cat. I can't even keep myself in beer. This is not the place. You won't be happy here. My work isn't authentic. I'm a minor artist." "The natural misfortune of our mortal and feeble condition is so wretched that when we consider it closely, nothing can console us," Sherry said. "That's Pascal." "I know," Peterson said, weakly. "Where is the john?" Louise asked. Ann marched into the kitchen and began to prepare, from supplies removed from her rucksack, something called *veal engagé.* "Kiss me," Sherry said, "I need love." Peterson flew to his friendly neighborhood bar, ordered a double brandy, and thrust himself into a telephone booth. "Miss Arbor? This is Hank Peterson. Listen, Miss Arbor, I can't do it. No, I mean really. I'm being punished horribly for even thinking about it. No, I mean it. You can't imagine what's going on around here. Please, get somebody else? I'd regard it as a great personal favor. Miss Arbor? Please?"

The other contestants were a young man in white pajamas named Arthur Pick, a karate expert, and an airline pilot in full uniform, Wallace E. Rice. "Just be natural," Miss Arbor said, "and of course be frank. We score on the basis of the validity of your answers, and of course that's measured by the polygraph." "What's this about a polygraph?" the airline pilot said. "The polygraph measures the validity of your answers," Miss Arbor said, her lips glowing whitely. "How else are we going to know if you're . . ." "Lying?" Wallace E. Rice supplied. The contestants were connected to the machine and the machine to a large illuminated tote board hanging over their heads. The master of ceremonies, Peterson noted without pleasure, resembled the President and did not look at all friendly.

The program began with Arthur Pick. Arthur Pick got up in his white pajamas and gave a karate demonstration in which he broke three half-inch pine boards with a single kick of his naked left foot. Then he told how he had disarmed a bandit, late at night at the A&P where he was an assistant manager, with a maneuver called a "rip-choong" which he demonstrated on the announcer. "How about that?" the announcer caroled. "Isn't that something? Audience?" The audience responded enthusiastically and Arthur Pick stood modestly with his hands behind his back. "Now," the announcer said, "let's play *Who Am I?* And here's your host, *Bill Lemmon!*" No, he doesn't look like the President, Peterson decided. "Arthur," Bill Lemmon said, "for twenty dollars—do you love your mother?" "Yes," Arthur Pick said. "Yes, of course." A bell rang, the tote board flashed, and the audience screamed. "He's lying!" the announcer shouted, "lying! lying! lying!" "Arthur," Bill Lemmon said, looking at his index cards, "the polygraph shows that the validity of your answer is . . . questionable. Would you like to try it again? Take another crack at it?" "You're crazy," Arthur Pick said. "Of course I love my mother." He was fishing around inside his pajamas for a handkerchief. "Is your mother watching the show tonight, Arthur?" "Yes, Bill, she is." "How long have you been studying karate?" "Two years, Bill." "And who paid for the lessons?" Arthur Pick hesitated. Then he said, "My mother, Bill." "They were pretty expensive, weren't they, Arthur?" "Yes, Bill, they were." "How expensive?" "Twelve dollars an hour." "Your mother doesn't make very much money, does she, Arthur?" "No, Bill, she doesn't." "Arthur, what does your mother do for a living?" "She's a garment worker, Bill. In the garment district." "And how long has she worked down there?" "All her life, I guess. Since my old man died." "And she doesn't make very much money, you said." "No But she *wanted* to pay for the lessons. She *insisted* on it." Bill Lemmon said, "She wanted a son who could break boards with his feet?" Peterson's liver leaped and the tote board spelled out, in huge, glowing white letters, the words BAD FAITH. The airline pilot, Wallace E. Rice, was led to reveal that he had been caught, on a flight from Omaha to Miami, with a stewardess sitting on his lap and wearing his captain's cap, that the flight engineer had taken a Polaroid picture, and that he had been given involuntary retirement after nineteen years of faithful service. "It was perfectly safe," Wallace E. Rice said, "you don't understand, the automatic pilot can fly that plane better than I can." He further confessed to a lifelong and intolerable itch after stewardesses which had much to do, he said, with the way their jackets fell just on top of their hips, and his own jacket with the three gold stripes on the sleeve darkened with sweat until it was black.

I was wrong, Peterson thought, the world is absurd. The absurdity is punishing me for not believing in it. I affirm the absurdity. On the other hand, absurdity is itself absurd. Before the emcee could ask the first question, Peterson began to talk. "Yesterday," Peterson said to the television audience, "in the typewriter in front of the Olivetti showroom on Fifth Avenue, I found a recipe for Ten Ingredient Soup that included a stone from a toad's head. And while I stood there marveling a nice old lady pasted on the elbow of my best Haspel suit a little blue sticker reading THIS

INDIVIDUAL IS A PART OF THE COMMUNIST CONSPIRACY FOR GLOBAL DOMINATION OF THE ENTIRE GLOBE. Coming home I passed a sign that said in ten-foot letters COWARD SHOES and heard a man singing "Golden Earrings" in a horrible voice, and last night I dreamed there was a shoot-out at our house on Meat Street and my mother shoved me in a closet to get me out of the line of fire." The emcee waved at the floor manager to turn Peterson off, but Peterson kept talking. "In this kind of a world," Peterson said, "absurd if you will, possibilities nevertheless proliferate and escalate all around us and there are opportunities for beginning again. I am a minor artist and my dealer won't even display my work if he can help it but minor is as minor does and lighting may strike even yet. Don't be reconciled. Turn off your television sets," Peterson said, "cash in your life insurance, indulge in a mindless optimism. Visit girls at dusk. Play the guitar. How can you be alienated without first having been connected? Think back and remember how it was." A man on the floor in front of Peterson was waving a piece of cardboard on which something threatening was written but Peterson ignored him and concentrated on the camera with the little red light. The little red light jumped from camera to camera in an attempt to throw him off balance but Peterson was too smart for it and followed wherever it went. "My mother was a royal virgin," Peterson said, "and my father a shower of gold. My childhood was pastoral and energetic and rich in experiences which developed my character. As a young man I was noble in reason, infinite in faculty, in form express and admirable, and in apprehension . . . " Peterson went on and on and although he was, in a sense, lying, in a sense he was not.

RON CARLSON

Bigfoot Stole My Wife

The problem is credibility.

The problem, as I'm finding out over the last few weeks, is basic credibility. A lot of people look at me and say, sure Rick, Bigfoot stole your wife. It makes me sad to see it, the look of disbelief in each person's eye. Trudy's disappearance makes me sad, too, and I'm sick in my heart about where she may be and how he's treating her, what they do all day, if she's getting enough to eat. I believe he's being good to her—I mean I feel it—and I'm going to keep hoping to see her again, but it is my belief that I probably won't.

In the two and a half years we were married, I often had the feeling that I would come home from the track and something would be funny. Oh, she'd say things: *One of these days I'm not going to be here when you get home*, things like that, things like everybody says. How stupid of me not to see them as omens. When I'd get out of bed in the early afternoon, I'd stand right here at this sink and I could see her working in her garden in her cut-off Levis and bikini top, weeding, planting, watering. I mean it was obvious. I was too busy thinking about the races, weighing the odds, checking the jockey roster to see what I now know: he was watching her too. He's probably been watching her all summer.

So, in a way it was my fault. But what could I have done? Bigfoot steals your wife. I mean: even if you're home, it's going to be a mess. He's big and not well trained.

When I came home it was about eleven-thirty. The lights were on, which really wasn't anything new, but in the ordinary mess of the place, there was a little difference, signs of a struggle. There was a spilled Dr. Pepper on the counter and the fridge was open. But there was something else, something that made me sick. The smell. The smell of Bigfoot. It was hideous. It was . . . the guy is not clean.

Half of Trudy's clothes are gone, not all of them, and there is no note. Well, I know what it is. It's just about midnight there in the kitchen which smells like some part of hell. I close the fridge door. It's the saddest thing I've ever done. There's a picture of Trudy and me leaning against her Toyota taped to the fridge door. It was taken last summer. There's Trudy in her bikini top, her belly brown as a bean. She looks like a kid. She was a kid I guess, twenty-six. The two times she went to the track with me everybody looked at me like how'd I rate her. But she didn't really care for the races. She cared about her garden and Chinese cooking and Buster, her collie, who I guess Bigfoot stole too. Or ate. Buster isn't in the picture, he was nagging my nephew Chuck who took the photo. Anyway I close the fridge door and it's like part of my life closed. Bigfoot steals your wife and you're in for some changes.

You come home from the track having missed the Daily Double by a neck, and when you enter the home you are paying for and in which you and your wife and your wife's collie live, and your wife and her collie are gone as is some of her clothing, there is nothing to believe. Bigfoot stole her. It's a fact. What should I do, ignore it? Chuck came down and said something like well if Bigfoot stole her why'd they take the Celica? Christ, what a cynic! Have you ever read anything about Bigfoot not being able to drive? He'd be cramped in there, but I'm sure he could manage.

I don't really care if people believe me or not. Would that change anything? Would that bring Trudy back here? Pull the weeds in her garden?

As I think about it, no one believes anything anymore. Give me one example of someone *believing* one thing. If dare you. After that we get into this credibility thing. No one believes me. I myself can't believe all the suspicion and cynicism there is in today's world. Even at the races, some character next to me will poke over at my tip sheet and ask me if I believe that stuff. If I believe? What is there to believe? The horse's name? What he did the last time out? And I look back at this guy, too cheap to go two bucks on the program, and I say: it's history. It is historical fact here. Believe. Huh. Here's a fact: I believe everything.

Credibility.

When I was thirteen years old, my mother's trailer was washed away in the flooding waters of the Harley River and swept thirty-one miles, ending right side up and nearly dead level just outside Mercy, in fact in the old weed-eaten parking lot for the abandoned potash plant. I know this to be true because I was inside the trailer the whole time with my pal, Nuggy Reinecker, who found the experience more life-changing than I did.

Now who's going to believe this story? I mean, besides me, because I was there. People are going to say, come on, thirty-one miles? Don't you mean thirty-one feet?

We had gone in out of the rain after school to check out a magazine that belonged to my mother's boyfriend. It was a copy of *Dude*, and there was a fold-out page I will never forget of a girl lying on the beach on her back. It was a color photograph. The girl was a little pale, I mean, this was probably her first day out in the sun, and she had no clothing on. So it was good, but what made it great was that they had made her a little bathing suit out of sand. Somebody had spilled a little sand just right, here and there, and the sand was this incredible gold color, and it made her look so absolutely naked it wanted to put your eyes out.

Nuggy and I knew there was flood danger in Griggs; we'd had a flood every year almost and it had been raining for five days on and off, but when the trailer bucked the first time, we thought it was my mother come home to catch us in the dirty book. Nuggy shoved the magazine under the bed and I ran out to check the door. It only took me a second and I hollered back *Hey no sweat, no one's here*, but by that time I returned to see what other poses they'd had this beautiful woman commit, Nuggy already had his pants to his ankles and was involved in what we knew was a sin.

If it hadn't been the timing of the first wave with this act of his, Nuggy might have gone on to live what the rest of us call a normal life. But the Harley had crested and the head wave, which they estimated to be three feet minimum, unmoored the trailer with a push that knocked me over the sofa, and threw Nuggy, already entangled in his trousers, clear across the bedroom.

I watched the village of Griggs as we sailed through. Some of the village, the Exxon station, part of it at least, and the carwash, which folded up right away, tried to come along with us, and I saw the front of Painters' Mercantile, the old porch and signboard, on and off all day.

You can believe this: it was not a smooth ride. We'd rip along for ten seconds, dropping and growling over rocks, and rumbling over tree stumps, and then wham! the front end of the trailer would lodge against a rock or something that could stop it, and whoa! we'd wheel around sharp as a carnival ride, worse really, because the furniture would be thrown against the far side and us with it, sometimes we'd end up in a chair and sometimes the chair would sit on us. My mother had about four thousand knickknacks in five big box shelves, and they gave us trouble for the first two or three miles, flying by like artillery, left, right, some small glass snail hits you in the face, later in the back, but that stuff all finally settled in the foot and then two feet of water which we took on.

We only slowed down once and it was the worst. In the railroad flats I thought we had stopped and I let go of the door I was hugging and tried to stand up and then swish, another rush sent us right along. We rammed along all day it seemed, but when we finally washed up in Mercy and the sheriff's cousin pulled open the door and got swept back to his car by water and quite a few of those knickknacks, just over an hour had passed. We had averaged, they figured later, about thirty-two miles an hour, reaching speeds of up to fifty at Lime Falls and the Willows. I was okay and walked out bruised and well washed, but when the sheriff's cousin pulled Nuggy out, he looked genuinely hurt.

"For godsakes," I remember the sheriff's cousin saying, "The damn flood knocked this boy's pants off!" But Nuggy wasn't talking. In fact, he never hardly talked to me again in the two years he stayed at the Regional School. I heard later, and I believe it, that he joined the monastery over in Malcolm County.

My mother, because she didn't have the funds to haul our rig back to Griggs, worried for a while, but then the mayor arranged to let us stay out where we were. So after my long ride in a trailer down the flooded Harley river with my friend Nuggy Reinecker, I grew up in a parking lot outside of Mercy, and to tell you the truth, it wasn't too bad, even though our trailer never did smell straight again.

Now you can believe all that. People are always saying: don't believe everything you read, or everything you hear. And I'm here to tell you. Believe it. Everything. Everything you read. Everything you hear. Believe your eyes. Your ears. Believe the small hairs on the back of your neck. Believe all of history, and all of the versions of history, and all the predictions for the future. Believe every weather forecast. Believe in God, the afterlife, unicorns, showers on Tuesday. Everything has happened. Everything is possible.

I come home from the track to find the cupboard bare. Trudy is not home. The place smells funny: hairy. It's a fact and I know it as a fact: Bigfoot has been in my house.

Bigfoot stole *my* wife.

She's gone.

Believe it.

I gotta believe it.

I am Bigfoot

That's fine. I'm ready.

I am Bigfoot. The Bigfoot. You've been hearing about me for some time now, seeing artists' renderings, and perhaps a phony photograph or two. I should say right here that an artist's rendering is one thing, but some trumped-up photograph is entirely another. The one that really makes me sick purports to show me standing in a stream in Northern California. Let me tell you something: Bigfoot never gets his feet wet. And I've only been to Northern California once, long enough to check out Redding and Eureka, both too quiet for the kind of guy I am.

Anyway, all week long, people (the people I contacted) have been wondering why I finally have gone public. A couple thought it was because I was angry at that last headline, remember: "Jackie O. Slays Bigfoot." No, I'm not angry. You can't go around and correct everybody who slanders you. (Hey, I'm not dead, and I only saw Jacqueline Onassis once, at about four hundred yards. She was on a horse.) And as for libel, what should I do, go up to Rockefeller Center and hire a lawyer? Please. Spare me. You can quote me on this: Bigfoot is not interested in legal action.

"Then, why?" they say. "Why climb out of the woods and go through the trouble of 'meeting the press,' so to speak?" (Well, first of all, I don't live in the woods *year round*, which is a popular misconception of my lifestyle. Sure, I like the woods, but I need action too. I've had some of my happiest times in the median of the Baltimore Belt-route, the orchards of Arizona and Florida, and I spent nearly five years in the corn country just outside St. Louis. So, it's not just the woods, okay?)

Why I came forward at this time concerns the truest thing I ever read about myself in the papers. The headline read "Bigfoot Stole My Wife," and it was right on the money. But beneath it was the real story: "Anguished Husband's Cry." Now I read the article, every word. Twice. It was poorly written, but it was all true. I stole the guy's wife. She wasn't the first and she wasn't the last. But when I went back and read that "anguished husband," it got me a little. I've been, as you probably have read, in all fifty states and eleven foreign countries. (I have never been to Tibet, in case you're wondering. That is some other guy, maybe the same one who was crossing that stream in Northern California.) *And*, in each place I've been, there's a woman. Come on, who is surprised by that? I don't always steal them, in fact, I never *steal* them, but I do *call them away,* and they come with me. I know my powers and I use my powers. And when I call a woman, she comes.

So, here I am. It's kind of a confession, I guess; kind of a warning. I've been around; I've been all over the world (except Tibet! I don't know if that guy is interested in women or not.). And I've seen thousands of women standing at their kitchen windows, their stare in the mid-afternoon goes a thousand miles; I've seen thousands of women, dressed to the nines, strolling the cosmetic counters in Saks and I. Magnin, wondering why their lives aren't like movies; thousands of women shuffling in the soft twilight of malls, headed for the Orange Julius stand, not really there, just biding time until things get lovely.

And things get lovely when I call. I cannot count them all, I cannot list the things these women are doing while their husbands are out there in another world, but one by one I'm meeting them on my terms. I am Bigfoot. I am not from Tibet. I go from village to town to city to village. At present, I am watching your wife. That's why I am here tonight. To tell you, fairly, man to man, I suppose, I am watching your wife and I know for a fact, that when I call, she'll come.

ANGELA CARTER

The Quilt Maker

One theory is, we make our destinies like blind men chucking paint at a wall; we never understand nor even see the marks we leave behind us. But not too much of the grandly accidental abstract expressionist about *my* life, I trust; oh, no. I always try to live on the best possible terms with my unconscious and let my right hand know what my left is doing and, fresh every morning, scrutinise my dreams. Abandon, therefore, or rather, deconstruct the blind-action painter metaphor; take it apart, formalise it, put it back together again, strive for something a touch more hard-edged, intentional, altogether less arty, for I do believe we all have the right to choose.

In patchwork, a neglected household art neglected, obviously, because my sex excelled in it—well, there you are; that's the way it's been, isn't it? Not that I have anything against fine art, mind; nevertheless, it took a hundred years for fine artists to catch up with the kind of brilliant abstraction that any ordinary housewife used to be able to put together in only a year, five years, ten years, without making a song and dance about it.

However, in patchwork, an infinitely flexible yet harmonious overall design is kept in the head and worked out in whatever material happens to turn up in the ragbag: party frocks, sackcloth, pieces of wedding-dress, of shroud, of bandage, dress shirts etc. Things that have been worn out or torn, remnants, bits and pieces left over from making blouses. One may appliqué upon one's patchwork birds, fruit and flowers that have been clipped out of glazed chintz left over from covering armchairs or making curtains, and do all manner of things with this and that.

The final design is indeed modified by the availability of materials; but not, necessarily, much.

For the paper patterns from which she snipped out regular rectangles and hexagons of cloth, the thrifty housewife often used up old love letters.

With all patchwork, you must start in the middle and work outward, even on the kind they call 'crazy patchwork,' which is made by featherstitching together arbitrary shapes scissored out at the maker's whim.

Patience is a great quality in the maker of patchwork.

The more I think about it, the more I like this metaphor. You can really make this image work for its living; it synthesises perfectly both the miscellany of experience and the use we make of it.

Born and bred as I was in the Protestant north working-class tradition, I am also pleased with the metaphor's overtones of thrift and hard work.

Patchwork. Good.

Somewhere along my thirtieth year to heaven—a decade ago now I was in the Greyhound Bus Station in Houston, Texas, with a man I was then married to. He gave me an American coin of small denomination (he used to carry about all our money for us because he did not trust me with it). Individual compartments in a large vending machine in this bus station contained various cellophane-wrapped sandwiches, biscuits and candy bars. There was a compartment with two peaches in it, rough-cheeked Dixie Reds that looked like Victorian pincushions. One peach was big. The other peach was small. I conscientiously selected the smaller peach.

'Why did you do that?' asked the man to whom I was married.

'Somebody else might want the big peach,' I said,

'What's that to you?' he said.

I date my moral deterioration from this point.

No; honestly. Don't you see, from this peach story, how I was brought up? It wasn't—truly it wasn't—that I didn't think I deserved the big peach. Far from it. What it was, was that all my basic training, all my internalised values, told me to leave the big peach there for somebody who wanted it more than I did.

Wanted it; desire, more imperious by far than need. I had the greatest respect for the desires of other people, although, at that time, my own desires remained a mystery to me. Age has not clarified them except on matters of the flesh, in which now I know very well what I want; and that's quite enough of that, thank you. If you're looking for true confessions of that type, take your business to another shop. Thank you.

The point of this story is, if the man who was then my husband hadn't told me I was a fool to take the little peach, then I would never have left him because, in truth, he was, in a manner of speaking, always the little peach to me.

Formerly, I had been a lavish peach thief, but I learned to take the small one because I had never been punished, as follows:

Canned fruit was a very big deal in my social class when I was a kid and during the Age of Austerity, food-rationing and so on. Sunday teatime; guests; a glass bowl of canned peach slices on the table. Everybody gossiping and milling about and, by the time my mother put the teapot on the table, I had surreptitiously contrived to put away a good third of those peaches, thieving them out of the glass bowl with my crooked forepaw the way a cat catches goldfish. I would have been shall we say, for the sake of symmetry—ten years old; and chubby.

My mother caught me licking my sticky fingers and laughed and said I'd already had my share and wouldn't get any more, but when she filled the dishes up, I got just as much as anybody else.

I hope you understand, therefore, how, by the time two more decades had rolled away, it was perfectly natural for me to take the little peach; had I not always been loved enough to feel I had some to spare? What a dangerous state of mind I was in, then!

As any fool could have told him, my ex-husband is much happier with his new wife; as for me, there then ensued ten years of grab, grab, grab didn't there, to make up for lost time.

Until it is like crashing a soft barrier, this collision of my internal calendar, on which dates melt like fudge, with the tender inexorability of time of which I am not, quite, yet, the ruins (although my skin fits less well than it did, my gums recede apace, I crumple like chiffon in the thigh). Forty.

The significance, the real significance, of the age of forty is that you are, along the allotted span, nearer to death than to birth. Along the lifeline I am now past the halfway mark. But, indeed, are we not ever, in some sense, past that halfway mark, because we know when we were born but we do not know . . .

So, having knocked about the four corners of the world awhile, the ex-peach thief came back to London, to the familiar seclusion of privet hedges and soiled lace curtains in the windows of tall, narrow terraces. Those streets that always seem to be sleeping, the secrecy of perpetual Sunday afternoons; and in the long, brick-walled back gardens, where the little town foxes who subsist off mice and garbage bark at night, there will be the soft pounce, sometimes, of an owl. The city is a thin layer on top of a wilderness that pokes through the paving stones, here and there, in tufts of grass and ragwort. Wood doves with mucky pink bosoms croon in the old trees at the bottom of the garden; we double-bar the door against burglars, but that's nothing new.

Next-door's cherry is coming out again. It's April's quick-change act: one day, bare; the next dripping its curds of bloom.

One day, once, sometime after the incident with the little peach, when I had put two oceans and a continent between myself and my ex-husband, while I was earning a Sadie Thompsonesque living as a barmaid in the Orient, I found myself, on a free weekend, riding through a flowering grove on the other side of the world with a young man who said: 'Me Butterfly, you Pinkerton.' And, though I denied it hotly at the time, so it proved, except, when I went away, it was for good. I never returned with an American friend, grant me sufficient good taste.

A small, moist, green wind blew the petals of the scattering cherry blossom through the open windows of the stopping train. They brushed his forehead and caught on his eyelashes and shook off on to the slatted wooden seats; we might have been a wedding party, except that we were pelted, not with confetti, but with the imagery of the beauty, the fragility, the fleetingness of the human condition.

'The blossoms always fall,' he said.

'Next year, they'll come again,' I said comfortably; I was a stranger here, I was not attuned to the sensibility, I believed that life was for living not for regret.

'What's that to me?' he said.

You used to say you would never forget me. That made me feel like the cherry blossom, here today and gone tomorrow; it is not the kind of thing one says to a person with whom one proposes to spend the rest of one's life, after all. And, after all that, for three hundred and fifty-two in each leap year, I never think of you, sometimes. I cast the image into the past, like a fishing line, and up it comes with a gold mask on the hook, a mask with real tears at the ends of its eyes, but tears which are no longer anybody's tears.

Time has drifted over your face.

The cherry tree in next-door's garden is forty feet high, tall as the house, and it has survived many years of neglect. In fact, it has not one but two tricks up its arboreal sleeve; each trick involves three sets of transformations and these it performs regularly as clockwork each year, the first in early, the second in late spring. Thus:

one day, in April, sticks; the day after, flowers; the third day, leaves.

Then—through May and early June, the cherries form and ripen until, one fine day, they are rosy and the birds come, the tree turns into a busy tower of birds admired by a tranced circle of cats below. (We are a neighbourhood rich in cats.) The day after, the tree bears nothing but cherry pits picked perfectly clean by quick, clever beaks, a stone tree.

The cherry is the principal monument of Letty's wild garden. How wonderfully unattended her garden grows all the soft months of the year, from April through September! Dandelions come before the swallow does and languorously blow away in drifts of fuzzy seed. Then up sprouts a long bolster of creeping buttercups. After that, bindweed distributes its white cornets everywhere, it climbs over everything in Letty's garden, it swarms up the concrete post that sustains the clothesline on which the lady who lives in the flat above Letty hangs her underclothes out to dry, by means of a pulley from her upstairs kitchen window. She never goes in to the garden. She and Letty have not been on speaking terms for twenty years.

I don't know why Letty and the lady upstairs fell out twenty years ago when the latter was younger than I, but Letty already an old woman. Now Letty is almost blind and almost deaf but, all the same, enjoys, I think, the changing colours of this disorder, the kaleidoscope of the seasons variegating the garden that neither she nor her late brother have touched since the war, perhaps for some now forgotten reason, perhaps for no reason.

Letty lives in the basement with her cat.

Correction. Used to live.

Oh, the salty realism with which the Middle Ages put skeletons on gravestones, with the motto: 'As I am now, so ye will be!' The birds will come and peck us bare.

I heard a dreadful wailing coming through the wall in the middle of the night. It could have been either of them, Letty or the lady upstairs, pissed out of their minds, perhaps, letting it all hang out, shrieking and howling, alone, driven demented by the heavy anonymous London silence of the fox-haunted night. Put my ear nervously to the wall to seek the source of the sound. 'Help!' said Letty in the basement. The cow that lives upstairs later claimed she never heard a cheep, tucked up under the eaves in dreamland sleep while I leaned on the doorbell for twenty minutes, seeking to rouse her. Letty went on calling 'Help!' Then I telephoned the police, who came flashing lights, wailing sirens, and double-parked dramatically, leaping out of the car, leaving the doors swinging; emergency call.

But they were wonderful. Wonderful. (We're not black, any of us, of course.) First, they tried the basement door, but it was bolted on the inside as a precaution against burglars. Then they tried to force the front door, but it wouldn't budge, so they smashed the glass in the front door and unfastened the catch from the inside. But Letty for fear of burglars, had locked herself securely in her basement bedroom, and her voice floated up the stairs: 'Help!'

So they battered her bedroom door open too, splintering the jamb, making a terrible mess. The cow upstairs, mind, sleeping sweetly throughout, or so she later claimed. Letty had fallen out of bed, bringing the bedclothes with her, knotting herself up in blankets, in a grey sheet, an old patchwork bedcover lightly streaked at one edge with dried shit, and she hadn't been able to pick herself up again, had lain in a helpless tangle on the floor calling for help until the coppers came and scooped her up and tucked her in and made all cosy. She wasn't surprised to see the police; hadn't she been calling: 'Help'? Hadn't help come?

'How old are you, love,' the coppers said. Deaf as she is, she heard the question, the geriatric's customary trigger. 'Eighty,' she said. Her age is the last thing left to be proud of. (See how, with age, one defines oneself by age, as one did in childhood.)

Think of a number. Ten. Double it. Twenty. Add ten again. Thirty. And again. Forty. Double that. Eighty. If you reverse this image, you obtain something like those Russian wooden dolls, in which big babushka contains a middling babushka who contains a small babushka who contains a tiny babushka and so on *ad infinitum.*

But I am further away from the child I was, the child who stole the peaches, than I am from Letty. For one thing, the peach thief was a plump brunette; I am a skinny redhead.

Henna. I have had red hair for twenty years. (When Letty had already passed through middle age.) I first dyed my hair red when I was twenty. I freshly henna'd my hair yesterday.

Henna is a dried herb sold in the form of a scum-green-coloured powder. You pour this powder into a bowl and add boiling water; you mix the powder into a paste using, say, the handle of a wooden spoon. (It is best not to let henna touch metal, or so they say.) This henna paste is no longer greyish, but now a dark vivid green, as if the hot water had revived the real colour of the living leaf, and it smells deliciously of spinach. You also add the juice of a half a lemon; this is supposed to 'fix' the final colour. Then you rub this hot, stiff paste into the roots of your hair.

(However did they first think of it?)

You're supposed to wear rubber gloves for this part of the process, but I can never be bothered to do that, so, for the first few days after I have refreshed my henna, my fingertips are as if heavily nicotine-stained. Once the green mud has been thickly applied to the hair, you wrap it in an impermeable substance—a polythene bag, or kitchen foil and leave it to cook. For one hour: auburn highlights. For three hours: a sort of vague russet halo around the head. Six hours: red as fire.

Mind you, henna from different *pays d'origines* has different effects—Persian henna, Egyptian henna, Pakistani henna, all these produce different tones of red, from that brick red usually associated with the idea of henna to a dark, burning, courtesan plum or cockatoo scarlet. I am a connoisseur of henna, by now, 'an unpretentious henna from the southern slope', that kind of thing. I've been every redhead in the book. But people think I am naturally redheaded and even make certain tempestuous allowances for me, as they did for Rita Hayworth, who purchased red hair at the same mythopoeic counter where Marilyn Monroe acquired her fatal fairness. Perhaps I first started dyeing my hair in order to acquire the privileged irrationality of redheads. Some men say they adore redheads. These men usually have very interesting psychosexual problems and shouldn't be let out without their mothers.

When I combed Letty's hair next morning, to get her ready for the ambulance, I saw telltale scales of henna'd dandruff lying along her scalp, although her hair itself is now a vague salt and pepper colour and, I hazard, has not been washed since about the time I was making the peach decision in the Houston, Texas, bus station. At that time, I had appropriately fruity—tangerine-coloured—hair in, I recall, a crewcut as brutal as that of Joan of Arc at the stake such as we daren't risk now, oh, no. Now we need shadows, my vain face and I; I wear my hair down to my shoulders now. At the moment, henna produces a reddish-gold tinge on me. That is because I am going grey.

Because the effect of henna is also modified by the real colour of the hair beneath. This is what it does to white hair:

In Turkey, in a small country town with a line of poplar trees along the horizon and a dirt-floored square, chickens, motorbikes, apricot sellers, and donkeys, a woman was haggling for those sesame-seed-coated bracelets of bread you can wear on your arm. From the back, she was small and slender; she was wearing loose, dark-blue trousers in a peasant print and a scarf wound round her head, but from beneath this scarf there fell the most wonderful long, thick, Rapunzel-like plait of golden hair. Pure gold; gold as a wedding ring. This single plait fell almost to her feet and was as thick as my two arms held together. I waited impatiently to see the face of this fairy-tale creature.

Stringing her breads on her wrist, she turned; and she was old.

'What a life,' said Letty, as I combed her hair.

Of Letty's life I know nothing. I know one or two things about her: how long she has lived in this basement—since before I was born, how she used to live with an older brother, who looked after her, an *older* brother. That he, last November, fell off a bus, what they call a 'platform accident', fell off the platform of a moving bus when it slowed for the stop at the bottom of the road and, falling, irreparably cracked his head on a kerbstone.

Last November, just before the platform accident, her brother came knocking at our door to see if we could help him with a light that did not work. The light in their flat did not work because the cable had rotted away. The landlord promised to send an electrician but the electrician never came. Letty and her brother used to pay two pounds fifty pence a week rent. From the landlord's point of view, this was not an economic rent; it would not cover his expenses on the house, rates etc. From the point of view of Letty and her late brother, this was not an economic rent, either; because they could not afford it.

Correction: Letty and her brother could not afford it because he was too proud to allow the household to avail itself of the services of the caring professions, social workers and so on. After her brother died, the caring professions visited Letty *en masse* and now her financial position is easier, her rent is paid for her.

Correction: *was* paid for her.

We know her name is Letty because she was banging out blindly in the dark kitchen as we/he looked at the fuse box and her brother said fretfully: 'Letty, give over!'

What Letty once saw and heard before the fallible senses betrayed her into a world of halftones and muted sounds is unknown to me. What she touched, what moved her, are mysteries to me. She is Atlantis to me. How she earned her living, why she and her brother came here first, all the real bricks and mortar of her life have collapsed into a rubble of forgotten past.

I cannot guess what were or are her desires.

She was softly fretful herself, she said: 'They're not going to take me away, are they?' Well, they won't let her stay here on her own, will they, not now she has proved that she can't be trusted to lie still in her own bed without tumbling out arse over tip in a trap of blankets, incapable of righting herself. After I combed her hair, when I brought her some tea, she asked me to fetch her porcelain teeth from a saucer on the dressing table, so that she could eat the biscuit. 'Sorry about that,' she said. She asked me who the person standing beside me was; it was my own reflection in the dressing-table mirror, but, all the same, oh, yes, she was in perfectly sound mind, if you stretch the definition of 'sound' only a very little. One must make allowances. One will do so for oneself.

She needed to sit up to drink tea, I lifted her. She was so frail it was like picking up a wicker basket with nothing inside it; I braced myself for a burden and there was none, she was as light as if her bones were filled with air like the bones of birds. I felt she needed weights, to keep her from floating up to the ceiling following her airy voice. Faint odour of the lion house in the bedroom and it was freezing cold, although, outside, a good deal of April sunshine and the first white flakes of cherry blossom shaking loose from the tight buds.

Letty's cat came and sat on the end of the bed. 'Hello, pussy,' said Letty.

One of those ill-kempt balls of fluff old ladies keep, this cat looks as if he's unravelling, its black fur has rusted and faded at the same time, but some cats are naturals for the caring professions—they will give you mute company long after anyone else has stopped tolerating your babbling, they don't judge, don't give a damn if you wet the bed and, when the eyesight fades, freely offer themselves for the consolation of still sentient fingertips. He kneads the shit-stained quilt with his paws and purrs.

The cow upstairs came down at last and denied all knowledge of last night's rumpus; she claimed she had slept so soundly she didn't hear the doorbell or the forced entry. She must have passed out or something, or else wasn't there at all but out on the town with her man friend. Or, her man friend was here with her *all the time* and she didn't want anybody to know so kept her head down. We see her man friend once or twice a week as he arrives crabwise to her door with the furtiveness of the adulterer. The cow upstairs is fiftyish, as well preserved as if she'd sprayed herself all over with the hair lacquer that keeps her bright brown curls in tight discipline.

No love lost between her and Letty. 'What a health hazard! What a fire hazard!' Letty, downstairs, dreamily hallucinating in the icy basement as the cow upstairs watches me sweep up the broken glass on the hall floor. 'She oughtn't to be left. She ought to be in a home.' The final clincher: 'For her *own good.*'

Letty dreamily apostrophised the cat; they don't let cats into any old people's homes that I know of.

Then the social worker came; and the doctor; and, out of nowhere, a great-niece, probably summoned by the social worker, a great-niece in her late twenties with a great-great-niece clutching a teddy bear. Letty is pleased to see the great-great-niece, and this child is the first crack that appears in the picture that I'd built up of Letty's secluded, lonely old age. We hadn't realised there were kin; indeed, the great-niece puts us in our place good and proper. 'It's up to family now,' she said, so we curtsy and retreat, and this great-niece is sharp as a tack, busy as a bee, proprietorial yet tender with the old lady. 'Letty, what have you got up to now?' Warding us outsiders off; perhaps she is ashamed of the shit-stained quilt, the plastic bucket of piss beside Letty's bed.

As they were packing Letty's things in an airline bag the great-niece brought, the landlord—by a curious stroke of fate—chose this very day to collect Letty's rent and perked up no end, stroking his well-shaven chin, to hear the cow upstairs go on and on about how Letty could no longer cope, how she endangered property and life on the premises by forcing men to come and break down doors.

What a life.

Then the ambulance came.

Letty is going to spend a few days in hospital.

This street is, as estate agents say, rapidly improving; the lace curtains are coming down, the round paper lampshades going up like white balloons in each front room. The landlord had promised the cow upstairs five thousand pounds in her hand to move out after Letty goes, so that he can renovate the house and sell it with vacant possession for a tremendous profit.

We live in hard-nosed times.

The still unravished bride, the cherry tree, takes flowering possession of the wild garden; the ex-peach thief contemplates the prospect of ripe fruit the birds will eat, not I. Curious euphemism 'to go', meaning death, to depart on a journey.

Somewhere along another year to heaven, I elicited the following laborious explanation of male sexual response, which is the other side of the moon, the absolute mystery, the one thing I can never know.

'You put it in, which isn't boring. Then you rock backwards and forwards. That can get quite boring. Then you come. That's not boring.'

For 'you', read 'him'.

'You come; or as we Japanese say, go.'

Just so. '*Ikimasu*,' to go. The Japanese orgasmic departure renders the English orgasmic arrival, as if the event were reflected in the mirror and the significance of it altogether different—whatever significance it may have, that is. Desire disappears in its fulfilment, which is cold comfort for hot blood and the reason why there is no such thing as a happy ending.

Besides all this, Japanese puts all its verbs at the ends of its sentences, which helps to confuse the foreigner all the more, so it seemed to me they themselves never quite knew what they were saying half the time.

'Everything here is arsy-varsy.'

'No. Where you are is arsy-varsy.'

And never the twain shall meet. He loved to be bored; don't think he was contemptuously dismissive of the element of boredom inherent in sexual activity. He adored and venerated boredom. He said that dogs, for example, were never bored, nor birds, so, obviously, the capacity that distinguished man from the other higher mammals, from the scaled and feathered things, was that of boredom. The more bored one was, the more one expressed one's humanity.

He liked redheads. 'Europeans are so colourful,' he said.

He was a tricky bugger, that one, a Big Peach, all right; face of Gérard Philipe, soul of Nechaev. I grabbed, grabbed and grabbed and, since I did not have much experience in grabbing, often bit off more than I could chew. Exemplary fate of the plump peach-thief; someone refuses to be assimilated. Once a year, when I look at Letty's cherry tree in flower, I put the image to work, I see the petals fall on a face that looked as if it had been hammered out of gold, like the mask of Agamemnon which Schliemann found at Troy.

The mask turns into a shining carp and flips off the hook at the end of the fishing line. The one that got away.

Let me not romanticise you too much. Because what would I do if you *did* resurrect yourself? Came knocking at my door in all your foul, cool, chic of designer jeans and leather blouson and your pocket stuffed with G.N.P., arriving somewhat late in the day to make an honest woman of me as you sometimes used to threaten that you might? 'When you're least expecting it . . .' God, I'm forty, now. Forty! I had you marked down for a Demon Lover; what if indeed you popped up out of the grave of the heart bright as a button with an American car purring outside waiting to whisk me away to where the lilies grow on the bottom of the sea? 'I am now married to a house carpenter,' as the girl in the song exclaimed hurriedly. But all the same, off she went with the lovely cloven-footed one. But I wouldn't. Not I.

And how very inappropriate too, the language of antique ballads in which to address one who knew best the international language of the jukebox. You'd have one of those Wurlitzer Cadillacs you liked, that you envied G.I.s for, all ready to humiliate me with; it would be bellowing out quadraphonic sound. The Everly Brothers. Jerry Lee Lewis. Early Presley. ('When I grow up,' you reveried, 'I'm going to Memphis to marry Presley.') You were altogether too much, you pure child of the late twentieth century, you person from the other side of the moon or mirror, and your hypothetical arrival is a catastrophe too terrifying to contemplate, even in the most plangent state of regret for one's youth.

I lead a quiet life in South London. I grind my coffee beans and drink my early cup to a spot of early baroque on the radio. I am now married to a house carpenter. Like the culture that created me, I am receding into the past at a rate of knots. Soon I'll need a whole row of footnotes if anybody under thirty-five is going to comprehend the least thing I say.

And yet . . . Going out into the back garden to pick rosemary to put inside a chicken, the daffodils in the uncut grass, enough blackbirds out to make a pie.

Letty's cat sits on Letty's windowsill. The blinds are drawn; the social worker drew them five days ago before she drove off in her little Fiat to the hospital, following Letty in the ambulance. I call to Letty's cat but he doesn't turn his head. His fluff has turned to spikes, he looks spiny as a horse-chestnut husk.

Letty is in hospital supping broth from a spouted cup and, for all my kind heart, of which I am so proud, my empathy and so on, I myself had not given Letty's companion another thought until today, going out to pick rosemary with which to stuff a roast for our greedy dinners.

I called him again. At the third call, he turned his head. His eyes looked as if milk had been poured into them. The garden wall too high to climb since now I am less limber than I was, I chucked half the contents of a guilty tin of cat food over. Come and get it.

Letty's cat never moved, only stared at me with its curtained eyes. And then all the fat, sleek cats from every garden up and down came jumping, leaping, creeping to the unexpected feast and gobbled all down, every crumb, quick as a wink. What a lesson for a giver of charity! At the conclusion of this heartless banquet at which I'd been the thoughtless host, the company of well-cared-for beasts stretched their swollen bellies in the sun and licked themselves, and then, at last, Letty's cat heaved up on its shaky legs and launched itself, plop on to the grass.

I thought, perhaps he got a belated whiff of cat food and came for his share, too late, all gone. The other cats ignored him. He staggered when he landed but soon righted himself. He took no interest at all in the stains of cat food, though. He managed a few doddering steps among the dandelions. Then I thought he might be going to chew on a few stems of medicinal grass; but he did not so much lower his head towards it as let his head drop, as if he had no strength left to lift it. His sides were caved-in under stiff, voluminous fur. He had not been taking care of himself. He peered vaguely around, swaying.

You could almost have believed, not that he was waiting for the person who always fed him to come and feed him again as usual, but that he was pining for Letty herself.

Then his hind legs began to shudder involuntarily. He so convulsed himself with shuddering that his hind legs jerked off the ground; he danced. He jerked and shuddered, shuddered and jerked, until at last he vomited up a small amount of white liquid. Then he pulled himself to his feet again and lurched back to the windowsill. With a gigantic effort, he dragged himself up.

Later on, somebody jumped over the wall, more sprightly than I and left a bowl of bread and milk. But the cat ignored that too. Next day, both were still there, untouched.

The day after that, only the bowl of sour sops, and cherry blossom petals drifting across the vacant windowsill.

Small sins of omission remind one of the greater sins of omission; at least sins of commission have the excuse of choice, of intention. However:

May. A blowy, bright-blue, bright-green morning; I go out on the front steps with a shifting plastic sack of garbage and what do I see but the social worker's red Fiat putter to a halt next door.

In the hospital they'd henna'd Letty. An octogenarian redhead, my big babushka who contains my forty, my thirty, my twenty, my ten years within her fragile basket of bones, she has returned, not in a humiliating ambulance, but on her own two feet that she sets down more firmly than she did. She has put on a little weight. She has a better colour, not only in her hair but in her cheeks.

The landlord, foiled.

Escorted by the social worker, the district nurse, the home help, the abrasive yet not ungentle niece, Letty is escorted down the unswept, grass-grown basement stairs into her own scarcely used front door that someone with a key has remembered to unbolt from inside for her return. Her new cockatoo crest—whoever henna'd her really understood henna—points this way and that way as she makes sure that nothing in the street has changed, even if she can see only large blocks of light and shadow, hear, not the shriking blackbirds, but only the twitch of the voices in her ear that shout: 'Carefully does it, Letty.'

'I can manage,' she said tetchily.

The door the policemen battered in closes upon her and her chattering entourage.

The window of the front room of the cow upstairs slams down, bang.

And what am I to make of that? I'd set it up so carefully, an enigmatic structure about evanescence and ageing and the mists of time, shadows lengthening, cherry blossom, forgetting, neglect, regret . . . the sadness, the sadness of it all. . .

But. Letty. Letty came home.

In the corner shop, the cow upstairs, mad as fire: 'They should have certified her'; the five grand the landlord promised her so that he could sell the house with vacant possession has blown away on the May wind that disintegrated the dandelion clocks. In Letty's garden now is the time for fierce yellow buttercups; the cherry blossom is over, no regrets.

I hope she is too old and too far gone to miss the cat.

Fat chance.

I hope she never wonders if the nice warm couple next door thought of feeding him.

But she has come home to die at her own apparently ample leisure in the comfort and privacy of her basement; she has exercised, has she not, her right to choose, she has turned all this into crazy patchwork.

Somewhere along my thirtieth year, I left a husband in a bus station in Houston, Texas, a town to which I have never returned, over a quarrel about a peach which, at the time, seemed to sum up the whole question of the rights of individuals within relationships, and, indeed, perhaps it did.

As you can tell from the colourful scraps of oriental brocade and Turkish homespun I have sewn into this bedcover, I then (call me Ishmael) wandered about for a while and sowed (or sewed) a wild oat or two into this useful domestic article, this product of thrift and imagination, with which I hope to cover myself in my old age to keep my brittle bones warm. (How cold it is in Letty's basement.)

But, okay, so I always said the blossom would come back again, but Letty's return from the clean white grave of the geriatric ward is *ridiculous*! And, furthermore, when I went out into the garden to pick a few tulips, there he is, on the other side of the brick wall, lolling voluptuously among the creeping buttercups, fat as butter himself—Letty's been feeding him up.

'I'm pleased to see *you*,' I said.

In a Japanese folk tale it would be the ghost of her cat, rusty and tactile as in life, the poor cat pining itself from death to life again to come to the back door at the sound of her voice. But we are in South London on a spring morning. Lorries fart and splutter along the Wandsworth Road. Capital Radio is braying from an upper window. An old cat, palpable as a second-hand fur coat, drowses among the buttercups.

We know when we were born but—

the times of our reprieves are equally random.

Shake it out and look at it again, the flowers, fruit and bright stain of henna, the Russian dolls, the wrinkling chiffon of the flesh, the old songs, the cat, the woman of eighty; the woman of forty, with dyed hair and most of her own teeth, who is *ma semblable, ma soeur*. Who now recedes into the deceptive privacy of a genre picture, a needlewoman, a quilt maker, a middle-aged woman sewing patchwork in a city garden, turning her face vigorously against the rocks and trees of the patient wilderness waiting round us.

The Little Knife

One Saturday in that last, interminable summer before his parents separated and the Washington Senators baseball team was expunged forever from the face of the earth, the Shapiros went to Nags Head, North Carolina, where Nathan, without planning to, perpetrated a great hoax. They drove down I-95, through the Commonwealth of Virginia, to a place called the Sandpiper—a ragged, charming oval of motel cottages painted white and green as the Atlantic, and managed by a kind, astonishingly fat old man named Colonel Larue, who smoked cherry cigars and would, if asked, play catch or keep-away. Outside his office, in the weedy gravel, stood an old red-and-radium-white Coke machine, which dispensed bottles from a vertical glass door that sighed when you opened it, and which reminded Nathan of the Automat his grandmother had taken him to once in New York City. The sight of the faded machine and of the whole Sandpiper—like that of the Automat—filled Nathan with a happy sadness, or, really, a sad happiness; he was not too young, at ten, to have developed a sense of nostalgia.

There were children in every cottage—with all manner of floats, pails, paddles, trucks, and flying objects—and his younger brother Ricky, to Nathan's envy, immediately fell in with a gang of piratical little boys with water pistols, who were always reproducing fart sounds and giggling chaotically when their mothers employed certain ordinary words such as "hot dog" and "rubber." The Shapiros went to the ocean every summer, and at the beginning of this trip, as on all those that had preceded it, Nathan and his brother got along better than they usually did, their mother broke out almost immediately in a feathery red heat rash, and their father lay pale and motionless in the sun, like a monument, and always forgot to take off his wristwatch when he went into the sea. Nathan had brought a stack of James Bond books and his colored pencils; there were board games—he and his father were in the middle of their Strat-O-Matic baseball playoffs—and miniature boxes of cereal; the family ate out every single night. But when they were halfway through the slow, dazzling week—which was as far as they were to get—Nathan began to experience an unfamiliar longing: He wanted to go home.

He awoke very early on Wednesday morning, went into the cottage's small kitchen, where the floor was sticky and the table rocked and trembled, and chose the last of the desirable cereals from the Variety pack, leaving for Ricky only those papery, sour brands with the scientific names—the sort that their grandparents liked. As he began to eat, Nathan heard, from the big bedroom down the hall, the unmistakable, increasingly familiar sound of his father burying his mother under a heap of scorn and ridicule. It was, oddly, a soft and pleading sound. Lately, the conversation and actions of Dr. Shapiro's family seemed to disappoint him terribly. His left hand was always flying up to smack his sad and outraged forehead, so hard that Nathan often thought he could hear his father's wedding ring crack against his skull. When they'd played their baseball game the day before—Nathan's Baltimore Bonfires against his father's Brooklyn Eagles—every decision Nathan made led to a disaster, and his father pointed out each unwise substitution and foolish attempt to steal in this new tone of miserable sarcasm, so that Nathan had spent the afternoon apologizing, and, finally, crying. Now he listened for his mother's voice, for the note of chastened shame.

The bedroom door slammed, and Mrs. Shapiro came out into the kitchen. She was in her bathrobe, a wild, sleepless smile on her face.

"Good morning, honey," she said, then hummed to herself as she boiled water and made a cup of instant coffee. Her spoon tinkled gaily against the cup.

"Where are you going, Mom?" said Nathan. She had taken up her coffee and was heading for the sliding glass door that led out of the kitchen and down to the beach.

"See you, honey," she sang.

"Mom!" said Nathan. He stood up—afraid, absurdly, that she might be leaving for good, because she seemed so happy. After a few seconds he heard her whistling, and he went to the door and pressed his face against the wire screen. His mother had a Disney whistle, melodious and full, like a Scotsman's as he walks across a meadow in a brilliant kilt. She paced briskly along the ramshackle slat-and-wire fence, back and forth through the beach grass, drinking from the huge white mug of coffee and whistling heartily into the breeze; her red hair rose from her head and trailed like a defiant banner. He watched her observe the sunrise—it was going to be a perfect, breezy day—then continued to watch as she set her coffee on the ground, removed her bathrobe, and, in her bathing suit, began to engage in a long series of yoga exercises—a new fad of hers—as though she were playing statues all alone. Nathan was soon lost, with the fervor of a young scientist, in contemplation of his pretty, whistling mother rolling around on the ground.

"Oh, how can she?" said Dr. Shapiro.

"Yes," said Nathan, gravely, before he blushed and whirled around to find his father, in pajamas, staring out at Mrs. Shapiro. His smile was angry and clenched, but in his eyes was the same look of bleak surprise, of betrayal, that had been there when Nathan took out Johnny Sain, a slugging pitcher, and the pinch-hitter, Enos Slaughter, immediately went down on strikes. There were a hundred new things that interested Nathan's mother—bonsai, the Zuni, yoga, real estate—and although Dr. Shapiro had always been a liberal, generous, encouraging man (as Nathan had heard his mother say to a friend), and had at first happily helped her to purchase the necessary manuals, supplies, and coffee-table books, lately each new fad seemed to come as a blow to him—a going astray, a false step.

"How can she?" he said again, shaking his big bearded head.

"She says it's really good for you," said Nathan.

His father smiled down on his son ruefully, and tapped him once on the head. Then he turned and went to the refrigerator, hitching up his pajama bottoms. They were the ones patterned with a blue stripe and red chevrons—the ones that Nathan always imagined were the sort worn by the awkward, doomed elephant in the Groucho Marx joke.

Later that day, as they made egg-salad sandwiches to carry down to the beach, Dr. and Mrs. Shapiro fought bitterly, for the fifth time since their arrival. In the cottage's kitchen was a knife—a small, new, foreign knife, which Mrs. Shapiro admired. As she used it to slice neat little horseshoes of celery, she praised it again. "Such a good little knife," she said. "Why don't you just take it?" said Dr. Shapiro. The air in the kitchen was suddenly full of sharp, caramel smoke, and Dr. Shapiro ran to unplug the toaster.

"That would be stealing," said Nathan's mother, ignoring her husband's motions of alarm and the fact that their lunch was on fire. "We are not taking this knife, Martin."

"Give it to me." Dr. Shapiro held out his hand, palm up.

"I'm not going to let you—make me—dishonest anymore!" said his mother. She seemed to struggle, at first, not to finish the sentence she had begun, but in the end she turned, put her face right up to his, and cried out boldly. After her outburst, both adults turned to look, with a simultaneity that was almost funny, at their sons. Nathan hadn't the faintest notion of what his mother was talking about.

"Don't steal, Dad," Ricky said.

"I only wanted it to extract the piece of toast," said their father. He was looking at their mother again. "God damn it." He turned and went out of the kitchen.

Her knuckles white around the handle of the knife, their mother freed the toast and began scraping the burnt surfaces into the sink. Because their father had said "God damn," Ricky wiggled his eyebrows and smiled at Nathan. At the slamming of the bedroom door, Nathan clambered up suddenly from the rickety kitchen table as though he had found an insect crawling on his leg.

"Kill it!" said Ricky. "What is it?"

"What is it?" said his mother. She scanned Nathan's body quickly, one hand half raised to swat.

"Nothing," said Nathan. He took off his glasses. "I'm going for a walk."

When he got to the edge of the water, he turned to look toward the Sandpiper. At that time in Nags Head there were few hotels and no condominiums, and it seemed to Nathan that their little ring of cottages stood alone, like Stonehenge, in the middle of a giant wasteland. He set off down the beach, watching his feet print and following the script left in the sand by the birds for which the motel was named. He passed a sand castle, then a heart drawn with a stick enclosing the names Jimmy and Beth. Sometimes his heels sank deeply into the sand, and he noticed the odd marks this would leave—a pair of wide dimples. He discovered that he could walk entirely on his heels, and his trail became two lines of big periods. If he took short steps, it looked as though a creature—a bird with two peg legs—had come to fish along the shore.

He lurched a long way in this fashion, watching his feet, and nearly forgot his parents' quarrel. But when at last he grew bored with walking on his heels and turned to go back, he saw that his mother and father had also decided to take a walk, and that they were, in fact, coming toward him—clasping hands, letting go, clasping hands again. Nathan ran to meet them, and they parted to let him walk between them. They all continued down the beach, stooping to pick up shells, glass, dead crabs, twine, and all the colored or smelly things that Nathan had failed to take note of before. At first his parents exclaimed with him over these discoveries, and his father took each striped seashell into his hands, to keep it safe, until there were two dozen and they jingled there like money. But after a while they seemed to lose interest, and Nathan found himself walking a few feet ahead of them, stooping alone, glumly dusting his toes with sand as he tried to eavesdrop on their careless and incomprehensible conversation.

"Never again," his mother said at last.

Dr. Shapiro let the shells fall. He rubbed his hands together and then stared at them as though waking from a dream in which he had been holding a fortune in gold. Straightening up so quickly that his head spun, Nathan let out a cry and pointed down at the sand beneath their feet, among the scattered shells. "Look at those weird tracks!" he cried.

They all looked down.

Speculation on the nature of the beast that went toeless down the shore went on for several minutes, and although Nathan was delighted at first, he soon began to feel embarrassed and, obscurely, frightened by the ease with which he had deceived his parents. His treachery was almost exposed when Ricky, carrying a long stick and wearing a riot of Magic Marker tattoos on his face and all down his arms, ran over to find out what was happening. The little boy immediately tipped back onto his heels, and would have taken a few steps like that had Nathan not grabbed him by the elbow and dragged him aside.

"Why do you have a dog on your face?" said Nathan.

"It's a jaguar," said Ricky.

Nathan bent to whisper into his brother's ear. "I'm tricking Mom and Dad," he said.

"Good," said Ricky.

"They think there's some kind of weird creature on the beach."

Ricky pushed Nathan away and then surveyed their mother and father, who were talking again, quietly, as though they were trying not to alarm their sons. "It can't be real," said Nathan's father.

Ricky's skin under the crude tattoos was tanned, his hair looked stiff and ragged from going unwashed and sea-tangled, and as he regarded their parents he held his skinny stick like a javelin at his side. "They're dumb," he said flatly.

Dr. Shapiro approached, stepping gingerly across the mysterious tracks, and then knelt beside his sons. His face was red, though not from the sun, and he seemed to have trouble looking directly at the boys. Nathan began to cry before his father even spoke.

"Boys," he said. He looked away, then back, and bit his lip. "I'm afraid—I'm sorry. We're going to go home. Your mom and I—don't feel very well. We don't seem to be well."

"No! No! It was Nathan!" said Ricky, laying down his spear and throwing himself into his father's arms. "It wasn't me. Make *him* go home."

Nathan, summoning up his courage, decided to admit that the curious trail of the crippled animal was his, and he said, "I'm responsible."

"Oh, no!" cried both his parents together, startling him. His mother rushed over and fell to her knees, and they took Nathan into their arms and said that it was never, never him, and they ruffled his hair with their fingers, as though he had done something they could love him for.

After they came back from dinner, the Shapiros, save Nathan, went down to the sea for a final, sad promenade. At the restaurant, Ricky had pleaded with his parents to stay through the end of the week—they had not even been to see the monument at Kitty Hawk, the Birthplace of Aviation. For Ricky's sake, Nathan had also tried to persuade them, but his heart wasn't in it—he himself wanted so badly to go home—and the four of them had all ended up crying and chewing their food in the brass-and-rope dining room of the Port O' Call; even Dr. Shapiro had shed a tear. They were going to leave that night. Nathan's family now stood, in sweatshirts, by the sliding glass door, his parents straining to adopt hard and impatient looks, and Nathan saw that they felt guilty about leaving him behind in the cottage.

"I'll pack my stuff," he said. "Just go." For a moment his stomach tightened with angry, secret glee as his mother and father, sighing, turned their backs on him and obeyed his small command. Then he was alone in the kitchen again, for the second time that day, and he wished that he had gone to look at the ocean, and he hated his parents, uncertainly, for leaving him behind. He got up and walked into the bedroom that he and Ricky had shared. There, in the twilight that fell in orange shafts through the open window, the tangle of their clothes and bedsheets, their scattered toys and books, the surfaces of the broken dresser and twin headboards seemed dusted with a film of radiant sand, as though the tide had washed across them and withdrawn, and the room was strewn with the seashells they had found. Nathan, after emptying his shoebox of baseball cards into his suitcase, went slowly around the room and harvested the shells with careful sweeps of his trembling hand. Bearing the shoebox back into the kitchen, he collected the few stray shards of salt-white and green beach glass that lay in a pile beside the electric can opener, and then added a hollow pink crab's leg in whose claw Ricky had fixed a colored pencil. When Nathan saw the little knife in the drainboard by the sink, he hesitated only a moment before dropping it into the box, where it swam, frozen, like a model shark in a museum diorama of life beneath the sea. Nathan chuckled. As clearly as if he were remembering them, he foresaw his mother's accusation, his father's enraged denial, and with an unhappy chuckle he foresaw, recalled, and fondly began to preserve all the discord for which, in his wildly preserving imagination, he was and would always be responsible.

PHILIP K. DICK

Beyond Lies the Wub

They had almost finished with the loading. Outside stood the Optus, his arms folded, his face sunk in gloom. Captain Franco walked leisurely down the gangplank, grinning.

"What's the matter?" he said. "You're getting paid for all this."

The Optus said nothing. He turned away, collecting his robes. The Captain put his boot on the hem of the robe.

"Just a minute. Don't go off. I'm not finished."

"Oh?" The Optus turned with dignity. "I am going back to the village." He looked toward the animals and birds being driven up the gangplank into the spaceship. "I must organize new hunts."

Franco lit a cigarette. "Why not? You people can go out into the veldt and track it all down again. But when we run halfway between Mars and Earth—"

The Optus went off, wordless. Franco joined the first mate at the bottom of the gangplank.

"How's it coming?" he asked. He looked at his watch. "We got a good bargain here."

The mate glanced at him sourly. "How do you explain that?"

"What's the matter with you? We need it more than they do."

"I'll see you later, Captain." The mate threaded his way up the plank, between the long-legged Martian go-birds, into the ship. Franco watched him disappear. He was just starting up after him, up the plank toward the port, when he saw *it*.

"My God!" He stood staring, his hands on his hips. Peterson was walking along the path, his face red, leading *it* by a string.

"I'm sorry, Captain," he said, tugging at the string. Franco walked toward him. "What is it?"

The wub stood sagging, its great body settling slowly. It was sitting down, its eyes half shut. A few flies buzzed about its flank, and it switched its tail.

It sat. There was slience.

"It's a wub," Peterson said. "I got it from a native for fifty cents. He said it was a very unusual animal. Very respected."

"This?" Franco poked the great sloping side of the wub. "It's a pig! A huge dirty pig!"

Philip K. Dick, "Beyond Lies the Wub" from Beyond Lies the Wub (Collected Stories: Volume 1). *Orion Publishing Group, 1988. Reprinted by permission of the author and the author's agents. Scovil Chichak Galen Literary Agency, Inc.*

"Yes sir, it's a pig. The natives call it a wub."

"A huge pig. It must weigh four hundred pounds." Franco grabbed a tuft of the rough hair. The wub gasped. Its eyes opened, small and moist. Then its great mouth twitched.

A tear rolled down the wub's cheek and splashed on the floor.

"Maybe it's good to eat," Peterson said nervously.

"We'll soon find out," Franco said.

The wub survived the takeoff, sound asleep in the hold of the ship. When they were out in space and everything was running smoothly, Captain Franco bade his men fetch the wub upstairs so that he might perceive what manner of beast it was.

The wub grunted and wheezed, squeezing up the passageway.

"Come on," Jones grated, pulling at the rope. The wub twisted, rubbing its skin off on the smooth chrome walls. It burst into the anteroom, tumbling down in a heap. The men leaped up.

"Good Lord," French said. "What is it?"

"Peterson says it's a wub," Jones said. "It belongs to him." He kicked at the wub. The wub stood up unsteadily, panting.

"What's the matter with it?" French came over. "Is it going to be sick?"

They watched. The wub rolled its eyes mournfully. It gazed around at the men.

"I think it's thirsty," Peterson said. He went to get some water. French shook his head.

"No wonder we had so much trouble taking off. I had to reset all my ballast calculations."

Peterson came back with the water. The wub began to lap gratefully, splashing the men.

Captain Franco appeared at the door.

"Let's have a look at it." He advanced, squinting critically. "You got this for fifty cents?"

"Yes, sir," Peterson said. "It eats almost anything. I fed it on grain and it liked that. And then potatoes, and mash, and scraps from the table, and milk. It seems to enjoy eating. After it eats it lies down and goes to sleep."

"I see," Captain Franco said. "Now, as to its taste. That's the real question. I doubt if there's much point in fattening it up any more. It seems fat enough to me already. Where's the cook? I want him here. I want to find out—"

The wub stopped lapping and looked up at the Captain.

"Really, Captain," the wub said. "I suggest we talk of other matters."

The room was silent.

"What was that?" Franco said. "Just now."

"The wub, sir," Peterson said. "It spoke."

They all looked at the wub.

"What did it say? What did it say?"

"It suggested we talk about other things."

Franco walked toward the wub. He went all around it, examining it from every side. Then he came back over and stood with the men.

"I wonder if there's a native inside it," he said thoughtfully. "Maybe we should open it up and have a look."

"Oh, goodness!" the wub cried. "Is that all you people can think of, killing and cutting?"

Franco clenched his fists. "Come out of there! Whoever you are, come out!"

Nothing stirred. The men stood together, their faces blank, staring at the wub. The wub swished its tail. It belched suddenly.

"I beg your pardon," the wub said.

"I don't think there's anyone in there," Jones said in a low voice. They all looked at each other.

The cook came in.

"You wanted me, Captain?" he said. "What's this thing?"

"This is a wub," Franco said. "It's to be eaten. Will you measure it and figure out—"

"I think we should have a talk," the wub said. "I'd like to discuss this with you, Captain, if I might. I can see that you and I do not agree on some basic issues."

The Captain took a long time to answer. The wub waited good-naturedly, licking the water from its jowls.

"Come into my office," the Captain said at last. He turned and walked out of the room. The wub rose and padded after him. The men watched it go out. They heard it climbing the stairs.

"I wonder what the outcome will be," the cook said. "Well, I'll be in the kitchen. Let me know as soon as you hear."

"Sure," Jones said. "Sure."

The wub eased itself down in the corner with a sigh. "You must forgive me," it said. "I'm afraid I'm addicted to various forms of relaxation. When one is as large as I—"

The Captain nodded impatiently. He sat down at his desk and folded his hands.

"All right," he said. "Let's get started. You're a wub? Is that correct?"

The wub shrugged. "I suppose so. That's what they call us, the natives, I mean. We have our own term."

"And you speak English? You've been in contact with Earthmen before?"

"No."

"Then how do you do it?"

"Speak English? Am I speaking English? I'm not conscious of speaking anything in particular. I examined your mind—"

"My mind?"

"I studied the contents, especially the semantic warehouse, as I refer to it—"

"I see," the Captain said. "Telepathy. Of course."

"We are a very old race," the wub said. "Very old and very ponderous. It is difficult for us to move around. You can appreciate anything so slow and heavy would be at the mercy of more agile forms of life. There was no use in our relying on physical defenses. How could we win? Too heavy to run, too soft to fight, too good-natured to hunt for game—"

"How do you live?"

"Plants. Vegetables. We can eat almost anything. We're very catholic. Tolerant, eclectic, catholic. We live and let live. That's how we've gotten along."

The wub eyed the Captain.

"And that's why I so violently objected to this business about having me boiled. I could see the image in your mind—most of me in the frozen food locker, some of me in the kettle, a bit for your pet cat—"

"So you read minds?" the Captain said. "How interesting. Anything else? I mean, what else can you do along those lines?"

"A few odds and ends," the wub said absently, staring around the room. "A nice apartment you have here, Captain. You keep it quite neat. I respect life-forms that are tidy. Some Martian birds are quite tidy. They throw things out of their nests and sweep them—"

"Indeed." The Captain nodded. "But to get back to the problem—"

"Quite so. You spoke of dining on me. The taste, I am told, is good. A little fatty, but tender. But how can any lasting contact be established between your people and mine if you resort to such barbaric attitudes? Eat me? Rather you should discuss questions with me, philosophy, the arts—"

The Captain stood up. "Philosophy. It might interest you to know that we will be hard put to find something to eat for the next month. An unfortunate spoilage—"

"I know." The wub nodded. "But wouldn't it be more in accord with your principles of democracy if we all drew straws, or something along that line? After all, democracy is to protect the minority from just such infringements. Now, if each of us casts one vote—"

The Captain walked to the door.

"Nuts to you," he said. He opened the door. He opened his mouth.

He stood frozen, his mouth wide, his eyes staring, his fingers still on the knob.

The wub watched him. Presently it padded out of the room, edging past the Captain. It went down the hall, deep in meditation.

The room was quiet.

"So you see," the wub said, "we have a common myth. Your mind contains many familiar myth symbols. Ishtar, Odysseus—"

Peterson sat silently, staring at the floor. He shifted in his chair.

"Go on," he said. "Please go on."

"I find in your Odysseus a figure common to the mythology of most self-conscious races. As I interpret it, Odysseus wanders as an individual aware of himself as such. This is the idea of separation, of separation from family and country. The process of individuation."

"But Odysseus returns to his home." Peterson looked out the port window, at the stars, endless stars, burning intently in the empty universe. "Finally he goes home."

"As must all creatures. The moment of separation is a temporary period, a brief journey of the soul. It begins, it ends. The wanderer returns to land and race. . . ."

The door opened. The wub stopped, turning its great head.

Captain Franco came into the room, the men behind him. They hesitated at the door.

"Are you all right?" French said.

"Do you mean me?" Peterson said, surprised. "Why me?"

Franco lowered his gun. "Come over here," he said to Peterson. "Get up and come here."

There was silence.

"Go ahead," the wub said. "It doesn't matter."

Peterson stood up. "What for?"

"It's an order."

Peterson walked to the door. French caught his arm.

"What's going on?" Peterson wrenched loose. "What's the matter with you?"

Captain Franco moved toward the wub. The wub looked up from where it lay in the corner, pressed against the wall.

"It is interesting," the wub said, "that you are obsessed with the idea of eating me. I wonder why."

"Get up," Franco said.

"If you wish." The wub rose, grunting. "Be patient. It is difficult for me." It stood, gasping, its tongue lolling foolishly.

"Shoot it now," French said.

"For God's sake!" Peterson exclaimed. Jones turned to him quickly, his eyes gray with fear.

"You didn't see him—like a statue, standing there, his mouth open. If we hadn't come down, he'd still be there."

"Who? The Captain?" Peterson stared around. "But he's all right now."

They looked at the wub, standing in the middle of the room, its great chest rising and falling.

"Come on," Franco said. "Out of the way."

The men pulled aside toward the door.

"You are quite afraid, aren't you?" the wub said. "Have I done anything to you? I am against the idea of hurting. All I have done is try to protect myself. Can you expect me to rush eagerly to my death? I am a sensible being like yourselves. I was curious to see your ship, learn about you. I suggested to the native—"

The gun jerked.

"See," Franco said. "I thought so."

The wub settled down, panting. It put its paws out, pulling its tail around it.

"It is very warm," the wub said. "I understand that we are close to the jets. Atomic power. You have done many wonderful things with it—technically. Apparently your scientific hierarchy is not equipped to solve moral, ethical—"

Franco turned to the men, crowding behind him, wide-eyed, silent.

"I'll do it. You can watch."

Franco nodded. "Try to hit the brain. It's no good for eating. Don't hit the chest. If the rib cage shatters, we'll have to pick bones out."

"Listen," Peterson said, licking his lips. "Has it done anything? What harm has it done? I'm asking you. And anyhow, it's still mine. You have no right to shoot it. It doesn't belong to you."

Franco raised his gun.

"I'm going out," Jones said, his face white and sick. "I don't want to see it."

"Me, too," French said. The men straggled out, murmuring. Peterson lingered at the door.

"It was talking to me about myths," he said. "It wouldn't hurt anyone."

He went outside.

Franco walked toward the wub. The wub looked up slowly. It swallowed.

"A very foolish thing," it said. "I am sorry that you want to do it. There was a parable that your Saviour related—"

It stopped, staring at the gun.

"Can you look me in the eye and do it?" the wub said. "Can you do that?"

The Captain gazed down. "I can look you in the eye," he said. "Back on the farm we had hogs, dirty razorback hogs. I can do it."

Staring down at the wub, into the gleaming, moist eyes, he pressed the trigger.

The taste was excellent.

They sat glumly around the table, some of them hardly eating at all. The only one who seemed to be enjoying himself was Captain Franco.

"More?" he said, looking around. "More? And some wine, perhaps."

"Not me," French said. "I think I'll go back to the chart room."

"Me, too." Jones stood up, pushing his chair back. "I'll see you later."

The Captain watched them go. Some of the others excused themselves.

"What do you suppose the matter is?" the Captain said. He turned to Peterson. Peterson sat staring down at his plate, at the potatoes, the green peas, and at the thick slab of tender, warm meat.

He opened his mouth. No sound came.

The Captain put his hand on Peterson's shoulder.

"It is only organic matter, now," he said. "The life essence is gone." He ate, spooning up the gravy with some bread. "I, myself, love to eat. It is one of the greatest things that a living creature can enjoy. Eating, resting, meditation, discussing things."

Peterson nodded. Two more men got up and went out. The Captain drank some water and sighed.

"Well," he said. "I must say that this was a very enjoyable meal. All the reports I had heard were quite true—the taste of wub. Very fine. But I was prevented from enjoying this in times past."

He dabbed at his lips with his napkin and leaned back in his chair. Peterson stared dejectedly at the table.

The Captain watched him intently. He leaned over.

"Come, come," he said. "Cheer up! Let's discuss things."

He smiled.

"As I was saying before I was interrupted, the role of Odysseus in the myths—"

Peterson jerked up, staring.

"To go on," the Captain said. "Odysseus, as I understand him—"

CHESTER HIMES

Prediction

The police parade was headed north up the main street of the big city. Of the thirty thousand policemen employed by the big city, six thousand were in the parade. It had been billed as a parade of unity to demonstrate the capacity of law enforcement and reassure the 'communities' during this time of suspicion and animosity between the races. No black policemen were standing for the simple reason that none had been asked to parade and none had requested the right to parade.

At no time had the races been so utterly divided despite the billing of unity given to the parade. Judging from the appearances of both the paraders and the viewers lining the street the word 'unity' seemed more applicable than the diffident allusion to the 'races,' for only the white race was on view and it seemed perfectly unified. In fact the crowd of all-white faces seemed to deny that a black race existed.

The police commissioner and the chiefs of the various police departments under him led the parade. They were white. The captains of the precinct stations followed, and the lieutenants in charge of the precinct detective bureaus and the uniformed patrolmen followed them. They were all white. As were all of the plain-clothes detectives and uniformed patrolmen who made up the bulk of the parade following. All white. As were the spectators behind the police cordons lining the main street of the big city. As were all the people employed on that street of the big city. As were all the people employed on that street in department stores and office buildings who crowded to doors and windows to watch the police parade pass.

There was only one black man along the entire length of the street at the time, and he wasn't in sight. He was standing in a small, unlighted chamber to the left of the entrance to the big city's big Catholic cathedral on the main street. As a rule this chamber held the poor box of the big cathedral from which the daily donations were collected by a preoccupied priest in the service of the cathedral at six p.m. each day. But now it was shortly past three o'clock and there were almost three hours before collection. The only light in the dark room came through two slots where the donations were made, one in the stone front wall opening onto the street and the other through the wooden door opening into the vestibule. The door was locked and the black man had the chamber to himself.

Chutes ran down from the slots into a closed coin box standing on legs. He had removed the chutes which restricted his movements and he now sat straddling the coin box. The slot in the stone front wall gave him a clear view of the empty street, flanked by crowds of white civilians, up which the policemen's parade would march. Beside him on the floor was a cold bottle of lemonade collecting beads of sweat in the hot humid air. In his arms he held a heavy-caliber blued steel automatic rifle of a foreign make.

The muzzle of the barrel rested on the inner edge of the slot in the stone wall and was invisible from without. He sat patiently, as though he had all the time in the world, waiting for the parade to come into sight. He had all of the remainder of his life. Subjectively, he had waited four hundred years for this moment and he was not in a hurry. The parade would come, he knew, and he would be waiting for it.

He knew his black people would suffer severely for this moment of his triumph. He was not an ignorant man. Although he mopped the floors and polished the pews of this white cathedral, he was not without intelligence. He knew the whites would kill him too. It was almost as though he were already dead. It required a mental effort to keep from making the sign of the cross, but he knew the God of this cathedral was white and would have no tolerance for him. And there was no black God nearby, if in fact there was one anywhere in the U.S. Now at the end of his life he would have to rely upon himself. He would have to assume the authority which controlled his life. He would have to direct his will which directed his brain which directed his finger to pull the trigger; he would have to do it alone, without comfort or encouragement, consoled only by the hope that it would make life safer for the blacks in the future. He would have to believe that the children of the blacks who would suffer now would benefit later. He would have to hope that the whites would have a second thought if it was their own blood being wasted. This decision he would have to take alone. He would have to control his thoughts to formulate what he wanted to think. There was no one to shape them for him. That is the way it should have been all along. To take the decisions, to think for himself, to die without application. And if his death was in vain and the whites would never accept the blacks as equal human beings, there would be nothing to live for anyway.

Through the slot in the front wall of the cathedral he saw the first row of the long police parade come into view. He could faintly hear the martial music of the band which was still out of sight. In the front row a tall, sallow-skinned man with gray hair, wearing a gray civilian suit, white shirt and black tie, walked in the center of four red-faced, gold-braided chief inspectors. The black man did not know enough about the police organization to identify the police departments from the uniforms of their chiefs, but he recognized the man in the civilian suit as the police commissioner from pictures he had seen in the newspapers. The commissioner wore highly polished spectacles with black frames which glinted in the rays of the afternoon sun, but the frosty blue eyes of the chief inspectors, squinting in the sun, were without aids.

The black man's muscles tightened, a tremor ran through his body. This was it. He lifted his rifle. But they had to march slightly farther before he could get them into his sights. He had waited this long, he could wait a few seconds longer.

The first burst, passing from left to right, made a row of entries in the faces of the five officers in the lead. The first officers were of the same height and holes appeared in their upper cheekbones just beneath the eyes and in the bridges of their noses. Snot mixed with blood exploded from their nostrils and their caps flew off behind, suddenly filled with fragments of their skulls and pasty gray brain matter streaked with capillaries like gobs of putty finely laced with red ink. The commissioner, who was slightly shorter, was hit in both temples and both eyes, and the bullets made star-shaped entries in both the lenses of his spectacles and the corneas of his eyeballs and a gelatinous substance heavily mixed with blood spurted from the rims of his eye sockets. He wore no hat to catch his brains and fragments of skull, and they exploded through the sunny atmosphere and splattered the spectators with goo, tufts of gray hair and splinters of bone. One skull fragment, larger than the others, struck a tall, well-dressed man on the cheek, cutting the skin and splashing brains against his face like a custard pie in a Mack Sennett comedy. The two chiefs on the far side, being a shade taller than the others caught the bullets in their teeth. These latter suffered worse, if such a thing was possible. Bloodstained teeth flew through the air like exotic insects, a shattered denture was expelled forward from a shattered jaw like the puking of plastic food. Jawbones came unhinged and dangled from shattered mouths. But the ultimate damage was that the heads were cut off just above the bottom jaws, which hung grotesquely from headless bodies spouting blood like gory fountains.

What made the scene so eerie was that the gunshots could not be heard over the blasting of the band and the soundproof stone walls of the cathedral. Suddenly the heads of five men were shattered into bits without a sound and by no agent that was immediately visible. It was like the act of the devil; it was uncanny. No one knew which way to run from the unseen danger but everyone ran in every direction. Men, women and children dashed about, panic-stricken, screaming, their blue eyes popping or squinting, their mouths open or their teeth gritting, their faces paper white or lobster red.

The brave policemen in the lines behind their slaughtered commissioner and chiefs drew their pistols and rapped out orders. Captains and lieutenants were bellowing to the plainclothes detectives and uniformed patrolmen in the ranks at the rear to come forward and do their duty. And row after row of the captains and lieutenants were shot down with their service revolvers in their hands. After the first burst the black man had lowered his sights and was now shooting the captains in the abdomen, riddling hearts and lings, livers and kidneys, bursting potbellies like paper sacks of water.

In a matter of seconds the streets were strewn with the carnage, nasty gray blobs of brains, hairy fragments of skull looking like sections of broken coconuts, bone splinters from jaws and facial bones, bloody, gristly bits of ears and noses, flying red and white teeth, a section of tongue; and slick and slimy with large purpling splashes and gouts of blood, squashy bits of exploded viscera, stuffed intestines bursting with half-chewed ham and cabbage and rice and gravy, were lying in the gutters like unfinished sausages before knotting. And scattered about in this bloody carnage were what remained of the bodies of policemen still clad in blood-clotted blue uniforms.

Spectators were killed purely by accident, by being caught in the line of fire, by bullets that had already passed through the intended victims. It was revealing that most of these were clean, comely matrons snugly fitting into their smooth white skins and little girl children with long blonde braids. Whether from reflex or design, most mature men and little boys had ducked for cover, flattening themselves to the pavement or rolling into doorways and underneath parked cars.

The black man behind the gun had not been seen nor had his hiding place been discovered. The front doors of the cathedral were closed and the stained glass windows high up in the front wall were sealed. The slot in the wall for donations to charity was barely visible from the street and then only if the gaze sought it out deliberately. And it was shaded by the architecture of the clerestory so that the dulled blued steel gun barrel didn't glint in the sun. As a consequence the brave policemen with their service revolvers in their hands were running helter-skelter with nothing to shoot at while being mown down by the black killer. The white spectators were fortunate that there were no blacks among them, despite the accidental casualties, for had these irate, nervous cops spied a black face in their midst there was no calculating the number of whites who would have been killed by them accidentally. But all were decided, police and spectators alike, that the sniper was a black man for no one else would slaughter whites so wantonly, slaughter them like a sadist stomping on an ant train. And in view of the history of all the assassinations and mass murders in the U.S., it was extraordinarily enlightening that all the thousands of whites caught in a deadly gunfire from an unseen assassin, white police and white civilians alike, would automatically agree that he must be black. Had they always experienced such foreboding? Was it a pathological portent? Was it inherited? Was it constant, like original sin? Was it a presentiment of the times? Who knows? The whites had always been as secretive of their fears and failing as had the blacks.

But it was the most gratifying episode of the black man's life. He experienced spiritual ecstasy to see the brains flying from those white men's heads, to see the fat arrogant bodies of the whites shattered and broken apart, cast into death. Hate served his pleasure; he thought fleetingly and pleasurably of all the humiliations and hurts imposed on him and all blacks by whites; in less than a second the complete outrage of slavery flashed across his mind and he could see the whites with a strange, pure clarity eating the flesh of the blacks and he knew at last that they were the only real cannibals who had ever existed. Cordite fumes stung his eyes, seared his lungs, choking him.

When he saw the riot tank rushing up the wide main street from police headquarters to kill him, he felt only indifference. He was so far ahead they could never get even now, he thought. He drew in the barrel of his gun to keep his position from being revealed and waited for his death, choking and almost blinded. He was ready to die. By then he had killed seventy-three whites, forty-seven policemen and twenty-six men, women and children civilians, and had wounded an additional seventy-five, and although he was never to know this figure, he was satisfied. He felt like a gambler who has broken the bank. He knew they would kill him quickly, but that was satisfactory too.

But, astoundingly, there remained a few moments of macabre comedy before his death arrived. The riot tank didn't know where to look for him. Its telescoped eye at the muzzle of the 20-mm. cannon stared right and left, looking over the heads and among the white spectators, over the living white policemen hopping about the dead, up and down the rich main street with its impressive stores, and in its frustration at not seeing a black face to shoot at it rained explosive 20-mm. shells on the black plaster of Paris mannequins displaying a line of beachwear in a department store window.

The concussion was devastating. Splintered plate glass filled the air like a sand-storm. Faces were split open and lacerated by flying glass splinters. One woman's head was cut completely off by a piece of flying glass as large as a guillotine. Varicolored wigs flew from white heads like frightened long-haired birds taking flight. And many others, men, women and children, were stripped stark naked by the force of the concussion.

On seeing bits of the black mannequins sailing past, a rookie cop loosed a fusillade from his .38-caliber police special. With a reflex that appeared shockingly human, on hearing itself shot upon from the rear, the tank whirled about and blasted two 20-mm. shells into the already panic-stricken policemen, instantly blowing twenty-nine of them to bits and wounding another one hundred and seventeen with flying shrapnel.

By then the screaming had grown so loud that suddenly motion ceased, as though a valve in the heart had stopped, and with the cessation of motion the screaming petered out to silence like the falling of a pall. Springing out of this motionless silence, a teenage youth ran across the blood-wet street and pointed with his slender arm and delicate hand at the coin slot in the front of the cathedral. All heads pivoted in that direction as though on a common neck, and the tank turned to stare at the stone wall with its blind eye also. But no sign of life was visible against the blank stone wall and the heavy wooden doors studded with brass. The tank stared a moment as if in deep thought, then 20-mm. cannon shells began to rain upon the stone, and people fled from the flying rock. It did not take long for the cannon to reduce the stone face of the cathedral to a pile of rubbish. But it took all of the following day to unearth the twisted rifle and a few scraps of bloody black flesh to prove the black killer had existed.

In the wake of this bloody massacre the stock market crashed. The dollar fell on the world market. The very structure of capitalism began to crumble. Confidence in the capitalistic system had an almost fatal shock. All over the world millions of capitalists sought means to invest their wealth in the Communist East.

Good night.

GISH JEN

Who's Irish?

In China, people say mixed children are supposed to be smart, and definitely my granddaughter Sophie is smart. But Sophie is wild, Sophie is not like my daughter Natalie, or like me. I am work hard my whole life, and fierce besides. My husband always used to say he is afraid of me, and in our restaurant, busboys and cooks all afraid of me too. Even the gang members come for protection money, they try to talk to my husband. When I am there, they stay away. If they come by mistake, they pretend they are come to eat. They hide behind the menu, they order a lot of food. They talk about their mothers. Oh, my mother have some arthritis, need to take herbal medicine, they say. Oh, my mother getting old, her hair all white now.

I say, Your mother's hair used to be white, but since she dye it, it become black again. Why don't you go home once in a while and take a look? I tell them, Confucius say a filial son knows what color his mother's hair is.

My daughter is fierce too, she is vice president in the bank now. Her new house is big enough for everybody to have their own room, including me. But Sophie take after Natalie's husband's family, their name is Shea. Irish. I always thought Irish people are like Chinese people, work so hard on the railroad, but now I know why the Chinese beat the Irish. Of course, not all Irish are like the Shea family, of course not. My daughter tell me I should not say Irish this, Irish that.

How do you like it when people say the Chinese this, the Chinese that, she say.

You know, the British call the Irish heathen, just like they call the Chinese, she say.

You think the Opium War was bad, how would you like to live right next door to the British, she say.

And that is that. My daughter have a funny habit when she win an argument, she take a sip of something and look away, so the other person is not embarrassed. So I am not embarrassed. I do not call anybody anything either. I just happen to mention about the Shea family, an interesting fact: four brothers in the family, and not one of them work. The mother, Bess, have a job before she got sick, she was executive secretary in a big company. She is handle everything for a big shot, you would be surprised how complicated her job is, not just type this, type that. Now she is a nice woman with a clean house. But her boys, every one of them is on welfare, or so-called severance pay, or so-called disability pay. Something. They say they cannot find work, this is not the economy of the fifties, but I say, Even the black people doing better these days, some of them live so fancy, you'd be surprised. Why the Shea family have so much trouble? They are white people, they speak English. When I come to this country, I have no money and do not speak English. But my husband and I own our restaurant before he die. Free and clear, no mortgage. Of course, I understand I am just lucky, come from a country where the food is popular all over the world. I understand it is not the Shea family's fault they come from a country where everything is boiled. Still, I say.

She's right, we should broaden our horizons, say one brother, Jim, at Thanksgiving. Forget about the car business. Think about egg rolls.

Pad thai, say another brother, Mike. I'm going to make my fortune in pad thai. It's going to be the new pizza.

I say, You people too picky about what you sell. Selling egg rolls not good enough for you, but at least my husband and I can say, We made it. What can you say? Tell me. What can you say?

Everybody chew their tough turkey.

I especially cannot understand my daughter's husband John, who has no job but cannot take care of Sophie either. Because he is a man, he say, and that's the end of the sentence.

Plain boiled food, plain boiled thinking. Even his name is plain boiled: John. Maybe because I grew up with black bean sauce and hoisin sauce and garlic sauce, I always feel something is missing when my son-in-law talk.

But, okay: so my son-in-law can be man, I am baby-sitter. Six hours a day, same as the old sitter, crazy Amy, who quit. This is not so easy, now that I am sixty-eight, Chinese age almost seventy. Still, I try. In China, daughter take care of mother. Here it is the other way around. Mother help daughter, mother ask, Anything else I can do? Otherwise daughter complain mother is not supportive. I tell daughter, We do not have this word in Chinese, *supportive*. But my daughter too busy to listen, she has too go to meeting, she has to write memo while her husband go to the gym to be a man. My daughter say otherwise he will be depressed. Seems like all his life he has this trouble, depression.

No one wants to hire someone who is depressed, she say. It is important for him to keep his spirits up.

Beautiful wife, beautiful daughter, beautiful house, oven can clean itself automatically. No money left over, because only one income, but lucky enough, got the baby-sitter for free. If John lived in China, he would be very happy. But he is not happy. Even at the gym things go wrong. One day, he pull a muscle. Another day, weight room too crowded. Always something.

Until finally, hooray, he has a job. Then he feel pressure.

I need to concentrate, he say. I need to focus.

He is going to work for insurance company. Salesman job. A paycheck, he say, and at least he will wear clothes instead of gym shorts. My daughter buy him some special candy bars from the health-food store. They say THINK! on them, and are supposed to help John think.

John is a good-looking boy, you have to say that, especially now that he shave so you can see his face.

I am an old man in a young man's game, say John.

I will need a new suit, say John.

This time I am not going to shoot myself in the foot, say John.

Good, I say.

She means to be supportive, my daughter say. Don't start the send her back to China thing, because we can't.

Sophie is three years old American age, but already I see her nice Chinese side swallowed up by her wild Shea side. She looks like mostly Chinese. Beautiful black hair, beautiful black eyes. Nose perfect size, not so flat looks like something fell down, not so large looks like some big deal got stuck in wrong face. Everything just right, only her skin is a brown surprise to John's family. So brown, they say. Even John say it. She never goes in the sun, still she is that color, he say. Brown. They say, Nothing the matter with brown. They are just surprised. So brown. Nattie is not that brown, they say. They say, It seems like Sophie should be a color in between Nattie and John. Seems funny, a girl named Sophie Shea be brown. But she is brown, maybe her name should be Sophie Brown. She never go in the sun, still she is that color, they say. Nothing the matter with brown. They are just surprised.

The Shea family talk is like this sometimes, going around and around like a Christmas-tree train. Maybe John is not her father, I say one day, to stop the train.

And sure enough, train wreck. None of the brothers ever say the word *brown* to me again.

Instead, John's mother, Bess, say, I hope you are not offended.

She say, I did my best on those boys. But raising four boys with no father is no picnic.

You have a beautiful family, I say.

I'm getting old, she say.

You deserve a rest, I say. Too many boys make you old.

I never had a daughter, she say. You have a daughter.

I have a daughter, I say. Chinese people don't think a daughter is so great, but you're right. I have a daughter.

I was never against the marriage, you know, she say. I never thought John was marrying down. I always thought Nattie was just as good as white.

I was never against the marriage either, I say. I just wonder if they look at the whole problem.

Of course you pointed out the problem, you are a mother, she say. And now we both have a granddaughter. A little brown granddaughter, she is so precious to me.

I laugh. A little brown granddaughter, I say. To tell you the truth, I don't know how she came out so brown.

We laugh some more. These days Bess need a walker to walk. She take so many pills, she need two glasses of water to get them all down. Her favorite TV show is about bloopers, and she love her bird feeder. All day long, she can watch that bird feeder, like a cat.

I can't wait for her to grow up, Bess say. I could use some female company.

Too many boys, I say.

Boys are fine, she say. But they do surround you after a while.

You should take a break, come live with us, I say. Lots of girls at our house.

Be careful what you offer, say Bess with a wink. Where I come from, people mean for you to move in when they say a thing like that.

Nothing the matter with Sophie's outside, that's the truth. It is inside that she is like not any Chinese girl I ever see. We go to the park, and this is what she does. She stand up in the stroller. She take off all her clothes and throw them in the fountain.

Sophie! I say. Stop!

But she just laugh like a crazy person. Before I take over as baby-sitter, Sophie has that crazy-person sitter, Amy the guitar player. My daughter thought this Amy very creative—another word we do not talk about in China. In China, we talk about whether we have difficulty or no difficulty. We talk about whether life is bitter or not bitter. In America, all day long, people talk about creative. Never mind that I cannot even look at this Amy, with her shirt so short that her belly button showing. This Amy think Sophie should love her body. So when Sophie take off her diaper, Amy laugh. When Sophie run around naked, Amy say she wouldn't want to wear a diaper either. When Sophie go *shu-shu* in her lap, Amy laugh and say there are no germs in pee. When Sophie take off her shoes, Amy say bare feet is best, even the pediatrician say so. That is why Sophie now walk around with no shoes like a beggar child. Also why Sophie love to take off her clothes.

Turn around! say the boys in the park. Let's see that ass!

Of course, Sophie does not understand. Sophie clap her hands, I am the only one to say, No! This is not a game.

It has nothing to do with John's family, my daughter say. Amy was too permissive, that's all.

But I think if Sophie was not wild inside, she would not take off her shoes and clothes to begin with.

You never take off your clothes when you were little, I say. All my Chinese friends had babies, I never saw one of them act wild like that.

Look, my daughter say. I have a big presentation tomorrow.

John and my daughter agree Sophie is a problem, but they don't know what to do.

You spank her, she'll stop, I say another day.

But they say, Oh no.

In America, parents not supposed to spank the child.

It gives them low self-esteem, my daughter say. And that leads to problems later, as I happen to know.

My daughter never have big presentation the next day when the subject of spanking come up.

I don't want you to touch Sophie, she say. No spanking, period.

Don't tell me what to do, I say.

I'm not telling you what to do, say my daughter. I'm telling you how I feel.

I am not your servant, I say. Don't you dare talk to me like that.

My daughter have another funny habit when she lose an argument. She spread out all her fingers and look at them, as if she like to make sure they are still there.

My daughter is fierce like me, but she and John think it is better to explain to Sophie that clothes are a good idea. This is not so hard in the cold weather. In the warm weather, it is very hard.

Use your words, my daughter say. That's what we tell Sophie. How about if you set a good example.

As if good example mean anything to Sophie. I am so fierce, the gang members who used to come to the restaurant all afraid of me, but Sophie is not afraid.

I say, Sophie, if you take off your clothes, no snack.

I say, Sophie, if you take off your clothes, no lunch.

I say, Sophie, if you take off your clothes, no park.

Pretty soon we are stay home all day, and by the end of six hours she still did not have one thing to eat. You never saw a child stubborn like that.

I'm hungry! she cry when my daughter come home.

What's the matter, doesn't your grandmother feed you? My daughter laugh.

No! Sophie say. She doesn't feed me anything!

My daughter laugh again. Here you go, she say.

She say to John, Sophie must be growing.

Growing like a weed, I say.

Still Sophie take off her clothes, until one day I spank her. Not too hard, but she cry and cry, and when I tell her if she doesn't put her clothes back on I'll spank her again, she put her clothes back on. Then I tell her she is good girl, and give her some food to eat. The next day we go to the park and, like a nice Chinese girl, she does not take off her clothes.

She stop taking off her clothes, I report. Finally!

How did you do it? my daughter ask.

After twenty-eight years experience with you, I guess I learn something, I say.

It must have been a phase, John say, and his voice is suddenly like an expert.

His voice is like an expert about everything these days, now that he carry a leather briefcase, and wear shiny shoes, and can go shopping for a new car. On the company, he say. The company will pay for it, but he will be able to drive it whenever he want.

A free car, he say. How do you like that.

It's good to see you in the saddle again, my daughter say. Some of your family patterns are scary.

At least I don't drink, he say. He say, And I'm not the only one with scary family patterns.

That's for sure, say my daughter.

Everyone is happy. Even I am happy, because there is more trouble with Sophie, but now I think I can help her Chinese side fight against her wild side. I teach her to eat food with fork or spoon or chopsticks, she cannot just grab into the middle of a bowl of noodles. I teach her not to play with garbage cans. Sometimes I spank her, but not too often, and not too hard.

Still, there are problems. Sophie like to climb everything. If there is a railing, she is never next to it. Always she is on top of it. Also, Sophie like to hit the mommies of her friends. She learn this from her playground best friend, Sinbad, who is four. Sinbad wear army clothes every day and like to ambush his mommy. He is the one who dug a big hole under the play structure, a foxhole he call it, all by himself. Very hardworking. Now he wait in the foxhole with a shovel full of wet sand. When his mommy come, he throw it right at her.

Oh, it's all right, his mommy say. You can't get rid of war games, it's part of their imaginative play. All the boys go through it.

Also, he like to kick his mommy, and one day he tell Sophie to kick his mommy too.

I wish this story is not true.

Kick her, kick her! Sinbad say.

Sophie kick her. A little kick, as if she just so happened was swinging her little leg and didn't realize that big mommy leg was in the way. Still I spank Sophie and make Sophie say sorry, and what does the mommy say?

Really, it's all right, she say. It didn't hurt.

After that, Sophie learn she can attack mommies in the playground, and some will say, Stop, but others will say, Oh, she didn't mean it, especially if they realize Sophie will be punished.

This is how, one day, bigger trouble come. The bigger trouble start when Sophie hide in the foxhole with that shovel full of sand. She wait, and when I come look for her, she throw it at me. All over my nice clean clothes.

Did you ever see a Chinese girl act this way?

Sophie! I say. Come out of there, say you're sorry.

But she does not come out. Instead, she laugh. Naaah, naah-na, naaa-naaa, she say.

I am not exaggerate: millions of children in China, not one act like this.

Sophie! I say. Now! Come out now!

But she know she is in big trouble. She know if she come out, what will happen next. So she does not come out. I am sixty-eight, Chinese age almost seventy, how can I crawl under there to catch her? Impossible. So I yell, yell, yell, and what happen? Nothing. A Chinese mother would help, but American mothers, they look at you, they shake their head, they go home. And, of course, a Chinese child would give up, but not Sophie.

I hate you! she yell. I hate you, Meanie!

Meanie is my new name these days.

Long time this goes on, long long time. The foxhole is deep, you cannot see too much, you don't know where is the bottom. You cannot hear too much either. If she does not yell, you cannot even know she is still there or not. After a while, getting cold out, getting dark out. No one left in the playground, only us.

Sophie, I say. How did you become stubborn like this? I am go home without you now.

I try to use a stick, chase her out of there, and once or twice I hit her, but still she does not come out. So finally I leave. I go outside the gate.

Bye-bye! I say. I'm go home now.

But still she does not come out and does not come out. Now it is dinnertime, the sky is black. I think I should maybe go get help, but how can I leave a little girl by herself in the playground? A bad man could come. A rat could come. I go back in to see what is happen to Sophie. What if she have a shovel and is making a tunnel to escape?

Sophie! I say.

No answer.

Sophie!

I don't know if she is alive. I don't know if she is fall asleep down there. If she is crying, I cannot hear her.

So I take the stick and poke.

Sophie! I say. I promise I no hit you. If you come out, I give you a lollipop.

No answer. By now I worried. What to do, what to do, what to do? I poke some more, even harder, so that I am poking and poking when my daughter and John suddenly appear.

What are you doing? What is going on? say my daughter.

Put down that stick! say my daughter.

You are crazy! say my daughter.

John wiggle under the structure, into the foxhole, to rescue Sophie.

She fell asleep, say John the expert. She's okay. That is one big hole.

Now Sophie is crying and crying.

Sophie, my daughter say, hugging her. Are you okay, peanut? Are you okay?

She's just scared, say John.

Are you okay? I say too. I don't know what happen, I say.

She's okay, say John. He is not like my daughter, full of questions. He is full of answers until we get home and can see by the lamplight.

Will you look at her? he yell then. What the hell happened?

Bruises all over her brown skin, and a swollen-up eye.

You are crazy! say my daughter. Look at what you did! You are crazy!

I try very hard, I say.

How could you use a stick? I told you to use your words!

She is hard to handle, I say.

She's three years old! You cannot use a stick! say my daughter.

She is not like any Chinese girl I ever saw, I say.

I brush some sand off my clothes. Sophie's clothes are dirty too, but at least she has her clothes on.

Has she done this before? ask my daughter. Has she hit you before?

She hits me all the time, Sophie say, eating ice cream.

Your family, say John.

Believe me, say my daughter.

A daughter I have, a beautiful daughter. I took care of her when she could not hold her head up. I took care of her before she could argue with me, when she was a little girl with two pigtails, one of them always crooked. I took care of her when we have to escape from China, I took care of her when suddenly we live in a country with cars everywhere, if you are not careful your little girl get run over. When my husband die, I promise him I will keep the family together, even though it was just two of us, hardly a family at all.

But now my daughter take me around to look at apartments. After all, I can cook, I can clean, there's no reason I cannot live by myself, all I need is a telephone. Of course, she is sorry. Sometimes she cry, I am the one to say everything will be okay. She say she have no choice, she doesn't want to end up divorced. I say divorce is terrible, I don't know who invented this terrible idea. Instead of live with a telephone, though, surprise, I come to live with Bess. Imagine that. Best make an offer and, sure enough, where she come from, people mean for you to move in when they say things like that. A crazy idea, go to live with someone else's family, but she like to have some female company, not like my daughter, who does not believe in company. These days when my daughter visit, she does not bring Sophie. Bess say we should give Nattie time, we will see Sophie again soon. But seems like my daughter have more presentation than ever before, every time she come she have to leave.

I have a family to support, she say, and her voice is heavy, as if soaking wet. I have a young daughter and a depressed husband and no one to turn to.

When she say no one to turn to, she mean me.

These days my beautiful daughter is so tired she can just sit there in a chair and fall asleep. John lost his job again, already, but still they rather hire a baby-sitter than ask me to help, even they can't afford it. Of course, the new baby-sitter is much younger, can run around. I don't know if Sophie these days is wild or not wild. She call me Meanie, but she like to kiss me too, sometimes. I remember that every time I see a child on TV. Sophie like to grab my hair, a fistful in each hand, and then kiss me smack on the nose. I never see any other child kiss that way.

The satellite TV has so many channels, more channels than I can count, including a Chinese channel from the Mainland and a Chinese channel from Taiwan, but most of the time I watch bloopers with Bess. Also, I watch the bird feeder—so many, many kinds of birds come. The Shea sons hang around all the time, asking when will I go home, but Bess tell them, Get lost.

She's a permanent resident, say Bess. She isn't going anywhere.

Then she wink at me, and switch the channel with the remote control.

Of course, I shouldn't say Irish this, Irish that, especially now I am become honorary Irish myself, according to Bess. Me! Who's Irish? I say, and she laugh. All the same, if I could mention one thing about some of the Irish, not all of them of course, I like to mention this: Their talk just stick. I don't know how Bess Shea learn to use her words, but sometimes I hear what she say a long time later. *Permanent resident. Not going anywhere.* Over and over I hear it, the voice of Bess.

DENIS JOHNSON

Work

I'd been staying at the Holiday Inn with my girlfriend, honestly the most beautiful woman I'd ever known, for three days under a phony name, shooting heroin. We made love in the bed, ate steaks at the restaurant, shot up in the john, puked, cried, accused one another, begged of one another, forgave, promised, and carried one another to heaven.

But there was a fight. I stood outside the motel hitchhiking, dressed up in a hurry, shirtless under my jacket, with the wind crying through my earring. A bus came. I climbed aboard and sat on the plastic seat while the things of our city turned in the windows like the images in a slot machine.

Once, as we stood arguing at a streetcorner, I punched her in the stomach. She doubled over and broke down crying. A car full of young college men stopped beside us.

"She's feeling sick," I told them.

"Bullshit," one of them said. "You elbowed her right in the *gut*."

"He did, he did, he did," she said, weeping.

I don't remember what I said to them. I remember loneliness crushing first my lungs, then my heart, then my balls. They put her in the car with them and drove away.

But she came back.

This morning, after the fight, after sitting on the bus for several blocks with a thoughtless, red mind, I jumped down and walked into the Vine.

The Vine was still and cold. Wayne was the only customer. His hands were shaking. He couldn't lift his glass.

I put my left hand on Wayne's shoulder, and with my right, opiated and steady, I brought his shot of bourbon to his lips.

"How would you feel about making some money?" he asked me.

"I was just going to go over here in the corner and nod out," I informed him.

"I decided," he said, "in my mind, to make some money."

"So what?" I said.

"Come with me," he begged.

"You mean you need a ride."

"I have the tools," he said. "All we need is that sorry-ass car of yours to get around in."

We found my sixty-dollar Chevrolet, the finest and best thing I ever bought, considering the price, in the streets near my apartment. I liked that car. It was the kind of thing you could bang into a phone pole with and nothing would happen at all.

Wayne cradled his burlap sack of tools in his lap as we drove out of town to where the fields bunched up into hills and then dipped down toward a cool river mothered by benevolent clouds.

All the houses on the riverbank—a dozen or so—were abandoned. The same company, you could tell, had built them all, and then painted them four different colors. The windows in the lower stories were empty of glass. We passed alongside them and I saw that the ground floors of these buildings were covered with silt. Sometime back a flood had run over the banks, cancelling everything. But now the river was flat and slow. Willows stroked the waters with their hair.

"Are we doing a burglary?" I asked Wayne.

"You can't burgulate a forgotten, empty house," he said, horrified at my stupidity.

I didn't say anything.

"This is a salvage job," he said. "Pull up to that one, right about there."

The house we parked in front of just had a terrible feeling about it. I knocked.

"Don't do that," Wayne said. "It's stupid."

Inside, our feet kicked up the silt the river had left here. The watermark wandered the walls of the downstairs about three feet above the floor. Straight, stiff grass lay all over the place in bunches, as if someone had stretched them there to dry.

Wayne used a pry bar, and I had a shiny hammer with a blue rubber grip. We put the pry points in the seams of the wall and started tearing away the Sheetrock. It came loose with a noise like old men coughing. Whenever we exposed some of the wiring in its white plastic jacket, we ripped it free of its connections, pulled it out, and bunched it up. That's what we were after. We intended to sell the copper wire for scrap.

By the time we were on the second floor, I could see we were going to make some money. But I was getting tired. I dropped the hammer, went to the bathroom. I was sweaty and thirsty. But of course the water didn't work.

I went back to Wayne, standing in one of two small empty bedrooms, and started dancing around and pounding the walls, breaking through the Sheetrock and making a giant racket, until the hammer got stuck. Wayne ignored this misbehavior.

I was catching my breath.

I asked him, "Who owned these houses, do you think?"

He stopped doing anything. "This is my house."

"It is?"

"It was."

He gave the wire a long, smooth yank, a gesture full of the serenity of hatred, popping its staples and freeing it into the room.

We balled up big gobs of wire in the center of each room, working for over an hour. I boosted Wayne through the trapdoor into the attic, and he pulled me up after him, both of us sweating and our pores leaking the poisons of drink, which smelled like old citrus peelings, and we made a mound of white-jacketed wire in the top of his former home, pulling it up out of the floor.

I felt weak. I had to vomit in the corner—just a thimbleful of grey bile. "All this work," I complained, "is fucking with my high. Can't you figure out some easier way of making a dollar?"

Wayne went to the window. He rapped it several times with his pry bar, each time harder, until it was loudly destroyed. We threw the stuff out there onto the mud-flattened meadow that came right up below us from the river.

It was quiet in this strange neighborhood along the bank except for the steady breeze in the young leaves. But now we heard a boat coming upstream. The sound curlicued through the riverside saplings like a bee, and in a minute a flat-nosed sports boat cut up the middle of the river going thirty or forty, at least.

This boat was pulling behind itself a tremendous triangular kite on a rope. From the kite, up in the air a hundred feet or so, a woman was suspended, belted in somehow, I would have guessed. She had long red hair. She was delicate and white, and naked except for her beautiful hair. I don't know what she was thinking as she floated past these ruins.

"What's she doing?" was all I could say, though we could see that she was flying.

"Now, that is a beautiful sight," Wayne said.

On the way to town, Wayne asked me to make a long detour onto the Old Highway. He had me pull up to a lopsided farmhouse set on a hill of grass.

"I'm not going in but for two seconds," he said. "You want to come in?"

"Who's here?" I said.

"Come and see," he told me.

It didn't seem anyone was home when we climbed the porch and he knocked. But he didn't knock again, and after a full three minutes a woman opened the door, a slender redhead in a dress printed with small blossoms. She didn't smile. "Hi," was all she said to us.

"Can we come in?" Wayne asked.

"Let me come onto the porch," she said, and walked past us to stand looking out over the fields.

I waited at the other end of the porch, leaning against the rail, and didn't listen. I don't know what they said to one another. She walked down the steps, and Wayne followed. He stood hugging himself and talking down at the earth. The wind lifted and dropped her long red hair. She was about forty, with a bloodless, waterlogged beauty. I guessed Wayne was the storm that had stranded her here.

In a minute he said to me, "Come on." He got in the driver's seat and started the car—you didn't need a key to start it.

I came down the steps and got in beside him. He looked at her through the windshield. She hadn't gone back inside yet, or done anything at all.

"That's my wife," he told me, as if it wasn't obvious.

I turned around in the seat and studied Wayne's wife as we drove off.

What word can be uttered about those fields? She stood in the middle of them as on a high mountain, with her red hair pulled out sideways by the wind, around her the green and grey plains pressed down flat, and all the grasses of Iowa whistling one note.

I knew who she was.

"That was her, wasn't it?" I said.

Wayne was speechless.

There was no doubt in my mind. She was the woman we'd seen flying over the river. As nearly as I could tell, I'd wandered into some sort of dream that Wayne was having about his wife, and his house. But I didn't say anything more about it.

Because, after all, in small ways, it was turning out to be one of the best days of my life, whether it was somebody else's dream or not. We turned in the scrap wire for twenty-eight dollars—each—at a salvage yard near the gleaming tracks at the edge of town, and went back to the Vine.

Who should be pouring drinks there but a young woman whose name I can't remember. But I remember the way she poured. It was like doubling your money. She wasn't going to make her employers rich. Needless to say, she was revered among us.

"I'm buying," I said.

"No way in hell," Wayne said.

"Come on."

"It is," Wayne said, "my sacrifice."

Sacrifice? Where had he gotten a word like sacrifice? Certainly I had never heard of it.

I'd seen Wayne look across the poker table in a bar and accuse—I do not exaggerate—the biggest, blackest man in Iowa of cheating, accuse him for no other reason than that he, Wayne, was a bit irked by the run of the cards. That was my idea of sacrifice, tossing yourself away, discarding your body. The black man stood up and circled the neck of a beer bottle with his fingers. He was taller than anyone who had ever entered that barroom.

"Step outside," Wayne said.

And the man said, "This ain't school."

"What the goddamn fucking piss-hell," Wayne said, "is that suppose to mean?"

"I ain't stepping outside like you do at school. Make your try right here and now."

"This ain't a place for our kind of business," Wayne said, "not inside here with women and children and dogs and cripples."

"Shit," the man said. "You're just drunk."

"I don't care," Wayne said. "To me you don't make no more noise than a fart in a paper bag."

The huge, murderous man said nothing.

"I'm going to sit down now," Wayne said, "and I'm going to play my game, and fuck you."

The man shook his head. He sat down too. This was an amazing thing. By reaching out one hand and taking hold of it for two or three seconds, he could have popped Wayne's head like an egg.

And then came one of those moments. I remember living through one when I was eighteen and spending the afternoon in bed with my first wife, before we were married. Our naked bodies started glowing, and the air turned such a strange color I thought my life must be leaving me, and with every young fiber and cell I wanted to hold on to it for another breath. A clattering sound was tearing up my head as I staggered upright and opened the door on a vision I will never see again: Where are my women now, with their sweet wet words and ways, and the miraculous balls of hail popping in a green translucence in the yards?

We put on our clothes, she and I, and walked out into a town flooded ankle-deep with white, buoyant stones. Birth should have been like that.

That moment in the bar, after the fight was narrowly averted, was like the green silence after the hailstorm. Somebody was buying a round of drinks. The cards were scattered on the table, face up, face down, and they seemed to foretell that whatever we did to one another would be washed away by liquor or explained away by sad songs.

Wayne was a part of all that.

The Vine was like a railroad club car that had somehow run itself off the tracks into a swamp of time where it awaited the blows of the wrecking ball. And the blows really were coming. Because of Urban Renewal, they were tearing up and throwing away the whole downtown.

And here we were, this afternoon, with nearly thirty dollars each, and our favorite, our very favorite, person tending bar. I wish I could remember her name, but I remember only her grace and her generosity.

All the really good times happened when Wayne was around. But this afternoon, somehow, was the best of all those times. We had money. We were grimy and tired. Usually we felt guilty and frightened, because there was something wrong with us, and we didn't know what it was; but today we had the feeling of men who had worked.

The Vine had no jukebox, but a real stereo continually playing tunes of alcoholic self-pity and sentimental divorce. "Nurse," I sobbed. She poured doubles like an angel, right up to the lip of a cocktail glass, no measuring. "You have a lovely pitching arm." You had to go down to them like a hummingbird over a blossom. I saw her much later, not too many years ago, and when I smiled she seemed to believe I was making advances. But it was only that I remembered. I'll never forget you. Your husband will beat you with an extension cord and the bus will pull away leaving you standing there in tears, but you were my mother.

DORIS LESSING

The Story of Two Dogs

Getting a new dog turned out to be more difficult than we thought, and for reasons rooted deep in the nature of our family. For what, on the face of it, could have been easier to find than a puppy once it had been decided: "Jock needs a companion, otherwise he'll spend his time with those dirty Kaffir dogs in the compound"? All the farms in the district had dogs who bred puppies of the most desirable sort. All the farm compounds owned miserable beasts kept hungry so that they would be good hunters for their meat-starved masters; though often enough puppies born to the cage-ribbed bitches from this world of mud huts were reared in white houses and turned out well. Jacob our builder heard we wanted another dog, and came up with a lively puppy on the end of a bit of rope. But we tactfully refused. The thin flea-bitten little object was not good enough for Jock, my mother said; though we children were only too ready to take it in.

Jock was a mongrel himself, a mixture of Alsatian, Rhodesian ridgeback, and some other breed—terrier?—that gave him ears too cocky and small above a long melancholy face. In short, he was nothing to boast of, outwardly: his qualities were all intrinsic or bestowed on him by my mother who had given this animal her heart when my brother went off to boarding school.

In theory Jock was my brother's dog. Yet why give a dog to a boy at that moment when he departs for school and will be away from home two-thirds of the year? In fact my brother's dog was his substitute; and my poor mother, whose children were always away being educated, because we were farmers, and farmers' children had no choice but to go to the cities for their schooling—my poor mother caressed Jock's too-small intelligent ears and crooned: "There, Jock! There, old boy! There, good dog, yes, you're a *good* dog, Jock, you're such a *good* dog. . . ." While my father said, uncomfortably: "For goodness sake, old girl, you'll ruin him, that isn't a house pet, he's not a lapdog, he's a farm dog." To which my mother said nothing, but her face put on a most familiar look of misunderstood suffering, and she bent it down close so that the flickering red tongue just touched her cheeks, and sang to him: "Poor old Jock then, yes, you're a poor old dog, you're not a rough farm dog, you're a good dog, and you're not strong, no you're delicate."

At this last word my brother protested; my father protested; and so did I. All of us, in our different ways, had refused to be "delicate"—had escaped from being

"The Story of Two Dogs" is reprinted with permission of Simon & Schuster Adult Publishing Group from African Stories *by Doris Lessing. Copyright © 1951, 1953, 1954, 1957, 1958, 1962, 1963, 1964, 1965, 1972, 1981 by Doris Lessing.*

"delicate"—and we wished to rescue a perfectly strong and healthy young dog from being forced into invalidism, as we all, at different times, had been. Also of course we all (and we knew it and felt guilty about it) were secretly pleased that Jock was now absorbing the force of my mother's pathetic need for something "delicate" to nurse and protect.

Yet there was something in the whole business that was a reproach to us. When my mother bent her sad face over the animal, stroking him with her beautiful white hands on which the rings had grown too large, and said: "There, good dog, yes Jock, you're such a gentleman—" well, there was something in all this that made us, my father, my brother and myself, need to explode with fury, or to take Jock away and make him run over the farm like the tough young brute he was, or go away ourselves forever so that we didn't have to hear the awful yearning intensity in her voice. Because it was entirely our fault that note was in her voice at all; if we had allowed ourselves to be delicate, and good, or even gentlemen or ladies, there would have been no need for Jock to sit between my mother's knees, his loyal noble head on her lap, while she caressed and yearned and suffered.

It was my father who decided there must be another dog, and for the expressed reason that otherwise Jock would be turned into a "sissy." (At this word, reminder of a hundred earlier battles, my brother flushed, looked sulky, and went right out of the room.) My mother would not hear of another dog until her Jock took to sneaking off to the farm compound to play with the Kaffir dogs. "Oh you bad dog, Jock," she said sorrowfully, "playing with those nasty dirty dogs, how could you, Jock!" And he would playfully, but in an agony of remorse, snap and lick at her face, while she bent the whole force of her inevitably betrayed self over him, crooning: "How could you, oh how could you, Jock?"

So there must be a new puppy. And since Jock was (at heart, despite his temporary lapse) noble and generous and above all well-bred, his companion must also possess these qualities. And which dog, where in the world, could possibly be good enough? My mother turned down a dozen puppies; but Jock was still going off to the compound, slinking back to gaze soulfully into my mother's eyes. This new puppy was to be my dog. I decided this: if my brother owned a dog, then it was only fair that I should. But my lack of force in claiming this puppy was because I was in the grip of abstract justice only. The fact was I didn't want a good noble and well-bred dog. I didn't know what I did want, but the idea of such a dog bored me. So I was content to let my mother turn down puppies, provided she kept her terrible maternal energy on Jock, and away from me.

Then the family went off for one of our long visits in another part of the country, driving from farm to farm to stop a night, or a day, or a meal, with friends. To the last place we were invited for the weekend. A distant cousin of my father, "a Norfolk man" (my father was from Essex), had married a woman who had nursed in the war (First World War) with my mother. They now lived in a small brick and iron house surrounded by granite *kopjes* that erupted everywhere from thick bush. They were as isolated as any people I've known, eighty miles from the nearest railway station. As my father said, they were "not suited," for they quarrelled or sent each other to Coventry all the weekend. However, it was not until much later that I thought about the pathos of these two people, living alone on a minute pension in the middle of the bush, and "not suited"; for that weekend I was in love.

It was night when we arrived, about eight in the evening, and an almost full moon floated heavy and yellow above a stark granite-bouldered *kopje*. The bush around was black and low and silent, except that the crickets made a small incessant din. The car drew up outside a small boxlike structure whose iron roof glinted off moonlight. As the engine stopped, the sound of crickets swelled up, the moonlight's cold came in a breath of fragrance to our faces; and there was the sound of a mad wild yapping. Behold, around the corner of the house came a small black wriggling object that hurled itself towards the car, changed course almost on touching it, and hurtled off again, yapping in a high delirious yammering which, while it faded behind the house, continued faintly, our ears, or at least mine, straining after it.

"Take no notice of that puppy," said our host, the man from Norfolk. "It's been stark staring mad with the moon every night this last week."

We went into the house, were fed, were looked after; I was put to bed so that the grownups could talk freely. All the time came the mad high yapping. In my tiny bedroom I looked out onto a space of flat white sand that reflected the moon between the house and the farm buildings, and there hurtled a mad wild puppy, crazy with joy of life, or moonlight, weaving back and forth, round and round, snapping at its own black shadow and tripping over its own clumsy feet—like a drunken moth around a candle flame, or like . . . like nothing I've ever seen or heard of since.

The moon, large and remote and soft, stood up over the trees, the empty white sand, the house which had unhappy human beings in it; and a mad little dog yapping and beating its course of drunken joyous delirium. That, of course, was my puppy; and when Mr. Barnes came out from the house saying: "Now, now, come now, you lunatic animal . . ." finally almost throwing himself on the crazy creature, to lift it in his arms still yapping and wriggling and flapping around like a fish, so that he could carry it to the packing case that was its kennel, I was already saying, as anguished as a mother watching a stranger handle her child: Careful now, careful, that's my dog.

Next day, after breakfast, I visited the packing case. Its white wood oozed out resin that smelled tangy in hot sunlight, and its front was open and spilling out soft yellow straw. On the straw a large beautiful black dog lay with her head on outstretched forepaws. Beside her a brindled pup lay on its fat back, its four paws sprawled every which way, its eyes rolled up, as ecstatic with heat and food and laziness as it had been the night before from the joy of movement. A crust of mealie porridge was drying on its shining black lips that were drawn slightly back to show perfect milk teeth. His mother kept her eyes on him, but her pride was dimmed with sleep and heat.

I went inside to announce my spiritual ownership of the puppy. They were all around the breakfast table. The man from Norfolk was swapping boyhood reminiscences (shared in space, not time) with my father. His wife, her eyes still red from the weeping that had followed a night quarrel, was gossiping with my mother about the various London hospitals where they had ministered to the wounded of the War they had (apparently so enjoyably) shared.

My mother at once said: "Oh my dear, no, not that puppy, didn't you see him last night? We'll never train him."

The man from Norfolk said I could have him with pleasure.

My father said he didn't see what was wrong with the dog, if a dog was healthy that was all that mattered: my mother dropped her eyes forlornly, and sat silent.

The man from Norfolk's wife said she couldn't bear to part with the silly little thing, goodness knows there was little enough pleasure in her life.

The atmosphere of people at loggerheads being familiar to me, it was not necessary for me to know *why* they disagreed, or in what ways, or what criticisms they were going to make about my puppy. I only knew that inner logics would in due course work themselves out and the puppy would be mine. I left the four people to talk about their differences through a small puppy, and went to worship the animal, who was now sitting in a patch of shade beside the sweet-wood-smelling packing case, its dark brindled coat glistening, with dark wet patches on it from its mother's ministering tongue. His own pink tongue absurdly stuck out between white teeth, as if he had been too careless or lazy to withdraw it into its proper place under his equally pink wet palate. His brown buttony beautiful eyes . . . but enough, he was an ordinary mongrelly puppy.

Later I went back to the house to find out how the battle balanced: my mother had obviously won my father over, for he said he thought it was wiser not to have that puppy: "Bad blood tells, you know."

The bad blood was from the father, whose history delighted my fourteen-year-old imagination. This district being wild, scarcely populated, full of wild animals, even leopards and lions, the four policemen at the police station had a tougher task than in places nearer town; and they had bought half a dozen large dogs to (a) terrorise possible burglars around the police station itself and (b) surround themselves with an aura of controlled animal savagery. For the dogs were trained to kill if necessary. One of these dogs, a big ridgeback, had "gone wild." He had slipped his tether at the station and taken to the bush, living by himself on small buck, hares, birds, even stealing farmers' chickens. This dog, whose proud lonely shape had been a familiar one to farmers for years, on moonlit nights, or in grey dawns and dusks, standing aloof from human warmth and friendship, had taken Stella, my puppy's mother, off with him for a week of sport and hunting. She simply went away with him one morning; the Barneses had seen her go; had called after her; she had not even looked back. A week later she returned home at dawn and gave a low whine outside their bedroom window, saying: I'm home; and they woke to see their errant Stella standing erect in the paling moonlight, her nose pointed outwards and away from them towards a great powerful dog who seemed to signal to her with his slightly moving tail before fading into the bush. Mr. Barnes fired some futile shots into the bush after him. Then they both scolded Stella who in due time produced seven puppies, in all combinations of black, brown and gold. She was no pure-bred herself, though of course her owners thought she was, or ought to be, being their dog. The night the puppies were born, the man from Norfolk and his wife heard a sad wail or cry, and arose from their beds to see the wild police dog bending his head in at the packing-case door. All the bush was flooded with a pinkish-gold dawn light, and the dog looked as if he had an aureole of gold around him. Stella was half wailing, half growling her welcome, or protest, or fear at his great powerful reappearance and his thrusting muzzle so close to her seven helpless pups. They called out, and he turned his outlaw's head to the window where they stood side by side in striped pyjamas and embroidered pink silk. He put back his head and howled, he howled, a mad wild sound that gave them gooseflesh, so they said; but I did not understand that until years later when Bill the puppy "went wild" and I saw him that day on the antheap howling his pain of longing to an empty listening world.

The father of her puppies did not come near Stella again; but a month later he was shot dead at another farm, fifty miles away, coming out of a chicken run with a fine white Leghorn in his mouth; and by that time she had only one pup left, they had drowned the rest. It was bad blood, they said, no point in preserving it, they had only left her that one pup out of pity.

I said not a word as they told this cautionary tale, merely preserved the obstinate calm of someone who knows she will get her own way. Was right on my side? It was. Was I owed a dog? I was. Should anybody but myself choose my dog? No, but . . . very well then, I had chosen. I chose this dog. I chose it. Too late, I *had* chosen it.

Three days and three nights we spent at the Barneses' place. The days were hot and slow and full of sluggish emotions; and the two dogs slept in the packing case. At nights, the four people stayed in the living room, a small brick place heated unendurably by the paraffin lamp whose oily yellow glow attracted moths and beetles in a perpetual whirling halo of small moving bodies. They talked, and I listened for the mad far yapping, and then I crept out into the cold moonlight. On the last night of our stay the moon was full, a great perfect white ball, its history marked on a face that seemed close enough to touch as it floated over the dark cricket-singing bush. And there on the white sand yapped and danced the crazy puppy, while his mother, the big beautiful animal, sat and watched, her intelligent yellow eyes slightly anxious as her muzzle followed the erratic movements of her child, the child of her dead mate from the bush. I crept up beside Stella, sat on the still-warm cement beside her, put my arm around her soft furry neck, and my head beside her alert moving head. I adjusted my breathing so that my rib cage moved up and down beside hers, so as to be closer to the warmth of her barrelly furry chest, and together we turned our eyes from the great staring floating moon to the tiny black hurtling puppy who shot in circles from near us, so near he all but crashed into us, to two hundred yards away where he just missed the wheels of the farm waggon. We watched, and I felt the chill of moonlight deepen on Stella's fur, and on my own silk skin, while our ribs moved gently up and down together, and we waited until the man from Norfolk came to first shout, then yell, then fling himself on the mad little dog and shut him up in the wooden box where yellow bars of moonlight fell into black dog-smelling shadow. "There now, Stella girl, you go in with your puppy," said the man, bending to pat her head as she obediently went inside. She used her soft nose to push her puppy over. He was so exhausted that he fell and lay, his four legs stretched out and quivering like a shot dog, his breath squeezed in and out of him in small regular wheezy pants like whines. And so I left them, Stella and her puppy, to go to my bed in the little brick house which seemed literally crammed with hateful emotions. I went to sleep, thinking of the hurtling little dog, now at last asleep with exhaustion, his nose pushed against his mother's breathing black side, the slits of yellow moonlight moving over him through the boards of fragrant wood.

We took him away next morning, having first locked Stella in a room so that she could not see us go.

It was a three-hundred-mile drive, and all the way Bill yapped and panted and yawned and wriggled idiotically on his back on the lap of whoever held him, his eyes rolled up, his big paws lolling. He was a full-time charge for myself and my mother, and, after the city, my brother, whose holidays were starting. He, at first sight of the second dog, reverted to the role of Jock's master, and dismissed my animal as altogether less valuable material. My mother, by now Bill's slave, agreed with him, but invited him to admire the adorable wrinkles on the puppy's forehead. My father demanded irritably that both dogs should be "thoroughly trained."

Meanwhile, as the nightmare journey proceeded, it was noticeable that my mother talked more and more about Jock, guiltily, as if she had betrayed him. "Poor little Jock, what will he say?"

Jock was in fact a handsome young dog. More Alsatian than anything, he was a low-standing, thick-coated animal of a warm gold colour, with a vestigial "ridge" along his spine, rather wolflike, or foxlike, if one looked at him frontways, with his sharp cocked ears. And he was definitely not "little." There was something dignified about him from the moment he was out of puppyhood, even when he was being scolded by my mother for his visits to the compound.

The meeting, prepared for by us all with trepidation, went off in a way which was a credit to everyone, but particularly Jock, who regained my mother's heart at a stroke. The puppy was released from the car and carried to where Jock sat, noble and restrained as usual, waiting for us to greet him. Bill at once began weaving and yapping around the rocky space in front of the house. Then he saw Jock, bounded up to him, stopped a couple of feet away, sat down on his fat backside and yelped excitedly. Jock began a yawning, snapping movement of his head, making it go from side to side in half-snarling, half-laughing protest, while the puppy crept closer, right up, jumping at the older dog's lifted wrinkling muzzle. Jock did not move away; he forced himself to remain still, because he could see us all watching. At last he lifted up his paw, pushed Bill over with it, pinned him down, examined him, then sniffed and licked him. He had accepted him, and Bill had found a substitute for his mother who was presumably mourning his loss. We were able to leave the child (as my mother kept calling him) in Jock's infinitely patient care. "You are such a good dog, Jock," she said, overcome by this scene, and the other touching scenes that followed, all marked by Jock's extraordinary forbearance for what was, and even I had to admit it, an intolerably destructive little dog.

Training became urgent. But this was not at all easy, due, like the business of getting a new puppy, to the inner nature of the family.

To take only one difficulty: dogs must be trained by their masters, they must owe allegiance to one person. And who was Jock to obey? And Bill: I was his master, in theory. In practice, Jock was. Was I to take over from Jock? But even to state it is to expose its absurdity: what I adored was the graceless puppy, and what did I want with a well-trained dog? Trained for *what?*

A watchdog? But all our dogs were watchdogs. "Natives"—such was the article of faith—were by nature scared of dogs. Yet everyone repeated stories about thieves poisoning fierce dogs, or making friends with them. So apparently no one really believed that watchdogs were any use. Yet every farm had its watchdog.

Throughout my childhood I used to lie in bed, the bush not fifty yards away all around the house, listening to the cry of the nightjar, the owls, the frogs and the crickets; to the tom-toms from the compound; to the mysterious rustling in the thatch over my head, or the long grass it had been cut from down the hill; to all the thousand noises of the night on the veld; and every one of these noises was marked also by the house dogs, who would bark and sniff and investigate and growl at all these; and also at starlight on the polished surface of a leaf, at the moon lifting itself over the mountains, at a branch cracking behind the house, at the first rim of hot red showing above the horizon—in short at anything and everything. Watchdogs, in my experience, were never asleep; but they were not so much a guard against thieves (we never had any thieves that I can remember) as a kind of instrument designed to measure or record the rustlings and movements of the African night that seemed to have an enormous life of its own, but a collective life, so that the falling of a stone, or a star shooting through the Milky Way, the grunt of a wild pig, and the wind rustling in the mealie field were all evidences and aspects of the same truth.

How did one "train" a watchdog? Presumably to respond only to the slinking approach of a human, black or white. What use is a watchdog otherwise? But even now, the most powerful memory of my childhood is of lying awake listening to the sobbing howl of a dog at the inexplicable appearance of the yellow face of the moon; of creeping to the window to see the long muzzle of a dog pointed black against a great bowl of stars. We needed no moon calendar with those dogs, who were like traffic in London: to sleep at all, one had to learn not to hear them. And if one did not hear them, one would not hear the stiff warning growl that (presumably) would greet a marauder.

At first Jock and Bill were locked up in the dining room at night. But there were so many stirrings and yappings and rushings from window to window after the rising sun or moon, or the black shadows which moved across whitewashed walls from the branches of the trees in the garden, that soon we could no longer stand the lack of sleep, and they were turned out on to the verandah. With many hopeful injunctions from my mother that they were to be "good dogs": which meant that they should ignore their real natures and sleep from sundown to sunup. Even then, when Bill was just out of puppyhood, they might be missing altogether in the early mornings. They would come guiltily up the road from the lands at breakfasttime, their coats full of grass seeds, and we knew they had rushed down into the bush after an owl, or a grazing animal, and, finding themselves farther from home than they had expected in a strange nocturnal world, had begun nosing and sniffing and exploring in practice for their days of wildness soon to come.

So they weren't watchdogs. Hunting dogs perhaps? My brother undertook to train them, and we went through a long and absurd period of "Down, Jock," "To heel, Bill," while sticks of barley sugar balanced on noses, and paws were offered to be shaken by human hands, etc., etc. Through all this Jock suffered, bravely, but saying so clearly with every part of him that he would do anything to please my mother—he would send her glances half proud and half apologetic all the time my brother drilled him, that after an hour of training my brother would retreat, muttering that it was too hot, and Jock bounded off to lay his head on my mother's lap. As for Bill he never achieved anything. Never did he sit still with the golden lumps on his nose, he ate them at once. Never did he stay to heel. Never did he remember what he was supposed to do with his paw when one of us offered him a hand. The truth was, I understood then, watching the training sessions, that Bill was stupid. I pretended of course that he despised being trained, he found it humiliating; and that Jock's readiness to go through with the silly business showed his lack of spirit. But alas, there was no getting around it. Bill simply wasn't very bright.

Meanwhile he had ceased to be a fat charmer; he had become a lean young dog, good-looking, with his dark brindled coat, and his big head that had a touch of Newfoundland. He had a look of puppy about him still. For just as Jock seemed born elderly, had respectable white hairs on his chin from the start; so Bill kept something young in him; he was a young dog until he died.

The training sessions did not last long. Now my brother said the dogs would be trained on the job: this to pacify my father, who kept saying that they were a disgrace and "not worth their salt."

There began a new regime, my brother, myself, and the two dogs. We set forth each morning, first, my brother, earnest with responsibility, his rifle swinging in his hand, at his heels the two dogs. Behind this time-honoured unit, myself, the girl, with no useful part to play in the serious masculine business, but necessary to provide admiration. This was a very old role for me indeed: to walk away on one side of the scene, a small fierce girl, hungry to be part of it, but knowing she never would be, above all because the heart that had been put to pump away all her life under her ribs was not only critical and intransigent, but one which longed so bitterly to melt into loving acceptance. An uncomfortable combination, as she knew even then—yet I could not remove the sulky smile from my face. And it *was* absurd: there was my brother, so intent and serious, with Jock the good dog just behind him; and there was Bill the bad dog intermittently behind him, but more often than not sneaking off to enjoy some side path. And there was myself, unwillingly following, my weight shifting from hip to hip, bored and showing it.

I knew the route too well. Before we reached the sullen thickets of the bush where game and birds were to be found, there was a long walk up the back of the *kopje* through a luxuriant pawpaw grove, then through sweet potato vines that tangled our ankles, and tripped us, then past a rubbish heap whose sweet rotten smell was expressed in a heave of glittering black flies, then the bush itself. Here it was all dull green stunted trees, miles and miles of the smallish, flattish, msasa trees in their second growth: they had all been cut for mine furnaces at some time. And over the flat ugly bush a large overbearing blue sky.

We were on our way to get food. So we kept saying. Whatever we shot would be eaten by "the house," or by the house's servants, or by "the compound." But we were hunting according to a newer law than the need for food, and we knew it and that was why we were always a bit apologetic about these expeditions, and why we so often chose to return empty-handed. We were hunting because my brother had been given a new and efficient rifle that would bring down (infallibly, if my brother shot) birds, large and small; and small animals, and very often large game like koodoo and sable. We were hunting because we owned a gun. And because we owned a gun, we should have hunting dogs, it made the business less ugly for some reason.

We were on our way to the Great Vlei, as distinct from the Big Vlei, which was five miles in the other direction. The Big Vlei was burnt out and eroded, and the waterholes usually dried up early. We did not like going there. But to reach the Great Vlei, which was beautiful, we had to go through the ugly bush "at the back of the *kopje*." These ritual names for parts of the farm seemed rather to be names for regions in our minds. "Going to the Great Vlei" had a fairy-tale quality about it, because of having to pass through the region of sour ugly frightening bush first. For it did frighten us, always, and without reason: we felt it was hostile to us and we walked through it quickly, knowing that we were earning by this danger the water-running peace of the Great Vlei. It was only partly on our farm; the boundary between it and the next farm ran invisibly down its centre, drawn by the eye from this outcrop to that big tree to that pothole to that antheap. It was a grassy valley with trees standing tall and spreading on either side of the watercourse which was a half-mile width of intense greenness broken by sky-reflecting brown pools. This was old bush, these trees had never been cut: the Great Vlei had the inevitable look of natural bush—that no branch, no shrub, no patch of thorn, no outcrop, could have been in any other place or stood at any other angle.

The potholes here were always full. The water was stained clear brown, and the mud bottom had a small movement of creatures, while over the brown ripples skimmed blue jays and hummingbirds and all kinds of vivid flashing birds we did not know the names of. Along the lush verges lolled pink and white water lilies on their water-gemmed leaves.

This paradise was where the dogs were to be trained.

During the first holidays, long ones of six weeks, my brother was indefatigable, and we set off every morning after breakfast. In the Great Vlei I sat on a pool's edge under a thorn tree, and daydreamed to the tune of the ripples my swinging feet set moving across the water, while my brother, armed with the rifle, various sizes of stick, and lumps of sugar and biltong, put the two dogs through their paces. Sometimes, roused perhaps because the sun that fell through the green lace of the thorn was burning my shoulders, I turned to watch the three creatures, hard at work a hundred yards off on an empty patch of sand. Jock, more often than not, would be a dead dog, or his nose would be on his paws while his attentive eyes were on my brother's face. Or he would be sitting up, a dog statue, a golden dog, admirably obedient. Bill, on the other hand, was probably balancing on his spine, all four paws in the air, his throat back so that he was flat from nose to tailtip, receiving the hot sun equally over his brindled fur. I would hear, through my own lazy thoughts: "Good dog, Jock, yes good dog. Idiot Bill, fool dog, why don't you work like Jock?" And my brother, his face reddened and sweaty, would come over to flop beside me, saying: "It's all Bill's fault, he's a bad example. And of course Jock doesn't see why he should work hard when Bill just plays all the time." Well, it probably was my fault that the training failed. If my earnest and undivided attention had been given, as I knew quite well was being demanded of me, to this business of the boy and the two dogs, perhaps we would have ended up with a brace of efficient and obedient animals, ever ready to die, to go to heel, and to fetch it. Perhaps.

By next holidays, moral disintegration had set in. My father complained the dogs obeyed nobody, and demanded training, serious and unremitting. My brother and I watched our mother petting Jock and scolding Bill, and came to an unspoken agreement. We set off for the Great Vlei but once there we loafed up and down the waterholes, while the dogs did as they liked, learning the joys of freedom.

The uses of water, for instance. Jock, cautious as usual, would test a pool with his paw, before moving in to stand chest deep, his muzzle just above the ripples, licking at them with small yaps of greeting or excitement. Then he walked gently in and swam up and down and around the brown pool in the green shade of the thorn trees. Meanwhile Bill would have found a shallow pool and be at his favourite game. Starting twenty yards from the rim of a pool he would hurl himself, barking shrilly, across the grass, then across the pool, not so much swimming across it as bouncing across it. Out the other side, up the side of the vlei, around in a big loop, then back, and around again . . . and again and again and again. Great sheets of brown water went up into the sky above him, crashing back into the pool while he barked his exultation.

That was one game. Or they chased each other up and down the four-mile-long valley like enemies, and when one caught the other there was a growling and a snarling and a fighting that sounded genuine enough. Sometimes we went to separate them, an interference they suffered; and the moment we let them go one or another would be off, his hind quarters pistoning, with the other in pursuit, fierce and silent. They might race a mile, two miles, before one leaped at the other's throat and brought him down. This game too, over and over again, so that when they did go wild, we knew how they killed the wild pig and the buck they lived on.

On frivolous mornings they chased butterflies, while my brother and I dangled our feet in a pool and watched. Once, very solemnly, as it were in parody of the ridiculous business (now over, thank goodness) of "fetch it" and "to heel," Jock brought us in his jaws a big orange and black butterfly, the delicate wings all broken, and the orange bloom smearing his furry lips. He laid it in front of us, held the still fluttering creature flat with a paw, then lay down, his nose pointing at it. His brown eyes rolled up, wickedly hypocritical, as if to say: "Look, a butterfly, I'm a *good* dog." Meanwhile, Bill leaped and barked, a small brown dog hurling himself up into the great blue sky after floating coloured wings. He had taken no notice at all of Jock's captive. But we both felt that Bill was much more likely than Jock to make such a seditious comment, and in fact my brother said: "Bill's corrupted Jock. I'm sure Jock would never go wild like this unless Bill was showing him. It's the blood coming out." But alas, we had no idea yet of what "going wild" could mean. For a couple of years yet it still meant small indisciplines, and mostly Bill's.

For instance, there was the time Bill forced himself through a loose plank in the door of the store hut, and there ate and ate, eggs, cake, bread, a joint of beef, a ripening guineafowl, half a ham. Then he couldn't get out. In the morning he was a swollen dog, rolling on the floor and whining with the agony of his overindulgence. "Stupid dog, Bill, Jock would never do a thing like that, he'd be too intelligent not to know he'd swell up if he ate so much."

Then he ate eggs out of the nest, a crime for which on a farm a dog gets shot. Very close was Bill to this fate. He had actually been seen sneaking out of the chicken run, feathers on his nose, egg smear on his muzzle. And there was a mess of oozing yellow and white slime over the straw of the nests. The fowls cackled and raised their feathers whenever Bill came near. First, he was beaten, by the cook, until his howls shook the farm. Then my mother blew eggs and filled them with a solution of mustard and left them in the nests. Sure enough, next morning, a hell of wild howls and shrieks: the beatings had taught him nothing. We went out to see a brown dog running and racing in agonised circles with his tongue hanging out, while the sun came up red over black mountains—a splendid backdrop to a disgraceful scene. My mother took the poor inflamed jaws and washed them in warm water and said: "Well now Bill, you'd better learn, or it's the firing squad for you."

He learned, but not easily. More than once my brother and I, having arisen early for the hunt, stood in front of the house in the dawn hush, the sky a high far grey above us, the edge of the mountains just reddening, the great spaces of silent bush full of the dark of the night. We sniffed at the small sharpness of the dew, and the heavy somnolent night-smell off the bush, felt the cold heavy air on our cheeks. We stood, whistling very low, so that the dogs would come from wherever they had chosen to sleep. Soon Jock would appear, yawning and sweeping his tail back and forth. No Bill—then we saw him, sitting on his haunches just outside the chicken run, his nose resting in a loop of the wire, his eyes closed in yearning for the warm delicious ooze of fresh egg. And we would clap our hands over our mouths and double up with heartless laughter that had to be muffled so as not to disturb our parents.

On the mornings when we went hunting, and took the dogs, we knew that before we'd gone half a mile either Jock or Bill would dash off barking into the bush; the one left would look up from his own nosing and sniffing and rush away too. We would hear the wild double barking fade away with the crash and the rush of the two bodies, and, often enough, the subsidiary rushings away of other animals who had been asleep or resting and just waiting until we had gone away. Now we could look for something to shoot which probably we would never have seen at all had the dogs been there. We could settle down for long patient stalks, circling around a grazing koodoo, or a couple of duikers. Often enough we would lie watching them for hours, afraid only that Jock and Bill would come back, putting an end to this particular pleasure. I remember once we caught a glimpse of a duiker grazing on the edge of a farmland that was still half dark. We got onto our stomachs and wriggled through the long grass, not able to see if the duiker was still there. Slowly the field opened up in front of us, a heaving mass of big black clods. We carefully raised our heads, and there, at the edge of the clod sea, a couple of arm's lengths away, were three little duikers, their heads turned away from us to where the sun was about to rise. They were three black, quite motionless silhouettes. Away over the other side of the field, big clods became tinged with reddish gold. The earth turned so fast towards the sun that the light came running from the tip of one clod to the next across the field like flames leaping along the tops of long grasses in front of a strong wind. The light reached the duikers and outlined them with warm gold. They were three glittering little beasts on the edge of an imminent sunlight. They then began to butt each other, lifting their hind quarters and bringing down their hind feet in clicking leaps like dancers. They tossed their sharp little horns and made short half-angry rushes at each other. The sun was up. Three little buck danced on the edge of the deep green bush where we lay hidden, and there was a weak sunlight warming their gold hides. The sun separated itself from the line of the hills, and became calm and big and yellow; a warm yellow colour filled the world, the little buck stopped dancing, and walked slowly off, frisking their white tails and tossing their pretty heads, into the bush.

We would never have seen them at all, if the dogs hadn't been miles away.

In fact, all they were good for was their indiscipline. If we wanted to be sure of something to eat, we tied ropes to the dogs' collars until we actually heard the small clink-clink-clink of guineafowl running through the bush. Then we untied them. The dogs were at once off after the birds who rose clumsily into the air, looking like flying shawls that sailed along, just above grass level, with the dogs' jaws snapping underneath them. All they wanted was to land unobserved in the long grass, but they were always forced to rise painfully into the trees, on their weak wings. Sometimes, if it was a large flock, a dozen trees might be dotted with the small black shapes of guineafowl outlined against dawn or evening skies. They watched the barking dogs, took no notice of us. My brother or I—for even I could hardly miss in such conditions—planted our feet wide for balance, took aim at a chosen bird and shot. The carcase fell into the worrying jaws beneath. Meanwhile a second bird would be chosen and shot. With the two birds tied together by their feet, the rifle, justified by utility, proudly swinging, we would saunter back to the house through the sun-scented bush of our enchanted childhood. The dogs, for politeness' sake, escorted us part of the way home, then went off hunting on their own. Guineafowl were very tame sport for them, by then.

It had come to this, that if we actually wished to shoot something, or to watch animals, or even to take a walk through bush where every animal for miles had not been scared away, we had to lock up the dogs before we left, ignoring their whines and their howls. Even so, if let out too soon, they would follow. Once, after we had walked six miles or so, a leisurely morning's trek towards the mountains, the dogs arrived, panting, happy, their pink wet tongues hot on our knees and forearms, saying how delighted they were to have found us. They licked and wagged for a few moments—then off they went, they vanished, and did not come home until evening. We were worried. We had not known that they went so far from the farm by themselves. We spoke of how bad it would be if they took to frequenting other farms—perhaps other chicken runs? But it was all too late. They were too old to train. Either they had to be kept permanently on leashes, tied to trees outside the house, and for dogs like these it was not much better than being dead—either that, or they must run free and take their chances.

We got news of the dogs in letters from home and it was increasingly bad. My brother and I, at our respective boarding schools where we were supposed to be learning discipline, order, and sound characters, read: "The dogs went away a whole night, they only came back at lunchtime." "Jock and Bill have been three days and nights in the bush. They've just come home, worn out." "The dogs must have made a kill this time and stayed beside it like wild animals, because they came home too gorged to eat, they just drank a lot of water and fell off to sleep like babies. . . ." "Mr. Daly rang up yesterday to say he saw Jock and Bill hunting along the hill behind his house. They've been chasing his oxen. We've got to beat them when they get home because if they don't learn they'll get themselves shot one of these dark nights. . . ."

They weren't there at all when we went home for the holidays. They had already been gone for nearly a week. But, or so we flattered ourselves, they sensed our return, for back they came, trotting gently side by side up the hill in the moonlight, two low black shapes moving above the accompanying black shapes of their shadows, their eyes gleaming red as the shafts of lamplight struck them. They greeted us, my brother and me, affectionately enough, but at once went off to sleep. We told ourselves that they saw us as creatures like them, who went off on long exciting hunts: but we knew it was sentimental nonsense, designed to take the edge off the hurt we felt because our animals, *our* dogs, cared so little about us. They went away again that night, or rather, in the first dawnlight. A week later they came home. They smelled foul, they must have been chasing a skunk or a wildcat. Their fur was matted with grass seeds and their skin lumpy with ticks. They drank water heavily, but refused food: their breath was fetid with the smell of meat.

They lay down to sleep and remained limp while we, each taking an animal, its sleeping head heavy in our laps, removed ticks, grass seeds, blackjacks. On Bill's forepaw was a hard ridge which I thought was an old scar. He sleep-whimpered when I touched it. It was a noose of plaited grass, used by Africans to snare birds. Luckily it had snapped off. "Yes," said my father, "that's how they'll end, both of them, they'll die in a trap, and serve them both right, they won't get any sympathy from me!"

We were frightened into locking them up for a day; but we could not stand their misery, and let them out again.

We were always springing gametraps of all kinds. For the big buck, the sable, the eland, the koodoo, the Africans bent a sapling across a path, held it by light string, and fixed on it a noose of heavy wire cut from a fence. For the smaller buck there were low traps with nooses of fine baling wire or plaited tree fibre. And at the corners of the cultivated fields or at the edges of waterholes, where the birds and hares came down to feed, were always a myriad tiny tracks under the grass, and often across every track hung a small noose of plaited grass. Sometimes we spent whole days destroying these snares.

In order to keep the dogs amused, we took to walking miles every day. We were exhausted, but they were not, and simply went off at night as well. Then we rode bicycles as fast as we could along the rough farm tracks, with the dogs bounding easily beside us. We wore ourselves out, trying to please Jock and Bill, who, we imagined, knew what we were doing and were trying to humour us. But we stuck at it. Once, at the end of a glade, we saw the skeleton of a large animal hanging from a noose. Some African had forgotten to visit his traps. We showed the skeleton to Jock and Bill, and talked and warned and threatened, almost in tears, because human speech was not dogs' speech. They sniffed around the bones, yapped a few times up into our faces—out of politeness, we felt; and were off again into the bush.

At school we heard that they were almost completely wild. Sometimes they came home for a meal, or a day's sleep, "treating the house," my mother complained, "like a hotel."

Then fate struck, in the shape of a bucktrap.

One night, very late, we heard whining, and went out to greet them. They were crawling towards the front door, almost on their bellies. Their ribs stuck out, their coats stared, their eyes shone unhealthily. They fell on the food we gave them; they were starved. Then on Jock's neck, which was bent over the food bowl, showed the explanation: a thick strand of wire. It was not solid wire, but made of a dozen twisted strands, and had been chewed through, near the collar. We examined Bill's mouth: chewing the wire through must have taken a long time, days perhaps: his gums and lips were scarred and bleeding, and his teeth were worn down to stumps, like an old dog's teeth. If the wire had not been stranded, Jock would have died in the trap. As it was, he fell ill, his lungs were strained, since he had been half strangled with the wire. And Bill could no longer chew properly, he ate uncomfortably, like an old person. They stayed at home for weeks, reformed dogs, barked around the house at night, and ate regular meals.

Then they went off again, but came home more often than they had. Jock's lungs weren't right: he would lie out in the sun, gasping and wheezing, as if trying to rest them. As for Bill, he could only eat soft food. How, then, did they manage when they were hunting?

One afternoon we were shooting, miles from home, and we saw them. First we heard the familiar excited yapping coming towards us, about two miles off. We were in a large vlei, full of tall whitish grass which swayed and bent along a fast regular line: a shape showed, it was a duiker, hard to see until it was close because it was reddish brown in colour, and the vlei had plenty of the pinkish feathery grass that turns a soft intense red in strong light. Being near sunset, the pale grass was on the verge of being invisible, like wires of white light; and the pink grass flamed and glowed; and the fur of the little buck shone red. It swerved suddenly. Had it seen us? No, it was because of Jock who had made a quick maneuvering turn from where he had been lying in the pink grass, to watch the buck, and behind it, Bill, pistoning along like a machine. Jock, who could no longer run fast, had turned the buck into Bill's jaws. We saw Bill bound at the little creature's throat, bring it down and hold it until Jock came in to kill it: his own teeth were useless now.

We walked over to greet them, but with restraint, for these two growling snarling creatures seemed not to know us, they raised eyes glazed with savagery, as they tore at the dead buck. Or rather, as Jock tore at it. Before we went away we saw Jock pushing over lumps of hot steaming meat towards Bill, who otherwise would have gone hungry.

They were really a team now; neither could function without the other. So we thought.

But soon Jock took to coming home from the hunting trips early, after one or two days, and Bill might stay out for a week or more. Jock lay watching the bush, and when Bill came, he licked his ears and face as if he had reverted to the role of Bill's mother.

Once I heard Bill barking and went to see. The telephone line ran through a vlei near the house to the farm over the hill. The wires hummed and sang and twanged. Bill was underneath the wires, which were a good fifteen feet over his head, jumping and barking at them: he was playing, out of exuberance, as he had done when a small puppy. But now it made me sad, seeing the strong dog playing all alone, while his friend lay quiet in the sun, wheezing from damaged lungs.

And what did Bill live on, in the bush? Rats, bird's eggs, lizards, anything *soft* enough? That was painful too, thinking of the powerful hunters in the days of their glory.

Soon we got telephone calls from neighbours: Bill dropped in, he finished off the food in our dog's bowl. . . . Bill seemed hungry, so we fed him. . . . Your dog Bill is looking very thin, isn't he? . . . Bill was around our chicken run—I'm sorry, but if he goes for the eggs, then . . .

Bill had puppies with a pedigreed bitch fifteen miles off: her owners were annoyed: Bill was not good enough for them, and besides there was the question of his "bad blood." All the puppies were destroyed. He was hanging around the house all the time, although he had been beaten, and they had even fired shots into the air to scare him off. Was there anything we could do to keep him at home? they asked; for they were tired of having to keep their bitch tied up.

No, there was nothing we could do. Rather, there was nothing we *would* do; for when Bill came trotting up from the bush to drink deeply out of Jock's bowl, and to lie for a while nose to nose with Jock, well, we could have caught him and tied him up, but we did not. "He won't last long anyway," said my father. And my mother told Jock that he was a sensible and intelligent dog; for she again sang praises of his nature and character just as if he had never spent so many glorious years in the bush.

I went to visit the neighbour who owned Bill's mate. She was tied to a post on the verandah. All night we were disturbed by a wild sad howling from the bush, and she whimpered and strained at her rope. In the morning I walked out into the hot silence of the bush, and called to him: Bill, Bill, it's me. Nothing, no sound. I sat on the slope of an antheap in the shade, and waited. Soon Bill came into view, trotting between the trees. He was very thin. He looked gaunt, stiff, wary—an old outlaw, afraid of traps. He saw me, but stopped about twenty yards off. He climbed halfway up another anthill and sat there in full sunlight, so I could see the harsh patches on his coat. We sat in silence, looking at each other. Then he lifted his head and howled, like the howl dogs give to the full moon, long, terrible, lonely. But it was morning, the sun calm and clear, and the bush without mystery. He sat and howled his heart out, his muzzle pointed away towards where his mate was chained. We could hear the faint whimperings she made, and the clink of her metal dish as she moved about. I couldn't stand it. It made my flesh cold, and I could see the hairs standing up on my forearm. I went over to him and sat by him and put my arm around his neck as once, so many years ago, I had put my arm around his mother that moonlit night before I stole her puppy away from her. He put his muzzle on my forearm and whimpered, or rather cried. Then he lifted it and howled. . . . "Oh my God, Bill, don't do that, please don't, it's not the slightest use, please, dear Bill. . . ." But he went on, until suddenly he leaped up in the middle of a howl, as if his pain were too strong to contain in sitting, and he sniffed at me, as if to say: That's you, is it, well, goodbye—then he turned his wild head to the bush and trotted away.

Very soon he was shot, coming out of a chicken run early one morning with an egg in his mouth.

Jock was quite alone now. He spent his old age lying in the sun, his nose pointed out over the miles and miles of bush between our house and the mountains where he had hunted all those years with Bill. He was really an old dog, his legs were stiff, and his coat was rough, and he wheezed and gasped. Sometimes, at night, when the moon was up, he went out to howl at it, and we would say: He's missing Bill. He would come back to sit at my mother's knee, resting his head so that she could stroke it. She would say: "Poor old Jock, poor old boy, are you missing that bad dog Bill?"

Sometimes, when he lay dozing, he started up and went trotting on his stiff old legs through the house and the outhouses, sniffing everywhere and anxiously whining. Then he stood, upright, one paw raised, as he used to do when he was young, and gazed over the bush and softly whined. And we would say: "He must have been dreaming he was out hunting with Bill."

He got ill. He could hardly breathe. We carried him in our arms down the hill into the bush, and my mother stroked and patted him while my father put the gun barrel to the back of his head and shot him.

SUSAN MINOT

Lust

Leo was from a long time ago, the first one I ever saw nude. In the spring before the Hellmans filled their pool, we'd go down there in the deep end, with baby oil, and like that. I met him the first month away at boarding school. He had a halo from the campus light behind him. I flipped.

Roger was fast. In his illegal car, we drove to the reservoir, the radio blaring, talking fast, fast, fast. He was always going for my zipper. He got kicked out sophomore year.

By the time the band got around to playing "Wild Horses," I had tasted Bruce's tongue. We were clicking in the shadows on the other side of the amplifier, out of Mrs. Donovan's line of vision. It tasted like salt, with my neck bent back, because we had been dancing so hard before.

Tim's line: "I'd like to see you in a bathing suit." I knew it was his line when he said the exact same thing to Annie Hines.

You'd go on walks to get off campus. It was raining like hell, my sweater as sopped as a wet sheep. Tim pinned me to a tree, the woods light brown and dark brown, a white house half hidden with the lights already on. The water was as loud as a crowd hissing. He made certain comments about my forehead, about my cheeks.

We started off sitting at one end of the couch and then our feet were squished against the armrest and then he went over to turn off the TV and came back after he had taken off his shirt and then we slid onto the floor and he got up again to close the door, then came back to me, a body waiting on the rug.

You'd try to wipe off the table or to do the dishes and Willie would untuck your shirt and get his hands up under in front, standing behind you, making puffy noises in your ear.

He likes it when I wash my hair. He covers his face with it and if I start to say something, he goes, "Shush."

For a long time, I had Philip on the brain. The less they noticed you, the more you got them on the brain.

My parents had no idea. Parents never really know what's going on, especially when you're away at school most of the time. If she met them, my mother might say, "Oliver seems nice" or "I like that one" without much of an opinion. If she didn't like them, "He's a funny fellow, isn't he?" or "Johnny's perfectly nice but a drink of water." My father was too shy to talk to them at all unless they played sports and he'd ask them about that.

The sand was almost cold underneath because the sun was long gone. Eben piled a mound over my feet, patting around my ankles, the ghostly surf rumbling behind him in the dark. He was the first person I ever knew who died, later that summer, in a car crash. I thought about it for a long time.

"Come here," he says on the porch.
    I go over to the hammock and he takes my wrist with two fingers.
    "What?"
    He kisses my palm then directs my hand to his fly.

Songs went with whichever boy it was. "Sugar Magnolia" was Tim, with the line "Rolling in the rushes/down by the riverside." With "Darkness Darkness," I'd picture Philip with his long hair. Hearing "Under My Thumb" there'd be the smell of Jamie's suede jacket.

We hid in the listening rooms during study hall. With a record cover over the door's window, the teacher on duty couldn't look in. I came out flushed and heady and back at the dorm was surprised how red my lips were in the mirror.

One weekend at Simon's brother's, we stayed inside all day with the shades down, in bed, then went out to Store 24 to get some ice cream. He stood at the magazine rack and read through *MAD* while I got butterscotch sauce, craving something sweet.

I could do some things well. Some things I was good at, like math or painting or even sports, but the second a boy put his arm around me, I forgot about wanting to do anything else, which felt like a relief at first until it became like sinking into a muck.

It was different for a girl.

When we were little, the brothers next door tied up our ankles. They held the door of the goat house and wouldn't let us out till we showed them our underpants. Then they'd forget about being after us and when we played whiffle ball, I'd be just as good as they were.

Then it got to be different. Just because you have on a short skirt, they yell from the cars, slowing down for a while, and if you don't look, they screech off and call you a bitch.

"What's the matter with me?" they say, point-blank.

Or else, "Why won't you go out with me? I'm not asking you to get married," about to get mad.

Or it'd be, trying to be reasonable, in a regular voice, "Listen, I just want to have a good time."

So I'd go because I couldn't think of something to say back that wouldn't be obvious, and if you go out with them, you sort of have to do something.

I sat between Mack and Eddie in the front seat of the pickup. They were having a fight about something. I've a feeling about me.

Certain nights you'd feel a certain surrender, maybe if you'd had wine. The surrender would be forgetting yourself and you'd put your nose to his neck and feel like a squirrel, safe, at rest, in a restful dream. But then you'd start to slip from that and the dark would come in and there'd be a cave. You make out the dim shape of the windows and feel yourself become a cave, filled absolutely with air, or with a sadness that wouldn't stop.

Teenage years. You know just what you're doing and don't see the things that start to get in the way.

Lots of boys, but never two at the same time. One was plenty to keep you in a state. You'd start to see a boy and something would rush over you like a fast storm cloud and you couldn't possibly think of anyone else. Boys took it differently. Their eyes perked up at any little number that walked by. You'd act like you weren't noticing.

The joke was that the school doctor gave out the pill like aspirin. He didn't ask you anything. I was fifteen. We had a picture of him in assembly, holding up an IUD shaped like a T. Most girls were on the pill, if anything, because they couldn't handle a diaphragm. I kept the dial in my top drawer like my mother and thought of her each time I tipped out the yellow tablets in the morning before chapel.

If they were too shy, I'd be more so. Andrew was nervous. We stayed up with his family album, sharing a pack of Old Golds. Before it got light, we turned on the TV. A man was explaining how to plant seedlings. His mouth jerked to the side in a tic. Andrew thought it was a riot and kept imitating him. I laughed to be polite. When we finally dozed off, he dared to put his arm around me, but that was it.

You wait till they come to you. With half fright, half swagger, they stand one step down. They dare to touch the button on your coat then lose their nerve and quickly drop their hand so you—you'd do anything for them. You touch their cheek.

The girls sit around in the common room and talk about boys, smoking their heads off.

"What are you complaining about?" says Jill to me when we talk about problems.

"Yeah," says Giddy. "You always have a boyfriend."

I look at them and think, As if.

I thought the worst thing anyone could call you was a cock-teaser. So, if you flirted, you had to be prepared to go through with it. Sleeping with someone was perfectly normal once you had done it. You didn't really worry about it. But there were other problems. The problems had to do with something else entirely.

Mack was during the hottest summer ever recorded. We were renting a house on an island with all sorts of other people. No one slept during the heat wave, walking around the house with nothing on which we were used to because of the nude beach. In the living room, Eddie lay on top of a coffee table to cool off. Mack and I, with the bedroom door open for air, sweated and sweated all night.

"I can't take this," he said at three A.M. "I'm going for a swim." He and some guys down the hall went to the beach. The heat put me on edge. I sat on a cracked chest by the open window and smoked and smoked till I felt even worse, waiting for something—I guess for him to get back.

One was on a camping trip in Colorado. We zipped our sleeping bags together, the coyotes' hysterical chatter far away. Other couples murmured in other tents. Paul was up before sunrise, starting a fire for breakfast. He wasn't much of a talker in the daytime. At night, his hand leafed about in the hair at my neck.

There'd be times when you overdid it. You'd get carried away. All the next day, you'd be in a total fog, delirious, absent-minded, crossing the street and nearly getting run over.

The more girls a boy has, the better. He has a bright look, having reaped fruits, blooming. He stalks around, sure-shouldered, and you have the feeling he's got more in him, a fatter heart, more stories to tell. For a girl, with each boy it's as though a petal gets plucked each time.

Then you start to get tired. You begin to feel diluted, like watered-down stew.

Oliver came skiing with us. We lolled by the fire after everyone had gone to bed. Each creak you'd think was someone coming downstairs. The silver loop bracelet he gave me had been a present from his girlfriend before.

On vacations, we went skiing, or you'd go south if someone invited you. Some people had apartments in New York that their families hardly ever used. Or summer houses, or older sisters. We always managed to find someplace to go.

We made the plan at coffee hour. Simon snuck out and met me at Main Gate after lights-out. We crept to the chapel and spent the night in the balcony. He tasted like onions from a submarine sandwich.

The boys are one of two ways: either they can't sit still or they don't move. In front of the TV, they won't budge. On weekends they play touch football while we sit on the sidelines, picking blades of grass to chew on, and watch. We're always watching them run around. We shiver in the stands, knocking our boots together to keep our toes warm, and they whizz across the ice, chopping their sticks around the puck. When they're in the rink, they refuse to look at you, only eyeing each other beneath low helmets. You cheer for them but they don't look up, even if it's a face-off when nothing's happening, even if they're doing drills before any game has started at all.

Dancing under the pink tent, he bent down and whispered in my ear. We slipped away to the lawn on the other side of the hedge. Much later, as he was leaving the buffet with two plates of eggs and sausage, I saw the grass stains on the knees of his white pants.

Tim's was shaped like a banana, with a graceful curve to it. They're all different. Willie's like a bunch of walnuts when nothing was happening, another's as thin as a thin hot dog. But it's like faces; you're never really surprised.

Still, you're not sure what to expect.

I look into his face and he looks back. I look into his eyes and they look back at mine. Then they look down at my mouth so I look at his mouth, then back to his eyes then, backing up, at his whole face. I think, Who? Who are you? His head tilts to one side.
  I say, "Who are you?"
  "What do you mean?"
  "Nothing."
  I look at his eyes again, deeper. Can't tell who he is, what he thinks.
  "What?" he says. I look at his mouth.
  "I'm just wondering," I say and go wandering across his face. Study the chin line. It's shaped like a persimmon.
  "Who are you? What are you thinking?"
  He says, "What the hell are you talking about?"

Then they get mad after, when you say enough is enough. After, when it's easier to explain that you don't want to. You wouldn't dream of saying that maybe you weren't really ready to in the first place.

Gentle Eddie. We waded into the sea, the waves round and plowing in, buffalo-headed, slapping our thighs. I put my arms around his freckled shoulders and he held me up, buoyed by the water, and rocked me like a sea shell.

I had no idea whose party it was, the apartment jam-packed, stepping over people in the hallway. The room with the music was practically empty, the bare floor, me in red shoes. This fellow slides onto one knee and takes me around the waist and we rock to jazzy tunes, with my toes pointing heavenward, and waltz and spin and dip to "Smoke Gets in Your Eyes" or "I'll Love You Just for Now." He puts his head to my chest, runs a sweeping hand down my inside thigh and we go loose-limbed and sultry and as smooth as silk and I stamp my red heels and he takes me into a swoon. I never saw him again after that but I thought, I could have loved that one.

You wonder how long you can keep it up. You begin to feel as if you're showing through, like a bathroom window that only lets in grey light, the kind you can't see out of.

They keep coming around. Johnny drives up at Easter vacation from Baltimore and I let him in the kitchen with everyone sound asleep. He has friends waiting in the car.

"What are you, crazy? It's pouring out there," I say.

"It's okay," he says. "They understand."

So he gets some long kisses from me, against the refrigerator, before he goes because I hate those girls who push away a boy's face as if she were made out of Ivory soap, as if she's that much greater than he is.

The note on my cubby told me to see the headmaster. I had no idea for what. He had received complaints about my amorous displays on the town green. It was Willie that spring. The headmaster told me he didn't care what I did but that Casey Academy had a reputation to uphold in the town. He lowered his glasses on his nose. "We've got twenty acres of woods on this campus," he said. "If you want to smooch with your boyfriend, there are twenty acres for you to do it out of the public eye. You read me?"

Everybody'd get weekend permissions for different places, then we'd all go to someone's house whose parents were away. Usually there'd be more boys than girls. We raided the liquor closet and smoked pot at the kitchen table and you'd never know who would end up where, or with whom. There were always disasters. Ceci got bombed and cracked her head open on the banister and needed stitches. Then there was the time Wendel Blair walked through the picture window at the Lowes' and got slashed to ribbons.

He scared me. In bed, I didn't dare look at him. I lay back with my eyes closed, luxuriating because he knew all sorts of expert angles, his hands never fumbling, going over my whole body, pressing the hair up and off the back of my head, giving an extra hip shove, as if to say *There*. I parted my eyes slightly, keeping the screen of my lashes low because it was too much to look at him, his mouth loose and pink and parted, his eyes looking through my forehead, or kneeling up, looking through my throat. I was ashamed but couldn't look him in the eye.

You wonder about things feeling a little off-kilter. You begin to feel like a piece of pounded veal.

At boarding school, everyone gets depressed. We go in and see the housemother, Mrs. Gunther. She got married when she was eighteen. Mr. Gunther was her high school sweetheart, the only boyfriend she ever had.

"And you knew you wanted to marry him right off?" we ask her.

She smiles and says, "Yes."

"They always want something from you," says Jill, complaining about her boyfriend.

"Yeah," says Giddy. "You always feel like you have to deliver something."

"You do," says Mrs. Gunther. "Babies."

After sex, you curl up like a shrimp, something deep inside you ruined, slammed in a place that sickens at slamming, and slowly you fill up with an overwhelming sadness, an elusive gaping worry. You don't try to explain it, filled with the knowledge that it's nothing after all, everything filling up finally and absolutely with death. After the briskness of loving, loving stops. And you roll over with death stretched out alongside you like a feather boa, or a snake, light as air, and you . . . you don't even ask for anything or try to say something to him because it's obviously your own damn fault. You haven't been able to—to what? To open your heart. You open your legs but can't, or don't dare anymore, to open your heart.

It starts this way:

You stare into their eyes. They flash like all the stars are out. They look at you seriously, their eyes at a low burn and their hands no matter what starting off shy and with such a gentle touch that the only thing you can do is take that tenderness and let yourself be swept away. When, with one attentive finger they tuck the hair behind your ear, you—

You do everything they want.

Then comes after. After when they don't look at you. They scratch their balls, stare at the ceiling. Or if they do turn, their gaze is altogether changed. They are surprised. They turn casually to look at you, distracted, and get a mild distracted surprise. You're gone. Their blank look tells you that the girl they were fucking is not there anymore. You seem to have disappeared.

WALTER MOSLEY

Pet Fly

I HAD BEEN SEEING Mona Donelli around the building since my first day working in interoffice mail. Mona laughing, Mona complaining about her stiff new shoes or the air conditioning or her boyfriend refusing to take her where she wanted to go. She's very pretty. Mona wears short skirts and giggles a lot. She's not serious at all. When silly Mona comes in she says hello and asks how you are, but before you get a chance to answer she's busy talking about what she saw on TV last night or something funny that happened on the ferry from Staten Island that morning.

I would see Mona almost every day on my delivery route—at the coffee-break room on the fifth floor or in a hallway, never at a desk. So when I made a rare delivery to the third-floor mortgage department and saw her sitting there, wearing a conservative sweater buttoned all the way up to her throat, I was surprised. She was so subdued, not sad but peaceful, looking at the wall in front of her and holding a yellow pencil with the eraser against her chin.

"Air conditioning too high again?" I asked, just so she'd know that I paid attention to the nonsense she babbled about.

She looked at me and I got a chill, because it didn't feel like the same person I saw flitting around the office. She gave me a silent and friendly smile, even though her eyes seemed to be wondering what my question meant.

I put down the big brown envelope addressed to her department and left without saying anything else.

Back in the basement, I asked my boss, Ernie, what was wrong with Mona.

"Nothing," he said. "I think she busted up with some guy or something. No, no, I'm a liar. She went out with her boyfriend's best friend without telling him. Now she doesn't get why the boyfriend's mad. That's what she said. Bitch. What she think?"

Ernie didn't suffer fools, as my mother would say. He was an older black man who had moved to New York from Georgia thirty-three years ago. He had come to work at Carter's Home Insurance three days after he arrived. "I would have been here on day one," he told me, "but my bus got in on Friday afternoon."

I'd been there for only three weeks. After I graduated from Hunter College, I didn't know what to do. I had a B.A. in poli sci, but I didn't really have any skills. Couldn't type or work a computer. I wrote all my papers in longhand and used a typing service. I didn't know what I wanted to do, but I had to pay the rent. When

Walter Mosley, "Pet Fly" originally published in The New Yorker, *December 13, 1999. Reprinted by permission of Walter Mosley and the Watkins/Loomis Agency.*

I applied for a professional-trainee position that Carter's Home had advertised at Hunter, the personnel officer told me that there was nothing available, but maybe if I took the mailroom position something might open up.

"They hired two white P.T.s the day after you came," Ernie told me at the end of the first week. I decided to ignore that. Maybe those people had applied before me, or maybe they had skills with computers or something.

I didn't mind my job. Big Linda Washington and Little Linda Brown worked with me. The Lindas had earphones and listened to music while they wheeled around their canvas mail carts. Big Linda liked rap and Little Linda liked R & B. Neither one talked to me much.

My only friend at work was Ernie. He was the interoffice mail director. He and I would sit in the basement and talk for hours sometimes. Ernie was proud of his years at Carter's Home. He liked the job and the company, but he had no patience for most of the bosses.

"Workin' for white people is always the same thing," Ernie would say.

"But Mr. Drew's black," I said the first time I heard his perennial complaint. Drew was the supervisor for all postal and interoffice communication. He was a small man with hard eyes and breath that smelled of vitamins.

"Used to be," Ernie said. "Used to be. But ever since he got promoted he forgot all about that. Used to be he'd come down here and we'd talk like you 'n' me doin'. But now he just stands at the door and grins and nods. Now he's so scared I'm gonna pull him down that he won't even sit for a minute."

"I don't get it," I once said to Ernie. "How can you like the job and the company if you don't like the people you work for?"

"It's a talent," he replied.

Why 'on't you tuck in your shirt?" Big Linda Washington said, sneering at me on the afternoon after I had seen Mona Donelli at her third-floor desk. "You look like some kinda fool, hangin' out all over the place."

Big Linda was taller than I, broader, too, and I'm pretty big. Her hair was straightened and frosted in gold. She wore dresses in primary colors, as a rule. Her skin was berry black. Her face, unless it was contorted from appraising me, was pretty.

We were in the service elevator, going up to the fifth floor. I tucked the white shirttails into my black jeans.

"At least you could make it even so the buttons go straight down," she remarked. "Just 'cause you light-skinned you can't go 'round lookin' like a mess."

I would have had to open up my pants to do it right, and I didn't want Big Linda to get any more upset than she already was.

She grunted and sucked a tooth.

The elevator opened, and she rolled out her cart. We had parallel routes, but I went in the opposite direction, deciding to take mail from the bottom of the stack rather than let her humiliate me.

The first person I ran into was Mona. Now she was wearing a one-piece deep red dress held up by spaghetti straps. Her breasts were free under the thin fabric, and her legs were bare. Mona was short, with thick black hair and green eyes. Her skin had a hint of olive but not so deep as what you think of as a Sicilian complexion.

"I can see why you were wearing that sweater at your desk," I said.

"What?" she replied, in a very unfriendly tone.

"That white sweater you were wearing," I said.

"What's wrong with you? I don't even own a white sweater."

She turned abruptly and clicked away on her red high heels. I wondered what had happened. I kept thinking that it was because of my twisted-up shirt. Maybe that's what made people treat me badly, maybe it was my appearance.

I continued along my route, pulling files from the bottom and placing them in the right "in" boxes.

"If the boxes ain't side by side, just drop it anywhere and pick up whatever you want to," Ernie had told me on my first day. "That's what I do. Mr. Averill put down the rules thirteen years ago, just before they kicked him upstairs."

Bernard Averill was the vice president in charge of all nonprofessional employees. He administered the cafeteria workers, the maintenance staff, secretarial services, and both the interoffice and postal mail departments. He was Ernie's hero because he was the only V.P. who had worked his way up from an entry-level position.

When I'd finished the route, I went through the exit door at the far end of the hall to get a drink of water. I planned to wait there long enough for Big Linda to have gone back down. While I was at the water fountain, a fly buzzed by my head. It caught my attention because not many flies made it into the air-conditioned buildings around Wall Street, even in summer.

The fly landed on my hand, then flew to the cold aluminum bowl of the water fountain. He didn't have enough time to drink before zooming up to the ceiling. From there he lit on the doorknob, then landed on the baby finger of my left hand. After that he buzzed down to the floor. He took no more than a second to enjoy each perch.

"You sure jumpy, Mr. Fly," I said, as I might have when I was a child. "But you might be a Miss Fly, huh?"

The idea that the neurotic fly could be a female brought Mona to mind. I hustled my cart toward the elevator, passing Big Linda on the way. She was standing in the hall, talking to another young black woman.

"I got to wait for a special delivery from, um, investigations," Big Linda explained.

"I got to go see a friend on three," I replied.

"Oh." Big Linda seemed relieved.

I realized that she was afraid I'd tell Ernie that she was idling with her friends. Somehow that stung more than her sneers.

She was still wearing the beaded sweater, but instead of the eraser she had a tiny Wite-Out brush in her hand, half an inch from a sheet of paper on her violet blotter.

"I bet that blotter used to be blue, huh?"

"What?" She frowned at me.

"That blotter—it looks violet, purple, but that's because it used to be blue but the sun shined on it, from the window."

She turned her upper torso to look out the window. I could see the soft contours of her small breasts against the white fabric.

"Oh," she said, turning back to me. "I guess."

"Yeah," I said. "I notice things like that. My mother says that's why I never finish anything. She says I get distracted all the time and don't keep my eye on the job."

"Do you have more mail for me?"

"No, uh-uh, I was just thinking."

She looked at the drying Wite-Out brush and then jammed it back into the small bottle that was in her other hand.

"I was thinking about when I saw you this morning," I continued. "About when I saw you and asked about the air conditioning and your sweater and you looked at me like I was crazy."

"Yes," she said, "why did you ask that?"

"Because I thought you were Mona Donelli," I said triumphantly.

"Oh." She sounded disappointed. "Most people figure out that I'm not Mona because my nameplate says Lana Donelli."

"Oh," I said, suddenly crushed. I could notice a blotter turning violet, but I couldn't read a nameplate.

Lana was amused.

"Don't look so sad," she said. "I mean, even when they see the name some people still call me Mona."

"They do?"

"Yeah. It's a problem having an identical twin. They see the name and think that Mona's a nickname or something. Isn't that dumb?"

"I didn't know you had a sister, but I saw Mona on the fifth floor in a red dress, and then I saw a fly that couldn't sit still, and then I knew that you had to be somebody else," I said.

"You're funny," Lana said, crinkling up her nose, as if she were trying to identify a scent. "What's your name?"

"Rufus Coombs."

"Hi, Rufus," she said.

"Hey," I said.

My apartment is on 168th Street, in Washington Heights. It's pretty much a Spanish-speaking neighborhood. I don't know many people there, but the rent is all I can afford. My apartment—living room with a kitchen alcove, a small bedroom, and a toilet with a shower—is on the eighth floor and looks out over the Hudson. The $458 a month includes heat and gas, but I pay my own electric. I took it because of the view. There was a cheaper unit on the second floor, but it had windows that look out on a brick wall and I was afraid I'd be burglarized.

"Do you own a TV or a stereo?" my mother asked when I was trying to decide which apartment to take.

"You know I don't."

"Then you ain't got nuthin' to burgle," she said. I had called her in California, where she lives with my uncle.

"But they don't know that," I said. "I might have a color TV with VCR and a bad sound system."

"Lord," my mother prayed.

I didn't own much; she was right about that. Single mattress on the floor, an old oak chair that I found on the street, and kitchen shelving that I bought from a liquidator, for bookshelves, propped up in the corner. I also have a rice pot, a frying pan, and a kettle, with cutlery and enough plates for two.

I have Rachel, an ex-girlfriend living in the East Village, who will call me back at work if I don't call her too often. My two other friends are Eric Chen and Willy Jones. They both live in Brooklyn and still go to school.

That evening, I climbed the seven flights up to my apartment. The elevator had stopped working a month ago. I sat in my chair and looked at the water. It was peaceful and relaxing. A fly was buzzing against the glass, trying to get out.

I got up to kill him. But up close I hesitated. His coloring was unusual, a metallic green. The dull red eyes seemed too large for the body, as though he were an intelligent mutant fly from some far-flung future on late-night television.

He buzzed against the pane, trying to get away from me. When I returned to my chair, he settled. The red sun was hovering above the cliffs of New Jersey. The green fly watched. I thought of the fly I'd seen at work. That bug had been black and fairly small by fly standards. Then I thought about Mona and then Lana. The smallest nudge of an erection stirred. I thought of calling Rachel, but I didn't have the heart to walk the three blocks to a phone booth. So I watched the sunset gleaming around the fly, who was now just a black spot on the window. I fell asleep in the chair.

At three A.M. I woke up and made macaroni and cheese from a mix. The fly came into the cooking alcove, where I stood eating my meal. He lit on the big spoon I'd used to stir the dinner and joined me for supper.

Ernie told me that mortgaging didn't get much interoffice mail.

"Most of their correspondence comes by regular mail," he explained.

"Aren't they on the newsletter list?"

"She a white girl?"

"So?"

"Nuthin'. But I want you to tell me what it's like if you get it."

I didn't answer him.

I began delivering invitations to office parties, sales force newsletters, and productivity tips penned by Mr. Averill to Lana Donelli. We made small talk for thirty seconds or so, then she'd pick up the phone to make a call. I always looked back as I rounded the corner to make sure she really had a call to make. She always did.

The following Monday, I bought a glass paperweight with the image of a smiling Buddha's face etched in the bottom. When I got to Lana's desk, she wasn't there. I waited around for a while but she didn't appear, so I wrote her a note that said "From Rufus to Lana" and put the leaded-glass weight on it.

I went away excited and half scared. What if she didn't see my note? What if she did and thought it was stupid? I was so nervous that I didn't go back to her desk that day.

"I really shouldn't have left it," I said that night to the green fly. He was perched peacefully on the rim of a small saucer. I had filled the inner depression with a honey-and-water solution. I was eating a triple cheeseburger with bacon and fries from Wendy's. My pet fly seemed happy with his honey water and buzzed my sandwich only a few times before settling down to drink.

"Maybe she doesn't like me," I said. "Maybe it's just that she was nice to me because she feels sorry for me. But how will I know if I don't try and see if she likes me?"

"Hi," I said to Lana the next morning. She was wearing a jean jacket over a white T-shirt. She smiled and nodded. I handed her Mr. Averill's productivity tips newsletter.

"Did you see the paperweight?"

"Oh, yeah," she said without looking me in the eye. "Thanks." Then she picked up the phone and began pressing buttons. "Hi, Tristan? Lana. I wanted to know if . . ." She put her hand over the receiver and looked at me. "Can I do something else for you?"

"Oh," I said. "No. No," and I wheeled away in a kind of euphoria.

It's only now, when I look back on that moment, that I can see the averted eyes, the quick call, and the rude dismissal for what they were. All I heard then was "Thanks." I even remember a smile. Maybe she did smile for a brief moment, maybe not.

On Tuesday and Wednesday, I left three presents for her. I left them when she was away from her desk. I got her a small box of four Godiva chocolates, a silk rose, and a jar of fancy rose-petal jelly. I didn't leave any more notes. I was sure that she'd know who it was.

On Thursday evening, I went to a nursery on the East Side, just south of Harlem proper. There I bought a bonsai, a crab apple tree, for $347.52. I figured I'd leave it during Lana's Friday lunch break, and then she'd be so happy that on Monday she'd have to have lunch with me, no matter what.

I suspected that something was wrong when my pet fly went missing. He didn't even show up when I started eating a Beef Burrito Supreme from Taco Bell. I checked the big spiderweb near the bathroom window, but there were no little bundles that I could see.

That evening I was on edge, thinking I saw flies flitting into every corner.

"What's that?" Ernie asked me the next morning when I came in with the tiny crab apple tree.

"It's a tree."

"Tree for what?"

"My friend Willy wanted me to pick it up for him. He wants it for his new apartment, and the only place he could get it is up near me. I'm gonna meet him at lunch and give it to him."

"Uh-huh," Ernie said.

"You got my cart loaded?" I asked him.

Just then the Lindas came out of the service elevator. Big Linda looked at me and shook her head, managing to express contempt and pity at the same time.

"There's your carts," Ernie said to them.

They attached their earphones and rolled back to the service elevator. Little Linda was looking me in the eye as the slatted doors closed. She was still looking at me as the lift rose.

"What about me?"

"That's all I got right now. Why don't you sit here with me?"

"Okay." I sat down, expecting Ernie to bring up one of his regular topics, either something about Georgia, white bosses, or the horse races, which he followed but never wagered on. But instead of saying anything he just started reading the *Post*.

After a few minutes I was going to say something, but the big swinging door opened. Our boss, Mr. Drew, leaned in. He smiled and nodded at Ernie and then pointed at me.

"Rufus Coombs?"

"Yeah?"

"Come with me."

I followed the dapper little man through the messy service hall to the passenger elevator, which the couriers rarely took. It was a two-man elevator, so Drew and I had to stand very close to each other. He wore too much cologne, but otherwise he was perfect for his supervisory job, wearing a light gray suit with a shirt that hinted at yellow. I knew that he must have been in his forties, but he could have passed for a graduate student. He was light-skinned, like me, with what my mother called good hair. There were freckles around his eyes. I could see all of that because Mr. Drew avoided my gaze. He wouldn't engage me in any way.

We got out on the second floor and went to his office, which was at the far end of the mail-sorting room.

I looked around the room as Drew was entering his office. I saw Mona looking at me from the crevice of a doorway. I knew it was Mona because she was wearing a skimpy dress that could have been worn on a hot date. I got only a glimpse of her before she ducked away.

"Come on in, Coombs," Drew said.

The office was tiny. Drew actually had to stand on the tips of his toes and hug the wall to get behind his desk. There was a stool in front of the desk, not a chair.

By the time he said, "Sir down," I had lost my nervousness. I gauged the power of Mr. Leonard Drew by the size of his office.

"You're in trouble, Rufus," he said, looking as somber as he could.

"I am?"

He lifted a pink sheet of paper and shook it at me.

"Do you recognize this?" he asked.

"No."

"This is a sexual-harassment complaint form."

"Yeah?"

"It names you on the complaint."

"I don't get it."

"Lana Donelli . . ." He went on to explain everything that I had been doing and feeling for the last week as if they were crimes. Going to Lana's desk, talking to her, leaving gifts. Even remarking on her clothes had been construed as if there was a sexual innuendo attached. By the time he was finished, I was worried that the police might be called in.

"Lana says that she's afraid to come in to work," Drew said, his freckles disappearing into angry lines around his eyes.

I wanted to say that I didn't mean to scare her, but I could see that my intentions didn't matter, that a small woman like Lana would be afraid of a big, sloppy mail clerk hovering over her and leaving notes and presents.

"I'm sorry," I said.

"Sorry doesn't mean much when it's got to this point," he said. "If it was up to me, I'd send you home right now. But Mr. Averill says he wants to talk to you."

"Aren't you supposed to give me a warning?" I asked.

Drew twisted up his lips, as if he had tasted something so foul that he just had to spit it out. "You haven't been here a month. You're on probation."

"Oh," I said.

"Well?" he asked after a few moments.

"What?"

"Go back to the mailroom and stay down there. Tell Ernie that I don't want you in the halls. You're supposed to meet Mr. Averill at one-forty-five, in his office. I've given him my recommendation to let you go. After something like this, there's really no place for you here. But he can still refer the matter to the police. Lana might want a restraining order."

I wanted to tell him that a restraining order was ridiculous. I wanted to go to Lana and tell her the same thing. I wanted to tell her that I bought her a rose because she wore rose toilet water, that I bought her the tree because the sun on her blotter could support a plant. I really liked her. But even while I was imagining what I could say, I knew that it didn't matter.

"Well?" Drew said. "Go."

Ernie made busywork for us that morning. He told me that he was upset about what had happened, that he'd told Drew to go easy.

"You know if you was white this wouldn't never have happened," Ernie said. "That girl just scared you some Mandingo gonna rape her. You know that's a shame."

I went up to the third floor a little before twelve. Lana was sitting at her desk, writing on a yellow legal pad. I walked right up to her and started talking so she couldn't ignore what I had to say.

"I just wanted to tell you that I'm sorry if you think I was harassing you. I didn't mean it, but I can see how you might have thought I was . . ."

Lana's face got hard.

". . . but I'm gonna get fired right after lunch and I just wanted to ask you one thing."

She didn't say anything, so I said, "Is it because I'm black that you're so scared'a me?"

"You're black?" she said. "I thought you were Puerto Rican or Spanish or something. I didn't know you were black. My boyfriend is black. You just give me the creeps. That's why I complained. I didn't think they were going to fire you."

She didn't care if I lived or died. She wasn't even scared, just disgusted. I thought I was in love, and I was about to be fired, and she'd never even looked close enough to see me.

I was so embarrassed that I went away without saying another word. I went down to the mailroom and sorted rubber bands until one-thirty-five.

Vice President Bernard Averill's office was on the forty-eighth floor of the Carter's Home Building. His secretary's office was larger by far than Mr. Drew's cubbyhole. The smiling blonde led me into Averill's airy room. Behind him was a giant window looking out over Battery Park, Ellis Island, and the Statue of Liberty. I would have been impressed if I wasn't empty inside.

Averill was on the phone.

"Sorry, Nick," he said into the receiver. "My one-forty-five is here."

He stood up, tall and thin. His gray suit looked expensive. His white shirt was crisp and bright under a rainbow tie. His gray hair was combed back, and his mustache was sharp enough to cut bread, as my mother is known to say.

"Sit down, Mr. Coombs."

He sat also. In front of him were two sheets of paper. At his left hand was the pink harassment form, at his right was a white form. Outside, the Budweiser blimp hovered next to Lady Liberty.

Averill brought his fingertips to just under his nose and gazed at a spot above my head.

"How's Ernie?" he asked.

"He's good," I said. "He's a great boss."

"He's a good man. He likes you."

I didn't know what to say to that.

Averill looked down at his desk. "This does not compute."

"What?"

He patted the white page. "This says that you're a college graduate, magna cum laude in political science, that you came here to be a professional trainee." He patted the pink sheet. "This says that you're an interoffice-mail courier who harasses secretaries in the mortgage department."

Averill reached into his vest pocket and came out with an open package of cigarettes. At orientation they'd told us that there was absolutely no smoking anywhere in the building, but he took one out anyway. He lit up and took a deep drag, holding the smoke in his lungs for a long time before exhaling.

"Is there something wrong with you?" he asked.

"I don't think so," I said, swallowing hard.

Averill examined me through the tobacco haze. He seemed disgusted.

Staring directly into my eyes, he said, "Do you see this desk?"

The question petrified me, but I couldn't say why. Maybe it was the intensity of his gaze.

"I could call five or six women into this office right now and have them right here on this desk. Right here." He jabbed the desk with his middle finger.

My heart was racing. I had to open my mouth to get enough air.

"They're not going to fill out any pink slips," he said. "Do you know why?"

I shook my head.

"Because I'm a man. I don't go running around leaving chocolates on empty desks like bait. I don't fake reasons to come skulking around with newsletters."

Averill seemed angry as well as offended. I wondered if he knew Lana, or maybe her family. Maybe he wanted to fight me. I wanted to quit right then, to stand up and walk out before anything else happened. I was already thinking of where I could apply for another job when Averill sat back and smiled.

"Why are you in the interoffice-mail room?" he asked, suddenly much friendlier.

"No P.T. positions were open when I applied," I said.

"Nonsense. We don't have a limit on P.T.s."

"But Ms. Worth said—"

"Oh." Averill held up his hand. "Reena. You know, Ernie helped me out when I got here, twenty-three years ago. I was just a little older than you. They didn't have the P.T. program back then, just a few guys like Ernie. He never even finished high school, but he showed me the ropes."

Averill drummed the fingers of his free hand between the two forms that represented me.

"I know this Lana's sister," he said. "Always wearing those cocktail dresses in to work. Her boss is afraid to say anything, otherwise he might get a pink slip, too." He paused to ponder some more. "How would you like to be a P.T. floater?"

"What's that?" I asked.

"Bumps you up to a grade seven and lets you move around in the different departments until you find a fit."

I was a grade B1.

"I thought you were going to fire me."

"That's what Drew suggested, but Ernie says that it's just a mixup. What if I talked to Lana? What if I asked her to hold this back, to give you a second chance?"

"I'd like that," I said. "Thanks."

"Probably be better if I let Drew fire you, you know," he said, standing up. I stood, too. "I mean if you fuck up once you'll probably just do it again, right?"

He held out his hand.

Watching the forbidden smoke curl around his head, I imagined that Averill was some kind of devil. When I thanked him and shook his hand, something inside me wanted to scream.

I found six unused crack vials a block from the subway stop near my apartment. I knew they were unused because they still had the little plastic stoppers in them.

When I got upstairs, I spent hours searching my place. I looked under the mattress and behind the toilet, under the radiator, and even down under the burners on the stove. Finally, after midnight, I decided to open the windows.

The fly had crawled down into the crack between the window frame and the sill in my bedroom. His green body had dried out, which made his eyes even bigger. He'd gone down there to die, or maybe, I thought, he was trying to get away from me. Maybe I had killed him. Later, I found out that flies have a very short life span. He probably died of old age.

I took his small, dried-out corpse and put it in one of the crack vials. I stoppered him in the tiny glass coffin and buried him among the roots of the bonsai crab apple.

"So you finally bought something nice for your house," my mother said after I told her about the changes in my life. "Maybe next you'll get a real bed."

ZZ PACKER

Brownies

By the end of our first day at Camp Crescendo, the girls in my Brownie troop had decided to kick the asses of each and every girl in Brownie Troop 909. Troop 909 was doomed from the first day of camp; they were white girls, their complexions like a blend of ice cream: strawberry, vanilla. They turtled out from their bus in pairs, their rolled-up sleeping bags chromatized with Disney characters—Sleeping Beauty, Snow White, Mickey Mouse—or the generic ones cheap parents bought— washed-out rainbows, unicorns, curly-eyelashed frogs. Some clutched Igloo coolers and still others held on to stuffed toys like pacifiers, looking all around them like tourists determined to be dazzled.

Our troop wended its way past their bus, past the ranger station, past the colorful trail guide drawn like a treasure map, locked behind glass.

"Man, did you smell them?" Arnetta said, giving the girls a slow once-over. "They smell like Chihuahuas. *Wet* Chihuahuas." Although we had passed their troop by yards, Arnetta raised her nose in the air and grimaced.

Arnetta said this from the very rear of the line, far away from Mrs. Margolin, who strung our troop behind her like a brood of obedient ducklings. Mrs. Margolin even looked like a mother duck—she had hair cropped close to a small ball of a head, almost no neck, and huge, miraculous breasts. She wore enormous belts that looked like the kind weight lifters wear, except hers were cheap metallic gold or rabbit fur or covered with gigantic fake sunflowers. Often these belts would become nature lessons in and of themselves. "See," Mrs. Margolin once said to us, pointing to her belt. "This one's made entirely from the feathers of baby pigeons."

The belt layered with feathers was uncanny enough, but I was more disturbed by the realization that I had never actually *seen* a baby pigeon. I searched for weeks for one, in vain—scampering after pigeons whenever I was downtown with my father.

But nature lessons were not Mrs. Margolin's top priority. She saw the position of troop leader as an evangelical post. Back at the A.M.E. church where our Brownie meetings were held, she was especially fond of imparting religious aphorisms by means of acrostics—Satan was the "Serpent Always Tempting And Noisome"; she'd refer to the Bible as "Basic Instructions Before Leaving Earth." Whenever she occasionally quizzed us on these at the beginning of the Brownie meeting, expecting to hear the acrostics parroted back to her, only Arnetta's correct replies soared over our vague mumblings. "Jesus?" Mrs. Margolin might ask expectantly, and Arnetta alone would dutifully answer, "Jehovah's Example, Saving Us Sinners."

Arnetta made a point of listening to Mrs. Margolin's religious talk and giving her what she wanted to hear. Because of this, Arnetta could have blared through a megaphone that the white girls of Troop 909 were "wet Chihuahuas" without arousing so much as a blink from Mrs. Margolin. Once Arnetta killed the troop goldfish by feeding it a French fry covered in ketchup, and when Mrs. Margolin demanded an explanation, Arnetta claimed that the goldfish had been eyeing her meal for *hours*, until—giving in to temptation—it had leapt up and snatched the whole golden fry from her fingertips.

"*Serious* Chihuahua," Octavia added—though neither Arnetta nor Octavia could *spell* "Chihuahua" or had ever *seen* a Chihuahua. Trisyllabic words had gained a sort of exoticism within our fourth-grade set at Woodrow Wilson Elementary. Arnetta and Octavia, compelled to outdo each other, would flip through the dictionary, determined to work the vulgar-sounding ones like "Djibouti" and "asinine" into conversation.

"*Caucasian* Chihuahuas," Arnetta said.

That did it. Drema and Elise doubled up on each other like inextricably entwined kites: Octavia slapped the skin of her belly; Janice jumped straight up in the air, then did it again, just as hard, as if to slam-dunk her own head. No one had laughed so hard since a boy named Martez had stuck his pencil in the electric socket and spent the whole day with a strange grin on his face.

"Girls, girls," said our parent helper, Mrs. Hedy. Mrs. Hedy was Octavia's mother. She wagged her index finger perfunctorily, like a windshield wiper. "Stop it now. Be good." She said this loudly enough to be heard, but lazily, nasally, bereft of any feeling or indication that she meant to be obeyed, as though she would say these words again at the exact same pitch if a button somewhere on her were pressed.

But the girls didn't stop laughing; they only laughed louder. It was the word "Caucasian" that had got them all going. One day at school, about a month before the Brownie camping trip, Arnetta had turned to a boy wearing impossibly high-ankled floodwater jeans, and said "What are *you*? *Caucasian?*" The word took off from there, and soon everything was Caucasian. If you ate too fast, you ate like a Caucasian; if you ate too slow, you ate like a Caucasian. The biggest feat anyone at Woodrow Wilson could do was to jump off the swing in midair, at the highest point in its arc, and if you fell (like I had, more than once) instead of landing on your feet, knees bent Olympic-gymnast-style, Arnetta and Octavia were prepared to comment. They'd look at each other with the silence of passengers who'd narrowly escaped an accident, then nod their heads, and whisper with solemn horror and haughtiness, "*Caucasian*."

Even the only white kid in our school, Dennis, got in on the Caucasian act. That time when Martez stuck the pencil in the socket, Dennis had pointed, and yelled, "That was *so* Caucasian!"

Living in the south suburbs of Atlanta, it was easy to forget about whites. Whites were like those baby pigeons: real and existing, but rarely thought about. Everyone had been to Rich's to go clothes shopping, everyone had seen white girls and their mothers coo-cooing over dresses; everyone had gone to the downtown library and seen white businessmen swish by importantly, wrists flexed in front of them to check the time on their watches as though they would change from Clark Kent into Superman any second. But those images were as fleeting as cards shuffled in a deck, whereas the ten white girls behind us—*invaders*, Arnetta would later call them—were instantly real and memorable, with their long shampoo-commercial hair, as straight as spaghetti from the box. This alone was reason for envy and hatred. The only black girl most of us had ever seen with hair that long was Octavia, whose hair hung past her butt like a Hawaiian hula dancer's. The sight of Octavia's mane prompted other girls to listen to her reverentially, as though whatever she had to say would somehow activate their own follicles. For example, when, on the first day of camp, Octavia made as if to speak, a silence began. "Nobody," Octavia said, "calls us niggers."

At the end of that first day, when half of our troop made its way back to the cabin after tag-team restroom visits, Arnetta said she'd heard one of the girls in Troop 909 call Daphne a nigger. The other half of the girls and I were helping Mrs. Margolin clean up the pots and pans from the ravioli dinner. When we made our way to the restrooms to wash up and brush our teeth, we met up with Arnetta midway.

"Man, I completely heard the girl," Arnetta reported. "Right, Daphne?"

Daphne hardly ever spoke, but when she did her voice was petite and tinkly, the voice one might expect from a shiny new earring. She'd written a poem once, for Langston Hughes Day, a poem brimming with all the teacher-winning ingredients—trees and oceans, sunsets and moons—but what cinched the poem for the grown-ups, snatching the win from Octavia's musical ode to Grandmaster Flash and the Furious Five, were Daphne's last lines:

> You are my father, the veteran
> When you cry in the dark
> It rains and rains and rains in my heart

She'd worn clean, though faded, jumpers and dresses when Chic jeans were the fashion, but when she went up to the dais to receive her prize journal, pages trimmed in gold, she wore a new dress with a velveteen bodice and a taffeta skirt as wide as an umbrella. All the kids clapped, though none of them understood the poem. I'd read encyclopedias the way others read comics, and I didn't get it. But those last lines pricked me, they were so eerie, and as my father and I ate cereal, I'd whisper over my Froot Loops, like a mantra, "*You are my father, the veteran. You are my father, the veteran, the veteran, the veteran,*" until my father, who acted in plays as Caliban and Othello and was not a veteran, marched me up to my teacher one morning, and said, "Can you tell me what the hell's wrong with this kid?"

I had thought Daphne and I might become friends, but she seemed to grow spooked by me whispering those lines to her, begging her to tell me what they meant, and I had soon understood that two quiet people like us were better off quiet alone.

"Daphne? Didn't you hear them call you a nigger?" Arnetta asked, giving Daphne a nudge.

The sun was setting through the trees, and their leafy tops formed a canopy of black lace for the flame of the sun to pass through. Daphne shrugged her shoulders at first, then slowly nodded her head when Arnetta gave her a hard look.

Twenty minutes later, when my restroom group returned to the cabin, Arnetta was still talking about Troop 909. My restroom group had passed by some of the 909 girls. For the most part, they had deferred to us, waving us into the restrooms, letting us go even though they'd gotten there first.

We'd seen them, but from afar, never within their orbit enough to see whether their faces were the way all white girls appeared on TV—ponytailed and full of energy, bubbling over with love and money. All I could see was that some rapidly fanned their faces with their hands, though the heat of the day had long passed. A few seemed to be lolling their heads in slow circles, half-purposefully, as if exercising the muscles of their necks, half-ecstatically, rolling their heads about like Stevie Wonder.

"We can't let them get away with that," Arnetta said, dropping her voice to a laryngitic whisper. "We can't let them get away with calling us niggers. I say we teach them a lesson." She sat down cross-legged on a sleeping bag, an embittered Buddha, eyes glimmering acrylic black. "We can't go telling Mrs. Margolin, either. Mrs. Margolin 'll say something about doing unto others and the path of righteousness and all. Forget that shit." She let her eyes flutter irreverently till they half closed, as though ignoring an insult not worth returning. We could all hear Mrs. Margolin outside, gathering the last of the metal campware.

Nobody said anything for a while. Arnetta's tone had an upholstered confidence that was somehow both regal and vulgar at once. It demanded a few moments of silence in its wake, like the ringing of a church bell or the playing of taps. Sometimes Octavia would ditto or dissent whatever Arnetta had said, and this was the signal that others could speak. But this time Octavia just swirled a long cord of hair into pretzel shapes.

"*Well?*" Arnetta said. She looked as if she had discerned the hidden severity of the situation and was waiting for the rest of us to catch up. Everyone looked from Arnetta to Daphne. It was, after all, Daphne who had supposedly been called the name, but Daphne sat on the bare cabin floor, flipping through the pages of the Girl Scout handbook, eyebrows arched in mock wonder, as if the handbook were a catalogue full of bright and startling foreign costumes. Janice broke the silence. She clapped her hands to broach her idea of a plan.

"They gone be sleeping," she whispered conspiratorially, "then we gone sneak into they cabin, then we gone put daddy longlegs in they sleeping bags. Then they'll wake up. Then we gone beat 'em up till they flat as frying pans!" She jammed her fist into the palm of her hand, then made a sizzling sound.

Janice's country accent was laughable, her looks homely, her jumpy acrobatics embarrassing to behold. Arnetta and Octavia volleyed amused, arrogant smiles whenever Janice opened her mouth, but Janice never caught the hint, spoke whenever she wanted, fluttered around Arnetta and Octavia futilely offering her opinions to their departing backs. Whenever Arnetta and Octavia shooed her away, Janice loitered until the two would finally sigh, "What *is* it, Miss Caucasoid? What do you want?"

"Oh shut up, Janice," Octavia said, letting a fingered loop of hair fall to her waist as though just the sound of Janice's voice had ruined the fun of her hair twisting.

"All right," Arnetta said, standing up. "We're going to have a secret meeting and talk about what we're going to do."

The word "secret" had a built-in importance. Everyone gravely nodded her head. The modifier form of the word had more clout than the noun. A secret meant nothing; it was like gossip: just a bit of unpleasant knowledge about someone who happened to be someone other than yourself. A secret *meeting*, or a secret *club*, was entirely different.

That was when Arnetta turned to me, as though she knew doing so was both a compliment and a charity.

"Snot, you're not going to be a bitch and tell Mrs. Margolin, are you?"

I had been called "Snot" ever since first grade, when I'd sneezed in class and two long ropes of mucus had splattered a nearby girl.

"Hey," I said. "Maybe you didn't hear them right—I mean—"

"Are you gonna tell on us or not?" was all Arnetta wanted to know, and by the time the question was asked, the rest of our Brownie troop looked at me as though they'd already decided their course of action, me being the only impediment. As though it were all a simple matter of patriotism.

Camp Crescendo used to double as a high school band and field hockey camp until an arching field hockey ball landed on the clasp of a girl's metal barrette, knifing a skull nerve, paralyzing the right side of her body. The camp closed down for a few years, and the girl's teammates built a memorial, filling the spot on which the girl fell with hockey balls, upon which they had painted—all in nail polish—get-well tidings, flowers, and hearts. The balls were still stacked there, like a shrine of ostrich eggs embedded in the ground.

On the second day of camp, Troop 909 was dancing around the mound of nail polish–decorated hockey balls, their limbs jangling awkwardly, their cries like the constant summer squeal of an amusement park. There was a stream that bordered the field hockey lawn, and the girls from my troop settled next to it, scarfing down the last of lunch: sandwiches made from salami and slices of tomato that had gotten waterlogged from the melting ice in the cooler. From the stream bank, Arnetta eyed the Troop 909 girls, scrutinizing their movements to glean inspiration for battle.

"Man," Arnetta said, "we could bum-rush them right now if that damn lady would *leave.*"

The 909 troop leader was a white woman with the severe pageboy hairdo of an ancient Egyptian. She lay sprawled on a picnic blanket. Sphinxlike, eating a banana, sometimes holding it out in front of her like a microphone. Beside her sat a girl slowly flapping one hand like a bird with a broken wing. Occasionally, the leader would call out the names of girls who'd attempted leapfrogs and flips, or of girls who yelled too loudly or strayed far from the circle.

"I'm just glad Big Fat Mama's not following us here," Octavia said. "At least we don't have to worry about her." Mrs. Margolin, Octavia assured us, was having her Afternoon Devotional, shrouded in mosquito netting, in a clearing she'd found. Mrs. Hedy was cleaning mud from her espadrilles in the cabin.

"I handled them." Arnetta sucked on her teeth and proudly grinned. "I told her we was going to gather leaves."

"Gather leaves," Octavia said, nodding respectfully. "That's a good one. They're so mad-crazy about this camping thing." She looked from ground to sky, sky to ground. Her hair hung down her back in two braids like a squaw's. "I mean, I really don't know why it's even called *camping*—all we ever do with Nature is find some twigs and say something like, 'Wow, this fell from a tree.'" She then studied her sandwich. With two disdainful fingers, she picked out a slice of dripping tomato, the sections congealed with red slime. She pitched it into the stream embrowned with dead leaves and the murky effigies of other dead things, but in the opaque water a group of small silver-brown fish appeared. They surrounded the tomato and nibbled.

"Look!" Janice cried. "Fishes! Fishes!" As she scrambled to the edge of the stream to watch, a covey of insects threw up tantrums from the wheatgrass and net-tle, a throng of tiny electric machines, all going at once. Octavia snuck up behind Janice as if to push her in. Daphne and I exchanged terrified looks. It seemed as though only we knew that Octavia was close enough—and bold enough—to actually push Janice into the stream. Janice turned around quickly, but Octavia was already staring serenely into the still water as though she were gathering some sort of courage from it. "What's so funny?" Janice said, eyeing them all suspiciously.

Elise began humming the tune to "Karma Chameleon," all the girls joining in, their hums light and facile. Janice began to hum, against everyone else, the high-octane opening chords of "Beat It."

"I love me some Michael Jackson," Janice said when she'd finished humming, smacking her lips as though Michael Jackson were a favorite meal. "I will marry Michael Jackson."

Before anyone had a chance to impress upon Janice the impossibility of this, Arnetta suddenly rose, made a sun visor of her hand, and watched Troop 909 leave the field hockey lawn.

"Dammit!" she said. "We've got to get them *alone*."

"They won't ever be alone," I said. All the rest of the girls looked at me. If I spoke even a word, I could count on someone calling me Snot, but everyone seemed to think that we could beat up these girls; no one entertained the thought that they might fight *back*. "The only time they'll be unsupervised is in the bathroom."

"Oh shut up, Snot," Octavia said.

But Arnetta slowly nodded her head. "The bathroom," she said. "The bathroom," she said, again and again. "The bathroom! The bathroom!" She cheered so blissfully that I thought for a moment she was joking.

According to Octavia's watch, it took us five minutes to hike to the restrooms, which were midway between our cabin and Troop 909's. Inside, the mirrors above the sinks returned only the vaguest of reflections, as though someone had taken a scouring pad to their surfaces to obscure the shine. Pine needles, leaves, and dirty flattened wads of chewing gum covered the floor like a mosaic. Webs of hair matted the drain in the middle of the floor. Above the sinks and below the mirrors, stacks of folded white paper towels lay on a long metal counter. Shaggy white balls of paper towels sat on the sink tops in a line like corsages on display. A thread of floss snaked from a wad of tissues dotted with the faint red-pink of blood. One of those white girls, I thought, had just lost a tooth.

The restroom looked almost the same as it had the night before, but it somehow seemed stranger now. We had never noticed the wooden rafters before, coming together in great V's. We were, it seemed, inside a whale, viewing the ribs of the roof of its mouth.

"Wow. It's a mess," Elise said.

"You can say that again."

Arnetta leaned against the doorjamb of a restroom stall. "This is where they'll be again," she said. Just seeing the place, just having a plan, seemed to satisfy her. "We'll go in and talk to them. You know, 'How you doing? How long will you be here?' that sort of thing. Then Octavia and I are gonna tell them what happens when they call any one of us a nigger."

"I'm going to say something, too," Janice said.

Arnetta considered this. "Sure," she said. "Of course. Whatever you want."

Janice pointed her finger like a gun at Octavia and rehearsed the line she'd thought up, "'We're gonna teach you a *lesson*.' That's what I'm going to say." She narrowed her eyes like a TV mobster. "'We're gonna teach you little girls a lesson!'"

With the back of her hand, Octavia brushed Janice's finger away. "You couldn't teach me to shit in a toilet."

"But," I said, "what if they say, 'We didn't say that. We didn't call anyone a N-I-G-G-E-R'?"

"Snot," Arnetta sighed. "Don't think. Just fight. If you even know how."

Everyone laughed while Daphne stood there. Arnetta gently laid her hand on Daphne's shoulder. "Daphne. You don't have to fight. We're doing this for you."

Daphne walked to the counter, took a clean paper towel, and carefully unfolded it like a map. With this, she began to pick up the trash all around. Everyone watched.

"C'mon," Arnetta said to everyone. "Let's beat it." We all ambled toward the restroom doorway, where the sunshine made one large white rectangle of light. We were immediately blinded and shielded our eyes with our hands, our forearms.

"Daphne?" Arnetta asked. "Are you coming?"

We all looked back at the girl, who was bending, the thin of her back hunched like a maid caught in stage limelight. Stray strands of her hair were lit nearly transparent, thin fiber-optic threads. She did not nod yes to the question, nor did she shake her head no. She abided, bent. Then she began again, picking up leaves, wads of paper, the cotton fluff innards from a torn stuffed toy. She did it so methodically, so exquisitely, so humbly, she must have been trained. I thought of those dresses she wore, faded and old, yet so pressed and clean; I then saw the poverty in them, I then could imagine her mother, cleaning the houses of others, returning home, weary.

"I guess she's not coming."

We left her, heading back to our cabin, over pine needles and leaves, taking the path full of shade.

"What about our secret meeting?" Elise asked.

Arnetta enunciated in a way that defied contradiction: "We just had it."

Just as we caught sight of our cabin, Arnetta violently swerved away from Octavia. "You farted," she said.

Octavia began to sashay, as if on a catwalk, then proclaimed, in a Hollywood-starlet voice, "My farts smell like perfume."

It was nearing our bedtime, but in the lengthening days of spring, the sun had not yet set.

"Hey, your mama's coming," Arnetta said to Octavia when she saw Mrs. Hedy walk toward the cabin, sniffling. When Octavia's mother wasn't giving bored, parochial orders, she sniffled continuously, mourning an imminent divorce from her husband. She might begin a sentence, "I don't know what Robert will do when Octavia and I are gone. Who'll buy him cigarettes?" and Octavia would hotly whisper "*Mama*" in a way that meant: Please don't talk about our problems in front of everyone. Please shut up.

But when Mrs. Hedy began talking about her husband, thinking about her husband, seeing clouds shaped like the head of her husband, she couldn't be quiet, and no one could ever dislodge her from the comfort of her own woe. Only one thing could perk her up—Brownie songs. If the rest of the girls were quiet, and Mrs. Hedy was in her dopey sorrowful mood, she would say, "Y'all know I like those songs, girls. Why don't you sing one?" Everyone would groan except me and Daphne. I, for one, liked some of the songs.

"C'mon, everybody," Octavia said drearily. "She likes 'The Brownie Song' best."

We sang, loud enough to reach Mrs. Hedy:

I've something in my pocket:
It belongs across my face.
And I keep it very close at hand in a most convenient place.
I'm sure you couldn't guess it
If you guessed a long, long while.
So I'll take it out and put it on—
It's a great big Brownie Smile!

"The Brownie Song" was supposed to be sung as though we were elves in a workshop, singing as we merrily cobbled shoes, but everyone except me hated the song and sang it like a maudlin record, played at the most sluggish of rpms.

"That was good," Mrs. Hedy said, closing the cabin door behind her. "Wasn't that nice, Linda?"

"Praise God," Mrs. Margolin answered without raising her head from the chore of counting out Popsicle sticks for the next day's session of crafts.

"Sing another one," Mrs. Hedy said, with a sort of joyful aggression, like a drunk I'd once seen who'd refused to leave a Korean grocery.

"God, Mama, get over it," Octavia whispered in a voice meant only for Arnetta, but Mrs. Hedy heard it and started to leave the cabin.

"Don't go," Arnetta said. She ran after Mrs. Hedy and held her by the arm. "We haven't finished singing." She nudged us with a single look. "Let's sing 'The Friends Song.' For Mrs. Hedy."

Although I liked some of the songs, I hated this one:

Make new friends
But keep the o-old,
One is silver
And the other gold.

If most of the girls in my troop could be any type of metal, they'd be bunched-up wads of tinfoil maybe, or rusty iron nails you had to get tetanus shots for.

"No, no, no," Mrs. Margolin said before anyone could start in on "The Friends Song." "An uplifting song. Something to lift her up and take her mind off all these earthly burdens."

Arnetta and Octavia rolled their eyes. Everyone knew what song Mrs. Margolin was talking about, and no one, no one, wanted to sing it.

"Please, no," a voice called out. "Not 'The Doughnut Song.'"

"Please not 'The Doughnut Song,'" Octavia pleaded.

"I'll brush my teeth twice if I don't have to sing 'The Doughnut—'"
"Sing!" Mrs. Margolin demanded.
We sang:

Life without Jesus is like a do-ough-nut!
Like a do-ooough-nut!
Like a do-ooough-nut!
Life without Jesus is like a do-ough-nut!
There's a hole in the middle of my soul!

There were other verses, involving other pastries, but we stopped after the first one and cast glances toward Mrs. Margolin to see if we could gain a reprieve. Mrs. Margolin's eyes fluttered blissfully, half-asleep.

"Awww," Mrs. Hedy said, as though giant Mrs. Margolin were a cute baby. "Mrs. Margolin's had a long day."

"Yes indeed," Mrs. Margolin answered. "If you don't mind, I might just go to the lodge where the beds are. I haven't been the same since the operation."

I had not heard of this operation, or when it had occurred, since Mrs. Margolin had never missed the once-a-week Brownie meetings, but I could see from Daphne's face that she was concerned, and I could see that the other girls had decided that Mrs. Margolin's operation must have happened long ago in some remote time unconnected to our own. Nevertheless, they put on sad faces. We had all been taught that adulthood was full of sorrow and pain, taxes and bills, dreaded work and dealings with whites, sickness, and death.

"Go right ahead, Linda," Mrs. Hedy said. "I'll watch the girls." Mrs. Hedy seemed to forget about divorce for a moment; she looked at us with dewy eyes, as if we were mysterious, furry creatures. Meanwhile, Mrs. Margolin walked through the maze of sleeping bags until she found her own. She gathered a neat stack of clothes and pajamas slowly, as though doing so were almost painful. She took her toothbrush, her toothpaste, her pillow. "All right!" Mrs. Margolin said, addressing us all from the threshold of the cabin. "Be in bed by nine." She said it with a twinkle in her voice, as though she were letting us know she was allowing us to be naughty and stay up till nine-fifteen.

"C'mon, everybody," Arnetta said after Mrs. Margolin left. "Time for us to wash up."

Everyone watched Mrs. Hedy closely, wondering whether she would insist on coming with us since it was night, making a fight with Troop 909 nearly impossible. Troop 909 would soon be in the bathroom, washing their faces, brushing their teeth—completely unsuspecting of our ambush.

"We won't be long," Arnetta said. "We're old enough to go to the restroom by ourselves."

Mrs. Hedy pursed her lips at this dilemma. "Well, I guess you Brownies are almost Girl Scouts, right?"

"Right!"

"Just one more badge," Drema said.

"And about," Octavia droned, "a million more cookies to sell." Octavia looked at all of us. *Now's our chance*, her face seemed to say, but our chance to do *what* I didn't exactly know.

Finally, Mrs. Hedy walked to the doorway where Octavia stood, dutifully waiting to say good-bye and looking bored doing it. Mrs. Hedy held Octavia's chin. "You'll be good?"

"Yes, Mama."

"And remember to pray for me and your father? If I'm asleep when you get back?"

"Yes, Mama."

When the other girls had finished getting their toothbrushes and washcloths and flashlights for the group restroom trip, I was drawing pictures of tiny birds with too many feathers. Daphne was sitting on her sleeping bag, reading.

"You're not going to come?" Octavia asked.

Daphne shook her head.

"I'm also gonna stay, too," I said. "I'll go to the restroom when Daphne and Mrs. Hedy go."

Arnetta leaned down toward me and whispered so that Mrs. Hedy, who had taken over Mrs. Margolin's task of counting Popsicle sticks, couldn't hear. "No, Snot. If we get in trouble, you're going to get in trouble with the rest of us."

We made our way through the darkness by flashlight. The tree branches that had shaded us just hours earlier, along the same path, now looked like arms sprouting menacing hands. The stars sprinkled the sky like spilled salt. They seemed fastened to the darkness, high up and holy, their places fixed and definite as we stirred beneath them.

Some, like me, were quiet because we were afraid of the dark; others were talking like crazy for the same reason.

"Wow," Drema said, looking up. "Why are all the stars out here? I never see stars back on Oneida Street."

"It's a camping trip, that's why," Octavia said. "You're supposed to see stars on camping trips."

Janice said, "This place smells like the air freshener my mother uses."

"These woods are *pine*," Elise said. "Your mother probably uses pine air freshener."

Janice mouthed an exaggerated "Oh," nodding her head as though she just then understood one of the world's great secrets.

No one talked about fighting. Everyone was afraid enough just walking through the infinite deep of the woods. Even without seeing anyone's face, I could tell this wasn't about Daphne being called a nigger. The word that had started it all seemed melted now into some deeper, unnameable feeling. Even though I didn't want to fight, was afraid of fighting, I felt as though I were part of the rest of the troop, as though I were defending something. We trudged against the slight incline of the path, Arnetta leading the way. I wondered, looking at her back, what she could be thinking.

"You know," I said, "their leader will be there. Or they won't even be there. It's dark already. Last night the sun was still in the sky. I'm sure they're already finished."

"Whose flashlight is this?" Arnetta said, shaking the weakening beam of the light she was holding. "It's out of batteries."

Octavia handed Arnetta her flashlight. And that's when I saw it. The bathroom was just ahead.

But the girls were there. We could hear them before we could see them.

"Octavia and I will go in first so they'll think there's just two of us. Then wait till I say, 'We're gonna teach you a lesson,'" Arnetta said. "Then bust in. That'll surprise them."

"That's what I was supposed to say," Janice said.

Arnetta went inside, Octavia next to her. Janice followed, and the rest of us waited outside.

They were in there for what seemed like whole minutes, but something was wrong. Arnetta hadn't given the signal yet. I was with the girls outside when I heard one of the Troop 909 girls say, "NO. That did NOT happen!"

That was to be expected, that they'd deny the whole thing. What I hadn't expected was *the voice* in which the denial was said. The girl sounded as though her tongue were caught in her mouth. "That's a BAD word!" the girl continued. "We don't say BAD words!"

"Let's go in," Elise said.

"No," Drema said. "I don't want to. What if we get beat up?"

"Snot?" Elise turned to me, her flashlight blinding. It was the first time anyone had asked my opinion, though I knew they were just asking because they were afraid.

"I say we go inside, just to see what's going on."

"But Arnetta didn't give us the signal," Drema said. "She's supposed to say, 'We're going to teach you a lesson,' and I didn't hear her say it."

"C'mon," I said. "Let's just go in."

We went inside. There we found the white girls, but about five girls were huddled up next to one big girl. I instantly knew she was the owner of the voice we'd heard. Arnetta and Octavia inched toward us as soon as we entered.

"Where's Janice?" Elise asked, then we heard a flush. "Oh."

"I think," Octavia said, whispering to Elise, "they're retarded."

"We ARE NOT retarded!" the big girl said, though it was obvious that she was. That they all were. The girls around her began to whimper.

"They're just pretending," Arnetta said, trying to convince herself. "I know they are."

Octavia turned to Arnetta. "Arnetta. Let's just leave."

Janice came out of a stall, happy and relieved, then she suddenly remembered her line, pointed to the big girl, and said, "We're gonna teach you a lesson."

"Shut up, Janice," Octavia said, but her heart was not in it. Arnetta's face was set in a lost, deep scowl. Octavia turned to the big girl, and said loudly, slowly, as if they were all deaf, "We're going to leave. It was nice meeting you, okay? You don't have to tell anyone that we were here. Okay?"

"Why not?" said the big girl, like a taunt. When she spoke, her lips did not meet, her mouth did not close. Her tongue grazed the roof of her mouth, like a little pink fish. "You'll get in trouble. I know. I know."

Arnetta got back her old cunning. "If you said anything, then you'd be a tattletale."

The girl looked sad for a moment, then perked up quickly. A flash of genius crossed her face: "I *like* tattletale."

"It's all right, girls. It's gonna be all right!" the 909 troop leader said. It was as though someone had instructed all of Troop 909 to cry at once. The troop leader had girls under her arm, and all the rest of the girls crowded about her. It reminded me of a hog I'd seen on a field trip, where all the little hogs would gather about the mother at feeding time, latching on to her teats. The 909 troop leader had come into the bathroom shortly after the big girl threatened to tell. Then the ranger came, then, once the ranger had radioed the station, Mrs. Margolin arrived with Daphne in tow.

The ranger had left the restroom area, but everyone else was huddled just outside, swatting mosquitoes.

"Oh. They *will* apologize," Mrs. Margolin said to the 909 troop leader, but Mrs. Margolin said this so angrily, I knew she was speaking more to us than to the other troop leader. "When their parents find out, every one a them will be on punishment."

"It's all right. It's all right," the 909 troop leader reassured Mrs. Margolin. Her voice lilted in the same way it had when addressing the girls. She smiled the whole time she talked. She was like one of those TV cooking show women who talk and dice onions and smile all at the same time.

"See. It could have happened. I'm not calling your girls fibbers or anything." She shook her head ferociously from side to side, her Egyptian-style pageboy flapping against her cheeks like heavy drapes. "It *could* have happened, see. Our girls are *not* retarded. They are *delayed* learners." She said this in a syrupy instructional voice, as though our troop might be delayed learners as well. "We're from the Decatur Children's Academy. Many of them just have special needs."

"Now we won't be able to walk to the bathroom by ourselves!" the big girl said.

"Yes you will," the troop leader said, "but maybe we'll wait till we get back to Decatur—"

"I don't want to wait!" the girl said. "I want my Independence patch!"

The girls in my troop were entirely speechless. Arnetta looked as though she were soon to be tortured but was determined not to appear weak. Mrs. Margolin pursed her lips solemnly and said, "Bless them, Lord. Bless them."

In contrast, the Troop 909 leader was full of words and energy. "Some of our girls are echolalic—" She smiled and happily presented one of the girls hanging on to her, but the girl widened her eyes in horror and violently withdrew herself from the center of attention, as though she sensed she were being sacrificed for the village sins. "Echolalic," the troop leader continued. "That means they will say whatever they hear, like an echo—that's where the word comes from. It comes from 'echo.'" She ducked her head apologetically. "I mean, not all of them have the most *progressive* of parents, so if they heard a bad word they might have repeated it. But I guarantee it would not have been *intentional.*"

Arnetta spoke. "I saw her say the word. I heard her." She pointed to a small girl, smaller than any of us, wearing an oversized T-shirt that read: EAT BERTHA'S MUSSELS.

The troop leader shook her head and smiled. "That's impossible. She doesn't speak. She can, but she doesn't."

Arnetta furrowed her brow. "No. It wasn't her. That's right. It was *her.*"

The girl Arnetta pointed to grinned as though she'd been paid a compliment. She was the only one from either troop actually wearing a full uniform: the mocha-colored A-line shift, the orange ascot, the sash covered with patches, though all the same one—the Try-It patch. She took a few steps toward Arnetta and made a grand sweeping gesture toward the sash. "See," she said, full of self-importance, "I'm a Brownie." I had a hard time imagining this girl calling anyone a "nigger"; the girl looked perpetually delighted, as though she would have cuddled up with a grizzly if someone had let her.

On the fourth morning, we boarded the bus to go home.

The previous day had been spent building miniature churches from Popsicle sticks. We hardly left the cabin. Mrs. Margolin and Mrs. Hedy guarded us so closely, almost no one talked for the entire day.

Even on the day of departure from Camp Crescendo, all was serious and silent. The bus ride began quietly enough. Arnetta had to sit beside Mrs. Margolin, Octavia had to sit beside her mother. I sat beside Daphne, who gave me her prize journal without a word of explanation.

"You don't want it?"

She shook her head no. It was empty.

Then Mrs. Hedy began to weep. "Octavia," Mrs. Hedy said to her daughter without looking at her, "I'm going to sit with Mrs. Margolin. All right?"

Arnetta exchanged seats with Mrs. Hedy. With the two women up front, Elise felt it safe to speak. "Hey," she said, then she set her face into a placid vacant stare, trying to imitate that of a Troop 909 girl. Emboldened, Arnetta made a gesture of mock pride toward an imaginary sash, the way the girl in full uniform had done. Then they all made a game of it, trying to do the most exaggerated imitations of the Troop 909 girls, all without speaking, all without laughing loud enough to catch the women's attention.

Daphne looked at her shoes, white with sneaker polish. I opened the journal she'd given me. I looked out the window, trying to decide what to write, searching for lines, but nothing could compare with the lines Daphne had written. "*My father, the veteran,*" my favorite line of all time. The line replayed itself in my head, and I gave up trying to write.

By then, it seemed as though the rest of the troop had given up making fun of the 909 girls. They were now quietly gossiping about who had passed notes to whom in school. For a moment the gossiping fell off, and all I heard was the hum of the bus as we sped down the road and the muffled sounds of Mrs. Hedy and Mrs. Margolin talking about serious things.

"You know," Octavia whispered, "why did *we* have to be stuck at a camp with retarded girls? You know?"

"*You* know why," Arnetta answered. She narrowed her eyes like a cat. "My mama and I were in the mall in Buckhead, and this white lady just kept looking at us. I mean, like we were foreign or something. Like we were from China."

"What did the woman say?" Elise asked.

"Nothing," Arnetta said. "She didn't say nothing."

A few girls quietly nodded their heads.

"There was this time," I said, "when my father and I were in the mall and—"

"Oh, shut up, Snot," Octavia said.

I stared at Octavia, then rolled my eyes from her to the window. As I watched the trees blur, I wanted nothing more than to be through with it all: the bus ride, the troop, school—all of it. But we were going home. I'd see the same girls in school the next day. We were on a bus, and there was nowhere else to go.

"Go on, Laurel," Daphne said to me. It was the first time she'd spoken the whole trip, and she'd said my name. I turned to her and smiled weakly so as not to cry, hoping she'd remember when I'd tried to be her friend, thinking maybe that her gift of the journal was an invitation of friendship. But she didn't smile back. All she said was, "What happened?"

I studied the girls, waiting for Octavia to tell me to "shut up" again before I even had a chance to utter another word, but everyone was amazed that Daphne had spoken. I gathered my voice. "Well," I said. "My father and I were in this mall, but *I* was the one doing the staring." I stopped and glanced from face to face. I continued. "There were these white people dressed like Puritans or something, but they weren't Puritans. They were Mennonites. They're these people who, if you ask them to do a favor, like paint your porch or something, they have to do it. It's in their rules."

"That sucks," someone said.

"C'mon," Arnetta said. "You're lying."

"I am not."

"How do you know that's not just some story someone made up?" Elise asked, her head cocked, full of daring. "I mean, who's gonna do whatever you ask?"

"It's not made up. I know because when I was looking at them, my father said, 'See those people. If you ask them to do something, they'll do it. Anything you want.'"

No one would call anyone's father a liar. Then they'd have to fight the person, but Drema parsed her words carefully. "How does your *father* know that's not just some story? Huh?"

"Because," I said, "he went up to the man and asked him would he paint our porch, and the man said, 'Yes.' It's their religion."

"Man, I'm glad I'm a Baptist," Elise said, shaking her head in sympathy for the Mennonites.

"So did the guy do it?" Drema asked, scooting closer to hear if the story got juicy.

"Yeah," I said. "His whole family was with him. My dad drove them to our house. They all painted our porch. The woman and girl were in bonnets and long, long skirts with buttons up to their necks. The guy wore this weird hat and these huge suspenders."

"Why," Arnetta asked archly, as though she didn't believe a word, "would someone pick a *porch*? If they'll do anything, why not make them paint the whole *house*? Why not ask for a hundred bucks?"

I thought about it, and I remembered the words my father had said about them painting our porch, though I had never seemed to think about his words after he'd said them.

"He said," I began, only then understanding the words as they uncoiled from my mouth, "it was the only time he'd have a white man on his knees doing something for a black man for free."

I remembered the Mennonites bending like Daphne had bent, cleaning the restroom. I remembered the dark blue of their bonnets, the black of their shoes. They painted the porch as though scrubbing a floor. I was already trembling before Daphne asked quietly, "Did he thank them?"

I looked out the window. I could not tell which were the thoughts and which were the trees. "No," I said, and suddenly knew there was something mean in the world that I could not stop.

Arnetta laughed. "If I asked them to take off their long skirts and bonnets and put on some jeans, they would do it?"

And Daphne's voice—quiet, steady: "Maybe they would. Just to be nice."

GRACE PALEY

Friends

To put us at our ease, to quiet our hearts as she lay dying, our dear friend Selena said, Life, after all, has not been an unrelieved horror—you know, I *did* have many wonderful years with her.

She pointed to a child who leaned out of a portrait on the wall—long brown hair, white pinafore, head and shoulders forward.

Eagerness, said Susan. Ann closed her eyes.

On the same wall three little girls were photographed in a schoolyard. They were in furious discussion: they were holding hands. Right in the middle of the coffee table, framed, in autumn colors, a handsome young woman of eighteen sat on an enormous horse—aloof, disinterested, a rider. One night this young woman, Selena's child, was found in a rooming house in a distant city, dead. The police called. They said, Do you have a daughter named Abby?

And with *him*, too, our friend Selena said. We had good times. Max and I. You know that.

There were no photographs of *him*. He was married to another woman and had a new, stalwart girl of about six, to whom no harm would ever come, her mother believed.

Our dear Selena had gotten out of bed. Heavily but with a comic dance, she soft-shoed to the bathroom, singing, "Those were the days, my friend . . . "

Later that evening, Ann, Susan, and I were enduring our five-hour train ride to home. After one hour of silence and one hour of coffee and the sandwiches Selena had given us (she actually stood, leaned her big soft excavated body against the kitchen table to make those sandwiches), Ann said, Well, we'll never see *her* again.

Who says? Anyway, listen, said Susan. Think of it. Abby isn't the only kid who died. What about that great guy, remember Bill Dalrymple—he was a non-cooperator or a deserter? And Bob Simon. They were killed in automobile accidents. Matthew, Jeannie, Mike. Remember Al Lurie—he was murdered on Sixth Street—and that little kid Brenda, who O.D.'d on your roof, Ann? The tendency, I suppose, is to forget. You people don't remember them.

What do you mean, "you people"? Ann asked. You're talking to *us*.

I began to apologize for not knowing them all. Most of them were older than my kids, I said.

Of course, the child Abby was exactly in my time of knowing and in all my places of paying attention—the park, the school, our street. But oh! It's true! Selena's Abby was not the only one of that beloved generation of our children murdered by cars, lost to war, to drugs, to madness.

Selena's main problem, Ann said—you know, she didn't tell the truth.

What?

A few hot human truthful words are powerful enough, Ann thinks, to steam all God's chemical mistakes and society's slimy lies out of her life. We all believe in that power, my friends and I, but sometimes . . . the heat.

Anyway, I always thought Selena had told us a lot. For instance, we knew she was an orphan. There were six, seven other children. She was the youngest. She was forty-two years old before someone informed her that her mother had *not* died in childbirthing her. It was some terrible sickness. And she had lived close to her mother's body—at her breast, in fact—until she was eight months old. Whew! said Selena. What a relief! I'd always felt I was the one who'd killed her.

Your family stinks, we told her. They really held you up for grief.

Oh, people, she said. Forget it. They did a lot of nice things for me too. Me and Abby. Forget it. Who has the time?

That's what I mean, said Ann. Selena should have gone after them with an ax.

More information: Selena's two sisters brought her to a Home. They were ashamed that at sixteen and nineteen they could not take care of her. They kept hugging her. They were sure she'd cry. They took her to her room—not a room, a dormitory with about eight beds. This is your bed, Lena. This is your table for your things. This little drawer is for your toothbrush. All for me? she asked. No one else can use it? Only me. That's all? Artie can't come? Franky can't come? Right?

Believe me, Selena said, those were happy days at Home.

Facts, said Ann, just facts. Not necessarily the *truth*.

I don't think it's right to complain about the character of the dying or start hustling all their motives into the spotlight like that. Isn't it amazing enough, the bravery of that private inclusive intentional community?

It wouldn't help not to be brave, said Selena. You'll see.

She wanted to get back to bed. Susan moved to help her.

Thanks, our Selena said, leaning on another person for the first time in her entire life. The trouble is, when I stand, it hurts me here all down my back. Nothing they can do about it. All the chemotherapy. No more chemistry left in me to therapeut. Ha! Did you know before I came to New York and met you I used to work in that hospital? I was supervisor in gynecology. Nursing. They were my friends, the doctors. They weren't so snotty then. David Clark, big surgeon. He couldn't look at me last week. He kept saying, Lena . . . Lena . . . Like that. We were in North Africa the same year—'44, I think. I told him, Davy, I've been around a long enough time. I haven't missed too much. He knows it. But I didn't want to make him look at me. Ugh, my damn feet are a pain in the neck.

Recent research, said Susan, tells us that it's the neck that's a pain in the feet.

Always something new, said Selena, our dear friend.

On the way back to the bed, she stopped at her desk. There were about twenty snapshots scattered across it—the baby, the child, the young woman. Here, she said to me, take this one. It's a shot of Abby and your Richard in front of the school—third grade? What a day! The show those kids put on! What a bunch of kids! What's Richard doing now?

Oh, who knows? Horsing around someplace. Spain. These days, it's Spain. Who knows where he is? They're all the same.

Why did I say that? I knew exactly where he was. He writes. In fact, he found a broken phone and was able to call every day for a week—mostly to give orders to his brother but also to say, Are you O.K., Ma? How's your new boyfriend, did he smile yet?

The kids, they're all the same, I said.

It was only politeness, I think, not to pour my boy's light, noisy face into that dark afternoon. Richard used to say in his early mean teens, You'd sell us down the river to keep Selena happy and innocent. It's true. Whenever Selena would say, I don't know, Abby has some peculiar friends, I'd answer for stupid comfort, You should see Richard's.

Still, he's in Spain, Selena said. At least you know that. It's probably interesting. He'll learn a lot. Richard is a wonderful boy, Faith. He acts like a wise guy but he's not.

You know the night Abby died, when the police called me and told me? That was my first night's sleep in two years. I *knew* where she was.

Selena said this very matter-of-factly—just offering a few informative sentences.

But Ann, listening, said, Oh!—she called out to us all, Oh!—and began to sob. Her straightforwardness had become an arrow and gone right into her own heart.

Then a deep tear-drying breath: I want a picture too, she said.

Yes. Yes, wait, I have one here someplace. Abby and Judy and that Spanish kid Victor. Where is it? Ah. Here!

Three nine-year-old children sat high on that long-armed sycamore in the park, dangling their legs on someone's patient head—smooth dark hair, parted in the middle. Was that head Kitty's?

Our dear friend laughed. Another great day, she said. Wasn't it? I remember you two sizing up the men. I *had* one at the time—I thought. Some joke. Here, take it. I have two copies. But you ought to get it enlarged. When this you see, remember me. Ha-ha. Well, girls—excuse me, I mean ladies—it's time for me to rest.

She took Susan's arm and continued that awful walk to her bed.

We didn't move. We had a long journey ahead of us and had expected a little more comforting before we set off.

No, she said. You'll only miss the express. I'm not in much pain. I've got lots of painkiller. See?

The tabletop was full of little bottles.

I just want to lie down and think of Abby.

It was true, the local could cost us an extra two hours at least. I looked at Ann. It had been hard for her to come at all. Still, we couldn't move. We stood there before Selena in a row. Three old friends. Selena pressed her lips together, ordered her eyes into cold distance.

I know that face. Once, years ago, when the children were children, it had been placed modestly in front of J. Hoffner, the principal of the elementary school.

He'd said, No! Without training you cannot tutor these kids. There are real problems. You have to know *how to teach.*

Our P.T.A. had decided to offer some one-to-one tutorial help for the Spanish kids, who were stuck in crowded classrooms with exhausted teachers among little middle-class achievers. He had said, in a written communication to show seriousness and then in personal confrontation to *prove* seriousness, that he could not allow it. And the Board of Ed. itself had said no. (All this no-ness was to lead to some terrible events in the schools and neighborhoods of our poor yes-requiring city.) But most of the women in our P.T.A. were independent—by necessity and disposition. We were, in fact, the soft-speaking tough souls of anarchy.

I had Fridays off that year. At about 11 a.m. I'd bypass the principal's office and run up to the fourth floor. I'd take Robert Figueroa to the end of the hall, and we'd work away at storytelling for about twenty minutes. Then we would write the beautiful letters of the alphabet invented by smart foreigners long ago to fool time and distance.

That day, Selena and her stubborn face remained in the office for at least two hours. Finally, Mr. Hoffner, besieged, said that because she was a nurse, she would be allowed to help out by taking the littlest children to the modern difficult toilet.

Some of them, he said, had just come from the barbarous hills beyond Maricao. Selena said O.K., she'd do that. In the toilet she taught the little girls which way to wipe, as she had taught her own little girl a couple of years earlier. At three o'clock she brought them home for cookies and milk. The children of that year ate cookies in her kitchen until the end of the sixth grade.

Now, what did we learn in that year of my Friday afternoons off? The following: Though the world cannot be changed by talking to one child at a time, it may at least be known.

Anyway, Selena placed into our eyes for long remembrance that useful stubborn face. She said, No. Listen to me, you people. Please. I don't have lots of time. What I want . . . I want to lie down and think about Abby. Nothing special. Just think about her, you know.

In the train Susan fell asleep immediately. She woke up from time to time, because the speed of the new wheels and the resistance of the old track gave us some terrible jolts. Once, she opened her eyes wide and said, You know, Ann's right. You don't get sick like that for nothing. I mean, she didn't even mention him.

Why should she? She hasn't even seen him, I said. Susan, you still have him-itis, the dread disease of females.

Yeah? And you don't? Anyway, he *was* around quite a bit. He was there every day, nearly, when the kid died.

Abby. I didn't like to hear "the kid." I wanted to say "Abby" the way I've said "Selena"—so those names can take thickness and strength and fall back into the world with their weight.

Abby, you know, was a wonderful child. She was in Richard's classes every class till high school. Good-hearted little girl from the beginning, noticeably kind—for a kid, I mean. Smart.

That's true, said Ann, very kind. She'd give away Selena's last shirt. Oh yes, they were all wonderful little girls and wonderful little boys.

Chrissy *is* wonderful, Susan said.

She *is*, I said.

Middle kids aren't supposed to be, but she is. She put herself through college— I didn't have a cent—and now she has this fellowship. And, you know, she never did take any crap from boys. She's something.

Ann went swaying up the aisle to the bathroom. First she said, Oh, all of them—just wohunderful.

I loved Selena, Susan said, but she never talked to me enough. Maybe she talked to you women more, about things. Men.

Then Susan fell asleep.

Ann sat down opposite me. She looked straight into my eyes with a narrow squint. It often connotes accusation.

Be careful—you're wrecking your laugh lines, I said.

Screw you, she said. You're kidding around. Do you realize I don't know where Mickey is? You know, you've been lucky. You always have been. Since you were a little kid. Papa and Mama's darling.

As is usual in conversations, I said a couple of things out loud and kept a few structured remarks for interior mulling and righteousness. I thought: She's never even met my folks. I thought: What a rotten thing to say. Luck—isn't it something like an insult?

I said, Annie, I'm only forty-eight. There's lots of time for me to be totally wrecked—if I live, I mean.

Then I tried to knock wood, but we were sitting in plush and leaning on plastic. Wood! I shouted. Please, some wood! Anybody here have a matchstick?

Oh, shut up, she said. Anyway, death doesn't count.

I tried to think of a couple of sorrows as irreversible as death. But truthfully nothing in my life can compare to hers: a son, a boy of fifteen, who disappears before your very eyes into a darkness or a light behind his own, from which neither hugging nor hitting can bring him. If you shout, Come back, come back, he won't come. Mickey, Mickey, Mickey, we once screamed, as though he were twenty miles away instead of right in front of us in a kitchen chair; but he refused to return. And when he did, twelve hours later, he left immediately for California.

Well, some bad things have happened in my life, I said.

What? You were born a woman? Is that it?

She was, of course, mocking me this time, referring to an old discussion about feminism and Judaism. Actually, on the prism of isms, both of those do have to be looked at together once in a while.

Well, I said, my mother died a couple of years ago and I still feel it. I think *Ma* sometimes and I lose my breath. I miss her. You understand that. Your mother's seventy-six. You have to admit it's nice still having her.

She's very sick, Ann said. Half the time she's out of it.

I decided not to describe my mother's death. I could have done so and made Ann even more miserable. But I thought I'd save that for her next attack on me. These constrictions of her spirit were coming closer and closer together. Probably a great enmity was about to be born.

Susan's eyes opened. The death or dying of someone near or dear often makes people irritable, she stated. (She's been taking a course in relationships *and* interrelationships.) The real name of my seminar is Skills: Personal Friendship and Community. It's a very good course despite your snide remarks.

While we talked, a number of cities passed us, going in the opposite direction. I had tried to look at New London through the dusk of the windows. Now I was missing New Haven. The conductor explained, smiling: Lady, if the windows were clean, half of you'd be dead. The tracks are lined with sharpshooters.

Do you believe that? I hate people to talk that way.

He may be exaggerating, Susan said, but don't wash the window.

A man leaned across the aisle. Ladies, he said, I do believe it. According to what I hear of this part of the country, it don't seem unplausible.

Susan turned to see if he was worth engaging in political dialogue.

You've forgotten Selena already, Ann said. All of us have. Then you'll make this nice memorial service for her and everyone will stand up and say a few words and then we'll forget her again—for good. What'll you say at the memorial, Faith?

It's not right to talk like that. She's not dead yet, Annie.

Yes, she is, said Ann.

We discovered the next day that give or take an hour or two, Ann had been correct. It was a combination—David Clark, surgeon, said—of being sick unto real death and having a tabletop full of little bottles.

Now, why are you taking all those hormones? Susan had asked Selena a couple of years earlier. They were visiting New Orleans. It was Mardi Gras.

Oh, they're mostly vitamins, Selena said. Besides, I want to be young and beautiful. Susan said, That's absolutely ridiculous. She made a joking pirouette.

But Susan's seven or eight years younger than Selena. What did she know? Because: People *do* want to be young and beautiful. When they meet in the street, male or female, if they're getting older they look at each other's face a little ashamed. It's clear they want to say, Excuse me, I didn't mean to draw attention to mortality and gravity all at once. I didn't want to remind you, my dear friend, of our coming eviction, first from liveliness, then from life. To which, most of the time, the friend's eyes will courteously reply, My dear, it's nothing at all. I hardly noticed.

Luckily, I learned recently how to get out of that deep well of melancholy. Anyone can do it. You grab at roots of the littlest future, sometimes just stubs of conversation. Though some believe you miss a great deal of depth by not sinking down down down.

Susan, I asked, you still seeing Ed Flores?

Went back to his wife.

Lucky she didn't kill you, said Ann. I'd never fool around with a Spanish guy. They all have tough ladies back in the barrio.

No, said Susan, she's unusual. I met her at a meeting. We had an amazing talk. Luisa is a very fine woman. She's one of the office-worker organizers I told you about. She only needs him two more years, she says. Because the kids—they're girls—need to be watched a little in their neighborhood. The neighborhood is definitely not good. He's a good father but not such a great husband.

I'd call that a word to the wise.

Well, you know me—I don't want a husband. I like a male person around. I hate to do without. Anyway, listen to this. She, Luisa, whispers in my ear the other day, she whispers, Suzie, in two years you still want him, I promise you, you got him. Really, I may still want him then. He's only about forty-five now. Still got a lot of spunk. I'll have my degree in two years. Chrissy will be out of the house.

Two years! In two years we'll all be dead, said Ann.

I know she didn't mean all of us. She meant Mickey. That boy of hers would surely be killed in one of the drugstores or whorehouses of Chicago, New Orleans, San Francisco. I'm in a big beautiful city, he said when he called last month. Makes New York look like a garbage tank.

Mickey! Where?

Ha-ha, he said, and hung up.

Soon he'd be picked up for vagrancy, dealing, small thievery, or simply screaming dirty words at night under a citizen's window. Then Ann would fly to the town or not fly to the town to disentangle him, depending on a confluence of financial reality and psychiatric advice.

How *is* Mickey? Selena had said. In fact, that was her first sentence when we came, solemn and embarrassed, into her sunny front room that was full of the light and shadow of windy courtyard trees. We said, each in her own way, How are you feeling, Selena? She said, O.K., first things first. Let's talk about important things. How's Richard? How's Tonto? How's John? How's Chrissy? How's Judy? How's Mickey?

I don't want to talk about Mickey, said Ann.

Oh, let's talk about him, talk about him, Selena said, taking Ann's hand. Let's all think before it's too late. How did it start? Oh, for godsakes talk about him.

Susan and I were smart enough to keep our mouths shut.

Nobody knows, nobody knows anything. Why? Where? Everybody has an idea, theories, and writes articles. Nobody knows.

Ann said this sternly. She didn't whine. She wouldn't lean too far into Selena's softness, but listening to Selena speak Mickey's name, she could sit in her chair more easily. I watched. It was interesting. Ann breathed deeply in and out the way we've learned in our Thursday-night yoga class. She was able to rest her body a little bit.

We were riding the rails of the trough called Park-Avenue-in-the-Bronx. Susan had turned from us to talk to the man across the aisle. She was explaining that the war in Vietnam was not yet over and would not be, as far as she was concerned, until we repaired the dikes we'd bombed and paid for some of the hopeless ecological damage. He didn't see it that way. Fifty thousand American lives, our own boys—we'd paid, he said. He asked us if we agreed with Susan. Every word, we said.

You don't look like hippies. He laughed. Then his face changed. As the resident face-reader, I decided he was thinking: Adventure. He may have hit a mother lode of late counterculture in three opinionated left-wing ladies. That was the nice part of his face. The other part was the sly out-of-town-husband-in-New-York look.

I'd like to see you again, he said to Susan.

Oh? Well, come to dinner day after tomorrow. Only two of my kids will be home. You ought to have at least one decent meal in New York.

Kids? His face thought it over. Thanks. Sure, he said. I'll come.

Ann muttered, She's impossible. She did it again.

Oh, Susan's O.K., I said. She's just right in there. Isn't that good?

This is a long ride, said Ann.

Then we were in the darkness that precedes Grand Central.

We're irritable, Susan explained to her new pal. We're angry with our friend Selena for dying. The reason is, we want her to be present when we're dying. We all require a mother or mother-surrogate to fix our pillows on that final occasion, and we were counting on her to be that person.

I know just what you mean, he said. You'd like to have someone around. A little fuss, maybe.

Something like that. Right, Faith?

It always takes me a minute to slide under the style of her public-address system. I agreed. Yes.

The train stopped hard, in a grinding agony of opposing technologies.

Right. Wrong. Who cares? Ann said. She didn't have to die. She really wrecked everything.

Oh, Annie, I said.

Shut up, will you? Both of you, said Ann, nearly breaking our knees as she jammed past us and out of the train.

Then Susan, like a New York hostess, began to tell that man all our private troubles—the mistake of the World Trade Center, Westway, the decay of the South Bronx, the rage in Williamsburg. She rose with him on the escalator, gabbing into evening friendship and, hopefully, a happy night.

At home Anthony, my youngest son, said, Hello, you just missed Richard. He's in Paris now. He had to call collect.

Collect? From Paris?

He saw my sad face and made one of the herb teas used by his peer group to calm their overwrought natures. He does want to improve my pretty good health and spirits. His friends have a book that says a person should, if properly nutritioned, live forever. He wants me to give it a try. He also believes that the human race, its brains and good looks, will end in his time.

At about 11:30 he went out to live the pleasures of his eighteen-year-old nighttime life.

At 3 a.m. he found me washing the floors and making little apartment repairs.

More tea. Mom? he asked. He sat down to keep me company. O.K., Faith. I know you feel terrible. But how come Selena never realized about Abby?

Anthony, what the hell do I realize about you?

Come on, you had to be blind. I was just a little kid, and *I* saw. Honest to God, Ma.

Listen, Tonto. Basically Abby was O.K. She was. You don't know yet what their times can do to a person.

Here she goes with her goody-goodies—everything is so groovy wonderful farout terrific. Next thing, you'll say people are darling and the world is *so* nice and round that Union Carbide will never blow it up.

I have never said anything as hopeful as that. And why to all our knowledge of that sad day did Tonto at 3 a.m. have to add the fact of the world?

The next night Max called from North Carolina. How's Selena? I'm flying up, he said. I have one early-morning appointment. Then I'm canceling everything.

At 7 a.m. Annie called. I had barely brushed my morning teeth. It was hard, she said. The whole damn thing. I don't mean Selena. All of us. In the train. None of you seemed real to me.

Real? Reality, huh? Listen, how about coming over for breakfast?—I don't have to get going until after nine. I have this neat sourdough rye?

No, she said. Oh Christ, no. No!

I remember Ann's eyes and the hat she wore the day we first looked at each other. Our babies had just stepped howling out of the sandbox on their new walking legs. We picked them up. Over their sandy heads we smiled. I think a bond was sealed then, at least as useful as the vow we'd all sworn with husbands to whom we're no longer married. Hindsight, usually looked down upon, is probably as valuable as foresight, since it does include a few facts.

Meanwhile, Anthony's world—poor, dense, defenseless thing—rolls round and round. Living and dying are fastened to its surface and stuffed into its softer parts.

He was right to call my attention to its suffering and danger. He was right to harass my responsible nature. But I was right to invent for my friends and our children a report on these private deaths and the condition of our lifelong attachments.

FRANCINE PROSE

Talking Dog

The dog was going to Florida. The dog knew all the best sleeping places along the side of the highway, and if my sister wanted to come along, the dog would be glad to pace himself so my sister could keep up. My sister told our family this when she came back to the dinner table from which Mother and I had watched her kneeling in the snowy garden, crouched beside the large shaggy white dog, her ear against its mouth.

My sister's chair faced the window, and when the dog first appeared in our yard, she'd said, "Oh, I know that dog," and jumped up and ran out the door. I thought she'd meant whose dog it was, not that she knew it to talk to.

"What dog?" My father slowly turned his head.

"A dog, dear," Mother said.

That year it came as a great surprise how many sad things could happen at once. At first you might think the odds are that one grief might exempt you, but that year I learned the odds are that nothing can keep you safe. So many concurrent painful events altered our sense of each one, just as a color appears to change when another color is placed beside it.

That year my father was going blind from a disease of the retina, a condition we knew a lot about because my father was a scientist and used to lecture us on it at dinner with the glittery detached fascination he'd once had for research gossip and new developments in the lap. Yet as his condition worsened he'd stopped talking about it; he could still read but had trouble with stairs andhad begun to touch the furniture. Out in daylight he needed special glasses, like twin tiny antique cameras, and he ducked his head as he put them on, as if burrowing under a cloth. I was ashamed for anyone to see and ashamed of being embarrassed.

My father still consulted part-time for a lab that used dogs in experiments, and at night he worked at home with a microscope and a tape recorder. "Slide 109," he'd say. "Liver condition normal." My sister had always loved animals, but no one yet saw a connection between my father dissecting dogs and my sister talking to them.

For several weeks before that night when the white dog came through our yard, my sister lay in bed with the curtains drawn and got up only at mealtime. Mother told the high school that my sister had bronchitis. At first my sister's friends telephoned, but only one, Marcy, still called. I'd hear Mother telling Marcy that my sister was much better, being friendlier to Marcy than she'd ever been before. Marcy had cracked a girl's front tooth and been sent to a special school. Each time Marcy telephoned, Mother called my sister's name and, when she didn't answer, said she must be sleeping. I believed my sister was faking it but even I'd begun to have the sickish, panicky feeling you get when someone playing dead takes too long getting up.

One night at dinner my sister told us that every culture but ours believed that ordinary household pets were the messengers of the dead.

"I don't know about that," my father said. "I don't know about *every* culture."

After that it was just a matter of time till she met the dog with a message. And we all knew who it was that my sister was waiting to hear from.

Her boyfriend, Jimmy Kowalchuk, had just been killed in Vietnam.

Mother had gone with my sister to Jimmy Kowalchuk's funeral. I was not allowed to attend, though I'd been in love with him, too. All day in school all I could think of was how many hours, how many minutes till they lowered him in the ground. It was a little like the time they executed Caryl Chessman and the whole school counted down the minutes till he died. The difference was that with Jimmy I was the only one counting, and I had to keep reminding myself that he was already dead.

Mother came home from the funeral in a bubbly, talkative mood. After my sister drifted off, Mother sat on the arm of my father's chair. She said, "They call this country a melting pot but if you ask me there's still a few lumps. Believe it or not, they had two priests—one Polish and one Puerto Rican. The minute I saw them I said to myself: This will take twice as long."

Mother had never liked it that Jimmy was half Polish, half Puerto Rican—if he couldn't be white Protestant, better Puerto Rican completely. She never liked it that our family knew someone name Jimmy Kowalchuk, and she liked it least of all that we knew someone fighting in Vietnam. Every Wednesday night Mother counseled draft resisters, and it made her livid that Jimmy had volunteered.

"Guess what?" Mother told us. "His name wasn't even Jimmy. It was Hymie. That's what the priests and the relatives kept saying. Hymie. Hymie. Hymie. Do you think she would have gone out with him if she had known that?"

"J pronounced Y," my father said. "J-A-I-M-E."

"Pedant," mumbled Mother, so softly only I heard.

"Excuse me?" my father said.

"Nothing," Mother said. "Maybe we should have got her that pony she nagged us about in junior high. Maybe we should have let her keep that falcon that needed a home."

To me she said, "This does not mean you, dear. You cannot have a bird or a pony."

But I didn't want a bird or a pony. I still wanted Jimmy Kowalchuk. And I alone knew that he and my sister had had a great love, a tragic love. For unlike my parents I had seen what Jimmy had gone through to win it.

The first time was on a wet gray day, winter twilight, after school. My parents were in the city, seeing one of my father's doctors, my sister was taking care of me, we were supposed to stay home. Jimmy came to take my sister out in his lemon-yellow '65 Malibu. My sister must have decided it was safer to bring me along—better an accomplice than a potential snitch. I felt like a criminal, like the Barrow Gang on the Jericho Turnpike, ready to hit the floor if I saw Mother's car in the opposite lane.

As Jimmy left the highway for smaller and smaller roads, I felt safer from my parents but more nervous about Jimmy. He was slight and tense and Latin with a wispy beard, dangerous and pretty, like Jesus with an earring. We drove past black trees, marshy scrub-pine lots, perfect for dumping bodies, not far from a famous spot where the Mafia often did. The light was fading and scraps of fog clung regretfully to the windshield.

Jimmy pulled off on the side of the road beside the bank of a frozen lake. "Ladies," he said, "I'll have to ask you to step outside for a minute." Leaning across my sister, he opened the door on her side and then arched back over the seat and opened mine for me.

A wet mist prickled our faces—tiny sharp needles of ice.

"I'm freezing," said my sister.

I said, "Do you think he'd leave us here?"

She said, "Stupid, why would my boyfriend leave us in the middle of nowhere?" I hadn't known for certain till then that Jimmy was her boyfriend. He hadn't even touched her leg when he'd reached down to shift gears.

Jimmy rammed the car in gear and pointed it at the lake and sped out onto the ice and hit the brake and spun. It was thrilling and terrifying to see a car whip around like a snake, and there was also a grace in it, the weightless skimming of a skater. The yellow car gathered the last of the light and cast a faint lemon glow on the ice.

Suddenly we heard the ice crack—first with a squeak, then a groan. My sister grabbed my upper arm and dug her fingers in.

Jimmy must have heard it, too, because the car glided to a stop and he gingerly turned it around and drove back in our direction. I stood up on tiptoe though I could see perfectly well. Then I looked at my sister as if she knew what was going to happen.

I was shocked by my sister's expression: not a trace of fear or concern, but an unreadable concentration and the sullen fixed anger I saw sometimes when we fought. She was very careful not to look like that out in the world, except if she saw a pet she thought was being mistreated. It was like watching a simmering pot, lid rattling, about to boil over, but her lids were halfway down and you couldn't see what was cooking. At the moment I understood that men would always like her better, prefer her smoky opacity to a transparent face like mine.

On the drive home Jimmy elaborated on his theory of danger. He said it was important for males to regularly test themselves against potentially fatal risks. He said it was like a checkup or maybe a vacation—you did it regularly for your health and for a hint on how you were doing.

"That's bullshit," my sister said.

"She thinks it's bullshit," Jimmy told me. "Do you think it's bullshit, kid?"

I knew he was inviting me to contradict my sister; it made me feel like a younger brother instead of an eighth-grade girl. I knew that if I agreed with him I might get to come along again. But that wasn't my reason for saying no. At that moment I believed him.

"The kid knows," Jimmy said, and I whispered: The kid. The kid. The kid.

"This danger thing," Jimmy told us, "is only about yourself. It would be criminal to take chances with somebody else's life. I would never go over the speed limit with you ladies in the car." I hunched my shoulders and burrowed into the fragrant back seat. I felt—and I think my sister felt—supremely taken care of.

My parents were often in the city with my father's doctors, occasionally staying over for tests, not returning till the next day. They told my sister to take care of me, though I didn't need taking care of.

Jimmy would drive over when he got through at Babylon Roofing and Siding. He loved his job and sometimes stopped to show us roofs he'd done. His plan was to have his own company and retire to Florida young and get a little house with grapefruit and mango trees in the yard. He said this to my sister. He wanted her to want it too.

My sister said, "Mangoes in Florida? You're thinking about Puerto Rico."

One night Jimmy parked in front of a furniture store and told us to slouch down and keep our eye on the dark front window. My sister and I were alone for so long I began to get frightened.

A light flickered on inside the store, the flame from Jimmy's lighter, bright enough to see Jimmy smiling and waving, reclining in a lounger.

When Jimmy talked about testing himself, he said he did it sometimes, but I began to wonder if he thought about it always. Just sitting in a diner, waiting for his coffee, he'd take the pointiest knife he could find and dance it between his fingers. I wondered what our role in it was. I wondered if he and my sister were playing a game of chicken: all she had to do was cry "Stop!" and Jimmy would have won. Once he ate a cigarette filter. Once he jumped off a building.

One evening Jimmy drove me and my sister over to his apartment. He lived in a basement apartment of a brick private house. It struck me as extraordinary: people lived in basement apartments. But it wasn't a shock to my sister, who knew where everything was and confidently got two beers from Jimmy's refrigerator.

Jimmy turned on the six o'clock news and the three of us sat on his bed. There was the usual Vietnam report: helicopters, gunfire. A sequence showed American troops filing through the jungle. The camera moved in for a close-up of the soldiers' faces, faces that I recognize now as the faces of frightened boys but that I mistook then for cruel grown men, happy in what they were doing.

My sister said, "Wow. Any one of those suckers could just get blown off that trail." On her face was that combustible mix of sympathy and smoldering anger, and in her voice rage and contempt combined with admiration. I could tell Jimmy was jealous that she looked like that because of the soldiers, and he desperately wanted her to look that way for him. I knew, even if he didn't, that she already had, and that she looked like that if she saw a dog in a parked car, in the heat.

Jimmy had a high draft number but he went down and enlisted. He said he couldn't sit back and let other men do the dying, an argument I secretly thought was crazy and brave and terrific. Mother said it was ridiculous, no one had to die, every kid she counseled wound up with a psychiatric 1-Y. And when Jimmy died she seemed confirmed; he had proved her right.

On the night of the funeral, Mother told us how Jimmy died. The friend who'd accompanied his body home had given a little speech. He said often at night Jimmy sneaked out to where they weren't supposed to be; once a flare went off and they saw him freaking around in the jungle. He said they felt better knowing that crazy Kowalchuk was out there fucking around.

Mother said, "That's what he said at the service. 'Out there fucking around.'"

But I was too hurt to listen, I was feeling so stupid for having imagined that Jimmy's stunts were about my sister and me.

Mother said, "Of course I think it's terrible that the boy got killed. But I have to say I don't hate it that now the two of them can't get married."

After that it was just a matter of time till my sister met the white dog that Jimmy had sent from the other world to take her to Florida.

My sister didn't go to Florida, or anyway not yet. Eventually she recovered—recovered or stopped pretending. Every night after dinner Mother said, "She's eating well. She's improving." Talking to strange dogs in the yard was apparently not a problem. Father's problem was a real problem; my sister's would improve. I knew that Mother felt this way, and once more she was right.

One night Marcy telephoned, Mother called my sister, and my sister came out of her room. She took the phone and told Marcy, "Sure, great. See you. Bye."

"Marcy knows about a party," she said.

Mother said, "Wonderful, dear," though in the past there were always fights about going to parties with Marcy.

We all stayed up till my sister came home, though we all pretended to sleep. My window was over the front door and I watched her on the front step, struggling to unlock the door, holding something bulky pressed against her belly. At last she disappeared inside. Something hit the floor with a thud. I heard my sister running. There was so much commotion we all felt justified rushing downstairs. Mother helped my father down, they came along rather quickly.

We found my sister in the kitchen. It was quiet and very dark. The refrigerator was open, not for food but for light. Bathed in its glow, my sister was rhythmically stroking a large iguana that stood poised, alert, its head slightly raised, on the butcher block by the stove.

In the equalizing darkness my father saw almost as well as we did. "Jesus Christ," he said.

My sister said, "He was a little freaked. You can try turning the light on."

Only then did we notice that the lizard's foot was bandaged. My sister said, "This drunken jerk bit off one of his toes. He got all the guys at the party to bet that he wouldn't do it. I just waded in and took the poor thing and the guy just gave it up. The asshole couldn't have cared very much if he was going to bite its toes off."

"Watch your language," Mother said. "What a cruel thing to do! Is this the kind of teenager you're going to parties with?"

"Animals," my father said. After that there was a silence, during which all of us thought that once my father would have unwrapped the bandage and taken a look at that foot.

"His name's Reynaldo," my sister said.

"Sounds Puerto Rican," said Mother.

Once there would have been a fight about her keeping the iguana, but like some brilliant general, my sister had retreated and recouped and emerged from her bedroom, victorious and in control. At that moment I hated her for always getting her way, for always outlasting everyone and being so weird and dramatic and never letting you know for sure what was real and what she was faking.

Reynaldo had the run of my sister's room, no one dared open the door. After school she'd lie belly down on her bed, cheek to cheek with Reynaldo. And in a way it was lucky that my father couldn't see that.

One night the phone rang. Mother covered the receiver and said, "Thank you, Lord. It's a boy."

It was a boy who had been at the party and seen my sister rescue Reynaldo. His name was Greg; he was a college student, studying for a business degree.

After he and my sister went out a few times, Mother invited Greg to dinner. I ate roast beef and watched him charm everyone but me. He described my sister grabbing the iguana out of its torturer's hands. He said, "When I saw her do that, I thought, This is someone I want to know better." He and my parents talked about her like some distant mutual friend. I stared hard at my sister, wanting her to miss Jimmy, too, but she was playing with her food, I couldn't tell what she was thinking.

Greg had a widowed mother and two younger sisters; he'd gotten out of the draft by being their sole support. He said he wouldn't go anyway, he'd go to Canada first. No one mentioned Reynaldo, though we could hear him scrabbling jealously around my sister's room.

Reynaldo wasn't invited on their dates and neither, obviously, was I. I knew Greg didn't drive onto the ice or break into furniture stores. He took my sister to Godard movies and told us how much she liked them.

One Saturday my sister and Greg took Reynaldo out for a drive. And when they returned—I waited up—the iguana wasn't with them.

"Where's Reynaldo?" I asked.

"A really nice pet shop," she said. And then for the first time I understood that Jimmy was really dead.

Not long after that my father died. His doctors had made a mistake. It was not a disease of the retina but a tumor of the brain. You'd think they would have known that, checked for that right away, but he was a scientist, they saw themselves in him and didn't want to know. Before he died he disappeared, one piece at a time. My sister and I slowly turned away so as not to see what was missing.

Greg was very helpful throughout this terrible time. Six months after my father died, Greg and my sister got married. By then he'd graduated and got a marketing job with a potato-chip company. Mother and I lived alone in the house—as we'd had, really, for some time. My father and sister had left so gradually that the door hardly swung shut behind them. Father's Buick sat in the garage, as it had since he'd lost his vision, and every time we saw it we thought about all that had happened.

My sister and Greg bought a house nearby; sometimes Mother and I went for dinner. Greg told us about his work and the interesting things he found out. In the Northeast they liked the burnt chips, the lumpy misshapen ones, but down South every chip had to be pale and thin and perfect.

"A racial thing, no doubt," I said, but no one seemed to hear, though one of Mother's favorite subjects was race relations down South. I'd thought my sister might laugh or get angry, but she was a different person. A slower, solid, heavier person who was eating a lot of chips.

One afternoon the doorbell rang, and it was Jimmy Kowalchuk. It took me a while to recognize him; he didn't have his beard. For a second—just a second—I was afraid to open the door. He was otherwise unchanged except that he'd got even thinner, and looked even less Polish and even more Puerto Rican.

He was wearing army fatigues. I was glad Mother wasn't home. He gave me a hug, my first ever from him, and lifted me off the ground. He said no, he was never dead, never even missing.

He said, "Some army computer glitch, some creep's clerical error." My father's death had made it easier to believe that people made such mistakes, and for one dizzying moment I allowed myself to imagine that maybe Jimmy's being alive meant my father was, too.

"You got older," Jimmy said. "This is like *The Twilight Zone*." And he must have thought so—that time had stopped in his absence. I invited him in, made him sit down, and then told him about my sister.

Jimmy got up and left the house. He didn't ask whom she'd married. He didn't ask where they lived, though I knew he was going to find her.

Once again I waited, counting down the hours. This time, although weeks passed, it was like counting one two three. Four—the phone rang. It was Greg. He had come home from the office and found my sister packed and gone.

A week later my sister called collect from St. Petersburg, Florida. She said Jimmy knew a guy, a buddy from Vietnam, he had found Jimmy a rental house and a job with a roofing company. They had hurricanes down there that would rip the top of your house off. She emphasized the hurricane part, as if that made it all make sense. In fact, she seemed so sure about the sensibleness of her situation that she made me promise to tell Mother and Greg she'd called and that she was fine.

Mother had less trouble believing that my sister had been kidnapped than that she'd left Greg and taken off with her dead boyfriend from Vietnam. It was a lot to process at once, she'd seen Jimmy buried. Greg had never heard of Jimmy, which made me wonder about my sister. I thought about Reynaldo, how forcefully she had seized him, how easily she'd let him go.

My sister had called from a pay phone. All she'd said was "St. Petersburg." Mother telephoned Mrs. Kowalchuk and got Jimmy's address from her. Afterwards Mother said, "The woman thinks it's a miracle. The army loses her son, she goes through hell, and she thinks it's the will of God."

Mother wrote my sister a letter. A month passed. There was no answer. By now Greg was in permanent shock, though he still went to work. One night he told us about a dipless chip now in the blueprint stage. Then even Mother knew we were alone, and her eyes filled with tears. She said, "Florida! It's warm there. When is your Easter vacation?"

We took my father's Buick, a decision that almost convinced us that some reason besides paralysis explained its still being in our garage. I sat up front beside Mother, scrunched low in the spongy seat. States went by. The highway was always the same. There was nothing to watch except Mother, staring furiously at the road. Though the temperature rose steadily, Mother wouldn't turn off the heat and by Florida I was riding with my head out the window, for air, and also working on a tan for Jimmy.

It was easy finding the address we got from Mrs. Kowalchuk. They were living in a shack, but newly painted white, and with stubby marigolds lining the cracked front walk.

"Tobacco Road," said Mother.

Then Mother and I saw Jimmy working out in the yard. His back was smooth and golden and muscles churned under his skin as he swayed from side to side, planing something—a door. Behind him a tree with shiny leaves sagged under its great weight of grapefruit, and sunlight dappled the round yellow fruit and the down on Jimmy's shoulders.

Jimmy stopped working and turned and smiled. He didn't seem surprised to see us. As he came toward us a large dog roused itself from the ground at his feet, a long-haired white dog so much like the one my sister spoke to in our yard that for a moment I felt faint and had to lean on Mother.

Mother shook me off. She hardly noticed the dog. She was advancing on Jimmy.

"I wasn't dead, it was a mistake." Jimmy sounded apologetic.

"Obviously," said Mother. Then she told me not to move and went into the house.

I couldn't have moved if I'd wanted. Every muscle had fused, every tiny flutter and tic felt grossly magnified and disgusting. I had never seen Jimmy without a shirt. I wanted to touch his back. He said, "I got my grapefruit tree."

"Obviously," I said in Mother's voice, and Jimmy grinned and we laughed. On the table lay a pile of tools. He wasn't stabbing them between his fingers. He must have gotten that out of his system, dying and coming back.

Even though it was Jimmy's house, we felt we couldn't go in. Every inch of space was taken up by what my mother and sister were saying. Where was Jimmy's Malibu? We walked to a cafeteria and stood in a line of elderly couples deciding between the baked fish and the chicken. Jimmy couldn't be served there, he wasn't wearing a shirt. The manager was sorry, it was a Florida law. Jimmy had gone to Vietnam and been lost in a computer and now couldn't even get a cup of cafeteria coffee. But I couldn't say that, my head was ringing with things I couldn't say—for example, that I had waited for him, and my sister hadn't.

Half a block from Jimmy's house, we saw an upsetting sight—my mother and sister in Mother's car with the engine running.

"Going for lunch?" Jimmy said. But we all knew they weren't.

Mother told me to get in back. Jimmy looked in and I saw him notice my sister's suitcase. He did nothing to stop us—that was the strangest part. He let me get in and let us take off and stood there and watched us go.

I never knew, I never found out what Mother said to my sister. Or maybe it wasn't what Mother said, perhaps it was all about Jimmy. Once again I thought of Reynaldo and my sister's giving him up. If I never knew what had happened with that, how could I ask about Jimmy? You assume you will ask the important questions, you will get to them sooner or later, an idea that ignores two things: the power of shyness, the fact of death.

That should have been the last time I saw Jimmy Kowalchuk—a wounded young god glowing with sun in a firmament of grapefruit. But there was one more time, nearer home, in the dead of winter.

Before that, Greg took my sister back. They went on as if nothing had happened. Greg got a promotion. They moved to a nicer house. I saw my sister sometimes. Jimmy was not a subject. I never asked about him, his name never came up. I would talk about school sometimes, but she never seemed to be listening. Once she said, out of nowhere, "I guess people want different things at different times in their lives."

I was a senior in high school when my sister was killed. Her car jumped a divider on the Sunrise Highway. It was a new car Greg kept well maintained, so it was nobody's fault.

On the way to the funeral Mother sat between me and Greg. When my sister went back to Greg, Mother had gone back to him, too. But that day, in the funeral car, she was talking to me.

"What was I doing?" Mother said. "I knew I couldn't make you girls happy. I was just trying to give you the chance to be happy if you wanted. I thought that life was a corridor with doors that opened and shut as you passed, and I was just trying to keep them from slamming on you."

The reality of my sister's death hadn't come home to me yet, and though my father's dying had taught me that death was final, perhaps Jimmy's reappearance had put that in some doubt. Guiltily I wondered if Jimmy would be at my sister's funeral, as if it were a party at which he might show up.

Jimmy came with his mother, a tiny woman in black. He was gritty, unshaven, tragically handsome in a wrinkled suit and dark glasses. He looked as if he'd hitchhiked or rode up on the Greyhound.

I went and stood beside Jimmy. No one expected that. After the service I left with him. Not even I could believe it. All the relatives watched me leave, Mother and Greg and my sister's friend Marcy. I wondered if this was how Jimmy felt, driving out onto the ice.

Jimmy was driving a cousin's rusted Chevy Nova. We dropped his mother at her house. Jimmy and I kept going. I could tell he'd been drinking. He must have given up on his rule about endangering other people. Finally I was alone with him, but it wasn't what I'd pictured. I wondered which friend I could call if I needed someone to pick me up.

I was starting college in the fall. I had some place I had to be. A new life was expecting me with its eye on the clock and no time and no patience for me to run away with Jimmy.

Jimmy drove to a crowded strip somewhere off Hempstead Turnpike. We stopped at the Shamrock, a dark, beery-smelling bar. Jimmy and I sat at a table. The bartender took our order. The regulars seemed too relaxed to pay any special attention to a Charlie Mansonesque Puerto Rican and a girl, below the drinking age, nervously sipping her beer.

Jimmy put away several boilermakers. He was getting drunker and drunker. He kept talking about my sister. He said some very unlikely things but nothing too strange to believe, especially when he repeated it, each time exactly the same.

He told me that the white dog had shown up the first day they moved to Florida. It ran up to my sister in the yard; they seemed to know each other. The dog, said my sister, had come to her after Jimmy died and personally guaranteed it that Jimmy was still alive. Jimmy said, "I had to wonder how the goddamn dog found out our Florida address."

The light in the Shamrock was fading. Jimmy blamed the war. He said, "I died and got through it halfway all right. But it gets you no matter what. I came back but it was too late. Your sister was talking to dogs."

I pictured Mother setting out silver platters of roast beef for the relatives who would be coming back after the funeral. I saw light wink off her coffee urn and the plates of little iced cakes and for one shaming moment a bright bubble shone and popped in the dusty fermented air of the bar.

It hadn't scared Mother but it had scared Jimmy, my sister talking to dogs. I remembered how unresistingly Jimmy had let Mother take her, as easily as my sister had let Reynaldo go. I had a vision of people pulling at each other, and of the people who loved them letting them slip through their hands and almost liking the silky feel of them sliding through their fingers.

Jimmy said my sister blamed herself for my father's death. She'd told Jimmy that when she realized he was looking at slides of dead dogs, she wished for something to happen so he would have to stop it. No matter how much my father told us about his disease, my sister believed that somehow she had caused it, and she had this pet iguana that was the only one she could tell. She told Jimmy the iguana had died in her arms and she blamed herself for that, too.

Tears welled up in Jimmy's eyes. He said, "The woman had powers."

For a fraction of a second I thought I might still want him. But I didn't want him. I just didn't want her to have him forever. I was shocked to be so jealous when death meant it could never be fixed. I didn't want it to be that way, but that was how it was.

I wanted to tell Jimmy that my sister didn't have powers. I wanted to say that her only power was the power to make everyone look, she'd had nothing, nothing to do with my father going blind, and she had lied to one of us about what happened to that iguana. I wanted to say she'd lied to us all, she'd faked it about the dog, as if it mattered whether the animal spoke, as if love were about the truth, as if he would love her less—and not more—for pretending to talk to a dog.

MARK RICHARD

Strays

AT NIGHT, stray dogs come up underneath our house to lick our leaking pipes. Beneath my brother and my's room we hear them coughing and growling, scratching their ratted backs against the boards beneath our beds. We lie awake, listening, my brother thinking of names to name the one he is setting out to catch. Salute and Topboy are high on his list.

I tell my brother these dogs are wild and cowering. A bare-heeled stomp on the floor off our beds sends them scuttling spine-bowed out the crawl-space beneath our open window. Sometimes, when my brother is quick, he leans out and touches one slipping away.

Our father has meant to put the screens back on the windows for spring. He has even hauled them out of the storage shed and stacked them in the drive. He lays them one by one over sawhorses to tack in the frames tighter and weave patches against mosquitoes. This is what he means to do, but our mother that morning pulls all the preserves off the shelves onto the floor, sticks my brother and my's Easter Sunday drawings in her mouth, and leaves the house through the field next door cleared the week before for corn.

Uncle Trash is our nearest relative with a car and our mother has a good half-day head start on our father when Uncle Trash arrives. Uncle Trash runs his car up the drive in a big speed, splitting all the screens stacked there from their frames. There is an exploded chicken in the grill of Uncle Trash's car. They don't even turn the motor off as Uncle Trash slides out and our father gets behind the wheel, backing back over the screens, setting out in search of our mother.

Uncle Trash finds out that he has left his bottle under the seat of his car. He goes into our kitchen, pulling out all the shelves our mother missed. Then he is in the towel box in the hall, looking, pulling out stuff in stacks. He is in our parents' room, opening short doors. He is in the storage shed, opening and sniffing a mason jar of gasoline for the power mower. Uncle Trash comes up and asks, Which way it is to town for a drink. I point up the road. Uncle Trash sets off, saying, Don't y'all burn the house down.

My brother and I hang out in the side yard, doing handstands until dark. We catch handfuls of lightning bugs and smear bright yellow on our shirts. It is late. I wash our feet and put us to bed. We wait for somebody to come back home but nobody ever does. Lucky for me when my brother begins to whine for our mother the stray dogs show up under the house. My brother starts making up lists of new names for them, naming himself to sleep.

Hungry, we wake up to something sounding in the kitchen not like our mother fixing us anything to eat.

It is Uncle Trash. He is throwing up and spitting blood into the pump-handled sink. I ask him did he have an accident and he sends my brother upstairs for merthiolate and Q-tips. His face is angled out from his head on one side so that-sided eye is shut. His good eye waters when he wiggles loose teeth with cut-up fingers.

Uncle Trash says he had an accident, all right. He says he was up in a card game and then he was real up in a card game, so up he bet his car, accidentally forgetting that our father had driven off with it in search of our mother. Uncle Trash says the man who won the card game went ahead and beat up Uncle Trash on purpose anyway.

All day Uncle Trash sleeps in our parents' room. We in the front yard can hear him snoring. My brother and I dig in the dirt with spoons, making roadbeds and highways for my tin metal trucks. In the evening, Uncle Trash comes down in one of our father's shirts, dirty, but cleaner than the one he had gotten beat up in. We have banana sandwiches for supper. Uncle Trash asks do we have a deck of cards in the house. He says he wants to see do his tooth-cut fingers still bend enough to work. I have to tell him how our mother disallows card-playing in the house but that my brother has a pack of Old Maid somewhere in the toy box. While my brother goes out to look I brag at how I always beat my brother out, leaving him the Old Maid, and Uncle Trash says, Oh, yeah? and digs around in his pocket for a nickel he puts on the table. He says, We'll play a nickel a game. I go into my brother and my's room to get the Band-Aid box of nickels and dimes I sometimes short from the collection plate on Sunday.

Uncle Trash is making painful faces, flexing his red-painted fingers around the Old Maid deck of circus-star cards, but he still shuffles, cuts, and deals a three-way hand one-handed—and not much longer, I lose my Band-Aid box of money and all the tin metal trucks of mine out in the front yard. Uncle Trash makes me go out and get them and put them on his side of the table. My brother loses a set of bowling pins and a stuffed beagle. In two more hands, we stack up our winter boots and coats with the hoods on Uncle Trash's side of the table. In the last hand, my brother and I step out of our shorts and underdrawers while Uncle Trash smiles, saying, And now, gentlemen, if you please, the shirts off y'all's backs.

Uncle Trash rakes everything my brother and I owned into the pillowcases off our bed and says let that be a lesson to me. He is off through the front porch door, leaving us buck-naked at the table, his last words as he goes up the road, shoulder-slinging his loot, Don't y'all burn the house down.

I am burning hot at Uncle Trash.

Then I am burning hot at our father for leaving us with him to look for our mother.

Then I am burning hot at my mother for running off, leaving me with my brother, who is rubber-chinning and face-pouting his way into a good cry.

There is only one thing left to do, and that is to take all we still have left that we own and throw it at my brother—and I do—and Old Maid cards explode on his face, setting him off on a really good howl.

I tell my brother that making so much noise will keep the stray dogs away, and he believes it, and then I start to believe it when it gets later than usual, past the crickets and into a long moon over the trees, but they finally do come after my brother finally does fall asleep, so I just wait until I know there are several strays beneath the bed boards, scratching their rat-matted backs and growling, and I stomp on the floor, what is my favorite part about the dogs, stomping and then watching them scatter in a hundred directions and then seeing them one by one collect in a pack at the edge of the field near the trees.

In the morning right off I recognize the bicycle coming wobble-wheeling into the front yard. It's the one the colored boy outside Cuts uses to run lunches and ice water to the pulpwood truck Mr. Cuts has working cut-over timber on the edge of town. The colored boy that usually drives the bicycle snaps bottlecaps off his fingers at my brother and I when we go to Cuts with our mother to make groceries. We have to wait outside by the kerosene pump, out by the tar-papered lean-to shed, the pop-crate place where the men sit around and Uncle Trash does his card work now. White people generally don't go into Cuts unless they have to buy on credit.

We at school know Mr. and Mrs. Cuts come from a family that eats children. There is a red metal tree with plastic-wrapped toys in the window and a long candy counter case inside to lure you in. Mr. and Mrs. Cuts have no children of their own. They ate them during a hard winter and salted the rest down for sandwiches the colored boy runs out to the pulpwood crew at noon. I count colored children going in to buy some candy to see how many make it back out, but generally our mother is ready to go home way before I can tell. Our credit at Cuts is short.

The front tire catches in one of our tin metal truck's underground tunnels and Uncle Trash takes a spill. The cut crate bolted to the bicycle handlebars spills brown paper packages sealed with electrical tape out into the yard along with a case of Champale and a box of cigars. Uncle Trash is down where he falls. He lays asleep all day under the tree in the front yard, moving only just to crawl back into the wandering shade.

We have for supper sirloins, Champale, and cigars. Uncle Trash teaches how to cross our legs up on the table after dinner, but says he'll go ahead and leave my brother and my's cigars unlit. There is no outlook for our toys and my Band-Aid can of nickels and dimes, checking all the packages, even checking twice again the cut crate bolted on the front of the bicycle. Uncle Trash shows us a headstand on the table while drinking a bottle of Champale, then he stands in the sink and sings "Gather My Farflung Thoughts Together." My brother and I chomp our cigars and clap but in our hearts we are low and lonesome.

Don't y'all burn down the house, says Uncle Trash, pedaling out the yard to Cuts.

My brother leans out our window with a rope coil and sirloin scraps strung on strings. He is in a greasy-fingered sleep when the strings slither like white snakes off our bed, over the sill, out into the fields beyond.

There's July corn and no word from our parents.

Uncle Trash doesn't remember the Fourth of July or the Fourth of July parade. Uncle Trash bunches cattails in the fenders of his bicycle and clips our Old Maid cards in the spokes and follows the fire engine through town with my brother and I in the front cut-out crate throwing penny candy to the crowds. What are you trying to be? the colored men at Cuts ask Uncle Trash when we end up the parade there. I spot a broken-wheeled tin metal truck of mine in a colored child's hand, driving it in circles by the Cuts front steps. Foolish, says Uncle Trash.

Uncle Trash doesn't remember winning Mrs. Cuts in a card game for a day to come out and clean the house and us in the bargain. She pushes the furniture around with a broom and calls us abominations. There's a bucket of soap to wash our heads and a jar of sour-smelling cream for our infected bites, fleas from under the house, and mosquitoes through the windows. The screens are rusty squares in the driveway dirt. Uncle Trash leaves her his razor opened as long as my arm. She comes after my brother and I with it to cut our hair, she says. We know better. My brother dives under the house and I am up a tree.

Uncle Trash doesn't remember July, but when we tell him about it, he says it sounds like July was probably a good idea at the time.

It is August with the brown, twisted corn in the fields next to the house. There is word from our parents. They are in the state capital. One of them has been in jail. Uncle Trash is still promising screens. We get from Cuts bug spray instead.

I wake up in the middle of a night. My brother floats through the window. Out in the yard, he and a stray have each other on the end of a rope. He reels her in and I make the tackle. Already I feel the fleas leave her rag-matted coat and crawl over my arms and up my neck. We spray her down with a whole can of bug spray until her coat lathers like soap. My brother gets some matches to burn a tick like a grape out of her ear. The touch of the match covers her like a blue-flame sweater. She's a fireball shooting beneath the house.

By the time Uncle Trash and the rest of town get there, the Fire Warden says the house is Fully Involved.

In the morning I see our parents drive past where our house used to be. I see them go by again until they recognize the yard. Uncle Trash is trying to bring my brother out of the trance he is in by showing him how some tricks work on the left-standing steps of the stoop. Uncle Trash shows Jack-Away, Queen in the Whorehouse, and No Money Down. Our father says for Uncle Trash to stand up so he can knock him down. Uncle Trash says he deserves that one. Our father knocks Uncle Trash down again and tells him not to get up. If you get up I'll kill you, our father says.

Uncle Trash crawls on all fours across our yard out to the road.

Goodbye, Uncle Trash, I say.

Goodbye, men! Uncle Trash says. Don't y'all burn the house down! he says, and I say, We won't.

During the knocking-down nobody notices our mother. She is a flat-footed running rustle through the corn all burned up by the summer sun.

MURIEL SPARK

The First Year of My Life

I was born on the first day of the second month of the last year of the First World War, a Friday. Testimony abounds that during the first year of my life I never smiled. I was known as the baby whom nothing and no one could make smile. Everyone who knew me then has told me so. They tried very hard, singing and bouncing me up and down, jumping around, pulling faces. Many times I was told this later by my family and their friends; but, anyway, I knew it at the time.

You will shortly be hearing of that new school of psychology, or maybe you have heard of it already, which after long and far adventuring research and experiment has established that all of the young of the human species are born omniscient. Babies, in their waking hours, know everything that is going on everywhere in the world; they can tune in to any conversation they choose, switch on to any scene. We have all experienced this power. It is only after the first year that it was brainwashed out of us; for it is demanded of us by our immediate environment that we grow to be of use to it in a practical way. Gradually, our know-all brain-cells are blacked out, although traces remain in some individuals in the form of E.S.P., and in the adults of some primitive tribes.

It is not a new theory. Poets and philosophers, as usual, have been there first. But scientific proof is now ready and to hand. Perhaps the final touches are being put to the new manifesto in some cell at Harvard University. Any day now it will be given to the world, and the world will be convinced.

Let me therefore get my word in first, because I feel pretty sure, now, about the authenticity of my remembrance of things past. My autobiography, as I very well perceived at the time, started in the very worst year that the world had ever seen so far. Apart from being born bedridden and toothless, unable to raise myself on the pillow or utter anything but farmyard squawks or police-siren wails, my bladder and my bowels totally out of control, I was further depressed by the curious behaviour of the two-legged mammals around me. There were those black-dressed people, females of the species to which I appeared to belong, saying they had lost their sons. I slept a great deal. Let them go and find their sons. It was like the special pin for my nappies which my mother or some other hoverer dedicated to my care was always losing. These careless women in black lost their husbands and their brothers. Then they came to visit my mother and clucked and crowed over my cradle. I was not amused.

'Babies never really smile till they're three months old,' said my mother. 'They're not *supposed* to smile till they're three months old.'

My brother, aged six, marched up and down with a toy rifle over his shoulder:

The grand old Duke of York
He had ten thousand men;
He marched them up to the top of the hill
And he marched them down again.

And when they were up, they were up.
And when they were down, they were down.
And when they were neither down nor up
They were neither up nor down.

'Just listen to him!'
'Look at him with his rifle!'
I was about ten days old when Russia stopped fighting. I tuned in to the Czar, a prisoner, with the rest of his family, since evidently the country had put him off his throne and there had been a revolution not long before I was born. Everyone was talking about it. I tuned in to the Czar. 'Nothing would ever induce me to sign the treaty of Brest-Litovsk,' he said to his wife. Anyway, nobody had asked him to.

At this point I was sleeping twenty hours a day to get my strength up. And from what I discerned in the other four hours of the day I knew I was going to need it. The Western Front on my frequency was sheer blood, mud, dismembered bodies, blistered crashes, hectic flashes of light in the night skies, explosions, total terror. Since it was plain I had been born into a bad moment in the history of the world, the future bothered me, unable as I was to raise my head from the pillow and as yet only twenty inches long. 'I truly wish I were a fox or a bird,' D. H. Lawrence was writing to somebody. Dreary old creeping Jesus. I fell asleep.

Red sheets of flame shot across the sky. It was 21st March, the fiftieth day of my life, and the German Spring Offensive had started before my morning feed. Infinite slaughter. I scowled at the scene, and made an effort to kick out. But the attempt was feeble. Furious, and impatient for some strength, I wailed for my feed. After which I stopped wailing but continued to scowl.

> The grand old Duke of York
> He had ten thousand men . . .

They rocked the cradle. I never heard a sillier song. Over in Berlin and Vienna the people were starving, freezing, striking, rioting and yelling in the streets. In London everyone was bustling to work and muttering that it was time the whole damn business was over.

The big people around me bared their teeth; that meant a smile, it meant they were pleased or amused. They spoke of ration cards for meat and sugar and butter. 'Where will it all end?'

I went to sleep. I woke and tuned in to Bernard Shaw who was telling someone to shut up. I switched over to Joseph Conrad who, strangely enough, was saying precisely the same thing. I still didn't think it worth a smile, although it was expected of me any day now. I got on to Turkey. Women draped in black huddled and chattered in their harems; yak-yak-yak. This was boring, so I came back to home base.

In and out came and went the women in British black. My mother's brother, dressed in his uniform, came coughing. He had been poison-gassed in the trenches. '*Tout le monde à la bataille!*' declaimed Marshal Foch the old swine. He was now Commander-in-Chief of the Allied Forces. My uncle coughed from deep within his lungs, never to recover but destined to return to the Front. His brass buttons gleamed in the firelight. I weighed twelve pounds by now; I stretched and kicked for exercise, seeing that I had a lifetime before me, coping with this crowd. I took six feeds a day and kept most of them down by the time the *Vindictive* was sunk in Ostend harbour, on which day I kicked with special vigour in my bath.

In France the conscripted soldiers leapfrogged over the dead on the advance and littered the fields with limbs and hands, or drowned in the mud. The strongest men on all fronts were dead before I was born. Now the sentries used bodies for barricades and the fighting men were unhealthy from the start. I checked my toes and fingers, knowing I was going to need them. *The Playboy of the Western World* was playing at the Court Theatre in London, but occasionally I beamed over to the House of

Commons which made me drop off gently to sleep. Generally, I preferred the Western Front where one got the true state of affairs. It was essential to know the worst, blood and explosions and all, for one had to be prepared, as the boy scouts said. Virginia Woolf yawned and reached for her diary. Really, I preferred the Western Front.

In the fifth month of my life I could raise my head from my pillow and hold it up. I could grasp the objects that were held out to me. Some of these things rattled and squawked. I gnawed on them to get my teeth started. 'She hasn't smiled yet?' said the dreary old aunties. My mother, on the defensive, said I was probably one of those late smilers. On my wavelength Pablo Picasso was getting married and early in that month of July the Silver Wedding of King George V and Queen Mary was celebrated in joyous pomp at St. Paul's Cathedral. They drove through the streets of London with their children. Twenty-five years of domestic happiness. A lot of fuss and ceremonial handing over of swords went on at the Guildhall where the King and Queen received a cheque for £53,000 to dispose of for charity as they thought fit. *Tout le monde à la bataille!* Income tax in England had reached six shillings in the pound. Everyone was talking about the Silver Wedding; yak-yak-yak, and ten days later the Czar and his family, now in Siberia, were invited to descend to a little room in the basement. Crack, crack, went the guns; screams and blood all over the place, and that was the end of the Romanoffs. I flexed my muscles. 'A fine healthy baby,' said the doctor; which gave me much satisfaction.

Tout le monde à la bataille! That included my gassed uncle. My health had improved to the point where I was able to crawl in my playpen. Bertrand Russell was still cheerily in prison for writing something seditious about pacifism. Tuning in as usual to the Front Lines it looked as if the Germans were winning all the battles yet losing the war. And so it was. The upper-income people were upset about the income tax at six shillings to the pound. But all women over thirty got the vote. 'It seems a long time to wait,' said one of my drab old aunts, aged twenty-two. The speeches in the House of Commons always sent me to sleep which was why I missed, at the actual time, a certain oration by Mr. Asquith following the armistice on 11th November. Mr. Asquith was a greatly esteemed former prime minister later to be an Earl, and had been ousted by Mr. Lloyd George. I clearly heard Asquith, in private, refer to Lloyd George as 'that damned Welsh goat.'

The armistice was signed and I was awake for that. I pulled myself on to my feet with the aid of the bars of my cot. My teeth were coming through very nicely in my opinion, and well worth all the trouble I was put to in bringing them forth. I weighed twenty pounds. On all the world's fighting fronts the men killed in action or dead of wounds numbered 8,538,315 and the warriors wounded and maimed were 21,219,452. With these figures in mind I sat up in my high chair and banged my spoon on the table. One of my mother's black-draped friends recited:

> I have a rendezvous with Death
> At some disputed barricade,
> When spring comes back with rustling shade
> And apple blossoms fill the air—
> I have a rendezvous with Death.

Most of the poets, they said, had been killed. The poetry made them dab their eyes with clean white handkerchiefs.

Next February on my first birthday, there was a birthday-cake with one candle. Lots of children and their elders. The war had been over two months and twenty-one days. 'Why doesn't she smile?' My brother was to blow out the candle. The elders were talking about the war and the political situation. Lloyd George and Asquith, Asquith and Lloyd George. I remembered recently having switched on to Mr. Asquith at a private party where he had been drinking a lot. He was playing cards and when he came to cut the cards he tried to cut a large box of matches by mistake. On another occasion I had seen him putting his arm around a lady's shoulder in a Daimler motor car, and generally behaving towards her in a very friendly fashion. Strangely enough she said, 'If you don't stop this nonsense immediately I'll order the chauffeur to stop and I'll get out.' Mr. Asquith replied, 'And pray, what reason will you give?' Well anyway it was my feeding time.

The guests arrived for my birthday. It was so sad, said one of the black widows, so sad about Wilfred Owen who was killed so late in the war, and she quoted from a poem of his:

What passing-bells for these who die as cattle?
Only the monstrous anger of the guns.

The children were squealing and toddling around. One was sick and another wet the floor and stood with his legs apart gaping at the puddle. All was mopped up. I banged my spoon on the table of my high chair.

But I've a rendezvous with Death
At midnight in some flaming town;
When spring trips north again this year,
And I to my pledged word am true,
I shall not fail that rendezvous.

More parents and children arrived. One stout man who was warming his behind at the fire, said, 'I always think those words of Asquith's after the armistice were so apt . . . '

They brought the cake close to my high chair for me to see, with the candle shining and flickering above the pink icing. 'A pity she never smiles.'

'She'll smile in time,' my mother said, obviously upset.

'What Asquith told the House of Commons just after the war,' said that stout gentleman with his backside to the fire, '—so apt, what Asquith said. He said that the war has cleansed and purged the world, by God! I recall his actual words: "All things have become new. In this great cleansing and purging it has been the privilege of our country to play her part . . . " '

That did it. I broke into a decided smile and everyone noticed it, convinced that it was provoked by the fact that my brother had blown out the candle on the cake. 'She smiled!' my mother exclaimed. And everyone was clucking away about how I was smiling. For good measure I crowed like a demented raven. 'My baby's smiling!' said my mother.

'It was the candle on her cake,' they said.

The cake be damned. Since that time I have grown to smile quite naturally, like any other healthy and house-trained person, but when I really mean a smile, deeply felt from the core, then to all intents and purposes it comes in response to the words uttered in the House of Commons after the First World War by the distinguished, the immaculately dressed and the late Mr. Asquith.

━━━◆◆◆━━━

JOHN UPDIKE

How Was It, Really?

INCREASINGLY, Don Fairbairn had trouble remembering how it had actually been in the broad middle stretch of his life, when he was living with his first wife and helping her, however distractedly, raise their children. His second marriage, which had once seemed so shiny and amazing and new, now was as old as his first had been—twenty-two years, exactly—when he had, one ghastly weekend, left it. His second wife and he lived in a house much too big for them yet so full of souvenirs and fragile inherited treasures that they could not imagine living elsewhere. In their present circle of friends, the main gossip was of health and death, whereas once the telephone wires had buzzed with word of affairs and divorces. His present wife, Vanessa, would set down the telephone to announce that Herbie Edgerton's cancer had come back and appeared to be into his lymph nodes and bones now; thirty years ago, his first wife, Alissa, would hang up and ask him if they were free for drinks and take-out pizza at the Langleys' this Saturday. Yes, she would go on, it was such short notice that it would have been rude from anybody but the Langleys. They were socially voracious, now that psychotherapy had helped them to see that they couldn't stand each other. Everybody's mental and marital health, as Don remembered it, was frail, so frail that woman, meeting, would follow their "How are you?" with "No, how are you *really*?"

And then—this with an averted glance and the hint of a blush from Alissa—she had seen Wendy Chace in the superette and impulsively asked her and Jim to drinks tomorrow evening. She had said yes, they'd love to, but they couldn't stay more than a minute, Jim had the Planning Commission meeting, they were fending off this evil out-of-state developer who was trying to turn the entire old Treadwell estate into Swiss-chalet-style condos. Just paraphrasing Jim's flighty, cause-minded wife made Alissa glow. This at least was vivid in Don's memory, the way his former wife's eyes would become livelier and her cheeks, a bit sallow normally, would redden and her lips, usually pursed and pensive, would dance into quips and laughter when Jim was near or in prospect. He couldn't blame her; he had been as bad as she, looking outside the home for strength to keep the home going. The formula had worked only up to a point—perhaps the point, somewhere in their forties, when they realized that life wasn't endless. The Fairbairns had been, actually, among the last in their old set to get divorced. They had stayed on the sinking ship while its deck tilted and its mast splintered and its sails flapped, whipping loose line everywhere.

A teetotaller now (weight, liver, conflicting pills), Don could remember the drinks—drinks on porches and docks, on boats and lawns, in living rooms and kitchens and dens. The high metallic sheen of gin, the slightly more viscid transparency of vodka, the grain-golden huskiness of bourbon, the paler, caustic timbre of Scotch, the sprig of mint, the slice of orange, the chunk of lime, the column of beer with its rising flutes of bubbles, the hemispheres of white and red wine floating above the table on their invisible stems, the little sticky-rimmed glasses of anisette and Cointreau and B & B and green Chartreuse that followed dinner, whirling the minutes toward midnight, while the more prudent, outsiderish guests peeked at their watches, thinking of the babysitter and tomorrow's sickly-sweet headache. Don remembered, from the viewpoint of a host, the magnanimous crunch of ice cubes broken out of their aluminum trays with an authoritative yank of the divider lever, and the pantry's round-shouldered array of half-gallon bottles from the liquor mart beside the superette, the cost of liquor a kind of dues you cheerfully paid for membership in the unchartered club of young couples. How curiously filling and adequate it was, the constant society of the same dozen or so people. Western frontiersmen, he remembered reading somewhere, said of buffalo meat that, strange to say, you never tired of eating it. The Fairbairns' friends would arrive for weekday drinks at six, harried and mussed, children in tow—the women bedraggled by a day of housework, the men fresh off the train with their city pallor—and be slowly transformed into ebullient charmers. Become dizzyingly confiding and glamorous and *intimes*, they would not leave much before eight, when the time had long passed to get the children, who had been devouring potato chips and Fig Newtons around the kitchen television, decently fed and into bed.

"How did you and Mom *do* it?" Don's sons and daughters asked him, with genuine admiration, of his old servantless four-child household. His children as they homed in on forty lived in city apartments or virtually gated New Jersey enclaves, with one or two children of their own whose nurture and protection required daily shifts of women of color—tag-team caregivers, one to achieve the dressing and the administration of breakfast and safe passage to nursery school, and another to supervise the evening meal and bath and bedtime video. Nevertheless, his daughters were exhausted by motherhood, which had come to them late, as a bit of progenitive moonlighting incidental to their thriving professional careers; conception had been rife with psychic tension and childbirth fraught with peril. His sons spoke solemnly, apprehensively to him about the education of their children and, even more remote, the job prospects available to these toddlers in the year 2020. They both, his two sons, performed some inscrutable monkey-business among computers and equities, and they thought in long-range demographic curves. Don had to laugh, being interviewed by them as a kind of pioneer, a survivor of a mythical age of domesticity, when giant parents strode the earth. "You were there," he reminded them. "You remember how it was. Our key concept was benign neglect." But they would not be put off and, indeed, half persuaded him that he had been an epic family man, chopping forests into cabins amid the wilderness of the baby boom.

Tracking their own children's progress, they asked him how old they had been when they first crawled, walked, talked, and read, and he was embarrassed to say that he could not remember. "Ask your mother," he told them.

"She says she doesn't remember, either. She says we were all wonderfully normal."

An only child, born in the Depression, Don had been honored at his birth with the purchase of a big white book, its padded cover proudly embossed *Baby's Book*, in which pages printed in dove-colored ink waited for the entry of his early achievements and the dates thereof. *July 20, 1935. Donald took his first step. A shaky one. September 6, 1938. Off to kindergarten! Donny clung and clung. Heartbreaking.* He was surprised to discover that his mother, in that little curly backward-slanting hand that seemed to his eyes the very distillation of methodical maternity, had entered everything up through his various graduations and his first wedding; she had noted her first two grandchildren but had not bothered with the second two or with his second nuptials. How odd it is, he thought, that America's present prosperity, based upon our outworking the Germans and the Japanese, has produced the same pinched, anxiously cherishing families as the Depression. His children's individual developments had become in his failing mind an amiable tangle while he daily dined on the social equivalent of buffalo meat.

The lack of recall almost frightened him. Did he help the kids with their homework? He must have. Did he and Alissa ever go grocery shopping together? He had no image of it. The beds, how had they got made, and the meals, how had they got onto the table for twenty-two years? Alissa must have done it all, somehow, while he was reading the sports page. Having the babies, now such a momentous rite of New Age togetherness and unembarrassed body-worship, was something else she had done alone, in the hospital, without complication or much complaint afterwards. The baby just appeared in a basket beside her bed, or at her breast, and in a few days he drove the two of them home, two where there had been one, a doubling of persons like a magic trick whose secret was too quick for the eye. The last childbirth, Don did remember, came on a winter midnight, and the obstetrician, awakened, had swung by in his car for her, and she had looked up smiling from the snowy street, like a Christmas caroller, and disappeared into the doctor's two-tone

Buick. Left alone with the residue of their children, he had been jittery, he remembered, and convinced that a burglar or crazed invader, sensing his family's moment of being vulnerably torn asunder, was in the big creaky house with him; Don had fallen asleep only after taking a golf club—a three-iron, in preference to a slower-swinging wood—into bed with him, for protection.

He tried to picture Alissa with a vacuum cleaner and couldn't, though he remembered himself, in the dining room of the first house they had lived in, wielding a wallpaper steamer, pressing the big square pan against the wall for a minute or two and stripping the paper with a broad putty knife and, in drenched shorts and T-shirt, wading through curling wet sheets of faded silver flowers. Once a week, in that same room, she would serve flank steak, it came to him, the brown meat nicely tucked around a core of peppery stuffing, and the whole platter, garnished with parsley and little red-skinned potatoes, redolent of bygone home economics, of those touching Fifties-born culinary ambitions that sought to perpetuate a sense of the family meal as a pious ceremony salted with the sweat of female labor. All those meals slavishly served, and in the end he had dismissed her like a redundant servant. Vanessa and he, with no children to feed, had become grazers, snackers, eaters-out, sometimes taking their evening meal separately, gobbling from microwave-safe containers while Peter Jennings injected his personal warmth into the news. She still had a fondness for pizza hot or cold.

"But what did you do about *sleep*? About children waking up all night?" the elder of his hard-working daughters, with tender blue shadows beneath her eyes, persisted.

"You all slept through, virtually from birth," he told her, suspecting he was lying but unable to locate the truth of it. There had been a child whimpering about an earache and falling asleep with the hurting ear pressed against the heat of a fresh-ironed dish towel. But was this himself as a child? He could not remember Alissa with an iron in her hand. He did remember getting up from bed in the pit of night and bringing a squalling armful of protoplasm back to bed and handing it to its mother, who was already sitting up with her nightie straps lowered, her bare chest shining. He would go back to sleep to the sound of tiny lips sucking, little feet softly kicking. He had been the baby, it seemed. Yet no social workers came to the door to rescue his children from abuse, no neighbors complained to the authorities, the children waited for the school bus dressed like the others—like little clowns in the space-age outfits of synthetic fabrics decades removed from the dark woollens, always damp, that he himself had worn—and ascended more or less smoothly through the passages of school and, like smart bombs, found colleges and mates and jobs, so he must have been an adequate parent and householder. "It frightens me," Don confessed to his daughter, "how little I remember."

The Saturday afternoons of it all, the masculine feats of maintenance, the changing of the storm windows to screens, the cellar workbench where spiders built webs across the clutter of rusting tools. The heating, electricity, telephone, and water bills—he could not see himself writing a single check, but he must have written many, all cashed, cancelled, and stored in Alissa's attic, along with the slides, the scrapbooks, the school reports and tinted school photographs that had accumulated over twenty-two years of days, each with its ups and downs, its mishaps, its sniffles, its excited tales told by children venturing toward adulthood, through a world that on every side was new to them. Don had lost the anatomy. He was like an astronomer before the Voyagers, before the Hubble telescope, working with blurs. He remembered being in love with one or another man's wife, getting drunk after dinner, telling Alissa to go to bed, and playing over and over again "Born to Lose," by Ray Charles, or maybe it was the Supremes' "Stop! in the Name of Love!," lifting the player arm from the LP repeatedly to regroove the band, and being told with a shy smile the next morning by his older son, "You sure listened to that song a lot last night." The curtains for a moment parted; there was a second of shamed focus. His son's bedroom was above the den where Don had sat mired in himself and the revolving grooves. He had kept the boy, who had to get up for school, awake.

And what of his girls' dating, that traditional tragicomedy, with its overtones of Attic patricide, in the age of the sitcom? His older daughter had gone off to boarding school when she was fifteen, and his younger daughter had been but twelve when he left the house. He could scarcely remember a single hot-rod swerving into the crackling driveway to carry off one of his trembling virgins.

Now this younger daughter invited him to have drinks on a boat. He didn't have to drink liquor, of course, she explained. More and more people didn't; it interfered with their training routines. She herself was slim and hard as a greyhound, and entered local marathons; her hair, which like Alissa's had begun to turn white early, was cut short as a boy's, to lower wind resistance, he supposed. The deal was this, Dad: the husband of a friend of theirs was turning forty, and she, the wife, was giving him as one of his presents a sunset cruise in the marshes, and since *his* parents were coming the friend, the wife—are you following this, Dad?—wanted some other members of the older generation to be there, so the question is could you and Vanessa come, since you know I guess the husband's father from apparently playing a few golf tournaments with him?

Actually, when he shook his peer's hand, under the canopy of the flat-bottomed cruise boat, he remembered him as an opponent who had illegally switched balls on the eighteenth green and then sunk the putt to win the match. At the time, he hadn't wished to undergo the social embarrassment of complaining to the officials, but he had avoided club tournaments ever since. Now the man—one of those odious exultant retirees with a face creased and thickened by an all-year tan—crowed over that remembered triumph. His wife, who was somewhat younger than he, and preeningly dressed in clothes that would have appeared less garish in Florida, fastened onto Vanessa as her only soulmate. Don drifted away, trying to hide among the drinking young couples, to whom he had nothing to say. Not drinking did that—it robbed you of things to say.

How strange it was to be once more at a party where the women were still menstruating. Lean, smart, they moved and twittered and struck poses with an electricity like that in silent movies, which look speeded-up. The men in their checked jackets and pastel slacks were boyish and broad—relatively clumsy foils for their wives' animation, which in the shuffle of the party kept sprouting new edges, abrupt new angles of slightly startled loveliness. Don inhaled, as if to extract from the salt air the scent of their secretions, their secrets. It had been at parties like this that he had gotten to know Vanessa Langley, her and her socially voracious husband. The similarity of her name to Alissa's had been one of the attractions; she would be a wife with "v" added, for vim and vigor, for vivacity and vagina and victory. He had fallen in love with her, she had fallen with him, and here they were, on board together, more than twenty years later.

The boat trundled, with its burden of canned music and clinking drinks and celebrating couples, out through the winding channel between the black-mud banks of the golden-green marsh toward the wider water, where islands crammed with shingled summer houses slowly changed position, starboard to port, as the captain put his craft through a scenic half-circle. There was a white lighthouse, and a stunning sunstruck slope where some American grandee of old had decreed a symmetrical pattern of trimmed shrubs like a great ideogram, and a marina whose pale masts stood as thick as wheat, and a nappy blue-green far stretch of wooded land miraculously yet undeveloped, and the eastward horizon of the open sea already darkening to receive its first starlight while the undulating land to the west basked under luminous salmon stripes, the lean remains of daylight. Don silently gazed outward at all this, and his fellow-passengers gave it moments of notice, but the main thrust of their attention was inward, toward each other, in bright and gnashing conversations growing shrill as the drinks sank in, a feast of love drowning out the canned music. That was how it was, how it had been, the living moment awash with beauty ignored in the quest for a better moment, slightly elsewhere, with some slightly differing other, while the weeds grew in the peony beds, and dust balls gathered beneath the sofa, and the children, unobserved, plotted their own escapes, their own elsewheres.

A few children had come along with their parents and, after being admonished not to fall overboard, fended for themselves. To one boy, rapt beside him at the rail, Don on the homeward swing pointed out a headland and a rosy mansion whose name he knew, beyond the marsh grasses now drinking in darkness as the tide slipped away from their roots. Vanessa, on the drive home, volunteered, "The birthday boy's father's wife and I have a number of mutual acquaintances, it turned out. She said an old college roommate of mine, Angela Hart, just had a double mastectomy." Don thought of confiding in turn how magically strange he had found it to be again among fertile women, with all the excitement that bred. He might in his youthful cruelty have once said something like this to Alissa—anything to get her to respond, to get the blood flowing—but between Vanessa and him there had come to prevail the tact of two cripples, linked victims of time.

IV | Catalysts

1. Sitting on a Bench

DISCUSSION

Looking for a character to star in your newest fiction? Look no farther than right outside of your head. Unless you are a hermit, self-sequestered in a cave, the chances are pretty good that you live among other humans. If this is the case, then the chances are even better that you live around characters just waiting to be studied: a post office, a town park, a shopping mall, a coffee shop—the possibilities are inexhaustible. All that is required for this exercise is a bench. In fact, a bench isn't even required. What is required is that you open your eyes and your ears and that you mindfully leave them open for the duration of this study.

Find a public place where you can observe people going about their daily activities. Try to choose a location where your presence won't be noticed, somewhere you can remain anonymous and unseen. Bring some books and your notebook. Remember: you are studying! These "props" will help you to feel more comfortable "spying" on those around you. If you are interested in studying dialogue, it is especially helpful to situate yourself in earshot of conversations. Don't worry. People won't notice you.

Now listen. Watch. Use all of your senses. Take in everything.

EXERCISE

Start naming strangers. Give them jobs. Give them marriages, happy or not. Give them children. Give them dogs. Give them what you think they might need. Or take something away from them. If you take away all of their money, what will they do? How will they feel? Imagine the broad spectrum of their lives. What do their houses look like? What do they think about when they can't sleep at night? How did their mothers love them? What are their earliest memories?

In short, build characters from the world around you.

Then give them something to do. Give them a plot. Where are they going? Who will they meet? Will they meet each other? Will they lose something along the way? And, if so, will they try to find it again?

Once you have characters, you are well on your way to writing a story. At the very least, this exercise will help you to practice the art of creating characters. And very few stories can exist without characters.

2. A Fish out of Water

DISCUSSION

"So an elephant walks into a bar," "So a priest walks into a brothel," "So this elderly man walks into a skateboard park." We are all familiar with this construction: someone is somewhere this someone should not be. In our somewhat orderly lives, we rarely find ourselves in situations where we are not among those who resemble us, understand us, and, often, ignore us. However, life throws us curve balls as the baseball fans will say, and we sometimes find ourselves in situations outside of our control. We find ourselves in places where we never hoped to be, often the very places we feared being the most.

It is in these moments that we come closest to discovering who we really are. This is why one of the greatest, most often recurring themes in our art is the theme of the "stranger." Consider the time-travelers, vampires, and aliens that make up so much of our collective imagination. Consider why we care so much about them. We are them. In our lives, we are all strangers at one time or another, and we respond to this situation of feeling alien quite viscerally.

EXERCISE

This exercise asks you to create one of these situations. Pick a character—someone who intrigues you—and spend some time considering this person. What is this character's name? His or her job? Where does this person come from? Where does this person think he or she is heading? What's his or her name? Sketch this out for yourself as fully as possible.

Now throw them into a situation that terrifies them. Or throw them into a situation that just simply baffles them, leaves them feeling confused or disoriented. Or send them somewhere where no one will recognize them but will surely take notice of them, a place where the character stands out.

Remember the old line that locals everywhere reserve for hapless strangers, "You're not from around here, are you?"

3. Mind Traveling: A Solitary Adventure

DISCUSSION

Let's say you're sitting on the bus. Or that you've got an hour-long drive. Let's say that, today, you forgot your newspaper. You have no headphones and you have nothing to read and no pen with which to write. You're staring at the back of the head in front of you. You're looking out the window to avoid making contact with the person sitting in the seat next to you. Where can you go from here? Nowhere.

Or everywhere. The human mind has such an incredible capacity for remembering and for creating that a mind-traveling bus rider can cover years in the space of a long ride. Or, more likely, the mind-traveler can journey in and out of a single event from countless perspectives, broken only by the interruptions of a bump in the road or a tap on the shoulder, someone waking you up.

EXERCISE

In this exercise, imagine yourself in a busy, but mostly inactive, situation. Maybe you're a bank teller. Maybe you're a fast-food server or toll-booth operator. What do you think about between customers? What do you do during the downtime?

Think now of something that may have happened weeks ago. Or years ago. Or maybe something that happened years ago but that informed something you did a week ago.

To write this story, you first set yourself in a place. Then you diverge from it . . . in your mind! See how far away from the central placement you can get, while returning to the central place on a regular basis to resolve interruptions.

Making Lines: Poetry

I | *Discussion of the Genre*

As a writer of poems, I've never had anything, really, except a good ear and a bad memory . . .

—Charles Wright

We believe there is at least one poem in everyone and that no two poems will or should ever be the same. We hope that you will find that this section of contemporary poems supports this belief. Just as there are many paths to and through short fiction or nonfiction, there are innumerable paths to and through poetry.

But, *what is a poem?* Does it rhyme? Does it surprise? Does it confess? *Yes, yes,* and *yes.* But, then again: *no.*

Not necessarily.

A poem is, essentially, a voice aware of itself in time, and it is a voice aware of itself not just as a retelling or a first telling of a tale, but as something meaning more than what it says. "Another way," suggested the poet William Stafford, "is to let the language itself begin to shape the event taking place by its means." The poem is, in fact, a difficult genre to introduce or discuss due to the very nature of poetry. How do you introduce an object that introduces itself?

A successful poem is, quite simply, the essential retelling of itself, of its moment in time. It can be necessary and evocative or elusive "*Perhaps*". Edgar Allan Poe stated that the reader should be able to complete a short story in a single sitting. We would argue that the poem should not only be able to be completed in a single sitting but ideally should be completed multiple times in a single sitting with multiple interpretations. The poem is inexhaustible.

Stafford, again, wrote in "A Way of Writing" (found in Section Five):

> If it happens that at this time in history and at this place in our own experience we happen on a word with a syllable that reverberates with many other syllables in contexts that reinforce what the immediate word is doing, we have "powerful language."

In this statement, "this time in history" does not mean this century, this epoch, or even this era. It means this very moment: the moment in which the reader of the poem is reading the poem, which is as real and as instant as that very moment in which the poet was writing the poem. "Here" is where *powerful language* appears.

Think of the reverie you experienced as a child, lying on your back watching clouds in the sky. To every cloud you looked and said, "What is that? Tiger? Elephant? Pony?" And each cloud changed as it moved across your field of vision: first tiger, then elephant, then pony. A poem should allow us, as careful readers, to experience the same reverie. Necessarily then, the writer of the poem should be in awe of its moment as well.

Maybe the definition of the poem is this simple: *it asks for your attention.* A short story may say to you, "Come along for the ride." An essay may say, "There's something to be learned here." A poem says essentially, "Pay attention to me. I've paid attention to what I have to say." It's a risky proposal, but, therein, lies the joy of making poetry. With the poem, we test our knowledge of ourselves or of the larger world in which we live. We test the ability of language to say the seemingly unsayable, and the poem provides the answer to our test.

The trick is to learn to write it down.

Poetry may occur as a day-dreamed narrative of two people you've never met. A poem may begin in you as a single sentence you can't forget. You might find the poem in an image through a car window. You may see a poem in another piece of writing, a moment that another writer seemed to miss. The trick is to learn to write it down— to recognize the moment.

The following selection of poems written by a diverse selection of poets in a veritable multitude of styles should spark in any reader a desire to write a poem of his or her own. Some will rhyme, most will not. Some will tell a narrative, some will not. Some will be primarily visual, some will be audible. Some are clear spoken, some are not.

Some are written by women, some by men. Some of them are angry, some sad. Some of them are angry and then sad and then resolved to happiness. Some are just happy.

Your poems and others' poems ultimately will ask of you only what, as a child, you asked of your own parents, what your children ask of you: that you pay them close attention, that you provide them with a loving environment in which to develop and to survive, and that you let them go as soon as they are able, to explore and to change in a world which they will now have helped create.

What is a poem?

Every poem you read and every poem you write must be allowed to answer that question with itself. In this, our garden of forking paths, we recognize that a poem is a crossroad, an intersection, and a point. The poem is nothing less than the inside of the poet laid bare.

II | A Quintessential: "Thinking About the Poet Larry Levis One Afternoon in Late May"

by Charles Wright

CHARLES WRIGHT

Thinking About the Poet Larry Levis One Afternoon in Late May

Rainy Saturday, Larry dead
                almost three weeks now,
Rain starting to pool in the low spots
And creases along the drive.
                  Between showers, the saying goes,
Roses and rhododendron wax glint
Through dogwood and locust leaves,
Flesh-colored, flesh-destined, spring in false flower, goodbye.

The world was born when the devil yawned,
                  the legend goes,
And who's to say it's not true,
Color of flesh, some inner and hidden bloom of flesh.
Rain back again, then back off,
Sunlight suffused like a chest pain across the tree limbs.
God, the gathering night, assumes it.

We haven't a clue as to what counts
In the secret landscape behind the landscape we look at here.
We just don't know what matters,
                May dull and death-distanced,

Sky half-lit and grackle-ganged—
It's all the same dark, it's all the same absence of dark.
Part of the rain has now fallen, the rest still to fall.

Discussion of a Quintessential

"Thinking About the Poet Larry Levis One Afternoon in Late May"

by Charles Wright

What is the primordial subject of poetry? It's somewhere between love and death. Love that must die. Death defeated by love. And so forth.

In Charles Wright's poem, "Thinking About the Poet Larry Levis One Afternoon in Late May," all of the questions that besiege the thinking universe seem to converge on a single man in a single moment: the contemplation of a friend's death by a lonely poet in the midst of the world in springtime. Everything in the poem happens, as the title proposes, in a specific instant in time and in a specific nearby place. But in the poem, the moment's arrival, the poet seems to escape time as he is digested by space. It is that rarest and most valuable sort of poem: it tells the truth about a truth whose existence we've always felt but never quite articulated. "We haven't a clue as to what counts," says Wright, "in the secret landscape behind the landscape we look at here."

Beginning in the very concrete and telling title, Wright informs the reader exactly where he or she is sitting in relation to this poem: the reader is sitting where the poet sits. "Rainy Saturday, Larry dead / almost three weeks now, / Rain starting to pool in the low spots / And creases along the drive." The simple cadence and the half-step down from "dead" to "almost" lead the reader slowly into the image of pooling rain in a driveway and a rain-drenched poet standing somewhere near it. As if to demonstrate the power of poetry to consecrate beauty, we hear the poet's mind move from the puddle to these lines:

> Between showers, the saying goes,
> Roses and rhododendron wax glint
> Through dogwood and locust leaves,
> Flesh-colored, flesh-destined, spring in false flower, goodbye.

Following so directly on the stark opening of this poem, this sequence of images leads the poet to interpret the flowering blooms of spring plants in a single word: "goodbye" and then leaves the reader to wonder how can so much sadness exist in a world of such beauty?

And the poet is asking just this question as well. But the poet never says so. The poem evokes a feeling, but the poem does not instruct in feeling.

After the seemingly careless hint of "the saying goes," we begin the second stanza with a half-broken line that reads "the legend goes," following a plain-spoken line, "The world was born when the devil yawned." Wright adds, as if almost yawning himself, "And who's to say it's not true." We have all had moments in our lives when our minds speak to us in direct sentences. Not commands: statements of reality. This poem records one of those moments. As sunset falls upon the writer and the dead, we encounter what certainly seems like truth:

> *Rain back again, then back off,*
> *Sunlight suffused like a chest pain across the tree limbs.*
> *God, the gathering night, assumes it.*

We don't have to have known the poet Larry Levis. We don't have to know whether Wright is a Christian or whether he believes in God. We don't have to know the physical circumstances of Levis' death. We don't have to know if Wright knows the physical circumstances of Levis' death. What we know from this passage is that the entire world in which the poet lives has been shaken and consumed by the fact of this death. The subtle and human detail of a chest pain should cause even the least attentive reader to say either "I know that pain" or "I fear that pain." This realization will be followed by "I too could be subject to that pain, and so could anybody I love."

Any poem, if it succeeds for any reader, does so by allowing the reader to recognize a truth within it that the reader has perhaps always known but never actually articulated or never articulated in the way that the poet has here. *The world was born when the devil yawned.*

The third and final stanza, as if shocked by what has just been stated in the previous stanza, begins "We haven't a clue as to what counts / In the secret landscape behind the landscape we look at here." Why this sudden discounting of what we think we know? Because the poet is not speaking to us with the hopes of simply telling us a teaching tale. No, the poet is offering us a time outside of time. A moment repeatable. The real truth is changing, "We just don't know what matters."

Real time is experienced emotionally, "May dull and death-distanced," and real space is the same, "Sky half-lit and grackle-ganged." While Wright has been blessed perhaps with eyes to see the inexhaustible poetry of the world, he has also been cursed with a heart that feels immeasurable loss. Fortunately, he has poetry within which to make peace with that loss.

> *It's all the same dark, it's all the same absence of dark.*
> *Part of the rain has now fallen, the rest still to fall.*

The world continues. The rain is yet to fall. The dark is the same for the poet as for his fallen friend. The poem goes on long after it ends, after it's been written, or read.

How does the poem go on?

We return to the title. We return to the first line. We continue. We read the poem again. How does he move from the driveway to the secret landscape behind the landscape? How does he see the wax glint of rhododendron leaves and still feel that the devil's yawning gave birth to the world? How does the name Larry seem to fall through the poem from the beginning to the end but is only mentioned once? How does God become the gathering night?

In poetry, we permit ourselves to make sense of the world by believing in our ability to make sense in the world. Sometimes, we have a simple feeling and we write a simple line. Sometimes we are confused and we write a confusing line. Sometimes we see a flower and we don't know why it is significant; we don't know what it means. But, sometimes we choose to write about that flower anyway, and we try to discover its meaning.

In poetry, we allow ourselves to ask questions, but we do not expect any answers—at least not easy answers. Sometimes we get answers, and sometimes we do not. Sometimes we read a poem a hundred times over and then we get an answer.

What we hope to get every time is a "feeling." "Sometimes," Emily Dickinson wrote, "a formal feeling comes." In Wright's remarkable poem, that feeling comes in waves. And those waves make lines we can revisit.

III | Reading Selections

RALPH ANGEL

Love's That Simple

At those who love you, who look up to you or just
    happen to feel like human beings
because of you. Even the moon would shed its skin,
the infant its shadow for you.

I mean you can if you want to,
in the face of, at whatever it is you think you can buy.
Money itself, or childhood, or somewhere to run to,
    someone impatient enough to speak for you.
You're no fool, you're entitled. And the only way
to avoid pain is to inflict it on somebody else.

But you *haven't* disappeared them,
though they're there for you. In gardens of sulfur,
    with blackened walls, until the heart is tamed and
    my lips bleed.
And intimacy, a taunt. And trust,
a stratagem. Your mama's racism.
Your daddy's legalese.

Here are the spiders that will crawl through your eyes.
Passion. Resilience. The wild, cold colors
of the Mediterranean. What if all you can do is despise
what you came for? The flawless. The seamless.
You've invented everyone!

Talk to them. What they think about and feel.
What they'll do the next time.

Ralph Angel, "Love's That Simple" from Neither World: Poems, *Miami University Press, 1995. Reprinted with permission of Ralph Angel and The Miami University Press.*

You, who are not responsible, chased by nothing, who
    limp nowhere. Tell them
about the mountain and the kingdom within.

And resentment. Betrayal. You had such high hopes
    for them.
The no one who takes a back seat to you,
who won't live up to whatever it was,
it's just too complicated.

We either forgive one another who we really are
or not.

MARVIN BELL

These Green-Going-to-Yellow

This year,
I'm raising the emotional ante,
putting my face
in the leaves to be stepped on,
seeing myself among them, that is;
that is, likening
leaf-vein to artery, leaf to flesh,
the passage of a leaf in autumn
to the passage of autumn,
branch-tip and winter spaces
to possibilities, and possibility
to God. Even on East 61st Street
in the blowzy city of New York,
someone has planted a gingko
because it has leaves like fans like hands,
hand-leaves, and sex. Those lovely
Chinese hands on the sidewalks

so far from delicacy
or even, perhaps, another gender of gingko—
do we see them?
No one ever treated us so gently
as these green-going-to-yellow hands
fanned out where we walk.
No one ever fell down so quietly
and lay where we would look
when we were tired or embarrassed,
or so bowed down by humanity
that we had to watch out lest our shoes stumble,
and looked down not to look up
until something looked like parts of people
where we were walking. We have no
experience to make us see the gingko
or any other tree,
and, in our admiration for whatever grows tall
and outlives us,
we look away, or look at the middles of things,
which would not be our way
if we truly thought we were gods.

EAVAN BOLAND

This Moment

A neighbourhood.
At dusk.

Things are getting ready
to happen
out of sight.

Stars and moths.
And rinds slanting around fruit.

But not yet.

One tree is black.
One window is yellow as butter.

A woman leans down to catch a child
who has run into her arms
this moment.

Stars rise.
Moths flutter.
Apples sweeten in the dark.

MICHAEL BURKARD

I Entered a House

I have this tremendous fear of dying, tomorrow,
whether I stay or go. I have this tremendous
fear of suffering in death, whether I shave or
don't shave, whether I kiss you, or you kiss me,
or no one kisses anyone for the time being.

I have this tremendous fear I entered a house
which forgot about me, and still forgets,
and the clocks are still suffering, waiting
for someone, anyone, to cross their legs, to
light a cigarette, to leave.

While, while. Anyone leaves. I had a dream
and now I can't find it. I am sleeping in a kiss,
my clothes are sleeping. It was still
raining, I was
walking out of my shoes.

SCOTT CAIRNS

Interval with Erato

That's what I like best about you, Erato sighed in bed, *that's why
you've become one of my favorites and why you will always be so.*
I grazed her ear with my tongue, held the salty lobe between my lips.

I feel like singing when you do that, she said with more than a hint
of music already in her voice. *So sing,* I said, and moved down
to the tenderness at the edge of her jaw. *Hmmm,* she said, *that's nice.*

Is there anything you don't like? I asked, genuinely meaning
to please. *I don't like poets in a hurry,* she said, shifting
so my lips might achieve the more dangerous divot of her throat.

Ohhhh, she said, as I pressed a little harder there. She held my face
in both hands. *And I hate when they get careless, especially
when employing second-person address.* She sat up, and my mouth

fell to the tip of one breast. *Yes,* she said, *you know how it can be—
they're writing "you did this" and "you did that" and I always
            assume,*
at first, that they mean me! She slid one finger into my mouth to
            tease

the nipple there. *I mean it's disappointing enough to observe
the lyric is addressed to someone else, and* then, *the poet spends
half the poem spouting information that the* you—*if she or he*

*were listening—would have known already, ostensibly as well as,
or better than, the speaker.* I stopped to meet her eyes. *I know just
what you mean,* I said. She leaned down to take a turn, working my
            chest

Scott Cairns, "Interval with Erato" from Philokalia: New and Selected Poems, *Zoo Press, 2002. Reprinted by
permission of the author.*

with her mouth and hands, then sat back in open invitation.
Darling, she said as I returned to the underside of her breast,
have you noticed how many poets talk to themselves, about them-
selves?

I drew one finger down the middle of her back. *Maybe they fear*
no one else will hear or care. I sucked her belly, cupped her sopping
vulva with my hand. *My that's delicious,* she said, lifting into me.

Are all poets these days so lonely? She wove her fingers with mine
so we could caress her there together. *Not me,* I said, and ran
my slick hands back up to her breasts. I tongued her thighs. I said,
I'm not

lonely now. She rubbed my neck, *No, dear, and you shouldn't be.*
She clenched, *Oh!*
a little early bonus, she said; *I like surprises.* Then, *So*
few poets appreciate surprises, so many prefer to speak

only what they, clearly, already know, or think they know. If I
were a poet . . . well, I wouldn't be one at all if I hadn't
found a way to get a little something for myself—something new

from every outing, no? Me neither, I said, if somewhat indistinctly.
Oh! she said. *Yes!* she said, and tightened so I felt her pulse against
my lips. She lay quietly for a moment, obviously thinking.

Sweetie, she said, *that's what I like best about you—you pay*
attention,
and you know how to listen when a girl feels like a little song.
Let's see if we can't find a little something now, especially for you.

HAYDEN CARRUTH

Of Distress Being Humiliated by the Classical Chinese Poets

Masters, the mock orange is blooming in Syracuse without scent,
      having been bred by patient horticulturists
To make this greater display at the expense of fragrance.
But I miss the jasmine of my back-country home.
Your language has no tenses, which is why your poems can never
      be translated whole into English;
Your minds are the minds of men who feel and imagine without
      time.
The serenity of the present, the repose of my eyes in the cool
      whiteness of sterile flowers.
Even now the headsman with his great curved blade and rank odor
      is stalking the byways for some of you.
When everything happens at once, no conflicts can occur.
Reality is an impasse. Tell me again
How the white heron rises from among the reeds and flies forever
      across the nacreous river at twilight
Toward the distant islands.

LUCILLE CLIFTON

11/10 again

some say the radiance around the body
can be seen by eyes latticed against

"Of Distress Being Humiliated by the Classical Chinese Poets by Hayden Carruth," from Tell Me Again How the
White Heron Rises and Flies Across the Nacreous River at Twilight Toward the Distant Islands, *copyright ©
1986 by Hayden Carruth. Reprinted by permission of New Directions Publishing Corp.*

Lucille Clifton, "11/10 again" from The Book of Light. *Copyright © 1993 by Lucille Clifton. Reprinted with the
permission of Copper Canyon Press, P.O. Box 271, Port Townsend, WA 98368-0271.*

all light but the particular. they say
you can notice something rise
from the houseboat of the body
wearing the body's face,
and that you can feel the presence
of a possible otherwhere.
not mystical, they say, but human,
human to lift away from the arms that
try to hold you (as you did then)
and, brilliance magnified,
circle beyond the ironwork
encasing your human heart.

KWAME DAWES

Libation

For Ellen

Here is the image of puppies sniffing aspens, garlanded
with rotten leaves so late in winter—Dogwoods, she says.
It's the season of Christ's bleeding, and those dogwoods were planted
as an epitaph to the old actor who howled his lines to empty houses—
before they bore him off on a stage flat, dead.

She tells me of the scarlet ooze of crushed dogwood roots,
this ink used to scratch out poems of lost love on the smooth
white of North Carolina birch. Here in the South
at the bleak end of February I turn bewildered, I find comfort
in the simple affinities of skin, sin, and suffering. I sing tentatively,
knowing too well the warm scent of blood-washed Baptist hymns.

In this fertile loam, new earth to me, the seeds I plant
grow too quickly into sores, septic melons bursting
into startling rot—like overfed guppies.

Libation from Midland *by Kwame Dawes. Reprinted with permission of Ohio University Press, Athens, Ohio, and Goose Lane Editions, Fredericton, New Brunswick, Canada.*

The dogwood in the wind speckles the bewildered puppies.
I pray among the leaves, pouring libation to thaw the earth.

NORMAN DUBIE

For Randall Jarrell, 1914–1965

What the wish wants to see, it sees.

All the dead are eating little yellow peas
Off knives under the wing of an owl
While the living run around, not aimlessly, but
Like two women in white dresses gathering
Hymnbooks out on a lawn with the first
Drops of rain already falling on them.

Once, I wrote a sudden and enormous sentence
At the bottom of a page in a notebook
Next to a sketch of a frog. The sentence
Described the gills of a sunfish
As being the color of cut rhubarb, or
Of basil if it is dried in a bundle
In a red kitchen with the last winter light
Showing it off, almost purple.

Anything approaching us we try to understand, say,
Like a lamp being carried up a lane at midnight.

Jeremy Taylor knew it watching an orange leaf
Go down a stream.
Self-taught, it came to us, I believe,
As old age to a panther who's about to
Spring from one branch to another, but suddenly
Thinks better of it.

Norman Dubie, "For Randall Jarrell, 1914–1965" from The Mercy Seat: Collected and New Poems
*1967–2001. Copyright © 1975 by Norman Dubie. Reprinted with the permission of Copper Canyon Press, P.O.
Box 271, Port Townsend, WA 98368-0271.*

She says to us from her tree,
"Please, one world at a time!" and leaps—

Making it, which could mean,
Into this world or some other. And between.

RUSSELL EDSON

The Fall

There was a man who found two leaves and came indoors holding them out saying to his parents that he was a tree.

To which they said then go into the yard and do not grow in the living-room as your roots may ruin the carpet.

He said I was fooling I am not a tree and he dropped his leaves.

But his parents said look it is fall.

JOHN ENGMAN

The Building I Live In Is Tipping Over

The archaeologist who digs deep enough,
through the rock and rolling tiers of ape man
and ape woman, will find my lowly bones
just as I left them, in rows like a xylophone.
She may play my ribs with her rubber mallet,
reviving a mood from ages ago, the haunted
little tunes of my carbon 14 content.

This is what she will know:
I was a homo sapiens with few employable traits,
not much data for the data base: American male,
biped and carnivore, a blameless five-foot-eight.
Perhaps she'll bring me home in a canvas sack
and stash my remains in a storage vault
as if she's collecting antiques. . .

I may be worth money someday!
My skeleton, the backbone of some new dream!
I doubt that, but imagine how pleased she'll be,
digging through the stream-of-consciousness rock
until she arrives at my flat, and petrified me,
caught in the act of whispering sweet nothings
through the fossil of a keyhole. . .

TESS GALLAGHER

Each Bird Walking

Not while, but long after he had told me,
I thought of him, washing his mother, his
bending over the bed and taking back
the covers. There was a basin of water
and he dipped a washrag in and
out of the basin, the rag
dripping a little onto the sheet as he
turned from the bedside to the nightstand
and back, there being no place

on her body he shouldn't touch because
he had to and she helped him, moving
the little she could, lifting so he could

Each Bird Walking copyright 1987 by Tess Gallagher. Reprinted from Amplitude: New and Selected Poems *with the permission of Graywolf Press, Saint Paul, Minnesota.*

wipe under her arms, a dipping motion
in the hollow. Then working up from
the feet, around the ankles, over the
knees. And this last, opening
her thighs and running the rag firmly
and with the cleaning thought
up through her crotch, between the lips,
over the V of thin hairs—

as though he were a mother
who had the excuse of cleaning to touch
with love and indifference
the secret parts of her child, to graze
the sleepy sexlessness in its waiting
to find out what to do for the sake
of the body, for the sake of what only
the body can do for itself.

So his hand, softly at the place
of his birth-light. And she, eyes deepened
and closed in the dim room.
And because he told me her death as
important to his being with her,
I could love him another way. Not
of the body alone, or of its making,
but carried in the white spires of trembling
until what spirit, what breath we were
was shaken from us. Small then,
the word *holy*.

He turned her on her stomach
and washed the blades of her shoulders, the
small of her back. "That's good," she said,
"that's enough."

On our lips that morning, the tart juice
of the mothers, so strong in remembrance, no
asking, no giving, and what you said, this
being the end of our loving, so as not to hurt
the closer one to you, made me look
to see what was left of us
with our sex taken away. "Tell me," I said,
"something I can't forget." Then the story of
your mother, and when you finished
I said, "That's good, that's enough."

JAMES GALVIN

Against the Rest of the Year

The meadow's a dream I'm working to wake to.
The real river flows under the river.
The real river flows
Over the river.
Three fishermen in yellow slickers
Stitch in and out of the willows
And sometimes stand for a long time, facing the water,
Thinking they are not moving.
*

Thoughts akimbo
Or watching the West slip through our hopes for it,
We're here with hay down,
Starting the baler, and a thunderhead
Stands forward to the east like a grail of milk.
*

The sky is cut out for accepting prayers.
Believe me, it takes them all.
Like empty barrels afloat in the trough of a swell
The stupid bales wait in the field.
The wind scatters a handful of yellow leaves
With the same sowing motion it uses for snow.
*

After this we won't be haying anymore.
Lyle is going to concentrate on dying for a while
And then he is going to die.
The tall native grasses will come ripe for cutting
And go uncut, go yellow and buckle under the snow
As they did before for thousands of years.
Of objects, the stove will be the coldest in the house.
The kitchen table will be there with its chairs,
Sugar bowl, and half-read library book.
The air will be still from no one breathing.
*

The green of the meadow, the green willows,
The green pines, the green roof, the water
Clear as air where it unfurls over the beaver dam
Like it isn't moving.

*

In the huge secrecy of the leaning barn
We pile the bodies of millions of grasses,
Where it's dark as a church
And the air is the haydust that was a hundred years.
The tin roof's a marimba band and the afternoon goes dark.
Hay hooks clink into a bucket and nest.
Someone lifts his boot to the running board and rests.
Someone lights a cigarette.
Someone dangles his legs off the back of the flatbed
And holds, between his knees, his hands,
As if they weighed fifty pounds.
Forever comes to mind, and peaks where the snow stays.

JACK GILBERT

Tear it Down

We find out the heart only by dismantling what
the heart knows. By redefining the morning,
we find a morning that comes just after darkness.
We can break through marriage into marriage.
By insisting on love we spoil it, get beyond
affection and wade mouth-deep into love.
We must unlearn the constellations to see the stars.
But going back toward childhood will not help.
The village is not better than Pittsburgh.
Only Pittsburgh is more than Pittsburgh.
Rome is better than Rome in the same way the sound
of raccoon tongues licking the inside walls
of the garbage tub is more than the stir
of them in the muck of the garbage. Love is not
enough. We die and are put into the earth forever.
We should insist while there is still time. We must
eat through the wildness of her sweet body already
in our bed to reach the body within that body.

ALBERT GOLDBARTH

This Cartography

I fell, I bled: it wasn't bad, just red
enough for Rae to say that I was spilling exquisitely
tiny maps of myself upon a public street

—an observation that's specific
to this Project Human Genome year,
although the idea of actuality represented

virtually and miniaturized is older,
I assume, than even the fist-wide bear
and finger-height of hunter on a Lascaux wall:

a map of a system of hungers (and red, by the way).
A sonnet's pattern is a map of the sky
of Shakespeare's day; a Beat howl,

the astronomy of a sky of holocaustal fires and void.
The acorn is, the duke's assassination is,
the way the rain cloud and the camel's hump are cousins

is . . . ; etc., including the way the gypsy reader takes
your hand as if its palm is an atlas of future time.
It's endless, this cartography,

the way *we're* endless: follow along the indicated
side road of your greatest fear or glory, and just
see if there's an end point; like that night

of sex's honey-coated hook, but also a gently misted
feeling of something spiritual on the horizon, and a porridge
of ethical quandary, and a repartee as hard as chrome,

until you needed to run from it all, and banged, or
we could say Big Banged, an elbow on the stony ledge
that fronted your suburban home, and a map of the cosmos

exploded into existence in that bony dome.

BECKIAN FRITZ GOLDBERG

Being Pharaoh

My grandmother turned into an old man,
deaf, with a hairy chin. It is August,

the damp panting of nights—I am
gradually building my own underworld

not just with prospective grief but
wires to hold up the asphodels.

Into it, a whole migration of shapes
skinned by light, pears gone

flat, and cars, and shadow like a floored heart.
They're the file of a river

and the Greeks had a river, the Romans.
The Egyptians who civilized the dead.

Tonight I am sick of every man
and his past. And the past is tired of his

request that it love him. I am trying
to make my bed. I am trying to keep

an angel from cracking my hip. The moon's
sleeve is flipped back in a drawer . . .

Thrush, you little singing spade—
I'm an unforgivably domestic mourner

and I might sleep through someone's
late supper, or hunger—just think how

Beckian Fritz Goldberg, "Being Pharaoh" from Never Be the Horse, *University of Akron Press, 1999. Reprinted by permission of the author.*

oblivious he will be. While I am in
the dark rustling my own inventory:

Each time we fall out of love we
say it wasn't really love at all as if

landing, a plane would say *no, not
actual sky*. While I am in the dark

getting fit for an afterlife. Admit
we never know the difference, like the woman

who stands up in the cinema and becomes
the black keyhole we peer into. I am

trying to keep her head down. So long
even her mother and mother's mother

turn blue. I am trying to keep
the ancestors out of the bedroom

so I can conceive a new face and new
arms, the feather trees across

the river, the curious shore dog.
Keep the distance simple like the top

deck of the parking garage from which
we can see the hospital. The present

may bond to any molecule, future
or past: My parents were kissing

while someone dragged the body past
the doorway, bag zipped to the chin

on the gurney, the head wound in white gauzes.
My father had taken off his mask, still

hissing oxygen, and mother was bent.
Of all things I've seen it was

old love that kept them from seeing.
Beautiful discretion, what moment will you

save from me? This should have been
a dream, something to wake from

but I never do. I am trying.
I will be pharaoh yet—

sealed with tiny boats and slavish
figurines. I am sick of every face

floating a sex by itself. Take in
this lampshade and these

curtains. Objects are memory.
As a child, I pictured the soul as a glass

wing, fluted, gelatinous, detached
as my voice under water. I made it up

a body—a paperweight—no snow
in the water, no water under the earth,

no music ever again in my hair, after
my hair. The dead will point to it,

What was the name for this, point to my hand,
What was the name for this? One life

has been mine so long, streets
and bicycles, monuments

descend in it. In the bedroom, a shirt
has fallen on shoes. Keep me

from seeing: Moon wanting into the dark
like the torn from—

the photograph—
It is August. One woman is so long

longing does not come out of her.
But this time I have loved you

so long I become
the boy you were. I must still

be alive, for everything is changing and
incomplete. Half a tree, half

drives its shadowy web near the shutters.
August has just turned September. The ancestors

want 4000-year-old grain, hard as quartz,
in grain jars. All I have are cigarettes.

What a night this is. What a night.
I'll lie down and my pillow will thrum

like a machine. I'll go barefoot
to the window, see if any light is

still on in any house. Who else
is afraid of missing something. Who else

knows one thing God can't enter
is my memory: I, a minor

twentieth-century poet, the first
of September, 4 A.M., finish one thing.

LINDA GREGG

The Letter

I am not feeling strong yet, but I am taking
good care of myself. The weather is perfect.
I read and walk all day and then walk to the sea.
I expect to swim soon. For now I am content.
I am not sure what I hope for. I feel I am
doing my best. It reminds me of when I was

sixteen dreaming of Lorca, the gentle trees outside
and the creek. Perhaps poetry replaces something
in me that others receive more naturally.
Perhaps my happiness proves a weakness in my life.
Even my failures in poetry please me.
Time is very different here. It is very good
to be away from public ambition.
I sweep and wash, cook and shop.
Sometimes I go into town in the evening
and have pastry with custard. Sometimes I sit
at a table by the harbor and drink half a beer.

JIM HARRISON

Rooster

to Pat Ryan

I have to kill the rooster tomorrow. He's being an asshole,
having seriously wounded one of our two hens with his insistent banging.
You walk into the barn to feed the horses and pick up an egg
or two for breakfast and he jumps her proclaiming she's mine she's mine.
Her wing is torn and the primary feathers won't grow back.
Chickens have largely been denatured, you know. He has no part
in those delicious fresh eggs. He crows on in a vacuum. He is
utterly pointless. He's as dumb as a tapeworm and no one cares
if he lives or dies. There. I can kill him
with an easy mind. But I'm still not up to it. Maybe I can hire
a weasel or a barn rat to do the job, or throw him to Justine,
the dog, who would be glad to rend him except the neighbors
have chickens too, she'd get the habit and we would have a beloved shot
dog to bury. So he deserves to die, having no purpose. We'll
have stewed barnyard chicken, closer to eating a gamebird than
that tasteless supermarket chicken born and bred in a caged

darkness. Everything we eat is dead except an occasional oyster
or clam. Should I hire the neighbor boy to kill him? Will the
hens stop laying out of grief? Isn't his long wavering crow
magnificent? Isn't the worthless rooster the poet's bird brother?
No. He's just a rooster and the world has no place for him.
Should I wait for a full wintry moon, take him to the top of the
hill after dropping three hits of mescaline and strangle him?
Should I set him free for a fox meal? They're coming back now
after the mange nearly wiped them out. He's like a leaking roof
with drops falling on my chest. He's the Chinese torture in the barn.
He's lust mad. His crow penetrates walls. His head bobs in lunar
jerks. The hens shudder but are bored with the pain of eggs.
What can I do with him? Nothing isn't enough. In the morning
we will sit down together and talk it out. I will tell him he
doesn't matter and he will wag his head, strut, perhaps crow.

BOB HICOK

AIDS

I tried visiting home.
They're such delicate people,
butterflies really,
quiet in a way
that reminds me of rain,
of the soft breath of sleep.
When Dad shook my hand
there was a tension to his skin
like exists inside every wind,
a desire to move forward and back
at the same time,
to touch and eradicate.
And when my mother kissed me
I cried in the way we sometimes do—
no tears, a burning force

Hicok, Bob. The Legend of Light. © 1995. Reprinted by permission of The University of Wisconsin Press.

behind the face,
pain turned upon itself,
a kind of emotional cannibalism—
because I felt
the slight trembling of her lips,
a stoic's most powerful expression
of fear and impotence.
We ate,
walked around the edge of the field,
talked about the season,
the neighbors,
the moon.
My mother swore
that through the years
it's become bigger,
and she laughed and said
   But maybe it's just my eyes.
I wanted to assure them
I'd been loved,
that there'd been someone
whose hand I'd held,
whose weaknesses I'd never betrayed.
How is it that people exist
so far apart,
that we stand a hand away
yet look upon each other
as ghosts,
as dust we love
yet cannot see or reach.
We looked at the stars come out,
in bunches, in leaps and swirls,
and I could say nothing,
could move no nearer,
no farther away.
I left the next morning,
afraid if I stayed
they'd cry,
cry and shatter
to look at me,
because I know they feel
it's somehow their fault,
that even this
they should have been able
to protect me from.
If only I could convince them,

could say something
which might work its way
into their sleep,
their hearts,
and soothe, and solace.
But all I can think of
is that you love as you have to
and die the best you can.

JANE HIRSCHFIELD

The Kingdom

At times
the heart
stands back
and looks at the body,
looks at the mind,
as a lion
quietly looks
at the not-quite-itself,
not-quite-another,
moving of shadows and grass.

Wary, but with interest,
considers its kingdom.

Then seeing
all that will be,
heart once again enters—
enters hunger, enters sorrow,
enters finally losing it all.
To know, if nothing else,
what it once owned.

TONY HOAGLAND

Jet

Sometimes I wish I were still out
on the back porch, drinking jet fuel
with the boys, getting louder and louder
as the empty cans drop out of our paws
like booster rockets falling back to Earth

and we soar up into the summer stars.
Summer. The big sky river rushes overhead,
bearing asteroids and mist, blind fish
and old space suits with skeletons inside.
On Earth, men celebrate their hairiness,

and it is good, a way of letting life
out of the box, uncapping the bottle
to let the effervescence gush
through the narrow, usually constricted neck.

And now the crickets plug in their appliances
in unison, and then the fireflies flash
dots and dashes in the grass, like punctuation
for the labyrinthine, untrue tales of sex
someone is telling in the dark, though

no one really hears. We gaze into the night
as if remembering the bright unbroken planet
we once came from,
to which we will never
be permitted to return.
We are amazed how hurt we are.
We would give anything for what we have.

LYNDA HULL

Counting in Chinese

Past midnight, September, and the moon dangles
mottled like a party lantern about to erupt
in smoke. The first leaves in the gutter eddy,
deviled by this wind that's traveled years,

whole latitudes, to find me here believing
I smell the fragrance of mock orange. For weeks
sometimes, I can go without thinking of you.
Crumpled movie handbills lift then skitter

across the pavement. They advertise the one
I've just seen—"Drunken Angel"—Kurosawa's
early film of occupied Japan, the Tokyo slums
an underworld of makeshift market stalls

and shacks where Matsu, the consumptive gangster,
dances in a zoot suit to a nightclub's swing band.
The singer mimes a parody of Cab Calloway
in Japanese. And later, as Matsu leans coughing

in a dance-hall girl's rented room, her painted
cardboard puppet etches shadows on the wall
that predict his rival's swift razor
and the death scene's slow unfurling, how

he falls endlessly it seems through a set
of doors into a heaven of laundry: sheets
on the line, the obis and kimonos stirring
with his passage. And all of this equals

a stark arithmetic of choices, his fate
the final sum. Why must it take so long
to value what's surrendered so casually?
I see you clearly now, the way you'd wait

Lynda Hull, "Counting in Chinese" reprinted from Star Ledger. *By the University of Iowa Press.*

for me, flashy beneath the Orpheum's
rococo marquee in your Hong Kong hoodlum's
suit, that tough-guy way you'd flick
your cigarette when I was late. You'd consult

the platinum watch, the one you'd lose
that year to poker. I could find again our room
above the Lucky Life Café, the cast-iron district
of sweatshop lofts. But now the square's deserted

in this small midwestern town, sidewalks
washed in the vague irreal glow of shopwindows,
my face translucent in the plate glass.
I remember this the way I'd remember a knife

against my throat: that night, after
the overdose, you told me to count, to calm
myself. You put together the rice-paper lantern
and when the bulb heated the frame it spun

shadows—dragon, phoenix, dragon and phoenix
tumbling across the walls where the clothes
you'd washed at the sink hung drying on
a nailed cord. The mock orange on the sill

blessed everything in that room
with its plangent useless scent. Forgive me.
I am cold and draw my sweater close. I discover
that I'm counting, out loud, in Chinese.

DAVID IGNATOW

At eighty I change my view

At age eighty to discover my illusion
about living in a hothouse of flowers.
Very well, I change my view:

David Ignatow, "At eighty I change my view" from Living Is What I Wanted: Last Poems. *Copyright © 1999 by Yaedi Ignatow. Reprinted with the permission of BOA Editions, Ltd., www.BOAEditions.org.*

a continual bombardment, Serbs in Bosnia,
and, under that constant bombardment, eat,
socialize and stroll in the streets.
A citizen of the town falls silently,
shot. In front and in the rear
we continue on our stroll and chatter
among ourselves, because, like good people,
we have adjusted
and carry an umbrella in the sun.

DENIS JOHNSON

The Veil

When the tide lay under the clouds
of an afternoon and gave them back to themselves
oilier a little and filled with anonymous boats,
I used to sit and drink at the very edge of it,
where light passed through the liquids in the glasses
and threw itself on the white drapes
of the tables, resting there like clarity
itself, you might think,
right where you could put a hand to it.
As drink gave way to drink, the slow
unfathomable voices of luncheon made
a window of ultraviolet light in the mind,
through which one at last saw the skeleton
of everything, stripped of any sense or consequence,
freed of geography and absolutely devoid
of charm; and in this originating
brightness you might see
somebody putting a napkin against his lips
or placing a blazing credit card on a plastic tray
and you'd know. You would know goddamn it. And never be able to say.

CAROLYN KIZER

To an Unknown Poet

I haven't the heart to say
you are not welcome here.
Your clothes smell of poverty, illness,
and unswept closets.
You come unannounced to my door
with your wild-faced wife and your many children.
I tell you I am busy.
I have a dentist's appointment.
I have a terrible cold.
The children would run mad
through our living room, with its collected
bibelots and objects of art.
I'm not as young as I was.
I am terrified of breakage.

It's not that I won't help you.
I'd love to send you a box
of hand-milled soap;
perhaps a check,
though it won't be enough to help.
Keep in mind that I came to your reading:
Three of us in the audience,
your wife, myself, and the bookstore owner,
unless we count the children who played trains
over your wife's knees in their torn jeans
and had to be hushed and hushed.

Next month I am getting an award
from the American Academy
and Institute of Arts and Letters.
The invitation came on hand-laid paper
thick as clotted cream.

I will travel by taxi
to 156th Street, where the noble old building,
as pale as the Acropolis,
is awash in a sea of slums.
And you will be far away, on the other Coast,
as far from our thoughts as Rimbaud
with his boy's face and broken teeth,
while we eat and drink and congratulate one another
in this bastion of culture.

BILL KNOTT

The Misunderstanding

I'm charmed yet chagrined by this misunderstanding
As when, after a riot my city's smashed-in stores appear all
Boarded up, billboarded over, with ads for wind-insurance.
Similarly, swimmingly, I miss the point. You too?

And my misunderstanding doesn't stop there, it grows—soon
I can't see why that sudden influx of fugitives,
All the world's escapees, rubbing themselves lasciviously against
    the Berlin Wall.
They stick like placards to it. Like napalm. Like ads for—

And me, I haven't even bought my biodegradable genitalia yet!
No. I was born slow, but picking up speed I run through
Our burnt-out streets, screaming, refusing to buy a house.
Finally, exasperated, the misunderstanding overtakes me,
    snatches up

Handcuffs. So now here I am, found with all you others
Impatiently craning, in this line that rumors out of sight up
    ahead somewhere,

Clutching our cash eager to purchase whatever it is, nervous
As if bombs were about to practice land-reform upon our
    bodies,

Redistribution of eyes, toes, arms, here we stand. Then, some
    new Age starts.

RUTH ELLEN KOCHER

Poem to a Jazz Man

My mother doesn't seem to remember
any of this, but the music must have been sweet,
cool jazz taking her like snake charm,
pleasure and desire, a warm July night.
The tall black man at the piano must have teased
the keys into filling that hot air with speak-easy
sugared sounds. She didn't have a chance.
Some poor white girl from the edge of town,
singing Saturdays to pay her rent,
could never have known what the music could do,
how the man and the piano, his fingers, his soul,
could so easily enter her, grow there
into a small, dark-eyed song.

Child, she would say, you are just like him.

Ruth Ellen Kocher, "Poem to a Jazz Man" from Desdemona's Fire: Poems, *Lotus Press, 1999. Reprinted by permission of the author.*

YUSEF KOMUNYAKAA

Believing in Iron

The hills my brothers & I created
Never balanced, & it took years
To discover how the world worked.
We could look at a tree of blackbirds
& tell you how many were there,
But with the scrap dealer
Our math was always off.
Weeks of lifting & grunting
Never added up to much,
But we couldn't stop
Believing in iron.
Abandoned trucks & cars
Were held to the ground
By thick, nostalgic fingers of vines
Strong as a dozen sharecroppers.
We'd return with our wheelbarrow
Groaning under a new load,
Yet tiger lilies lived better
In their languid, August domain.
Among paper & Coke bottles
Foundry smoke erased sunsets,
& we couldn't believe iron
Left men bent so close to the earth
As if the ore under their breath
Weighed down the gray sky.
Sometimes I dreamt how our hills
Washed into a sea of metal,
How it all became an anchor
For a warship or bomber
Out over trees with blooms
Too red to look at.

STANLEY KUNITZ

Day of Foreboding

Great events are about to happen.
I have seen migratory birds
in unprecedented numbers
descend on the coastal plain,
picking the margins clean.
My bones are a family in their tent
huddled over a small fire
waiting for the uncertain signal
to resume the long march.

LARRY LEVIS

The Poem Returning as an Invisible Wren to the World

Once, there was a poem. No one read it & the poem
Grew wise. It grew wise & then it grew thin,
No one could see it perched on the woman's
Small shoulders as she went on working beside

The gray conveyor belt with the others.
No one saw the poem take the shape of a wren,
A wren you could look through like a window,
And see all the bitterness of the world

In the long line of shoulders & faces bending
Over the gleaming, machined parts that passed
Before them, the faces transformed by the grace
And ferocity of a wren, a wren you could look

Through, like a lens, to see them working there.
This is not about how she threw herself into the river,
For she didn't, nor is it about the way her breasts
Looked in moonlight, nor about moonlight at all.

This is about the surviving curve of the bridge
Where she listened to the river whispering to her,
When the wren flew off & left her there,
With the knowledge of it singing in her blood.

By which the wind avenges. By which the rain avenges.
By which even the limb of a dead tree leaning
Above the white, swirling mouth of an eddy
In the river that once ran beside the factory window

Where she once worked, shall be remembered
When the dead come back, & take their places
Beside her on the line, & the gray conveyor belt
Starts up with its raspy hum again. Like a heaven's.

THOMAS LUX

The Man Inside the Chipmunk Suit

isn't very tall, 4 ft.
11½ inches, and can't speak
all day but waves a lot,
bobs to left and right, nods,
a little happy leap now
and then (his suit weighs 30 lbs.),

and a hundred snapshots a day
is the norm—a child or two or three enclosed
in his arms and paws. When asked
a question, as he often is, most often
about Uncle Owl,
his pal and the bigger star
in the cartoon from which the characters
are derived, he can't talk
but shrugs, hands out and open,
up to each side. He can't talk
because Chester Chipmunk
can't talk and he *is* Chester Chipmunk.
There are no small parts,
only small actors,
his high school drama teach said
and then said *That didn't come out*
the way I meant.
The man inside the chipmunk suit
wants to be inside the bunny suit,
or better, the monkey suit: there are sounds
to make, the part's a stretch.
His Method lessons have prepared him.
The man inside the chipmunk suit
has dreams just like you,
or her, or me, or them.
Above his sink is pinned
a picture of a minor movie star.

CLARENCE MAJOR

The Swine Who's Eclipsed Me

I, the alleged culprit, have a case.
I, the alleged captive criminal,
deny these very words: this
is a tirade against my own claim,
my existence. Hold these words

up to light, they will burn the page.
A Machiavellian of moral poison,
he holds my arm twisted
behind my back. I know
of no forthcoming parole.
My one chance is to reach out
and wrap his neck in confetti,
then crawl out through the tail end
of my own metamorphosis.
Yet I hear the action: the poison
arrow I drive into his heart
may be my own first step
to pushing up tulips
on a grassy mound.
We pay the toll as one.
Drawbridge guards do not tax us
as two. I, the alleged salient spirit,
am the true wise one; I am reliable,
moral, able to catch myself
even before I am thrown.

WILLIAM MATTHEWS

A Happy Childhood

*Babies do not want to hear about
babies; they like to be told of giants
and castles.*

Dr. Johnson

No one keeps a secret so well as a child.

Victor Hugo

My mother stands at the screen door, laughing.
"Out out damn Spot," she commands our silly dog.
I wonder what this means. I rise into adult air

like a hollyhock, I'm so proud to be loved
like this. The air is tight to my nervous body.
I use new clothes and shoes the way the corn-studded

soil around here uses nitrogen, giddily.
Ohio, Ohio, Ohio. Often I sing
to myself all day like a fieldful of August

insects, just things I whisper, really,
a trance in sneakers. I'm learning
to read from my mother and soon I'll go to school.

I hate it when anyone dies or leaves and the air
goes slack around my body and I have to hug myself,
a cloud, an imaginary friend, the stream in the road-

side park. I love to be called for dinner.
Spot goes out and I go in and the lights
in the kitchen go on and the dark,

which also has a body like a cloud's,
leans lightly against the house. Tomorrow
I'll find the sweatstains it left, little grey smudges.

Here's a sky no higher than a streetlamp,
and a stack of morning papers cinched by wire.
It's 4:00 A.M. A stout dog, vaguely beagle,

minces over the dry, fresh-fallen snow;
and here's our sleep-sodden paperboy
with his pliers, his bike, his matronly dog,

his unclouding face set for paper route
like an alarm clock. Here's a memory
in the making, for this could be the morning

he doesn't come home and his parents
two hours later drive his route until
they find him asleep, propped against a streetlamp,

his papers all delivered and his dirty paper-
satchel slack, like an emptied lung,
and he blur-faced and iconic in the morning

air rinsing itself a paler and paler blue
through which a last few dandruff-flecks
of snow meander casually down.

The dog squeaks in out of the dark,
snuffling *me too me too.* And here he goes
home to memory, and to hot chocolate

on which no crinkled skin forms like infant ice,
and to the long and ordinary day,
school, two triumphs and one severe

humiliation on the playground, the past
already growing its scabs, the busride home,
dinner, and evening leading to sleep

like the slide that will spill him out, come June,
into the eye-reddening chlorine waters
of the municipal pool. Here he goes to bed.

Kiss. Kiss. Teeth. Prayers. Dark. Dark.
Here the dog lies down by his bed,
and sighs and farts. Will he always be

this skinny, chicken-bones?
He'll remember like a prayer
how his mother made breakfast for him

every morning before he trudged out
to snip the papers free. Just as
his mother will remember she felt

guilty never to wake up with him
to give him breakfast. It was Cream
of Wheat they always or never had together.

It turns out you are the story of your childhood
and you're under constant revision,
like a lonely folktale whose invisible folks

are all the selves you've been, lifelong,
shadows in fog, grey glimmers at dusk.
And each of these selves had a childhood

it traded for love and grudged to give away,
now lost irretrievably, in storage
like a set of dishes from which no food,

no Cream of Wheat, no rabbit in mustard
sauce, nor even a single raspberry,
can be eaten until the afterlife,

which is only childhood in its last
disguise, all radiance or all humiliation,
and so it is forfeit a final time.

In fact it was awful, you think, or why
should the piecework of grief be endless?
Only because death is, and likewise loss,

which is not awful, but only breathtaking.
There's no truth about your childhood,
though there's a story, yours to tend,

like a fire or garden. Make it a good one,
since you'll have to live it out, and all
its revisions, so long as you all shall live,

for they shall be gathered to your deathbed,
and they'll have known to what you and they
would come, and this one time they'll weep for you.

The map in the shopping center has an X
signed "you are here." A dream is like that.
In a dream you are never eighty, though

you may risk death by other means:
you're on a ledge and memory calls you
to jump, but a deft cop talks you in

to a small, bright room, and snickers.
And in a dream, you're everyone somewhat,
but not wholly. I think I know how that

works: for twenty-one years I had a father
and then I became a father, replacing him
but not really. Soon my sons will be fathers.

Surely, that's what middle-aged means,
being father and son to sons and father.
That a male has only one mother is another

story, told wherever men weep wholly.
Though nobody's replaced. In one dream
I'm leading a rope of children to safety,

through a snowy farm. The farmer comes out
and I have to throw snowballs well to him
so we may pass. Even dreaming, I know

he's my father, at ease in his catcher's
squat, and that the dream has revived
to us both an old unspoken fantasy:

we're a battery. I'm young, I'm brash,
I don't know how to pitch but I can
throw a lamb chop past a wolf. And he

can handle pitchers and control a game.
I look to him for a sign. I'd nod
for anything. The damn thing is hard to grip

without seams, and I don't rely only
on my live, young arm, but throw by all
the body I can get behind it, and it fluffs

toward him no faster than the snow
in the dream drifts down. Nothing
takes forever, but I know what the phrase

means. The children grow more cold
and hungry and cruel to each other
the longer the ball's in the air, and it begins

to melt. By the time it gets to him we'll be
our waking ages, and each of us is himself
alone, and we all join hands and go.

    Toward dawn, rain explodes on the tin roof
like popcorn. The pale light is streaked by grey
and that green you see just under the surface

of water, a shimmer more than a color.
Time to dive back into sleep, as if into
happiness, that neglected discipline. . . .

In those sixth-grade book reports
you had to say if the book was optimistic
or not, and everyone looked at you

the same way: how would he turn out?
He rolls in his sleep like an otter.
Uncle Ed has a neck so fat it's funny,

and on the way to work he pries the cap
off a Pepsi. Damn rain didn't cool one weary
thing for long; it's gonna be a cooker.

The boy sleeps with a thin chain of sweat
on his upper lip, as if waking itself,
becoming explicit, were hard work.

Who knows if he's happy or not?
A child is all the tools a child has,
growing up, who makes what he can.

CHRISTOPHER MERRILL

Three Boats

Proud of its burden, the tugboat's a father
On the night shift, loading cement for his son
Who wants to be a singer or a priest;
An overseer watering his fields,
His daughters, and his slaves; a novelist
Leashed to his desk, wreathed in pipe smoke, and worn
Down by the words asleep on the last page,
Who groans, like the tug bellowing its horn

Until it finds the lane down which to tow
Its barge, its fruits, into the teeming harbor.

And the purse seine works in pairs—bride and groom,
Fence post and rail. It believes in cornerstones;
In sacraments of closure—eyelids, knots;
And in the woman following her husband
To another city and another set
Of circles to crack, islands to explore
And colonize before his lungs give out,
Before his creditors foul their air and water;—
Theirs is a marriage of necessity,
A balancing of nets, accounts, and soundings.

But the hydroplane delights in revelation.
Like the divine, it works in quick, sheer strokes;
Like money, it disappears before we know it.
It skims the Sound for the main points, ignoring
All the particulars—schooners, skiffs, kelp,
The buried reef; it scores the sheet of water,
Like a glass cutter, and then the sun applies
Its thumbprint till a window splits apart,
Revealing an old mariner and his secret
—The cache of emeralds hidden in the waves.

JANE MILLER

Poetry

Invited onto the grounds of the god,
who decides what words mean,
we are amazed at the world
perfect at last. Gold fish, gold finches, gold watches,
trash blasted into crystal, all
twilights supporting one final sunset
with slender fingers of consolation.

Jane Miller, "Poetry" from Memory at These Speeds: New and Selected Poems. *Copyright © 1996 by Jane Miller. Reprinted with the permission of Copper Canyon Press, P.O. Box 271, Port Townsend, WA 98368-0271*

A little reality goes a long way,
far off in the distance the weak sea
beaches its blue whales, the small sky
melds the stars into one
serious fire, burning eternally
out of control, our earth.
But here we are visiting
the plutonium factory dazzling
to the eye, the one good one remaining
to us in our wisdom. We have concluded
that automatic, volcanic sunrises and sunsets
where light trips on the same cardboard vine
are blinding, and we would rather fail
painfully slowly than survive a copy
of the world perfect at last. Yet we are
impressed by the real thing, which we walk
like dew upon flesh, suddenly lubricated and translucent
beyond our dreamiest desires, hard-pressed
to object. Consoled that there is so little
difference between the terrible and the real,
we admire the powerful appleseeds bobbing
in the dewy pools, we cannot help
but enjoy their greeny spring, and it is only by resting
on the miraculous grass, wildly uniform, mildly serene,
that we sense
with our secret selves, the little bit we left behind and
remember, that we are out of our element, that we are
being made into words even as we speak.

NAOMI SHIHAB NYE

Blood

"A true Arab knows how to catch a fly in his hands,"
my father would say. And he'd prove it,

Naomi Shihab Nye, "Blood" from The Words Under the Words: Selected Poems, *Eighth Mountain Press, 1995. Reprinted by permission of the author.*

cupping the buzzer instantly
while the host with the swatter stared.

In the spring our palms peeled like snakes.
True Arabs believed watermelon could heal fifty ways.
I changed these to fit the occasion.

Years before, a girl knocked,
wanted to see the Arab.
I said we didn't have one.
After that, my father told me who he was,
"Shihab"— "shooting star"—
a good name, borrowed from the sky.
Once I said, "When we die, we give it back?"
He said that's what a true Arab would say.

Today the headlines clot in my blood.
A little Palestinian dangles a truck on the front page.
Homeless fig, this tragedy with a terrible root
is too big for us. What flag can we wave?
I wave the flag of stone and seed,
table mat stitched in blue.

I call my father, we talk around the news.
It is too much for him,
neither of his two languages can reach it.
I drive into the country to find sheep, cows,
to plead with the air:
Who calls anyone *civilized?*
Where can the crying heart graze?
What does a true Arab do now?

ADRIENNE RICH

Amends

Nights like this: on the cold apple-bough
a white star, then another

exploding out of the bark:
on the ground, moonlight picking at small stones

as it picks at greater stones, as it rises with the surf
laying its cheek for moments on the sand
as it licks the broken ledge, as it flows up the cliffs,
as it flicks across the tracks

as it unavailing pours into the gash
of the sand-and-gravel quarry
as it leans across the hangared fuselage
of the crop-dusting plane

as it soaks through cracks into the trailers
tremulous with sleep
as it dwells upon the eyelids of the sleepers
as if to make amends

TOMAZ SALAMUN

I Have a Horse

I have a horse. My horse has four legs.
I have a record player. On my record player I sleep.
I have a brother. My brother is a sculptor.
I have a coat. I have a coat to keep me warm.
I have a plant. I have a plant to have green in my room.
I have Maruška. I have Maruška because I love her.
I have matches. With matches I light cigarettes.
I have a body. With a body I do the most beautiful things that I do.
I have destruction. Destruction causes me many troubles.
I have night. Night comes to me through the window of my room.
I have fun racing cars. I race cars because car racing is fun.
I have money. With money I buy bread.

I have six really good poems. I hope I will write more of them.
I am twenty-seven years old. All these years have passed like
　lightning.
I am relatively courageous. With this courage I fight human stupidity.
I have a birthday March seventh. I hope March seventh will be a nice
　day.
I have a friend whose daughter's name is Breditza. In the evening
　when they put her to bed she says Salamun and falls asleep.

JEANNINE SAVARD

Transfer

in memory of Rudy Dahl

You're standing irresistibly with a frozen glass
Of Jim Beam in the sand, your flight suit buckled
And helmet tucked like a dinosaur egg
Above your slow right hip. A goat steps
Forward dripping bloody milk, half-digested
Secret codes and live nerve from its teeth. Gold beads
Fill your footsteps, dragged earth ends and sun here
In the ripened mind of night. Songs
You sang follow the snake tracks
Into invisibility and out again. Your breastbone
Heaves, dusk purple, in its extreme desire
To stay resurrected for this newest war.
Your hand drifts and tics the glowing
Altimeter. Everyone's mouth on the distant screen
Jiggles open and shut like the slot machines
You played in Nevada. What will
You do now the morning star
Is full over, alternate strips of knowing
And unknowing, silver and black
Icebag smoke over the designated targets, oil fields

Reprinted from Trumpeter: *"Transfer" by permission of Carnegie Mellon University Press.* © *1993 by Jeannine Savard.*

Burning, your leg aching and hard
To bend. You say, "I'll leave it behind." You find
A key chained to your neck and run
To the hatch, the wings skimmed with rain, moon cloth
Over the throttle—nose up and up, near to the full,
Closer to the bright virgin no one's ever seen.

DENNIS SCHMITZ

About Night

    It's a blindness
the barn owl has memorized in order
to see: when the owl doubts

or loathes its
compromise, it goes heavy in the familiar
pine woods, & simple light
(though here on Inverness
ridge light's only mongrel greens & grays

less gray) will not hold the bird up.
It's almost night
by the time the short-pants hikers queue
for the last Point Reyes bus,

chatting Gortex & freeze-dried stews.
Rain off the Pacific's begun to thin
all colors, whipping up
the thrift-store smell of old eucalyptus

trees around the ranger post,
coating equally prey & raptor.
How I love going blind

Dennis Schmitz, "About Night" from About Night: Selected and New Poems, *Oberlin College Press,* © 1993.
Reprinted by permission of the publisher.

into this ride,
the bus headlights smearing
into firs & the greedy
laurels that for sun have twisted themselves
ugly between bigger trees,
our windows slowly taking the darkness

of the world outside.
An hour to San Raphael—
I'm over a rear wheel, taking the road,
wading into it with my legs
fighting the cramped seat, waiting for sleep
to smudge everything,
my wings, of course, only metaphor.

CHARLES SIMIC

Dream Broker

You may find yourself with my help
Taking small, apprehensive steps
In a cabal of side streets,
Doorways on the lurk, dim store signs.
Insomnia Detective Agency, restorers
Of defaced and mislaid memories,
Are at your discreet service:

Here then are the small beads of rain
Rapping against the windowpane
The day your grandmother died.
Here's the chained dog whipped by a man
In full view of the evening train,

And the girl with a white blindfold
Feeling her way in the empty museum.

You expected her hidden companions
To burst after her merrily,
But nobody did. It got dark
For the saint pierced by arrows
And for you, too, chump,
But nobody else came along.

WILLIAM STAFFORD

Not Very Loud

Now is the time of the moths that come
in the evening. They are around, just being
there, at windows and doors. They crowd
the lights, planing in from dark fields
and liking it in town. They accept each other
as they fly or crawl. How do they know
what is coming? Their furred flight,
softer than down, announces a quiet
approach under whatever is loud.

What are moths good for? Maybe they offer
something we need, a fluttering
near the edge of our sight, and they may carry
whatever is needed for us to watch
all through those long nights in our still,
vacant houses, if there is another war.

JEAN VALENTINE

Silences: A Dream of Governments

From your eyes I thought
we could almost move   almost speak
But the way your face
held there, in the yellow air,
And that hand, writing down our names—
And the way the sun
shone right through us
Done with us

       Then
the plain astonishment—the air
broken open: just ourselves
sitting, talking; like always;
the kitchen window
propped open by the same
blue-gray dictionary.
August.   Rain.   A Tuesday.

Then, absence. The open room
suspended   The long street
gone off   quiet, dark.
The ocean floor.   Slow
shapes glide by

Then, day
keeps beginning again: the same
stubborn pulse against the throat,
the same
listening for a human voice—
your name, my name

"Silences: A Dream of Governments" from Door In the Mountain: New and Collected Poems, *Wesleyan, 2004.*
Reprinted by permission of the author.

BRUCE WEIGL

Anniversary of Myself

A lifetime ago

I squatted down on a curb
in a frozen twilight parking lot

some fucking where

and looked up into the near
apartment's windows
and at the lives going on
behind them in the light.

The fingers of my gloves had holes.
I don't know what I was doing.
There had been a war
and my people
had grown disenchanted.

I had a fifth of somebody's
whiskey in my pocket. That night
the liquor kept me warm. Now
I flitter branch to branch outside your window,
lit with a thousand watts of something
I can taste and feel but cannot see.

I am moth wing in summer sky,
night bird not blinded or butchered
by your unkempt, sleepless dogs.

Bruce Weigl, "Anniversary of Myself" from Archeology of the Circle: New and Selected Poems, Grove Press,
1999. Reprinted by permission of the author.

DAVID WOJAHN

Cold Glow: Icehouses

Because the light this morning is recondite
like figures behind curtains from a long way off,
because the morning is cold and this room is heatless,
I've gone without sleep, I brood.
The protocol of memory: the faucet dripping
into a sponge, then thinking of the way
I saw White Bear Lake freeze over
twenty years ago in Minnesota, the carp oblivious below.

I thought last night of Solomon Petrov,
a Ukrainian rabbi in my college science books
afflicted with total recall, a pathological memory
that made perspective impossible.
Once for doctors he *remembered* running for a train
in Petersburg in winter. They recorded
his quickened pulse, body temperature plunging.
The death by fever of his first wife Tania
was not remembered, but continually relived.

And memory is not accomplishment.
Last night again you described for me
our child pulled dead from your womb. In sleep you talked
to yourself and the child, who passed unnamed
wholly into memory. Now you wanted peace,
some distance. And every memory, said Solomon Petrov,
must proceed unchanged in the mind, going on
like smoke to designate itself again
like a second floor window where I stood as a boy
to watch the fishermen park their cars
on the lake, icehouse lights in the evening below.

Or our child whose name is only ash,
is only a thought too hurtful to free.

Mornings like these, he floats at the window, waiting
and mouthing his name, there through a tangent of ice,
his face and hands ashimmer.

C. D. WRIGHT

only the crossing counts

It's not how we leave one's life. How go off
the air. You never know do you. You think you're ready
for anything; then it
happens, and you're not. You're really
not. The genesis of an ending, nothing
but a feeling, a slow movement, the dusting
of furniture with a remnant of the revenant's shirt.
Seeing the candles sink in their sockets; we turn
away, yet the music never quits. The fire kisses our face.
O phthsis, o lotharian dead eye, no longer
will you gaze on the baize of the billiard table. No more
shooting butter dishes out of the sky. Scattering light.
Between snatches of poetry and penitence you left
the brumal wood of men and women. Snow drove
the butterflies home. You must know
how it goes, known all along what to expect,
sooner or later . . . the faded cadence of anonymity.
Frankly, my dear, frankly, my dear, frankly

AL YOUNG

Desert Footage: Three Dissolves

Egypt, Israel, Palestine & Arizona—
all in one heady spring season

1/

Crossing, we arrive, we change up, we come back
inside the original oasis, that quivering water, its
cool-holed message no mirage; a power-mirror. Ours.

2/

Brushes with sages, lifetime leads, unload, unjam
right here, where now don't need no start, don't need
no count; where lust, like dusty first-impressions, suns
up, suns down & falls away by twists & blazing turns.

Stopped cold by night, excitement slows. Zigzag,
the jazz of cactus fuzz & insect buzz & lizards whizzing
every whichway nowhere & buzzards minding their own
lazy business zooms, the horizon a shining rim-shot.

3/

Bowled over by blue, by light & cooling cloud, desert
can reach its peaks & depths, its flats & sharps,
with singular, insular pleasure. And treasures
we always haul back lack the track-record market value
wealth-wish we've been air-conditioned to cherish.

In malls & designer back alleys of urgent dreaming,
desire grinds & bumps & tallies & bills. But back here
at home, back smack in the desert, silence & space
ease in & replace get-&-gimme, mucho & gotcha.
Or is it we who get erased? The thrill of peace enthrones
out here, where water walks & kings don't mean a thing.

Al Young, "Desert Footage: Three Dissolves" from The Sound of Dreams Remembered: Poems 1990–2000,
2001. Reprinted by permission of the author.

IV | *Catalysts*

1. In Search of the Image

DISCUSSION

An image is a thing outside of ourselves that we conjure into consciousness through our senses. We then internalize this "thing" in order to experience, remember, and imagine it, all the while having both cerebral reactions—the thoughts and ideas about the image—as well as the vast expanse of emotional responses—all of the *feelings*—that the image evokes.

An image might take form as a physical object. It might be something more ethereal such as sound. Or an image might be a gesture or a movement. The smell of your mother's hair, the first notes of your favorite song, a treasured photograph, the fifteen seconds of floating as a leaf falls from the tree to the ground, a horse drinking from a creek—all of these are images because they can be "imagined," experienced externally, and integrated into an internal experience.

What is most important for the writer to know is that the image is at the heart of nearly all poetry or perhaps even of all literature.

So how do we find images and how will finding images help us to write poems? Based on the above definition, they are everywhere. Becoming acquainted with imagery is really a matter of becoming aware of the world around us. And often the poem itself is born out of the image.

EXERCISE

This exercise is focused on the visual image. It requires a bit of research, some snooping around those places where images are plentiful: *the world of visual art.* Historically, poetry and visual art have maintained a healthy connection to one another. First, you need to find a wealth of images. Go to a nearby museum or gallery, or visit virtual museums on the Internet. Go to the library and browse the stacks of art books. Visit your local bookstore and look through some photography magazines. Your options for finding visual art are endless.

Spend a good deal of time studying the images you see. Find one that speaks to you, draws you closer, causes you to dwell within it. Try to experience the image on multiple levels. What does it make you think about? How does your body feel when you look at it? What kinds of emotions does it elicit?

Now it is time to "write the image," to put its visual elements into language. You will use description, adjectives, precisely chosen words, and even similes. You will think of the things that are "like" the image. You will notice the microscopic details of the image. You will allow the image to become something other than its visual representation. You will explore what is *not* present in the image. Perhaps you have chosen a painting of a woman drinking coffee. Who is watching her? What is she thinking about? How much coffee is left in the cup? Is it warm? Did she add cream? If there is a window behind her, what is outside that window? When she finishes her coffee, what will she do?

Asking these questions is the work of the poet. The answers are the work of the poem. At times, the questions will need to be left unanswered. Simply being conscious of the questions might be enough to bring the image to life and to conjure the poem into being.

2. The Narrative Poem

DISCUSSION

Narrative permeates nearly every aspect of our lives. We communicate using narrative on an hourly basis. We all have stories to tell, and some of us feel the compulsion to write down those stories. Most likely, it is with story writing that we first approach creative writing. Surely, if we struggle to read poems, then the writing of poems is an even more daunting activity. Yet, contemporary poetry has blessed us with the lyrical narrative, the poem that finds a balance between carefully chosen language and images and a finely spun tale.

The poet's challenge is the necessity of choice. Once the poet decides that a particular story should occur in a poem rather than in a piece of prose—perhaps because the story will be best told with holes, missing pieces, with the transcendence of time—then the poet must make some decisions based on the economy of form. The poem will utilize line breaks, leaving more white space on the page. What kinds of silences will the unwritten or unspoken evoke? Which details must be included? Which details must be omitted?

Like the fiction writer, the narrative poet might ask the story to tell itself slightly out of the order in which it occurred. When certain factual details fail the story, the story might require embellishment. The poet might decide to lie. The narrative poet, unlike the fiction writer, often leaps outside the narrative in order to find another perspective.

EXERCISE

For this exercise, you'll need to choose a story, either fictional or factual, with a chronological series of events or circumstances that for some reason seems worthy of record. Try writing the narrative to its fullest extent, but write it in prose. Use images, character development, dialogue, and avoid breaking lines.

Once you have several pages, go through and begin crossing things out. Begin making choices. Ask yourself which words, phrases, or sentences can be left out.

Now, on a separate sheet of paper, write down what you have left. Experiment with line breaks, paying attention to the rhythm and integrity of each line. Can each line exist without the others? Where are the natural pauses? Where would you like your reader to dwell, to linger?

Finally, force yourself to leap outside the narrative. Find one element in the story, an object or a character, and try approaching the story from its perspective. If there is a dog in your story, perhaps not a central character but included nonetheless, what might the dog be experiencing? If one of your characters sits in a rocking chair, take the chair outside the story itself and explore what else the object might evoke.

3. The Newspaper Poem

DISCUSSION

Politics and poetry have had an inextricable relationship for centuries. One could argue that Homer was a political poet, both documenting and editorializing current events such as the Trojan War and the fall of Troy. Shakespeare's histories, poetical interpretations of the political, are surely evidence of this connection. The political poetry of the twentieth and twenty-first centuries can seem didactic at times, leaning more toward activism and less toward art.

You don't have to be a political poet in order to capture cultural and historical turning points. You don't have to stand on a soapbox to turn headlines into a meaningful expression of the human experience. In fact, transforming real world events into artistic events can illuminate meaning where before there was little. With art, we are able to *feel* in a more immediate way than the minimalism and fact offering provided by newspapers.

Not only does daily newspaper reading help keep our brains attuned to language and the written word, it also provides a valuable source of writing material.

EXERCISE

For this exercise, you'll need to pick up a recent newspaper and begin turning its pages. Like any other instance in which you are consciously observing with the intention of finding material for your writing, you will want to be aware of your visceral reactions to what you read and what you see. Pay attention to the headlines, the stories themselves, quotes taken from those interviewed, and the accompanying photographs. Take notes. Write down interesting words and phrases.

You will most likely find that the articles are thrifty, sparse even, with their use of language. Facts are important here. But it is exactly this simplicity that leaves room for your poem to emerge. You are looking for a skeleton, just the scaffolding on which you can build a poem.

Once you have chosen a particular news story and a few resonant lines from it, use your poetic license to fill in the gaps, to tell your version of the truth, your perspective, maybe even your fabrication. Try to ask questions about the situation that the journalist would not ask! If a plane crashed in the Alaskan wilderness, what if a fisherman witnessed it? What was the experience like for that person? If a scientific discovery is made, how might it relate to something very specific about your life? If a politician makes a statement, what was he *really* thinking, what did he *want* to say but couldn't?

Your job is to give the news story a life beyond itself. Your job is to speculate and make connections in unpredictable ways. Your job is also to personalize events which, most times, remain on the periphery of our lives. Your job is to humanize, to help your reader find an emotional connection to what is typically a very intellectual experience.

Evolving Worlds and Disoriented Words: Experimental Writing

I | *Discussion of the Genre*

All writing is experimental. We poke, prod, and process with language. A short story might, in many cases, know that it wants to be a short story when it grows up but it will, in all probability, not know just how that will occur. A poem may want to be three five-lined stanzas with indented lines but neither will it know just what those lines will say in most instances. The memoirist? One never knows what one will discover about oneself. Every act of writing is a brave experiment and, sometimes, the actual form of the writing may be part of that experiment. The paths only fork when some brave and perhaps careless wanderer wanders off the beaten way and into a new direction away from the garden and back into the forest.

A poem may start out as a poem and turn into a letter. Maybe a single paragraph will end up feeling just like a poem. An essay on an art exhibit may begin simply as that and then evolve into an essay about one's experience of art at various points in one's life or into many different points of one life. A short story may include a poem. *And why shouldn't it?*

This book has attempted to provide you with a representative collection of the established writing genres and to open a discussion about when an essay will be appropriate, when a poem seems right, or when a fictional story needs to be told. Regardless of what form the writer chooses, whether the poem is a poem or the short story a short story, what will ultimately affect the reader is its language and its message, its translatable meaning. In this section, we hope to leave you with the impression that writing takes as many forms as there are writers, that alternatives to all accepted forms exist, and that every writer has access to these forms. Remember, the garden is yours, and the paths must follow your own movement.

The work collected here demonstrates that a prose piece might not adhere to a single narrative or to any narrative at all and that poetry will occur even in the absence of line breaks. The writer writes, essentially, to communicate and to engage the reader. The writer writes to invite the reader into a fearlessly experimental place and into the act of creation itself, to invite the reader into the world of a work-in-progress, a work in the processes of bringing itself into being. If we read to discover, we must write to discover as well.

With experimental forms, with alternatives to established genres, the writer does not escape the need for his or her writing to take on meaning or for that writing to elicit meaning. Great writing is both evocative and provocative. It both opens our eyes and moves our minds. To achieve this, you must ask yourself some important questions: *Will I attempt to do something new? What do I need to say? How should I say it?*

There are no easy answers to the latter two questions, of course, if the answer to the first question is "yes."

What we hope you will find in this section is breathing room, room to stretch your legs in your mind full of ideas. Thus far, we've examined and discussed the potential offered by traditional modes of writing. We've suggested that writing is a varied and constantly evolving art. We've collected what we consider to be the finest examples of a myriad of styles and voices. In this section, we ask you to put it all together and make something new. Poet Michael McFee considers the youth of Jesus Christ. E. Ethelbert Miller remembers watching television with his father. Michael Palmer is a computer screen. The selections here range from hilarious to despondent, brief to expansive.

In his novel about a novel, *Wonderboys*, Michael Chabon writes about the "midnight disease," an affliction suffered by those strange folk who feel compelled to write creatively, who feel like they are "tossing on a restless pillow in a world full of sleepers." To be a creative writer, tirelessly experimental, sometimes you might need to pinch your arm to stay awake. An experimental form might be just the pinch you need.

In reading the following selections, ask yourself, "Why?" "Why did he or she make this choice?" Maybe you'll find an answer, maybe not.

The next time you sit down to write something new, we hope you'll be able to ask yourself, "Why would I make this choice that I'm about to make?"

Prose poetry. Sudden fiction. Call them what you like. Remember this: the novel was once an experiment. The written poem was as well. Forms that seem to be radical today may seem essential tomorrow.

II | A Quintessential: "The Colonel"

by Carolyn Forché

What you have heard is true. I was in his house. His wife carried a tray of coffee and sugar. His daughter filed her nails, his son went out for the night. There were daily papers, pet dogs, a pistol on the cushion beside him. The moon swung bare on its black cord over the house. On the television was a cop show. It was in English. Broken bottles were embedded in the walls around the house to scoop the kneecaps from a man's legs or cut his hands to lace. On the windows there were gratings like those in liquor stores. We had dinner, rack of lamb, good wine, a gold bell was on the table for calling the maid. The maid brought green mangoes, salt, a type of bread. I was asked how I enjoyed the country. There was a brief commercial in Spanish. His wife took everything away. There was some talk then of how difficult it had become to govern. The parrot said hello on the terrace. The colonel told it to shut up, and pushed himself from the table. My friend said to me with his eyes: say nothing. The colonel returned with a sack used to bring groceries home. He spilled many human ears on the table. They were like dried peach halves. There is no other way to say this. He took one of them in his hands, shook it in our faces, dropped it into a water glass. It came alive there. I am tired of fooling around he said. As for the rights of anyone, tell your people they can go fuck themselves. He swept the ears to the floor with his arm and held the last of his wine in the air. Something for your poetry, no? he said. Some of the ears on the floor caught this scrap of his voice. Some of the ears on the floor were pressed to the ground.

Discussion of a Quintessential

"The Colonel"
by Carolyn Forché

"There is no other way to say this," declares the poet Carolyn Forché, as an unnamed San Salvadoran colonel empties a bag of human ears on a table before her. There is no precedented way to say that a colonel in the army of an American-backed and UN-recognized government could possess a grocery bag full of the stolen ears of his country's citizens and that, as the culminating act of a dinner party, he would present them to his guest, a visiting American poet.

357

To report this act would necessarily be an act of violence as well. This paradox begs the question: *how does the writer write this in a way that befits without belittling the suffering of human lives?* To do so, she must engage in a dangerous and, ultimately, necessary experiment.

"What you have heard is true," begins Forché's brief and powerful prose piece. Everything leading up to this moment has been reality. The moment of this poem begins in a moment of clarity and utter honesty. "What you have heard is true. I was in his house."

In this extraordinary work, the poet eschews line breaks and any other trappings of poetry in order to let the event of the poem speak for itself. "There were daily papers, pet dogs, a pistol on the cushion beside him. The moon swung bare on its black cord over the house." The setting itself speaks to the writer of the violence that underscores every second of this encounter. A pistol. A moon hung in the galleys. "Broken bottles were embedded in the walls around the house to scoop the kneecaps from a man's legs or cut his hands to lace."

What we are presented with is a real-time meeting of culture and depravity. The civilized and the primal: an adult human male not only with an ability to enjoy TV and mangoes but also able to "serve" torture to those whose politics differ from his own. A dictator and a man. An executioner and a dinner host.

Perhaps the form of Forché's remembrance of this moment is determined less by her will than by the force of the colonel's character. In order for a piece of writing to contain this character, the writing must be more than one thing at once: poetry and prose, memoir and journal, observance and meditation, criticism and reportage.

Consider this: "We had dinner, rack of lamb, good wine, a gold bell was on the table for calling the maid. The maid brought green mangoes, salt, a type of bread. I was asked how I enjoyed the country." Taken out of context, this passage would mean something entirely different. But the context of this moment is everything: an expression of cultural richness and hospitality in the home of a man capable of primitive cruelty. The horrific uniqueness of this moment requires an expression as unique as it is horrible, the execution of a terrifying experiment in the written word. Thus, Forché presents us with a prose poem, a mini report, an expressionistic news brief.

As we move through the poem toward its inevitable emptying of the canvas bag on the table, we feel the weight of each observation pile one upon another. Not given line breaks in which to catch our breath, nor character background to bolster our presence, nor a chronological sequence which would offer us any hope of conclusion, we are forced to sit in Forché's seat and endure, as she did, the unendurable. When at last the bag is emptied, and the severed ears of human prisoners tumble onto the table before us, we finally have some inclination of how far this experiment will take us. It is as if we discover the limits of our own tolerance by living within the limits of the writer's. It is, simply, as if we are there at the table in her place, attempting along with her to discover a way of saying these things she is compelled to say.

Perhaps this moment could have been rendered by a poem. Perhaps, it could also have been recreated in an essay. Surely, it could have been told in a letter to a magazine or newspaper editor. That it comes to us as a poetic work of short prose, or as a prosaic work of imagistic and narrative poetry, is testament to the truth that Carolyn Forché—the only person present whose experience as a writer called her to bring it forth—could offer it only in the form that we have before us.

Was it true? Was she there? Is this accurate?

Who can say?

No one but Forché or the colonel. If it is a fiction, no one but Forché can say. What matters most is the truth that has been successfully conveyed: *man's cruelty to man will remain mostly unspeakable and wholly unfathomable.* Therefore, it is an act of sheer courage to attempt to express such horror and an act of great worth to have transformed it into art. This is not the triumph of mere experiment; this is a testament to the power of creative writing.

III | *Reading Selections*

KIM ADDONIZIO

Survivors

He and his lover were down to their last few T cells and arguing over who was going to die first. He wanted to be first because he did not want to have to take care of his lover's parrot or deal with his lover's family, which would descend on their flat after the funeral, especially the father, who had been an Army major and had tried to beat his son's sexual orientation out of him with a belt on several occasions during adolescence; the mother, at least, would be kind but sorrowful, and secretly blame him, the survivor—he knew this from her letters, which his lover had read to him each week for the past seven years. He knew, too, that they all—father, mother, two older brothers—would disapprove of their flat, of the portrait of the two of them holding hands that a friend had painted and which hung over the bed, the Gay Freedom Day poster in the bathroom, all the absurd little knickknacks like the small plastic wind-up penis that hopped around on two feet; maybe, after his lover died, he would put some things away, maybe he would even take the parrot out of its cage and open the window so it could join the wild ones he'd heard of, that nested in the palm trees on Delores Street, a whole flock of bright tropical birds apparently thriving in spite of the chilly Bay Area weather—he would let it go, fly off, and he would be completely alone then; dear God, he thought, let me die first, don't let me survive him.

Kim Addonizio, "Survivors" from In The Box Called Pleasure: Stories, *Northwestern University Press, 1999. Reprinted by permission of the author.*

CATHRYN ALPERT

That Changes Everything

I

This feeling that something is deeply wrong. Not basically, as some people might say, but deeply, as in to the core. Blood and bone. As in this is the stuff we're made of and there's no getting away.

II

Brush one hundred times before you go to bed. Rise at eight and scrape cornflakes off the counter. Put your makeup on in a different order and the day may hold surprises.

III

"Be thankful for what you've got," he says, spreading mustard on his bun. He means two eyes, of course, 'cause he lost one in Vietnam. He means two of everything that's supposed to come in twos, like heartbeats, and footsteps, and yes, even people.

And I want to tell him it's different than that. But how do you say this to a man who's stared down shrapnel?

IV

When he lost his eye, he lost his depth perception. He'd reach for a beer and grab thin air. He once cracked his forehead on a doorway. "It comes back," he told me. "It takes a while, but the brain relearns to see things in perspective."

V

Each morning I make a list of things to do. At night, whatever is left undone I transfer to another list which I keep in a bedroom drawer. This other list is ten pages long. At the top it says, "Box baby clothes." I have them all in boxes, but they aren't the right boxes for storing clothes you want to save for your grandchildren.

Cathryn Alpert, "That Changes Everything" from Sudden Fiction: American Short-Short Stories, *Robert Shapard and James Thomas, eds., G. M. Smith, 1986. Reprinted by permission of the author.*

VI

You can tell which one isn't real by the way it sits in its socket, staring blankly into the world like the eye of a gaffed mackerel. I like to look at it, this ball of sightless glass. When the light is right, I can see myself in its reflection.

VII

I lie in bed after midnight and count stars through our open window. They arc slowly across a cloudless sky. Last night there were fifty-seven.

VIII

Years ago he wore a patch, but gave it up when he saw the women it attracted. "Earth mothers," he told me. Women who wiped soup from his beard and clipped the dead skin from around his toenails. In bed, they rode him like a stick pony.

He chose me, he said, because I seemed indifferent.

IX

Some mornings, after the kids have gone to school, I sit in bed and watch steam rise from my coffee. It has purpose, steam. It knows what to do.

X

He bites hard into his burger. Hunches close to the table. Looks up at me with half an eye.

And I want to tell him I know I am loved. And that that changes everything.

And it would be such an easy lie.

TOM ANDREWS

Cinema Vérité

THE DEATH OF ALFRED, LORD TENNYSON

The camera pans a gorgeous snow-filled landscape: rolling hills, large black trees, a frozen river. The snow falls and falls. The camera stops to find Tennyson, in an armchair, in the middle of a snowy field.

Tennyson:
It's snowing. The snow is like . . . the snow is like crushed aspirin,
like bits of paper . . . no, it's like gauze bandages, clean teeth, shoelaces,
    headlights . . . no,
I'm getting too old for this, it's like a huge T-shirt that's been chewed on
    by a dog,
it's like semen, confetti, chalk, sea shells, woodsmoke, ash, soap, trillium,
    solitude, daydreaming . . . Oh hell,
you can see for yourself! That's what I hate about film!

He dies.

WILLIAM MAKEPEACE THACKERAY FOLLOWS HIS BLISS

The Fairfield County Fair in Lancaster, Ohio. Shots of Thackeray on the Ferris Wheel, the bumper cars, at the livestock auction, drinking beer at the demolition derby. Cut to Thackeray at the concession stand.

THACKERAY: I can't make up my mind between Elephant Ears and a chili dog.
CONCESSIONAIRE: Oh, go ahead, Mr. Thackeray, get both. You deserve it.

Tom Andrews, "Cinema Vérité: The Death of Alfred Lord Tennyson, Cinema Vérité: William Makepeace Thackeray Follows His Bliss, Cinema Vérité: Jacques Derrida and God's TSIMTSUM" from Field: Contemporary Poetry and Poetics, Number 48, Spring 1993. Reprinted by permission of Oberlin College Press.

THACKERAY: You're right! What the hell, Elephant Ears and chili dogs for everyone! They're on me!

ASSEMBLED PASSERSBY [IN CHORUS]: Oh boy! Thank you, William Makepeace Thackeray, possessor of one of the strangest middle names in history!

The fair comes to a halt as Thackeray is lifted and carried through the streets of Lancaster . . .

JACQUES DERRIDA AND GOD'S TSIMTSUM

An intensely exciting montage of Macchu Picchu, erupting volcano, North Pole glaciers, cells multiplying, Brazilian rainforests, $E = MC^2$, 200 MeV, undersea vistas, the Milky Way, etc., eventually leading us to the Mount of Olives, where God and Derrida loaf, the latter holding a Camcorder.

GOD: I withdrawal from Myself into Myself to provide a space and an occasion for all creation.

DERRIDA [FLUSTERED, SHAKING THE CAMCORDER]: Wait a minute . . . Which button do I press? . . .

Videotape streams and spills out of the Camcorder . . .

DONALD BARTHELME

The Glass Mountain

1. I was trying to climb the glass mountain.
2. The glass mountain stands at the corner of Thirteenth Street and Eighth Avenue.
3. I had attained the lower slope.
4. People were looking up at me.

5. I was new in the neighborhood.

6. Nevertheless I had acquaintances.

7. I had strapped climbing irons to my feet and each hand grasped a sturdy plumber's friend.

8. I was 200 feet up.

9. The wind was bitter.

10. My acquaintances had gathered at the bottom of the mountain to offer encouragement.

11. "Shithead."

12. "Asshole."

13. Everyone in the city knows about the glass mountain.

14. People who live here tell stories about it.

15. It is pointed out to visitors.

16. Touching the side of the mountain, one feels coolness.

17. Peering into the mountain, one sees sparkling blue-white depths.

18. The mountain towers over that part of Eighth Avenue like some splendid, immense office building.

19. The top of the mountain vanishes into the clouds, or on cloudless days, into the sun.

20. I unstuck the righthand plumber's friend leaving the lefthand one in place.

21. Then I stretched out and reattached the righthand one a little higher up, after which I inched my legs into new positions.

22. The gain was minimal, not an arm's length.

23. My acquaintances continued to comment.

24. "Dumb motherfucker."

25. I was new in the neighborhood.

26. In the streets were many people with disturbed eyes.

27. Look for yourself.

28. In the streets were hundreds of young people shooting up in doorways, behind parked cars.

29. Older people walked dogs.

30. The sidewalks were full of dogshit in brilliant colors: ocher, umber, Mars yellow, sienna, viridian, ivory black, rose madder.

31. And someone had been apprehended cutting down trees, a row of elms broken-backed among the VWs and Valiants.

32. Done with a power saw, beyond a doubt.

33. I was new in the neighborhood yet I had accumulated acquaintances.

34. My acquaintances passed a brown bottle from hand to hand.

35. "Better than a kick in the crotch."

36. "Better than a poke in the eye with a sharp stick."

37. "Better than a slap in the belly with a wet fish."

38. "Better than a thump on the back with a stone."

39. "Won't he make a splash when he falls, now?"

40. "I hope to be here to see it. Dip my handkerchief in the blood."

41. "Fart-faced fool."

42. I unstuck the lefthand plumber's friend leaving the righthand one in place.

43. And reached out.

44. To climb the glass mountain, one first requires a good reason.

45. No one has ever climbed the mountain on behalf of science, or in search of celebrity, or because the mountain was a challenge.

46. Those are not good reasons.

47. But good reasons exist.

48. At the top of the mountain there is a castle of pure gold, and in a room in the castle tower sits . . .

49. My acquaintances were shouting at me.

50. "Ten bucks you bust your ass in the next four minutes!"

51. . . . a beautiful enchanted symbol.

52. I unstuck the righthand plumber's friend leaving the lefthand one in place.

53. And reached out.

54. It was cold there at 206 feet and when I looked down I was not encouraged.

55. A heap of corpses both of horses and riders ringed the bottom of the mountain, many dying men groaning there.

56. "A weakening of the libidinous interest in reality has recently come to a close." (Anton Ehrenzweig)

57. A few questions burned in my mind.

58. Does one climb a glass mountain, at considerable personal discomfort, simply to disenchant a symbol?

59. Do today's stronger egos still *need* symbols?

60. I decided that the answer to those questions was "yes."

61. Otherwise what was I doing there, 206 feet above the power-sawed elms, whose white meat I could see from my height?

62. The best way to fail to climb the mountain is to be a knight in full armor—one whose horse's hoofs strike fiery sparks from the sides of the mountain.

63. The following-named knights had failed to climb the mountain and were groaning in the heap: Sir Giles Guilford, Sir Henry Lovell, Sir Albert Denny, Sir Nicholas Vaux, Sir Patrick Grifford, Sir Gisbourne Gower, Sir Thomas Grey, Sir Peter Coleville, Sir John Blunt, Sir Richard Vernon, Sir Walter Willoughby, Sir Stephen Spear, Sir Roger Faulconbridge, Sir Clarence Vaughan, Sir Hubert Ratcliffe, Sir James Tyrrel, Sir Walter Herbert, Sir Robert Brakenbury, Sir Lionel Beaufort, and many others.

64. My acquaintances moved among the fallen knights.

65. My acquaintances moved among the fallen knights, collecting rings, wallets, pocket watches, ladies' favors.

66. "Calm reigns in the country, thanks to the confident wisdom of everyone." (M. Pompidou)

67. The golden castle is guarded by a lean-headed eagle with blazing rubies for eyes.

68. I unstuck the lefthand plumber's friend, wondering if—

69. My acquaintances were prising out the gold teeth of not-yet-dead knights.

70. In the streets were people concealing their calm behind a façade of vague dread.

71. "The conventional symbol (such as the nightingale, often associated with melancholy), even though it is recognized only through agreement, is not a sign (like the traffic light) because, again, it presumably arouses deep feelings and is regarded as possessing properties beyond what the eye alone sees." (*A Dictionary of Literary Terms*)

72. A number of nightingales with traffic lights tied to their legs flew past me.

73. A knight in pale pink armor appeared above me.

74. He sank, his armor making tiny shrieking sounds against the glass.

75. He gave me a sideways glance as he passed me.

76. He uttered the word "*Muerte*" as he passed me.

77. I unstuck the righthand plumber's friend.

78. My acquaintances were debating the question, which of them would get my apartment?

79. I reviewed the conventional means of attaining the castle.

80. The conventional means of attaining the castle are as follows: "The eagle dug its sharp claws into the tender flesh of the youth, but he bore the pain without a sound, and seized the bird's two feet with his hands. The creature in terror lifted him high up into the air and began to circle the castle. The youth held on bravely. He saw the glittering palace, which by the pale rays of the moon looked like a dim lamp, and he saw the windows and balconies of the castle tower. Drawing a small knife from his belt, he cut off both the eagle's feet. The bird rose up in the air with a yelp, and the youth dropped lightly onto a broad balcony. At the same moment a door opened, and he saw a courtyard filled with flowers and trees, and there, the beautiful enchanted princess." (*The Yellow Fairy Book*)

81. I was afraid.

82. I had forgotten the Band-Aids.

83. When the eagle dug its sharp claws into my tender flesh—

84. Should I go back for the Band-Aids?

85. But if I went back for the Band-Aids I would have to endure the contempt of my acquaintances.

86. I resolved to proceed without the Band-Aids.

87. "In some centuries, his [man's] imagination has made life an intense practice of all the lovelier energies." (John Masefield)

88. The eagle dug its sharp claws into my tender flesh.

89. But I bore the pain without a sound, and seized the bird's two feet with my hands.

90. The plumber's friends remained in place, standing at right angles to the side of the mountain.

91. The creature in terror lifted me high in the air and began to circle the castle.

92. I held on bravely.

93. I saw the glittering palace, which by the pale rays of the moon looked like a dim lamp, and I saw the windows and balconies of the castle tower.

94. Drawing a small knife from my belt, I cut off both the eagle's feet.

95. The bird rose up in the air with a yelp, and I dropped lightly onto a broad balcony.

96. At the same moment a door opened, and I saw a courtyard filled with flowers and trees, and there, the beautiful enchanted symbol.

97. I approached the symbol, with its layers of meaning, but when I touched it, it changed into only a beautiful princess.

98. I threw the beautiful princess headfirst down the mountain to my acquaintances.

99. Who could be relied upon to deal with her.

100. Nor are eagles plausible, not at all, not for a moment.

MICHAEL BENEDIKT

The Meat Epitaph

This is what it was: Sometime in the recent but until now unrecorded past, it was decided by cattle-ranchers that since people were increasingly insistent that "you are what you eat," all cattle on the way to market were to be marked with brief descriptive tags noting the favorite food of each beast, and how much they ate of it. This, it was felt, would both delight the diner and comfort the consumer: people would be able to tell exactly what kind of flavor and texture beef they were purchasing beforehand, and always secure exactly the kind of product most likely to delight their taste (it was something a little like our present-day system of catering to preferences for light and dark meat in chicken). The system set up seemed ideally efficient: first, they attached the tag to each beast on its last day on the ranch, just before the two or three days required for shipment to the slaughterhouse—during which travel time the animal customarily doesn't eat anything, anyway.

Once at the slaughterhouse, they carefully removed the tags; and during the slaughtering, duplicated the so-called "parent tag" numerous times, preparing perhaps hundreds of tiny tags for each animal. Directly after, at the packing plant, these were affixed to the proper parts, each section of each animal being separately and appropriately tagged, as if with an epitaph. But something went wrong with this means of augmenting the diner's delight, and of comforting the consumer. At first, quite predictably, the tags came out reading things like "Much grass, a little moss, medium grain" and "Much grass, much grain, generally ate a lot." And this, as one might expect, proved a great pleasure to the consumer. But then tags began coming through reading things like "A little grass, small grain, many diverse scraps from the table"; and "She was our favorite, gave her all we had to give"; and one (featured at dinnertime one evening on national television) saying: "Goodbye, Blackie Lamb, sorry you had to grow up—we'll miss you." Gradually, despite its efficiency, this system somehow ceased to delight the diner, and comfort the consumer. And this is how the practice of the meat epitaph began to become generally neglected during the course of time; and how people came to eat their meat, as they generally do today, partially or wholly blindfolded.

KENNETH BERNARD

Sister Francetta and the Pig Baby

Let me get right into it. When Sister Francetta was a little girl she looked into a baby carriage one day and saw a baby with a pig head. It wore dainty white clothes, had little baby hands and feet, a baby's body. Of course the sounds it made were strange, but the main thing was the pig head. It lay there on its back, kicking its feet, waving its arms, and staring at the world through a pig head. Now Sister Francetta taught us her morality through stories. For example, little boys and girls who put their fingers in forbidden places sometimes found that their fingers rotted away. That was the moral of a story about a boy who picked his nose. However, rotting fingers were a comparatively mild consequence. Sister Francetta's childhood world was filled with sudden and horrible attacks of blindness, deafness, and dumbness. Ugly purple growths developed overnight anywhere inside or outside of people's bodies. Strange mutilations from strange accidents were common. It absolutely did not pay to be bad. Sinful thoughts were the hardest to protect

Kenneth Bernard, "Sister Francetta and the Pig Baby" from Iowa Review *(Spring, 1978). Reprinted by permission.*

against. Prayer and confession were the surest remedies. As I grew older, Sister Francetta's tales gradually subsided into remote pockets of my mind, occasionally to crop up in dream or quaint reminiscence. Except for the pig baby. The pig baby is still with me. It was different from her other stories. For example, it had no moral, it was just there: there had once been a baby with a pig head. Also, whereas Sister Francetta told her other stories often, and with variations, she told the story of the pig baby only once. And she told it differently, as if she herself did not understand it but nevertheless felt a tremendous urgency to reveal it. The other stories she told because they were *useful*. The story of the pig baby she told because she had *faith* in it. It captured my imagination totally. I tried to find out more, but she usually put me off. And I thought a great deal about it. Since Sister Francetta is dead now, I suppose I am the only expert in the world on the pig baby, and what I know can be listed very quickly:

1. The pig baby was apparently Caucasian.
2. Its parents were proud of it and in public seemed totally unaware of its pig head.
3. I do not know how long it lived. It apparently never went to school.
4. It always snorted noticeably but never let out any really piglike sounds like *oink*.
5. It ate and drank everything a regular baby ate and drank.
6. Its parents were not Catholic.
7. Everyone pretended not to notice that the baby had a pig head. For some reason it was not talked about either.
8. At some early point the family either moved away or disappeared.
9. No one said anything about that either.

Sister Francetta died a few years after I had her as a teacher. She was still young. It was whispered among us that she had horrible sores all over her body. I became an excellent student and went on to college. There I developed more sophisticated ideas about the pig baby, the two most prominent of which were 1. that Sister Francetta herself was the pig baby, and 2. that the pig baby was Jesus Christ. There is no logic to either conclusion. Since college I have more or less given up the pig baby. Nevertheless it is a fact that I never look into a carriage without a flush of anxiety. And I cannot get rid of the feeling that Sister Francetta is angry with me.

MARILYN CHIN

The True Story of Mr. and Mrs. Wong

Mrs. Wong bore Mr. Wong four children, all girls. One after the other, they dropped out like purple plums. Years passed. One night after long hours at the restaurant and a bad gambling bout Mr. Wong came home drunk. He kicked the bedstead and shouted, "What do you get from a turtle's rotten womb but rotten turtle eggs?" So, in the next two years he quickly married three girls off to a missionary, a shell-shocked ex-Marine, and an anthropologist. The youngest ran away to Hollywood and became a successful sound specialist.

Mr. Wong said to Mrs. Wong, "Look what happened to my progeny. My ancestors in heaven are ashamed. I am a rich man now. All the Chinese restaurants in San Jose are named Wong. Yet, you couldn't offer me a healthy son. I must change my fate, buy myself a new woman. She must have fresh eggs, white and strong." So, Mr. Wong divorced Mrs. Wong, gave her a meager settlement, and sent her back to Hong Kong, where she lived to a ripe old age as the city's corpse beautician.

Two years ago, Mr. Wong became a born-again Christian. He now loves his new wife, whose name is Mrs. Fuller-Wong. At first she couldn't conceive. Then, the Good Lord performed a miracle and removed three large polyps from her womb. She would bear Mr. Wong three healthy sons who would all become corporate tax accountants.

MICHAEL CHITWOOD

Hard Surface Road

That summer they took off a corner of the cemetery. I watched from behind the stone where the lamb folded its forelegs in marble. The men drank water from Mason jars they asked me to fill. A brass basket spilled its roses on a stone rolled

Marilyn Chin, "The True Story of Mr. and Mrs. Wong," Micro Fiction: An Anthology of Really Short Stories, *Jerome Stern, Ed., W.W. Norton, 1996. Reprinted by permission of the author.*

Michael Chitwood, "Hard Surface Road" from Salt Works: Poems, *Ohio Review Books, 1992. Used by permission of the author.*

like a settee cushion and dented where someone slept: "Gone but not forgotten." The men shaved the graveyard bank. "The crooked shall be made straight," one said, handing back the jar smeared with his finger dirt. I rode the gate of the Perdue plot, raising the latch and going in slow. It took all of June for them to make the turn and go down the Thurman road. The dust followed every truck and powdered the stones like talc. I could go only as far as the graveyard, and they piled the jars like rocks, the mouths open in all directions. They chimed and shifted when I picked one up. When the crew moved out of sight, the dust was settled and would fly no more.

LYDIA DAVIS

This Condition

In this condition: stirred not only by men but by women, fat and thin, naked and clothed; by teenagers and children in latency; by animals such as horses and dogs; by vegetables such as carrots, zucchinis, eggplants, and cucumbers; by fruits such as melons, grapefruits, and kiwis; by plant parts such as petals, sepals, stamens, and pistils; by the bare arm of a wooden chair, a round vase holding flowers, a little hot sunlight, a plate of pudding, a person entering a tunnel in the distance, a puddle of water, a hand alighting on a smooth stone, a hand alighting on a bare shoulder, a naked tree limb; by anything curved, bare, and shining, as the limb or bole of a tree; by any touch, as the touch of a stranger handling money; by anything round and freely hanging, as tassels on a curtain, as chestnut burrs on a twig in spring, as a wet teabag on its string; by anything glowing, as a hot coal; anything soft or slow, as a cat rising from a chair; anything smooth and dry, as a stone, or warm and glistening; anything sliding, anything sliding back and forth; anything sliding in and out with an oiled surface, as certain machine parts; anything of a certain shape, like the state of Florida; anything pounding, anything stroking; anything bolt upright, anything horizontal and gaping, as a certain sea anemone; anything warm, anything wet, anything wet and red, anything turning red, as the sun at evening; anything wet and pink; anything long and straight with a blunt end, as a pestle; anything coming out of anything else, as a snail from its shell, as a snail's horns from its head; anything opening; any stream of water running, any stream running, any stream spurting, any stream spouting; any cry, any soft cry, any grunt; anything going into anything else, as a hand searching in a purse; anything clutching, anything grasping; anything rising, anything tightening or filling, as a sail; anything dripping, anything hardening, anything softening.

STEPHEN DIXON

Flying

She was fooling around with the plane's door handle. I said "Don't touch that, sweetheart, you never know what can happen." Suddenly the door disappeared and she flew out and I yelled "Judith" and saw her looking terrified at me as she was being carried away. I jumped out after her, smiled and held out my arms like wings and yelled "Fly like a bird, my darling, try flying like a bird." She put out her arms, started flying like me and smiled. I flew nearer to her and when she was close enough I pulled her into my body and said "It's not so bad flying like this, is it? It's fun. You hold out one arm now and I'll hold out one of mine and we'll see where we can get to." She said "Daddy, you shouldn't have gone after me, you know that," and I said "I wouldn't let you out here all alone. Don't worry, we'll be okay if we keep flying like this and once we're over land, get ourselves closer and closer to the ground."

The plane by now couldn't be seen. Others could, going different ways, but none seemed to alter their routes for us no matter how much waving I did. It was a clear day, blue sky, no clouds, the sun moving very fast. She said "What's that?" pointing down and I said "Keep your arm up, we have to continue flying." She said "I am, but what's that?" and I said "Looks like a ship but's probably an illusion." "What's an illusion?" and I said "What a time for word lessons; save them for when we get home. For now just enjoy the flying and hope for no sudden air currents' shifts." My other arm held her tightly and I pressed my face into hers. We flew like that, cheek to cheek, our arms out but not moving. I was worried because I hadn't yet come up with any idea to help us make a safe landing. How do we descend, how do we land smoothly or crash-land without breaking our legs? I'll hold her legs up and just break mine if it has to come to that. She said "I love you, Daddy, I both like you and love you and always will. I'm never going to get married and move away from home." I said "Oh well, one day you might, not that I'll ever really want you

Dixon, Stephen. "Flying" from LONG MADE SHORT, pp. 32–35. © 1993 by The Johns Hopkins University Press. Originally published in North American Review. *Reprinted with permission of The Johns Hopkins University Press and the author.*

to. And me too to you, sweetie, with all that love. I'm glad we're together like this. A little secret though. For the quickest moment in the plane I thought I wouldn't jump out after you, that something would hold me back. Now nothing could make me happier than what I did."

We left the ocean and were over cliffs and then the wind shifted and we were being carried north along the coast. We'd been up at almost the same distance from water and land for a long time and I still had no idea how to get down. Suddenly along the coastal road I saw my wife driving our car. Daniel was in the front passenger seat, his hand sticking out the window to feel the breeze. The plane must have reported in about the two people sucked out of the plane, and when Sylvia heard about it she immediately got in the car and started looking for us, thinking I'd be able to take care of things in the air and that the wind would carry us East.

"Look at them, sweetheart, Mommy and Daniel. He should stick his arm in; what he's doing is dangerous." She said "There aren't any other cars around, so it can't hurt him." "But it should be a rule he always observes, just in case he forgets and sticks it out on a crowded highway. And a car could suddenly come the other way. People drive like maniacs on these deserted roads and if one got too close to him his arm could be torn off." "But the car would be going the other way, wouldn't it? so on Mommy's side, not his," and I said "Well, the driver of another car going their way could suddenly lose his head and try and pass on the right and get too close to Daniel's arm.—Daniel," I screamed, "put your arm back right now. This is Daddy talking." His arm went back in. Sylvia stopped the car, got out and looked up and yelled "So there you are. Come back now, my darlings; you'll get yourselves killed." "Look at her worrying about us, Judith—that's nice, right?—Don't worry, Sylvia," I screamed, "we're doing just fine, flying. There's no feeling like it in the world, we're both quite safe, and once I figure out a way to get us down, we will. If we have to crash-land doing it, don't worry about Judith—I'll hold her up and take the whole brunt of it myself. But I think it's going to be some distance from here, inland or on the coast, so you just go home now and maybe we'll see you in time for dinner. But you'll never be able to keep up with us the way this wind's blowing, and I don't know how to make us go slower." "You sure you'll be all right?" she yelled and I said "I can hardly hear you anymore, but yes, I think I got everything under control."

We flew on, I held her in my arm, kissed her head repeatedly, thinking if anything would stop her from worrying, that would. "You sure there's nothing to worry about, Daddy?—I mean about what you said to Mommy," and I said "What are you doing, reading my mind? Yes, everything's okay, I'm positive." We continued flying, each with an arm out, and by the time night came we were still no closer or farther away from the ground.

RUSSELL EDSON

Ape and Coffee

Some coffee had gotten on a man's ape. The man said, animal did you get on my coffee?

No no, whistled the ape, the coffee got on me.

You're sure you didn't spill on my coffee? said the man.

Do I look like a liquid? peeped the ape.

Well you sure don't look human, said the man.

But that doesn't make me a fluid, twittered the ape.

Well I don't know what the hell you are, so just stop it, cried the man.

I was just sitting here reading the newspaper when you splashed coffee all over me, piped the ape.

I don't care if you are a liquid, you just better stop splashing on things, cried the man.

Do I look fluid to you? Take a good look, hooted the ape.

If you don't stop I'll put you in a cup, screamed the man.

I'm not a fluid, screeched the ape.

Stop it, stop it, screamed the man, you are frightening me.

MOLLY GILES

The Poet's Husband

He sits in the front row, large, a large man with large hands and large ears, dry lips, fresh-cut hair, pink skin, clear eyes that don't blink, a nice man, calm, that's the impression he gives, a quiet man who knows how to listen; he is listening now as

Russell Edson, "Ape and Coffee" from The Tunnel: Selected Poems, *Oberlin College Press,* © 1994. *Reprinted by permission of the publisher.*

Molly Giles, "The Poet's Husband" from Micro Fiction: An Anthology of Really Short Stories, *Jerome Stern, Ed., W.W. Norton, 1996. Molly Giles is the author of a novel,* Iron Shoes, *and two award winning collections of short stories,* Rough Translations *and* Creek Walk. *She teaches fiction writing at the University of Arkansas in Fayetteville.*

she sways on the stage in a short black dress and reads one poem about the time she slit her wrists and another poem about a man she still sees and a third poem about a cruel thing he himself said to her six years ago that she never forgot and never understood, and he knows that when she is finished everyone will clap and a few, mostly women, will come up and kiss her, and she will drink far too much wine, far too quickly, and all the way home she will ask, "What did you think, what did you really think?" and he will say, "I think it went very well"—which is, in fact, what he does think—but later that night, when she is asleep, he will lie in their bed and stare at the moon through a spot on the glass that she missed.

✦✦✦✦✦✦✦✦

T I M O T H Y K E L L Y

Babe Ruth Pointing

When Babe Ruth points, the whole table stops eating. What is it, Babe. Mustard? Salt? Mrs. Ruth says Pass Babe the salt.

No. Not salt. Babe Ruth, the Sultan of Swat, stands up in his retired Yankee pinstripes, and points. Mrs. Ruth is on her feet, Please Babe, what. The window? The street? There's nothing in the street.

George Herman Ruth, Bambino Babe, ignores her; he lifts his frenchbread at arm's length and points. His cap sits low on his bulldog head; his cleats dig automatically into the linoleum.

Nova Scotia says Babe. It was always Nova Scotia, always.

Eventually the Babe slumps back to his chair, embarrassed silence around the table. A nice place, pipes Mrs. Ruth, Nova Scotia. Mountains, rivers, the ocean, I'm sure it's just delightful, Babe—

The Babe leans over to me. Nova Scotia, he says, is the cat's ass.

Timothy Kelly, "Babe Ruth Pointing" from Models of the Universe: An Anthology of the Prose Poem, *Stuart Friebert and David Young, eds., Oberlin College Press, 1995. Reprinted by permission of the author.*

JAMAICA KINCAID

Girl

Wash the white clothes on Monday and put them on the stone heap; wash the color clothes on Tuesday and put them on the clothesline to dry; don't walk barehead in the hot sun; cook pumpkin fritters in very hot sweet oil; soak your little cloths right after you take them off; when buying cotton to make yourself a nice blouse; be sure that it doesn't have gum on it; because that way it won't hold up well after a wash; soak salt fish overnight before you cook it; is it true that you sing benna in Sunday school?; always eat your food in such a way that it won't turn someone else's stomach; on Sundays try to walk like a lady and not like the slut you are so bent on becoming; don't sing benna in Sunday school; you mustn't speak to wharf-rat boys; not even to give directions; don't eat fruits on the street—flies will follow you; *but I don't sing benna on Sundays at all and never in Sunday school*; this is how to sew on a button; this is how to make a buttonhole for the button you have just sewed on; this is how to hem a dress when you see the hem coming down and so to prevent yourself from looking like the slut I know you are so bent on becoming; this is how you iron your father's khaki shirt so that it doesn't have a crease; this is how you iron your father's khaki pants so that they don't have a crease; this is how you grow okra—far from the house; because okra tree harbors red ants; when you are growing dasheen; make sure it gets plenty of water or else it makes your throat itch when you are eating it; this is how you sweep a corner; this is how you sweep a whole house; this is how you sweep a yard; this is how you smile to someone you don't like very much; this is how you smile to someone you don't like at all; this is how you smile to someone you like completely; this is how you set a table for tea; this is how you set a table for dinner; this is how you set a table for dinner with an important guest; this is how you set a table for lunch; this is how you set a table for breakfast; this is how to behave in the presence of men who don't know you very well; and this way they won't recognize immediately the slut I have warned you against becoming; be sure to wash every day; even if it is with your own spit; don't squat down to play marbles—you are not a boy; you know; don't pick people's flowers—you might catch something; don't throw stones at blackbirds; because it might not be a blackbird at all; this is how to make a bread pudding; this is how to make doukona; this is how to make pepper pot; this is how to make a good medicine for a cold; this is how to make a good medicine to throw away a child before it even becomes a child; this is how to catch a fish; this is how to throw back a fish you don't like, and that way something bad won't fall on you; this is how to bully a man; this is how a man bullies you; this is how to love a man, and if this doesn't work there are other ways, and if they don't work don't feel too bad about giving up; this is how to spit up in the air if you feel like it, and this is how to move quick so that it doesn't fall on you; this is how to make ends meet; always squeeze bread to make sure it's fresh; *but what if the baker won't let me feel the bread?*; you mean to say that after all you are really going to be the kind of woman who the baker won't let near the bread?

PHILIP LEVINE

Travelling Music

for my brother

The suitcase is weary of being used, of hiding your clothes and all their dusts and waters. Of holding so many appointments, so many bruises, so many cartridges and feathers. It has fallen open on the bed you told it to ignore. There's the pencil you wrote no one with, the paper your lies bled into, the boot without a brother, the sock without a foot, even the rag bearing your three colors for everyone to see.

A man who rides a horse is still a man. Sooner or later he will have to dismount. He will have to eat. Bowing his head before the plate, breaking the piece of bread, reaching for water or wine, he will be shorter than you. Later he may even talk too much and have to sleep. If you put your ear to his heart you will hear the beating of hooves, the rolling of the earth, waves crashing on a far shore.

Once you bite into the piece of bread it can never be whole again. You can put it on the altar and go away for a lifetime. When you come back it may be alive with ants or the color of earth or surrounded by roses. One corner may be tipped with wine the way a white cheek purples in winter. The little dark seeds of its crust will bear nothing except rage or more hunger.

You come into your room and hang your jacket on the door. It smells of work, the leather has swallowed so much grease, so much salt, so many hours when the clock

Philip Levine, "Travelling Music" from Models of the Universe: An Anthology of the Prose Poem, *Stuart Friebert and David Young, eds., Oberlin College Press, 1995. Reprinted by permission of the author.*

wouldn't move. But now it dozes. You roll up your sleeves and run water into the sink. The harsh green soap, the little black brush, the warm water, they take away the dust, the chips of salt, the slivers of metal. The dirt is you. There's no towel. You shake off your hands. You reach for the coat.

GORDON LISH

Fear:

Four Examples

My daughter called from college. She is a good student, excellent grades, is gifted in any number of ways.

"What time is it?" she said. I said, "It is two o'clock." "All right," she said. "It's two now. Expect me at four—four by the clock that said it's two." "It was my watch," I said. "Good," she said.

It is ninety miles, an easy drive.

At a quarter to four, I went down to the street. I had these things in mind—look for her car, hold a parking place, be there waving when she turned into the block.

At a quarter to five, I came back up. I changed my shirt. I wiped off my shoes. I looked into the mirror to see if I looked like someone's father.

She presented herself shortly after six o'clock.

"Traffic?" I said. "No," she said, and that was the end of that.

Just as supper was being concluded, she complained of insufferable pain, and doubled over on the dining-room floor.

"My belly," she said. "What?" I said. She said, "My belly. It's agony. Get me a doctor."

There is a large and famous hospital mere blocks from my apartment. Celebrities go there, statesmen, people who must know what they are doing.

With the help of a doorman and an elevator man, I got my daughter to the hospital. Within minutes, two physicians and a corps of nurses took the matter in hand.

I stood by watching. It was hours before they had her undoubled and were willing to announce their findings.

A bellyache, a rogue cramp, a certain nonspecific seizure of the abdomen—vagrant, indecipherable, a mystery not worth further inquiry.

We left the hospital unassisted, using a succession of tunnels in order to shorten the distance home. The exposed distance, that is—since it would be four in the morning on the city streets, and though the blocks would be few, each one of them could be catastrophic. So we made our way along the system of underground passageways that link the units of the hospital until we were forced to surface and exit. We came out onto a street with not a person on it—until we saw him, the young man who was going from car to car. He carried something under his arm. It looked to me to be a furled umbrella—black fabric, silver fittings. It could not have been what it looked to be—but instead a tool of entry disguised as an umbrella!

He turned to us as we stepped along, and then he turned back to his work—going from car to car, trying the doors, and sometimes using the thing to dig at the windows.

"Don't look," I said. My daughter said, "What?" I said, "There's someone across the street. He's trying to jimmy open cars. Just keep on walking as if you don't see him."

My daughter said, "Where? I don't see him."

I put my daughter to bed and the hospital charges on my desk and then I let my head down onto the pillow and listened.

There was nothing to hear.

Before I surrendered myself to sleep, there was only this in my mind—the boy in the treatment room across the corridor from my daughter's, how I had wanted to cry out each time he had cried out as a stitch was sutured into his hand.

"Take it out! Take it out!"

This is what the boy was shrieking as the doctor worked to close the wound.

I thought about the feeling in me when I had heard that awful wailing. The boy wanted the needle out. I suppose it hurt worse than the thing that had inspired them to sew him up.

But then I considered the statement for emergency services—translating the amount first into theater tickets, then into hand-ironed shirts.

Cows in Trouble

These were not the average "contented" cows. They were cows born for trouble. They were not cows who could stand by and let people call them "bossy." They were cows who could not hang around all day lowing. They were cows who could be just as happy chewing someone else's cud as their own. These were renegade cows.

My first experience with the renegade cows began one day as I was admiring a particularly attractive cow at Johnson's Weed Farm. As I stood there watching her sultry body moving lithely through the rushes, I noticed several other cows staring at me through the weeds, giving me that look that only a cow can give.

Later that night, I was at home thinking over the day's events. The Rubber Duck Throwing Contest, the parade that followed: bands and floats and baton-tossing girls all marching down the middle of the Missouri River. I *should* have been analyzing the glare of those cows I'd seen earlier that day.

The doorbell rang. I opened the door, glad to have a visitor, but found myself face to face with three renegade cows. I could not see their eyes behind the dark glasses.

They ambled in and I did not try to stop them.

That night they just stood around my bed and watched me sleep, much the same way my potatoes do, and I guess you might say I learned my lesson: *Don't fool with renegade cows.*

The Halo

When Jesus was born, I thought he had a caul; but with his first cry, it began to glow. That was the halo—always in the way, poking my breast when he nursed, nicking Joseph when he'd bend to kiss the boy good night. But if we reached to take

Steve Martin, "Cows in Trouble" from Cruel Shoes. Reprinted by permission of International Creative Management, Inc. Copyright © 1977 by Steve Martin.

Michael McFee, "The Halo" from Micro Fiction: An Anthology of Really Short Stories, Jerome Stern, Ed., W.W. Norton, 1996. Reprinted by permission of Michael McFee.

it off, somehow it wasn't there: it was a mirage, a shadow, a little golden cloud we couldn't quite touch.

Jesus could remove it, though. He'd fly it like a kite, the sun on a string. He'd skip it across the lake and it would always return. He'd even work it into his juggling routine, pieces of fruit landing on a dazzling plate, ta-dah!

Joseph was embarrassed. Maybe the halo reminded him of what he wasn't. So he built it a fine cedar box, and made Jesus take it off and lock it inside and bury it out back under the fig tree and promise not to dig it up. Joseph told him he could have it back one day, when he was a man.

And so Jesus grew up a normal boy, and everybody forgot about the halo.

But last night I dreamed that a couple of thieves dug up the box. And when they opened it, the fig tree burst into golden fruit, hundreds of sweet halos and not a snake in sight.

E. ETHELBERT MILLER

Changing the Channel

My father and I have pillows behind our backs. The television is on but we talk without looking at each other. It is better this way, easier for my father to find words, which interrupt his breath like commercials. It is one of those strange moments when our small apartment in the Bronx is empty. My sister is on a date with a boy she can't bring home. My brother is at church lighting candles and saying prayers which will not lengthen his life. My mother is selecting lamb chops over pork in a nearby store, and the price has nothing to do with our health. Now is the time when my father has a good job in the post office and this miracle of rest is what we share while watching old movies that offer no resemblance to who we are.

E. Ethelbert Miller, "Changing the Channel" from Micro Fiction: An Anthology of Really Short Stories, *Jerome Stern, Ed., W.W. Norton, 1996. Reprinted by permission of E. Ethelbert Miller.*

RICK MOODY

Primary Sources[1]

Abbé, William Parker.[2] *A Diary of Sketches.* Concord, N.H.: St. Paul's School, 1976.
Bangs, Lester. *Psychotic Reactions and Carburetor Dung.*[3] Edited by Greil Marcus.
  New York: Knopf, 1987.
Barnes, Djuna. *Interviews.* Washington, D.C.: Sun & Moon, 1985.

---

[1]Born 10.18.61 in NYC. Childhood pretty uneventful. We moved to the suburbs. I always read a lot. I did some kid stuff, but mostly I read. So this sketchy and selective bibliography—this list of some of the books I have around the house now—is really an autobiography.

[2]Art instructor at St. Paul's School when I was there ('75–'79). Abbé was an older, forgetful guy when I met him. He was in his late sixties probably. He lived alone in an apartment above the infirmary at SPS, an apartment that had burned once. The fire took a lot of Abbé's paintings, and I believe this accounted for the halo of sadness around him. He could also be infectiously happy, though. His house was full of jukeboxes, dolls, and electrical toys. Games of every kind.

One time I showed him my *Sgt. Pepper's* picture disc—remember those collector's gimmicks that revolutionized the LP for a few minutes in the seventies? The famous jacket art was printed on the vinyl. Abbé laughed for a good long time over that. He sat in the old armchair in my room, the one with the stuffing coming out of it and laughed. He loved that kind of thing. He had a lot of Elvis on his jukeboxes.

[3]Lester's last published piece, in the Voice, appeared in my senior year of college. I moved back to NYC a little later, after six months in California, where it was too relaxed. By the time I got to New York, the East Village galleries were already disappearing. Lester was dead. The Gap had moved in on the N.W. corner of St. Mark's and Second Avenue.

Barrett, Syd.[4] "Golden Hair." On *The Madcap Laughs.* EMI Cassette C4-46607, 1990 (reissue).

Barthes, Roland. *A Lover's Discourse.*[5] Translated by Richard Howard. New York: Hill & Wang, 1978.

Bernhard, Thomas. *The Lime Works.* Chicago: Univ. of Chicago Press, 1986 (reprint of New York: Knopf, 1973).

Book of Common Prayer and Administration of the Sacraments and Other Rites and Ceremonies of the Church, According to the Use of the Protestant Episcopal Church[6] *in the United States of America, The.* New York: Harper & Brothers, 1944.

Borges, Jorge Luis. *Labyrinths.*[7] Edited by Donald A. Yates and James E. Irby. New York: New Directions, 1964.

Breton, André. *Manifestoes of Surrealism.*[8] Ann Arbor, Mich.: Univ. of Michigan Press (Ann Arbor Paperbacks), 1969.

Carroll, Lewis. *The Annotated Alice.* Edited with an introduction and notes[9] by Martin Gardner. New York: Clarkson N. Potter (Bramhall House), 1960.

Carter, Angela.[10] *The Bloody Chamber and Other Adult Tales.* New York: Harper &

---

[4]In 1978, back at SPS, I took six hits of "blotter" acid and had a pretty wrenching bad trip. Eternal damnation, shame, humiliation, and endless line of men in clown costumes chanting my name and laughing. That kind of thing. I turned myself in, confessed, to a master I liked, the Rev. Alden B. Flanders. Somewhere in the middle of the five or six hours it took to talk me down, I asked him if he thought I would remember this moment for the rest of my life.

[5]"The necessity for this book is to be found in the following consideration: that the lover's discourse is today *of an extreme solitude.* . . . Once a discourse is thus . . . exiled from all gregarity, it has no recourse but to become the site, however exiguous, of an *affirmation.*"

[6]I didn't get baptized until I was fifteen. The minister, who had buried my grandparents and my uncle and performed my mother's remarriage, couldn't remember my name. Right then, the church seemed like the only thing that would get me through adolescence. I was going to get confirmed later, too, but instead I started drinking.

[7]Cf., "Eco, Umberto," and also n. 9, below.

[8]The band I played in in college was called Forty-five Houses. We got our name from the first Surrealist manifesto: "Q. 'What is your name?' A. 'Forty-five houses.' (Ganser syndrome, or beside-the-point replies)." Our drummer, Kristen, preferred women to men, but I sort of fell in love with her anyway. After we graduated she gave me a ride on her motorcycle. It was the first time I ever rode one. I held tight around her waist.

[9]See n. 20, below.

Carter, Angela.[10] *The Bloody Chamber and Other Adult Tales*. New York: Harper & Row, 1979.

Cheever, John. *The Journals of John Cheever*.[11] New York: Knopf, 1991.

―――. *The Wapshot Chronicle*. New York: Harper & Brothers, 1957.

Coover, Robert. *In Bed One Night & Other Brief Encounters*. Providence, R.I.: Burning Deck, 1983.

Daniels, Les. *Marvel: Five Fabulous Decades of the World's Greatest Comics*.[12] With an introduction by Stan Lee. New York: Abrams, 1992.

Danto, Arthur C. *Encounters and Reflections: Art in the Historical Present*. New York: FSG, 1990.

"Darmok."[13] *Star Trek: The Next Generation*. Paramount Home Video, 1991, 48 minutes.

Davis, Lydia. *Break It Down*. New York: FSG, 1986.

De Montaigne, Michel. *The Complete Essays of Montaigne*. Translated by Donald M. Frame. Stanford, Calif.: Stanford Univ. Press, 1958.

Derrida, Jacques. *Of Grammatology*.[14] Translated by Gayatri Chakravorty Spivak. Baltimore, Md.: Johns Hopkins, 1976 (originally published as *De la Grammatologie* [Paris: Editions de Minuit, 1967]).

---

[10]The first day of Angela's workshop in college a guy asked her what her work was like. She said, "My work cuts like a steel blade at the base of a man's penis." Second semester, there was a science fiction writer in our class who sometimes slept through the proceedings—and there were only eight or nine of us there. One day I brought a copy of *Light in August* to Angela's office hours and she said, "I wish I was reading *that* [Faulkner], instead of *this* [pointing to a stack of student work]."

[11]As a gift for graduating boarding school, my dad gave me a short trip to Europe. Two weeks. I was a little bit afraid of travel, though, as I still am, and in London I spent much of the time in Hyde Park, in a chair I rented for 15p a day. The sticker that is my proof of purchase still adorns my copy of *The Stories of John Cheever*, also given to me by my dad. I haven't been back to the U.K. since.

[12]We moved a lot when I was a kid. In eighth grade I had a calendar on which I marked off the days until I'd be leaving Connecticut forever. My attachments weren't too deep. I spent a lot of time with Iron Man, the Incredible Hulk, and the Avengers. I also liked self-help books and Elton John records.

[13]Picard and the crew of the *Enterprise* attempt to make contact with a race of aliens, the Children of Tama, who speak entirely in an allegorical language. Picard doesn't figure out the language until the captain of the Tamarians is already dead. A big episode for those who realize how hard communicating really is.

[14]One guy I knew in college actually threw this book out a window. Here are some excerpts from my own marginalia: "Function of art is supplementalism though devalorization of weighted side of oppositions"; "Attendance as performance: more absence creates more real presence." I'm not sure what I meant, but I loved Derrida's overheated analogies: "Writing in the common sense is the dead letter, it is the carrier of death. It exhausts life. On the other hand, on the other face of the same proposition, writing in the metaphoric sense, natural, divine, and living writing, is venerated" (p. 17).

Elkin, Stanley. *The Franchiser*. Boston: Godine (Nonparel Books), 1980 (reprint of New York: FSG, 1976).

"Erospri." In *The Whole Earth 'Lectronic Link*,[15] modem: (415) 332-6106, Sausalito, Calif., 1986–.

Feelies, The. *The Good Earth*.[16] Coyote TTC 8673, 1986.

Fitzgerald, F. Scott. *The Crack-Up*. New York: New Directions, 1959.

Foucault, Michel. *Discipline and Punish: The Birth of the Prison*. New York: Vintage, 1979 (reprint of New York: Random House, 1977; originally published as *Surveiller et Punir* [Paris: Gallimard, 1975]).

Gaddis, William. *The Recognitions*.[17] New York: Penguin, 1985 (reprint of New York: Harcourt, Brace, 1955).

Genet, Jean. *The Thief's Journal*. New York: Bantam, 1965 (reprint of New York: Grove, 1964; originally published as *Journal du Voleur* [Paris: Gallimard, 1949]).

Gyatso, Tenzin, the 14th Dalai Lama. *Freedom in Exile*. New York: HarperCollins, 1990.

Hawkes, John.[18] *Second Skin*. New York: New Directions, 1964.

----

[15]The *Well*—as it is abbreviated—has a really good Star Trek conference too. This private conference is about *sex*. I started messing with computers in junior high when my grades got me out of study hall. Which was good because people used to threaten me if I didn't let them copy my homework. It was on the *Well* that I learned both the address for a mail-order catalogue called *Leather Toys* and how to affix clothespins.

[16]My drinking got really bad in graduate school. In the mid-eighties. I was in love with a woman who was living in Paris and I took the opportunity, at the same time, to get mixed up with a friend in New York. Kate, the second of these women, first played this record for me. The snap of the snare that begins *The Good Earth* has a real tenderness to it, for me. I was playing this record when I was really ashamed of myself and also afterwards when I was hoping for forgiveness.

[17]At the end of my drinking, when I was living in Hoboken, I started writing my first novel, *Garden State*. Later, through a chain of kindnesses, someone managed to slip a copy of it to William Gaddis, the writer I most admired, then and now. Much later, long after all of this, I got to know Gaddis's son Matthew a little bit, and he said that the book had probably gotten covered up with papers, because that's the way his dad's desk is. But maybe there was one afternoon when it was on top of a stack.

[18]The last day of class with Jack Hawkes we were standing out on one of those Victorian porches in Providence—a bunch of us, because there was always a crowd of people trying to get into Jack's classes (and they were usually really talented)—firing corks from champagne bottles out into the street. We got a couple that made it halfway across. Hawkes was mumbling something about how sad it was that so many writers were so afflicted by drink. In less than a week I was going to graduate.

Hawthorne, Nathaniel. *Hawthorne's Short Stories.*[19] Edited with an introduction by Newton Arvin. New York: Knopf, 1946.

Hogg, James. *The Private Memoirs and Confessions of a Justified Sinner.* New York: Penguin, 1976.

Johnson, Denis. *Angels.* New York: Vintage, 1989 (reprint of New York: Knopf, 1983).

Joyce, James. *Ulysses.* New York: Vintage, 1961.

Jung, C. G. "Individual Dream Symbolism in Relation to Alchemy." In *Collected Works*, Vol. 12, Part II. Translated by R. F. C. Hull. Princeton, N.J.: Princeton Univ. Press (Bollingen Series), 1968.

Kapuscinski, Ryszard. *The Emperor.* New York: Vintage, 1989 (reprint of New York: HBJ), 1983.

Lewis, James. "Index."[20] *Chicago Review* 35 (1 [autumn 1985]): 33–35.

Marcus, Greil. *Lipstick Traces: A Secret History of the Twentieth Century.*[21] Cambridge, Mass.: Harvard Univ. Press, 1989.

Marx, Groucho. *The Groucho Letters: Letters from and to Groucho Marx.*[22] New York: Fireside, 1987.

Mitchell, Stephen. *The Gospel According to Jesus.* New York: HarperCollins, 1991.

Pagels, Elaine. *The Gnostic Gospels.*[23] New York: Vintage, 1989 (reprint of New York: Random House, 1979).

---

[19]"Another clergyman in New England, Mr. Joseph Moody, of York, Maine, who died about eighty years since, made himself remarkable by the same eccentricity that is here related of the Reverend Mr. Hooper. In his case, however, the symbol had a different import. In early life he had accidentally killed a beloved friend; and from that day till the hour of his own death, he hid his face from men."

[20]See n. 7, above.

[21]During the period when I was finishing my first novel I had an office job in publishing, from which I was later fired. I judged everything against the books I loved when I was a teenager, *The Crying of Lot 49*, Beckett's *Murphy, One Hundred Years of Solitude*, etc. Besides Lester Bangs (see above), Marcus's *Lipstick Traces* was one of the only recently published books I liked. Another was *Responses: On Paul de Man's Wartime Journalism* (Univ. of Nebraska Press).

[22]In 1987, I institutionalized myself. At that moment, Thurber and Groucho Marx and anthologies of low comedy seemed like the best literature had to offer. I thought I was going to abandon writing—something had to give—but I didn't. I felt better later.

[23]"The accusation that the gnostics invented what they wrote contains some truth: certain gnostics openly acknowledged that they derived their *gnosis* from their own experience. . . . The gnostic Christians . . . assumed that they had gone far beyond the apostles' original teaching."

Paley, Grace. *Enormous Changes at the Last Minute.* New York: FSG, 1974.

Pärt, Arvo. *Tabula Rasa.*[24] ECM new series 817 (1984).

Peacock, Thomas Love. *Headlong Hall and Gryll Grange.* Oxford: Oxford Univ. Press (The World's Classics), 1987.

Plato. *Great Dialogues of Plato.* Edited and translated by W. H. D. Rouse. New York: Mentor, 1956.

"Polysexuality." *Semiotexte.*[25] 4 (1 [1981]).

Sacks, Oliver. *Awakenings.* 3rd ed. New York: Summit, 1987.

Schulz, Bruno. *Sanatorium Under the Sign of the Hourglass.*[26] Translated by Celina Wieniewska. New York: Penguin, 1979.

Sebadoh. *Sebadoh III.*[27] Homestead HMS 168–4, 1991.

Thomas à Kempis. *The Imitation of Christ.* New York: Penguin, 1952.

W., Bill. "Step Seven." In *Twelve Steps and Twelve Traditions.*[28] New York: Alcoholics Anonymous World Services, 1986.

---

[24]And Cage's book, *Silence*; and *Music for Airports*; and LaMonte Young's "The Second Dream of the High Tension Line Step Down Transformer from the Four Dreams of China"; and Ezra Pound after St. Elizabeth's, and *Be Here Now* and Mark Rothko.

[25]The back cover of this issue consists of a newspaper photo of a man in a wedding gown slumped over on a toilet, his skin ribbed with gigantic blisters. He's really destroyed, this guy. The photo, supposedly, was from *The Daily News*. And since my grandfather worked for the *News*, the luridness of this horror struck close. This, I learned, was an act of *pleasure*.

[26]Angela Carter assigned this book to us in sophomore year. I was taking a lot of quaaludes that spring. One night I stayed up all night on Methadone and wrote a story, cribbed from Bruno Schulz, about a guy who lives in a house that *is actually his grandmother*. Later, when I told Angela that I'd written the story high, she said, "Quaaludes, the aardvark of the drug world."

[27]"All these empty urges must be satisfied."

[28]"The chief activator of our defects has been self-centered fear—primarily fear that we would lose something we already possessed or would fail to get something we demanded."

Williams, William Carlos. *The Collected Poems of William Carlos Williams.*[29] Volume II: 1939–1962. Copyright © 1962 by William Carlos Williams. Reprinted by permission of New Directions Publishing.

Zappa, Frank, Captain Beefheart and the Mothers of Invention. *Bongo Fury.* Barking Pumpkin D4-74220, 1975,[30] 1989.

---

[29]"Sick as I am / confused in the head / I mean I have / endured this April so far / visiting friends" (p. 428). *Garden State* was published in spring of 1992. I was already pretty far into my second book, *The Ice Storm*. I left Hoboken for good.

[30]There was a time when I was an adolescent when I didn't feel like I had a dad, even though he didn't live that far away and I saw him on Sundays. This is an admission that won't please him or the rest of my family. The way I see it, though, there has never been a problem between me and my *actual* dad. But dads make the same tentative decisions we sons make. Once my father said to me, "I wonder if you kids would have turned out differently if I had been around to kick some ass." This was during one of those long car rides full of silences. The question didn't even apply to me. He might have been there, he might not have. Didn't matter. I was looking elsewhere for the secrets of ethics and home. I was looking.

MICHAEL ONDAATJE

7 or 8 Things I Know About Her— A Stolen Biography

THE FATHER'S GUNS

After her father died they found nine guns in the house. Two in his clothing drawers, one under the bed, one in the glove compartment of the car, etc. Her brother took their mother out onto the prairie with a revolver and taught her to shoot.

THE BIRD

For a while in Topeka parrots were very popular. Her father was given one in lieu of a payment and kept it with him at all times because it was the fashion. It swung above him in the law office and drove back with him in the car at night. At parties friends would bring their parrots and make them perform what they had been taught: the first line from *Twelfth Night*, a bit of Italian opera, cowboy songs, or a surprisingly good rendition of Russ Colombo singing 'Prisoner of Love.' Her father's parrot could only imitate the office typewriter, along with the *ching* at the end of each line. Later it broke its neck crashing into a bookcase.

THE BREAD

Four miles out of Topeka on the highway—the largest electrical billboard in the State of Kansas. The envy of all Missouri. It advertised bread and the electrical image of a knife cut slice after slice. These curled off endlessly. 'Meet you at the bread,' 'See you at the loaf,' were common phrases. Aroused couples would park there under the stars on the open night prairie. Virtue was lost, 'kissed all over by every boy in Wichita.' Poets, the inevitable visiting writers, were taken to see it, and it hummed over the seductions in cars, over the nightmares of girls in bed. Slice after slice fell towards the earth. A feeding of the multitude in this parched land on the way to Dorrance, Kansas.

FIRST CRITICISM

She is two weeks old, her mother takes her for a drive. At the gas station the mechanic is cleaning the windshield and watches them through the glass. Wiping his hands he puts his head in the side window and says, 'Excuse me for saying this but I know what I'm talking about—that child has a heart condition.'

LISTENING IN

Overhear her in the bathroom, talking to a bug: 'I don't want you on me, honey.' 8 a.m.

SELF-CRITICISM

'For a while there was something about me that had a dubious quality. Dogs would not take meat out of my hand. The town bully kept handcuffing me to trees.'

FANTASIES

Always one fantasy. To be travelling down the street and a man in a clean white suit (the detail of 'clean' impresses me) leaps into her path holding flowers and sings to her while an invisible orchestra accompanies his solo. All her life she has waited for this and it never happens.

REPRISE

In 1956 the electric billboard in Kansas caught fire and smoke plumed into a wild sunset. Bread on fire, broken glass. Birds flew towards it above the cars that circled round to watch. And last night, past midnight, her excited phone call. Her home town is having a marathon to benefit the symphony. She pays $4 to participate. A tuxedoed gentleman begins the race with a clash of cymbals and she takes off. Along the route at frequent intervals are quartets who play for her. When they stop for water a violinist performs a solo. So here she comes. And there I go, stepping forward in my white suit, with a song in my heart.

MICHAEL PALMER

"A Word Is Coming Up on the Screen . . ."

A word is coming up on the screen, give me a moment. In the meantime let me tell you a little something about myself. I was born in Passaic in a small box flying over Dresden one night, lovely figurines. Things mushroomed after that. My cat has twelve toes, like poets in Boston. Upon the microwave she sits, hairless. The children they say, you are no father but a frame, waiting for a painting. Like, who dreamed you up? Like, gag me with a spoon. Snow falls—winter. Things are aglow. One hobby is Southeast Asia, nature another. As a child I slept beneath the bed, fists balled. A face appeared at the window, then another, the same face. We skated and dropped, covering our heads as instructed. Then the music began again, its certainty intact. The true dancers floated past. They are alive to this day, as disappearing ink. After the storm we measured the shore, I grew to four feet then three. I drove a nail through the page and awoke smiling. That was my first smile. In a haze we awaited the next. You said, "Interior colors." You said, "Antinucleons." You said, "Do not steal my words for your work." Snow falls—winter. She hands out photographs of the Union dead. Things are aglow. I traded a name for what followed it. This was useless. The palace of our house has its columns, its palms. A skull in a handcart. I removed a tongue and an arm, but this was useless. On Tuesday Freud told me, "I believe in beards and women with long hair. Do not fall in love." Is there discourse in the tropics? Does the central motif stand out clearly enough? In this name no letters repeat, so it cannot be fixed. Because it's evening I remember memory now. Your English I do not speak. A word is coming up on the screen.

Pumpkins

There is a terrible accident. A truck full of Halloween pumpkins is speeding around a curve and fails to see another car unwisely making a U-turn. In the car is a young woman, married, the mother of three, who, when the vehicles collide, is killed.

Actually, she is beheaded, her body thrown from the car and decapitated with such force that the head sails through the air and lands in a pile of pumpkins spilled out onto the road.

Her husband is spared this detail until the next day, when it appears in a front page story in the local paper.

This newspaper is bought by a woman about to leave home on a trip. The tragedy so unhinges her that she rushes off the train and calls her husband at work. When she mentions the pumpkin-truck accident, he says, Pumpkin-truck accident? precisely like their five-year-old son saying, Bubble gum on the couch?

The woman begins to tremble, realizing now what she should have realized (and because she is in therapy, she thinks, she *did* realize, no wonder she was upset!). The accident occurred more or less exactly in front of the house of a woman with whom her husband had a love affair but has promised he has stopped seeing.

She senses that her husband knows about this accident—and not from reading the newspaper. That is why he sounds guilty. Perhaps he was with his lover when it happened, perhaps this woman called him for comfort, just as she is calling him now. As she confronts him with this, her husband keeps interrupting to answer questions at his office.

The next morning the woman sees her therapist on an emergency basis. She tells him the whole story; from buying the paper and reading about the pumpkin-truck to calling her husband to her husband moving out again last night.

The therapist says he is sorry; he cannot talk about this. He tells her that, coincidentally, one of his patients is the husband of the woman killed by the pumpkin-truck. It is, after all, a small town. The therapist says he has been dealing with this tragedy for two days—on a *real* crisis basis, a *real* emergency basis—and frankly he cannot stand to hear it treated as another subplot in this woman's continuing romantic imbroglio.

The woman bursts into tears. The therapist apologizes for his unprofessional behavior; he says the whole thing has unnerved him in ways even he doesn't understand.

That night the therapist tells his wife about this. For ethical reasons he leaves out the names. Still, he repeats what the woman told him and what he said and what happened.

Except that this time, instead of saying "pumpkins," he says "Christmas trees." "Christmas trees?" says his wife. "Did I say Christmas trees?" he says. "How funny. I meant pumpkins." Naturally he realizes that this slip of the tongue is a clue to why this incident so disturbs him.

Later, in bed, he considers his mistake. And before long it comes to him. Because for once the truth is not submerged, but bobs on the surface, like a buoy, tied to a time he often revisits in looking back on his life.

At five he suffered a case of mumps which turned into something more serious. He remembers running to his parents' room, his cheeks swinging like sacks of flesh from his face. He remembers falling. After that he was sick for months—from autumn through early winter. The symbolism is so obvious: pumpkin time when he became ill, Christmas when he recovered.

Now his wife gets into bed, but he doesn't notice. For he is feeling, as never before, how much of his life has passed: all the years that separate him from that swollen-faced boy. He thinks how sweet that period was, the rhythm of those days, sleep, radio, chilled canned pears, the kingdom of the blanket, the kingdom of ice outside it.

For an instant he nearly recaptures that haze of safety, confusion and boredom, when he fell asleep looking at pumpkins and awoke seeing a Christmas tree, when nothing scared him, not even time, it was all being taken care of. Then it recedes like the plots of dreams he wakes up already forgetting.

It is like the experience of speeding along a highway, and some broken sign or ruined cafe will suddenly recall his past, but before he can tell his wife, they have already driven by. He knows that if he turns and goes back, what caught his eye will have vanished—though perhaps he may catch a glimpse of it, fleeing from him down the road.

BRUCE HOLLAND ROGERS

Murder, Mystery

Okay, this is a murder mystery. The victim is lying in a field not far from U.S. 36. Face down.

It's early morning. Along the eastern horizon there's a band of clouds, though the sky overhead is blue. The sun is up, but still hidden. Here's what I want you to see: to the west, another cloud bank lies against the Flatirons, with just the jagged tops of the first and third Flatirons jutting through. I've already said the sky is blue, but I don't think you've really seen it. Brilliant blue? Piercing blue? At this distance, you can see the summits of Longs Peak and Mount Meeker, capped with snow and orange in the early light.

See it? See the bright orange mountains against the blue sky? See the clouds hugging the Flatirons? Can you sense what the light is like for someone standing in this field? (There is no one standing there, of course. There's just the body, and the body is lying down.) A western meadowlark sings. They only sing at certain levels of light, early in the day and early in the evening. The song is like this: three bright, slow notes, then a flurry of song too fast and complex to describe. You can hold the sound in your mind for only a moment, then the memory of it melts away.

I know what you're thinking.

We'll get to the body, I promise. But first I want to be certain you can see the light, the two banks of clouds, the orange mountains, the blue sky behind them. It's spring. The foothills are green. Soon the sun will rise a little more and burn those clouds from the Flatirons. You'll see just how green the hills are. The western meadowlark will stop singing.

There's heavy traffic on U.S. 36, but no one has seen the body. Cars swish by. Anyone could spot this body. It's right here in the field.

It looks as if the dead man was shot in the back and fell forward. There's not much blood around the hole in the back of his shirt. The exit wound is probably another story.

Was he killed here? Did he expect it? Were there two men holding his arms while another pointed the gun? What caliber of gun was it? Was he a drug dealer? Witness to another crime? Jealous husband? The lover? Maybe the wife killed him. Maybe he didn't expect it. Maybe he was killed somewhere else and brought here, dumped here.

The soil in the field is soft. There are footprints. Someone will be able to tell the story, or part of it, anyway, by looking at those footprints. They'll figure out the caliber of the gun. They'll identify the man and unravel his history, interview suspects.

But we won't.

This is not that kind of mystery.

His face is against the ground, but turned a little.

At this time of year, at this time of morning, there's something about the smell of earth and growing grass.

The man's lips are parted. His tongue juts a little between his teeth. It's as if he's tasting the dew on the grass.

That's not a symbol or anything. That's just the way it is.

I wish I had a word for the blue of the sky.

CHARLES SIMIC

From Dime–Store Alchemy

POETICS OF MINIATURE

Perhaps the ideal way to observe the boxes is to place them on the floor and lie down beside them.

It is not surprising that child faces stare out of the boxes and that they have the dreamy look of children at play. Theirs is the happy solitude of a time without clocks when children are masters of their world. Cornell's boxes are reliquaries of days when imagination reigned. They are inviting us, of course, to start our childhood reveries all over again.

VAUDEVILLE DE LUXE

My baby's got a black cat bone.

—HOP WILSON

A fetish, so the dictionaries tell us, is a spirit attached to a material object. "Hide your God, He's your strength," advised the poet Paul Valéry, and the same goes for the fetish. It's usually kept out of sight.

Cornell's boxes are like witch doctors' concoctions. They contain objects that have sacred and magical properties. The box is a little voodoo temple with an altar. Love medicine or medicine of immortality is being prepared.

In the meantime, you've got to whisper to the black cat bone if you want it to make it do its thing.

UNTITLED (WHITE BALLS IN COTS), CA. MID-1950

This box has the appearance of a game board, a puzzle, or perhaps some abacuslike calculating machine. The balls have stopped randomly on their own, or they were moved by an invisible hand. Whichever is the case, this is their position now. In other boxes of the same series, balls may be replaced by blocks and their position varies.

It's been a long time since the balls were in motion, one thinks. Besides, some of them appear to be missing. Here's an image of infinity, not as extension, but as division into equal and anonymous parts.

How's this terrifying game to be played?

Charles Simic, excerpt from "Dime–Store Alchemy" from Dime–store Alchemy: The Art of Joseph Cornell, *pp. 37–44. Ecco Press, 1992. Reprinted by permission of the author.*

CHESSBOARD OF THE SOUL

Around the boxes I can still hear Cornell mumble to himself. In the basement of the quiet house on Utopia Parkway he's passing the hours by changing the positions of a few items, setting them in new positions relative to one another in a box. At times the move is no more than a tenth of an inch. At other times, he picks the object, as one would a chess figure, and remains long motionless, lost in complicated deliberation.

Many of the boxes make me think of those chess problems in which no more than six to seven figures are left on the board. The caption says: "White mates in two moves," but the solution escapes the closest scrutiny. As anyone who attempts to solve these problems knows, the first move is the key, and it's bound to be an unlikely appearing move.

I have often cut a chess problem from a newspaper and taped it to the wall by my bed so that I may think about it first thing in the morning and before turning off the lights at night. I have especially been attracted to problems with minimum numbers of figures, the ones that resemble the ending of some long, complicated, and evenly fought game. It's the subtlety of two minds scheming that one aims to recover.

At times, it may take months to reach the solution, and in a few instances I was never able to solve the problem. The board and its figures remained as mysterious as ever. Unless there was an error in instructions or position, or a misprint, there was no way in hell the white could mate in two moves. And yet . . .

At some point my need for a solution was replaced by the poetry of my continuous failure. The white queen remained where it was on the black square, and so did the other figures in the original places, eternally, whenever I closed my eyes.

THE TRUTH OF POETRY

A toy is a trap for dreamers. The true toy is a poetic object.

There's an early sculpture of Giacometti's called Palace at 4 A.M. (1932). It consists of no more than a few sticks assembled into a spare scaffolding, which the mysterious title makes haunting and unforgettable. Giacometti said that it was a dream house for him and the woman with whom he was in love.

These are dreams that a child would know. Dreams in which objects are renamed and invested with imaginary lives. A pebble becomes a human being. Two sticks leaning against each other make a house. In that world one plays the game of being someone else.

This is what Cornell is after, too. How to construct a vehicle of reverie, an object that would enrich the imagination of the viewer and keep him company forever.

GARY SNYDER

The Ship in Yokohama

They made me fireman at first, because 12 men missed the ship in Yokohama—I never saw such drunks or brawls or loons on any ship or anything; guys eating snakes alive & tales of port before that, Sasebo, half the crew drunk ashore ten days running naked down the streets & diving off piers, knocking over cabbage-stands & breaking barwindows, paying for it all, throwing ashtrays & buggering crewmembers with naked chairlegs leaning on bartables. But old ship got sort of straightened out after I came aboard, with new Captain & new Chief Engineer just arrived, only a few fights with wrenches all over the engineroom etc. Went to Ceylon & saw snakecharmer, walked alone in the jungle by gray mother monkeys & hoped a cobra would scare me, climbed jungly tree to look on blue bay waters, sitting in tree crotch with neat pile of dry monkeyshit placed there, & drank beer in dingy dirtfloor place with print color pictures of the life of Gotama on the walls, little dirty children & shiftless men & chickens & white cows. From Ceylon back to Guam, discharged half our oil there, picked up new true firemen & demoted me to regular wiper's job, & took on four Guamanian boys to fill out our crew—they look like Indians, have Spanish names & speak some dialect of Malayo-Polynesian, Mariana Isles are Micronesian; then went clear out mid-Pacific to Midway to give up the rest of our oil, Albatross island & Navy base, a dismal scene but for contract Hawaiian workers with wood shed booze hall every night three days gambling & drinking can beer, them brown tanned tattered & bearded guys the happiest, Chinamen, French, Polynesian, everything blood mixed & grownup there. We turned right around & sailed on 48 days to Bahrain Persia for more oil, green slick waters of Singapore & phosphorescent Indian Sea, Arabia Deserta. That load of oil in arched around the southern coast of Araby a long scarp barren cliffs & splendid rockforms, through Suez full of greasy thieves in bumboats sneak alongside & steal whatever, out into Mediterranean choppy & cool now after Red Sea nights, one morning past Crete & then port in Sicily, a rocky fortress town called Augusta, also took train & walked a day around Catania, Europe & heavy Church of Italy, the streets deserted-looking after Japan, olive tree & cactus, somehow too tired for me.

Gary Snyder, "The Ship in Yokohama" from MODELS OF THE UNIVERSE: An Anthology of the Prose Poem, Stuart Friebert and David Young, eds., Oberlin College Press, 1995. © Gary Snyder 1995. Reprinted by permission of the author.

JEROME STERN

Morning News

I get bad news in the morning and faint. Lying on tile, I think about death and see the tombstone my wife and I saw twenty years ago in the hilly colonial cemetery in North Carolina: *Peace at last.* I wonder, where is fear? The doctor, embarrassed, picks me up off the floor and I stagger to my car. What do people do next?

I pick up my wife. I look at my wife. I think how much harder it would be for me if she were this sick. I remember the folk tale that once seemed so strange to me, of the peasant wife beating her dying husband for abandoning her. For years, people have speculated on what they would do if they only had a week, a month a year to live. Feast or fast? I feel a failure of imagination. I should want something fantastic—a final meal atop the Eiffel Tower. Maybe I missed something not being brought up in a religion that would haunt me now with an operatic final confrontation between good and evil—I try to imagine myself a Puritan fearful of damnation, a saint awaiting glory.

But I have never been able to take seriously my earnestly mystical students, their belief that they were heading to join the ringing of the eternal spheres. So my wife and I drive to the giant discount warehouse. We sit on the floor like children and, in five minutes, pick out a 60-inch television, the largest set in the whole God damn store.

JAMES TATE

Distance from Loved Ones

After her husband died, Zita decided to get the face-lift she had always wanted. Halfway through the operation her blood pressure started to drop, and they had to stop. When Zita tried to fasten her seat belt for her sad drive home, she threw out her shoulder. Back at the hospital the doctor examined her and found cancer run

Jerome Stern, "Morning News" from Micro Fiction: An Anthology of Really Short Stories, Jerome Stern, Ed., W.W. Norton, 1996. Reprinted by permission of the Estate of Jerome Stern.

"Distance from Loved Ones" by James Tate, from Distance From Loved Ones (Wesleyan University Press, 1990). © 1990 by James Tate. Reprinted by permission of Wesleyan University Press.

rampant throughout her shoulder and arm and elsewhere. Radiation followed. And, now, Zita just sits there in her beauty parlor, bald, crying and crying.

My mother tells me all this on the phone, and I say: Mother, who is Zita?

And my mother says, I am Zita. All my life I have been Zita, bald and crying. And you, my son, who should have known me best, thought I was nothing but your mother.

But, Mother, I say, I am dying. . . .

ELIZABETH TORNES

Sleep

If you *must*, then touch it. But only with a long pole of exhaustion, only if you're wrapped in grey feathers. Wear them like a cloak as you enter the valley, otherwise, you are trespassing. If you expect sleep, like a huge elephant, or oak tree, to take you on: you'll see an elephant dancing on a toothpick. Expect lightning, and a small luminous insect arches, back and forth, across a black sky. Expect revelation, and your thoughts swarm up in a smokescreen.

But wear grey into the valley, lie quietly under the oak: you will be taken to a river you can slide deep into, given the stone of a dream that will never rise up.

CHARLES WRIGHT

The Poet Grows Older

It seemed, at the time, so indifferent an age that I recall nothing of it except an infinite tedium to be endured. I envied no one, nor dreamed of anything in particular as, unwillingly, I enveloped myself in all of the various disguises of a decent childhood.

"Sleep" is reprinted by permission of the author. Elizabeth Tornes is a poet and writer living in Lac du Flambeau, Wisconsin. She recently edited a collection of oral histories entitled Memories of Lac du Flambeau Elders *(University of Wisconsin Press).*

Charles Wright, "The Poet Grows Older" published originally in The Grave of the Right Hand, *Wesleyan University Press (1970). Reprinted by permission of the author.*

Nothing now comes to mind of ever embarking upon famous voyages to the usual continents; of making, from the dark rooms and empty houses of my imagination, brilliant escapes from unnatural enemies; or, on rainy winter afternoons in an attic, of inventing one plot or counterplot against a prince or a beast. . . . Instead, it must have been otherwise.

I try to remember, nevertheless, something of all that time and place, sitting alone here in a room in the middle of spring, hearing the sound of a rain which has fallen for most of April, concerned with such different things, things done by others. . . . I read of the aimless coups in the old dynasties from Africa to Afghanistan, their new republics whose lists of war lords alone are enough to distress the Aryan tongue; of intricate rockets in search of a planet, soon, perhaps to land in a country somewhere outside the pedestrian reach of reason; of the latest, old sailor's account of a water dragon seen bathing off the grizzled coast of Scotland. . . . It is at times such as this, and without thinking, really, clothed in my goat's-wool robes, that I steal a camel from an outlying Arabian stable, gather together my clansmen, and gallop for days along the miraculous caravan trails to Asia.

DAVID YOUNG

Four About Metaphysics

1.

Who can hold a fire in his hand? You spread your fingers. Ideally, they should be a substance like cork, and your palm a substance like hooves. Or antlers. A stag can poke his horns right into a furnace, can't he? Even if he can't, he probably thinks he can, whereas we feel vulnerable in the presence of vast spaces, extreme conditions. That far-flung glitter through which the midget spaceship floats. Or the frosty Caucasus. Or the snapped axle of a covered wagon halfway across the desert. Or the excitement of seeing whales surface by lanternlight. All around you. In the dark Pacific. If you didn't have to consider the boat capsizing and the light going out. If you were the boat and your hand its own unquenchable lantern.

David Young, "Four About Metaphysics" from Models of the Universe: An Anthology of the Prose Poem, *Stuart Friebert and David Young, eds., Oberlin College Press, © 1995. Reprinted by permission of the publisher.*

2.

A glass of water and an onion for his supper, the Spanish visionary sat at his table in the future. Ultimate secrets were streaming from the monastery. A rowboat was crossing the very blurred lake. Sex, for him, was just an impolite kind of staring. But the blue-eyed countess did not seem to mind. Millions of things sought to claim his attention, and he tried to look beyond them. Remembering this sentence: "The sea is as deepe in a calme as in a storme."

3.

To one side a thin church, flying a flag or a pair of pants. In the distance a castle from which a flock of rooks streams up in a spreading wedge. Someone fumbling with a barrel. And at a long table before a peeling house, people are talking, eating, fighting, kissing. Noticed by a dog, one man is vomiting. A group of musicians can be seen through the smoke from the cooking fire. About to appear from over the hill, someone like Tamburlaine or Genghis Khan.

4.

"How fortunate for Alabama," I thought. I was turning the pages of a book that resembled a piece of ice. Rapidly, as if I feared it would melt. I passed the song, the recipe, the sermon, the code, and the questionnaire. I passed the sketch of the wrestler, flexing his muscles and sobbing. I passed the poem about shooting stars and puritan names. I was searching for the story that begins: "God was not even allowed to touch Mary. It seemed to him sometimes that if he could just take her face in his hands, the world would reassemble itself with excitement. But he did not. Meanwhile, the seed. . . ." And so on. I could not find that story. I came instead to this.

IV | *Catalysts*

1. This Is Just to Say: The Poem Disguised as a Letter

DISCUSSION

Consider William Carlos Williams' famous poem "This Is Just to Say," in which a note left tacked to a refrigerator admits to the theft of a plum. This tiny note, this minor admission, when rendered in the truest and simplest words possible, placed within the empty space of a page, and broken consciously into lines of poetry surely becomes more than just a note. The form of Williams' poem rises primarily out of the need for one human being to confess a transgression to another human being, but the poem also rises out of a need for the commonplace to become meaningful, for the accepted to become experimental.

Williams' simple declaration of a minor domestic transgression has resonated with countless readers as an echo of their own home lives. The note says something more like, *forgive me but we've grown so far apart.* It is a profoundly sad poem and a profoundly beautiful realization. What Williams' refrigerator confession can also say to each of us as writers is this: *everything can eventually become a piece of creative writing: if it has intent, if it has an intended audience, and if we give it the attention it deserves.*

EXERCISE

In this exercise, we ask you to consider revealing something to someone that you've never had the nerve to reveal before. Tell your mother that you "borrowed" her car once without asking or ever confessing. Tell your boss about the time that you "were sick" but you actually spent the day rolling in the grass with your dogs. Or tell your best friend about the time you . . . well, you get the idea. Write the note.

Write it on a piece of note paper. Write it in pencil. Next, draw lines to indicate line breaks after each complete phrase. Count the number of total lines and decide on the stanza length that can come closest to dividing equally the number of complete phrases. Then, type your letter.

Chances are you'll have a very clear and very moving confessional poem disguised as a letter.

Now, a second experiment. You get a second poem from the first. Take the note you have just written and find the central object or location in the note that is not *you* and is not your intended recipient. For instance, in Williams' poem, the plums would be the central objects or the kitchen his location.

Rewrite the piece from the perspective of this object or location. Recast your actions in the third person. In short, write a note in which the object of the confession "rats you out."

Once you have these two perspectives, put them away for a few days. Then return to them and embellish at will. You may even find that the two pieces can be synthesized into one piece.

2. The Interrupted Radio Broadcast: The Nonfiction Collage

DISCUSSION

It is rare that an experiment occurs out of thin air. It is difficult to make something out of nothing; physics and religion both agree on this. However, it is much easier, and often just as rewarding, to take something that already exists and transform it into an entirely new entity.

EXERCISE

Begin with a single first-person account of an event in your own life or an event in the life of a fictional character you've either created or have encountered in another's work. Attempt to be as brief as possible in recounting this experience, keeping in mind the importance of descriptive language and an engaging voice. Write only a paragraph, no more than approximately 100 words in length.

When you are done with this piece, set it aside.

Now, go to a national news source: a newspaper, a website, or the television. For instance, go to CNN, the *New York Times*, or *Newsweek*. Find an article that interests you and write a summary of it, being as concise and factual as possible, which is approximately as long as your first paragraph. Be careful to note specific words or phrases that caught your attention in the original piece.

Now, go to a local or regional news source—your local paper, your town's chamber of commerce, your school paper—and again briefly summarize a story that intrigues you.

Now, here is the trickiest part: take the three exercises you've just done, turn the pages over, and set them aside. Take another sheet of paper and *free write* for as long as it takes to get a fourth and final piece which is approximately the same length as the first three. Consider yourself encouraged to fragment your sentences, to repeat yourself, to write nonsense, to diverge wildly. If you get stumped, change subjects as quickly as you can and keep writing.

Here is where the fun starts. You should have about 400 words of seemingly disconnected topics all coming from the same world and being interpreted on the fly by the same mind. Imagine that you are transcribing a radio broadcast of all four writings simultaneously and that you are constantly switching the dial back and forth between. Sure there will be static and there will be wild transitions that seem to be meaningless or even nonsensical, but there will also be a strange cohesion as each story spirals into the other.

To achieve this interrupted broadcast, type one or two sentences from the first exercise, your paragraph of memoir. Then, start a new paragraph. Type one or two sentences from the second exercise, the national news story. Again, start a new paragraph. Type one or two sentences from the third exercise, the local news story. Continue alternating from exercise to exercise until you have exhausted them all. Feel free to fragment at any point along the way.

After you have completed this, set it aside for a day or so.

Then, return to it and see what you have!

3. In the Midst: Short-Shorts, Flash Fiction, and Prose Poems

DISCUSSION

This exercise is quite simple and its requirements are very definite: write a *short-short*, or a *flash fiction*, or a *prose poem*. Whatever you want to call it, and it has been called many things, this little work of art can give you immense pleasure and can also prove to be the seed for a much larger, more elaborate work in the future. The prose poem, the short-short, the flash fiction (whatever you want to call it) admits from the outset that there isn't much time to complete the thought. How many places can the writer get to in a short-short space?

EXERCISE

Here are the guidelines:

(1) Begin in the midst of the story by writing a single sentence about *what just happened*. . . . For instance, write perhaps about a steaming pile of rubble, or about an awful conversation that has just ended in silence, or maybe a baby has just been born.

(2) Write two sentences in which the setting is described, providing one sensory detail for each. For instance: *The room was sickly blue. A ceiling fan knocked against the ceiling.*

(3) Write a single sentence in which the main character reacts to the event of the first sentence. For instance, describe a body movement or a facial gesture, a spoken voice or an internal monologue, even a grimace or perhaps a shriek.

(4) Now, write a single sentence in which another character, an antagonist, reacts to the same event in a nearly opposite manner. For instance, the antagonist laughs as the main character cries.

(5) Give the main character a single sentence in which to reply in a manner appropriate to his or her first action. If she spoke, then she speaks again. If he grimaced, then perhaps he should shake his head. In short, introduce a conflict.

(6) Now recount a change that occurs in the setting of the first sentence. For example, the rubble is cleared away, someone begins to laugh, or the baby suddenly stops crying.

Hopefully, after completing this exercise, you will have a single paragraph of prose which contains as much emotional and narrative tension, release, and recovery as the most successful short stories or narrative poems.

The Mapmaker's Unmade Map: Writing about Writing

I | *Discussion of the Genre*

Writing is a process of dealing with not-knowing, a forcing of what and how.
—Donald Barthelme, from "Not-Knowing"

Think about a mapmaker venturing through unmapped terrain with a blank page open and a pen in hand. The landscape is, if not familiar, understandable. The foliage is reminiscent of that from other locales; the geography, a faint recollection. The garden is far behind yet the path goes on and on, endlessly forking. The mapmaker has a lifetime's worth of experience to utilize, a wealth of previously seen lands, but he or she has never been *here* before. The mapmaker moves forward into an unknown but graspable future, interpreting the path on the move.

The writing process never repeats itself exactly, but the act of writing is repeated countless times, every day, every minute, around the world. It is both a fundamental human struggle and a fundamental human skill. This desire to record is as essential and instinctual as the first urge to speak, or to ponder a problem, or to remember a moment, or to repeat a moment. In this section you will find essays that cover exactly these moments, these ponderances, and these repetitions.

Where do you start? Where do you want to go? What do you want to find? A traveling mapmaker would carry a rucksack full of tools. What about you? What will you bring to your new uncharted discovery? What will ensure both your progress and, if necessary, your return? You will bring your pen or your keyboard, your memory, and the infinite possibilities of your imagination.

In this section, you will find the ruminations of novelists, poets, and memoirists on one single subject: *Where does the creative impulse begin?* There are, of course, many answers. There are, of course, many paths. The essays in this section will open doors to the back rooms of every writer's mind, and these doors will open into unfamiliar spaces. This is as true for poets as it is for painters, for philosophers as well as novelists, for scientists as well as spiritualists.

In these essays, you will encounter contradictions, similarities, and wild surprises. You will find poets with photographic memories and memoirists who lie out of necessity. You will find writers such as Patricia Hampl, who admits, "It still comes as a shock to realize that I don't write about what I know: I write in order to find out what I know." None of these essays, however, will claim to teach you how to write, how to be creative, or how to tell the truth.

What this work may tell you is where to begin looking for writing within your own life, even if where to begin looking is where there is no writing already. Characters, plot lines, moving images, and impeccable dialogue exist all around those who are careful to listen for them. Like the mapmaker, the pathfinder, a writer must come to understand that no detail is insignificant. The effectiveness of a written work will depend on accuracy of observation and authenticity of recording.

The reader balances these expectations with an understanding that no piece of writing will be exact in every detail. As you move through these essays, remember the old Zen teachers who say, "I can point to the moon, but I cannot make you see it." You will find essays which encourage you to read, but no one can force you to do so. These essays can point you toward the act of writing and will serve you well as valuable maps to the authors' various writing consciousnesses. When all is said and done, however, you will have to find your own path on your own blank page.

You will have to confront your own unknown. The garden is dark and forks wildly; you will not know where you're heading until you arrive. As you will find in the following pages, writers don't necessarily set out to write about the act of writing. Often, they stumble onto the subject while failing to complete something else. This understanding supports another powerful and rewarding notion in the writing process: *nothing is ever wasted.*

Paths cross, paths return. The garden forks back onto itself. We end at the beginning and then we begin again.

II | *A Quintessential: "Memory and Imagination"*
by Patricia Hampl

When I was seven, my father, who played the violin on Sundays with a nicely tortured flair which we considered artistic, led me by the hand down a long, unlit corridor in St. Luke's School basement, a sort of tunnel that ended in a room full of pianos. There, many little girls and a single sad boy were playing truly tortured scales and arpeggios in a mash of troubled sound. My father gave me over to Sister Olive Marie, who did look remarkably like an olive.

Her oily face gleamed as if it had just been rolled out of a can and laid on the white plate of her broad, spotless wimple. She was a small, plump woman; her body and the small window of her face seemed to interpret the entire alphabet of olive: Her face was a sallow green olive placed upon the jumbo ripe olive of her habit. I trusted her instantly and smiled, glad to have my hand placed in the hand of a woman who made sense, who provided the satisfaction of being what she was: an Olive who looked like an olive.

My father left me to discover the piano with Sister Olive Marie so that one day I would join him in mutually tortured piano-violin duets for the edification of my mother and brother who sat at the table spooning in the last of their pineapple sherbet until their part was called for: They put down their spoons and clapped while we bowed, while the sweet ice in their bowls melted, while the music melted, and we all melted a little into one another for a moment.

But first Sister Olive must do her work. I was shown middle C, which Sister seemed to think terribly important. I stared at middle C, and then glanced away for a second. When my eye returned, middle C was gone, its slim finger lost in the complicated grasp of the keyboard. Sister Olive struck it again, finding it with laughable ease. She emphasized the importance of middle C, its central position, a sort of North Star of sound. I remember thinking, Middle C is the belly button of the piano, an insight whose originality and accuracy stunned me with pride. For the first time in my life I was astonished by metaphor. I hesitated to tell the kindly Olive for some reason; apparently I understood a true metaphor is a risky business, revealing of the self. In fact, I have never, until this moment of writing it down, told my first metaphor to anyone.

Sunlight flooded the room; the pianos, all black, gleamed. Sister Olive, dressed in the colors of the keyboard, gleamed; middle C shimmered with meaning and I resolved never—never—to forget its location: It was the center of the world.

Then Sister Olive, who had had to show me middle C twice but who seemed to have drawn no bad conclusions about me anyway, got up and went to the windows on the opposite wall. She pulled the shades down, one after the other. The sun was too bright, she said. She sneezed as she stood at the windows with the sun shedding its glare over her. She sneezed and sneezed, crazy little convulsive sneezes, one after another, as helpless as if she had the hiccups.

"The sun makes me sneeze," she said when the fit was over and she was back at the piano. This was odd, too odd to grasp in the mind. I associated sneezing with colds, and colds with rain, fog, snow, and bad weather. The sun, however, had caused Sister Olive to sneeze in this wild way, Sister Olive who gleamed benignly and who was so certain of the location of the center of the world. The universe wobbled a bit and became unreliable. Things were not, after all, necessarily what they seemed. Appearance deceived: Here was the sun acting totally out of character, hurling this woman into sneezes, a woman so mild that she was named, so it seemed, for a bland object on a relish tray.

I was given a red book, the first Thompson book, and told to play the first piece over and over at one of the black pianos where the other children were crashing away. This, I was told, was called practicing. It sounded alluringly adult, practicing. The piece itself consisted mainly of middle C, and I excelled, thrilled by my savvy at being able to locate that central note amidst the cunning camouflage of all the other white keys before me. Thrilled too by the shiny red book that gleamed, as the pianos did, as Sister Olive did, as my eager eyes probably did. I sat at the formidable machine of the piano and got to know middle C intimately, preparing to be as tortured as I could manage one day soon with my father's violin at my side.

But at the moment Mary Katherine Reilly was at my side, playing something at least two or three lessons more sophisticated than my piece. I believe she even struck a chord. I glanced at her from the peasantry of single notes, shy, ready to pay homage. She turned toward me, stopped playing, and sized me up.

Sized me up and found a person ready to be dominated. Without introduction she said, "My grandfather invented the collapsible opera hat."

I nodded, I acquiesced, I was hers. With that little stroke it was decided between us—that she should be the leader and I the sidekick. My job was admiration. Even when she added, "But he didn't make a penny from it. He didn't have a patent"— even then, I knew and she knew that this was not an admission of powerlessness, but the easy candor of a master, of one who can afford a weakness or two. With the clairvoyance of all fated relationships based on dominance and submission, it was decided in advance: That when the time came for us to play duets, I should always play second piano, that I should spend my allowance to buy her the Twinkies she craved but was not allowed to have, that finally, I should let her copy from my test paper, and when confronted by our teacher, confess with convincing hysteria that it was I, I who had cheated, who had reached above myself to steal what clearly belonged to the rightful heir of the inventor of the collapsible opera hat. . . .

There must be a reason I remember that little story about my first piano lesson. In fact, it isn't a story, just a moment, the beginning of what could perhaps become a story. For the memoirist, more than for the fiction writer, the story seems already *there*, already accomplished and fully achieved in history ("in reality," as we naively say). For the memoirist, the writing of the story is a matter of transcription.

That, anyway, is the myth. But no memoirist writes for long without experiencing an unsettling disbelief about the reliability of memory, a hunch that memory is not, after all, *just* memory. I don't know why I remembered this fragment about my first piano lesson. I don't, for instance, have a single recollection of my first arithmetic lesson, the first time I studied Latin, the first time my grandmother tried to teach me to knit. Yet these things occurred too and must have their stories.

It is the piano lesson that has trudged forward, clearing the haze of forgetfulness, showing itself bright with detail decades after the event. I did not choose to remember the piano lesson. The experience was simply there, like a book that has always been on the shelf, whether I ever read it or not, the binding and title showing as I skim across the contents of my life. On the day I wrote this fragment I happened to take that memory, not some other, from the shelf and paged through it. I found more detail, more event, perhaps a little more entertainment that I had expected, but the memory itself was there from the start. Waiting for me.

Wasn't it? When I reread the piano lesson vignette just after I finished it, I realized that I had told a number of lies. I *think* it was my father who took me the first time for my piano lesson, but maybe he only took me to meet my teacher and there was no actual lesson that day. And did I even know then that he played the violin—didn't he take up his violin again much later as a result of my piano playing and not the reverse? And is it even remotely accurate to describe as "tortured" the musicianship of a man who began every day by belting out "Oh What a Beautiful Morning" as he shaved? More: Sister Olive Marie did sneeze in the sun, but was her name Olive? As for her skin tone—I would have sworn it was olivelike. I would have been willing to spend the better part of a morning trying to write the exact description of an imported Italian or Greek olive her face suggested: I wanted to get it right.

But now, were I to write that passage over, it is her intense black eyebrows I would see, for suddenly they seem the central fact of that face, some indicative mark of her serious and patient nature. But the truth is, I don't remember the woman at all. She's a sneeze in the sun and a finger touching middle C.

Worse: I didn't have the Thompson book as my piano text. I'm sure of that because I remember envying children who did have this wonderful book with its pictures of children and animals printed on the pages for music.

As for Mary Katherine Reilly. She didn't even go to grade school with me (and her name isn't Mary Katherine Reilly—but I made that change on purpose). I met her in Girl Scouts and only went to school with her later, in high school. Our relationship was not really one of leader and follower; I played first piano most of the time in duets. She certainly never copied anything from a test paper of mine: She was a better student, and cheating just wasn't a possibility for her. Though her grandfather (or someone in her family) did invent the collapsible opera hat and I remember that she was proud of this fact, she didn't tell me this news as a deft move in a childish power play.

So, what was I doing in this brief memoir? Is it simply an example of the curious relation a fiction writer has to the material of her own life? Maybe. But to tell the truth (if anyone still believes me capable of the truth), I wasn't writing fiction. I was writing memoir—or was trying to. My desire was to be accurate. I wished to embody the myth of memoir: to write as an act of dutiful transcription.

Yet clearly the work of writing a personal narrative caused me to do something very different from transcription. I am forced to admit that memory is not a warehouse of finished stories, not a gallery of framed pictures. I must admit that I invented. But why?

Two whys: Why did I invent and, then, if memory inevitably leads to invention, why do I—why should anybody—write memoir at all?

I must respond to these impertinent questions because they, like the bumper sticker I saw the other day commanding all who read it to QUESTION AUTHORITY, challenge my authority as a memoirist and as a witness.

It still comes as a shock to realize that I don't write about what I know, but in order to find out what I know. Is it possible to convey the enormous degree of blankness, confusion, hunch, and uncertainty lurking in the act of writing? When I am the reader, not the writer, I too fall into the lovely illusion that the words before me which read so inevitably, must also have been written exactly as they appear, rhythm and cadence, language and syntax, the powerful waves of the sentences laying themselves on the smooth beach of the page one after another faultlessly.

But here I sit before a yellow legal pad, and the long page of the preceding two paragraphs is a jumble of crossed-out lines, false starts, confused order. A mess. The mess of my mind trying to find out what it wants to say. This is a writer's frantic, grabby mind, not the poised mind of a reader waiting to be edified or entertained.

I think of the reader as a cat, endlessly fastidious, capable by turns of mordant indifference and riveted attention, luxurious, recumbent, ever poised. Whereas the writer is absolutely a dog, panting and moping, too eager for an affectionate scratch behind the ears, lunging frantically after any old stick thrown in the distance.

The blankness of a new page never fails to intrigue and terrify me. Sometimes, in fact, I think my habit of writing on long yellow sheets comes from an atavistic fear of the writer's stereotypic "blank white page." At least when I begin writing, my page has a wash of color on it, even if the absence of words must finally be faced on a yellow sheet as much as on a blank white one. We all have our ways of whistling in the dark.

If I approach writing from memory with the assumption that I know what I wish to say, I assume that intentionality is running the show. Things are not that simple. Or perhaps writing is even more profoundly simple, more telegraphic and immediate in its choices than the grating wheels and chugging engine of logic and rational intention suppose. The heart, the guardian of intuition with its secret, often fearful intentions, is the boss. Its commands are what a writer obeys—often without knowing it.

This is the beauty of the first draft. And why it's worth pausing a moment to consider what a first draft really is. By my lights, the piano lesson memoir is a first draft. That doesn't mean it exists here exactly as I first wrote it. I like to think I've cleaned it up from the first time I put it down on paper. I've cut some adjectives here, toned down the hyperbole there (though not enough), smoothed a transition, cut a repetition—that sort of housekeeperly tidying up.

But the piece remains a first draft because I haven't yet gotten to know it, haven't given it a chance to tell me anything. For me, writing a first draft is a little like meeting someone for the first time. I come away with a wary acquaintanceship, but the real friendship (if any) is down the road. Intimacy with a piece of writing, as with a person, comes from paying attention to the revelations it is capable of giving, not by imposing my own notions and agenda, no matter how well intentioned they might be.

I try to let pretty much anything happen in a first draft. A careful first draft is a failed first draft. That may be why there are so many inaccuracies in the piano lesson memoir: I didn't censor, I didn't judge. I just kept moving. But I would not publish this piece as a memoir on its own in its present state. It isn't the "lies" in the piece that give me pause, though a reader has a right to expect a memoir to be as accurate as the writer's memory can make it.

The real trouble: The piece hasn't yet found its subject; it isn't yet about what it wants to be about. Note: What *it* wants, not what I want. The difference has to do with the relation a memoirist—any writer—has to unconscious or half-known intentions and impulses in composition.

Now that I have the fragment down on paper, I can read this little piece as a mystery which drops clues to the riddle of my feelings, like a culprit who wishes to be apprehended. My narrative self (the culprit who invented) wishes to be discovered by my reflective self, the self who wants to understand and make sense of a half-remembered moment about a nun sneezing in the sun.

We store in memory only images of value. The value may be lost over the passage of time (I was baffled about why I remembered my sneezing nun), but that's the implacable judgment of feeling: *This*, we say somewhere within us, is something I'm hanging on to. And, of course, often we cleave to things because they possess heavy negative charges. Pain has strong arms.

Over time, the value (the feeling) and the stored memory (the image) may become estranged. Memoir seeks a permanent home for feeling and image, a habitation where they can live together. Naturally, I've had a lot of experiences since I packed away that one from the basement of St. Luke's School; that piano lesson has been effaced by waves of feeling for other moments and episodes. I persist in believing the event has value—after all, I remember it—but in writing the memoir I did not simply relive the experience. Rather, I explored the mysterious relationship between all the images I could round up and the even more impacted feelings that caused me to store the images safely away in memory. Stalking the relationship, seeking the congruence between stored image and hidden emotion—that's the real job of memoir.

By writing about that first piano lesson, I've come to know things I could not know otherwise. But I only know these things as a result of reading this first draft. While I was writing, I was following the images, letting the details fill the room of the page and use the furniture as they wished. I was their dutiful servant—or thought I was. In fact, I was the faithful retainer of my hidden feelings which were giving the commands.

I really did feel, for instance, that Mary Katherine Reilly was far superior to me. She was smarter, funnier, more wonderful in every way—that's how I saw it. Our friendship (or she herself) did not require that I become her vassal, yet perhaps in my heart that was something I sought. I wanted a way to express my admiration. I suppose I waited until this memoir to begin to find the way.

Just as, in the memoir, I finally possess that red Thompson book with the barking dogs and bleating lambs and winsome children. I couldn't (and still can't) remember what my own music book was, so I grabbed the name and image of the one book I could remember. It was only in reviewing the piece after writing it that I saw my inaccuracy. In pondering this "lie," I came to see what I was up to: I was getting what I wanted. Finally.

The truth of many circumstances and episodes in the past emerges for the memoirist through details (the red music book, the fascination with a nun's name and gleaming face), but these details are not merely information, not flat facts. Such details are not allowed to lounge. They must work. Their labor is the creation of symbol. But it's more accurate to call it the *recognition* of symbol. For meaning is not "attached" to the detail by the memoirist; meaning is revealed. That's why a first draft is important. Just as the first meeting (good or bad) with someone who later becomes the beloved is important and is often reviewed for signals, meanings, omens, and indications.

Now I can look at that music book and see it not only as "a detail" but for what it is, how it acts. See it as the small red door leading straight into the dark room of my childhood longing and disappointment. That red book *becomes* the palpable evidence of that longing. In other words, it becomes symbol. There is no symbol, no life-of-the-spirit in the general or the abstract. Yet a writer wishes—certainly we all wish—to speak about profound matters that are, like it or not, general and abstract. We wish to talk to each other about life and death, about love, despair, loss, and innocence. We sense that in order to live together we must learn to speak of peace, of history, of meaning and values. The big words.

We seek a means of exchange, a language which will renew these ancient concerns and make them wholly, pulsingly ours. Instinctively, we go to our store of private associations for our authority to speak of these weighty issues. We find, in our details and broken, obscured images, the language of symbol. Here memory impulsively reaches out and embraces imagination. That is the resort to invention. It isn't a lie, but an act of necessity, as the innate urge to locate truth always is.

All right. Invention is inevitable. But why write memoir? Why not call it fiction and be done with it? And if memoir seeks to talk about "the big issues," of history and peace, death and love—why not leave these reflections to those with expert or scholarly knowledge? Why let the common or garden variety memoirist into the club? I'm thinking again of that bumper sticker: Question Authority. Why?

My answer, naturally, is a memoirist's answer. Memoir must be written because each of us must possess a created version of the past. Created: that is, real in the sense of tangible, made of the stuff of a life lived in place and in history. And the downside of any created thing as well: We must live with a version that attaches us to our limitations, to the inevitable subjectivity of our points of view. We must acquiesce to our experience and our gift to transform experience into meaning. You tell me your story, I'll tell you mine.

If we refuse to do the work of creating this personal version of the past, some-one else will do it for us. That is the scary political fact. "The struggle of man against power," Milan Kundera's hero in *The Book of Laughter and Forgetting* says, "is the struggle of memory against forgetting." He refers to willful political forget-ting, the habit of nations and those in power (Question Authority!) to deny the truth of memory in order to disarm moral and ethical power.

It is an efficient way of controlling masses of people. It doesn't even require much bloodshed, as long as people are entirely willing to give over their personal memories. Whole histories can be rewritten. The books which now seek to deny the existence of the Nazi death camps now fill a room.

What is remembered is what becomes reality. If we "forget" Auschwitz, if we "forget" My Lai, what then do we remember? And what is the purpose of our remembering? If we think of memory naively, as a simple story, logged like a docu-mentary in the archive of the mind, we miss its beauty but also its function.

The beauty of memory rests in its talent for rendering detail, for paying homage to the senses, its capacity to love the particles of life, the richness and idio-syncrasy of our existence. The function of memory, while experienced as intensely personal, is surprisingly political.

Our capacity to move forward as developing beings rests on a healthy relation with the past. Psychotherapy, that widespread method for promoting mental health, relies heavily on memory and on the ability to retrieve and organize images and events from the personal past. We carry our wounds and perhaps even worse, our capacity to wound, forward with us. If we learn not only to tell our stories but to listen to what our stories tell us—to write the first draft and then return for the second draft—we are doing the work of memory.

Memoir is the intersection of narration and reflection, of storytelling and essay writing. It can present its story *and* consider the meaning of the story. The first commandment of fiction—Show, Don't Tell—is not part of the memoirist's faith. Memoirists must show *and* tell. Memoir is a peculiarly open form, inviting broken and incomplete images, half-recollected fragments, all the mass (and mess) of detail. It offers to shape this confusion—and, in shaping, of course, it necessarily creates a work of art, not a legal document. But then, even legal documents are only valiant attempts to consign the truth, the whole truth, and nothing but the truth to paper. Even they remain versions.

Locating touchstones—the red music book, the olive Olive, my father's violin playing—is satisfying. Who knows why? Perhaps we all sense that we can't grasp the whole truth and nothing but the truth of our experience. Just can't be done.

What can be achieved, however, is a version of its swirling, changing wholeness. A memoirist must acquiesce to selectivity, like any artist. The version we dare to write is the only truth, the only relationship we can have with the past. Refuse to write your life and you have no life. That is the stern view of the memoirist.

Personal history, logged in memory, is a sort of slide projector flashing images on the wall of the mind. And there's precious little order to the slides in the rotating carousel. Beyond that confusion, who knows who is running the projector? A memoirist steps into this darkened room of flashing, unorganized images and stands blinking for a while. Maybe for a long while. But eventually, as with any attempt to tell a story, it is necessary to put something first, then something else. And so on, to the end. That's a first draft. Not necessarily the truth, not even *a* truth sometimes, but the first attempt to create a shape.

The first thing I usually notice at this stage of composition is the appalling inaccuracy of the piece. Witness my first piano lesson draft. Invention is screamingly evident in what I intended to be transcription. But here's the further truth: I feel no shame. In fact, it's only now that my interest in the piece quickens. For I can see what isn't there, what is shyly hugging the walls, hoping not to be seen. I see the filmy shape of the next draft. I see a more acute version of the episode or—this is more likely—an entirely new piece rising from the ashes of the first attempt.

The next draft of the piece would have to be true re-vision, a new seeing of the materials of the first draft. Nothing merely cosmetic will do—no rouge buffing up the opening sentence, no glossy adjective to lift a sagging line, nothing to attempt covering a patch of gray writing.

I can't say for sure, but my hunch is the revision would lead me to more writing about my father (Why was I so impressed by that ancestral inventor of the collapsible opera hat? Did I feel I had nothing as remarkable in my own background?). I begin to think perhaps Sister Olive is less central to this business than she appears to be. She is meant to be a moment, not a character. I'm probably wasting my time on her, writing and writing around her in tight descriptive circles, waiting for the real subject to reveal itself. My father!

So I might proceed, if I were to undertake a new draft of the memoir. I begin to feel a relationship developing between a former self and me.

And even more important, a relationship between an old world and me. Some people think of autobiographical writing as the precious occupation of the unusually self-absorbed. Couldn't the same accusation be hurled at a lyric poet, at a novelist—at anyone with the audacity to present a personal point of view? True memoir is written, like all literature, in an attempt to find not only a self but a world.

The self-absorption that seems to be the impetus and embarrassment of autobiography turns into (or perhaps always was) a hunger for the world. Actually, it begins as hunger for *a* world, one gone or lost, effaced by time or a more sudden brutality. But in the act of remembering, the personal environment expands, resonates beyond itself, beyond its "subject," into the endless and tragic recollection that is history. We look at old family photographs in which we stand next to black, boxy Fords, and are wearing period costumes, and we do not gaze fascinated because there we are young again, or there we are standing, as we never will again in life, next to our mother. We stare and drift because there we are historical. It is the dress, the black car that dazzle us now and draw us beyond our mother's bright arms which once caught us. We reach into the attractive impersonality of something more significant than ourselves. We write memoir, in other words. We accept the humble position of writing a version, the consolation prize for our acknowledgment we cannot win "the whole truth and nothing but."

I suppose I write memoir because of the radiance of the past—it draws me back and back to it. Not that the past is beautiful. In our communal memoir, in history, the darkness we sense is not only the dark of forgetfulness. The darkness is history's tunnel of horrors with its tableaux vivants of devastation. The blasted villages, the hunted innocents, the casual acquiescence to the death camps and tiger cages are back there in the fetid holes of history.

But still, the past is radiant. It sheds the light of lived life. One who writes memoir wishes to step into that light, not to see one's own face—that is not possible—but to feel the length of shadow cast by the light. No one owns the past, though typically the first act of new political regimes, whether of the left or the right, is an attempt to rewrite history, to grab the past and make it over so the end comes out right. So their power looks inevitable.

No one owns the past, but it is a grave error (another age would have said a grave sin) not to inhabit memory. Sometimes I think it is all we really have. But that may be melodrama, the bad habit of the memoirist, coming out. At any rate, memory possesses authority for the fearful self in a world where it is necessary to claim authority in order to Question Authority.

There may be no more pressing intellectual need in our culture than for people to become sophisticated about the function of memory. The political implications of the loss of memory are obvious. The authority of memory is a personal confirmation of selfhood, and therefore the first step toward ethical development. To write one's life is to live it twice, and the second living is both spiritual and historical, for a memoir reaches deep within the personality as it seeks its narrative form and it also grasps the life-of-the-times as no political analysis can.

Our most ancient metaphor says life is a journey. Memoir is travel writing, then, notes taken along the way, telling how things looked and what thoughts occurred. Show *and* tell. But I cannot think of the memoirist as a tourist. The memoir is no guide book. This traveler lives the journey idiosyncratically, taking on mountains, enduring deserts, marveling at the lush green places. Moving through it all faithfully, not so much a survivor with a harrowing tale to tell as that older sort of traveler, the pilgrim, seeking, wondering.

Discussion of a Quintessential

"Memory and Imagination"
by Patricia Hampl

It is a daunting task to write about the act of writing and a challenge to consider the vast worlds of the imagination, memory, and creativity. Scholars spend entire careers investigating the mind's creative operations and still the subject remains mysterious. For the writer, this is an especially precarious activity. We fear that, in uncovering the secrets of the creative process, we may lose the ability to engage in it. Yet, there are those brave souls, such as Patricia Hampl, who eagerly present perspectives on creativity from which we, as readers and writers, can benefit in meaningful ways.

In this provocative essay, Hampl offers a comprehensive and honest investigation into the writer's creative process. She does so by presenting her own experience as a writer, revealing both the stages of her writing process and her approach to discovering and discerning meaning and insight in her own unguarded work. Hampl presents a vivid exploration of the unconscious mind, storing and then attempting to retrieve consequential images from memory. The imagination conjures these images from the past into a present experience, and Hampl shows how our relationship to memory and our ability to imagine memory can intensely impact creative processes and be impacted by creative processes. In short, the memoir writer should remain suspect of his or her cherished memories. They are often, if not always, creations of our imagination working in past tense.

She begins the essay with a generous portion of memoir, in order to illustrate several important phenomena which occur during her creative process. With rich detail and emotional depth, she reveals to the reader a time in her youth when the world existed for her in simple and vivid terms: *Sister Olive, the Middle C, tortured piano-violin duets with her father*. Reading this passage, one can almost feel the ivory key beneath one's finger. And Sister Olive is a fantastic character who sits beside the reader and points him or her through the memory.

Then, Hampl reveals that those memories are false. None were exactly the truth. And the truth is nothing if not exact. She admits to the fabrication of details and argues convincingly for the necessity of imagined truth, the creative lie. "Here," she shows us, "memory impulsively reaches out and embraces imagination. That is the resort to invention. It isn't a lie, but an act of necessity, as the innate urge to locate truth always is." These inventions offer writers the opportunity to revise history and to retroactively create realities that the writer desired. However, the important work remains: understanding how the inaccuracies of our memory function and what these unintended lies tell us about the truths of our present experience.

Hampl says, "I try to let pretty much anything happen in a first draft." She believes that it is best for the writer to relinquish control and to let the writing itself communicate and teach. It is best to "keep moving" and allow memory and the imagination to unveil the mysteries of the unconscious mind. "That may be," she says, "why there are so many inaccuracies in the piano lesson memoir: I didn't censor, I didn't judge. I just kept moving." The memory often chooses itself.

Although Hampl's focus is on the act of writing memoir, the ideas she presents can and should be carried forward into every genre of writing. She reminds us that all literature is written "in attempt to find not only a self but a world." As she illustrates, the writer's development of every idea begins as an intensely internal experience involving personal memories and distinctive imaginative moments, and then evolves into an external one, a work of art that succeeds in illustrating commonalities of the human condition. Hampl shares with us one human's progress from the unconscious self to the conscious self and how that process impacts every human's relationship with his or her world. "For meaning," she says, "is not 'attached' to the detail by the memoirist; meaning is *revealed*." [italics ours]

Ultimately, she concludes, this is a pilgrim's quest: "Moving through it all faithfully, not so much a survivor with a harrowing tale to tell as . . . [a] pilgrim, seeking, wondering." The memoirist, like all writers, seeks to rediscover and remember the past, but, when necessary, may resort to creating the past. In this essay, Patricia Hampl performs a valuable service to all writers by examining the inventions of her own past and by honestly revealing her fictions.

We leave you now with three final powerful lessons distilled from this quintessentially firsthand study of the writing process:

1. Trust in the endlessly creative potential of your memory.
2. Allow everything you encounter to enter your first drafts, but never trust your memory to be completely accurate.
3. Never trust a draft until you've explored and revised it.

III | *Reading Selections*

A. R. AMMONS

A Poem Is a Walk

Nothing that can be said
in words is worth saying.

LAOTSE

I don't know whether I can sustain myself for thirty minutes of saying I know nothing—or that I need to try, since I might prove no more than you already suspect, or, even worse, persuade you of the fact. Nothingness contains no images to focus and brighten the mind, no contrarieties to build up muscular tension; it has no place for argumentation and persuasion, comparison and contrast, classification, analysis. As nothingness is more perfectly realized, there is increasingly less (if that isn't contradictory) to realize, less to say, less need to say. Only silence perfects silence. Only nothingness contributes to nothingness. The only perfect paper I could give you would be by standing silent before you for thirty minutes. But I am going to try this imperfect, wordy means to suggest why silence is finally the only perfect statement.

I have gone in for the large scope with no intention but to make it larger; so I have had to leave a lot of space "unworked," have had to leave out points the definition of any one of which could occupy a paper longer than this. For though we often need to be restored to the small, concrete, limited, and certain, we as often need to be reminded of the large, vague, unlimited, unknown.

I can't tell you where a poem comes from, what it is, or what it is for: nor can any other man. The reason I can't tell you is that the purpose of a poem is to go past telling, to be recognized by burning.

I don't, though, disparage efforts to say what poetry is and is for. I am grateful for—though I can't keep up with—the flood of articles, theses, and textbooks that mean to share insight concerning the nature of poetry. Probably all the attention to poetry results in some value, though the attention is more often directed to lesser than to greater values.

Once every five hundred years or so, a summary statement about poetry comes along that we can't imagine ourselves living without. The greatest statement in our language is Coleridge's in the *Biographia*. It serves my purpose to quote only a fragment from the central statement: that the imagination—and, I think, poetry— "reveals itself in the balance or reconciliation of opposite or discordant qualities." This suggests to me that description, logic, and hypothesis, reaching toward higher and higher levels of generality, come finally to an antithesis logic can't bridge. But poetry, the imagination, can create a vehicle, at once concrete and universal, one and many, similar and diverse, that is capable of bridging the duality and of bringing us the experience of a "real" world that is also a reconciled, a unified, real world. And this vehicle is the only expression of language, of words, that I know of that contradicts my quotation from Laotse, because a poem becomes, like reality, an existence about which nothing that can be said in words is worth saying.

Statement can also achieve unity, though without the internal suspension of variety. For example, All is One, seems to encompass or erase all contradiction. A statement, however, differs from a work of art. The statement, All is One, provides us no experience of manyness, of the concrete world from which the statement derived. But a work of art creates a world of both one and many, a world of definition and indefinition. Why should we be surprised that the work of art, which over-reaches and reconciles logical paradox, is inaccessible to the methods of logical exposition? A world comes into being about which any statement, however revelatory, is a lessening.

Knowledge of poetry, which is gained, as in science or other areas, by induction and deduction, is likely to remain provisional by falling short in one of two ways: either it is too specific, too narrow and definite, to be widely applicable—that is, the principles suggested by a single poem are not likely to apply in the same number or kind in another poem: or, the knowledge is too general, too abstract and speculative, to fit precisely the potentialities of any given poem. Each poem in becoming generates the laws by which it is generated: extensions of the laws to other poems never completely take. But a poem generated by its own laws may be unrealized and bad in terms of so-called objective principles of taste, judgment, deduction. We are obliged both to begin internally with a given poem and work toward generalization *and* to approach the poem externally to test it with a set— and never quite the same set—of *a priori* generalizations. Whatever we gain in terms of the existence of an individual poem, we lose in terms of a consistent generality, a tradition: and vice versa. It is Scylla and Charybdis again. It is the logically insoluble problem of one and many.

To avoid the uncertainty generated by this logical impasse—and to feel assured of something definite to teach—we are likely to prefer one side or the other—either the individual poem or the set of generalizations—and then to raise mere preference to eternal verity. But finally, nothing is to be gained by dividing the problem. A teacher once told me that every line of verse ought to begin with a capital letter. That is definite, teachable, mistaken knowledge. Only by accepting the uncertainty of the whole can we free ourselves to the reconciliation that is the poem, both at the subconscious level of feeling and the conscious level of art.

One step further before we get to the main business of the paper. Questions structure and, so, to some extent predetermine answers. If we ask a vague question, such as, What is poetry?, we expect a vague answer, such as, Poetry is the music of words, or Poetry is the linguistic correction of disorder. If we ask a narrower question, such as, What is a conceit?, we are likely to get a host of answers, but narrower answers. Proteus is a good figure for this. You remember that Proteus was a minor sea god, a god of *knowledge*, an attendant on Poseidon. Poseidon is the ocean, the total view, every structure in the ocean as well as the unstructured ocean itself. Proteus, the god of knowledge, though, is a minor god. Definite knowledge, knowledge specific and clear enough to be recognizable as knowledge, is, as we have seen, already limited into a minor view. Burke said that a clear idea is another name for a little idea. It was presumed that Proteus knew the answers—and more important The Answer—but he resisted questions by transforming himself from one creature or substance into another. The more specific, the more binding the question, the more vigorously he wrestled to be free of it. Specific questions about poetry merely turn into other specific questions about poetry. But the vague question is answered by the ocean which provides distinction and non-distinction, something intellect can grasp, compare, and structure, and something it can neither grasp, compare, nor structure.

My predisposition, which I hope shortly to justify, is to prefer confusion to over-simplified clarity, meaninglessness to neat, precise meaning, uselessness to over-directed usefulness. I do not believe that rationality can exhaust the poem, that any scheme of explanation can adequately reflect the poem, that any invented structure of symbology can exceed and thereby replace the poem.

I must stress here the point that I appreciate clarity, order, meaning, structure, rationality: they are necessary to whatever provisional stability we have, and they can be the agents of gradual and successful change. And the rational, critical mind is essential to making poems: it protects the real poem (which is non-rational) from blunders, misconceptions, incompetences; it weeds out the second rate. Definition, rationality, and structure are ways of seeing, but they become prisons when they blank out other ways of seeing. If we remain open-minded we will soon find for any easy clarity an equal and opposite, so that the sum of our clarities should return us where we belong, to confusion and, hopefully, to more complicated and better assessments.

Unlike the logical structure, the poem is an existence which can incorporate contradictions, inconsistencies, explanations and counter-explanations and still remain whole, unexhausted and inexhaustible; an existence that comes about by means other than those of description and exposition and, therefore, to be met by means other than, or in addition to, those of description and exposition.

With the hope of focusing some of these problems, I want now to establish a reasonably secure identity between a poem and a walk and to ask how a walk occurs, what it is, and what it is for. I say I want a reasonably secure identity because I expect to have space to explore only four resemblances between poems and walks and no space at all for the differences, taking it for granted that walks and poems are different things. I'm not, of course, interested in walks as such but in clarification or intensification by distraction, seeing one thing better by looking at something else. We want to see the poem.

What justification is there for comparing a poem with a walk rather than with something else? I take the walk to be the externalization of an interior seeking, so that the analogy is first of all between the external and the internal. Poets not only do a lot of walking but talk about it in their poems: "I wandered lonely as a cloud," "Now I out walking," and "Out walking in the frozen swamp one grey day." There are countless examples, and many of them suggest that both the real and the fictive walk are externalizations of an inward seeking. The walk magnified is the journey, and probably no figure has been used more often than the journey for both the structure and concern of an interior seeking.

How does a poem resemble a walk? First, each makes use of the whole body, involvement is total, both mind and body. You can't take a walk without feet and legs, without a circulatory system, a guidance and co-ordinating system, without eyes, ears, desire, will, need: the total person. This observation is important not only for what it includes but for what it rules out: as with a walk, a poem is not simply a mental activity; it has body, rhythm, feeling, sound, and mind, conscious and subconscious. The pace at which a poet walks (and thinks), his natural breath-length, the line he pursues, whether forthright and straight or weaving and medita-tive, his whole "air," whether of aimlessness or purpose—all these things and many more figure into the "physiology" of the poem he writes.

A second resemblance is that every walk is unreproducible, as is every poem. Even if you walk exactly the same route each time—as with a sonnet—the events along the route cannot be imagined to be the same from day to day, as the poet's health, sight, his anticipations, moods, fears, thoughts cannot be the same. There are no two identical sonnets or villanelles. If there were, we would not know how to keep the extra one: it would have no separate existence. If a poem is each time new, then it is necessarily an act of discovery, a chance taken, a chance that may lead to fulfillment or disaster. The poet exposes himself to the risk. All that has been said about poetry, all that he has learned about poetry, is only a partial assur-ance.

The third resemblance between a poem and a walk is that each turns, one or more times, and eventually *returns*. It's conceivable that a poem could take out and go through incident after incident without ever returning, merely ending in the poet's return to dust. But most poems and most walks return. I have already quoted the first line from Frost's "The Wood-Pile." Now, here are the first three lines:

Out walking in the frozen swamp one grey day,
I paused and said, "I will turn back from here.
No, I will go on farther—and we shall see."

The poet is moving outward seeking the point from which he will turn back. In "The Wood-Pile" there is no return: return is implied. The poet goes farther and farther into the swamp until he finds by accident the point of illumination with which he closes the poem.

But the turns and returns or implied returns give shape to the walk and to the poem. With the first step, the number of shapes the walk might take is infinite, but then the walk begins to "define" itself as it goes along, though freedom remains total with each step: any tempting side-road can be turned into on impulse, or any wild patch of woods can be explored. The pattern of the walk is to come true, is to be recognized, discovered. The pattern, when discovered, may be found to apply to the whole walk, or only a segment of the walk may prove to have contour and therefore suggestion and shape. From previous knowledge of the terrain, inner and outer, the poet may have before the walk an inkling of a possible contour. Taking the walk would then be searching out or confirming, giving actuality to, a previous intuition.

The fourth resemblance has to do with the motion common to poems and walks. The motion may be lumbering, clipped, wavering, tripping, mechanical, dance-like, awkward, staggering, slow, etc. But the motion occurs only in the body of the walker or in the body of the words. It can't be extracted and contemplated. It is non-reproducible and non-logical. It can't be translated into another body. There is only one way to know it and that is to enter into it.

To summarize, a walk involves the whole person; it is not reproducible; its shape occurs, unfolds; it has a motion characteristic of the walker.

If you were brought into a classroom and asked to teach walks, what would you teach? If you have any idea, I hope the following suggestions will deprive you of it.

The first thought that would occur to you is, What have other people said about walks? You could collect all historical references to walks and all descriptions of walks, find out the average length of walks, through what kind of terrain they have most often proceeded, what kind of people have enjoyed walks and why, and how walks have reflected the societies in which they occurred. In short, you could write a history of walks.

Or you could call in specialists. You might find a description of a particularly disturbing or interesting walk and then you might call in a botanist to retrace that walk with you and identify all the leaves and berries for you: or you might take along a sociologist to point out to you that the olive trees mentioned were at the root—forgive me—of feudal society: or you might take along a surveyor to give you a close reading in inches and degrees: or you might take a psychoanalyst along to ask good questions about what is the matter with people who take walks: or you might take a physiologist to provide you with astonishment that people can walk at all. Each specialist would no doubt come up with important facts and insights, but your attention, focused on the cell structure of the olive leaf, would miss the main event, the walk itself.

You could ask what walks are good for. Here you would find plenty: to settle the nerves, to improve the circulation, to break in a new pair of shoes, to exercise the muscles, to aid digestion, to prevent heart attacks, to focus the mind, to distract the mind, to get a loaf of bread, to watch birds, to kick stones, to spy on a neighbor's wife, to dream. My point is clear. You could go on indefinitely. Out of desperation and exasperation brought on by the failure to define the central use or to exhaust the list of uses of walks, you would surrender, only to recover into victory by saying, Walks are useless. So are poems.

Or you could find out what walks mean: do they mean a lot of men have unbearable wives, or that we must by outward and inward motions rehearse the expansion and contraction of the universe; do walks mean that we need structure—or, at an obsessive level, ritual in our lives? The answer is that a walk doesn't mean anything, which is a way of saying that to some extent it means anything you can make it mean—and always more than you can make it mean. Walks are meaningless. So are poems.

There is no ideal walk, then, though I haven't taken the time to prove it out completely, except the useless, meaningless walk. Only uselessness is empty enough for the presence of so many uses, and only through uselessness can the ideal walk come into the sum total of its uses. Only uselessness can allow the walk to be totally itself.

I hope you are now, if you were not before, ready to agree with me that the greatest wrong that can be done a poem is to substitute a known part for an unknown whole and that the choice to be made is the freedom of nothingness: that our experience of poetry is least injured when we accept it as useless, meaningless, and non-rational.

Besides the actual reading in class of many poems, I would suggest you do two things: first, while teaching everything you can and keeping free of it, teach that poetry is a mode of discourse that differs from logical exposition. It is the mode I spoke of earlier that can reconcile opposites into a "real" world both concrete and universal. Teach that. Teach the distinction.

Second, I would suggest you teach that poetry leads us to the unstructured sources of our beings, to the unknown, and returns us to our rational, structured selves refreshed. Having once experienced the mystery, plenitude, contradiction, and composure of a work of art, we afterwards have a built-in resistance to the slogans and propaganda of over-simplification that have often contributed to the destruction of human life. Poetry is a verbal means to a non-verbal source. It is a motion to no-motion, to the still point of contemplation and deep realization. Its knowledges are all negative and, therefore, more positive than any knowledge. Nothing that can be said about it in words is worth saying.

RICHARD BAUSCH

So Long Ago

Indulge me, a moment.

I have often said glibly that the thing which separates the young from the old is the knowledge of what Time really is; not just how fast, but how illusive and arbitrary and mutable it is. When you are twenty, the idea of twenty years is only barely conceivable, and since that amount of time makes up one's whole life, it seems an enormous thing—a vast, roomy expanse, going on into indefiniteness. One arrives at forty with a sense of the error in this way of seeing, and maturity, um, can be said to have set in.

And the truest element of this aspect of the way we experience time, of course, is the sense of the nearness of time past.

I have a memory of being bathed by my father on my seventh birthday. Morning, rainy light at a window. The swish and wash of lukewarm water. My own body, soft-feeling and small under the solid strong hands, lathered with soap. I said, "Well, I guess I'm a big boy now."

He said, "No, not quite."

I remember feeling a bit surprised, perhaps even downcast, that he didn't simply agree with me, as most of the adults in our large family usually did. He ran the towel over me, ruffled my hair with it, drying me off. I went across the hall into my room, and dressed for the April day. Baseball season was starting.

Let me go back there for a little while, to that bath, my seventh birthday. At the time, I wasn't old enough to understand the difference between the humoring of children, which is a large part of any talk with them, and truth telling, which is what my father did. I loved his rough hands on me, and the smell of him— aftershave, and cigarettes, and sometimes the redolence of my mother's Chanel.

He hated lies, and lying. He was a storyteller, and he must have learned early how to exaggerate and heighten things, to make the telling go better, to entertain and enthrall. He was so good at it. He could spin it out and do all the voices and set the scene and take you to the laughs, and there simply *had* to have been elements that he fabricated. And yet he hated lies. Any trouble you ever got into in our house always had to do with that: you learned very early that even if you *had* done something wrong, something for which you wanted some kind of an excuse, or explanation, it had better not involve telling a lie.

I was often in some kind of mischief at school—my twin, Robert, and I had a talent for making other kids laugh, and for imitating our teachers' gestures and voice mannerisms. Well, we were the sons of a storyteller. Neither of us liked school very much; and the teachers, the nuns of Saint Bernadette's, knew it. They kept tabs on us. They were at some pains to discipline us. And whenever we got into a scrape at school, we lived in dread that our father would ask us, that evening, how things had gone at school. I remember sitting at the dinner table as he and my mother told stories, or commented happily on the various people—friends and family—who inhabited our lives then. Bobby and I would sit there in awful anticipation of the question: "How was school today?" You couldn't gloss over anything—you couldn't use a cover-all word like *fine*. You had to be specific, and you had to tell it all, the truth. You were *compelled* to do so by what you knew of the value he set upon the truth. And never mind philosophical truth, or the truth of experience, really; he wanted to know what happened in the day, what was said and done, and how it went—*that* kind of truth.

I have no memory—not even a glimmer—of how and when we learned that this was what he expected from us, and that the surest way to earn his displeasure was by lying to him. I don't have much of a memory of him telling us this; I recall him talking about how it was a thing *his* father expected, but by then I was in my teens, and I understood it then as an echo of a kind, a source.

All right.

I remember being surprised that in my father's truthful opinion I was not a big boy yet. I remember that we had two boys our age living next door to us, and that this took place on Kenross Avenue in Montgomery County, Maryland. I know intellectually that the year was 1952, and that Truman was still president. I could not have said who Truman was then, and I recall that a few months later, in the summer, when the Republican Convention was on our little General Electric black-and-white television, I saw all those people in the arena, with Eisenhower standing there on the podium, and I guessed the number to be everyone in the world. "No," my father said, "It's not even a small fraction of the number." I didn't know the word *fraction* and yet I understood what he meant.

Sometime around then I saw film of the war that had just ended, and I was told by my mother that another war was going on, in Korea. A summer evening—we were driving past an army post, and I had seen the antiaircraft guns, the olive drab barrels aimed at the sky. I wondered aloud why we couldn't hear the guns.

"It's on the other side of the world, honey. Thousands of miles away."

In 1952, my mother was thirty-four years old. Now, I'm almost twenty years older than that, and this is the math I'm always doing—have been doing, like a kind of mental nerve-tic, since I was twenty-seven years old, and a father for the first time myself.

When my son Wes was fourteen months old, we moved to Iowa, where I attended the Writers' Workshop. I spent a lot of time with him that year, and as he grew slightly older I decided to conduct a sort of experiment: I'd see if I could manage to keep in his memory the times we had at Iowa—the swing set and sandbox outside the Hawkeye Court Apartments, the little amusement park by the river in Iowa City, with its Ferris wheel and its kiddie train. I'd ask him about it, almost daily: "Do you remember the swing set? The sandbox? Do you remember how I used to push you on the swings, and you didn't want to go in the house? Remember the summer nights when it would be getting dark, and we'd go to that park and ride in the kiddie train?" Yes, he remembered. He was three, and then four, and then five, and he remembered. He offered elements of that time, so he wasn't merely remembering *my* memory: yes, the swing set and the sandbox—but did I remember the red wagon that got stuck there, and then buried there by the other children? I did. Yes, the kiddie train, but remember the buffalo? Yes, there had been a small enclosure with Bison standing in it; the big Ferris wheel, yes, but did I remember riding it and being stopped at the very top?

Oh, yes.

I had begun to think I might be able to help my son carry that part of his life with him into his own adulthood—earliest memories that have chronological shape. It became important that he have it all to keep. And then one winter evening, as we were riding in the car on the way to a movie, I asked him about Iowa again, and he recalled nothing—it was all simply gone. I asked him about the swing set, the sandbox, the park, the train, the Ferris wheel, even the buffalo. To each one he said, "No." Innocently, simply, without the slightest trace of perplexity or anything of what I was feeling, which was sorrow. You could see him striving to get something of it back, but it was like a game, and there was nothing. No, he had no recollection of any of it. I don't think it had been more than a week or two since we had gone through this little litany of memory, and even so it had all disappeared from his mind, and my description of it was only a story, now.

When I was fifteen, my great-grandmother, Minnie Roddy, died. Minnie had for the most part raised my mother, because Minnie's daughter had had to go to work for the government when my mother was still a baby. They all lived with my aunt Daisy, Minnie's sister, in a big sprawling Victorian house with a wide porch that had blue-gray painted boards and white trim. When Minnie began to fail, my mother went over there, and we later learned, through the talk of the adults in the rooms of the two houses, that she was holding the old woman in her arms in the last moments. Minnie used to tell me stories, sitting in the breakfast nook, by the windows where younger children ran. Summer evenings, the cousins and aunts and uncles out on the lawn, throwing horseshoes. The bell-like clang of the metal on metal when someone hit one of the posts, or scored a ringer or a leaner. Fireflies rising in the shallow pools of shade in the spaces between the houses, in the cloud-shaped willow tree—you couldn't see its trunk for the drooping filamental mass of its branches—at the edge of the property. Minnie talking, telling me about coming from Ireland on a ship; about her husband—who had come to America after killing a man in a fight one afternoon in a pub in Dublin. Her voice would trail off, and the louder voices out the window would distract me. I'd nod and pretend to listen. I was always reading books, as Bobby was, but it showed more on me, and I was the one, after all, who believed that I had a vocation. I was planning for the priesthood. Minnie Roddy would say, "You'll grow up and tell these stories. You'll grow up and be a writer."

And she would go on talking, unscrolling her memory of earlier days, of my mother as a young girl; of Ireland, and a childhood spent, for the most part, in the latter part of the nineteenth century. I didn't hear most of it. I nodded and pretended to listen, while this woman—this tiny slip of a lady with her wire-framed glasses and her clear large blue eyes—tried to give me treasure, something to store up, for the arrival of a season I was not and am not ready for.

When she died, it was decided that Bobby and I were old enough to attend the funeral. I felt a strange detached curiosity about the whole thing: I was actually going to see a dead person. I told one of the other boys in my class, speaking it out with a sort of quiet, fake-brave shrug. "I'm going to see a dead person today."

"Who?"

"My great-grandmother."

"Jesus, no kidding?"

I was, I suppose, even a little proud of the fact. Minnie had lived to great age, and her going seemed natural enough, and so far away from my own life and world that I could only think of it in a sort of abstract haze. I was still young enough and egocentric enough to be unable quite to imagine my own demise.

The day of the funeral was bright and chilly. I don't recall whether it was spring or fall. It wasn't summer, because I was in school. I think it was fall. We rode with our parents to the funeral home, and I was like a secret traveler in the backseat, planning my exploration of this curiosity, death, this unreal element of the life I was in so permanently. I was wildly curious; I understood, according to the tenets of the faith I had been raised in that Minnie Roddy would not be there, but only her body, the empty vessel she had vacated. She was in that blue elsewhere that I associated with the sky, and we could now pray to her.

Blue is the important color, here.

Standing over the box where she lay, looking like a bad likeness of herself, I saw the forking, colorless veins in her bony hands, the fingers of which were wound with a black rosary; and I saw the blue place at her earlobe, where blue did not belong. I marked it, and knew that I would never forget it.

This sounds as though I were marking things with the flaccid, nervous sensitivity of one of those pretentious people who like to think of themselves as a romantic central figure in their own drama: the incipient artist, observing everything with the intention of later recording it. I do not mean it this way at all, and it was not like that at all. I was a child, still. I knew next to nothing about anything, especially about myself. And I don't know that I have learned much since then, either.

I suppose I have to admit that it might just be impossible to have it both ways: to claim that I was not that hypersensitive romantic figure, the artist-as-a-young-man, and still report the impressions of a moment like that one, standing over the body of a woman who had lived a life so separate from mine, and nothing like mine, and whose reality could not have anticipated that she would be a figure in my speech, a character in a story I would tell, even as she told me about all the living she had seen and done, and I pretended to listen. In any case, I do not mean this the way it will sound. I mean to express the quality of a memory, in order to say something about this life we live, so much of which is fugitive, so much of which is lost in the living of it.

The room we were in was banked with flowers, and there were chairs in rows, as though someone might give a lecture, or a homily. Minnie's coffin looked to have been where it was long enough for this prodigious wall of flowers to grow up on three sides of it. There was a dim light, a candle burning at one end. The light was brightest where she lay, with her eyes shut in a way that made you understand they would not open again. The skin looked oddly transparent, like the synthetic skin of a doll. And there was the blue place at the ear, the place, I knew, where the cosmetics of the mortician hadn't quite taken. I stood there and looked with a kind of detached, though respectful silence at this, aware of it not as death, quite, but death's signature. I was conscious of the difference. I spent my minute there, head bowed, and then walked back to my seat at the rear of the room, with the other young people, all in their early teens, like me. I saw my mother and my aunt

Florence come from where I had just been, and my mother had a handkerchief that she held to her nose. She sobbed, once. Earlier, when we had arrived, Florence had come up to my mother and said, "You scared the bejesus out of me." I don't know—or I don't remember—what this was about; I think it had something to do with what had gone on last night, at the viewing. Perhaps my mother had gotten woozy, or swooned. It was the first time I had ever heard the word *bejesus*.

Florence and my mother sat down, and a priest led us in the rosary. If he said anything about the woman who lay behind him in the long box, I don't recall it. We were in the room for a time, and then people began to file out. I remained in my seat, and I have no idea why. Others crossed in front of me, and maybe I was saying my own prayers—it seems to me now that I must have felt some pang of guilt for my oddly remote observation of everything, and was trying to say the words of a prayer, repeating them inwardly in an attempt to say them not out of automatic memory but actually to enter into the meaning of them:

> Hail Mary, full of grace, the Lord is with thee. Blessed art thou among women and blessed is the fruit of thy womb, Jesus. Holy Mary, Mother of God, pray for us sinners, now and at the hour of our death, Amen.

The others were all filing quietly out of the long room, and I saw the mortician step to the side of the casket, where we had each stood only moments before. With a practical sureness, the nearly offhand familiarity of experience, he reached into the white satin that ringed Minnie Roddy's head, and pushed downward on it, a tucking motion, and Minnie slipped from her sleeping pose. Her head dropped down into that box like a stone.

Something must have shown in my face; and the mortician's wife—let us call them the Hallorans, because I no longer recall the name—saw the change in my features. Later, as I was getting into the back of my father's car, Aunt Florence leaned in and said, "Honey, Mrs. Halloran wanted me to tell you that Mr. Halloran was only making it so Minnie could rest better."

I nodded. I don't believe I said anything. It was almost as if I had stumbled upon someone in a privy act; I felt the same kind of embarrassment. But there was something else in it, too, a kind of species-thrill: this was the human end, a reality I was not expecting. I am trying to express this as exactly as I can, and it is finally inexpressible. I know that all my fascination was gone, and I sat there in the back of the car, looking out at the sunny streets of Washington, D.C., and felt numb, far down.

That memory is as present to me as the moment, almost a decade earlier, when I said to my father that I was a big boy, and he told me the truth, that I was not a big boy. Not yet. And those memories are as near as the memory of asking, in the first line of this story, for your indulgence.

Of course, this is not an original perception; yet one arrives at it in life—doesn't one?—with the sense of having had a revelation: one's personal past is a *place*, and everything that resides there does so in contemporaneous time. What then, of the collective past? The collective memory? That is where chronology really is. We come from the chaos of ourselves to the world, and we yearn to know what happened to all the others who came before us. So we impose Time on the flow of events, and call it history. For me, Memory is always *story*. True memory is nothing like the organized surface of a story, yet that is all we have to tell it, and know it, and experience it again: but if we are doomed to put our remembered life into stories, we are blessed by it, too.

I never spoke to my mother and father, or even to my brothers and sisters, about what I had seen at the funeral home. I don't know why, now. I can't recall why. Perhaps it was too private, finally; and perhaps I did not want to have it in memory, didn't want to fix it there in the telling. But it has never left me. It is with all the others, large and small, important and meaningless, all waiting in the same timeless dark, to drift toward the surface when I write, or daydream, or sleep.

CHARLES BAXTER

Shame and Forgetting in the Information Age

We have transformed information into a form of garbage.

NEIL POSTMAN

1. In Memory of Tom, My Brother

In April 1998, my brother Tom died, at the age of fifty-nine. He died in his sleep, of a heart attack, one day after his fifty-ninth birthday. He had been afflicted with bad health for some time, including congestive heart failure, renal failure, diabetes, cancer, and narcolepsy. He once fell asleep at the wheel and had to crawl out of his wrecked car and a drainage ditch to the nearest house. His financial affairs were a calamity. Faced with these problems, he was almost perversely upbeat. Every week over the phone I'd ask him how he was, and he'd say, "Not too bad for an old man!"

Charles Baxter, "Shame and Forgetting in the Information Age" from The Business of Memory: The Art of Remembering in an Age of Forgetting, *Charles Baxter, ed., Graywolf Press, 1999. Courtesy of Darhansoff, Verrill, Feldman Literary Agency.*

Tom was an outcast of the information age. Perhaps every family has one. He was ours. He had trouble in school (and he went to a lot of schools) because he could not learn printed information easily. Reading and writing often defeated him, and they did so before the culture had begun to employ the phrase "learning disability," and before this society had become dependent on computers. He had a computer and claimed he didn't know how to use it. For years, long after I had begged him to stop, he would introduce himself exuberantly as "the dumb brother." I was stricken by this phrase, made heart-sick by it, and by his efforts to turn this source of shame into an identifying badge.

Forgetting was shameful to him, and he felt it marked him for life.

His spelling was atrocious. He wrote in a scrawl. Much of my writing made very little sense to him, except for the stories that he recognized and in which he figured, and there were many. I wrote about him all the time. He was my muse for a while. He never forgot anyone he ever met, and he never forgot a story, witnessed or heard. He listened to stories and told them expressively, with awe and wonder. As long as he could function in the world, he was a salesman, a manufacturer's rep, a job in which he could put his storytelling capacities to use. He didn't—almost everyone said this about him—have a mean bone in his body.

His father—his and mine—died in 1948 when Tom was nine years old, and at the funeral some man, some friend of the family, told Tom, "You're *not* going to cry, are you." It wasn't a question; it was an order. "He told me to stuff it," Tom said later. And stuff it he did, with food.

Where do you go, what do you do, if you can't manage the printed information that we churn out? What becomes of you? What if you can't stand it? Melville's Bartleby starved in the Tombs. My brother took the opposite tack. He ate. He over-ate. He took it, the food, all in. He became large and unseemly; he became so big that when he came into the room, any room anywhere, people helplessly stared at this huge tottering man. He stuffed it and then he went on stuffing it. He absorbed it. He fought his shame (he always ate in secret, out of sight, preferably in the dark) by eventually calling attention to it: He began wearing pink sportshirts and kelly green trousers and rainbow suspenders. By his mid-to-late forties, he was unemployable, defeated by his exasperated difficulties with his appearance and with the printed word.

He was among the ranks of those who cannot easily process written information, the data-disabled. There's a large number of these people around, and no one likes to talk about them. They are a great scandal to our sensibilities. We have a myth that education will help them get on their feet. For some of them, yes. But for many, many others, education is the wall they can't get over, or through.

My brother had a storehouse of stories. If an experience had been witnessed and reported to him, he could remember the narrative in detail and tell it again. I'll repeat this for emphasis: he never forgot anyone. He loved to tell stories about how he had recognized someone who couldn't recognize him, who had forgotten who he was. It was his special triumph never to forget a name or a face, and he was amused by my own difficulty in remembering names. He thought it was a telling commentary on the sort of person I was, and am, that I had such difficulties. He was amused that I forgot human beings but remembered what I had read. However, if it—the information—arrived on paper, or on a screen, he'd lose track of the content. It wouldn't stick. With me, it did.

Nevertheless, he once could recite the words that Charley speaks over Willy Loman's grave, "a salesman don't put a bolt to a nut" speech, by heart. "All I have," my brother would say, "is a smile and a shoeshine." When I see him now, he is sitting at a table, telling an amazing story, a story that may or may not be true. He didn't always care if a story was literally true, but it had to be narratively useful and explain something that needed explaining.

By some miracle he never became embittered. He loved the world and loved God in a way that I refused to. He found the world quite wonderful, a fit place for stories. He was the first person to take me into a public library and to explain to me that each card represented a book. I didn't believe him. When I was eleven, I pestered him with questions about what happened on a date between the girl and the boy (I was completely mystified), and so, with his girlfriend's permission, he took me along the next time they went out, so he could show me how the thing was done. She let me hold her hand at the movie.

A few years ago he was officially put on the rolls of the disabled. He had been disabled almost from the start, and his various ambitions (to be ordained, to host a radio program) were frustrated by quizzes, tests, exams. All this terrible writing! It was inescapable. He even flunked out of radio school. Toward the end of his life—I can still hardly believe it—he became a freelance writer on the subjects of boating and outdoor recreation. It was a brave choice. It was like pitching your tent in the camp of the enemy. I don't know if he ever earned any money from it—I don't think he did—but it kept him busy.

He wanted to be remembered. To this end, he was horribly, shockingly, punitively generous to everyone. He was always giving something away. It was in his nature to do so, but it was also a request: please remember me; after all, I remember you. Every gift from him was a remembrance. He went bankrupt twice, mostly because he gave everything away.

When we went into his apartment after his death, the papers—all the documents and letters and magazines and bank statements and computer printouts and postcards and newspapers and ranks of unread how-to manuals and books and directories and reference books—were stacked and stashed everywhere. It rose, in great piles, almost to the ceiling. The air was bad. The papers had absorbed all the oxygen, and there was a rank smell of paper oxidizing, turning brown, like the smell of food cooking. He lived amid these documents. They surrounded him, like the foetid documentary accumulations in *Bleak House*. The apartment was stuffed with written material, all the paperwork of a lifetime, very little of it thrown out or recycled. It had befriended him. Because he couldn't hold it in his head, he kept it around and had learned to live with it. Besides, he couldn't bend over to pick it up.

We searched through it all. There was no will. He hadn't written one. As they say: all he had left behind were our memories of him. That, and the papers.

2. *Memory, Shame, and Forgetting: An Introduction*

Ann Arbor, Michigan, where I happen to live, is a small and rather tightly wound city where information processing is a major industry. Surrounded by farmland, the area is nevertheless dominated by the University of Michigan and by its intellectual, artistic, and athletic productions. A barn, not two miles from where I live, has M GO BLUE patterned on its roof shingles.

People here often take considerable pride in their minds and more particularly in their memories. The town is full of Know-It-Alls. It has to be. Standing in front of others, sporting their expensive ties and slightly askew accessories in classrooms or outside of them, my colleagues rattle off facts and figures and concepts and patterns while their students take notes. The virtuosi of knowledge, they are presumed to have—they *do* have—some authority because of what they know and what they remember. Their lives and their authority depend upon their ability to remember, and to remember their subjects in public. Having a private memory in a place like this one might be pleasant, but it is certainly beside the point, at least professionally. Private memories stay at home, or end up in a therapist's office.

The business of Ann Arbor (or Madison, or Berkeley, or Bloomington, any college or university town) is memory, cultural memory. Software, in every sense.

This may explain why I perked up, some months ago, as I was sitting in a local restaurant, when I heard two women in the next booth talking about memory. I bent over to eavesdrop, which is, in part, what I do for a living.

"How much memory have you got?" one of them asked the other.

"I don't know."

"You don't *know*?" the first one asked. "You don't know how much memory you have? Didn't you ask the salesman?"

Of course they were not talking about their own minds. But it was an extraordinary conversation because its tone was so offhand, what one of my students once called "so *lunchtime*." In a way that even Marshall McLuhan might not have predicted, the mechanical extensions of humans have now apparently extended to our brains, and more particularly to our memories. "Your memory" can now in casual conversation refer to your computer's memory rather than your own.

This usage signals a conflation in the way that we think about the data we remember, as opposed to what we would call "our memories." "Our memories" are memories of our experiences in narrative form. They are probably not in the external computer unless we are keeping a journal or writing a memoir, in which case only the words are there. Data, by contrast, the proliferating facts and figures, can easily be stored.

Confusion about the two forms of memory is spreading and manifesting itself in peculiar ways, most peculiarly in what might seem to be its opposite, a huge desire or need to forget, a kind of fetishizing of amnesia. *Strategic amnesia* might be an appropriate phrase to describe how we are coping with information-glut, what David Shenk in a recent book on the subject called "data smog."

Strategic amnesia has everything to do with the desire to create or destroy personal histories. It has everything to do with the way we tell stories. As I write, it is smearing into unintelligibility the daily tableaux of public and political life. In this sense, narrative dysfunction and strategic amnesia are conniving, and have joined hands.

This is complicated and perplexing and needs to be approached slowly and with caution, not to say alarm.

We read and are told every day that our industrial economy has shifted in the last two decades toward the production of information. The manufacture of goods has been exported to a large degree and displaced by the mass production of data. The technology of data processing has increased exponentially year by year, resulting in high-speed forms of planned obsolescence in software programs (Windows, etc.) and in the computers themselves. The only frustrating limit to this technology, one CEO told me, is the speed of light, which is now too slow.

The easy mass access to the Internet has resulted in the rapid trading of information and the public postings of semiprivate and occasionally lurid materials in homepages and web sites. Furthermore, a large proportion of the population works with, or is at least familiar with, information technology. We are all (well, most of us) computer users now. Many of us have to spend the day in front of screens, moving the information around or creating new information.

There is more information all the time. No one can absorb all the information. No one wants to. The day ends, not with physical exhaustion, but with data-fatigue or data-nausea. Information on a screen is subtly different from information gleaned from books, although no one has been completely clear about the nature of this difference. Because there's always more information, an information explosion, but a limited capacity to absorb it or even to know what information is essential and what information is trivial, anxiety often results, data-anxiety. What do you need to know, what do you need to absorb, what do you need to remember? Who can say? No one can keep up. No one is in a position to tell you.

Given such a situation, every place where computers reign is like Ann Arbor. You can process information perfectly well in a farmhouse in North Dakota. In an information society, large sectors of the population, to survive, have had to acquire some competency in handling data, organizing it, moving it around, displaying it, and disposing of it.

A proliferation of information causes information-inflation. That is, every individual piece of information loses some value given the sheer quantity of other information. Some information turns quickly into garbage. Bad information may well force out good, in a Gresham's Law of data processing.

The tremendous quantities of data—much of it trivial or even subtrivial—have created new forms of competency, having to do with both arranging the data and remembering it.

Remembering data and remembering an experience are two very different activities. It is possible that the quantity of data we are supposed to remember has reduced our capacity to remember or even to have experiences; this turn of events was predicted by Walter Benjamin in the 1930s.

What meaning does forgetfulness possess in an information age?

Is It Forgetfulness Or Is It Alzheimer's?

Advertisement headline in the *New York Times*
for a prescription drug, Cognex, to aid memory

The signs of anxiety over forgetfulness have been turning up everywhere lately, but most prominently, for me, in television commercials and newspaper ads. One recent such commercial, shown nationally, begins with documentary footage of a young woman in a large stadium singing the Canadian national anthem. After about ten seconds, she begins to fluff her lines. A pause, while she looks embarrassed and shamefaced. She then stops singing. Cut to a voice-over, an announcer saying, "Everybody needs a good night's sleep to perform well." On the screen, we see a shot of the product: a mattress. Memory-anxiety makes for good business.

Prescription drugs that aid the memory, so-called "cognitive enhancers," are touted in full-page ads in the *New York Times*.

The phobia about forgetting has entered the run of daily conversation. A colleague in my department, forgetting my name as we meet in the hallway, turns beet red from embarrassment and says that it must be the onset of Alzheimer's. Another friend, having forgotten her keys in her office, says that she is in fact worried not so much about the keys but about her memory slips. These slips are commonplace, she says, but they are causing her depressive spells. She can't stop talking about it. Clearly she is obsessing about her mental competence. Time and again, I have seen friends and colleagues lose their trains of thought in meetings and then blush and stammer and apologize, as if their professional standing had suddenly been endangered.

Many people seem to believe that remembering is simply a matter of willpower.

During an enormous stadium concert by the band R.E.M., Michael Stipe, the lead singer, apologizes to the audience, thousands of us, for having the lyric sheets to the songs he sings placed on a music stand in front of him.

In an information age, forgetfulness is a sign of debility and incompetence. It is taken as weakness, an emblem of losing one's grip. For anyone who works with quantities of data, a single note of forgetfulness can sound like a death knell. To remember is to triumph over loss and death; to forget is to form a partnership with oblivion. And in our time, the former president, Ronald Reagan, has become the central figure, the genius loci, the brawny poster-child, of forgetfulness.

Reagan's most recognizable feature during his administration involved the conjunction of ahistoricism, rigid beliefs, self-indulgence, and intractable memory loss about details. When it suited him, and sometimes when it didn't, Reagan forgot. It was characteristic of Reagan to say, "I don't remember." Reagan's tendency to get history wrong, to render it imaginary, to discredit history altogether, slides imperceptibly into his double-dealing in the Iran-Contra affair, his forgetfulness and disavowals of responsibility, his social ethos of self-interest and selfishness, and, ultimately, into his final data-free twilight. In this sense, Reagan managed to contradict the principle that I laid out a few paragraphs ago: his forgetfulness, far from making him incompetent, *enabled* him to be the sort of president he was; it set him free from responsibility for his actions. For a while, he made forgetfulness *work*. Forgetfulness means that your mind may have crashed. It may, paradoxically, set you free.

Reaganism, understood as the proving ground of historical amnesia, strategically ignored the past in favor of a wasteful and a self-indulgent present. With Reaganism, forgetting aided and abetted power.

> Don't stop thinking about tomorrow.
> Don't stop—it'll soon be here. . .
> Yesterday's gone, yesterday's gone.
>
> "Don't Stop" by Fleetwood Mac's Christine McVie Played during the Democratic Convention Nominating Bill Clinton

With respect to the past, Clinton carries on the tradition started by Reagan. The disavowals of responsibility (Clinton denies; he never forgets) give to the Clintonian past the same aura as the Reagan past: it becomes unreadable and unintelligible. In a sort of postmodern political version of *Les Misérables*, Clinton turns into a presidential Jean Valjean pursued by the relentless Inspector Javert, Kenneth Starr. But this time around, there is something fishy about Clinton's pose of innocence and Starr's pose of righteousness. Starr, whatever his political associations might be, is in the position of trying to reconstruct and narrativize Clinton's past not for the purposes of truth but to serve political ends, and Clinton, like Reagan before him, seems to be eager to make that past go away. The Starr Report, not surprisingly, makes the case against Clinton by constructing what it calls "The Narrative."

Clinton is a representative figure of our time because he remembers huge quantities of data but also seems eager to slip large sections of the past into the trash icon, so that he can indulge himself. Clinton seems to be able to bury the past without demonstrating visible shame. (Nixon, at least, dependably broke out into a sweat whenever the cameras were trained on him.) After each new revelation, Clinton goes back on TV, smiling, looking the same as ever. "Yesterday's gone" is a phrase from political progressivism and, in this case, from the recent and excitingly narcotic political rhetoric of debauchery and deniability, just like the now-classic "mistakes were made." His high approval ratings suggest that nobody really minds, that, in fact, the American people secretly approve. Clinton has become a hero of selective data management.

3. On Information and Memory: Walter Benjamin

In his essay "The Storyteller" (1936), collected in *Illuminations*, Walter Benjamin makes a series of points about the relation between information and experience. In a calm tone that belies his apocalyptic intent, Benjamin argues that the explosion of information in the Modern Age is denying us something precious: "the ability to exchange experiences." That is, storytelling.

"Experience," Benjamin says, "has fallen in value." To paraphrase his argument: you don't want to hear about my experiences anymore. Nor am I usually in a mood to tell you about them. Why? First of all, because much of my experience feels blank, terrible, or unchanging. Benjamin here uses the example of mute shell-shocked soldiers coming back from World War I. Secondly, I'm not having experiences in my day-to-day life: instead, I'm absorbing or processing information. "Information," Benjamin says, "proves incompatible with the spirit of storytelling. If the art of storytelling has become rare, the dissemination of information has had a decisive share in this state of affairs."

Benjamin goes on, in a wonderfully suggestive but somewhat unclear manner, to differentiate between a memory for information and a memory for experiences. His implication is that the coming information-glut will force experience— and storytelling generally—into a corner and additionally force it to resort to extremes.

Imagine a person who spends all day in a windowless office or cubicle, copying or moving information. Let us whimsically call this person Ms. Bartleby. Ms. Bartleby must go to sales conferences and talk about all the new ideas and theories and projections, and she must be absolutely current in the resources and techniques of data management and document preparation and presentation, and she must remember much of what has been said to her over her cell phone and what has appeared on her computer screen, and she must check her pager every half hour. Whatever the job is that she must do, they want it done yesterday.

Nevertheless, Ms. Bartleby comes home, at the end of the day, feeling blank. The only experiences she has had, during the whole week, are those that seem to be empty of actual experiential content (unless you count that turbulence that her flight encountered over—what was it?—Cleveland?). The data leaves no experience-memory in her head. She comes to the end of the week craving a drink or a drug. At least that's an experience. Maybe she wants to do an extreme sport for a few hours on Saturday. She may have spiritual yearnings but no particular outlet for them. But she doesn't really want to talk about her work because she can't converse about it. She can only make statements about it. There aren't any stories there, unless her coworkers are seducing or cheating or harassing each other, always a possibility.

Benjamin's point about this is that our experiences have been reduced in number at the same time that the available mental space for them has shrunk. In an information age, our representative figure, Ms. Bartleby, is rich in information and poor in experience. She sits all day in front of screens at work, and then she sits in front of screens at home. If she has a baby, there's half a chance that the father will not aid the birth, but videotape it. Instead of trusting his own memory, he'll record the event by means of mechanical reproduction, turning it into a spectacle on TV. Returning to Ms. Bartleby: she is going to put a huge amount of psychic pressure on the quality of whatever relationships she has, and there may be quite a few, as a result. She will feel terrible shame if she forgets any of the data she is supposed to master. And yet, if her life feels inadequate and shallow to her, that very forgetting, that very shame, may, through a quasi-Freudian reversal, also seem immensely attractive.

Forgetting and shame might just serve, under the immediate surface of consciousness, as an escape route of sorts.

Not "I prefer not to," but "I don't remember." Or, "I prefer not to" in the form of "I don't remember." Not remembering locates itself as an act of sabotage against mere data, of rebellion at the local level. It is memory's version of the Freudian slip.

Bartleby would only feel shame at not remembering if she felt that her job was really worth doing. If the job wasn't especially worth doing, if it was a Dilbert job, or if she had messed up and wanted to cover her tracks, forgetfulness would take on a positively Elysian aspect. It would put her right back into childhood. And there would be the example of Reagan. Reagan's forgetfulness gave him a certain innocence, a head-shaking self-deprecatory boyishness.

Clinton's boyishness has been remarked upon by everyone, and quite acidly by Bob Dole, who never looked much like a boy even when he was one.

4. Shame, Innocence, and the Memoir

The recent proliferation of memoirs has been viewed with alarm by literary and cultural pundits, who have claimed that all these memoirs are yet another manifestation of the ubiquitous viral narcissism at work in the American cultural body, identified by Christopher Lasch and several others. Well, maybe. But if we follow the lines sketched out decades ago by Benjamin, we might discover that the literary memoir is, like therapy, a local antidote to information-poisoning. It's a perfectly reasonable response to the devaluation and even destruction of personal experience. The memoir (along with journal writing) is one of the few places where experience-memory goes to take shelter and to be increased in value. The memoir is memory's revenge upon info-glut. Television cannot do it; movies cannot do it. If anything, they stand against the intimacy of personal experience in favor of spectacle.

Every memoir argues that a personal memory is precious. No other artistic form makes that argument with the same specificity or urgency.

After all, if you have a personal memory, what can you do with it? You can carry it around, or you can try to dispose of it. But the chances are that your memories will feel precious to you, and you may want to share them by narrating them. They constitute the story of your life, the key to your own narrative. Traumatic memories may be the exceptions. I will have more to say about this later.

Because of their value, personal memories are rarely treated with irony by the person who has them, at least in America. Irony, by metaphorically negating what has actually happened, would render your own memories and your life inchoate. Irony would be an auto-inflicted calamity when applied to one's own memories: it would be like putting oneself into liquidation. Memoirs tend to be earnest, even when they are lyric and comic. They exhibit loyalty to one's own past. Even

Nabokov was dead serious about his past in *Speak, Memory*, no matter how much he applied the filigree. No one treasured a personal past more than he did.

What you remember is the key to who you are. This commonplace formulation excludes dismissive irony and the mere piling-up of information as techniques for memoir writing. Personal information must be converted into experience if it is to communicate anything, methodically disproving the bleakest of Benjamin's prophecies. If any writer can tell the story of his or her life, s/he has a chance of escaping from the suffering of a dysfunctional personal narrative. S/he is seeking to understand that suffering and to turn it into something readable and coherent and functional in a time of data-glut. As a result, *a memoir cannot be summarized*. It only works if it includes the details. There's no intimacy otherwise, and any memoir requires intimacy to convey its experiences.

American memoirs of the past two decades are some of the most powerful literary documents that we have created during this period, in part, I think, because they have taken seriously the condition of innocence and the subsequent corruption or fall from that innocence, and seen it in relation to storytelling. The memoir has saved a place for childhood and adult experience when everyone else in the professional-managerial class was trying to get rid of it. Memoirs are deeply involved with rites of initiation and with education. This is classic memoir territory, familiar from Augustine and Rousseau. To quote Robert Hass, "All the new thinking is about loss./In this it resembles all the old thinking."

And yet these inquiries into innocence and its loss often appear to have another common theme. It is natural that a writer would want to write about parents, but recent memoirs seem to have reserved a special place for missing or empty or vacated or just bad fathers. Something has gone wrong with the fathers; there is something either shameful or absent about them.

Gertrude Stein, a sort of one-woman early-warning system, was one of the first to notice this phenomenon. In *Everybody's Autobiography*, published in 1937, she writes that, following the death of God, we are about to go into the era of the Bad Father. She names Hitler and Stalin as examples. "There is too much fathering going on just now and there is no doubt about it fathers are depressing."

Stein's own *The Making of Americans* is father haunted. So is Paul Auster's *The Invention of Solitude*, Mary Karr's *The Liars' Club*, Kathryn Harrison's *The Kiss*, Michael Ryan's *Secret Life*, Geoffrey Wolff's *The Duke of Deception*, Tobias Wolff's *This Boy's Life*, and Mary Gordon's *The Shadow Man: A Daughter's Search for Her Father*. Perhaps this is all historical coincidence. But I think not; I think something else is going on.

The fathers or stepfathers in most of these books are elusive. They distort their own histories, or empty them out, or tell tall tales, in order to create dysfunctional narratives, thereby increasing their own power and confusing their children. They take on the role of the storyteller in order to create puzzles and mazes rather than histories. To recapitulate my argument from a previous essay on the subject, narrative dysfunction (the phrase is C. K. Williams's) is the process by which we lose track of the story of ourselves, the story that tells us who we are supposed to be and how we are supposed to act. In a dysfunctional narrative, true accountability vanishes. No one seems to be responsible for anything, or else the wrong people are accused of what may not, in fact, have happened at all. This is usually a complex response to shame: incest (*The Kiss*), alcoholism (*Secret Life*), repressed family histories (*The Invention of Solitude*), or ethnic identity (*The Shadow Man, The Duke of Deception*). Shame comes first, but strategic forgetting follows closely behind.

In most of these books, the author is at pains to investigate history in order to understand it, to tell the truth after a father has lied about it or simply said nothing or pretended to forget it. What the fathers in these books have done is to gain the upper hand by telling an odd story or by staying silent. They remain figures of sometimes diabolical authority as long as the stories they tell falsify history or drain it of content.

Evading their own lives, they manage by means of dysfunctional narratives to disable the lives of their children, their listeners. Strategic amnesia replaces paternal accountability.

We are back to Reagan. These fathers institute a form of Reaganism at the local, domestic level.

If your memory of your experiences is precious, *then your father has, at least in a patriarchal culture, a special and almost sacred power to confirm a history.* He can also distort or corrupt history and the past and your place in it. The rise of the memoir, then, is not so much a sign of literary narcissism as it is an antidote to the widespread practice of dysfunctional narration within the family. Every memoir seeks to make a narrative functional again, to tell the truth about experience.

5. *"Maybe Erasure is Necessary": The Literature of Forgetting*

The literature of the first three-quarters of this century is distinguished thematically by its efforts to go in search of lost time. A large number of the great texts of this century are, typically, heroic efforts at historical remembrance, reconstruction, recollection. Against our zest for destruction, they preserve the personal memory and the cultural artifact. They reconstruct. They hold on. They are our epics of conservation in the face of certain loss.

You would think that forgetting, the erasure of the specific, would be antiliterary and antihistorical—a counternarrative practice. You would think that there could be no such thing as a literature of forgetting, no such thing as a great epic of amnesia. The pages, by necessity, would all be blank. *Tout oublier, c'est tout . . . quelque chose.*

Everything would dissolve into a haze. It might begin as trauma or comedy but it would certainly end as nightmare.

Nevertheless, it's just possible that in the last part of the twentieth century, we are pioneering a new kind of literature, a literature of amnesia, as we assemble the fragmentary texts of forgetting. This new literature is probably one side effect of data-nausea, of which narrative minimalism may be another. If memory stands against death, forgetting stands against data. It's also one solution to the problem of trauma.

The first novel I remember reading that used forgetting as a consistent narrative device was Edmund White's *Forgetting Elena* (1973), much admired by Nabokov. After two hundred pages of comic antinarrative, the narrator, following the beautiful and mysterious Elena's death, remembers himself and his apparent storytelling task. Does he want to deliver the eulogy for Elena? His answer is, "I remember nothing. Who is Elena?" The end. It's as if Nick Carraway, after struggling unsuccessfully for two hundred pages to remember who Gatsby *was*, conclusively asked, in a moment of brilliant slack-jawed obtuse blankness, "Who is Gatsby?" The question isn't rhetorical; the character, by being forgotten, is gone, and the book, thank God, is over. It's a sort of camp triumph over Proustian monumentalism.

We stand here in the shadow of Beckett, the plays and novels made out of loss and emptiness and absence, of stories and texts for nothing, of *Imagination Dead Imagine*, of Beckett's claim that James Joyce had used the resources of memory and history, and that he, Beckett, would take the opposite course, the way of forgetting. We stand in the shadow of Maeterlinck's Mélisande in *Pelléas and Mélisande*, perpetually vague and beautiful, without any discernible history, demanding attention and love from everybody, unconversant, resigned, quiet, a catalyst for violence, erotic, and mutely hysterical.

In one form or another, writers of talent have devised a fictional poetics of forgetting, of momentary stories without a past: Douglas Cooper in *Amnesia*, Steve Erickson in *Amnesiascope*, Lydia Davis in *Almost No Memory*, to name only a few examples. Dennis Cooper's narrator, at the end of *Guide*, says, untellingly, in his last sentence, following 176 pages of narrative, "You can basically forget about us." Meaning: you *should* forget about us. If you can. Just try.

The shame of forgetting. The necessity of it. What help is the data if you don't—if you can't and won't—remember the story? My last example is drawn from Tim O'Brien's 1994 novel *In the Lake of the Woods*. O'Brien's novel doesn't answer these questions, but it poses them ingeniously. The book's narrative is absolutely and conclusively dysfunctional: there's a way into it but no way out. Its characters disappear and ultimately vanish, and the book's project is to make their disappearances unanswerable and invisible. There may be an art, even a high art, to evasion; if so, this book practices it. The book is constructed to be unintelligible at its most crucial points, and I don't mean that as criticism.

In all truth, *In the Lake of the Woods* is a strange novel. It gives off an odor of sulphur. Its protagonist, John Wade, also known as "Sorcerer," has been in Vietnam and has been involved with the butchery at Thuan Yen, a place commonly known as My Lai. After his return to the United States, he runs for political office but is defeated when his past catches up with him. Following his defeat at the polls, he takes his wife Kathy up to Minnesota's Lake of the Woods. There, something happens to Kathy. She disappears. She may (or may not) have been killed by her husband, who may (or may not) have poured boiling water out of a teakettle all over her. He can't remember. In any case, John dutifully and despairingly searches for her once she's gone. At the end of the novel, he, too, disappears, hunting for her (the book, one might say, is *about* hunting), across the vast expanse of that lake. He vanishes over the horizon line of the narrative, and the prose ends, or maybe just stops, with a blizzard of questions.

Those are the bones of the story, and I have recounted them in a somewhat glib and offhanded manner, because they don't really account for much in the book. There is no final accounting here. It is as if every element in the tale had become hypothetical. The author is constantly disclaiming his own authority, yanking back events and episodes that were posited as actual. The protagonist and the narrative reel from one event to the next, blank-faced, almost criminally obsessive, traumatized.

In this novel, trauma everywhere infects the narrative order. The only certainty is that John Wade went to Vietnam and saw something there. Beyond that, epistemological frenzy, narrated in a somewhat deadpan manner, is the rule rather than the exception. Does John really love Kathy? The novel claims that he does, but the examples of this love are persistently hollow and overmiked, like someone shouting into a public-address system. Did he kill her? The implied narrator, at one point, finds this possibility *distasteful*. What are John's experiences? Whatever they are, they are so terrible—and the novel is quite clear about this particular fracturing—that they cannot be held in the memory. We arrive, by a tortuous and circuitous route, back at shame, as catalyst and curse.

As if to compensate for all this narrative vacancy, these holes in the story, the novel applies an interesting strategy, designed to fail. Using the narrator as a sort of classic investigator on the scene of the crime, the book at first subtly and then quite openly begins to subdivide, like a paramecium. One part of the book remains a traditional if evasive narrative of John and Kathy's experiences. The second part contains testimony and facts. To the trauma of the story, the book supplies evidence, testimony, witnesses, and tragicomic footnotes. The footnotes, of course, give the appearance of explaining something by providing pivotal evidence and data. "Pivotal evidence," however, is woefully insufficient. So is the data. Because the entire novel is in the form of an unsolved mystery, the footnotes constitute a wild-goose chase. There are intensely interesting discoveries along the way, but the whole journey eventuates in a mystifying absence.

The book, halfway through, begins to experience its own data-smog, a self-generated info-glut. Very cannily, it places this data-smog next to a traumatized and piecemeal history, which is both John Wade's and, by extension, America's. It's as if our recent annals are shot through, not with momentous events occurring in a stately historical manner, but with trauma: assassinations, massacres, unthinkable horrors enacted on a daily basis. Yet another child enters yet another school and methodically kills his classmates, and the townspeople, on camera, say that it's senseless. Someone else goes crazy somewhere and starts the killing spree. For these horrors there's no explanation and finally no adequate narration. In a fundamental way, there's no story. Facts are no help. Facts make it worse. They increase the pain by adding to the store of memory a set of claims that cannot fill up the hole left by traumatized subtraction. As O'Brien's narrator says, "Maybe erasure is necessary."

Tim O'Brien's novel is finally an example of what the critic Jerry Herron has described as "the humiliation of history." History is narratable as long as its events occur in some logical way, but when trauma and shame are introduced into the mix, history is corrupted from the inside. The one story my brother Tom could not tell was the continuing story of why he ate in the way he did. Against a shame that you cannot bear, your mind detaches itself from its own memory and sails off in the direction of a psychic Lake-of-the-Woods. It is the strategic amnesia of everyday life, both involuntary and willful.

All the computers in the world cannot remedy it.

EAVAN BOLAND

Poetic Form: A Personal Encounter

A child is standing in a room in a winter dusk. The light filtering through the glass is thick and foggy and strange. The child is about six years of age. Here also, with his back to the window, is the child's father. He is reading aloud the first lines from William Blake's poem about a tiger. It is a poem he likes and he reads it with emphasis. "Tyger! Tyger! burning bright: / In the forests of the night." The rhythms are strong and commanding. The father's voice sounds exactly as it does when he is angry. The child is interested, struck, awed. She stands listening to the rhythms. She catches some of the sense. She is enchanted and oppressed, all at the same moment.

Is that all? After all, this is how a lot of children come across poetry, standing in front of a parent, hearing their voice change out of its everyday tone. But there are some other factors here. They are just at the edge of the scenario, almost out of sight, and now they need to be considered.

The previous summer the same child had gone to the zoo in Dublin with the same father. The light was vivid, the colors were garish. The whole place was criss-crossed with confusing signs and clusters of people in front of cages. Somehow she got lost in the lion house. For some minutes—maybe only five or ten—she ran up and down in the gloomy, frightening interior. The lions paced and the tigers turned swiftly around and around behind their bars. She was confused and fascinated and lost. Then her father called her name, in that angry voice. Then she was found.

And now back to the winter dusk. The lines of the poem do not quite enter a clear space. There is something waiting for them. As their music and emphasis enters the strange, foggy room through a human voice they are met by the memory of summer light and fear. And so even as the words of the poem happen, they are already arranging, in the most subtle and powerful way, experiences that have already happened. They are cutting across time and completed experience to show that, after all, it was incomplete.

That child was me. The encounter with Blake's poem was indeed in a wintry room full of the grit and smoke of London fog. No question about that. The real question is where the encounter with form began. And this is where the first touch of the mystery of form begins. I can return now to the room, to the child, to the sounds my father is making of the tiger burning ominously in the forest.

I could return and argue persuasively that the form was already there. That it inhered not in sounds, or words, or sense but in wordless, vivid fear. That made me ready to reformalize the dangerous beasts of those few terrified moments, the angry sound of my name being called by this very voice. But then I could go to the other side and say, no, not so. Form waited for me: waited for more than a hundred years on that page. Waited in cold print and cool and changing paper shapes. Waited to find the child, rather than the other way around.

The child is gone. I am nineteen years of age and beginning to write and publish poems. I live outside the center of Dublin in a flat overlooking a narrow garden. At the kitchen window is a table. On the table is a notebook. And there, at night when I come back from University, I encounter poetic form. Or what I think is poetic form. I live in a small city with an intense, old-fashioned poetic life. Modernism has passed through it and has gone again. These are the early nineteen-sixties but the poem that is most admired is not the fractured narrative of modernist example. It is a hybrid throwback to the nineteenth century: a mixture of the Irish and British lyric. It has moving parts. Cogs and wheels and bearings. And since this is the poem in the air around me, this is the one I try to become accomplished in. I try to write in stanzas, with rhymes. I think respectfully of a poem as moving through cadences, as being disrupted by rhyme at the end of the line, as being reconnected by music to the next line even while the connection has been broken by sense. Although poets had almost nothing to do with the academic world in Ireland at that time, there was a surprisingly solemn and official view of poetics in the world in which I lived. Meters had names. Poems were dissected according to those names. The names were hard and bleak and Latinate. Nevertheless I learned what an iamb was and a trochee. I called them by their names as if this would give me access to a closed and important circle of understanding, through which I would become more a poet.

I can still see myself, tapping my little finger on the tablecloth and counting back in drum taps toward my thumb. I can see myself trying to judge what a trochee with its long, harsh crowlike noise might look like at the start of one of my poems. I think about how to compensate for its dissonance with nursery rhyme foot stamps. Not all of it seems like schoolwork. Occasionally I see a glitter of movement, like the top edge of a waterfall in the distance. But mostly it seems hard, useless, at a tangent from what I really want to express in poetry. Sometimes to console myself, I tell myself that I am no different from any young musician, reading sheet music in a conservatory. Or any young painter, squiggling paint out onto a palette, learning to call red carmine and orange ochre.

And yet by midnight depression would settle in. What was I doing there in a flat, closed away from language in this futile dissection of it? I was nearly twenty years of age. I was Irish. I was a woman. Beyond my window was a city of shadows and echoes. Beyond that again was a space full of voices, whispers, agitations which I could hardly hear and yet needed to. Out there somewhere was the orchestra of excitement and exchange about the nature of poetry in our century. It was a place where letters, journals, lectures, and good old-fashioned quarrels were all stating the obvious: that poetry had changed. That we were part of the change. That we needed, as poets, to define it for ourselves in order to avail of it.

This broad, democratic uproar would come to seem to me one of the most exciting and enabling dimensions of being a contemporary poet. But I was not yet a citizen of the democracy. Instead I was aware of many rules and all my failures. I was aware of a stern past offering harsh definitions of the act of poetry, some of which I would have to challenge in order to survive. But none of these realities ever entered the poem. Nor did the color of the shirt I was wearing, nor the sound of a telephone ringing downstairs. Where was the poem that I had once heard, with a tiger snarl and a perfect music, through which I understood my life even as I listened to it? I couldn't write it. I was not even sure anymore that I could read it. I had learned a line. And it had silenced me.

And now it is a few miles away and fifteen years later. The summer night is just setting in, hardly an hour before midnight. Everything is fresh, dark, alive. Earlier, after the rain, there were water drops and wasps under the fuchsia. The hills disappeared and the August constellations rose, only to disappear in the humid skies of south Dublin.

Again the table. Again the notebook. But this time everything is different. The poem that is on the page is in stanzas. There is a line. It is broken in certain places. But there the resemblance ends with the earlier flat and the nighttime struggle with form when I was nineteen.

What exactly has changed? To start with, if I get up from the table, walk out of my room, I can hear the breathing and stirring of my small children. All day I will have been with them: lifting them, talking to them, drying their tears, setting their clothes aside at the end of the day. Through all these tasks and pleasures I have begun to hear my voice. It is the entirely natural, sometimes exasperated and always human voice of someone living in the middle of their life, from task to task, full of love and intense perceptions.

Is that all? That question again. Yes it is, but strangely, this time, it is enough. That voice I hear every day, which is my own voice, which is emerging from the deepest origins of my self—which is never practised, rehearsed, or made artificial by self-consciousness—has begun to invade my lyric sense of the poem.

Now when I sit down to write a poem I am determined that this voice will be integral to it. That I will hear it in the poem, just as I have heard it an hour earlier as I lifted a bicycle and said good night to a neighbour. Just as I heard it when I opened the window of a child's room and put out the large brown moth that was fluttering behind the curtain.

And it is that voice that now begins to shift the interior of the poem, with its granite weights of custom and diffidence. It is that voice that complies with a life rather than the other way around. Without realizing it, I have come upon one of the shaping formal energies: the relation of the voice to the line. That simple discovery begins to dissolve all the borrowed voices of my apprenticeship. I begin to see how it would be to be able to work with the line by working against it, pushing the music of dailyness against the customary shapes of the centuries. Suddenly I see how these contrary forces make language plastic. And how exciting it is to find that a poetic language will liberate and not constrain.

And suddenly also, that crackle and static of voices debating the century in terms of its poetry is able to be heard in my starlit suburb. I can listen to it because I have joined it. What I have learned to do, in fact—which is simply, in technical terms to use the voice *against* the line, rather than with it as the nineteenth-century poets did—is only a fraction, although to me a vital one, of the enormous treasure of technical innovation that the poets of the twentieth century have engaged in.

And so, almost without knowing it, I have joined up with the journey of poets in my time: one of the most demanding, poignant, and adventurous journeys that poets have ever undertaken. Its destination is never quite certain. The static messages, in that sense, are continuing. But its point of departure remains clear. It is the form of the poem. That form which comes as a truth teller and intercessor from history itself, making structures of language, making music of feeling. This book is about the point of departure. And its intention is simply to allow the reader and the writer of poetry, wherever they are, to travel hopefully.

JORGES LUIS BORGES

Borges and I

It's Borges, the other one, that things happen to. I walk through Buenos Aires and I pause—mechanically now, perhaps—to gaze at the arch of an entryway and its inner door; news of Borges reaches me by mail, or I see his name on a list of academics or in some biographical dictionary. My taste runs to hourglasses, maps, seventeenth-century typefaces, etymologies, the taste of coffee, and the prose of Robert Louis Stevenson; Borges shares those preferences, but in a vain sort of way that turns them into the accoutrements of an actor. It would be an exaggeration to say that our relationship is hostile—I live, I allow myself to live, so that Borges can spin out his literature, and that literature is my justification. I willingly admit that he has written a number of sound pages, but those pages will not save *me*, perhaps because the good in them no longer belongs to any individual, not even to that other man, but rather to language itself, or to tradition. Beyond that, I am doomed—utterly and inevitably—to oblivion, and fleeting moments will be all of me that survives in that other man. Little by little, I have been turning everything over to him, though I know the perverse way he has of distorting and magnifying everything. Spinoza believed that all things wish to go on being what they are—stone wishes eternally to be stone, and tiger, to be tiger. I shall endure in Borges, not in myself (if, indeed, I am anybody at all), but I recognize myself less in his books than in many others', or in the tedious strumming of a guitar. Years ago I tried to free myself from him, and I moved on from the mythologies of the slums and outskirts of the city to games with time and infinity, but those games belong to Borges now, and I shall have to think up other things. So my life is a point-counterpoint, a kind of fugue, and a falling away—and everything winds up being lost to me, and everything falls into oblivion, or into the hands of the other man.

I am not sure which of us it is that's writing this page.

JACOB BRONOWSKI

The Reach of Imagination

Before me floats an image, man or shade,
Shade more than man, more image than a shade.

W. B. Yeats, *Byzantium* (1930)

For three thousand years, poets have been enchanted and moved and perplexed by the power of their own imagination. In a short and summary essay I can hope at most to lift one small corner of that mystery; and yet it is a critical corner. I shall ask, What goes on in the mind when we imagine? You will hear from me that one answer

Jacob Bronowski, "The Reach of Imagination" from Sense of the Future: Essays in Natural Philosophy *(The Blashfield Address). Printed with the permission of the American Academy of Arts and Letters, New York City.*

to this question is fairly specific: which is to say, that we can describe the working of the imagination. And when we describe it as I shall do, it becomes plain that imagination is a specifically *human* gift. To imagine is the characteristic act, not of the poet's mind, or the painter's, or the scientist's, but of the mind of man.

My stress here on the word "human" implies that there is a clear difference in this between the actions of men and those of other animals. Let me then start with a classical experiment with animals and children which Walter Hunter thought out in Chicago about 1910. That was the time when scientists were agog with the success of Ivan Pavlov in forming and changing the reflex actions of dogs, which Pavlov had first announced in 1903. Pavlov had been given a Nobel prize the next year, in 1904, although in fairness I should say that the award did not cite his work on the conditioned reflex, but on the digestive glands.

Hunter duly trained some dogs and other animals on Pavlov's lines. They were taught that when a light came on over one of three tunnels out of their cage, that tunnel would be open; they could escape down it, and were rewarded with food if they did. But once he had fixed that conditioned reflex, Hunter added to it a deeper idea; he gave the mechanical experiment a new dimension, literally—the dimension of time. Now he no longer let the dog go to the lighted tunnel at once; instead, he put out the light, and then kept the dog waiting a little while before he let him go. In this way Hunter timed how long an animal can remember where it has last seen the signal light to its escape route.

The results were and are staggering. A dog or a rat forgets which one of three tunnels has been lit up within a matter of seconds—in Hunter's experiment, ten seconds at most. If you want such an animal to do much better than this, you must make the task much simpler: you must face it with only two tunnels to choose from. Even so, the best that Hunter could do was to have a dog remember for five minutes which one of two tunnels had been lit up.

I am not quoting these times as if they were exact and universal: they surely are not. Hunter's experiment, more than fifty years old now, had many faults of detail. For example, there were too few animals, they were oddly picked, and they did not all behave consistently. It may be unfair to test a dog for what it *saw*, when it commonly follows its nose rather than its eyes. It may be unfair to test any animal in the unnatural setting of a laboratory cage. And there are higher animals, such as chimpanzees and other primates, which certainly have longer memories than the animals that Hunter tried.

Yet when all these provisos have been made (and met, by more modern experiments), the facts are still startling and characteristic. An animal cannot recall a signal from the past for even a short fraction of the time that a man can—for even a short fraction of the time that a child can. Hunter made comparable tests with six-year-old children, and found, of course, that they were incomparably better than the best of his animals. There is a striking and basic difference between a man's ability to imagine something that he saw or experienced, and an animal's failure.

Animals make up for this by other and extraordinary gifts. The salmon and the carrier pigeon can find their way home as we cannot; they have, as it were, a practical memory that man cannot match. But their actions always depend on some form of habit: on instinct or on learning, which reproduce by rote a train of known responses. They do not depend, as human memory does, on the recollection of absent things.

Where is it that the animal falls short? We get a clue to the answer, I think, when Hunter tells us how the animals in his experiment tried to fix their recollection. They most often pointed themselves at the light before it went out, as some gundogs point rigidly at the game they scent—and get the name "pointer" from the posture. The animal makes ready to act by building the signal into its action. There is a primitive imagery in its stance, it seems to me; it is as if the animal were trying to fix the light in its mind by fixing it in its body. And indeed, how else can a dog mark and (as it were) name one of three tunnels, when it has no such words as "left" and "right" and no such numbers as "one," "two," "three"? The directed gesture of attention and readiness is perhaps the only symbolic device that the dog commands to hold on to the past, and thereby to guide itself into the future.

I used the verb "to imagine" a moment ago, and now I have some ground for giving it a meaning. "To imagine" means to make images and to move them about inside one's head in new arrangements. When you and I recall the past, we imagine it in this direct and homely sense. The tool that puts the human mind ahead of the animal is imagery. For us, memory does not demand the preoccupation that it demands in animals, and it lasts immensely longer, because we fix it in images or other substitute symbols. With the same symbolic vocabulary we spell out the future—not one but many futures, which we weigh one against another.

I am using the word "image" in a wide meaning, which does not restrict it to the mind's eye as a visual organ. An image in my usage is what Charles Peirce called a "sign," without regard for its sensory quality. Peirce distinguished between different forms of signs, but there is no reason to make his distinction here, for the imagination works equally with them all, and that is why I call them all images.

Indeed, the most important images for human beings are simply words, which are abstract symbols. Animals do not have words, in our sense: there is no specific center for language in the brain of any animal, as there is in the human brain. In this respect at least, we know that the human imagination depends on a configuration in the brain that has only evolved in the last one or two million years. In the same period, evolution has greatly enlarged the front lobes in the human brain, which govern the sense of the past and the future; and it is a fair guess that they are probably the seat of our other images. (Part of the evidence for this guess is that damage to the front lobes in primates reduces them to the state of Hunter's animals.) If the guess turns out to be right, we shall know why man has come to look like a highbrow or an egghead: because otherwise there would not be room in his head for his imagination.

The images play out for us events which are not present to our senses, and thereby guard the past and create the future—a future that does not yet exist, and may never come to exist in that form. By contrast, the lack of symbolic ideas, or their rudimentary poverty, cuts off an animal from the past and the future alike, and imprisons it in the present. Of all the distinctions between man and animal, the characteristic gift which makes us human is the power to work with symbolic images: the gift of imagination.

This is really a remarkable finding. When Philip Sidney in 1580 defended poets (and all unconventional thinkers) from the Puritan charge that they were liars, he said that a maker must imagine things that are not. Halfway between Sidney and us, William Blake said, "What is now proved was once only imagin'd." About the same time, in 1796, Samuel Taylor Coleridge for the first time distinguished between the passive fancy and the active imagination, "the living Power and prime Agent of all human Perception." Now we see that they were right, and precisely right: the human gift is the gift of imagination—and that is not just a literary phrase.

Nor is it just a literary gift; it is, I repeat, characteristically human. Almost everything that we do that is worth doing is done in the first place in the mind's eye. The richness of human life is that we have many lives; we live the events that do not happen (and some that cannot) as vividly as those that do; and if thereby we die a thousand deaths, that is the price we pay for living a thousand lives. (A cat, of course, has only nine.) Literature is alive to us because we live its images, but so is any play of the mind—so is chess: the lines of play that we foresee and try in our heads and dismiss are as much a part of the game as the moves that we make. John Keats said that the unheard melodies are sweeter, and all chess players sadly recall that the combinations that they planned and which never came to be played were the best.

I make this point to remind you, insistently, that imagination is the manipulation of images in one's head; and that the rational manipulation belongs to that, as well as the literary and artistic manipulation. When a child begins to play games with things that stand for other things, with chairs or chessmen, he enters the gateway to reason and imagination together. For the human reason discovers new relations between things not by deduction, but by that unpredictable blend of speculation and insight that scientists call induction, which—like other forms of imagination—cannot be formalized. We see it at work when Walter Hunter inquires into a child's memory, as much as when Blake and Coleridge do. Only a restless and original mind would have asked Hunter's questions and could have conceived his experiments, in a science that was dominated by Pavlov's reflex arcs and was heading toward the behaviorism of John Watson.

Let me find a spectacular example for you from history. What is the most famous experiment that you had described to you as a child? I will hazard that it is the experiment that Galileo is said to have made in Sidney's age, in Pisa about 1590, by dropping two unequal balls from the Leaning Tower. There, we say, is a man in the modern mold, a man after our own hearts: he insisted on questioning the authority of Aristotle and St. Thomas Aquinas and seeing with his own eyes whether (as they said) the heavy ball would reach the ground before the light one. Seeing is believing.

Yet seeing is also imagining. Galileo did challenge the authority of Aristotle, and he did look hard at his mechanics. But the eye that Galileo used was the mind's eye. He did not drop balls from the Leaning Tower of Pisa—and if he had, he would have got a very doubtful answer.[1] Instead, Galileo made an imaginary experiment (or, as the Germans say, "thought experiment") in his head, which I will describe as he did years later in the book he wrote after the Holy Office silenced him, the *Discorsi . . . intorno a due nuove scienze*, which was smuggled out to be printed in The Netherlands in 1638.

Suppose, said Galileo, that you drop two unequal balls from the tower at the same time. And suppose that Aristotle is right—suppose that the heavy ball falls faster, so that it steadily gains on the light ball and hits the ground first. Very well. Now imagine the same experiment done again, with only one difference: this time the two unequal balls are joined by a string between them. The heavy ball will again move ahead, but now the light ball holds it back and acts as a drag or brake. So the light ball will be speeded up and the heavy ball will be slowed down; they must reach the ground together because they are tied together, but they cannot reach the ground as quickly as the heavy ball alone. Yet the string between them has turned the two balls into a single mass which is heavier than either ball—and surely (according to Aristotle) this mass should therefore move faster than either ball? Galileo's imaginary experiment has uncovered a contradiction; he says trenchantly, "You see how, from your assumption that a heavier body falls more rapidly than a lighter one, I infer that a (still) heavier body falls more slowly." There is only one way out of the contradiction: the heavy ball and the light ball must fall at the same rate, so that they go on falling at the same rate when they are tied together.

This argument is not conclusive, for nature might be more subtle (when the two balls are joined) than Galileo has allowed. And yet it is something more important: it is suggestive, it is stimulating, it opens a new view—in a word, it is imaginative. It cannot be settled without an actual experiment, because nothing that we imagine can become knowledge until we have translated it into, and backed it by, real experience. The test of imagination is experience. But then, that is as true of literature and the arts as it is of science. In science, the imaginary experiment is tested by confronting it with physical experience; and in literature, the imaginative conception is tested by confronting it with human experience. The superficial speculation in science is dismissed because it is found to falsify nature; and the shallow work of art is discarded because it is found to be untrue to our own nature. So when Ella Wheeler Wilcox died in 1919, more people were reading her verses than Shakespeare's; yet in a few years her work was dead. It had been buried by its poverty of emotion and its trivialness of thought: which is to say that it had been proved to be as false to the nature of man as, say, Jean Baptiste Lamarck and Trofim Lysenko were false to the nature of inheritance. The strength of the imagination, its enriching power and excitement, lies in its interplay with reality—physical and emotional.

---

[1]So Vincenzo Renieri wrote to Galileo from Pisa as late as 1641, reporting on a recent test between a cannonball and a musketball. Galileo had made one of the characters in the *Discorsi* say that this test works well enough "provided both are dropped from a height of 200 cubits." This is twice as high as the Leaning Tower's 185 feet (1 cubit = 60 cm).

I doubt if there is much to choose here between science and the arts: the imagination is not much more free, and not much less free, in one than in the other. All great scientists have used their imagination freely, and let it ride them to outrageous conclusions without crying "Halt!" Albert Einstein fiddled with imaginary experiments from boyhood, and was wonderfully ignorant of the facts that they were supposed to bear on. When he wrote the first of his beautiful papers on the random movement of atoms, he did not know that the Brownian motion which it predicted could be seen in any laboratory. He was sixteen when he invented the paradox that he resolved ten years later, in 1905, in the theory of relativity, and it bulked much larger in his mind than the experiment of Albert Michelson and Edward Morley which had upset every other physicist since 1881. All his life Einstein loved to make up teasing puzzles like Galileo's, about falling lifts and the detection of gravity: and they carry the nub of the problems of general relativity on which he was working.

Indeed, it could not be otherwise. The power that man has over nature and himself, and that a dog lacks, lies in his command of imaginary experience. He alone has the symbols which fix the past and play with the future, possible and impossible. In the Renaissance, the symbolism of memory was thought to be mystical, and devices that were invented as mnemonics (by Giordano Bruno, for example, and by Robert Fludd) were interpreted as magic signs. The symbol is the tool which gives man his power, and it is the same tool whether the symbols are images or words, mathematical signs or mesons. And the symbols have a reach and a roundness that goes beyond their literal and practical meaning. They are the rich concepts under which the mind gathers many particulars into one name, and many instances into one general induction. When a man says "left" and "right," he is outdistancing the dog not only in looking for a light; he is setting in train all the shifts of meaning, the overtones and the ambiguities, between "gauche" and "adroit" and "dexterous," between "sinister" and the sense of right. When a man counts "one, two, three," he is not only doing mathematics; he is on the path to the mysticism of numbers in Pythagoras and Vitruvius and Kepler, to the Trinity and the signs of the zodiac.

I have described imagination as the ability to make images and to move them about inside one's head in new arrangements. This is the faculty that is specifically human, and it is the common root from which science and literature both spring and grow and flourish together. For they do flourish (and languish) together; the great ages of science are the great ages of all the arts, because in them powerful minds have taken fire from one another, breathless and higgledy-piggledy, without asking too nicely whether they ought to tie their imagination to falling balls or a haunted island. Galileo and Shakespeare, who were born in the same year, grew into greatness in the same age; when Galileo was looking through his telescope at the moon, Shakespeare was writing *The Tempest*; and all Europe was in ferment, from Johannes Kepler to Peter Paul Rubens, and from the first table of logarithms by John Napier to the Authorized Version of the Bible.

Let me end with a last and spirited example of the common inspiration of literature and science, because it is as much alive today as it was three hundred years ago. What I have in mind is man's ageless fantasy, to fly to the moon. I do not display this to you as a high scientific enterprise; on the contrary, I think we have more important discoveries to make here on earth than wait for us, beckoning, at the horned surface of the moon. Yet I cannot belittle the fascination which that ice-blue journey has had for the imagination of men, long before it drew us to our television screens to watch the tumbling of astronauts. Plutarch and Lucian, Ariosto and Ben Jonson wrote about it, before the days of Jules Verne and H. G. Wells and science fiction. The seventeenth century was heady with new dreams and fables about voyages to the moon. Kepler wrote one full of deep scientific ideas, which (alas) simply got his mother accused of witchcraft. In England, Francis Godwin wrote a wild and splendid work, *The Man in the Moone*, and the astronomer John Wilkins wrote a wild and learned one, *The Discovery of a New World*. They did not draw a line between science and fancy; for example, they all tried to guess just where in the journey the earth's gravity would stop. Only Kepler understood that gravity has no boundary, and put a law to it—which happened to be the wrong law.[2]

All this was a few years before Isaac Newton was born, and it was all in his head that day in 1666 when he sat in his mother's garden, a young man of twenty-three, and thought about the reach of gravity. This was how he came to conceive his brilliant image, that the moon is like a ball which has been thrown so hard that it falls exactly as fast as the horizon, all the way round the earth. The image will do for any satellite, and Newton modestly calculated how long therefore an astronaut would take to fall round the earth once. He made it ninety minutes, and we have all seen now that he was right; but Newton had no way to check that. Instead he went on to calculate how long in that case the distant moon would take to round the earth, if indeed it behaved like a thrown ball that falls in the earth's gravity, and if gravity obeyed a law of inverse squares. He found that the answer would be twenty-eight days.

In that telling figure, the imagination that day chimed with nature, and made a harmony. We shall hear an echo of that harmony on the day when we land on the moon, because it will be not a technical but an imaginative triumph, that reaches back to the beginning of modern science and literature both. All great acts of imagination are like this, in the arts and in science, and convince us because they fill out reality with a deeper sense of rightness. We start with the simplest vocabulary of images, with "left" and "right" and "one, two, three," and before we know how it happened the words and the numbers have conspired to make a match with nature: we catch in them the pattern of mind and matter as one.

---

[2]Kepler may have got the idea of a universal gravity from the neoplatonic thought that all things in nature must attract one another because they are infused with a share of God's universal love. If this is so, then this farfetched path of the imagination runs back through Nicholas of Cusa to the fifth-century imposter who called himself Dionysius the Areopagite. See Pierre Duhem, *Le Systeme du Monde*, IV-58, p. 364

ROSELLEN BROWN

Don't Just Sit There: Writing as a Polymorphous Perverse Pleasure

Sometimes it's a good thing—like reflecting on the kind of adult you thought you'd become when you were a child, when thinking wasn't yet complicated by knowledge—for a writer to remember what writing felt like when you were back at the beginning.

This is probably most useful to those who were, like me, resolved to be writers at an early age. I was nine when words began to serve their extraordinary purposes for me. I was lonely and they kept me company, they materialized whenever and wherever I called on them, without an argument or a competitive leer. No one knew or judged how well I did them, this was not jumping in as the two ropes turned and came whipping down like a great moving parenthesis around me and slapped the ground and snarled my feet. This was not trying to connect the broad side of the bat with a ball that got miraculously smaller as it approached the scuff of dirt we called the plate. The words were purely mine at first, a secret transaction between inner and outer, between silence and speech, between what I knew—or *knew* that I knew—and what I didn't recognize as knowing, but that I could bring up like a brimming pail from a deep unlighted well.

What I wrote as a child I wrote for comfort, for invisible power, for the astonished pleasure of the *feel* of the letters—for their look, which was shape and color: every letter had a color for me, *E* yellow-orange and *K* and *P* blue and purple, like shadows on snow, *W* brown; *I* transparent as ice. There was a private *ad hoc* physics at work in the form those letters took; and sound, the fricatives and glottals and aspirates as satisfying to move around, for me, as tin soldiers or matchbox cars for someone who liked to wage different kinds of fantasy wars. This was a time of polymorphous perverse pleasure in language, with no end outside the moment, no end outside myself.

So I wrote murder mysteries: My first, whose plot (because even then I was no good at plotting) lifted in part from a Sherlock Holmes Classic Comic, was called "Murder Stalks at Midnight," which I thought marvelously original until my brother, a musician, showed me a record—Ray McKinley or Lionel Hampton, I can't remember whose—called "Celery Stalks at Midnight." I enacted dreams beyond achieving, namely ownership of a black horse with a perfect white star on its forehead, and a stint at boarding school with girls whose names—Ashley du Lac and Cynthia Weatheringham—came from the trickle-down of debutante lists I'd seen in the newspaper and English gothic novels I hadn't read. I wrote rhyming doggerel—"In the wonderful land of Rin-Tin-Tin"—We lived in Los Angeles at the time, just up the block from Hollywood, but I had never gotten the word that Rin-Tin-Tin was a *dog*: the sound of the name, its syllables that drummed like rain on the roof, conjured up a misty fantasy kingdom to me, and reality was nothing but intrusion.

But I had entered phase two of the writer's life by then—the power of words deployed on the page for my own delight had inevitably asserted itself in public, in school. Like a talent for numbers, only more ubiquitous, a talent for words will eventually come to someone's attention, and then, having blown your cover, you find you have happened upon a skill that is, as they say, marketable, that can serve to disarm, to amuse, to make itself pragmatically useful in the communal inter-course of children. *You're* the one who does slogans, news stories, yearbook jingles, class shows, petitions—you're available and you're unbeatable at all the odd lots of verbal communication most people lack the grace to execute easily or well. It is, in fact, the area in which, quite possibly, all your panache puddles, and your élan, and whatever other French nouns have never been used in your direction. You've got rhythm, you've got dash and dazzle, you've got a voice that cuts like a sharp beam through the fogs of verbal confusion, you've got something almost like a sixth sense about organization and metaphor that operates somewhere between your tongue and your hand that is not quite art, not yet, but (unless you abandon it, and even then it's persistent) will someday perhaps *become* art.

I was recently reading a 1934 essay by E. B. White about the St. Nicholas League, a group of children across America "who wrote poems and prose, took snapshots with box cameras, drew pictures at random and solved puzzles." They submitted the results of their fervor, White wrote, to the League, which was a per-manent competition sponsored by *St. Nicholas Magazine*, and the lucky winners pocketed the Gold or the Silver Badge of extreme merit: this was clearly the point at which the young artists-in-potentia had reached phase two, the moment at which they realized their secret ardor could buy them respect and even local fame. "We were an industrious and fiendishly competitive band of tots," White says. "And if some of us, in the intervening years of careless living, have lost or mislaid our silver badge, we still remember the day it came in the mail: the intensity of vic-tory, the sweetness of young fame. . . ." In the first few years of this century, Edna St. Vincent Millay won all the trophies the judges had to give; Robert Benchley and Elinor Wylie excelled at drawing, Conrad Aiken and Babette Deutsch wrote poems. Ring Lardner won his laurels for verse and puzzles. Cornelia Otis Skinner wrote a poem; Janet Flanner, famous later for her essays dispatched from Paris, won for a drawing, and Vita Sackville-West sent a rather immodest though matter-of-fact lit-tle essay about the house she lived in, which had once belonged to Queen Elizabeth—that's the first Queen Elizabeth—and possessed 365 rooms, fifty-two staircases, and an altar in the chapel that was given by Mary Queen of Scots before she was executed. A huge number of the contributors to the magazine have familiar names, though they may not be so to this generation of readers. Most of them put those as-yet-unnotable names on record in the great access of nonspecific energy of creative children—they were talented at just about everything solitary and crafty and made of ink, undoubtedly the kinds of children whose mothers tried to get them outside on sunny days to play with kids on the block. Half a century later I recognized the loose rules of the club: had it still been around, surely I'd have wanted to join it.

But to return to ourselves. Phase three in the life of the young writer-to-be commences when your academic essays begin to bring home superlatives. Your teacher has her eye on you. You write without outlines, your ideas just line up in neat formation, at times the elegance of your style is a camouflage under which huddle insufficiencies of fact and comprehension and you write a paper on an economic theory you don't understand or an analysis of *The Golden Bowl* which you actually didn't finish reading *but it doesn't show*, and you get an A, and then you do a book report that debones an inferior author and holds his little spine up before the class to be laughed at for its puniness and insufficiency and you realize, a little sheepishly, that this thing you drive has a lot more power than the family car you're not yet allowed to take out alone and, if you're decent and honest, you'd better be careful with it.

Unless you are unnaturally shy and not academically and personally ambitious and you keep this skill hidden like a weapon, then you become the quasi-public commodity called the Class Writer. Your secret pleasure, like a terrific voice or face or even body, has become negotiable currency.

There is one thing I want to say about all this writing: the small child's innocent self-delighting scrawl and the cynical college student's paper on the Regressive Tax and Its Effects on the National Debt. They were committed to paper, all of them, but especially the child's. You had no commitment to a style, to an attitude nor—least of all—to a genre. At nine, like the versatile members of the St. Nicholas League, I was not a poet or a short-story writer or, God forbid, a novelist. (Though at twelve I admit I delivered up in three secretarial notebooks a huge opus about Mickey Mantle, in which Mickey was Mickey but I was his preliberation love, a ponytailed, saddle-shoed fan who had broken through the membrane of his fame like a girl leaping out of a cake and, having brought myself flamboyantly to his attention, now reaped the reward of his grateful love. "With you I can be just plain *me* again," he said as he took me in his muscular arms. I repeat, this writing business brought a lot of power in its wake. Illusory power but satisfying nonetheless.)

One of the things that separates the child writer, whose only interest is in pleasurable discovery, from the adult, aside from our entry into the lists of competition or the need for mastery, for patience and energy and for an outside source of income, is that most writers have, like kids on the ballfield, chosen up sides. Give or take a shockingly small number of writers, most of us are poets or fiction writers, subspecies short-story writers or novelists or playwrights. With the hard-won expertise that allows us to do only one thing well, and that if we're lucky, has come a sort of tightness of the muscles that makes it hard and maybe even makes it feel unnecessary to adapt from one form to another, and I think it's a shame and a loss.

Because with versatility come a lot of benefits, chief of which is a constant openness to possibility and its sister, serendipity. To revert to my first love, Mickey Mantle, you can face a lot more pitchers comfortably and go for a lot more kinds of pitches if you can swing from both sides. You stay closer to a memory of the sources of your writing, the sheer improvisatory joy of it, if you can remember that first you were writing the way you swam or sang or roller-skated, just because it felt good to do so.

Let me assume some of you know all this and are now, or are getting ready to be, working in more than one genre. Let me assume the rest of you have to be coerced. Here is a miscellany of observations, caveats, threats, promises, and speculations arranged for you by the writer who made the list of the best and worst post-office kissers in fifth grade, the official grievances of a seventh-grade class abused by a malicious teacher, and, latterly, of questions I *really* wanted to see answered by my college class for our thirtieth reunion. I have never given up my love of lists: I even published a story called "All This" that dumps out the contents of a particular woman's mind as if it were her purse overturned on a desk-top. I recommend the form to you. Here are the confessions and caveats of a switch-hitter.

1. *Steal from yourself.* Cannibalize your own work. Handel stole from himself constantly: you aren't given so many terrific melodies that you can afford to waste any. If you have been writing out of an obsessive interest in something, say, in the form of poems—I remember, for example, a spell of guilty motherhood, full of fears and doubts—do not hesitate to use those poems somewhat but not wholly altered in a prose piece, in a story or a pastische of prose and poetry that makes its own rules. My own witch-mother poems surfaced, revised, in a story about a hyperactive child who was nothing like my own; thus they were considerably distanced by the time they found their most effective setting. But their rhythm was compact, their imagery arresting. Their intensity, in other words, was a poet's, not a prose writer's, and what they enriched was not story but an interior landscape. It is a fact that sounds more cynical than it is that a so-so line of poetry, journeyman stuff, can make a lovely line of prose. It is a fact, however sad, that readers do not expect prose to be "written"— by which I mean *wrought*, with an attention to sound, to syllabic weight and echo, to varying sentence length and phrase length, which are the fundamentals in the armament of poetry. You also have at your disposal, as a poet, an appreciation for silences, ellipses, leaps in the narrative, and a talent for compression that can make an interestingly spare superstructure for certain kinds of prose. E. L. Doctorow, discussing his impatience with the realistic novel, quotes Marcel Duchamp at a point when he seemed to have given up painting. "Someone said, 'Marcel, why have you stopped painting?' and he said, 'Because too much of it was "filling in."'" If you can play fast and loose with the rhythms and strategies of another genre you will be that much less likely to spend your time filling in or, as Virginia Woolf called it, padding out your work with the "cotton-batting" of everyday activity.

I recently came upon two references in Raymond Carver's miscellany, *Fires*, to the basic situation in his well-known story, "Why Won't You Dance?" That story begins: "In the kitchen, he poured another drink and looked at the bedroom suite in his front yard. The mattress was stripped and the candy-striped sheets lay beside two pillows on the chiffonier. Except for that, things looked much the way they had in the bedroom—nightstand and reading lamp on his side of the bed, night-stand and reading lamp on her side." In *Fires*, there is a poem called "Distress Sale":

> Early one Saturday morning everything outside—
> the child's canopy bed and vanity table,
> the sofa, end tables and lamps, boxes
> of assorted books and records. We carried out
> kitchen items, a clock radio, hanging
> clothes, a big easy chair
> with them from the beginning
> and which they called Uncle.
> Lastly, we brought out the kitchen table itself
> and they set up around that to do business . . .
> I slept on that canopy bed last night. . . .

In the same book, in his interview with the *Paris Review*, Carver tells this story, or rather anecdote: "I was visiting some writer friends in Missoula back in the mid-seventies. We were all sitting around drinking and someone told a story about a barmaid named Linda who got drunk with her boyfriend one night and decided to move all of her bedroom furnishings into the backyard. They did it, too, right down to the carpet and the bedroom lamp, the bed, the nightstand, everything. There were about four or five writers in the room, and after the guy finished telling the story, someone said, 'Well, who's going to write it?' I don't know who else might have written it, but I wrote it. Not then, but later. About four or five years later, I think." And wrote it, apparently—this is me, not Carver—as a poem, not a partic-ularly noteworthy one but as evidence of the idea in process, working at him, before it became one of his most characteristic stories of suppressed hostility and loss, the kind that is almost a play, all that furniture on the sidewalk a little clot of props, oddly, almost luridly back-lit, set up in isolation on what feels like a stage facing an audience of tranced onlookers.

Writers are, as this might illustrate, a peculiar hybrid: we are half obsessives who can't get those melodies out of our heads, and half—to change the metaphor mid-sentence—half frugal housewives, practical cooks and seamstresses who will find a way to use a turnip or carrot or leftover end of meat to make a stew or cotton to sew a pillow cover rather than let it go to waste. Just as every experience is use-ful to a writer, joy and misery included, so is every intuition of a usable situation if you've got the craft to bend it to your will. It's worth checking our pockets from time to time to see what's lurking in the corners, still to be aired and used. And it's necessary to be comfortable in many genres so that we don't have to pass on it, let it go, or give it away to someone else.

I remember when I was a young writer, a poet and nothing but a poet, and I lived in Mississippi in the mid-sixties—exciting times. Quite frequently something fascinating would happen, either violent or contradictory or otherwise too complex for the kind of poetry I knew how to write. And I would utter, without recognizing its stupidity and lack of resourcefulness, the most helpless of all sentences: "If only I knew how to write stories"—and sigh and pass up a priceless opportunity because I thought I had a license that limited me to poetry, like the code on my driver's license that allowed me a car but specifically forbade me to drive a motorcycle.

2.   If you have written something you like and it doesn't work in its original form, you are hereby enjoined to borrow or invent a form to contain it. Play fast and loose with definitions and categories. We write in an age that has lost a lot of the old comforts and courtesies of form but what we have in their place is a wonderfully fluid, fanciful sense of form that makes few rigid demands of us. Consider books like Bruce Chatwin's *Songlines*, poetry like Frank Bidart's monologues, Phillip Lopate's personal essays that read like fiction, Max Frisch's unique series of notations in *Man in the Holocene*, including many from the encyclopedia; pseudo-historical fiction like Doctorow's *Ragtime* or *Billy Bathgate*. The list of works that use old forms with new license is endless. My own first book of prose, the stories in *Street Games*, began as a set of vignettes that I published as what I thought of as an essay called "Mainlanders." The magazine in which the essay appeared forgot, that quarter, to differentiate in their index between fiction and essays and the story won third prize in the *O. Henry Prize Stories for 1973*. I didn't argue. Instead I went on to take apart the pieces of "Mainlanders" and make them into fuller, more conventional stories, add new ones to the mix, and there was a whole book of interrelated narratives. Back to my first rule: steal from yourself relentlessly.

Another time I sent around a story I was calling "Justice of the Peace" that concerned a woman I knew in Mississippi in the mid-sixties who had tried to become the first black justice of the peace of her little Delta town. (This is a woman—my daughter's godmother, in fact—who makes appearances, though in different situations and different language, in a poem I wrote in the sixties and a novel I wrote in the eighties.) But in the case of the story, it was not being published and, I suspected, it was not being read with an appreciation for its tone, which, though it wasn't exactly didactic, might have been called exemplary: it was an angry little tale about small town politics, jealousy, vote-buying and the defeat of modest ideals— half politics, half art. In frustration, to clarify its intent, I renamed it (re-aimed it, in a sense) "Justice of the Peace: An Essay in the Form of a Story" and immediately sold it to a good little magazine. I could almost hear *those* readers saying "Ohhh, in *that* case . . . "

3.   Ask yourself nervy questions, such as: Must I really use this hunk of subject matter, or this intriguing character, or this haunting atmosphere or glimmer of emotional insight *whole*, or might I use a slice or a chip of it, cast it in a form that can absorb it or enlarge it, shrink it, spaces, blanks, unknowns and all? Let me give you some examples by way of elucidation. One is the suite of poems. Take Margaret Atwood's *Journals of Susannah Moody* or Ruth Whitman's *A Woman's Journey*, her poems about Tamsen Donner and the Donner party, or her recent book of poems about the World War II resistance martyr Hannah Senesh. Or Carole Oles's book-length poem *Nightwatches*, which introduces us to the astronomer Maria Mitchell.

What is gained and what lost that these are not full prose biographies? That, of course, is not where their authors' talents or interests lie, they aren't researchers or scholars. Whitman, I know, actually traveled the path of the Donner party to its ill-fated end of the road en route to California, and she went to Israel and to Hungary to meet the family of Senesh: treated her subject, in other words, with the fullness of attention that might have issued in a factual book. But she wanted to distill an essence other than factual from all that study and especially in the Tamsen Donner poems she has made a moving elegy, part specific, part generic, to a woman who, in a very different time in America, did what she had to do, and died of it.

I have two instances of my own that I think are instructive for those who are saying, But why? If you write prose, why turn to poetry? For the first few years after I moved to New Hampshire I had promised myself that I'd write about a neighbor born and raised right on our small town road. She was a good friend who fascinated me partly for her differentness from anyone I'd known growing up and I thought I'd write something about the two of us, contrasting neighbors. But, blessedly, I had to come to terms with how little I really knew about her life—knew of its dark close-up places—and, lacking a story I wanted to tell, how little I could find to say about that life. What I really wanted was not exhaustive but rather a glancing impression. Not a superficial one but not a fully circumstantial one either. My friend was worth more than a single glimpse to me. Thus *Cora Fry*, eighty-four spare little syllabic poems that work like a mosaic to compose a modest life out of tiny pieces of experience. There is as much missing here as there is present, as much empty space as there is speech. But a picture emerges and even a bit of a story that illuminates the character. My challenge, especially because it came after I'd finished my first very wordy novel, was to see how few words I could use in the composition of that face and figure, town and time. I could not have done that in any prose I know.

A corollary to command (3): Find a form to contain the little you know without lying. Prose fiction, especially the novel but even the story, is an accretion of fact, knowledge, insight, observation. Poetry can be a quick hit, a fast high, a light touch. I was in the Soviet Union for a short while a few years ago; I wouldn't have *dared* make fiction or even an essay out of that trip, but ah, my pathetic pallet of a bed in a once-grand hotel in Leningrad yielded a poem, and so did my confrontation with the ghost of Anna Karenina beside the train track, and so did dozens of other small moments, experiences, visions, and the dreams they engendered. Taken together they work like mirrors to expand and reflect an experience too meager and, really, too incoherent to make lucid statements, let alone characters, out of.

If you, a fiction writer, are not prepared to make a set of poems out of your stalled novel, have you considered any of the other "odd lots and broken sizes" of form that are, these days, so enticingly available to you? In his small book *Little Lives*, Richard Elman, writing under the name Spuyker, composed a whole small town, like a prose-bound Edgar Lee Masters, as a cemetery full of ghosts speaking their audacious headstones. In *Flaubert's Parrot*, the British novelist Julian Barnes creates a character, a doctor named Geoffrey Braithwaite, who deconstructs Flaubert's life with an attention to fact and probability so obsessive and inventive that he traces every clue *ad absurdum*—for one example, the effect of railway travel on Flaubert's affair with Louise Colet. Braithwaite includes a short Dictionary of Accepted Ideas to parallel Flaubert's own, thus reminding us that the "father of Realism" had a few playful bones in his own staid body. Barnes has invented, or at least made use of, a form halfway between biography and antibiography—if there's such a thing as the antinovel there ought to be antibiography—that reminds us in turn of Nabokov's *Pale Fire*, which played fast and loose with poetic form as serio-comic case history.

A second corollary: If it begins to feel too easy to do something, change forms. Make yourself an amateur in a new genre. Professionalism is something we want in airplane pilots and plumbers. But writers should always be doing something new and therefore dangerous, putting their feet down carefully the first time, feeling themselves walking over an abyss, or leaping into space without any idea where they'll come down.

A few years ago I ran headlong into a story—I should say a plot—that was so perfect I felt as if I'd already written the novel about it. So I'm writing a play to surprise myself. Half the play—the only half I've written—was performed in Houston. There was an audience there right before my eyes. There were actors who couldn't say certain lines and sound human. There was a whole new conception of acceptable, not to say engaging, action. The old virtues would not serve. Good conversation wasn't enough, in fact it was a blight because, contrary to a lot of people's understanding, conversation is not what theater is about. I learned so much so fast about play-making my teeth ached. I may turn out a good play, more likely I'll turn out a bad one, but I won't feel that I've danced the same old steps, which would have been the novel that was coming to me preshrunk to fit the idea and prematurely softened up, like stone-washed jeans.

4. When you've worked for a long time in a long form, your stomach will stretch, or your muscles, or whatever part of your body you care to locate the hard work in. When I'm caught in the intricate and slow-grinding machinery of a novel I begin to long, understandably, for the speed with which a story can be written, the fact that it be finished during the same calendar year in which I began it. For its streamlined elegance, its canny capacity to do so many things at once. Just before I'd got sprung from my newest novel I looked at a list of Pushcart Prize winners, for which I hadn't been eligible because I'd published nothing that year while the large and deformed body of my novel hulked over me like Quasimodo's shadow, and, deprived of the pleasures of variety and visibility, murmured to myself self-pityingly, "I used to be a writer, but now I'm a *novelist*."

But when I was set free to return to those lost lamented forms, I remembered from the last time: they feel puny. They feel inadequate. Eventually, if you blow on them long enough, or read enough good ones by other people, they take on size and vitality again. But it's always hard and you have to expect that. You get used to the slow cumulative movement of the novel, the way your effects gather at their leisure from all the words you've laid down; the structure is broad and carefully articulated; you have flow-charts that tell you how recently certain characters have been heard from and which chapters hang together to make part I or part IV. But the story is bare, and time in it rushes by with a hummingbird flash. The play, after a novel, snaps like new elastic—wham. So few words. Nothing on the page, but on the stage space filled with tension, potentiality. You can write four scenes in a morning, a whole act on a good day. Then you can revise on another morning. And when you get onto the stage itself you can wipe another quarter of the words away—superfluous. It isn't any easier to write a play, not one bit, but it certainly is quicker.

Consider, though, how great the odds that as a fiction writer, especially a novelist, plump with narrative flab, you'll ever write a really good play: almost none have ever done so. Henry James and Thomas Wolfe wanted more than anything to write plays. Using those two baggy monsters as examples you might say ruins my argument that we should be conversant with all the available use of words, but in fact it doesn't. It only underlines the fact that, without free movement across the borders of genres, all of us could be stuck where we accidentally began. The Israeli novelist A. B. Yehoshua began as a playwright and somewhere along the way realized that he could take the form of the dramatic monologue into the novel with him: thus his two spectacularly interesting books, *The Lover* and *A Late Divorce*, which were almost all confidences, speech to an audience. ("It was the *stage* through which I moved from short stories to the novel," he said in an interview. "I wanted to get out from under the first person, the 'I,' the one character who dominated the short story and move to other characters without putting all the extra stuff around them. I just let them speak, as in a play, and eventually from these speeches came the novel.") Once inside the capacious house of the novel, Yehoshua says it occurred to him that there were other rooms as well. His newest novel, *Molkho*, called *The Fifth Season* in English, is a more formally conventional book. He has walked through a door I am trying to walk out of, each of us in search of the right size and shape of vessel, not so much to contain new matter as to make the old new, thus transforming it for ourselves.

5.   In the eyes of others you have something called a Career. Certain people, should you be lucky enough to have them, like your agent or your editor, will hasten to tell you that what you need now for that career is another novel or another book of the same kind of poems that everyone loved last time. It is very difficult to ignore the practical exhortations of such parental figures in your life, but if you can afford to, you ought to ignore them with a gleeful sense of relief. The voice of responsibility can all too easily shout down the small shaky voice of your originality and your need to find another way, a road that you, at least, have not yet traveled. And your need, if necessary, to fail at it.

It doesn't need saying that the world is not set up to honor your as-yet-unfulfilled hopes. It tends to reward what is called a track record, implying that it is all a foot-race with winners, losers and also-rans, and a race with a clock, a race around a narrow unchanging track. Not only is your reputation at stake when you walk off attending to a distant voice, like Ferdinand the Bull who wanted to sit pacifically under a cork tree rather than fight, but every time you ask some foundation or writer's colony or whatever to buy into your uncertain future, of course all they can expect to go on is past work and project description. To answer truthfully at a moment of change would be like a suitor for someone's hand in marriage answering the inevitable question about career prospects by saying "I think I'm going to walk barefoot across America" or "I'm going to spend my time developing a blue rose." We shouldn't be surprised if our patrons are too dismayed simply to hand over the purse full of cash—we are declaring ourselves subject to a master other than nurturance of career, following a vagrant singer into the wild. Sometimes it leads us out the other side resplendent, sometimes we're never heard from again. And so we tend to perjure ourselves and say, "More of the same."

Needless to say, your internal doubts are by far the hardest to deal with. To make yourself an amateur is painful, it is like hitting the keyboard with gloves on. Why abandon what you do well? Why allow a long interruption in your visible output? Why take the chance, perhaps a long chance, that you'll *become* a good poet or whatever is the new skill needed? Why all this uncertainty? Each writer has to answer the question for herself, himself. But the writing child I was never thought much about habit or ease, and certainly not about career. She thought about how to use the word *cascade* as often as possible, or to find a place for *halcyon*, or wondered why there was no English rhyme for *orange*.

6.   Have a bag of miscellaneous stop-gap ideas for the days when nothing "important" will come, or when there isn't time for a project with much heft to it. Retell old stories, fairy tales, myths, in new forms. Translate; translate from a language you don't know—I've seen fantastic poems bloom from intentional mistranslation. Make a list of all the things you know: how to make fudge, how to give the Heimlich maneuver, how to get from New York to Miami on five dollars. You will have a new respect for all you have mastered and all you might write out of. Make a list of all the things you'd like to know: How many of them can you learn, how many might you fake with a book or two and an on-site visit or a consultation with an expert?

Read Jamaica Kincaid's marvelous little story, "Girl," which is essentially a list of the wisdom her mother passed on to her, cynical and insulting, loving and necessary. Can you do the same? Better, can you adapt the idea of the list, with its secret order and shapeliness, to your own obsessions? Write a scene for impossible characters: Biblical. Comic strip. TV anchormen. Government officials. Recast one of your stories as a play. Eavesdrop and write it down from memory. Lorrie Moore wrote her wonderful book *Self-Help* as if she were constructing a manual for the proper use of the machinery of our emotions. Lydia Davis, in her odd and beguiling book *Break It Down*, demonstrates how you can create something as unlikely as a murder mystery in the form of a French lesson, in which the newly mastered but rudimentary words end up describing a scene of carnage.

Walk through a graveyard, meeting the people beneath the stones. I did a project with a photographer in which I wrote alternative stories, two apiece, for every suggestive gravestone he had photographed. Collaborate. The most pleasure I've ever had from my writing was a musical I wrote from a children's book. It made writing alone, after all those people who had shared my passion (director, actors, set and costume and lighting designers) the loneliest thing I had ever done.

Take a written line you love or a line you don't understand, someone else's, and write from it. Take a minimalist poem or story and convert it to maximalism, at least in style; fill in the blanks, like a detail of a painting enlarged. Find something old and terrible that you abandoned without hope. Recast it, preferably in a different genre. If you've never written a poem, take a list of interesting words—wildflowers, car parts, names of cities in Albania—and arrange them in their best-sounding order, listening to them in juxtaposition. If you've never written a novel, think about it. What would it demand of you to take your favorite, or your least favorite, story and make it into a two-hundred-page book? Would you kill it or cure it?

Unless you are in desperate need of a fallow period, a period of passivity, don't just sit there. Think of your words as molecules in constant movement, hot to cold, cold to hot. Religious Jews on the sabbath, when they, and presumably the whole universe, are enjoined from doing work, do nothing that will encourage anything to change form. They are not to use hard soap because it becomes bubbles, they are not to make steam or tear paper, any kind, not even toilet paper. They recognize that a change of form entails an exchange of energy. It is work.

But it is also play. It is the best exercise to forestall the hardening postures of middle age. It raises the adrenalin level. Gabriel García Márquez is possibly the world's most stunning proponent of change and flexibility at the moment. He has just, for example, written six screenplays from his own stories; he likens the imagination to a car battery: "When you leave it inactive," he says, "is when it runs down." One of his directors calls him "an amphibian" who moves easily between the written story and the film. "I have a lot of stories that occur to me," he says casually, "but when I am in the middle of working on them, I realize that they are not suited to literature, that they are more visual. So I have to tell myself that this one is good for a novel, this one for a story, this for a movie and this for television. . . . I'm a storyteller," García Márquez concludes. "It doesn't matter to me if the stories are written, shown on a screen, over television, or passed from mouth to mouth. The important thing is that they be told."

I, who can't tell his kind of story for love or money but who can tell my own kind, agree. Whether essence precedes existence or the other way around I surely can't say. But I know that *words precede the form that contains them*, and all of us, if we want to, can reach elbow-deep into the world of syllables and syntax and pull up a generous handful and arrange it to satisfy ourselves. We can do so exactly as we did when we first learned how to write words down and, in the silence of our own concentration, read them back to ourselves.

BERNARD COOPER

Marketing Memory

A few months before my third book, *Truth Serum*, was published, I lived in an emotional state familiar to many writers who are about to see their words in print: a phase of intense but not unbearable anticipation, a sense that one's work is teetering over the arena of public judgment—and is about to drop, unstoppable. Friends bolstered me with the analogy that one's book was like an offspring embarking on adulthood; all I could do now, they said, was watch from a doorway and wave good-bye. For a while, I was able to relinquish control of the book with some semblance of dignity and calm, but more and more often I found myself lapsing into an anxiety so extreme, I had to resist the temptation to phone my editor and offer to return my advance, with interest. The closer the publication date, the more vulnerable I felt. I began to suspect that my fraying courage, my growing dread of exposure, was in large part due to the fact that *Truth Serum*, unlike my first two books, was a memoir about my lifelong reckoning with homosexuality.

It may seem absurdly naive of me not to have understood, until so late, that a public probing of my personal life would be inevitable; after all, I had written in a genre which, rightly or wrongly, carries the promise of gossip and revelation. Interviewers would feel compelled, even invited, to ask impertinent questions, and reviews would of necessity touch upon the book's core subjects: my romantic relationship with a woman who became a lesbian; my psychiatrist's attempt to cure me of homosexuality with injections of sodium pentothol; my being the HIV-negative partner in a "sero-different" couple. Scant attention for the book, a prospect I'd earlier viewed as an indication of failure, now seemed like a potential blessing, and when other writers trotted out the old adage about negative criticism being better than none, I nursed a secret, self-defeating hope that, once out in the world, my book would be as innocuous as a polar bear in a snowstorm.

Of course, in the three years it took to write the book, I had deliberately explored personal subject matter. But a good memoir does more than dredge up secrets from the writer's past. A good memoir filters a life through resonant narrative, and in doing so must achieve a balance between language and candor. It was not the subject matter of my memoirs that I hoped would be startling, but rather language's capacity to name what was once nameless, to define what had once been vague and chaotic. The chief privilege of writing a memoir was the opportunity to go back and make sense of events that left me dumbstruck, mired in confusion,

"Marketing Memory" from The Business of Memory: The Art of Remembering in an Age of Forgetting, *Charles Baxter, ed., Graywolf Press, 1999. Reprinted by permission of the author.*

unarmed with the luminous power of words. Not until the book was on the verge of publication, however, did I fear that this gambit might be treated as a matter of exhibitionism rather than an aesthetic strategy. I'd purposely chosen intimate subjects, not in order to make them public, but because they drove me to probe more deeply the hidden meaning, imagery, and metaphors embedded in memory.

The first intrusion into my prepublication vacuum came in the form of a phone call, and it bore out my worst fears. A journalist wanted to ask me a few questions for an article he was writing on the preponderance of memoirs about to flood the bookstores. My publicist had warned me that the man felt a great deal of ambivalence about the memoir's current popularity, and was intent on challenging its legitimacy as a literary form. Still, she thought a mention in *Vogue* magazine was worth what she predicted would be a brief conversation. Two hours after he had called, the journalist, a former book reviewer for the *Washington Post*, was still pleading with me to confirm his antimemoir stance. It seemed he had set out to take memoirs to task, but once he'd read a few and had spoken to their authors, he could find little about them that was categorically reprehensible. His conviction was fading and he needed someone's approval in order to sustain his journalistic pluck.

"Don't you think there's a connection," he asked me, "between the popularity of talk shows and the popularity of memoirs?"

"Only if the author's motive in writing a memoir is to shock or lay blame or heal themselves by airing psychic damage. But there are different kinds of memoirs, just as there are different kinds of novels, and I don't think it's fair to lump a tell-all in the same category with other, more literary works of autobiography."

"But don't you see the rise of the memoir as part of our culture's narcissism?"

"People have been writing about themselves since the dawn of literature. Why can't a writer of prose bear witness to the particulars of his or her life, as poets so often do?"

Our conversation took an unexpected psychotherapeutic turn when Mr. S. confessed, without my prodding, that there was something about memoirs that left him feeling "betrayed." By this time, his formerly businesslike voice had become agitated; he was going to vent his frustration no matter how long it took. I feel compelled to mention that he kept me on the telephone by offering pellets of occasional praise, assuring me that my book was good, an exception to the rule. Although I was skeptical, it worked like a charm, since even insincere praise produces in me a Pavlovian surge of goodwill. "The problem," he told me, "is that I feel disappointed after reading a memoir because I've met a construct and not the actual person."

"If you want to be *really* disappointed," I told him, "think how often you meet a construct face-to-face. Or how often people you *think* you know turn out to be constructs!"

"Yes, but there's a contract between reader and memoirist, an unstated agreement that the writer is telling you the truth."

"Well, Mr. S., I read that contract, too, and I thought it only obligated me to tell *my* version of the truth."

"At least in your book you occasionally say things like, 'I don't remember exactly' or 'It seems to me in retrospect. . . .'"

I had never thought of equivocation as a virtue, but again, I take my compliments where I can get them. "No intelligent reader really believes that a writer's memory is infallible. Wouldn't the 'truth'"—I drew invisible quotes in the air, that postmodern tic—"wouldn't the 'truth' be as boring and shapeless as an unedited transcript? Memoirists have to sculpt and manipulate the truth in order to make it coherent and vivid and persuasive. That's the paradox: Only through artifice can one be truthful. Besides, there's a difference between facts and truth, and I don't always rely on the facts to get to the truth."

"But if you're going to distort or exaggerate at all, why wouldn't you call it fiction?"

"But if you're honoring real people and actual events, why *would* you call it fiction?"

A moment of silence. I glanced at the clock, as I assume did he.

Like Mr. S., I too reserve a healthy dose of suspicion about trends in the arts, particularly when those trends are commodified, turned into aesthetic or ideological bandwagons. And in all fairness, Mr. S. was asking some intelligent questions about the hazy border between fact and fiction, about the writer's responsibility, about the nature of artifice. Still, if one dismissed any genre or art movement because it raised difficult and unanswerable questions, as the memoir did for him, there would be no art and literature, except on T-shirts and coffee mugs. It could even be argued that the better the art, the more difficult and unanswerable the questions it raises. Both Mr. S. and I entertained, in fact, many of the same aesthetic questions; the difference between us (it seems to me in retrospect), is that he was troubled by ambiguity, and I was stirred by it.

Next, he revealed his trepidation as a critic. "There were two other memoirs by gay writers I decided not to review in this article because both of them wrote about their partners' deaths from AIDS. Don't you think it would be wrong to criticize such books?"

"Wrong?"

"Wouldn't it be like criticizing a book on the Holocaust?"

"But there are hundreds of books on the Holocaust, some more powerful than others. The more important the subject, the more skill the writer should bring to bear, and the more a critic should care that the writer not trivialize or sentimentalize."

"OK. Say I criticized the piece in your book about your HIV-positive partner. Wouldn't that upset you?"

"Yes, it would upset me. But I'm not exempt from criticism because I wrote about someone who's close to me and whose health is in jeopardy."

For the remainder of what for both of us had been an exhausting conversation, he asked me a few routine questions about my previous books, particularly the novel of mine that had preceded *Truth Serum*, and was based, I informed him, on the death of my older brother from leukemia. When the conversation finally ended, I sensed in his voice the disappointment and betrayal he spoke of earlier; all our philosophical footwork, all our aesthetic sparring, hadn't won me over to his side.

My conversation with Mr. S. was a joy compared to my reaction to the prepublication reviews. The first, I'm happy to report, was a starred review in *Kirkus*, and not since kindergarten have five-pointed stars seemed like such radiant geometric marvels. When my agent read me the review, I remember that my shoulders, which for weeks had been arching toward my ears, fell gently earthward. The wait, I believed, was over, my worry vindicated by sweet hyperbole. I clung to the review's last line, which urged the widest possible readership because of *Truth Serum's* craftsmanship. The very next day, however, my agent called with the review from *Publishers Weekly*. My agent is a tactful soul, and it pained me to hear his stoic tone when duty forced him to pelt me with insults. This reviewer claimed that my book *might* be of interest to "gay professionals" (by which I thought he really meant "professional gays") but that its craftless rambles were an attempt to claim that life, "when played in a homosexual key, is somehow more heroic."

No review has ever made me so miserable. It was bad enough to be accused of homosexual chauvinism, but worse was my resulting defensiveness. Late at night, in the midst of a fitful sleep, my thoughts would boil down to something plaintive, childlike, primal: "He hates me because I'm a big sissy." It was like being catapulted back though the decades and reliving every assault on my soft, unguarded, newly forming self. My life, I realized in the pale light of dawn, was open to jibes and scrutiny from all quarters. And because that life went undisguised, any reproach about the book, regardless how timid, would feel like an attack against me.

I brooded over this review for weeks. Although I had no proof, I assumed the reviewer was a straight man because heterosexual males, as a group, are more likely to engage in what psychologists call "protest behavior"—making vociferous public distinctions between oneself and an ostracized "other." For all I knew, the reviewer could have been a woman or another gay man, but I needed a well-defined and admittedly convenient figure toward whom to aim my protestations, which consisted chiefly of insisting that I abhor any art that makes a claim for group superiority. An account of the secrecy and self-deceit that is part of queer experience may seem, to unsympathetic ears, like "special pleading," or so I had to remind myself over and over.

During this period of relentless internal monologues, I received another phone call from Mr. S. "I've finished the article," he announced brightly.

I chose "Oh" from the menu of appropriate noises, but couldn't understand why he had called to tell me this.

"I felt I should warn you," he continued, "that although I say yours was one of the few memoirs I liked, I'm going to criticize you for not mentioning the death of your brother. I didn't know you had a brother until you mentioned him in our phone conversation, and anyone reading *Truth Serum* would think that you were an only child." He cleared his throat. "Is that OK?"

No detonated inside my head, but I heard myself say, "You're the critic."

In fact, I had three brothers, all of whom died from various ailments, a sibling history that strains even my credulity. I'd written about the death of my brothers in two previous books, and had consciously chosen not to cover that ground again in *Truth Serum*. My brothers were much older than I (there was a fifteen-year difference between the youngest of my older brothers and myself) and they lived away from home for the bulk of my youth. Very early in the writing of *Truth Serum*, I knew that a book concerned with homosexual awakening would sooner or later deal with AIDS and the population of friends I've lost to the disease. I also suspected I would write about my HIV-positive partner, Brian. To be blunt, I decided to limit the body count in this book in order to prevent it from collapsing under the threat of death. For the most part, however, this decision was personal rather than literary: there is only so much loss I can stand to place at the center of the daily rumination that writing requires. Were it only possible to contain in a single book the vast, senseless matrix of these deaths, but what skills I have jam and sputter and, ultimately, fail in the face of it. Only when the infinite has edges am I capable of making art.

I did my best to convey this reasoning to Mr. S., sighing with such a mix of melancholy and exasperation that my dog Zack walked over and planted himself at my side, as if to offer a sedative of warm fur and steady breath. "Would anything I'm telling you," I asked mid-explanation, "make a difference?"

"Well, no," he said. "I've already handed in the article. But I did say something positive about your discretion. I mean, being gay is no big deal these days. But in *Secret Life*, for example, the writer Michael Ryan writes about having sex with his dog! You wouldn't do that . . . would you?"

When I looked down at Zack, he raised his brown eyes and thumped his tail in a most appealing way.

Soon after the book came out, my publisher sent me on a small book tour. After a reading, people would sometimes commend me for my "honesty" and "courage" in writing about sexuality. (An ironic compliment for someone who had faced the prospect of his book tour with all the backbone of a sponge.) I thanked these people, but tried to explain that I felt neither honest nor brave when I worked with personal subjects because the rigors of shaping sentences and paragraphs overwhelmed any sense that I was dealing with risky or revealing subject matter. In the end, my history became so much raw material to temper in the forge of craft. In fact, the very familiarity of autobiographical material freed me up to concentrate on the sensual and emotional effects of language (for me the most pleasurable part of writing) instead of on the invention of story. I'd never flattered myself that my personal history is more exceptional or fascinating than most, but rather have seen it as a readily accessible source from which to write. Since "honesty" in writing is so often artless and indulgent, and since mere audacity so often masquerades as "courage," I was actually a little bothered by the suggestion that these were the work's most notable qualities. I'd hoped that the formal aspects of my autobiographical writing—its structure, language, and juxtaposition of images—were what made it worthwhile.

This "aesthetic distance," I began to see, had lulled me into a state of illusory safety while the memoir was being written. An illusion reinforced by the fact that I inhabit the realm of the midlist writer, a no-man's-land of chronic modesty and lowered expectations. The possibility that my book would garner much attention seemed fairly remote. At most I thought that, since the surge of memoirs by American writers was a topic of debate among people in the book business, some stray interest might fall my way. But once the tour was underway, it surprised me how frequently I was called upon to be a spokesperson for the memoir in general, or for the gay memoir in particular. For the first time in my career, I was part of a trend, and I found myself struggling against the prevailing current more often than swimming with it. It has always been hard enough for me to act as an advocate for my square inch of literary territory, and suddenly people expected me to answer questions about the literary marketplace, about the motives of other memoirists, about the suicide rate among gay youth, or the societal ramifications of same-sex marriage—issues I could not pretend to address with any degree of expertise. In other words, people expected me to be a generalist because I employ the public medium of language, when in fact language has always brought me closer to the exception, the sui generis, the self in its nearly inexpressible complexity.

Toward the end of my book tour, I took part in a panel discussion on the memoir, and discovered that I was not the only writer subjected to baffling questions. After we six panelists briefly discussed our memoirs, the moderator announced that she would take questions from the audience. Hands waved like a field of wheat. For the next forty minutes we heard what amounted to a single inquiry: *Should I hire an attorney?* This question was usually preceded by the synopsis of a memoir-in-progress: the psychotic sister inducted into a cult in Honolulu; the computer hacker who tapped into the Pentagon; the parent guilty of moral trespasses that were passionately hinted at but never named. It began to seem as if we live in a country virtually erupting with prosecutable secrets. We panelists took turns balking at questions like: *What kind of disclosures constitute libel? What's the necessity of changing names if a book's subject is deceased? Does the statute of limitations really matter when it comes to a small-press book? How reliable are the inhouse lawyers that publishers hire to give manuscripts a legal reading?* It was like a bad dream in which I'd gone to participate in an informal literary talk but ended up taking the Bar exam.

In San Francisco, as had happened throughout the book tour, people periodically came up to me and inquired about Brian's health. I often couldn't tell, for a disorienting instant, if these were people I knew, or who knew Brian; perfect strangers possessed a vague familiarity *because* of their concern. This interest in the well-being of my beloved was heartening; it allowed me to believe my writing had been intimate and engaging enough to create allies in what has sometimes been for us an isolating despair. And yet, I was taken aback each time it happened, reminded anew how this potential connection with a reader is, in the writer's long hours of solitude and uncertainty, at most a fond hope.

Understandably, Brian was not at all prepared to hear from those who learned about his HIV status from my book. One night, in fact, he came home from work and told me that someone had rushed up to him on the street, arms outstretched, to say he'd read that Brian was "dying." In fact, Brian was quite robust, and it upset me to think that I'd unwittingly dragged him into a spectacle of public sympathy that was the price—some might say the punishment—of having written frankly about our relationship. Aesthetic concerns had blinded me to the repercussions of frankness; more than writing *about* our relationship, I felt I was writing *through* our relationship; I'd tried to trace the day-by-day reclamation of our erotic life after Brian's diagnosis, not in order to describe us as a couple, or to boast about our passion, but in order to examine desire, which is protean, adaptable, and enduring.

Before the book was published, Brian and I had discussed at length how he might feel when the book came out, to what degree he was willing to have himself discussed in interviews, and even whether it would be advisable to withhold his last name from the dedication page, a request I was glad to honor. And yet, last name or no, he too was struck by the downright surreality of my, of our, fleeting brush with literary celebrity. The burden of responsibility weighed heavily on me during the writing of that section—I had to convey Brian's extraordinary optimism without glossing over his fear and physical suffering—and I continued to maintain a protective stance toward him after it appeared in print. And yet, each time he described some disconcerting encounter with someone who'd read about him in *Truth Serum*, it was all I could do not to interrupt and ask—forgive my writer's undernourished ego!—whether the person had liked my book.

During the brief spate of readings and reviews, people began to materialize from my past. An Armenian girl from the second grade whose sprightly manner I'd wanted desperately to emulate, phoned to say that she'd recognized herself in one memoir (she's now a district court judge and mother of two) and was curious to know what I'd been up to for the last forty years. The flamboyant arts and crafts teacher from my junior high school thrust out a now age-spotted hand and introduced himself before a reading. These were impromptu, dreamlike reunions; it had been so long since I'd last seen these people, and I'd resuscitated their memory through such an effort of will, that it stunned me to realize they were real after all—the flesh-and-blood bases, and not the products, of my imagination.

It could be argued that people from a fiction writer's past are just as likely to appear out of the blue when a novel is published. But typically these people have not populated the book one is promoting. One's characters, a sane writer would be quick to agree, do not call with congratulations, or surprise you by showing up at a book signing, a little worn around the edges and eager to catch up on old times.

It can also be argued that the experience of having *any* book enter the world leaves the author open to unforeseen reactions, and to the discomfort those reactions might cause. And yet, no matter how fervently the memoirists believe they can distinguish themselves from the thing they've made, it's not an altogether autonomous product that's held beneath the magnifying glass of critical assessment—it is, in essence, the sum of one's life.

The process of writing a memoir is insular, ruminative, a mining of privacies; once published, however, the book becomes an act of extroversion, an advertisement to buy, a performance of self rather than its articulation. The gap between these two experiences—the creation of a memoir and the ramifications of having written one—is wide enough, it seems to me, to bewilder even the most poised and gregarious among us. "No one who writes an autobiography can possibly know what they're in for," said Geoffrey Wolff, "until that book comes out."

Of all the surprises, however, the greatest for me has been this: by writing a memoir I've refashioned my past. *Truth Serum* has virtually supplanted my memories, so that, when asked about my personal history, I conjure up some section of the book. After all that labor, after worrying every sentence into being, those passages are deeply rooted, closely known. Most scenes, in fact, are far more vivid than the inklings, speculations, and stabs at accuracy from which they originated. It's as if some distillate of memory flooded the pages and turned them sanguine, leaving all that isn't recalled in that book pale and anemic.

The Polish writer Bruno Schultz said, "Memory is a filament around which our sense of the world has crystallized." Memoirs too are like those filaments; dipped in the cloudy solution of the past, words gather and congeal into books, and those books assume a life more intricate and erie than the writer could second-guess.

MARK DOTY

From Still Life with Oysters and Lemon

A sharp cracking cold day, the air of the Upper East Side full of rising plumes of smoke from furnaces and steaming laundries, exhaust from the tailpipes of idling taxis, flapping banners, gangs of pigeons. Here on the museum steps a flock suddenly chooses to take flight, the sound of their ascent like no other except maybe the rush of air a gas stove makes, when the oven suddenly ignites, only with the birds that sudden suck of air is followed by a rhythmic hurry of wings that trails away almost immediately as the flock moves into the air. Their ascent echoes back from the solidity of the museum's columns and heavy doors, the wide stairway where even in the cold people are smoking and shifting their chilly weight from side to side, eating pretzels, hunching over blue and white paper cups of coffee.

I have a backache, I'm travel weary, and it couldn't matter less, for this whole scene—the crowd and hustle on the museum steps, which seem alive all day with commerce and hurry, with gatherings and departures—is suffused for me with warmth, because I have fallen in love with a painting. Though that phrase doesn't seem to suffice, not really—rather it's that I have been drawn into the orbit of a painting, have allowed myself to be pulled into its sphere by casual attraction deepening to something more compelling. I have felt the energy and life of the painting's will; I have been held there, instructed. And the overall effect, the result of looking and looking into its brimming surface as long as I could look, is love, by which

I mean a sense of tenderness toward experience, of being held within an intimacy with the things of the world.

That sense has remained with me as I moved out through the dark stone lobby of the museum, with its huge vase of flowers looming over the information desk in the center of the room, and out into the sudden winter brightness—the gray brightness of Manhattan in January—onto the museum steps. There, stepping outside into the day, where nothing is framed or bounded as things in the museum are, suddenly the sense of intimacy and connection I've been feeling flares out, as if my painting had been a hearth, a heated and glowing place deep in the museum interior, and I'd carried the warmth of it with me out into the morning. Is it morning still? The sky's a huge crystal, cracked and alive with fractures, contrails, cloudy patches, huge distances.

But nothing seems truly remote to me, no chill too intractable. Because I have stepped from a warm suspension out into the shatteringly cold air, something of that suspension remains within me, or around me. It is the medium in which I and my fellow citizens move. We are all moving, just now, in the light that has come toward me through a canvas the size of a school notebook; we all walking in the light of a wedge of lemon, four oysters, a half-glass of wine, a cluster of green grapes with a few curling leaves still attached to their stem. This light is enough to reveal us as we are, bound together, in the warmth and good light of habitation, in the good and fleshly aliveness of us.

How is it possible?

It's a simple painting, really, *Still Life with Oysters and Lemon*, by one Jan Davidsz de Heem, painted in Antwerp some three hundred and fifty years ago, and displayed today—after who knows what places it has been—in a glass case at the Metropolitan, lying flat, so that one bends and looks down into its bronzy, autumnal atmosphere. Half-filled *roemer* (an old Dutch drinking glass, with a knobby base) with an amber inch of wine, dewy grapes, curl of a lemon peel. Shimmery, barely solid bodies of oysters, shucked in order to allow their flesh to receive every ministration of light. It *is* an atmosphere; the light lovingly delineating these things is warm, a little fogged, encompassing, tender, ambient. As if, added to the fragrance evoked by the sharp pulp of the lemon, and the acidic wine, and the salty marsh-scent of the oysters, were some fragrance the light itself carried.

Simple, and yet so firm in its assertions.

I'll try to name them.

That this is the matrix in which we are held, the generous light binding together the fragrant and flavorful productions of vineyard, marsh, and orchard— where has that lemon come from, the Levant?

That the pleasures of what can be tasted and smelled are to be represented, framed, set apart; that pleasure is to be honored.

That the world is a dialogue between degrees of transparency—globes of the grapes, the wine in the glass equally penetrated by light but ever so slightly less clear than the vessel itself, degrees of reflectivity.

That the world of reflection implicates us, as well—there, isn't that the faintest image of the painter in the base of the glass, tilted, distorted, lost in the contemplation of his little realm? Looking through things, as well, through what he's made of them, toward us?

That there can never be too much of reality; that the attempt to draw nearer to it—which will fail—will not fail entirely, as it will give us not the fact of lemons and oysters but this, which is its own fact, its own brave assay toward what is.

That description is an inexact, loving art, and a reflexive one; when we describe the world we come closer to saying what we are.

And something else, of course; there's always more, deep in art's pockets, far down in the chiaroscuro on which these foodstuffs rest: everything here has been transformed into feeling, as if by looking very hard at an object it suddenly comes that much closer to some realm where it isn't a thing at all but something just on the edge of dissolving. Into what? Tears, gladness—you've felt like this before, haven't you? Taken far inside. When? Held. Maybe that's what the darkness behind these things, that warm brown ground, is: the dark space within an embrace.

Intimacy, says the phenomenologist Gaston Bachelard, is the highest value.

I resist this statement at first. What about artistic achievement, or moral courage, or heroism, or altruistic acts, or work in the cause of social change? What about wealth or accomplishment? And yet something about it rings true, finally— that what we want is to be brought into relation, to be inside, within. Perhaps it's true that nothing matters more to us than that.

But then why resist intimacy, why seem to flee it? A powerful countercurrent pulls against our drive toward connection; we also desire individuation, separateness, freedom. On one side of the balance is the need for home, for the deep solid roots of place and belonging; on the other is the desire for travel and motion, for the single separate spark of the self freely moving forward, out into time, into the great absorbing stream of the world.

A fierce internal debate, between staying moored and drifting away, between holding on and letting go. Perhaps wisdom lies in our ability to negotiate between these two poles. Necessary to us, both of them—but how to live in connection without feeling suffocated, compromised, erased? We long to connect; we fear that if we do, our freedom and individuality will disappear.

One would not expect to turn to still life for help with these questions. But I think of the familiar phrase about there being "more than meets the eye"; in these paintings, the "more" *does* meet the eye; they suggest that knowledge is visible, that it might be seen in the daily world. They think, as it were, through things.

In my Jan Davidsz de Heem, for instance, there is a spectacular spiral of lemon peel, a flourish of painterly showing-off. The rind has been sliced in a single strip, and it curls in the air, resting atop the *roemer*; one of its coils dips inside, toward the wine, so that we see it now plainly, now veiled by the slightly gray cast of the glass. Now the pebbly yellow, as it twists through air, now the white pith that lay between that outer skin and the body of the fruit. Shadows lie in the twisting helix, in the curling hollows—like the socket of an armpit, or the hollows at the base of the neck, the twin wells of the collarbone. These are fleshy, erotic shadows, and they stand in contrast to the brilliance raking across the peel, cut so thin as to be translucent, a slice of the warmth and energy pouring into this room we'll never see.

This is by no means the only bravura lemon in Dutch painting of the seventeenth century. They are, in fact, everywhere, in pictures by Pieter de Ring, Abraham van Beyeren, Willem Kalf, Jan Jansz den Uyl, and Adriaen van Utrecht, to name just a few. These lemons seem to leap to the foreground; the stippled, textured surface of the paint—noticeably thickened beside the glazed surface used elsewhere for silver cups and pewter plates, or bowls of porcelain—gives the eye a focal point and therefore makes the peel appear closer to us.

They are, in a way, nudes, always in dishabille, partly undraped, the rind peeled away to allow our gaze further pleasure—to see the surface, and beneath that another surface. Often the pith is cut away as well, the fruit faceted so that we can see its wet translucence, a seed just beneath, and sometimes another seed or two is tossed to the side of the plate on which this odalisque rests, diminutive seeds just as precise as the fruit and its pulpy sections; nothing is too tiny for the attentive eye.

The lemons are built, in layers, out of lead tin yellow, which the Italians called *giallo di Fiandria*, a warm canary made by heating lead and tin oxides together, which was also the preferred pigment for the petals of daffodils, and out of *luteolum Neapolitanum*, or Naples yellow, and of a glowing but unstable pigment called orpiment. Often these colors are glazed with yellow glazes made of broom or berries. Alchemists' work, turning tin and arsenic and vegetable juices into golden fruit painted with a kind of showy complication and variety that suggests there must have been competition among the painters of lemons. How to paint a lemon with a freedom and inventiveness that sets it apart? Jacob von Hulsdonck specialized in citrus partially ripe, the stippled surface of the fruit blushed with that acidy green which indicates the peel's only recently yellowed. Whose half-peeled fruit could be most complexly faceted, like a gemstone, in order to reveal nuances of transparency and reflectivity, the seeds resting within the revealed sections? Who could give the coiled peel the greatest sense of heft and curve, or spiral it down from the edge of a table, with the most convincing sense of gravity's pull? In Cornelis de Heem's *The Flute of Wine*, a swoop of lemon peel occupies the very center of the picture, looping down into the space below the edge of the table and back up again to end in a flourish of curl, impossibly long, as if the little fruit had yielded an unlikely bounty of peel to serve the painter's purposes. Whose peel could be cut the thinnest, barely there at all, a translucent yellow interruption in the air?

In another canvas of Jan Davidsz de Heem's, the lavishly wealthy *Nautilus Cup with Silver Vessels*, the painter seems to strut, to take the lemon competition as far as it might reasonably go, even a little farther. Here a strip of peel is shown alone, detached from its fruit, at the corner of a table shrouded in a dark cloth. The peel coils intricately, impossibly—a baroque bit of ribboning made to show us exactly what this painter could do.

Lemons: all freedom, all ego, all vanity, fragrant with scent we can't help but imagine when we look at them, the little pucker in the mouth. And redolent, too, of strut and style. Yet somehow they remain intimate, every single one of them: only lemons, only that lovely, perishable, ordinary thing, held to scrutiny's light, fixed in a moment of fierce attention. As if here our desire to be unique, unmistakable, and our desire to be of a piece were reconciled. Isn't that it, to be yourself and somehow, to belong? For a moment, held in balance.

To think through things, that is the still life painter's work—and the poet's. Both sorts of artists require a tangible vocabulary, a worldly lexicon. A language of ideas is, in itself, a phantom language, lacking in the substance of worldly things, those containers of feeling and experience, memory and time. We are instructed by the objects that come to speak with us, those material presences. Why should we have been born knowing how to love the world? We require, again and again, these demonstrations.

My first resonant, instructive thing?

Hypnotist's wheel, red swirl blazoned on a hard white candy ground, spinning even when it isn't moving; that's the life of the spiral, it seems to whirl even when it's at rest. Peppermints, each wrapped in a shiny square of cellophane which twists at the ends into little flourishes. They emerge, one after the other, endless, pouring out; perhaps they come into being the way matter is said to do, from the collapsed bodies of dead stars, streaming out into the world. But the dark from whence they emerge is the unfathomable void of my grandmother's glossy black pocketbook.

Her name is Lona, though I don't know that, and won't for years. Because this is East Tennessee, in the second half of the nineteen fifties, she is called Mamaw, and that's the only name I have ever called her.

Mamaw wears a thin flowered dress of rayon or some other slippery stuff, and a white crocheted cardigan sweater, also thin, that keeps riding up her skinny, intricately mottled wrists; the sleeves of her sweaters are never long enough, and somehow this underlines the fact that everything about her is thin, both delicate and peculiarly sturdy at once.

Those wrists are a wonder: veins and splotches, just at the back of the hand, rhyme with her liver-colored "age spots." Together we've heard a commercial on her radio for a cream that claimed to make them fade and then *vanish* (magician's verb: something pops out of sight, out of being, like a silver dollar or a dove). The adjective the radio chose for the spots was "horrid": interesting clear sound, immediately calling up, for some reason, a chain of scents—vomit, calamine lotion, peculiar odor of a cigar box filled with rubber bands, girdle folded in a drawer.

When Mamaw stands up with the sun behind her you can see through the dress to her legs, and I am the perfect height to study the outline of the elastic stockings she wears, folded over at the top into a kind of cuff, which makes a darker band beneath her knees. My grandfather wears these, too; they seem part of a vocabulary of age, one of the assembly of items binding what would otherwise sag or separate or fall: elastic things, rubber things, corsets and belts and lifts, stays and trusses. All tend toward the beige region of the spectrum, and though they are called "flesh" they're the color of no one's skin, but the hue of mannequins or dolls. Beneath her stockings are thick black shoes; their chunky short heels bear the hallmark of necessity rather than style.

Her ensemble is completed by the pocketbook; the word seems as capacious and black as the thing it represents, which is square, shiny, carried by a double strap, and closed with an irresistible pair of prongs that must be snapped one over the other, so that the pocketbook opens and closes with a satisfying click: slight reverberation of metal, the nice feel of fingers firm against patent leather.

What can't the pocketbook contain? Certainly it holds far more than I know; it is not for me to delve into its contents, many of which I doubtless couldn't name if I saw them. But she brings things up and into the light as they are needed, or simply in order to entertain with their startling variety. Which includes a plastic rain bonnet of see-through vinyl that folds up, growing increasingly opaque as it is doubled and tripled into a tiny rectangle and slipped into a plastic envelope. A paper fan, the stiff oblong sort printed with a religious picture and mounted on a wooden handle. These change periodically as new ones are provided in church, but this week's scene—the week we are going to see the bears!—pictures Jesus in the garden of Gethsemane. His face turned upward, long hair flowing, he kneels at a convenient stone, pale countenance tilted toward the moon. Or is he suffering the children to come unto him? Maybe it's Easter, and everything is lilies and lilies. Whatever the case, there is more: an exquisite little change purse, whose labial folds increase to catch and sort coins, its top sealed by another of those tempting closures. Doan's Pills. Lavender water. Smelling salts in a tiny glass ampule, to be broken when absolutely needed. Round tin of snuff, since she likes the occasional pinch. A tiny red edition of the New Testament, tissues in small packets, a sparkly pair of multifaceted earrings whose clasp has long ago broken; short, dull-tipped pencils; a cluster of the ubiquitous, potentially useful rubber bands; a scrap of ribbon snipped from the flowers at whose grave? And then, the item to which my attention is repeatedly drawn, to which all the other items are merely ancillary: those red, pinwheeled peppermints.

We're in the backseat of the green Studebaker, driving to see the bears. It isn't a long drive, really, from our house up into the Smokies, but, heavens, the preparations and consideration, the work of getting everyone ready for the Sunday drive. I am in the backseat with my grandfather, who has his cane standing upright between his legs and is wearing a brown felt fedora with a black ribbon above the brim. And then me, in the middle, though I do not turn toward him but toward Mamaw, who has the window seat (as well as a cardboard box from the store in which she last bought one of those flowered dresses) in case of car sickness. She has a brown paper sack containing pears, some pieces of fried chicken individually wrapped in foil, her Geritol, and a quantity of triangular sandwiches, consisting of nothing but butter on white bread. These she loves. For me there is apple butter, dark and resinous, on the same white triangles—like little sails or game pieces.

Memory, which has so thoroughly costumed and illuminated the aspect of the old woman to my right, has not had resources left over to do much with the rest of that automobile's interior. My father's driving; my sister is beside him, probably thirteen or fourteen, and the metal bar dividing the windshield in half seems to spring right out of the center of her blond head; my mother is in the right-hand half of the view. Certainly there is discussion, perhaps songs, does someone turn from the front seat to the back and tell me to be still? No narrative here, but suddenly we're in Gatlinburg, whose salient feature is bears: little stuffed black bears, toys the size of my head or my paired hands, each wearing a vest or belt of red vinyl. They are lovable in their multiplicity, rows and rows of bears hanging from shelves, porch rails, the sides of tables of souvenirs: snow globes, ashtrays, thermometers, salt and pepper shakers, plaques of sliced and varnished wood with mottoes inscribed beneath the glaze. Boxes of candy, shaped like leaves or snowflakes. I want a bear.

Which I cannot have, because we are going on to see the real bears. The mountains are pale blue, in memory, like those misty and indeterminate landscapes in the backdrops of Leonardos; we are driving and driving on curving roads, we are stopping for vistas, we are lined up and photographed, in my face that lingering regret for the embraceable entity of the furry black toy with its vinyl vest and its small and friendly gaze. Then we are parked at a turnout, on the side of the high, two-lane road, not on the slope side, which is all air and distance, but on the side where the trees are, cool and towering, and out of the dark spaces between the pines have come the bears. They are walking toward us, coming on all fours in a scamper or standing up, on two legs, a bit less gracefully, lumbering a little, but their faces are open and eager; they are coming to see us, and suddenly I know I have been so lonely. That is why I wanted my parents to buy me that small bear; I wanted to embrace the animal, wanted to carry the lustrous black beast in my arms, sit him beside me on the car seat. And now, I think, I want to live with the bears, want to be back in their company—why "back"? Was I in their company sometime before? It seems like a homecoming, to be with them, and maybe Mamaw feels it too, which is why she opens the pocketbook and produces the beautiful candies and lays them out on the low stone wall that marks the border between the turnout and the woods. Does she unwrap the peppermints? I can't recall—only the red swirls set out on the rough surface of the piled stones, and the gesture of her hand reaching down into invisibility and coming up with two or three of the little pinwheels and holding them out toward the eager black faces drawing nearer.

And soon we were in the car, all of us, with the windows closed, and the tall figures standing around us, rocking back and forth a little, their forepaws raised in the air, their tongues touching their teeth and lips, and Mamaw was still rummaging in her pocketbook saying, *There must be more in here somewheres.*

RUSSELL EDSON

Portrait of the Writer as a Fat Man
Some Subjective Ideas or Notions on the Care
and Feeding of Prose Poems

. . . At first the fat man, who has seen himself only as the expanded borders of one larger than most, yet containing a consciousness of average size, perhaps smaller by the squeeze of his flesh, seeks now an episodic prose work, the novel; that harmony of diverse materials, his life. His novel is to be about a writer writing a novel about a writer writing a novel about a writer writing a novel, and so forth; a novel within a novel within a novel; an image reflected between two mirrors back and forth in ever receding smaller mirrors. . . .

He is a very fat person, more, simply than the bulk of flesh, he vaguely sees this, though classed with others of such heft; his soul is also fatted with the lack of ability.

Yes, he is a very fat person because there are thin people. It is relative. He supposes that there are fatter people than he. Of course there are; and probably fatter people than those who are fatter than he.

This is silly, I am simply a fat man whose eyes are of average size, from where I look out from my flesh like anyone else.

And so it is that he wants to write about a fat man such as himself, who now commits himself to composition, growing itchy in his bed, not only from his constant eating, much of which takes place in his bed for lack of love, but because of ideas, excellent fictives, which give rise to an increased heartbeat, and an optimism not fully justified by talent or metabolic levels. But of course this is no longer of moment. Talent is, as he would say, a dilettante measure in my new frame of mind. He casts it out as a silly ornament.

All is will and power, both growing from the other like a single club, with which I shall force a fiction—as though I scrubbed floors to send my son through college that he might get a high paying job and buy me a castle to live in, where I spend my remaining days simpering and whimpering about how I went down on my knees with a scrub-pail to send my son through college. . . .

Russell Edson, "Portrait of the Writer as a Fat Man: Some Subjective Ideas or Notions on the Care and Feeding of Prose Poems" from Field: Contemporary Poetry and Poetics, number 13, Fall 1975. Reprinted by permission of the author.

2

The fat man sat down to his typewriter almost as though he were sitting down to a dinner, his face set with that same seriousness that must attend all his sittings down to dinner, like a huge transport vessel taking on fuel; a gluttony that has grown far beyond simple self-indulgence.

3

The fat man sat before his typewriter and wrote, the fat man sat before his typewriter and wrote, the fat man sat before his typewriter and wrote: It was better to find a single defensible place, a philosophy, if not a material barrier, that by its very nature offered no challenge to anyone.

To live in the refuse of others is to live in the negative of their desire. Assuming all the while that existence itself is the highest premium. Therefore, that I go unchallenged is the platform upon which I build my durance.

The fat man wrote: Many species have outlived their tormentors simply by offering no challenge, but living where their tormentors would not, by eating what their tormentors felt not fit for those in the position of seemingly perfect choice.

The fat man wrote: The tormentor grows into dilettantism. The tormentor finds existence more an art than a practical concern. Nature becomes a drawing room where the fine music of bees is heard among the flowers, and the lisp of cool drink flows from glaciered mountains; and life with all its easy fruit becomes a boudoir of death. For nature is not constant, and turns like a restless sleeper in her bed; the earthquake, the flood. The clock of expectation cracks. The air is all in smoke, the hardy are run to gas, and the stink is everywhere. A stratum of complacency lays down its bones in the earth like a shredded lace.

The fat man wrote: There was a microbe that lived in the droppings of the great. The microbe had a much different set of values than the great, those who indulged themselves down the avenues of dependency, where only the rarest of flowers, mingled with the hissing of champagne, and a touch of indirect lighting in the warm summer evenings, gave moment to the endless ease. . . .

The fat man wrote: The young microbe worked the fields of refuse. . . .

The fat man wrote: Yet, the fat man may be the very one floundering in the easy avenue. . . .

4

Is the typewriter not like the console of some giant musical instrument designed to ruin one's head? wrote the fat man writing about a fat man.

. . . A sudden rush of dream figures pulls the head's womb inside out. . . . Belly of soft plumbing, unhappy fat man. . . .

The typewriter is the keyboard of an organ; the pipes run up through the world, contrived through trees and telephone poles . . .

5

. . . It was as if to buy a farm you bought a cabbage. The fat man smiled and fell out of his head. The moon had risen. . . . What of that? . . . The pulse of days, moon-thud, sun-thud, regularity, even if one's own has gone. One becomes used to living in areas of time. Islands of memory surrounded by nothing.

The twentieth century, a country someplace in the universe; my species suffocating itself to death with its groin. Piling its redundancy beyond love or renewal; stool and child dropped with equal concern . . . We were our own excrement.

Our young meant no more to us than mosquitoes. We burnt them, we starved them. We let the universe know that we meant nothing to ourselves. We hated God for igniting us with neuronic tissue. We created God as he had us. Why not, he didn't stop us? If we were made in his image, so was he also imprisoned in ours. . . .

6

The human intelligence sees itself as the only thing different from all things else in the universe; an isolated witness to a seemingly endless cosmological process, ever burgeoning as galaxies and morning glories. Human intelligence recognizing its frail root and utter dependency on the physical universe. . . . That out of the vast mindlessness was it born. . . . Must look upon its situation as absurd. Intelligence is in the care of mindlessness. . . .

7

The fat man comes to this: That the artifice of the novel is impossible for him; he has not enough faith to build a cathedral. He must work toward bits and pieces formed from memory . . . And yet, experience remains hidden and less important than the inscape it has formed. To find a prose free of the self-consciousness of poetry; a prose more compact than the storyteller's; a prose removed from the formalities of *literature*. . . .

8

. . . A prose that is a cast-iron aeroplane that can actually fly, mainly because its pilot doesn't seem to care if it does or not. Nevertheless, this heavier-than-air prose monstrosity, this cast-iron toy will be seen to be floating over the trees.

It's all done from the cockpit. The joy stick is made of flesh. The pilot sits on an old kitchen chair before a table covered with oilcloth. The coffee cups and spoons seem to be the controls.

But the pilot is asleep. You are right, this aeroplane seems to fly because its pilot dreams. . . .

We are not interested in the usual literary definitions, for we have neither the scholarship nor the ear. We want to write free of debt or obligation to literary form or idea; free even from ourselves, free from our own expectations. . . . There is more truth in the act of writing than in what is written. . . .

9

. . . Growing your own writing without going to the Iowa Writers Workshop, and without sending your work to known poets—your own garden, your own medita-tion—isolation!—Painful, necessary!. . . Finally the golden bubble of delight, one is saved by one's own imagination.

One comes to the writing table with one's own hidden life, the secret of the fat man; not dragging Pound's *Cantos*. . . .

The trouble with most who would write poetry is that they are unwilling to throw their lives away. . . . They are unwilling. . . .

How I hate little constipated lines that are afraid to be anything but correct, without an ounce of humor, that gaiety that death teaches!

What we want is a poetry of miracles—minus the "I" of ecstasy! A poem that as many people who read it each reads a different poem. A poetry freed from its time. A poetry that engages the Creation, which we believe is still in process, and that it is entirely an imaginative construction, which our creative acts partake of, and are necessary to. We are all helping to imagine the Universe.

Which means a poetry not caught and strangled on particular personalities. A poetry that can see itself beyond its obvious means.

And we wish above all to be thought of as "beneath contempt" by the pompous, those who have stood their shadows over the more talented.

How I despise the celebrity poet!

10

. . . The self-serious poet with his terrible sense of mission, whose poems are grad-ually decaying into sermons of righteous anger; no longer able to tell the difference between the external abstraction and the inner desperation; the inner life is no longer lived or explored, but converted into public anger.

Beware of serious people, for their reality is flat; and they have come to think of themselves as merely flat paste-ons. Their rage at the flatness of their lives knows no end; and they keep all their little imitators scared to death. . . .

And they are meddlers, they try to create others in their own image because theirs is failing. . . .

11

Poems of celebration in praise of the given reality are written by prayer writers and decorators. They, of course, have heaven in mind. In their bones they think they are securing a place next to God.

This kind of poet neglects content for form; always seeking the *way* to write; thus, in extremity, form becomes content. The ersatz sensibility that crushes vitality; the how-to poets with their endless discussion of breath and line; the polishing of the jewel until it turns to dust.

Of course this kind of poem must try to express itself as celebration and ecstasy, which is the empty mirror of soliloquy, the "I" poem, where the poet can't get past himself.

This is boring because it is not creative, it is middle-class mercantile morality. It is for those who in the name of craft, their hope of heaven, refuse to write poetry. Because at the heart of the "I" poem is little imagination and a total lack of humor; only the sensitive, self-serious soliloquist, who seems so dated and tiny in the box of mirrors he has built up around himself.

12

Being a fat man one must depend on external structures for support, walls, doorways, furniture; but this does not necessarily mean that one needs external support for one's vision. A fat man may have to make his mind do what his body cannot, more perhaps than others with more physical function. In the limitation is found both the bridge and the barrier, which is as necessary as friction to walking. I don't wish here to create a perfect box. But I do wish to suggest that beyond the sense that all is lost is yet the real hope, the excitement of knowing that there is always a little more; and that *little more* is the joyous place from where one writes.

This is the sense of nothingness, that life is always poised on the edge of decay, that seemingly solid structures long to become dust, that time adores the future more than the present, and only man holds the past with any tenderness. The sense that all is passing away, even as I write this, that in a way the *new* means death; this sense creates the Angel of Joy, which is for me the true Muse. The fat man who has nothing to lose is allowed to be silly, the Angel of Joy prescribes it. . . .

13

. . . A poetry freed from the definition of poetry, and a prose free of the necessities of fiction; a personal form disciplined not by other literature but by unhappiness; thus a way to be happy. Writing is the joy when all other joys have failed. Else, but for the unsavory careerists, why write? It is good fun to ruin the surface of a piece of paper; to, as it were, run amuck. One hurts no one, and paper is cheap enough.

The idle man finds symbolic work. And more, the fat man is only capable of symbolic work. You do agree, I hope? Men are happy when they are working. Even idle men are made happy by thinking of work, even if only thinking of others at work. It is always a pleasure to see the naughty little hands of man engaged in something other than scratching.

Thus the work is found. The writer comes to blank paper. The difficulty is *what to write about*? Believe it or not, subject matter is the first concern of the beginning writer, and will remain the concern of the *real* writer.

Subject matter? Well, of course it's the psychic material that longs to be substance. It is not simply a hook on which to hang form.

In other words, speaking of writing, the way a thing is written is far less important than what the thing is about. This may sound very unliterary, but, after all, the object of creative writing is not literature; at least it shouldn't be, for that is a worldly measure that has so little to do with the work at hand.

We say the *how* comes into being by virtue of the *what*. Surely, if the subject matter is fully imagined, its physicalness fully grasped, then the subject matter will predict its form. Nothing can exist without a shape. But form does not exist without substance. The *how* is merely, or should be, the shape of the *what*. If it is not, the writing is boring. BORING!

If a writer cannot collect his psyche into a physical reality, he ought to think seriously of trying something other than writing.

14

. . . Then the prose poem: Superficially a prose poem should look somewhat like a page from a child's primer, indented paragraph beginnings, justified margins. In other words, the prose poem should not announce that it is a special prose; if it is, the reader will know it. The idea is to get away from obvious ornament, and the obligations implied therein. Let those who play tennis play their tennis.

A good prose poem is a statement that seeks sanity whilst its author teeters on the edge of the abyss. The language will be simple, the images so direct, that oftentimes the reader will be torn with recognitions inside himself long before he is conscious of what is happening to him.

Regular poetry, even when it is quite empty of content, the deep psychic material, can manage with its ornaments of song and shape to be dimensional; which is to say, the ability to define space, which is very necessary to all the arts. Such a regular poem may seem the near "perfect object," albeit a beautiful box with nothing in it. Which is good enough; anything brought out of the abyss is to be honored. But *is* it good enough?! Isn't static predictability just rather boring?

As to the dimensional quality necessary to art, we mean depth, volume, in a word, shape; substance with a texture of parts that define space and durance. In the prose poem this sense of dimension is given by humor. The prose poem that does not have some sense of the funny is flat and uninformed, and has no more life than a shopping list. I don't mean the banal, high-schoolish snickering that one sees so often in so-called prose poems, but the humor of the deep, uncomfortable metaphor.

15

To come back to the prose poem. What makes us so fond of it is its clumsiness, its lack of expectation or ambition. Any way of writing that isolates its writer from worldly acceptance offers the greatest creative efficiency. Isolation from other writers, and isolation from easy publishing. This gives one that terrible privacy, so hard to bear, but necessary to get past the idea one has of oneself in relation to the world. I'm not talking about breaking oneself as a monk or a nun might, causing all desire and creativity to become the thick inky darkness that freezes function, but that the writer ought to look to himself, to his own means, that he may get past those means.

It is the paradox, that it is through ourselves we get to that place that is not ourselves; that is, in fact, all of us.

The fear of being alone is sometimes expressed in the elitist nonsense that the poet is some kind of special person owing something to the "inarticulate masses" (who in heaven ever coined that?), which is the same old messianic crap, that same old paranoia wrapped in the same old sentimental rags!

Oh where has the ideal of the ivory tower gone?

16

The prose poem is an approach, but certainly not a form; it is art, but more general than most of the other arts. This may sound odd because we know prose poems as things written on paper. But it is only incidental that they are written out; the spirit or approach which is represented in the prose poem is not specifically literary. My personal convenience is best served by writing only because writing is the fastest way. This kind of creation needs to be done as rapidly as possible. Any hesitation causes it to lose its believability, its special reality; because the writing of a prose poem is more of an experience than a labor toward a product. If the finished prose poem is considered a piece of literature, this is quite incidental to the writing. This kind of creating should have as much ambition as a dream, which I assume most of us look upon, meaning our nightly dreams, as throwaway creations, not things to be collected in a book of poems.

Abundance is also important. The re-working of something that might be saved is no good; better to go on and make something else, and then something else. Prose poems cannot be perfected, they are not literary constructions, unless anything written is to be so considered; prose poems have no place to go. Abundance and spontaneity; spontaneous abundance in imitation of the joy and energy of general creation and substance.

Goatfoot, Milktongue, Twinbird
The Psychic Origins of Poetic Form

When we pursue the psychic origins of our satisfaction with poetic form, we come to the end of the trail. It is deep in the woods, and there is a fire; Twinbird sits quietly, absorbed in the play of flame that leaps and falls; Goatfoot dances by the fire, his eyes reflecting the orange coals, as his lean foot taps the stone. Inside the fire there is a mother and child, made one, the universe of the red coal. This is Milktongue.

1. Some Premises

First, in connection with oppositions:

1.   Any quality of poetry can be used for a number of purposes, including opposed purposes. Thus, concentration on technique has often been used to trivialize content, by poets afraid of what they will learn about themselves. But concentration on technique can absorb the attention while unacknowledged material enters the language; so technique can facilitate inspiration.

On the other hand, a poet can subscribe to an antitechnical doctrine of inspiration in a way that simply substitutes one technique for another. Surrealism can become as formulaic as a pastoral elegy.

2.   When a poet says he is doing *north*, look and see if he is not actually doing *south*. Chances are that his bent is so entirely *south* that he must swear total allegiance to *north* in order to include the globe.

3.   Energy arises from conflict. Without conflict, no energy. Yin and yang. Dark and light. Pleasure and pain. No synthesis without thesis and antithesis. Conflict of course need not be binary but may include a number of terms.

4.   Every present event that moves us deeply connects in our psyches with something (or things) in the past. The analogy is the two pieces of carbon that make an arc light. When they come close enough, the spark leaps across. The one mourning is all mourning; "After the first death, there is no other." This generalization applies to the composition of poems (writing), and to the recomposition of poems (reading).

Donald Hall, "Goatfoot, Milktongue, Twinbird" from Breakfast Served Any Time All Day, *University of Michigan Press, 2003. Reprinted by permission of Donald Hall.*

5.   The way out is the same as the way in. To investigate the process of making a poem is not merely an exercise in curiosity or gossip, but an attempt to understand the nature of literature. In the act of reading, the reader undergoes a process—largely without awareness, as the author was largely without intention—which resembles, like a slightly fainter copy of the original, the process of discovery or recovery that the poet went through in his madness or inspiration.

And then, more general:

6.   A poem is human inside talking to human inside. It may *also* be reasonable person talking to reasonable person, but if it is not inside talking to inside, it is not a poem. This inside speaks through the second language of poetry, the unintended language. Sometimes, as in surrealism, the second language is the only language. It is the ancient prong of carbon in the arc light. We all share more when we are five years old than when we are twenty-five; more at five minutes than at five years. The second language allows poetry to be universal.

7.   *Lyric poetry, typically, has one goal and one message, which is to urge the condition of inwardness, the "inside" from which its own structure derives.*

2. Form: The Sensual Body

There is the old false distinction between *vates* and *poiein*. It is a boring distinction, and I apologize for dragging it out again. I want to use it in its own despite.

The *poiein*, from the Greek verb for making or doing, becomes the poet—the master of craft, the maker of the labyrinth of epic or tragedy or lyric hymn, tale-teller and spell-binder. The *vates* is bound in his own spell. He is the rhapsode Socrates patronizes in *Ion*. In his purest form he utters what he does not understand at all, be he oracle or André Breton. He is the visionary, divinely inspired, who like Blake may take dictation from voices.

But Blake's voices returned to dictate revisions. The more intimately we observe any poet who claims extremes of inspiration or of craftsmanship, the more we realize that his claims are a disguise. There is no *poiein* for the same reason that there is no *vates*. The claims may be serious (they may be the compensatory distortion which allows the poet to write at all) and the claims may affect the looks of the poem—a surrealist poem and a neoclassic Imitation of Horace *look* different—but the distinction becomes trivial when we discover the psychic origins of poetic form.

I speak of the psychic origins of poetic *form*. Psychologists have written convincingly of the origins of the *material* of arts, in wish-fulfillment and in the universality of myth. We need not go over ideas of the poet as daydreamer, or of the collective unconsciousness. Ernst Kris's "regression in the service of the ego" names an event but does not explain how it comes about. But one bit of Freud's essay on the poet as daydreamer has been a clue in this search. At the end of his intelligent, snippy paper, Freud says that he lacks time now to deal with form, but that he suspects that formal pleasure is related to forepleasure. Then he ducks through the curtain and disappears. Suppose we consider the implications of his parting shot. Forepleasure develops out of the sensuality of the whole body which the infant experiences in the pleasure of the crib and of the breast. The connection between forepleasure and infancy is the motion from rationality to metaphor.

But to begin our search for the psychic origins of poetic form, we must first think of what is usually meant by the word "form," and then we must look for the reality. So often form is looked upon only as the fulfillment of metrical expectations. Meter is nothing but a loose set of probabilities; it is a trick easily learned; anyone can learn to arrange one-hundred-and-forty syllables so that the even syllables are louder than the odd ones, and every tenth syllable rhymes: the object will be a sonnet. But only when you have forgotten the requirements of meter do you begin to write poetry in it. The resolutions of form which ultimately provide the wholeness of a poem—resolutions of syntax, metaphor, diction, and sound—are minute and subtle and vary from poem to poem. They vary from sonnet to sonnet, or, equally and not more greatly, from sonnet to free verse lyric.

Meter is no more seriously binding than the frame we put around a picture. But the *form* of free verse is as binding and as liberating as the *form* of a rondeau. Free verse is simply less predictable. Yeats said that the finished poem made a sound like the click of the lid on a perfectly made box. One-hundred-and-forty syllables, organized into a sonnet, do not necessarily make a click; the same number of syllables, dispersed in asymmetric lines of free verse, will click like a lid if the poem is good. In the sonnet and in the free verse poem, the poet improvises toward that click, and achieves his resolution in unpredictable ways. The rhymes and line lengths of the sonnet are too gross to contribute greatly to that sense of resolution. The click is our sense of lyric *form*. This pleasure in resolution is Twinbird.

The wholeness and identity of the completed poem, the poem as object in time, the sensual body of the poem—this wholeness depends upon a complex of unpredictable fulfillments. The satisfying resolutions in a sonnet are more subtle than rhyme and meter, and less predictable. The body of sound grows in resolutions like assonance and alliteration, and in near-misses of both; or in the alternations, the going-away and coming-back, of fast and slow, long and short, high and low. The poem—free verse or meter, whatever—may start with lines full of long vowels, glide on diphthong sounds like "eye" and "ay" for instance, move to quick alternative lines of short vowels and clipped consonants, and return in a coda to the long vowels "eye" and "ay." The assonance is shaped like a saucer.

The requirements of fixity are complex, and the conscious mind seldom deals with them. Any poet who has written metrically can write arithmetically correct iambic pentameter as fast as his hand can move. In improvising toward the click, the poet is mostly aware of what sounds right and what does not. When something persists in not sounding right, the poet can examine it bit by bit—can analyze it—in the attempt to consult his knowledge and apply it.

This knowledge is habitual. It is usually not visible to the poet, but it is available for consultation. When you learn something so well that you forget it, you can begin to do it. You dance best when you forget that you are dancing. Athletics—a tennis stroke, swimming, a receiver catching a football—is full of examples of actions done as if by instinct, which are actually learned procedure, studied and practiced until they become "second nature." So it is with poetry. The literary form of poems is created largely by learning—in collaboration with the unconscious by a process I will talk about later. Possible resolutions of metaphor, diction, and sound are coded into memory from our reading of other poets, occasionally from our reading of criticism, from our talk with other poets, and from our revisions of our own work, with the conscious analysis that this revision sometimes entails. New resolutions are combinations of parts of old ones, making new what may later be combined again and made new again.

When the experienced reader takes a poem in, his sense of fixity comes also from memory. He too has the codes in his head. The new poem fulfills the old habits of expectation in some unexpected way. The reader does not know why—unless he bothers to analyze; then probably not fully—he is pleased by the sensual body of the poem. He does not need to know why, unless he must write about it. The pleasure is sufficient. Since the poet's madness is the reader's madness, the resolution of the mad material is the reader's resolution as well as the poet's. The way in is the same as the way out.

Whatever else we may say of a poem we admire, it exists as a sensual body. It is beautiful and pleasant, manifest content aside, like a worn stone that is good to touch, or like a shape of flowers arranged or accidental. This sensual body reaches us through our mouths, which are warm in the love of vowels held together, and in the muscles of our legs which as in dance tap the motion and pause of linear and syntactic structure. These pleasures are Milktongue and Goatfoot.

There is a nonintellectual beauty in the moving together of words in phrases—"the music of diction"—and in resolution of image and metaphor. The sophisticated reader of poetry responds quickly to the sensual body of a poem, before he interrogates the poem at all. The pleasure we feel, reading a poem, is our assurance of its integrity. (So Pound said that technique is the test of sincerity.) We will glance through a poem rapidly and if it is a skillful fake we will feel repelled. If the poem is alive and honest, we will feel assent in our quickening pulse—though it might take us some time to explain what we were reacting to.

The soi-disant *vates* feels that he speaks from the unconscious (or with the voice of the God), and the *poiein* that he makes all these wholenesses of shape on purpose. Both of them disguise the truth. All poets are *poiein* and *vates*. The *poiein* comes from memory of reading, and the *vates* from memory of infancy. The sensual body of the poem derives from memory of reading most obviously, but ultimately it leads us back further—to the most primitive psychic origins of poetic form.

3. Conflict Makes Energy

People frequently notice that poetry concerns itself with unpleasant subjects: death, deprivation, loneliness, despair, if love then the death of love, and abandonment. Of course there are happy poems, but in English poetry there are few which are happy through and through—and those few tend to be light, short, pleasant, and forgettable. Most memorable happy poems have a portion of blackness in them. Over all—Keats, Blake, Donne, Yeats, Eliot, Shakespeare, Wordsworth— there is more dark than light, more elegy than celebration. There is no great poem in our language which is simply happy.

Noticing these facts, we reach for explanations: maybe to be happy is to be a simpleton; maybe poets are morbid; maybe life is darker than it is light; maybe when you are happy you are too busy being happy to write poems about it and when you are sad, you write poems in order to *do* something. There may be half-truths in these common ideas, but the real explanation lies in the structure of a poem; and, I suggest, in the structure of human reality.

Energy arises from conflict.

A) The sensual body of a poem is a pleasure separate from any message the poem may contain.

B) If the poem contains a message which is pleasurable (a word I have just substituted for "happy"), then the two pleasures walk agreeably together for a few feet, and collapse into a smiling lethargy. The happy poem sleeps in the sun.

C) If the message of the poem, on the whole, is terrifying—that They flee from me, that one time did me seek; that I am sick, I must die; that On Margate Sands / I can connect / Nothing with nothing; that Things fall apart, the center will not hold—then pain of message and pleasure of body copulate in a glorious conflict-dance of energy. This alternation of pleasure and pain is so swift as to seem simultaneous, to *be* simultaneous in the complexity both of creation and reception, a fused circle of yin and yang, a oneness in diversity.

The pain is clear to anyone. The pleasure is clear (dear) to anyone who loves poems. If we acknowledge the pleasure of the sensual body of the poem, we can see why painful poems are best: conflict makes energy and resolves our suffering into ambivalent living tissue. If human nature is necessarily ambivalent, then the structure of the energetic poem resembles the structure of human nature.

The sensual body, in poems, is not simply a compensation for the pain of the message. It is considerably more important, and more central to the nature of poetry. When we pursue the psychic origins of our satisfaction with poetic form, we come to the end of the trail. It is deep in the woods, and there is a fire; Twinbird sits quietly, absorbed in the play of flame that leaps and falls; Goatfoot dances by the fire, his eyes reflecting the orange coals, as his lean foot taps the stone. Inside the fire there is a mother and child, made one, the universe of the red coal. This is Milktongue.

4. Goatfoot, Milktongue, Twinbird

Once at a conference on creativity, a young linguist presented a model of language. Xeroxed in outline, it was beautiful like a concrete poem. I looked for language as used in poems and looked a long time. Finally I found it, under "autistic utterance," with the note that this utterance might later be refined into lyric poetry.

It reminded me of another conference I had attended a year or two earlier. A psychoanalyst delivered a paper on deriving biographical information about an author from his fiction. He distributed mimeographed copies of his paper, which his secretary had typed from his obscure handwriting; he began his remarks by presenting a list of errata. The first correction was, "For 'autistic,' read 'artistic' throughout."

The newborn infant cries, he sucks at the air until he finds the nipple. At first he finds his hand to suck by accident—fingers, thumb; then he learns to repeat that pleasure. Another mouth-pleasure is the autistic babble, the "goo-goo," the small cooing and purring and bubbling. These are sounds of pleasure; they are without message, except that a parent interprets them as "happy": pleasure is happy. Wittgenstein once said that we could sing the song with expression or without expression; very well, he said, let us have the expression without the song. (He was being ironic; I am not.) The baby's autistic murmur is the expression without the song. His small tongue curls around the sounds, the way his tongue warms with the tiny thread of milk that he pulls from his mother. This is Milktongue, and in poetry it is the deep and primitive pleasure of vowels in the mouth, of assonance and of holds on adjacent long vowels; of consonance, mmmm, and alliteration. It is Dylan Thomas and the curlew cry; it is That dolphin-torn, that gong-tormented sea; it is Then, in a wailful choir, the small gnats mourn.

As Milktongue mouths the noises it curls around, the rest of his body plays in pleasure also. His fists open and close spasmodically. His small bowed legs, no good for walking, contract and expand in a rhythmic beat. He has begun the dance, his muscles move like his heartbeat, and Goatfoot improvises his circle around the fire. His whole body throbs and thrills with pleasure. The first parts of his body which he notices are his hands; then his feet. The strange birds fly at his head, waver, and pause. After a while he perceives that there are two of them. They begin to act when he wishes them to act, and since the *mental* creates the *physical*, Twinbird is the first magic he performs. He examines these independent/dependent twin birds. They are exactly alike. And they are exactly unalike, mirror images of each other, the perfection of opposite-same.

As the infant grows, the noises split off partly into messages. "Mmm" can be milk and mother. "Da-da" belongs to another huge shape. He crawls and his muscles become useful to move him toward the toy and the soda cracker. Twinbird flies more and more at his will, as Milktongue speaks, and Goatfoot crawls. But still he rolls on his back and his legs beat in the air, Still, the sister hands flutter at his face. Still, the noises without message fill the happy time of waking before hunger, and the softening down, milktongue full, into sleep. The growing child skips rope, hops, dances to a music outside intelligence, rhymes to the hopscotch or jump rope, and listens to the sounds his parents please him with:

Pease porridge hot
Pease porridge cold
Pease porridge in-the-pot
Five days old.

Or himself learns:

> Bah, bah, black sheep
> Have you any wool;
> Yes, sir, yes, sir,
> Three bags full.
> One for my master,
> One for my dame
> And one for the little boy
> That lives down the lane.

The mouth-pleasure, the muscle-pleasure, the pleasure of match-unmatch.

But "Shades of the prison house begin to close / Upon the growing boy." Civilized humans try gradually to cut away the autistic component in their speech. Goatfoot survives in the dance, Twinbird in rhyme and resolution of dance and noise. Milktongue hides itself more. It ties us to the mother so obviously that men are ashamed of it. Tribal society was unashamed and worshipped Milktongue in religion and history. Among the outcast in the modern world, Milktongue sometimes endures in language, as it does in the American black world, and in the world of the poor Southern whites. In Ireland where the mother (and the Virgin) are still central, Milktongue remains in swearing and in the love of sweet speech. Probably, in most of the modern world, Milktongue exists only in smoking, eating, and drinking; and in oral sexuality.

But Milktongue and Goatfoot and Twinbird have always lived in the lyric poem, for poet and for reader. They are the ancestors, and they remain the psychic origins of poetic form, primitive both personally (back to the crib) and historically (back to the fire in front of the cave). They keep pure the sensual pleasure that is the dark secret shape of the poem. We need an intermediary to deal with them, for a clear reason: Goatfoot and Milktongue and Twinbird, like other figures that inhabit the forest, are wholly preverbal. They live before words.

They approach the edge of the clearing, able to come close because the Priestess has no eyes to frighten them with. The Priestess, built of the memory of old pleasures, only knows how to select and order. The Priestess does not know what she says, but she knows that she says it in dactylic hexameter. Goatfoot and Milktongue and Twinbird leave gifts at the edge of the forest. The Priestess picks up the gifts, and turns to the light, and speaks words that carry the dark mysterious memory of the forest and the pleasure.

The poet writing, and the reader reading, lulled by Goatfoot and Milktongue and Twinbird into the oldest world, become able to think as the infant thinks, with transformation and omnipotence and magic. The form of the poem, because it exists separately from messages, can act as trigger or catalyst or enzyme to activate not messages but types of mental behavior. Coleridge spoke of meter as effecting the willing suspension of disbelief. They are the three memories of the body—not only meter; and they are powerful magic—not only suspension of disbelief. The form of the poem unlocks the mind to old pleasures. Pleasure leaves the mind vulnerable to the content of experience before we have intellectualized the experience and made it acceptable to the civilized consciousness. The form allows the mind to encounter real experience, and so the real message is permitted to speak—but only because the figures in the forest, untouched by messages, have danced and crooned and shaped.

The release of power and sweetness! Milktongue also remembers hunger, and the cry without answer. Goatfoot remembers falling, and the ache that bent the night. Twinbird remembers the loss of the brother, so long he believed in abandonment forever. From the earliest times, poetry has existed in order to retrieve, to find again, and to release. In the man who writes the poem, in the reader who lives it again, in the ideas, the wit, the images, the doctrines, the exhortations, the laments and the cries of joy, the lost forest struggles to be born again inside the words. The life or urge and instinct, that rages and coos, kicks and frolics, as it chooses only without choosing—this life is the life the poem grows from, and leans toward.

JANE HIRSHFIELD

Poetry and the Mind of Concentration

Every good poem begins in language awake to its own connections—language that hears itself and what is around it, sees itself and what is around it, looks back at those who look into its gaze and knows more perhaps even than we do about who and what we are. It begins, that is, in the body and mind of concentration.

By concentration, I mean a particular state of awareness: penetrating, unified, and focused, yet also permeable and open. This quality of consciousness, though not easily put into words, is instantly recognizable. Aldous Huxley described it as the moment the doors of perception open; James Joyce called it epiphany. The experience of concentration may be quietly physical—a simple, unexpected sense of deep accord between yourself and everything. It may come as the harvest of long looking and leave us, as it did Wordsworth, amid thought "too deep for tears." Within action, it is felt as a grace state: time slows and extends, and a person's every movement and decision seem to partake of perfection. Concentration can be also placed into things—it radiates undimmed from Vermeer's paintings, from the small marble figure of a lyre-player from prehistoric Greece, from a Chinese three-footed bowl—and into musical notes, words, ideas. In the wholeheartedness of concentration, world and self begin to cohere. With that state comes an enlarging: of what may be known, what may be felt, what may be done.

A request for concentration isn't always answered, but people engaged in many disciplines have found ways to invite it in. A ninth-century Zen monk, Zuigan, could be heard talking to himself rather sternly each morning: "Master Zuigan!" he would call out. "Yes?" "Are you here?" "Yes!" Violinists practicing scales and dancers repeating the same movements over decades are not simply warming up or mechanically training their muscles. They are learning how to attend unswervingly, moment by moment, to themselves and their art; learning to come into steady presence, free from the distractions of interest or boredom.

Writers, too, must find a path into concentration. Some keep a fixed time of day for writing, or engage in small rituals of preparation and invitation. One may lay out exactly six freshly sharpened pencils, another may darken the room, a third may develop as odd a routine as Flaubert, who began each workday by sniffing a drawer of aging apples. Immersion in art itself can be the place of entry, as Adam Zagajewski points out in "A River": "Poems from poems, songs / from songs, paintings from paintings." Yet however it is brought into being, true concentration appears—paradoxically—at the moment willed effort drops away. It is then that a person enters what scientist Mihaly Csikszentmihalyi has described as "flow" and Zen calls "effortless effort." At such moments, there may be some strong emotion present—a feeling of joy, or even grief—but as often, in deep concentration, the self disappears. We seem to fall utterly into the object of our attention, or else vanish into attentiveness itself.

This may explain why the creative is so often described as impersonal and beyond self, as if inspiration were literally what its etymology implies, something "breathed in." We refer, however metaphorically, to the Muse, and speak of profound artistic discovery as revelation. And however much we may come to believe that "the real" is subjective and constructed, we still feel art is a path not just to beauty, but to truth: if "truth" is a chosen narrative, then new stories, new aesthetics, are also new truths.

Difficulty itself may be a path toward concentration—expended effort weaves us into a task, and successful engagement, however laborious, becomes also a labor of love. The work of writing brings replenishment even to the writer dealing with painful subjects or working out formal problems, and there are times when suffering's only open path is through an immersion in what is. The eighteenth-century Urdu poet Ghalib described the principle this way: "For the raindrop, joy is in entering the river— Unbearable pain becomes its own cure."

Difficulty then, whether of life or of craft, is not a hindrance to an artist. Sartre called genius "not a gift, but the way a person invents in desperate circumstances." Just as geological pressure transforms ocean sediment to limestone, the pressure of an artist's concentration goes into the making of any fully realized work. Much of beauty, both in art and in life, is a balancing of the lines of forward-flowing desire with those of resistance—a gnarled tree, the flow of a statue's draped cloth. Through such tensions, physical or mental, the world in which we exist becomes itself. Great art, we might say, is thought that has been concentrated in just this way: honed and shaped by a silky attention brought to bear on the recalcitrant matter of earth and of life. We seek in art the elusive intensity by which it knows.

Concentration's essence is kinetic, and the dictionary shows the verb as moving in three directions. The first definition of "to concentrate" is *to direct toward a common center*. This form of concentration pulls a poem together, making of its disparate parts a single event. A lyric poem can be seen as a number of words that, taken as a whole, become a new, compound word, whose only possible definition is the poem itself. That unity of purpose is a poem's integrity and oneness, drawing it inward and toward coherence.

The second definition is *to focus one's attention*; this aspect of concentration faces outward, and has to do with the feeling of clarity a good poem brings to both writer and reader. Clarity does not mean simplicity, or even ease of understanding—at times, only the most complex rendering can do justice to an experience, and other times, ambiguity itself is a poem's goal. Still, one of Ezra Pound's definitions of poetry was "the best words in the best order." Walt Whitman wrote, "The fruition of beauty is no chance of hit or miss. . . . It is inevitable as life . . . exact and plumb as gravitation." This second kind of concentration moves then into exactitude, a precise connecting. Focusing on its object, it rinses clean and grounds both poem and world.

The third definition is *to increase in strength or density*, as in concentrating a salt solution. The direction of movement here is in another dimension entirely, neither inward nor outward: it is our own state of being that alters. Concentration of this kind relates to the way a poem's presentation of meaning opposes not chaos—which is just a stage of transformation—but the laziness and entropy of ordinary mind.

This intensification is one reason certain words persist at the center of our lives. Through poetry's concentration great sweeps of thought, emotion, and perception are compressed to forms the mind is able to hold—into images, sentences, and stories that serve as entrance tokens to large and often slippery realms of being. Consider William Butler Yeats's "The Second Coming"—its "rough beast, slouching toward Bethlehem," or, from the same poem, the lines, "The best lack all conviction, while the worst / Are full of passionate intensity." Whether image or abstract statement, these words hold fast in the mind, seeded with the surplus of beauty and meaning that is concentration's mark.

Finally, concentration is one translation of *dhyana*, the Sanskrit term—source of the Chinese *chan* and Japanese *zen*—that describes the one-pointed mind of meditation. In the Western word's etymology, we find a related concept, *kentron*: the Greek word for the sharp point at the center, from a verb meaning "to prick." When you go to concentration's center, you are pricked, which should mean you wake up—exactly what a good poem helps you do.

The forms concentration can take when placed into the words of poems are probably infinite. Still, six emerge as central energies through which poetry moves forward into the world it creates—the concentrations of music, rhetoric, image, emotion, story, and voice. Not all work at the same level, and in any particular poem each will always coexist with at least some of the others; yet each can at times stand at the core of a poem's speaking.

Poetry has historically been defined as particular ways of organizing thought through sound, and its music remains the point where any good poem begins. We take our first, sheer joy in audible language before birth, as we listen from within the womb to the particular murmur of life in a human community and body. Heard speech remains a doorway and invitation throughout our lives, and every poem, whether traditional or free verse, must feel alive and grounded in its speaking before it will live in any other way.

The musical qualities of verse create their own concentration. Prosody draws the mind into a heightened alertness in which other powers of insight and imagination may also come into being; its forms bring a poem together, urging the memorable compression in which poetry begins. But a poem's interweavings of sound do something else as well: they signal the way every part of a poem affirms its connection with all the rest, each element speaking to and with every other. A glittering, multifaceted expression of interconnection is among poetry's central gifts.

One way poetry connects is across time. Saying a poem aloud, or reading it silently if we do so with our full attention, our bodies as well as our minds enter the rhythms present at that poem's conception. We breathe as the author breathed, we move our own tongue and teeth and throat in the ways they moved in the poem's first making. There is a startling intimacy to this. Some echo of a writer's physical experience comes into us when we read her poem; if the poem is our own, it is our own past that reinhabits our bodies, at least in part. Shaped language is strangely immortal, living in a meadowy freshness outside of time.

But it also lives in the moment, in us. Emotion, intellect, and physiology are inseparably connected in the links of a poem's sound. It is difficult to feel intimacy while shouting, to rage in a low whisper, to skip and weep at the same time. The cadences and music a poem makes within us join to create its feeling-tone as well. The difference between irony and sincerity, for instance, is conveyed by subtle verbal cues, small shifts of pitch and rhythm. A good measure of content can live in such distinctive patterns of sound.

The repetition and changes of a poem's prosody are the outward face of inner transformation. Unfolding their tensions and resolutions, a poem's sounds make of experience a shapeliness, with beginning, middle, and end. And under every poem's music, whether in form or free verse, lies the foundational heartbeat, its drum and assurance accompanying us through our lives. One of prosody's promises, then, is of a continuing, coherent existence. Some readers object to formal verse for just this reason. They feel in it a worldview too orderly for the chaos and uncertainty of contemporary life. Yet to write in a traditional form is to find that a regular returning in one dimension can bring unexpected turns in another: hunting a rhyme, the mind falls on a wholly surprising idea. This balancing between expected and unforeseen, both in aesthetic and cognitive structures, is near the center of every work of art. Through the gate of concentration, defining yet open, both aspects enter.

A poem's music affects us whether or not we make it conscious; still, to study sound's workings reawakens both ear and poem. Generalization cannot teach this alertness. It is learned only by saying one poem at a time aloud, completely. Voicing it repeatedly, feeling its weights and measures, sounding its vowels; noticing where in the body each syllable comes to rest; tasting the consonants' motion through lips and tongue. Then saying it yet again, this time hearing the meaning, and hearing how music and content not only support one another but are indistinguishably one. A good choice is Yeats's "The Lake Isle of Innisfree." A work that sounds like water over rocks or wind in trees, it holds not only the music of human thought and feeling but also the music of earth in its words.

The Lake Isle of Innisfree

I will arise and go now, and go to Innisfree,
And a small cabin build there, of clay and wattles made:
Nine bean rows will I have there, a hive for the honeybee,
And live alone in the bee-loud glade.

And I shall have some peace there, for peace comes dropping slow,
Dropping from the veils of the morning to where the cricket sings;
There midnight's all a glimmer, and noon a purple glow,
And evening full of the linnet's wings.

I will arise and go now, for always night and day
I hear lake water lapping with low sounds by the shore;
While I stand on the roadway, or on the pavements grey,
I hear it in the deep heart's core.

This poem's form is traditional; still, as with any good poem, its musical strength lies in its subtler workings. The regular rhyme scheme plays against large variations of meter; stresses and rhythms continually shift. Iambs move into spondees, lines with caesuras' internal pauses turn into lines that flow unobstructed to their end. And most powerfully, the changing vowels and consonants carry music's literal informing: ss and l sounds bind the poem together while the light vowels of "glimmer" and "linnet" give way to the long as and os of the final stanza.

Any few sentences can scarcely describe how Yeats's prosody weaves a world; readers must finish the exercise for themselves. Yet even on a first hearing, by the time "I hear lake water lapping with low sounds by the shore" arrives, it is the lake itself to which we listen. Then comes the slow and slowing rhythm of "deep heart's core." Those three strong beats, holding the long e that is the poem's bass note, bring us to the close of the poem far within our own being, plunged into the longing for such a place, where only the essential asks our attention. It is a place of solitude's beauty and silence, of thought beyond words—that words' music has made.

Before we can concentrate easily, we need to know where we stand. This is the work of rhetoric, to locate words and reader in time and place, in situation and point of view. Sound invites concentration by engaging the body and the emotions; rhetoric draws in and focuses the cognitive mind. Traditionally defined as the art of choosing the words that will best convey the speaker's intent, rhetoric's concern is the precise and beautiful movement of mind in language.

Americans distrust artful speech, believing that sincerity and deliberation cannot coexist. The sentiment has roots in the last century: "A line will take us hours, maybe; / Yet if it does not seem a moment's thought, / Our stitching and unstitching has been naught," Yeats wrote in "Adam's Curse." Romantic temperament, he knew, equates spontaneity and truth. But the word *art* is neighbor to *artifice*, and in human culture, as in the animal and vegetable worlds, desirability entails not only the impulse of the moment but also enhancement, exaggeration, rearrangement, and deception. We don't find the fragrance of night-scented flowering tobacco or the display of a peacock's tail insincere—by such ruses this world conducts its erotic business. To acknowledge rhetoric's presence in the beauty of poems, or any other form of speech, is only to agree to what already is.

Rhetoric persuades at a level so immediate it is scarcely conscious, and spelling out its workings can often seem tedious: the mind moves more quickly than that. Yet this potent, subliminal grounding is nonetheless chosen and worth exploring, and so the first tool lifted in rhetoric's shop is a basic question: "Who is speaking to whom, and toward what end?" The question's simplicity is deceptive: in its answering, many shadow devices of meaning-making step into light.

In poetry, though, one element precedes even this: that a poem is a poem is itself essential rhetorical information. The organization of white space and ink or the vocal tones that signal "poetry" are instructions to reader or listener to enter the changed consciousness that poetry asks. Each element of a poem is expected to be meaningful, part of a shaped and shaping experience of a whole: a word's placement on the page is significant, not accidental; sound qualities matter; even punctuation is thoroughly alive, responsive to itself and its context. To feel how, reading poetry, we shift instinctively into these altered expectations and assumptions, consider "found" poems. Just as Duchamp's urinal changed in nature when placed in a gallery setting, a newspaper article or recipe placed into poetry's lines is recast; the new form signals us, in reading it, to listen for concentration's transforming arc.

The power of "The Lake Isle of Innisfree" lies in its marriage of music and meaning, and rhetoric too plays its role in our encounter with that poem. First comes the visual (or auditory) recognition that what we are entering is a poem. Next, we absorb the title's message that these words concern a place, and immediately we wait to see how that place will be filled—in poetry, a landscape is never only outer, it is also a portrait of a state of soul. With the text's first word, we discover the poem is in the first person; with the second, we find the speaker making a statement about the future. Already, we are intuiting what kind of "I" this may be, probably guessing it is the poet speaking directly. (The other possibility is a more fictional "I," familiar from first-person novels or from dramatic monologues such as Robert Browning's "My Last Duchess.")

While forming a hypothesis about the speaker, we listen at the same time for some idea of whom the "I" may address. Two possibilities come to mind. One is that the poet speaks to a specific person, present in the poet's mind if not on the page. In some poems, this implied listener turns out to be the reader himself. But here it seems most likely the poem is a private meditation, spoken by the self to the self and "overheard" by the reader. This second interpretation, though odd when described in the abstract, is the rhetoric of many first-person lyric poems—since before the advent of literacy, poetry has served as a vessel in which solitary thought might occur.

As the reader makes his way through a poem, these initial hypotheses are tested and either confirmed or revised. Also continually held in the mind is the third part of rhetoric's basic question: Why am I being told these things? What will I know by the end of this poem I did not know before? For in the realm of poetry, the answer to the question, Toward what end? is almost always twofold: an ostensible speaker and listener and reason for speaking appear within the context of the poem, but another dialogue also takes place, between writer and reader. Here the *who* is the poet, the *whom* is the reader, and the *end* is the experience we take from the poem, the reason for speech rather than silence. (Occasionally, the two rhetorical frames may meet, as they do when the reader of a love poem is the beloved to whom it is addressed, or when the author of a private meditative lyric reads her own work.)

Every reading reflects not only the poem but also the reader, and so answers to the third part of rhetoric's question will differ. For me, "The Lake Isle of Innisfree" haunts first with the image of a life stripped down to the grace of essentials; it speaks of the sustenance and mystery of the simple; of the chance that, by paying attention to only what matters, one may find the heart's deep hungers and daily existence joined together and made whole. But good poems always hold more than one knowledge, and Yeats's words speak as well the impossibility of such a life. The poet proclaims his departure, yet the last stanza finds him standing undeparted, amid Dublin's streets: he listens to the siren call while remaining in place, as he has, night and day, for some time. The island of Innisfree is irresistible and unobtainable, a dream simultaneously praised and mourned. It is a figure, perhaps, for the fate of everything we desire and cannot have. This unease about the poem's outcome tugs half-recognized beneath its sureness of surface. That undertow is no small part of how a seemingly simple poem carries in the end so mysteriously powerful an effect.

Rhetoric's various devices make a vast contribution to a poem's meaning, power, and grace. For instance, if a poem's basic grammatical strategy is changed, its meaning will shift as well. Imagine the first line of Yeats's poem to read "You must arise and go now," or "Yesterday I arose and went"—either would lead to an entirely different work.

Similarly important is the order in which a poem's elements arrive: order shapes not only the rhythms of a poem's unfolding, but also its statement. When William Carlos Williams writes of the importance of the common by describing a red wheelbarrow "glazed with rain / water // beside the white / chickens," it makes a difference that the chickens, those unpoetic creatures, are what we meet last—if its endnote were the more "poetic" image of rain, rather than chickens, the poet's meaning would be undercut. Similarly Williams's many line breaks work to slow the mind, to focus the attention on a brief poem; the placement of free verse on the page has rhetorical as well as musical meaning.

Apparently minor grammatical choices can have large rhetorical effects—the choice of a pronoun, for example, or of the definite or indefinite article. Again, a small experiment makes it clear: compare "Outside my window, I saw the bird" with "Outside the window, I saw a bird." In the first sentence, we are in a place the speaker considers home, seeing a bird with which there is or will be a particular relationship; in the second, none of this is true. And while we might assume the more particularizing grammar will always be "better," some statements require exactly the second, general grammatical strategy. When Emily Dickinson begins, "A bird came down the walk," we know immediately what is familiar to her, what new; that author and bird are strangers makes a difference, for both the opening and the end of her poem.

Beginnings are useful places to feel how rhetoric engages the cognitive mind. As soon as we've heard Shakespeare's "Shall I compare thee to a summer's day?" we lean to hear how the rest of the sonnet will fulfill the comparison. A strong opening proposition is another way to snare the attention, as in W. H. Auden's "Musée des Beaux Arts": "About suffering they were never wrong, / The Old Masters. . . " We can be called to wakefulness by a puzzle, as in Czeslaw Milosz's statements: "Rivers grow small. Cities grow small. And splendid gardens / show what we did not see there before: crippled leaves and dust." By their interest or strangeness, such openings raise a question, an anticipation in the mind. How does a river or city grow small? What is it the Old Masters knew about suffering? These unanswered questions carry the reader forward, alert and curious, into the poem. Even so small a gesture as opening a poem with a prepositional phrase ("In the garden" or "At dawn") has its effect—the reader enters the poem both grounded in physical being and in motion, situated in time or place and looking for what comes next.

Finally, there are poems whose rhetoric consists of an undisguised manipulation of grammar. Gwendolyn Brooks, in "A Lovely Love," rings sorrowful, imperative stage directions directly into the reader's ear: "Let it be alleys. Let it be a hall / Whose janitor javelins epithets and thought / To cheapen hyacinth darkness. . . " This is a poet creating reality by force of will. Philip Levine, too, characteristically moves his poems by deliberate changes of grammar. His poem "What Work Is," for example, alternates between the second-person "you," in which the speaker addresses the reader, and the "you" that is a colloquial substitute for "I." When at the poem's close they become one, the synthesis is no small part of the poem's power, though it is doubtful readers will have spelled out for themselves just what has occurred.

To be aware of a poem's effects—aware of the expectations raised by each new word and aware of how the poem satisfies and changes those expectations throughout its course—does not require naming every moment's strategic gesture. It requires only our alert responsiveness, our presence to each shift in the currents of language with an answering shift in our own being. Poems, despite the ways they are sometimes taught, are not crossword-puzzle constructions; first drafts, and many stages of revision, take place at a level closer to daydream. But daydream with an added intensity: while writing, the mind moves between consciousness and the unconscious in the effortless effort of concentration. The result, if the poet's intensity of attention is sufficient, will be a poem that brims with its own knowledge, water trembling as if miraculously above the edge of a cup. Such a poem will be perfect in the root sense of the word: "thoroughly done."

In the concentration of poetry, rhetoric not only reflects intention but shapes it: the clarity of the writer and the clarities of syntax, word choice, and grammar are not one-directional, but two. Making a poem is neither a wholly conscious activity nor an act of unconscious transcription—it is a way for new thinking and feeling to come into existence, a way in which disparate modes of meaning and being may join. This is why the process of revising a poem is no arbitrary tinkering, but a continued honing of the self at the deepest level. Yeats describes revision's work in an untitled quatrain, epigraph to his 1908 *Collected Poems*:

> The friends that have it I do wrong
> when ever I remake a song,
> Should know what issue is at stake:
> it is myself that I remake.

In *ABC of Reading*, Ezra Pound describes poetic meaning as taking three primary forms. First, he names melopoeia, a poem's music. Second, there is logopoeia, a poem's intellectual component. We come now to his third power: phanopoeia, the making of images.

Image's concentration, like sound's, is a field where the energies of mind and body meet. The deepest of image's meanings is its recognition of our continuity with the rest of existence: within a good image, outer and subjective worlds illumine one another, break bread together, converse. In this way, image increases both vision and what is seen. Keeping one foot braced in the physical and the other in the realm of inner experience, image enlivens both.

How does this interconnection of animate and inanimate, exterior and interior, work? Consider two images from Philip Larkin's "Here" (a portrait of the English city of Hull), each intermingling abstraction and felt life: "Here silence stands / like heat" and "Here is unfenced existence: / Facing the sun, untalkative, out of reach." Though the poem describes Hull's oppression and dullness, in each sentence the inanimate quickens, breathes. Silence, given a body through both synaesthesia and verb choice, takes on a muscular presence. Existence, even less sensory, is brought also into the world's woven fabric, first by being "unfenced" (the fence is there, splintery and palpable, even when placed into consciousness within the negative) and then by being situated, as silence has been, in familiar bodily life—"facing the sun" and "untalkative" are human attributes. Still, these images are no simplistic personification. They are forms that let us inhabit abstraction as if from within, and so begin to know our kinship with the wide field of being. They show the way poetry moves consciousness toward empathy.

Intelligence and receptivity are connected—human meaning is made by seeing into what is. Larkin's images show how the outer world can be transformed by a subjectively infused vision; inner event placed into the language of the physical takes on an equally mysterious addition. This comes in part from the way image summons the body into a poem. It comes as well from the surplus of perception a good image emits, like an extra light: in one set of words, more than one knowledge resides. "Evening full of the linnet's wings" is physical description. It is also Yeats's imagination of a possible state of inner life. Each reading enriches and magnifies the other.

Image-making, wrote Wallace Stevens, "is primarily a discipline of rightness." In a good image, something previously unformulated (in the most literal sense) comes into the realm of the expressed. Without precisely this image, we feel, the world's store of truth would be diminished; and conversely, when a writer brings into language a new image that is fully right, what is knowable of existence expands. A new image transforms, but its rightness is rooted in what already exists—the senses' witness. Image is taken up by the reaching mind, but also within the welcoming ears, the tongue's four recognitions, the muscles' familiar surge of kinship. "With my whole body I taste these peaches," wrote Stevens, and it is by our own bodies that we know what this means.

Thinking within the fields of image, the mind crosses also into the knowledge the unconscious holds—into the shape-shifting wisdom of dream. Poetic concentration allows us to bring the dream-mind's compression, displacement, wit, depth, and surprise into our waking minds. It is within dreamlife we first learn to read rain as grief, or the way that a turtle's walking may speak of containment and an awkward, impeccable fortitude. The need for such entrance to the unconscious may be why the story of Orpheus requires Eurydice's death—it brings the singer into the underworld journey necessary for poetry's work. Her loss causes as well the outpouring of longing and grief that companion our knowledge that beauty cannot be possessed; a longing and grief that, having nowhere else to go, become in Orpheus, as in Yeats, the source of song.

To investigate the image at work, here are two poems; the first is an early poem of mourning, by Sharon Olds.

The Winter After Your Death

The long bands of mellow light
across the snow
narrow slowly.
The sun closes her gold fan
and nothing is left but black and white—
the quick steam of my breath, the dead
accurate shapes of the weeds, still, as if
pressed in an album.

Deep in my body my green heart
turns, and thinks of you. Deep in the
pond, under the thick trap
door of ice, the water moves,
the carp hangs like a sun, its scarlet
heart visible in its side.

The poem begins in the wholly literal world, but moves quickly into the imaginal with the appearance of the female sun. This personification, more conspicuous than Larkin's, risks pulling the poem into sentimentality; yet it does not, perhaps because the sun of the poem's closing image is so stark. In any case, this sun folding her gold fan is also a rather lovely and old-fashioned image, introducing the colors that carry the poem's emotion forward as they shift from gold to black and white, then into the startling green heart of the poet and the equally startling scarlet one of the carp.

The poem (whose fourteen lines, with a shift between the first eight and the last six, signal us that it is vestigially a sonnet) moves through four sentences, each more inward in nature. From simple and outward visual description, both grammar and imagery move into a realm more complex and more personal: the sun of the second sentence is feminine; the poet appears in the white steam of breath; the weeds, both directly and through their comparison with pressed flowers, speak of the death that goes otherwise unmentioned in the poem's body. The third sentence is again grammatically simple, yet its surreal green heart contains tremendous power. And as the heart turns, the poem turns, into the interior transparencies of the fourth sentence, where ice and water and carp are equal presences.

The images of "The Winter After Your Death" embody the twin depths, literal and figurative, of internal and external worlds. Everything pulls in two directions: the ice that is not only a trap door but also, because of the line break, a trap that is not a door; the visible heart of the fish that becomes not only life, but also—because what is ordinarily hidden within is now seen—the body's fragile mortality. The whole poem is a passage into the underworld made through the eyes, but one that returns us as well to the living. The displacement of loss into simile allows outer seeing to shift into the inner world, where what has vanished can still be known. Weeds pass from the actual into the realm of memory. The sun vanished from the beginning of the poem returns, transformed. That blood-red image offers only a vulnerable salvation, but it is one that must do.

In "The Winter After Your Death," every detail is multiple in meaning, as with the images in dream; however actual it seems at the start, the landscape of the poem becomes metaphor, entirely the terrain of mourning. But the world of objects can appear in poems in plainer ways as well, staying close to how we live in ordinary relationship with things—to the way bedsheet, shoes, window, cup, and fork are our constant and given companions. Here, a shoe is a shoe. Yet these images too can open us into a wider understanding, as in "The Fishing-Tackle," written by Bertolt Brecht when he was a refugee in southern California during World War II.

It is a poem that investigates the objective world as it is, rather than transformed to another purpose, and that is part of the point. Keeping faithful to primary life was Brecht's ethic as well as his aesthetic.

The Fishing-Tackle

In my room, on the whitewashed wall
Hangs a short bamboo stick bound with cord
With an iron hook designed
To snag fishing nets from the water. The stick
Came from a second-hand store downtown. My son
Gave it to me for my birthday. It is worn.
In salt water the hook's rust has eaten through the binding.
These traces of use and of work
Lend great dignity to the stick. I
Like to think that this fishing-tackle
Was left behind by those Japanese fishermen
Whom they have now driven from the West Coast into camps
As suspect aliens; that it came into my hands
To keep me in mind of so many
Unsolved but not insoluble
Questions of humanity.

(trans. Lee Baxendall)

Like "The Winter After Your Death," "The Fishing-Tackle" begins with straight-forward description. We are given a room with a whitewashed wall, on which hangs what was once an implement of work and is now an ornament. The tool is described simply, but at some length: by the duration of his interest as much as by what he says, Brecht shows this object as worthy of attention. Its substance, the story of how it came to him, the way it is rusted and worn—more than half the poem stays rooted in this factual realm. Only then are we told the questions the tool's presence raises in the poet's mind, and only the most subtle hint, the phrase "that it came into my hands," signals us to remember Brecht's own relationship to the story. To remember, that is, a great deal: Brecht's position as a refugee from another country with which America is at war. Our knowledge that he too has been forced to abandon his primary work. The difference between the poet's own freedom and the previous owner's confinement in a camp. The question of what happens to a thing (or a person) forcibly removed from its living context. Brecht leaves the reader to name for herself these "unsolved but not insoluble questions," and this too is a sign of respect. The poet trusts we will choose to ponder with him the harsh koan of how we treat one another and why.

As "The Winter After Your Death" leaves much of its meaning unspoken, so, too, does "The Fishing-Tackle." In each poem, the reader is given the data of image and only enough information to understand what terrain he is in, then left to complete the work himself: to furnish what has been left out with his own awareness, poetic concentration, and knowledge of inner and outer worlds. Olds has placed the background information into her title, while Brecht has put his into the body of the poem; but if we doubt that the concentration of image is as much the core of the latter poem as the former, we have only to try an experiment. First, give it the title "Considering the Japanese Fishermen Put into Camps," and cut the poem to its first seven lines. While the result is another work than the actual version, it remains a poem, both meaningful and moving. But try to read "The Fishing-Tackle" starting with "I like to think" and it oddly evaporates, all its power vanished. In this test we begin to feel the work image performs in poems.

While difficult to consider in isolation, passion is another fundamental energy in the making of poems. Strong emotion is concentrating by definition: overtaken by passion, we think of nothing else. Powerful feeling rushes language forward in distinctive and recognizable ways. Think of Christopher Smart's "Jubilate Agno," Allen Ginsberg's "Howl," Emily Dickinson's "Wild Nights, Wild Nights"—rather than holding Wordsworth's "emotion recollected in tranquility," these poems are vivid, present-moment enactments, and different as they are, there are qualities of speaking they share. The best descriptive poetry falls also into this category, I believe. What Pablo Neruda once referred to as "the furious blood" of his poems makes not only the poems of love, anger, and political rage swell with the vision of genius, but also his poems on tomatoes and wristwatches. Poems of strong feeling flood, overspill; however much the poet may have worked them, they taste of the unrestrainable, of outburst.

Two ways of speaking, singly or together, create this effect. The first is the music of forceful repetition, both in rhythms and words. Anaphora—repetition at a line's or sentence's beginning—is especially pervasive: strong feeling stutters forward. The second is the frequent inclusion of lists and the mounding up of detail; here, strength of emotion bursts forth as if by its own abundance. What poems of this type will not show is markedly visible logopoeia. Passion does not make careful arguments: it declares itself, and that is enough.

Both these earmarks of passionate feeling appear in Sylvia Plath's "Zoo Keeper's Wife." The poem begins with the lines, "I can stay awake all night, if need be— / Cold as an eel, without eyelids." Here is its final stanza:

> How our courtship lit the tindery cages—
> Your two-horned rhinoceros opened a mouth
> Dirty as a bootsole and big as a hospital sink
> For my cube of sugar: its bog breath
> Gloved my arm to the elbow.
> The snails blew kisses like black apples.
> Nightly now I flog apes owls bears sheep
> Over their iron stile. And still don't sleep.

Plath's rage unleashes itself in a rush of accumulating surreal detail, both distorting and accurate; her parade of animals has a nightmare's wildness of reach. The distinctive music of emotion-driven poetry is present as well—these lines press forward with percussive, insistent rhythm; hard consonants clip; alliteration and assonance thicken until the words reel. Then the blunt rhyme of the final two lines slams the poem shut, violence of feeling palpable in its every part.

A different emotion appears in the closing section of Theodore Roethke's "The Shape of the Fire." Here, at the end of a long poem that has been wildly disordered, the healing power of the natural replenishes the psyche in a wealth of closely focused images, in the anaphoric murmur of infinitive verbs, and in the more subtle, but still audible, rhyme of both the first and last words in each of the final two lines. The poem unfurls wonder, gratitude, the amazement that fulfillment is possible:

> To have the whole air!
> The light, the full sun
> Coming down on the flowerheads,
> The tendrils turning slowly,
> A slow snail-lifting, liquescent;
> To be by the rose
> Rising slowly out of its bed,
> Still as a child in its first loneliness;
> To see cyclamen veins become clearer in early sunlight,
> And mist lifting out of the brown cattails;
> To stare into the after-light, the glitter left on the lake's surface,
> When the sun has fallen behind a wooded island;
> To follow the drops sliding from a lifted oar,
> Held up, while the rower breathes, and the small boat drifts
>   quietly shoreward;
> To know that light falls and fills, often without our knowing,
> As an opaque vase fills to the brim from a quick pouring,
> Fills and trembles at the edge yet does not flow over,
> Still holding and feeding the stem of the contained flower.

Repetition and list can also be used to convey extremity of feeling within the context of its restraint. In a mastery probably unchosen, but no less achieved, what we feel in such poems is the effort it costs the writer simply to speak at all. Elizabeth Bishop's villanelle "One Art" is a consummate example, a calm and formal listing of losses—houses, rivers, a mother's watch, the poem's simple, heartbreaking "you"—in which the poet's control is broken by only a single moment of struggle: "It's evident / the art of losing's not too hard to master / though it may look like (*Write* it!) like disaster."

Another poet of restraint is Constantin Cavafy. Homosexual love and the condition of religious or linguistic outcastness (both historically and in his own early twentieth-century Alexandria) occupy much of his work. His sonnet "Hidden Things" is a work stripped even more bare than Bishop's villanelle; it may be no accident that both these poets chose to work frequently within the binding framework of form. As with Bishop, a keening comes through the poet's ostensible control: even amid irony, Cavafy's quiet repetitions communicate the strict fierceness of his grief.

Hidden Things

From all I did and all I said
let no one try to find out who I was.
An obstacle was there that changed the pattern
of my actions and the manner of my life.
An obstacle was often there
to stop me when I'd begin to speak.
From my most unnoticed actions,
my most veiled writing—
from these alone will I be understood.
But maybe it isn't worth so much concern,
so much effort to discover who I really am.
Later, in a more perfect society,
someone else made just like me
is certain to appear and act freely.

(TRANS. EDMUND KEELEY AND PHILIP SHERRARD)

Next comes the concentration of narrative, in which event itself is the sinew that moves a poem forward. Storytelling, like rhetoric, pulls us in through the cognitive mind as much as through the emotions. It answers both our curiosity and our longing for shapely forms: our profound desire to know what happens, and our persistent hope that what happens will somehow make sense. Narrative instructs us in both these hungers and their satisfaction, teaching us to perceive and to relish the arc of moments and the arc of lives. If shapeliness is illusion, it is one we require— it shields against arbitrariness and against chaos's companion, despair. And story, like all the forms of concentration, connects. It brings us to a deepened coherence with the world of others and also within the many levels of the self.

Much of the cultural work once performed by poetic narrative has been taken on by film and works in prose; one reason will be explored later in this book. Yet story remains a basic human path toward the discovery and ordering of meaning and beauty, and the narrative lyric, especially, continues to flourish. An example is Tess Gallagher's poem written after the death of her father, "Black Silk":

She was cleaning—there is always
that to do—when she found,
at the top of the closet, his old
silk vest. She called me
to look at it, unrolling it carefully
like something live
might fall out. Then we spread it
on the kitchen table and smoothed
the wrinkles down, making our hands
heavy until its shape against Formica

came back and the little tips
that would have pointed to his pockets
lay flat. The buttons were all there.
I held my arms out and she
looped the wide armholes over
them. "That's one thing I never
wanted to be," she said, "a man."
I went into the bathroom to see
how I looked in the sheen and
sadness. Wind chimes
off-key in the alcove. Then her
crying so I stood back in the sink-light
where the porcelain had been staring. Time
to go to her, I thought, with that
other mind, and stood still.

The energies of poetry's concentrations do not exist in isolation from one another, and this poem is suffused with sound and images, with precisely deployed grammar and passionate feeling. The vest—what is still here, with each of its buttons intact—is made present with all the sensuous particularity of the mind of image. The grammatical concentration of rhetoric is here as well: we are left to infer the vastness of what is not here—the father—solely through the subjunctive phrase, "the little tips that *would have* pointed to his pockets." Then there is the subtle displacement of "like something live might fall out," in whose colloquial diction we hear the echo of this grown daughter's childhood. Reading the words, we think first of what moths or spiders might live on the high shelves of a rarely opened closet; only afterward do we realize the deeper resonance of the phrase.

Still, "Black Silk" is not so much about grief in its overwhelming first arrival as it is about how we continue living with grief once it has entered our lives in an irreversible way. That is why the heart of the poem lies in narrative, in its telling of what this mother and daughter do and fail to do. By describing without commentary or judgment what is found, what is said, what is thought and done, Gallagher succeeds in being both tactful and entirely revealing. Such reticence is one of narrative's strengths: story, at its best, becomes a canvas to which the reader as well as the writer must bring the full range of memory, intellect, and imaginative response. The best stories are almost mythlike in their ability to support alternative readings, different conclusions—for instance, nothing within this poem tells us that it is about a nuclear family, and the poem is equally moving if read in other ways. The words of a poem are not ends, but means into an exploration without limit.

Narrative carries the knowledge of our alteration through the shifting currents of circumstance and time. What then is the core perception of "Black Silk"? It is a poem about the ways that love both binds and changes us over time, and about the solitude the grief of maturity finally brings. In separation from the father lies an irrevocable separation from the mother as well: holding out her arms, the poet is given not the comfort of familial love, but what Gallagher has described elsewhere as "the arm holes of absence." This daughter who slips her body into roles the mother would not choose is also a daughter who experiences the material weight of each side of the family drama. She slips, too, into the word-sewn fabric of her own life—its stories of luminous sheen, sadness, loneliness, anger; its bright self-knowledge and dark threads of strength.

The final poetic concentration to consider is voice—not the grammatical voice of rhetoric, but the lived inhabitance a good poem gives off. Voice is not a matter of subject, nor of the activity a poem undertakes; it is another level of content, equally essential to a poem's realization, infusing each choice and gesture a poem makes. Voice is the underlying style of being that creates a poem's rounding presence, making it continuous, idiosyncratic, and recognizable.

A person's heard voice is replete with information. So it is with the voice of a poem, directing us in myriad ways into the realm it inhabits—a realm more or less formal, more or less argumentative, more or less emotional, linear, textured. As we gauge a person's kindness by tone, regardless of what she is saying, we similarly recognize a poem's tenderness or harshness toward the world around it; its engagement or detachment; whether it is ironic, comic, fantastic, serious, compassionate, irreverent, or philosophical. We intuit these things as a dog intuits another dog's friendly or challenging disposition.

Voice in this sense is the body language of a poem—the part that cannot help but reveal what it is. Everything that has gone into making us who we are is held there. Yet we also speak of writers "finding their voice." The phrase is both meaningful and odd, a perennial puzzle: how can we "find" what we already use? The answer lies, paradoxically, in the quality of listening that accompanies self-aware speech: singers, to stay in tune, must hear not only the orchestral music they sing with, but also themselves. Similarly, writers who have "found a voice" are those whose ears turn at once inward and outward, both toward their own nature, thought patterns, and rhythms, and toward those of the culture at large.

Sometimes, as with Emily Dickinson or William Blake, a writer's ear will lean far toward the inner; the risk then is that his or her voice will be incomprehensible to others, at least for a time. But there is risk, too, for the writer who turns only outward, toward the speech and thought of the commons: such language, though comprehensible, has not been dipped in the stubborn ink of one person's uniqueness. Even the ostensibly "plain" language of early William Carlos Williams, of William Bronk, or of Robert Creeley is in some way also a heightening, a paring and framing—that is what makes their words poems. The effects of voice can be seen most easily, though, at the other end of the spectrum, as in Gerard Manley Hopkins's "Carrion Comfort":

> Not, I'll not, carrion comfort, Despair, not feast on thee;
> Not untwist—slack as they may be—these last strands of man
> In me ór, most weary, cry *I can no more*. I can;
> Can something, hope, wish day come, not choose not to be.

But ah, but O thou terrible, why wouldst thou rude on me
Thy wring-world right foot rock? lay a lionlimb against me? scan
With darksome devouring eyes my bruisèd bones? and fan,
O in turns of tempest, me heaped there; me frantic to avoid thee
    and flee?

Why? That my chaff might fly; my grain lie, sheer and clear.
Nay in all that toil, that coil, since (seems) I kissed the rod,
Hand rather, my heart lo! lapped strength, stole joy, would
    laugh, cheer.

Cheer whóm though? Thé hero whose héaven-handling flúng me,
    fóot tród
Me? or mé that fóught him? O which one? is it eách one? That níght,
    that year
Of now done darkness I wretch lay wrestling with (my God!)
    my God.

The poem's rhetorical frame is an address, directed to the second-person Despair; yet however rooted it is in the gestures of speech, this sonnet's language comes to a music wholly original and poetry-born. Halting and rushing at once, inventive, pressured, elliptical, from its first phrase the poem stands removed from the ordinary orders of meaning. Yet once the reader agrees to its ways, she can imagine no other vessel for what is here said; disrupted word order, new compounds, and self-correction become the marks of the onslaught of which the poem speaks. This is language that marries rhetorical, intellectual, and theologically inquiring mind with the thick-laid sounds and images of the poetry of feeling. It is an alchemy not seen before, made by the genius of Hopkins's concentration.

Though voice dominates in "Carrion Comfort," every realized poem has a carriage unmistakably its own. One of the ways we come to recognize the work of individual writers is by developing a sense for their characteristic ways of addressing the world and of moving a poem. Recall Elizabeth Bishop's similes, honed by the self-correction she may have learned from Hopkins; Dickinson's staccato rhythms of insight; Jorie Graham's fracturings, gaps, and mixing of abstraction with concrete detail ("the sleek whiskey-colored slice of time"); Galway Kinnell's encyclopedic lyrical reach and the occasional turns of humor in even his most serious poems. Each of these modes of speaking both mirrors and creates a self—at least the self of the poems and, quite possibly, as Yeats implied in the quatrain quoted earlier, of the life as well.

No matter how carefully we read or how much attention we bring to bear, a good poem can never be completely entered, completely known. If it is the harvest of true concentration, it will know more than can be said in any other way. And because it thinks by music and image, by story and passion and voice, poetry can do what other forms of thinking cannot: approximate the actual flavor of life, in which subjective and objective become one, in which conceptual mind and the inexpressible presence of things become one.

Letting this wideness of being into ourselves, as readers or as writers, while staying close to the words themselves, we begin to find in poems a way of entering both language and being on their own terms. Poetry leads us into the self, but also away from it. Transparency is part of what we seek in art, and in art's mind of concentration that is both capacious and focused. Free to turn inward and outward, free to remain still and wondering amid the mysteries of mind and world, we arrive, for a moment, at a kind of fullness that overspills into everything. One breath taken completely; one poem, fully written, fully read—in such a moment, anything can happen. The pressed oil of words can blaze up into music, into image, into the heart and mind's knowledge. The lit and shadowed places within us can be warmed.

***

RICHARD HUGO

Writing off the Subject

I often make these remarks to a beginning poetry-writing class.

You'll never be a poet until you realize that everything I say today and this quarter is wrong. It may be right for me, but it is wrong for you. Every moment, I am, without wanting or trying to, telling you to write like me. But I hope you learn to write like you. In a sense, I hope I don't teach you how to write but how to teach yourself how to write. At all times keep your crap detector on. If I say something that helps, good. If what I say is of no help, let it go. Don't start arguments. They are futile and take us away from our purpose. As Yeats noted, your important arguments are with yourself. If you don't agree with me, don't listen. Think about something else.

When you start to write, you carry to the page one of two attitudes, though you may not be aware of it. One is that all music must conform to truth. The other, that all truth must conform to music. If you believe the first, you are making your job very difficult, and you are not only limiting the writing of poems to something done only by the very witty and clever, such as Auden, you are weakening the justification for creative-writing programs. So you can take that attitude if you want, but you are jeopardizing my livelihood as well as your chances of writing a good poem.

If the second attitude is right, then I still have a job. Let's pretend it is right because I need the money. Besides, if you feel truth must conform to music, those of us who find life bewildering and who don't know what things mean, but love the sounds of words enough to fight through draft after draft of a poem, can go on writing—try to stop us.

One mark of a beginner is his impulse to push language around to make it accommodate what he has already conceived to be the truth, or, in some cases, what he has already conceived to be the form. Even Auden, clever enough at times to make music conform to truth, was fond of quoting the woman in the Forster novel who said something like, "How do I know what I think until I see what I've said."

A poem can be said to have two subjects, the initiating or triggering subject, which starts the poem or "causes" the poem to be written, and the real or generated subject, which the poem comes to say or mean, and which is generated or discovered in the poem during the writing. That's not quite right because it suggests that the poet recognizes the real subject. The poet may not be aware of what the real subject is but only have some instinctive feeling that the poem is done.

Young poets find it difficult to free themselves from the initiating subject. The poet puts down the title: "Autumn Rain." He finds two or three good lines about Autumn Rain. Then things start to break down. He cannot find anything more to say about Autumn Rain so he starts making up things, he strains, he goes abstract, he starts telling us the meaning of what he has already said. The mistake he is making, of course, is that he feels obligated to go on talking about Autumn Rain, because that, he feels, is the subject. Well, it isn't the subject. You don't know what the subject is, and the moment you run out of things to say about Autumn Rain start talking about something else. In fact, it's a good idea to talk about something else before you run out of things to say about Autumn Rain.

Don't be afraid to jump ahead. There are a few people who become more interesting the longer they stay on a single subject. But most people are like me, I find. The longer they talk about one subject, the duller they get. Make the subject of the next sentence different from the subject of the sentence you just put down. Depend on rhythm, tonality, and the music of language to hold things together. It is impossible to write meaningless sequences. In a sense the next thing always belongs. In the world of imagination, all things belong. If you take that on faith, you may be foolish, but foolish like a trout.

Never worry about the reader, what the reader can understand. When you are writing, glance over your shoulder, and you'll find there is no reader. Just you and the page. Feel lonely? Good. Assuming you can write clear English sentences, give up all worry about communication. If you want to communicate, use the telephone.

To write a poem you must have a streak of arrogance—not in real life I hope. In real life try to be nice. It will save you a hell of a lot of trouble and give you more time to write. By arrogance I mean that when you are writing you must assume that the next thing you put down belongs not for reasons of logic, good sense, or narrative development, but because you put it there. You, the same person who said that, also said this. The adhesive force is your way of writing, not sensible connection.

The question is: how to get off the subject, I mean the triggering subject. One way is to use words for the sake of their sounds. Later, I'll demonstrate this idea.

The initiating subject should trigger the imagination as well as the poem. If it doesn't, it may not be a valid subject but only something you feel you should write a poem about. Never write a poem about anything that ought to have a poem written about it, a wise man once told me. Not bad advice but not quite right. The point is, the triggering subject should not carry with it moral or social obligations to feel or claim you feel certain ways. If you feel pressure to say what you know others want to hear and don't have enough devil in you to surprise them, shut up. But the advice is still well taken. Subjects that ought to have poems have a bad habit of wanting lots of other things at the same time. And you provide those things at the expense of your imagination.

I suspect that the true or valid triggering subject is one in which physical characteristics or details correspond to attitudes the poet has toward the world and himself. For me, a small town that has seen better days often works. Contrary to what reviewers and critics say about my work, I know almost nothing of substance about the places that trigger my poems. Knowing can be a limiting thing. If the population of a town is nineteen but the poem needs the sound seventeen, seventeen is easier to say if you don't know the population. Guessing leaves you more options. Often, a place that starts a poem for me is one I have only glimpsed while passing through. It should make impression enough that I can see things in the town—the water tower, the bank, the last movie announced on the marquee before the theater shut down for good, the closed hotel—long after I've left. Sometimes these are imagined things I find if I go back, but real or imagined, they act as a set of stable knowns that sit outside the poem. They and the town serve as a base of operations for the poem. Sometimes they serve as a stage setting. I would never try to locate a serious poem in a place where physical evidence suggests that the people there find it relatively easy to accept themselves—say the new Hilton.

The poet's relation to the triggering subject should never be as strong as (must be weaker than) his relation to his words. The words should not serve the subject. The subject should serve the words. This may mean violating the facts. For example, if the poem needs the word "black" at some point and the grain elevator is yellow, the grain elevator may have to be black in the poem. You owe reality nothing and the truth about your feelings everything.

Let's take what I think is a lovely little poem, written in 1929 by a fine poet who has been unjustly ignored.

Rattlesnake

I found him sleepy in the heat
And dust of a gopher burrow,
Coiled in loose folds upon silence
In a pit of the noonday hillside.
I saw the wedged bulge
Of the head hard as a fist.
I remembered his delicate ways:
The mouth a cat's mouth yawning.
I crushed him deep in dust,
And heard the loud seethe of life

In the dead beads of the tail
Fade, as wind fades
From the wild grain of the hill.*

I find there's much to be learned about writing from this excellent poem. First I think it demonstrates certain truths that hold for much art. The poem grows from an experience, either real or imagined—I only recently found out that this particular experience was real. The starting point is fixed to give the mind an operating base, and the mind expands from there. Often, if the triggering subject is big (love, death, faith) rather than localized and finite, the mind tends to shrink. Sir Alexander Fleming observed some mold, and a few years later we had a cure for gonorrhea. But what if the British government had told him to find a cure for gonorrhea? He might have worried so much he would not have noticed the mold. Think small. If you have a big mind, that will show itself. If you can't think small, try philosophy or social criticism.

The need for the poem to have been written is evident in the poem. This is a strong example of the notion that all good serious poems are born in obsession. Without this poem the experience would have been neither validated nor completed.

The poem has elements of melodrama. All art that has endured has a quality we call schmaltz or corn. Our reaction against the sentimentality embodied in Victorian and post-Victorian writing was so resolute writers came to believe that the further from sentimentality we got, the truer the art. That was a mistake. As Bill Kittredge, my colleague who teaches fiction writing, has pointed out: if you are not *risking* sentimentality, you are not close to your inner self.

The poem is located in a specific place. You don't know where, but you know the poet knows where. Knowing where you are can be a source of creative stability. If you are in Chicago you can go to Rome. If you ain't no place you can't go nowhere.

The snake is killed gratuitously. The study of modern psychology may have helped some of us become better people. We may treat our children better because we have gained some rudimentary notion of cause and effect in behavior. But in art, as seemingly in life, things happen without cause. They just happen. A poem seldom finds room for explanations, motivations, or reason. What if the poem read

Because I knew his poison
Was dangerous to children
I crushed him deep in dust . . . ?

The poet would be making excuses for himself, and the fierce honesty with which he faces his raw act of murder would be compromised. Nothing in the drama *King Lear* can possibly serve as explanation of the shattering cruelty of Regan and Cornwall when they blind Gloucester. From a writer's standpoint, a good explanation is that Shakespeare knew a lot of creeps walk this earth.

---

*From Brewster Ghiselin, *Against the Circle* (New York: Dutton, 1946), p. 60. Reprinted with permission of the author.

But there's more to be learned from this poem than just artistic principles. They are always suspect anyway, including those I think I find here. Let's move on to the language of the poem.

Generally, in English multisyllabic words have a way of softening the impact of language. With multisyllabic words we can show compassion, tenderness, and tranquillity. With multisyllabic words we become more civilized. In the first four lines of the poem, seven of the twenty-six words, slightly better than one out of four, are two-syllable words. This is a fairly high count unless you are in politics. The snake is sleepy. He presents no threat to the speaker. His dwelling is that of a harmless creature, a gopher. It's almost as if the snake were a derelict, an orphan, a vagabond who sleeps wherever he can. The words "noonday hillside" suggest that the world does not have rigid topography but optional configurations. At 4 P.M. it might not be a hillside at all. We take our identities from our relationships, just as the earth takes its configurations from the time of day, the position of the source of light. This is a warm, fluid world.

With single-syllable words we can show rigidity, honesty, toughness, relentlessness, the world of harm unvarnished. In lines five and six, the snake is seen as a threat, the lines slam home heavy as the fist the poet sees as simile for the head of the snake. But of course, men, not snakes, have fists, and so we might ask: where does the danger really lie here?

The speaker then has a tender memory of the snake in lines seven and eight, and we get two three-syllable words and a long two-syllable word, "yawning." You might note that the poet is receptive to physical similarities of snakes and domestic cats—they look much alike when yawning—just as later he sees and hears the similarity of rattlesnakes to wheat (grain), the way the tail looks like the tassle, the way the rattle sounds like wind in the grain.

In the final five lines the poet kills the snake, faces himself and the moral implications of his act without a flinch or excuse, and we get no multisyllabic words in the entire passage. All single-syllable words, and the gaze is level, the whole being of the speaker honestly laid out, vulnerable on his private moral block. If one acts on the rigid prejudicial attitudes expressed in lines five and six (which the speaker did), and not on the fluid, tender, humane attitudes expressed in the first four lines and lines seven and eight, then in return one is faced with the fully developed, uncompromising picture of what one has done. Forever.

In this poem the triggering subject remains fully in view until late in the poem, whereas the generated object, what the poem is saying, just begins to show at the end but is nonetheless evident. The snake as such is being left behind, and attitudes about life are starting to form. The single-syllable words in the last five lines relentlessly drive home the conviction that all life is related, and that even if life isn't sacred, we might be better off if we acted as if it were. In this case the poet got off the initiating subject late.

I mentioned that one way of getting off the subject, of freeing yourself from memory if you will, is to use words for the sake of sound. Now I must use four lines from an early poem of mine, simply because I can't verify any other poet's process. I know what mine was at the time. These are the first four lines of the fourth stanza of an early poem called "At the Stilli's Mouth."

With the Stilli this defeated and the sea
turned slough by close Camano, how can water die
with drama, in a final rich cascade,
a suicide, a victim of terrain, a martyr?

When I was a young poet I set an arbitrary rule that when I made a sound I felt was strong, a sound I liked specially, I'd make a similar sound three to eight syllables later. Of course it would often be a slant rhyme. Why three to eight? Don't ask. You have to be silly to write poems at all.

In this case the word "cascade" fell lovingly on my ear and so, soon after, "suicide." I wasn't smart enough to know that I was saying that my need to see things dramatically was both childish and authentic. But "suicide" was right and led to "victim of terrain" and "martyr," associative notions at least, but also words that sound like other words in the passage, "martyr" like "drama" and "water," "victim" like "final" and "Stilli" (Northwest colloquial for Stilliguamish, the river). Instead of "suicide" I might have hit on "masquerade," but that would have been wrong and I hope I would have known it. I might have simply because "masquerade" sounds *too much* like "cascade," calls attention to itself, and to my ear is less interesting. What I'm trying to tell you is that by doing things like this I was able to get off the subject and write the poem. The fact that "suicide" sounds like "cascade" is infinitely more important than what is being said.

It isn't of course, but if you think about it that way for the next twenty-five years you could be in pretty good shape.

◄━━━◆◆◆◆◆━━━►

ERICA JONG

My Grandmother on My Shoulder

So much of childhood lies buried in the mysteries of the synapses. Repressed because unbearable—perhaps because it conflicts with some necessary myth we have constructed to explain our ancestors. Or perhaps simply because it pains us to remember.

So much of self-knowledge is just recovering memory. This is one of the saving graces of aging. Memory sails back through the seas of dying gray matter and we grow sane enough to bear our own consciousness. Short-term memory, the old ones tell us, dies away like melody on a summer night. But ancient buried chords

Erica Jong, "My Grandmother on My Shoulder" from Writers on Writing: A Breadloaf Anthology, *Eds. Robert Pack and Jay Parini, Middlebury College Press, 1991. Reprinted by permission of Erica Jong.*

return, as if played on a harpsichord with some strings broken. A recitative with words missing, a partial transcript of an unrecoverable conversation.

I grew up in an old-fashioned European family in New York. Perhaps that is one reason I feel so much at home in Italy. Grandmother, Grandfather, Mother, Father, three sisters, housekeeper—we might as well have been a family of the last century.

My grandparents came from Russia and spoke Russian and Yiddish when they did not want the children to understand. My parents were called by their first names, like children; my grandparents were "Mama" and "Papa."

Papa painted in the tall studio facing north toward the Museum of Natural History (in one of those turrets, I later learned, Margaret Mead, one of my heroines, wrote). As befitting the patriarch, he had the only studio. My mother, also a painter, folded and unfolded her easel as the time to work permitted. And my grandmother? She cooked and baked and worried over us. I never thought of her as having creativity at all—and I never learned her recipe for brisket or apple pie or even roast potatoes.

I painted still lives with my grandfather, but it was my grandmother who taught me, in some mysterious way, to be a woman. It was my grandmother who taught me to be the second sex. It was my grandmother I had to kill before I could become a writer.

Every woman artist has to kill her own grandmother. She perches on our shoulder whispering: "Write nice things. Don't embarrass the family." But "nice things" are rarely true things. The truth about human beings is rarely "nice."

And so we are divided—we creators of the female gender. In some way we identify with the patriarch—or how would we have become creators at all? And in some way we identify with the murderer; the one we murder—"Mama"—is ourselves.

I have asked myself again and again how is it possible that the women's revolution has started and stopped so many times in history—beginning with the suddenness of an earthquake and often dying away just as quickly. Women spill oceans of ink, change some laws, change some expectations—and then subside, and become their grandmothers again. What is this dialectic that drives them? What is their guilt that causes them to sabotage their own gains?

It is not merely biology—the softening effect of estrogen on the human female—and the years of bearing and rearing. For we no longer bear and rear for all our lives, and often we are stronger and more determined for every child we bear. The secret is to be found, rather, in the long dependency of the human creature and the many years it takes to form those curious mosaics we call our memories. In those mosaics there are both "male" and "female" forms. Onto the "female" we project all that we must repress, stifle, kill within ourselves. Onto the "male" we project all that we must assert in ourselves in order to create.

If this were conscious, everything would be easy—including change. But it is far from conscious. We do not *know* that we value the male and devalue the female. We do not *know* that we are divided against ourselves. We do not *know* we have internalized "Papa" as right and "Mama" as wrong.

So we twist in the wind: identify with Mama and we deny our creativity; identify with Papa and we need to kill our grandmothers in order to assert ourselves.

Every book I have written has been written on the bleeding corpse of my grandmother. Every book has been written with guilt, powered by pain. Every book has been a baby I did not bear, 10,000 meals I did not cook, 10,000 beds I did not make. I wish, above all, to be undivided, to be whole (this, in fact, is the theme of all my work), but I remain divided. Like a person who once committed a terrible crime that went unpunished, I always wait for the ax to fall.

My grandmother died in 1969. Ten years later I wrote this poem, attempting to capture something of the feelings her example raised in me:

Woman Enough

Because my grandmother's hours
were apple cakes baking,
& dust motes gathering,
& linens yellowing
& seams and hems
inevitably unraveling—
I almost never keep house—
though really I *like* houses
& wish I had a clean one.

Because my mother's minutes
were sucked into the roar
of the vacuum cleaner,
because she waltzed with the washer-dryer
& tore her hair waiting for repairmen—
I send out my laundry,
& live in a dusty house,
though really I *like* clean houses
as well as anyone.

I am woman enough
to love the kneading of bread
as much as the feel
of typewriter keys
under my fingers—
springy, springy.
& the smell of clean laundry
& simmering soup
are almost as dear to me
as the smell of paper and ink.

I wish there were not a choice;
I wish I could be two women.

I wish the days could be longer.
But they are short.
So I write while
the dust piles up.

I sit at my typewriter
remembering my grandmother
& all my mothers,
& the minutes they lost
loving houses better than themselves—
& the man I love cleans up the kitchen
grumbling only a little
because he knows
that after all these centuries
it is easier for him
than for me.

Now, a decade later, these feelings are even stronger.

Seeing the hatred and envy that women have of other women, the passionate denunciation of female progress, I have often wondered, where does the intensity of the hatred come from and why are women so bitter toward those among themselves who press for change?

If you have been a good girl all your life and have adhered to good-girl rules, mustn't you attack the bad girl, the one who breaks rules and gets away with it? Cheated by life with grandma on one shoulder, cheated by playing by rules invented by man to keep us meek, we often attack the very ones who seek to free us—a case of wanting to kill the messenger.

Unless this dialectic changes, women will never progress. They will begin their revolution but never complete it. They will win freedoms only to have their daughters give them back.

In the sixties and seventies, we thought it was only a case of having enough women in power. What we had not bargained for is that often women in power do not advance the cause of their own sex.

Identified with the male because the male in our culture means assertion, often women in power behave like men—or worse.

Nancy Reagan, Imelda Marcos, Margaret Thatcher, Leona Helmsley—these are not women who advance the cause of women. These are women who have imitated all the worst aspects of male power and have cut off not one breast (like the Amazons of old), but two.

A truly revolutionary movement of women would be one that asserted and glorified the real strengths of the female—nurturance, the ability to connect with emotion, the ability to make human beings connect with and nurture one another. It is a false feminism that abandons the strengths of womanhood for an unbecoming imitation of the arrogance of the male. It is a false feminism that dictates that women become artificial men in order to assert their power.

Where does this leave the female creator? In a quandary, usually. The quandary I have described above. My grandmother sits on my shoulder and I seek to kill her. Is there an alternative way to be a woman artist? Is there an androgynous freedom beyond female and male?

A memory from childhood drifts back through the synapses. I am lying in the big bed between my parents. Perhaps I am four or five. I have awakened with a nightmare and my sleepy father has carried me into bed and placed me between himself and my mother.

Bliss. A foretaste of heaven. A memory of the amniotic ocean—the warmth of my mother's body on one side and of my father's on the other. (Freudians would say I am happy to separate them—and maybe they are right—but let us shelve that question for now.) Suffice it to say that I am happy to be here in the primeval cave. Suffice it to say that I am bathed in the radiance of paradiso.

Back, back in time. I lie on my back and the ceiling seems a kaleidoscope of diced peas and carrots—nursery food—comforting and warm. My parents' mingled smells and mine. Family pheromones. Familiar smells out of which we are born. For the moment, there is no world but this, no siblings, no teachers, no streets, no cars. Eden is here between my sleeping parents and there is no banishment in sight. I deliberately hold myself awake to savor this heaven as long as I can. I fight off sleep to savor the moment of *paradiso* threading through the *purgatorio* of everyday life, the *inferno* of school and sisters, of competitive sandbox wars, and the cruelty of other children.

This is where we all begin—in the paradiso of childhood. And it is to this place that poetry seeks to return us. Poetry and love. We seek them all our lives. The poles of our being—love and death: the parental bed and the grave. Our passage is from one to the other.

My grandmother on my shoulder is upset. She doesn't want me to write these things. She believes the course of wisdom in a woman's life is to keep silent about all the truth she knows. It is dangerous, she has learned, to parade intimate knowledge. The clever woman smiles and keeps mum. My problem is that books don't get written that way. Especially not books containing truth.

So we come back, inevitably, to the problem of women writing the truth. We must write the truth in order to validate our own feelings, our own lives, and we have only very recently earned those rights. Dictators burn books because they know that books help people claim their feelings and that people who claim their feelings are harder to crush.

Patriarchal society has put a gag on women's public expression of feelings because silence compels obedience. My grandmother thinks she wants to protect me. She doesn't want to see me stoned in the marketplace. She doesn't want me pilloried for my words. She wants me safe so that I can save the next generation. She has a matriarch's interest in keeping our family alive.

Hush, Mama, the world has changed. We are claiming our own voices. We will speak not only for ourselves but also for you. And our daughters, we hope, will never have to kill *their* grandmothers.

Two more memories drift back through the decades. The first is of you washing my little hands between your own and saying that you were "washing away the

Germans"—with its pun on "germs." The second is of the children—me, my older sister Susannah, and the baby, Claudia, hiding in the cave of the linen closet and playing "Running away from the Nazis." The war is already long over. It is 1947—but in our memories, the war is never over. Three little Jewish girls in New York City, in a world where anti-Semitism seems the remotest possibility, are playing as if Anne Frank's fate applied to them. (And, in some way, of course it does.)

I make a foray into the kitchen for bread and butter sandwiches while my older sister holds the fort (and the baby).

"What are you doing?" asks my Grandmother.

"Oh, nothing," I say, running back for cover with the sandwiches.

"Children!" calls my Grandmother. "Children!"

We pretend not to hear her.

"*Children*," she calls, "What are you playing?"

"Oh, nothing," we say, munching our sandwiches in the closet, hiding from imaginary Nazis.

We cannot say that we are playing love and death. We would not even know how to form the words. But we are playing for our lives, playing for time, and playing as a way of learning life.

My older sister who originated this game was born in 1937. The world was on the edge of war when she first emerged into it, and she absorbed the threat of danger with her mother's milk. I followed her lead, as second children do. The details obsessed me: the baby bundled in the doll carriage; my mission to the kitchen to snatch the sandwiches (bread, butter, applesauce, and powdered sugar); my mad dash back down the hall through imaginary woods filled with imaginary Nazis, shouldering imaginary machine guns; my sense of my own importance as a survivor, provider, purveyor of food.

"In dreams begin responsibilities," says the great Irish poet Yeats. In games begin the serious business of our lives. Still the messenger, still the provider, I am still hiding in the scented cave of the linen closet to write, then rushing out to gather sustenance from the world, then running back to feed the baby and myself.

The baby that I feed is sometimes my daughter, sometimes myself, sometimes my books. But the model of frenzied survival is clear. I alternate between periods of calm and periods of maximum stress. The second World War still rages in my head.

I try to imagine my grandmother's life compared to my own. Born in the 1880s in Russia, raised in Odessa, she came to England in her teens, married, and had two daughters before the first World War began. In the twenties, she raising two small children in New York, having survived pogroms, prerevolutionary unrest, the influenza epidemic, the first World War, displacement, emigration, two new languages, two new lands. And I, the second daughter of a second daughter of a second daughter, bear all these burdens and disruptions in my soul.

I seize them all as opportunities. I embrace the courage and tenacity she passed along to me. But I have won the right to speak of it—a right she never dreamed.

Mama—the world will silence us soon enough. Let us not conspire by silencing ourselves. "The snow falls over all the living and all the dead," said James Joyce. Let us unbury ourselves while we still have breath and life to do it. The world is not so dangerous if we surrender our fear. Think of all we have lived through collectively—we second daughters of second daughters . . . and we are still alive! Let us raise our voices in celebration of that amazing fact of survival. Let us never accept silence as our fate again!

WILLIAM MATTHEWS

A Note on Prose, Verse and the Line

"Lack of a firm sense of the line is a handicap," writes John Haines ("Further Reflections on Line and the Poetic Voice"), and asks, "Is this why the prose poem is so much in evidence these days? There you don't have to justify your lines, just make the paragraph and let it go."

Haines uses "justify" not in its typesetter's meaning, but in its religious meaning; writers of prose poems are like the lilies of the field.

I imagine one is drawn to write prose poems not by sloth, more purely practiced in hammocks, but by an urge to participate in a different kind of psychic energy than verse usually embodies.

Here are excerpts from etymologies of "prose" and "verse" in Webster's Third New International Dictionary. Prose is "fr. L *prosa*, fem. of *prosus* straightforward, direct." Verse is "fr. L *versus* row, line, verse; akin to L *vertere* to turn."

So the line in prose is like a fishing line, cast out as far as it will go, straightforward. And the line in verse goes out from the margin, turns back, goes out again, etc. Thus poetry is often linked to dance. The serpentine line of verse goes more down the page than across it.

I think of the long lines tending toward prose in Blake's prophetic books. Whitman, visionary passages from Ginsberg and Roethke. Such poems are questing, tentative, discursive—fr. L *discursus* ("past part. of *discurrere* to run about")—rather than direct. But in them the line takes on some of the characteristics we stereotypically associate with prose.

Short-lined, rhyming, metrically regular poems would presumably accommodate a different kind of psychic energy.

But counter-examples abound. I don't intend to propose laws, rather to notice tendencies. And to suggest that such tendencies, familiar to poets from memories—conscious and unconscious—of reading poems, are among the many factors influencing their decisions about lines.

William Matthews, "A Note on Prose, Verse and the Line" from Field *#10 (Spring) 1974. Reprinted by permission of the Estate of William Matthews.*

THOMAS McGRATH

Language, Power, and Dream

"The history of all hitherto existing society is the history of class struggles." And the history of history is language, and *in* language. There are the fossils (even from the time before class struggle) that are benign. There are others, later, like the Homeric "honor," like seventeenth century "honor," "honor" among thieves, the white confederate "honor" of Jefferson Davis—these fossils contain poisons that are still active and some deadly. There are words like *moon* and *labor* which, if we look inside, contain more rings of growth than even the oldest tree.

Language is, perhaps, only a moment of the growth of what became consciousness and will go beyond it, but it is our machine for separating ourselves from the world in order to create it (as Adam did by naming the beasts and herbs). In creating the world we also *appropriate* it. The world then is internalized. Now we can make maps; the demons of the four cardinal compass points (Cham to Amaymon) are born and the Age of Exploration (external and internal) begins.

Any of these roads would take us back or forward to Eden, but the class struggle in the form of the Angel blocks the way back with a flaming sword. There would still be no problem if language *still and only* belonged to the workers—we would simply shove the sword up the ass of the angel and march on in. But with *division*— so important in separating ourselves from the world in order to see it, know it, and, finally, change it—that same necessitous Angel, who symbolizes also the class struggle, has put up signs: *Eden—Detour 3 miles south by way of route 66*. Or: (to put it in another way:) if direction is discovered, misdirection becomes possible, i.e., the tree blazed on the wrong side, newspapers, education-with-Ph.D. theses-on-Marxist-poets, foxfire, "the book with one thousand false addresses"—a general production of false consciousness even by men who think they are men of good will.

"Make it new," said Pound. But Pound, like Eliot and Yeats, was essentially a pre-nineteenth-century man and his thinking was, in part at least, that of an even earlier ruling class. The language of these poets generates (among other things) a fog of false consciousness in which platoons of professors are still wandering, sending out plaintive cries about the "depth," the "profundity" of the bogs they have fallen into. But, it is true, there *is* something there: pain, above all. About which the old masters were never wrong, or so we have been told. Their pain is of the loss of the "centre" of "tradition" of "virtue" and *virtu*—a loss of aristocratic values already knocked in the head by the bourgeoisie. These "modernists" are really belated medieval writers—they followed the signs out of their own century. But that is why

Thomas McGrath, "Language, Power, and Dream" from Claims for Poetry. *Reprinted by permission of Copper Canyon Press.*

they have such a modern sound. The strategies, the successes and failures, of this holy trinity, point to the reasons why we have not yet had a great *bourgeois* poem of the twentieth century. In English. And never will have.

To go back to the Angel. The law is: the owners will put up the signs and most of them will point in the wrong direction. If language can delude, it will first delude the user. We must try to remember the revolutionary axiom: In the beginning was the *world!*

Everyone wants to reform language. Reformers can be dangerous: they begin by wanting to purify the language of the tribe but may end (as Shaw had it) slaughtering multitudes over an extra vowel. Things turn to their opposites. The liberating purification of language which begins with Wordsworth becomes constrictive, becomes protectionist, buys guard dogs and chainlink fences, wants law and order, is in favor of high tariffs. Or to take examples from our own times—either Pound or Williams will do—they begin as revolutionaries, knocking down the inflated and bankrupt language of the American survivors of Victorianism. And indeed it *was* liberating to see those apparitional faces, and interesting to see the chickens and the red wheelbarrow, though the "so much" that is said to depend upon them turns out to be not (as Williams supposed) the validity of the whole visible world of objects but merely the temporality of a consumer society.

Metaphysical consumerism! As the Williams tradition runs down in the work of the less talented of his followers, the object becomes All, becomes the One. Things (but not goods) are hypostatized and so any thing is as good as anything else and a beer can equals the Mona Lisa. This mock materialism is essentially puritan. Feelings are muted or excised and objects proliferate. This is what Freud called anal and Marx called petty bourgeois or commodity fetishism and it is where the search for purity has led a lot of poets and novelists: to things rather than feelings about them, to situations without people, to aesthetics pretending to be politics.

Out of so much of this temporary "war politics" rises a terrible spiritual smell which signals to the enemy: "I'm not really like this. Just stop bombing Hanoi and I will go back to my primary interests: flowers, early cockcrow, the Holy Ghost, wheelbarrows, the letter G, inhabitable animals, the sacred mysteries of the typewriter keyboard, and High Thought including the Greater, the Lesser, and High, Low, Jack-and-the-goddam-game mysticism." Worthy enough subjects in themselves. . . .

Language is always a little out of date and so it always needs reforming: because the world changes; because the real landscape that underlies the landscape of the poem erodes and alters; because our consciousness changes to catch up with the changes in the world; because the world is never adequate to our needs and desires and so we must change it—and by doing so change our needs and desires. The best poets find the new words for this new world of change and need. They may not be understood or felt until we see that the world is changing and "filling in" their words. Then "illusion" is transformed into "reality."

The search for purity and limit in language is often a hedge against anxiety—anxiety that results from a glimpse of the flux and change that is the world. A poet feeling this often sets up a metaphysical system of absolutes, values derived from picking the bones of various systems, to set against the flux. Or, if less honest, he buries his absolutes. His poems, like the pointer on a compass, always turn to these magnets. True North is always under his feet! He has found the still point of the turning world and there, locked in the chastity belt of "purified" language, he remains.

I prefer the impure. There is, after all, in our time, another tradition of language—that leading from Hart Crane and others. What we want and need, in my view, *now*, is not this questionable purity but a language, to paraphrase Louis Simpson, like the belly of a shark, a language that can digest *anything*.

Language is part of the forces of production for the poets—it is what they use to create their poetic "goods." The language chosen by or given to some poets, like certain kinds of machines, can produce variety: "aphorisms, epigrams, songs, song-like poems and so on" as Roethke had it, the tremendous range of "impure poetry" in Neruda's term. Alas, our time tends toward specialization. But if you want to make wood for the winter a chain saw is better than a stone axe.

If we continue the analogy we will see that even more important than the forces are the *relations* of production. If the poet thinks he *owns* the means of production (that language factory where the private vision must be socialized into the public myth) when in fact he only uses what has been given to him (*any* tradition within the bourgeois limit) he will produce a consciousness that is at least in part false. The American worker thinks he is free, but he is chained to the machine. So "politics must be in command." We must try to find our real relationship to things.

Language gives us perception and orientation—which includes the possibility of lying signposts, false consciousness. Through language we appropriate the world and our selves, existence creating essence in a process that can never be complete. History—that is, class struggle—begins with alienation and exile when we were cast out of Eden. History *is* alienation as it appears to consciousness. It is the sense of division, of duality, which the fig leaves symbolized, the pain of being incomplete. When we return to Eden we will possess full consciousness and alienation will end.

Satori, those "mystical" returns to what was and will be, can only be realized individually. They are returns to the Eden of the time before the snake. They are brief because Eden is not big enough for all of us and complete consciousness cannot be merely *personal*—the appropriation and internalization of the world through action, art, and language is a social process. What we feel now is the pain of duality and conflict: man vs. the world (which is men struggling with themselves, nature and other men). In the beginning was the world. But in transcendence subject and object will become the Word: Mannature. Then love must change its form—when the Flesh is made Word—and death, for the unalienated, will have to be reinvented. . . .

Somebody writes to ask: "Are you still working on that long poem about North Dakota?" But I'm not writing a poem about North Dakota as such, though there is a lot in the poem that involves experiences, past and present, from places *in* North Dakota.

"North Dakota is everywhere," the poem says. This provoked indignation in an English reviewer, who seemed appalled at the idea. But the line was written in Skyros, was set off by the suicide of an impoverished and destroyed fisherman, and referred to a *condition*. And North Dakota is a condition, or a part of one. North Dakota—or Montana or New Mexico or wherever, so long as it is not the East, the city—is an experience which many poets are now having. If the experience could be easily described perhaps it would not be necessary for us to write about it in poems. But the poems are discovering the experience, creating it, destroying false consciousness, creating the new. . . .

What is in that experience? Here are two reactions to the West from the November 21, 1971, issue of the *New York Times Book Review*. The first is from Shirley Schoonover, writing from Nebraska. What is Nebraska? Once, she notes, there were buffalo and Indians; now there are beef and farmers. The state is physically beautiful, she says, and she responds to the terrific weather. As for culture, "Insurance companies have made cement monuments where long ago the Indians came to talk peace or war." (*That* is right on, but she can't see where it leads.) Art "is fine for covering that crack over the fireplace." The Nebraska football team has a huge coliseum but the University Theater goes begging. Etc., etc. (It's still Mainstreet, seen at this level.) As for the lot of writers "I've already indicated that the three most famous Nebraska writers went East and stayed there. That should tell you a lot." The writers she refers to are Willa Cather, Mari Sandoz, and Wright Morris. She is getting out herself. "That's Nebraska. Beautiful but killingly lonely for the writer."

Perhaps she is doing the right thing—I don't know her work and maybe there is nothing she could learn from the Genius of the place, even if she could get in contact with that restless spirit. But loneliness can be greatly valuable—surely it was valuable to Cather and Morris. And in any case the three writers *took the place along with them*—Nebraska is everywhere. Miss Schoonover noticed a few blazes that might have led to something interesting, but in general she seems to have seen only real estate. The author's note says that she now lives in Rochester, New York.

The second reaction is that of William Eastlake, from Arizona. The piece is a fanciful dialogue between Eastlake and "my Indian writer friend, Many Bitter Songs." It is full of jokes, but some things seem to be said with considerable seriousness. Many Bitter Songs asks why Eastlake writes in the West:

"Because, as you said, the West has never been written about. Never until your time. The West is just being discovered," I said.

"There have been several white geniuses in America. Why didn't they write about the West?"

"Because," I said, "they were cowards. They could not face the horrors of the West. The extermination of the Indian, the murder of the land. The terrific beauty. They sat in New York and polished old sayings . . . America is too terrible a subject for an American. . . ."

"Then we can forget the West."

"No, no. We cannot forget the West. There is no America outside the West, and there never will be. It is the dream, and that dream is the only hope. No, we cannot forget the West. Where all the races meet in a place of beauty, not in a place of blood. The land cannot grant amnesty."

That meeting in a place of beauty rather than of blood has to be in "the dream." The time surely has not arrived yet. It won't be arrived at either until we come to terms with "the extermination of the Indian," until we understand the exploitations and rip-offs that have been practiced against all ethnic groups, until we can square these rip-offs and those against the working class as well. This must enter—and is entering—our consciousness and our politics. All this great "West" is a place of wounds. All of *America* is such a place, but the East has paved over them. If we see this, "Nebraska" can be intensely dramatic for a writer. We certainly don't want an art to "cover that crack over the fireplace." *Do not bandage these wounds!*

What is there, out here on the edge, that makes our experience different from that of the city poet? First there is the land itself. It has been disciplined by machines but it is still not dominated. The plow that broke the plains is long gone and the giant tractor and the combine are here, but the process of making a living is still a struggle and a gamble—it is not a matter of putting raw materials in one end of a factory and taking finished products out of the other. Weather, which is only a nuisance in the city, takes on the power of the gods here, and vast cycles of climate, which will one day make all the area a dust bowl again and finally return it to grass, make all man's successes momentary and ambiguous. Here man can never think of himself, as he can in the city, as the master of nature. Like it or not he is subject to the ancient power of seasonal change; he cannot avoid being *in* nature; he has a heroic adversary that is no abstraction. At a level below immediate consciousness we respond to this, are less alien to our bodies, to human and natural time.

The East is much older than these farther states, has more history. But I believe that that history no longer functions, has been forgotten, has been "paved over." In the East man begins every day from himself. Here, the past is still alive and close at hand—the arrowheads we turn up may have been shot at our grandfathers. I am not thinking of any romantic frontier. The past out here was bloody, and full of injustice, though hopeful and heroic. It is very close here—my father took shelter with his family at Fort Ransom during an Indian scare when he was a boy. Later he heard of the massacre at Wounded Knee. Most of us are haunted by the closeness of that past, and by the fact that we are only a step from the Indian, whose sense of life so many of the younger people are trying to learn.

Not long ago, if one wanted to be an artist of any kind, it was necessary to leave these parts. Lenin spoke of "the idiocy of the villages," and in the nineteenth and early twentieth centuries if one wanted to experience his own time he *had* to go to the cities. The city was, in fact, being remade—out of factory production, class struggle, the growth of the city working class, the rise of revolutionary politics. And of course, even if the artist was unaware of these vast and radical social changes, the city was the repository of art and culture. So the artist *had* to go to the city, where he/she was successful, or failed and disappeared, or returned defeated.

That old pattern has changed. The young would-be artist may still go to the city; but more and more frequently now he returns—to Nebraska or Arizona or wherever. Part of this is the result of our "affluence" and "mobility." If he wants to make another run to San Francisco or Seattle (would-be *poets* from west of Chicago never seem to go to New York any more) he can always do so. The result of this "return" (a part of all initiation rites) is only now being felt. God knows what will come of it, but the waste places are being populated by long-haired poets, and little magazines turn up like toadstools after a rain.

Why do they return? In part, I think, because they find the unknown lands in which they were born dramatic for the reasons I have tried to sketch out above. Also, I think, they are reacting against the deracination they feel in the city artist, who, unless he is a revolutionary or third world person, must find his materials in that very deracination (a field well worked for a century) or in the frayed remnants of a cosmopolitan tradition. What does the young writer need? The central experience of his time, whatever it may be. Beyond that, books and talk with others in his craft. These he can now find as easily out in the backlands as in the city—and not just young poets like himself but older ones like Bly, or Stafford, or Hugo, who have been in the city and left it. The result will be, I think, a poetry which, for a time at least, finds the city irrelevant. But, since these poets have had their wanderjahre and are not parochial or simply regional, it will be a poetry which is both local *and* international.

> Without a terrain in which, to which, I belong,
> language itself is my one home, my Jerusalem. . . .

This is Denise Levertov in her generous and courageous poem "To Stay Alive." It is a terrifying idea, because language has a history, can never be up in the air—the very "Jerusalem" she refers to is not just that spiritual home and terminal of longing: it is also now a particular city within the system of international imperialism. History has added a new meaning to the word. It is hard to see this if we try to make language itself our home, and perhaps it is some realization of this which leads more and more poets to a sense of the necessity of place: a place to turn around in, ground under our feet, a base to operate from, a blaze on a tree that lets us locate ourselves on the map of ourselves and our time.

I think this is our "Yenan" period, (I'm *not* using the term in the way that James Moore has used it recently) and that it will be necessary to reenter the city. Supposing he already knows the facts of life and the class struggle, the poet has nothing to learn from the city. Where once it was a liberating place, it is now a stultifying one. Only in the ghettos is something "happening," as the great proliferation of black, Chicano, and Indian poetry shows. For such poets the ghettos are a source of strength. But the white poet can enter the ghetto only with great difficulty and in any case the ghettos are only beginning to work through to revolutionary politics. At the moment they are still involved (with important exceptions) in cultural and political nationalism, dead ends which it seems must be explored before a serious politics becomes possible. When that time comes the cities will again be the place of the central experience of the time and the poets will have to go back. But when that time comes, a new revolutionary consciousness will have solved many old problems and created new ones.

The point is to find, during these years of "wandering in the desert," the link with the revolutionary past in order to create, invent, rescue, restructure, resurrect that past. This may be our gift to the city. But we cannot find that "place we went wrong" without a knowledge of the ground under our feet. So place is important.

And for me, two places. Where I began—still there and still changeless, the little river and the coulee hills, enduring under the accumulating strata of change and history. To quote Joseph Smeall, "Of the purgative and cathartic emotions that are a chief business of poetry, Aristotle says, that they start amid near things."

So I begin with that place and my life. But, again I say, not my *personal life as such*. All of us live twice at the same time—once uniquely and once representatively. I am interested in those moments when my unique personal life intersects with something bigger, when my small brief moment has a part in "fabricating the legend."

So there has to be a second "place" and it is anywhere *outside this window* where I am writing, i.e., the world in large. The writing itself is part of the subject of the poem, the act, impossible to accomplish, of bringing the two masks of the world into line, of solving the social, personal, and political riddles I see all around. Looking out that window, I see that North Dakota *is* everywhere.

ROGER ROSENBLATT

"I Am Writing Blindly"

Besides the newsworthy revelation of Lieut. Captain Dimitri Kolesnikov's dying message to his wife recovered from the husk of the sunken submarine *Kursk*—that 23 of the 118 crewmen had survived in an isolated chamber for a while, in contradiction to claims by Russian officials that all had perished within minutes of the accident—there was the matter of writing the message in the first place.

In the first place, in the last place, that is what we people do—write messages to one another. We are a narrative species. We exist by storytelling—by relating our situations—and the test of our evolution may lie in getting the story right.

What Kolesnikov did in deciding to describe his position and entrapment, others have also done—in states of repose or terror. When a JAL airliner went down in 1985, passengers used the long minutes of its terrible, spiraling descent to write letters to loved ones. When the last occupants of the Warsaw Ghetto had finally seen their families and companions die of disease or starvation, or be carried off in trucks to extermination camps, and there could be no doubt of their own fate, still they took scraps of paper on which they wrote poems, thoughts, fragments of lives, rolled them into tight scrolls, and slipped them into the crevices of the ghetto walls.

Why did they bother? With no countervailing news from the outside world, they assumed the Nazis had inherited the earth; that if anyone discovered their writings, it would be their killers, who would snicker and toss them away. They wrote because, like Kolesnikov, they had to. The impulse was in them, like a biological fact.

So enduring is this storytelling need that it shapes nearly every human endeavor. Businesses depend on the stories told of past failures and successes and on the myth of the mission of the company. In medicine, doctors increasingly rely on a patient's narrative of the progress of an ailment, which is inevitably more nuanced and useful than the data of machines. In law, the same thing. Every court case is a competition of tales told by the prosecutor and defense attorney; the jury picks the one it likes best.

All these activities derive from essential places in us. Psychologist Jerome Bruner says children acquire language in order to tell the stories that are already in them. We do our learning through storytelling processes. The man who arrives at our door is thought to be a salesman because his predecessor was a salesman. When the patternmaking faculties fail, the brain breaks down. Schizophrenics suffer from a loss of story.

The deep proof of our need to spill, and keep on spilling, lies in reflex, often in desperate circumstances. A number of years ago, Jean-Dominique Bauby, the editor of *Elle* magazine in Paris, was felled by a stroke so destructive that the only part of his body that could move was his left eyelid. Flicking that eyelid, he managed to signal the letters of the alphabet, and proceeded to write his autobiography, *The Diving Bell and the Butterfly*, with the last grand gesture of his life.

All this is of acute and consoling interest to writers, whose odd existences are ordinarily strung between asking why we do it and doing it incessantly. The explanation I've been able to come up with has to do with freedom. You write a sentence, the basic unit of storytelling, and you are never sure where it will lead. The readers will not know where it leads either. Your adventure becomes theirs, eternally recapitulated in tandem—one wild ride together. Even when you come to the end of the sentence, that dot, it is still strangely inconclusive. I sometimes think one writes to find God in every sentence. But God (the ironist) always lives in the next sentence.

It is this freedom of the message sender and receiver that connects them— sailor to wife, the dying to the living. Writing has been so important in America, I think, because communication is the soul and engine of democracy. To write is to live according to one's terms. If you ask me to be serious, I will be frivolous. Magnanimous? Petty. Cynical? I will be a brazen believer in all things. Whatever you demand I will not give you—unless it is with the misty hope that what I give you is not what you ask for but what you want.

We use this freedom to break the silence, even of death, even when—in the depths of our darkest loneliness—we have no clear idea of why we reach out to one another with these frail, perishable chains of words. In the black chamber of the submarine, Kolesnikov noted, "I am writing blindly." Like everyone else.

MICHAEL RYAN

Tell Me a Story

When I was little boy, my father told me bedtime stories about the Greenies. The Greenies were a race of tiny people—three feet tall—who lived inside the earth. My father had discovered them when he was my age exploring caves in the Ozarks where he grew up on a dirt farm. He'd entertain himself climbing deep down in the dark, among bats and stalagmites and stalactites, further down than anyone had ever gone. One day, he saw an odd light coming through a crack above a ledge high up in the cave wall, almost hidden by rocks. He climbed up and by moving the rocks he saw an opening just large enough for him to squeeze through. There was a ledge on the other side, too, and there in the great cavern beneath him, in a shining city made of emeralds, diamonds, platinum, and gold, he saw the Greenies, all scurrying this way and that like ants. It was terrifically hot and damp, the stones around him radiated heat. When he climbed down closer he could see their pale green skin tough as rhinoceros hide and their corkscrew-tipped heads that could drill through granite. There was a good Greenie king, a gorgeous Greenie princess who was in love with my father (gorgeous, I guess, despite her corkscrew-tipped head), bad Greenies who had left the city and threatened it with raids, and assorted natural cataclysms and fantastic monsters.

The detail I remember best was incidental to the big battles and epic struggle for racial survival. After my father had helped the Greenies and been accepted and honored by them, he was given full access to their kingdom, permission never before granted to an outsider. He could roam about wherever he wanted and treat whatever they had as his own—the latter privilege he didn't exercise except for the three modest, perfect diamonds he took for his mother, for the woman he would someday marry (this diamond could be found in my mother's engagement ring), and for himself (here was his, in the gold ring on his right hand; he said someday, when he was dead, it would be mine). One quiet day in the kingdom, happy and content with these harmonious, gentle people, he was exploring its outer reaches by himself and, in a grotto on the other side of a stream, he came upon a goat with a head exactly like the lampshade on the floor lamp next to my bed—narrow at the top and opening out—and, behind the goat, emerging from the shadows, the most beautiful woman he had ever seen, completely naked. Then the grotto began pulsing with a strange light. They stared at him, woman and goat. He knew if he crossed the stream his life would be changed. He'd never see his parents again, or maybe even the Greenies. The woman smiled invitingly but the goat hissed and out of its lampshade skull came poison smoke. My father turned and ran, onto the next wonder and adventure. Although I'm sure I asked about them, they never appeared in the stories again.

After that I couldn't look at the lamp without seeing the goat. It had two simultaneous beings. In the daylight, it was the lamp *and* the goat or the goat functioning as a lamp, and at night when the light was turned out it became the goat, perfectly still, an immobile outline permanently suspended in the instant before it would start to move and spume poison smoke. It sent a chill through me from toes to scalp, an awful thrill that was finally too much, and made me feel like I was spinning wildly in outer space. But when my father was sitting on the edge of the bed with his elbows on his knees, I could see his white shirt in the dark, I could feel the pressure of his hips, and that contact grounded me enough so that no matter how scared or crazy I became I wanted him to keep telling me the stories.

He didn't tell them often—each time had to be a special treat. And each time, before he would begin, he'd ask me if I believed in the Greenies. I had to say yes to get a story, to say I believed that this fabulous world was going on inside the earth even as he spoke. I didn't believe it, then I said I did, and as the word left my mouth I believed and didn't believe at the same time—like the goat-lamp. It was secret life. It was my father's secret life. He had made it from the basic stuff of the Old Testament, Buck Rogers, and H. Rider Haggard (*King Solomon's Mines*)—his favorite author—but also from his own childhood memories, probably some of the fondest he had, of being brave and adventurous, exploring caves by himself. Although he was the storyteller in our family, he almost never told me anything about *his* father, who was an alcoholic (like himself)—his father's absence from his stories only now seems significant to me. The stories were cautionary and instructional, exemplifying courage I was meant to emulate, invariably dramatizing his lonely battle with the world. He was always alone in them. Clearly, that was his memory of himself—or, more accurately, my memory of his memory of himself, communicated to me most powerfully in the Greenie stories (hybrids of memory and fantasy that they were): the hero against a hostile world. My dad was the hero. I absorbed the message like a soft little sponge, the way only a child can. I wanted to be like my dad. I wanted to be the hero, too.

But why tell this story of these stories? In a remarkable essay about his father in his almost-forgotten book of autobiographical essays, *Court of Memory*, James McConkey writes, "Memory, which gives us our identities, can, by an act of grace, release us from ourselves to an outpouring of its most hidden contents." My father's stories—his memory and identity—wounded me almost too deeply for words but also gave me life. They are engraved in me. Stories are the way we articulate ourselves to ourselves, as well as to one another. We tell hundreds of stories every day. Through their agency we make the amorphous, inexhaustible inner into the shapely, provisional outer. They are an irreplaceable way of knowing and mode of social intercourse (notwithstanding our dominant "efficient" scientific models of knowledge and social organization). Their material is the material of memory, which is generative, not a passive lump of stuff. One does not take a memory and make it into a story. Memory itself makes the story—and, as McConkey implies, we can be released not only *by* its story but also *to* it. Memory is both the subject and predicate of which we are the objects.

In this regard, the only difference between fiction and nonfiction is how faithful the writer must be to memory and how willing he is to rein it in when it gallops toward fantasy, for which it's also the source. Surely writing fiction—and reading it—can also produce that graceful release McConkey is talking about. Every reader of this essay has experienced the rapture of reading a piece of writing that *takes* you, an experience of art that probably reproduces an experience in life—of being "flooded" by memory, of tapping into an underground stream that seems simply to burst forth. But memory is always there, implicitly telling us what to feel and think, what we like and don't, who we are. "Memory . . . gives us our identities": we don't have memory: it has us—as if it were a container and an engine in which we are also contained, by which we are driven. How deeply we are formed by what happens to us, whom we're born to, the previous generations who live in us. We are probably also what happened to them, even if we don't know what that is or even who they were, shards embedded in stories and chromosomes. No wonder we are such mysteries to ourselves. Our feelings are grounded in sources that will elude us no matter what reductive psychoanalytic explanations we construct to manage them or how many ingenious drugs are designed to alter them. "The eye sees what it has been given to see by concrete circumstances," wrote Flannery O'Connor, "and the imagination reproduces what, by some related gift, it is able to make live." How that moment of seeing the goat-lamp shaped me exceeds my powers of analysis, but, in O'Connor's terms, maybe not the power of imagination—by becoming part of a story.

The discipline of writing includes a special opportunity for the writer as a person to make an interpersonal object that not only expresses his feelings but also embodies them, that makes them both accessible to him and strangely independent of him. This is writing's gift to the writer and, like all large gifts, it carries a large obligation. O'Connor again: "In the act of writing, one sees that the way a thing is made controls and is inseparable from the whole meaning of it. The form of a story gives it meaning which any other form would change." It's precisely this that distinguishes rendering from remembering—or reporting, which is merely remembering with a pen in your hand (a tape recorder, in the case of the celebrity memoir). To use Henry James's favorite term for it, the writer has to "do" the thing he writes about. Through this "doing," the writer's unfathomable, private feelings are transformed into apprehensible, shared language. Such a complete transformation could happen in talk if talk weren't ephemeral, local, and unrevisable, if what was discovered in talk were worked over and made palpable (the way James worked over dinner-party-conversation "donnees" into novels). It's this lack of writing's discipline applied to subjects that require the utmost discipline that make bad memoirs so bad and afternoon talk shows so embarrassing—not, as some newspaper book critics have asserted, the subjects themselves. Shame becomes a circus act on Jenny Jones, but in the hands of a writer like Kafka (or O'Connor, or James, or Chekhov, or Shakespeare—the list could be extended to every great writer we have) it is an essential and inexhaustible subject, given a shape we can understand and deeply need to understand. It becomes social, public, part of shared culture, and thereby takes on significance. Whereas, left to fester and gnaw one isolated psyche, shame is only murderous. Did Kafka save his life by writing? Maybe not, but he has helped to save others. Mine, for one.

The most surprising personal aspect of writing my autobiography was discovering the emotional weight of events I had thought not so important to me. Because they were important to the story, they demonstrated how important they were to me. People I knew only briefly affected me more than I had ever guessed. It was as if the story itself called them up from the depths and showed me how to see them. Some of them I had almost forgotten, submerged in that underground stream of memory that the daily concentration of writing tapped into. My narrative—"the telling of events in time"—formed itself from the events memory had to tell.

But I also shaped the narrative, and, in this regard, I was continuously interacting with memory. By reading what I wrote, I perceived certain subjects—shame (and its compulsive sexual expression) prominent among them; growing up male, Catholic, and white in America; the hellish economic pressure on a middle-class family; a boy's love/hate of his alcoholic father—and these subjects became the book's subject much more than what happened to me, which matters only as illustration, one instance of how these subjects impinged on one of many individual and unrepeatable lives: a testimony not a confession. The subjects became a principle of selection from the mass of all that happened to me, all the people I knew, all that was said or thought; and this principle, if I may call it that, pushed and pulled against incidents and characters that insisted on being part of the story. As Nabokov put it, "The following of thematic designs through one's life should be the true purpose of autobiography." This requires the exercise of the autobiographer's critical faculties, and the more talented a critic he is of his own life the better his book is likely to be—a talent he must exercise more explicitly than the novelist, and more certainly, since his misconceptions will be everywhere evident. In

O'Connor's words, "The writer has to judge himself with a stranger's eye and a stranger's severity. . . . No art is sunk in the self, but rather, in art the self becomes self-forgetful in order to meet the demands of the thing seen and the thing being made."

But is this really possible when the writer's own life is the subject? Can autobiography ever be "self-forgetful," as O'Connor rightly asserts art must be? It can only if the life of the story is the main thing—the life of the story, paradoxically, *not* the life of the autobiographer, which is merely the raw material of the story. The autobiographer must be mindful of the prerogatives and imperatives of the story in every way a novelist must be, and must be equally faithful to it, and finally no less able to enter the points of view of the characters at their specific times and places, especially his own. My task was not only to make the reader feel how it felt to be me; it was to make me feel how it felt to be me. In the act of writing, I relived the experience I was writing about—and I also didn't, because it was also becoming language, with the frustration and exhilaration which always accompanies that. When I lived those experiences as a child and teenager and young man there was plenty of frustration and precious little exhilaration, and none of it of the writerly kind. I felt lost and indeed was lost, never for a moment imagining that it all would someday become "material." Now the conditions of my life had changed. I was an adult (finally), no longer literally at the mercy of the conditions I was dramatizing. The writing helped me to be no longer at the mercy of these conditions emotionally, either—the release McConkey calls an act of grace. I needed the task of rendering my life, a contract with the reader which obliged me to honor the facts. I knew the gift of the story was wrapped in what actually happened (as memory remembered it and writing might render it)—the gift of the story to me and, I hoped, to the reader. "The reader" was oddly and exclusively *in* the act of writing itself. I wrote to the book, to the story, not to any person, real, imagined, or hypostatized. The aesthetic and ethical relationships between me and this reader-in-the-writing were identical: getting it down right was right.

Needless to say, however, this put me in conflict with myself—between me as a writer and as a person—over the revelations the story contained, that this story had to contain in order to be told. There was no avoiding that. As William Maxwell said in an interview,

> Sometimes I have suffered the torments of the damned in describing real people, where I was sure that I was, perhaps, causing pain. And in this struggle the artist won out. There was a point at which I would not give up something that I knew was right. Aesthetically. And artistically.

And he was talking about fiction, with its built-in ethical safety valve. No reader confuses Ishmael with Melville, or Nick Carraway with F. Scott Fitzgerald, or the unhappy husband who narrates "The Kreutzer Sonata" with Tolstoy (except the U.S. Post Office Department, which wouldn't deliver the American newspapers that serialized it, and State Senator Theodore Roosevelt who denounced its author as a "sexual moral pervert"). But the narrator of an autobiography, in the reader's mind, *is* the author—not just the writer, but also the person, in the flesh, who pays his taxes and shops for bagels.

This identification for the writer is both aesthetically and ethically perilous. "How could this guy publish this about his wife?" is not a question that occurs these days to most readers of "The Kreutzer Sonata." But such questions naturally do occur to readers of autobiographies, and they are much muddled at present in this atmosphere of promiscuous exposure à la Jenny Jones and the shame circus, the deadbolt linkage of information and promotion that pervades our media culture, in which what people are saying seems invariably connected to something they're selling (vide the Author Book Tour, apparently pioneered in our era by—who else?—Jacqueline Susann). Why should autobiographers be expected to be disinterested when nobody else seems to be? Much less about the representation of one's self and one's life, with its potential effects on one's well-being? Why should we not read autobiographies, especially ones that deal with intimate subjects and personal revelations, as mere "tell-alls," "domestic confessionals," and "autopathographies" (to cite just three hostile journalistic coinages): an inherently repugnant form of narcissistic merchandising, self-display, and self-promotion?

The book itself has to answer such questions—formally, in *its* character and tone—not the writer, on talk shows or anywhere else. If the writer's privacy is sacrificed for the book's intimacy, it may be worth it if the book is worth it, although that will not relieve "the torments of the damned" he may suffer, since how can he ever be sure his book is worth it? How can he compare his family's feelings to the good his book does and is? Books and people are not comparable. But the terms of art and life are deeply entangled, as they are in the writer himself as an artist and a human being. In my experience, there are no formulas to answer the ethical questions that arise when publishing an autobiography, except to ask for the permission of the people whose lives are exposed by it, much less the questions that arise while writing it, at moments when the ethical wages unconditional war on the aesthetic. The autobiographer's failure to win the reader's suspension of disbelief is perhaps even more deadly than the novelist's. He is condemned to tell his story in the first person, which complicates his problems no end. Just getting off center stage so the story can speak is a daunting technical and temperamental challenge that demands, among other things, preternatural psychological tact. Self-consciousness is as fatal as the lack of it, especially in the intricate business of self-portrayal. An excessively proprietary interest in his main character (himself) will sink his story like a pair of concrete boots. Any autobiographer who does not constantly torment himself with the question, "Is this interesting to anyone else?" is probably going to write a book that isn't. Without invention, he must fascinate us as much as a novelist with the endlessly interesting interactions between character (people) and plot (what happens to them), just as we are fascinated in and by our own lives.

How intimate should a story be? As intimate as it has to be, is the only answer I know. Each age has its idea of decorum, although we have come to expect art to violate it, so that the violation is sometimes now mistaken for the art and romanticized as "transgression." On the other side, the genteel tradition of criticism has always confused the beautiful and the agreeable, and the value of privacy with the conventions of secrecy. Maybe because most of my childhood reading was done in bed, alone in the halo of a small overhead lamp that seemed to define the circumference of the world, and I had heard my father's stories about the Greenies in a dim nightlight-lit bedroom, storytelling will forever be to me a most intimate act: the writer's voice is inside my head, inside me. The writer's consideration for me is shown not in sparing me his shame but in rendering his story clearly and palpably—"immediately, instantaneously graspable," in Chekhov's words—so that, most paradoxically in the case of autobiography, the writer seems to disappear into the details. "Released to an outpouring," "self-forgetful in order to meet the demands of the thing seen and the thing being made," he becomes his book, the story itself.

I haven't read Kathryn Harrison's *The Kiss* or Frank McCourt's *Angela's Ashes*, but I do know that Harrison's book is "about" incest and McCourt's is "about" his impoverished childhood in Limerick with his alcoholic mother (and includes her incestuous affair with her cousin). I know this despite not watching television or afternoon talk shows. This sort of sound-bite information seems to be in the air itself. Unfortunately, it's mistaken for knowledge—a natural mistake since we are forced to process so much information all the time. Humans, the learning animal, have adapted to this condition of daily life in most of the world. But it's a particularly unfortunate mistake when applied to books, although publishers encourage it and apparently believe they have to (and have to include marketing directors in their publishing decisions). Such information says less about a book than a Pepsi commercial says about Pepsi because a book is a more complicated mental and emotional experience than a soft drink, but the mechanism is the same, and this kind of thinking—this adaptation to info-glut—may now be the largest single obstacle between the writer and reader: It may be keeping some of the best books from being bought, published, and even written, and almost certainly affects how people read (or, more often, don't). To know Kathryn Harrison's book is about incest is to know almost nothing about it. Other books, especially fiction and poetry without identifiable and startling subjects, are less easily mistranslated into information and therefore do not enter the air at all.

This said, once a book is in a reader's hands, its relationship to him seems potentially the same as it ever was. It can teach not what to think and feel but how to think and feel. That some readers seek personal stories in reaction to a depersonalized culture in which institutional sources of authority are suspect may partially account for the so-called "memoir explosion." Autobiography is only more obviously "personal" than poetry or fiction, but it is finally always about memory, and as much about the moment of recollection as the moment being recalled—the presentness of the past and the pastness of the present, which every person must work out for himself over and over again if he wants a chance to be happy or useful or available to the ordinary pleasures of life. Other people's lives are interesting to us, but in this singular respect every good autobiography is also our own, a tale of the tribe that does for us what stories have always done.

WILLIAM STAFFORD

A Way of Writing

A writer is not so much someone who has something to say as he is someone who has found a process that will bring about new things he would not have thought of if he had not started to say them. That is, he does not draw on a reservoir; instead, he engages in an activity that brings to him a whole succession of unforeseen stories, poems, essays, plays, laws, philosophies, religions, or—but wait!

Back in school, from the first when I began to try to write things, I felt this richness. One thing would lead to another; the world would give and give. Now, after twenty years or so of trying, I live by that certain richness, an idea hard to pin, difficult to say, and perhaps offensive to some. For there are strange implications in it.

One implication is the importance of just plain receptivity. When I write, I like to have an interval before me when I am not likely to be interrupted. For me, this means usually the early morning, before others are awake. I get pen and paper, take a glance out of the window (often it is dark out there), and wait. It is like fishing. But I do not wait very long, for there is always a nibble—and this is where receptivity comes in. To get started I will accept anything that occurs to me. Something always occurs, of course, to any of us. We can't keep from thinking. Maybe I have to settle for an immediate impression: it's cold, or hot, or dark, or bright, or in between! Or—well, the possibilities are endless. If I put down something, that thing will help the next thing come, and I'm off. If I let the process go on, things will occur to me that were not at all in my mind when I started. These things, odd or trivial as they may be, are somehow connected. And if I let them string out, surprising things will happen.

If I let them string out. . . . Along with initial receptivity, then, there is another readiness: I must be willing to fail. If I am to keep on writing, I cannot bother to insist on high standards. I must get into action and not let anything stop me, or even slow me much. By "standards" I do not mean "correctness"—spelling, punctuation, and so on. These details become mechanical for anyone who writes for a while. I am thinking about such matters as social significance, positive values, consistency, etc. I resolutely disregard these. Something better, greater, is happening! I am following a process that leads so wildly and originally into new territory that no judgment can at the moment be made about values, significance, and so on. I am making something new, something that has not been judged before. Later others—and maybe I myself—will make judgments. Now, I am headlong to discover. Any distraction may harm the creating.

So, receptive, careless of failure, I spin out things on the page. And a wonderful freedom comes. If something occurs to me, it is all right to accept it. It has one

William Stafford, "A Way of Writing" from Field: Contemporary Poetry and Poetics, *number 2, Spring 1970 Reprinted by permission of Oberlin College Press.*

justification: it occurs to me. No one else can guide me. I must follow my own weak, wandering, diffident impulses.

A strange bonus happens. At times, without my insisting on it, my writings become coherent; the successive elements that occur to me are clearly related. They lead by themselves to new connections. Sometimes the language, even the syllables that happen along, may start a trend. Sometimes the materials alert me to something waiting in my mind, ready for sustained attention. At such times, I allow myself to be eloquent, or intentional, or for great swoops (Treacherous! Not to be trusted!) reasonable. But I do not insist on any of that; for I know that back of my activity there will be the coherence of my self, and that indulgence of my impulses will bring recurrent patterns and meanings again.

This attitude toward the process of writing creatively suggests a problem for me, in terms of what others say. They talk about "skills" in writing. Without denying that I do have experience, wide reading, automatic orthodoxies and maneuvers of various kinds, I still must insist that I am often baffled about what "skill" has to do with the precious little area of confusion when I do not know what I am going to say and then I find out what I am going to say. That precious interval I am unable to bridge by skill. What can I witness about it? It remains mysterious, just as all of us must feel puzzled about how we are so inventive as to be able to talk along through complexities with our friends, not needing to plan what we are going to say, but never stalled for long in our confident forward progress. Skill? If so, it is the skill we all have, something we must have learned before the age of three or four.

A writer is one who has become accustomed to trusting that grace, or luck, or—skill.

Yet another attitude I find necessary: most of what I write, like most of what I say in casual conversation, will not amount to much. Even I will realize, and even at the time, that it is not negotiable. It will be like practice. In conversation I allow myself random remarks—in fact, as I recall, that is the way I learned to talk—so in writing I launch many expendable efforts. A result of this free way of writing is that I am not writing for others, mostly; they will not see the product at all unless the activity eventuates in something that later appears to be worthy. My guide is the self, and its adventuring in the language brings about communication.

This process-rather-than-substance view of writing invites a final, dual reflection:

1. Writers may not be special—sensitive or talented in any usual sense. They are simply engaged in sustained use of a language skill we all have. Their "creations" come about through confident reliance on stray impulses that will, with trust, find occasional patterns that are satisfying.

2. But writing itself is one of the great, free human activities. There is scope for individuality, and elation, and discovery, in writing. For the person who follows with trust and forgiveness what occurs to him, the world remains always ready and deep, an inexhaustible environment, with the combined vividness of an actuality and flexibility of a dream. Working back and forth between experience and thought, writers have more than space and time can offer. They have the whole unexplored realm of human vision.

LUISA VALENZUELA

Writing with the Body

As I leave the ambassador's residence in Buenos Aires early one morning in 1977, at the height of my country's military dictatorship, and walk through the dark, tree-lined streets, I think I am being followed. I have been hearing political testimony from people who sought asylum in the Mexican embassy. Enemies of the de facto government. I think that I can be abducted at any moment. Yet I feel immensely vital, filled with an inexplicable strength that may come from my having reached some kind of understanding. I walk back home through those streets that appear to be empty, and take all the precautions I can to make sure that I'm not being followed, that I'm not being aimed at from some doorway, and I feel alive. I would say happy.

Now I know why.

The answer is simple, now, so many years later. I felt—at this moment, I feel—happy because I was—am—writing with the body. Writing that lingers in the memory of my pores. Writing with the body? Yes. I am aware of having done this throughout my life, at intervals, although it may be almost impossible for me to describe. I'm afraid that it's a matter of a secret action or a mode of being that may be ineffable.

But I don't believe in the ineffable. The struggle of every person who writes, of every true writer, is primarily against the demon of that which resists being put into words. It is a struggle that spreads like an oil stain. Often, to surrender to the difficulty is to triumph, because the best text can sometimes be the one that allows words to have their own liberty.

While writing with the body one also works with words, sometimes completely formed in one's mind, sometimes barely suggested. Writing with the body has nothing to do with "body language." It implies being fully committed to an act which is, in essence, a literary act.

At the Mexican embassy that night in 1977, I had just spoken at length with an ex-president who was a political refugee, as well as with a terrorist who had also sought asylum. Both men were sitting at the same table; we were all somewhat drunk and, because of that, more sincere. Then I walked down the streets and as I was walking, I was writing with the body. And not just because of a letter that I was mentally addressing to my friend, Julio Cortázar. I was telling him in the letter—because I knew that I was risking my life and was afraid—that I don't want to play "duck": when I get into the water, I choose to get wet.

Luisa Valenzuela, "Writing with the Body" from The Writer on Her Work, *edited by Janet Sternburg Vol. 2: New Essays in New Territory, W.W. Norton. Reprinted by permission of Luisa Valenzuela.*

I was writing with the body, and fear had much to do with this.

Fear.

I was the kind of child who always poked around wherever there was fear: to see what kind of a creature fear was. I played at being a snake, a snail, or a hippopotamus in a warm African river. Among the animals I avoided was the ostrich. I wanted nothing to do with hiding my head in the sand. I don't know what crazy, morbid impulse made me run through the dark long hallways to the foyer at the entrance of my house, in the middle of the night, when the clock—controlled by witches—struck the hour. Nor do I know what made me go to the terrace where there was supposed to be a two-headed eagle, or behind the house where all kinds of dangers were lurking. I would have preferred hiding my head under the covers. But then who would reassure me? How could my eyes face daylight if they couldn't face shadows in the night? This is why I would go to look, and maybe because I looked came the need, sometime much later, to tell what I had seen.

Why?

Because of surprise

Because of adventure

Because of a question, and a gut rejection of any answers.

You tend to ask yourself why write with your entire body when you have that simple upper extremity which, thanks to the evolution of the species, has an opposable thumb especially made for holding a pen.

You also ask yourself—and this is really overwhelming—why write at all? In my case, I belong, body and soul and mind, to the so-called Third World where certain needs exist that are not at all literary.

Then other responses (or perhaps they are excuses) come to mind. The need to preserve collective memory is undoubtedly one of them.

There is yet another good excuse: writing as one's destined vocation. But I don't know if literature was my destiny. I wanted to be a physicist, or a mathematician, and, before that, an archaeologist or anthropologist, and for a long time I wanted to be a painter. Because I was raised in a house full of writers and that wasn't for me. No, ma'am. No thanks.

Fernando Alegría now describes that moment and place as the Buenos Aires Bloomsbury and this description isn't as crazy as it may appear. In our old house in the Belgrano section of town, the habitués were named Borges, Sábato, Mallea. My mother, the writer Luisa Mercedes Levinson, was the most sociable person in the world when she wasn't in bed, writing.

When I was a child, I would look from the door of her room and she would be in her bed surrounded by papers, all day until sunset when the others arrived. I would watch her with admiration and with the conviction that that life wasn't for me. I wanted a different future.

Disguises I chose for Carnivals:

Aviatrix

Woman Explorer

Robin Hood

Those were the masks that belonged to the official Carnival. But other masks at other times also took the shape of exploration and adventure. I would climb onto the roofs of the neighboring houses to try and reach the end of the block, something which was impossible to do because of the gardens in between. On those days when I felt really daring, I would climb up to a stone angel that clung to a column and that needed my presence, because otherwise no one would ever see it. I would also sneak into empty lots, or explore an abandoned house around the block. I was always looking for treasures that changed according to my ambitions: colorful figurines, stamps, coins. There was an old guard at the abandoned house who would let us in and was our friend. Until one afternoon, after exploring the basement looking for secret passages—at that time we pretended that the house belonged to German spies or was it a smuggler's hideout?—the old guard greeted us with his fly open and all those strange things hanging out. I ran away with my best friend in tow. I never went back, but years, thousands of years later, I wondered if that was the treasure for which we searched.

Now I know: with that small adventure around the block and with those big stories I made up, I began the slow learning process of writing with the body

Because

pores or ink, it is the same thing

the same stakes.

Clarice Lispector knew it and in her books focused on that love-hate, that happiness-misfortune we call literature. Her novels appear to be about love and the search for knowledge but they are also different ways of speaking about writing.

One's happiness is greatest when the story flows like a stream of clear water, even if the worst abominations are being narrated. It is only during the reading of those passages that the fear of what has flowed from one's own pen takes over.

There is another misfortune in writing and it is perhaps the most painful. It is inscribed during times of silence, when nothing is written with the body or mind or hand. Periods of drought which seem to be of nonexistence.

This is why I say sometimes that writing is a full-time curse.

I also say that, in its best moments, writing a novel is a euphoric feeling, like being in love.

And to think that my mother, the writer, is to blame for all of this. Not because of the example she set, not because of my emulation of her, which I acknowledge. She is to blame because when I was in the sixth grade in elementary school, my teacher asked her to help me with my compositions. "Your daughter is so bright in science," my teacher told her, "it's a shame that her grade should go down because she can't write." So my mother, overzealous in trying to help me, wrote a composition as she thought a tender eleven-year-old would.

I didn't think it was a very dignified text. From that moment on, I decided to assume the responsibility of my own writings. And that's how things are.

Because writing is the path that leads to the unknown. The way back is made of reflection, trying to come to terms with yourself and with that which has been produced. I strongly believe in the fluctuation from intuition to understanding. Placing ourselves right there

at the border
between two currents
at the center of the whirlpool,
the eye of the tornado?

"You are too intelligent to be beautiful" is what many of us have been told at some time by a man we've loved. Or, supposing literature is your profession: "You are too intelligent to be a good writer." Contrasting, of course, that ugly, masculine thing which is intelligence with female intuition. You wouldn't tell that to Susan Sontag is what someone with clearer ideas would reply. But those marks were made on young and tender skin, and from that moment on, one will always have a feeling of inadequacy.

Incapable, inactive, unproductive. I think all of us, from the time we're very young, feel at some time what could be called a nostalgia for imprisonment: the crazy, romantic fantasy that a prisoner has all the time to herself, to write. Only later do we realize that writing is an exercise of liberty.

From exigencies and from temptations, the stuff of literature is made. And from reflection, also. From everything. There is no unworthy material, although a great deal must be discarded.

When I was seventeen years old, I started working in journalism. For many years it was the perfect combination, one that allowed me to be part of all the disciplines, to go everywhere, and, at the same time, to write. A gift of ubiquity wrapped in words. I had the tremendous luck, almost a miracle, of having a boss who was a true teacher. Ambrosio Vencino was not a journalist; he was a displaced man of letters. To him I owe my obsessive precision with language.

I owe my travels to myself, to my need to touch the world with my own hands. I never paid attention to the premise that you don't have to leave your own bedroom to know the world. I traveled, I continue traveling, and I sometimes think that in all those displacements, parts of my self are being left behind.

Rodolfo Walsh, the Argentine writer and activist, once told me when I was complaining about how much I went from one place to the next and how little I wrote: "Your writing is also made from your travels."

Many years later, my writing was also made from another of Rodolfo Walsh's lessons to which I didn't pay much attention at the time. One day he showed me the difficult physical exercises that Cuban guerrillas practiced then in the Sierra Maestra. That physical guerrilla wisdom seemed to stand me in good stead in 1975 and 1976, when I sat in the cafes of Buenos Aires, devastated by state terrorism, and wrote stories that were, in a way, guerrilla exercises.

I put my body where my words are.

The physical loss hasn't been as great for me as it has been for others. I haven't been tortured, beaten, or persecuted. Knock on wood. I've been spared, perhaps because my statements aren't frontal; they are visions from the corner of my eye, oblique. I think we must continue writing about the horrors so that memory isn't lost and history won't repeat itself.

As a teenager, I was a voracious reader and I bragged about it but there were two books that I read in secret: *Freud* by Emil Ludwig and *The Devil in the Flesh*

(*Le Diable au Corps*) by Raymond Radiguet. With these two books I may not have gone very far in terms of pornographic material but it's clear that my libido was already acting up.

That writing with the body known as the act of love happened later, as it should have, and turned out quite well, with great style, but with more of an inclination toward the short story than the novel.

I love the short story for being round, suggestive, insinuating, microcosmic. The story has both the inconvenience and the fascination of new beginnings.

The novel, on the other hand, requires more concentration, more time, a state of grace. I love it because of the joy in opening new paths as words progress.

Paths to the unknown, the only interesting ones.

What I already know bores me, makes me repetitive. This is why whenever I have had a good plot that was clearly thought out, I was forced to give it up or at least to compress it, trying to squeeze out the juice that wasn't visible at first sight.

If I had to write my creed, I would first mention humor:

I believe in having a sense of humor at all costs
I believe in sharp, black humor
I believe in the absurd
in the grotesque

in everything which allows us to move beyond our limited thinking, beyond self-censorship and the censorship by others, which tends to be much more lethal. Taking a step to one side to observe the action as it is happening. A necessary step so that the vision of political reality is not contaminated by dogmas or messages.

I have nothing to say.

With luck, something will be said through me, despite myself, and I might not even realize it.

It is said that women's literature is made of questions.

I say that women's literature consequently is much more realistic.

Questions, uncertainties, searches, contradictions.

Everything is fused, and sometimes confused, and implicates us. The true act of writing with the body implies being fully involved. I am my own bet; I play myself, as though lying on the roulette table, calling out "All or nothing!"

What is interesting about the literary wager is that we do wager everything, but we don't know against what.

They say that women's literature is made of fragments.

I repeat that it is a matter of realism.

It is made of rips, shreds of your own skin which adhere to the paper but are not always read or even legible. Shreds that can be of laughter, of sheer delight.

Sometimes while writing, I have to get up to dance, to celebrate the flow of energy transforming itself into words. Sometimes the energy becomes words that are not printed, not even with the delicate line of a fountain pen, which is the most voluptuous in the act of writing. You must always celebrate when—whether in a cafe or subway—a happy combination of words, a fortuitous allusion, elicits associations that unwind the mental thread of writing without a mark. The mark comes next. And I will do my best to retain the freshness of that first moment of awe and transformation.

TRANSLATED FROM THE SPANISH BY CYNTHIA VENTURA AND JANET STERNBURG

IV | *Catalysts*

1. Gift Memories: A Meditative Essay on the Recollection of Borrowed Images

Discussion

Our early memories are usually driven by things, objects, people, scenes, smells, tastes, and sounds, and these childhood recollections are often fragmented. We may recall a piece of a story but be unable to form an entire narrative. Interestingly, many of our childhood memories, both images and discontinuous narratives, are formed as a result of other people, family members and friends, telling us about ourselves as children. For example, your mother shows you a photograph of yourself at age two and tells you a story about the image. You allow the photographic image and the narrative you've heard to become a part of your imagination. You begin creating more images as a result of hearing your mother's narrative.

Before you know it, you have formed a memory. And this memory relies on both the storytelling of another and your own ability to imagine yourself. Sometimes when this phenomenon has occurred in the distant past, we are unable to determine which memories we recorded firsthand and which ones we "borrowed" from others. Yet, the distinction between these two types of memory can offer insight into how memory functions and its impact on the creative process, especially the process of writing.

Exercise

As a way of understanding the operations of your memory, your past, try to recall some of your earliest memories. Remember that these memories will be mostly imagistic and fairly incomplete in their narrative sense. First, try writing about them in present tense. Be as illustrative as possible, including every available detail, every sensation, and as many images as you can.

Sit with those memories for a while and try not to rush through them. When you feel ready, attempt to identify which of the memories are actually your recollections, your stored information, and which of them you believe are "gifts," images that you have acquired from someone else. Once you have determined which memories are "yours" and which are "borrowed," write about your relationship to both kinds of memory.

Now construct a meditative essay which describes each of these early recollections in vivid detail. As you describe these memories, discuss the operation of your memory and your imagination at the same time. Be aware of your imagination's push to create the world of your past as you wanted it and also of your memory's attempt to be accurate. Explore how these two kinds of memory affect your emotional reaction or connection to your past; describe your ability to *feel* your childhood.

2. The First House of Memory: Images in Hiding

Discussion

Poet and essayist Mark Doty sometimes uses a variation of this next exercise in his creative writing classes as a way of exploring the functions of childhood memory as explained by Gaston Bachelard in his book, *Poetics of Space*. Bachelard believes that the images we have stored, especially those images which exist in our childhood hiding places, the forts we built, the nooks, crannies, and alcoves, have the greatest power and potential of insight into our unconscious minds. By returning to those secret spaces, we allow our imagination to re-experience the sensations of childhood reverie. In this state we are sometimes able to uncover material from our past, from our memory, which has been unavailable to us for quite some time.

Exercise

Begin by thinking of the first house in which you can actually remember living. Draw a rough sketch of that house's floor plan, labeling the rooms, doors, windows. As you draw, you will most likely find yourself attracted to one area of the house, often one room. Identify this space and spend a bit of time drawing and labeling objects that you remember existing there.

When you feel that you have spent enough time focused on this particular area, begin listing as many details as you can about the space on a separate sheet of paper. Try to move quickly through the list and don't allow yourself to think too intensely about your list; just keep writing.

Once you have exhausted your listing possibilities, imagine yourself in this space, but try to imagine your childhood self there. From the perspective of yourself at this young age and in present tense, begin to write what it is like to be there. You may find that this exercise provides the setting for a piece of memoir and that your present-tense exploration begins to shape itself into a narrative. Also, this activity may result in a conceptual discovery in which you begin to understand and write about the importance of place, the recollection of meaningful imagery, and how our re-imagined returns to childhood can impact our creative processes.

3. I and I: Addressing the Self

Discussion

Argentinean Jorge Luis Borges is arguably the greatest Spanish-language writer of the twentieth century. A prolific essayist, speaker, author of short stories, and poet, Borges, a slowly becoming blind librarian, pushed the boundaries of writing with every new work he produced. Combining a lifetime of scholarship with an urgent imagination, Borges blurred the lines between truth and fiction with dizzying detail, relentless focus, and an uncanny sense of humor.

In his short work "Borges and I," he addresses the reader and explains that, actually, "It's Borges, the other one, that things happen to . . . news of Borges reaches me by mail, or I see his name on a list of academics or in some biographical dictionary." It's "the other one," he tells us: we're after the wrong guy. He wants us to understand that the characters we create, portray, or enact are changing entities and certainly are not as simple as they seem. Nor as truthful.

If we accept every "I" an author offers at face value, we are missing a great deal. In fact, he points out, the person who parades around looking and acting just like Borges is just an actor acting like Borges. An actor named Borges. This tiny essay, one full paragraph and a single closing sentence, has enticed readers for decades; the punch line being, of course, "I'm not sure which it is of us that's writing this page." Why is this short piece so successful? *Because the author is forced to speak outside of himself.*

The following exercise is quite simple and seemingly inexhaustible: *introduce yourself to the reader in third person.* Sound simple? It is. There's one catch: *introduce yourself to your reader by telling the reader stories about what you've done, not by describing your chosen character traits.* Remember the time you jumped from a thirty-foot tree into water below? Remember the time you wrecked your bicycle? Remember the many times you did something in your life that you never thought you would do?

Exercise

Brainstorm first on these memories from your past, and jot them down on a piece of paper as fast as you can. Give yourself from ten to twenty minutes to think of as many active moments in your life as possible.

Then describe yourself to the reader, as the writer of "Borges and I" describes Borges. Talk about your relationship with this person you call yourself. Refer to this character by your own name. Be on the lookout for mistruths and exaggerations. They may provide new insights!

Finally, talk about the writing that your namesake has done. Try to explain to the reader why and how you do it. Do you remember the first time you wrote a poem? A song? A story? A letter? A name? Describe this experience, again addressing yourself as a third person, then describe the process you've just undergone. Write about yourself writing about yourself writing. What have you learned?

Index